MICROSOFT CERTIFIED SYSTEMS ENGINEER

MCSE Windows® 2000

Certification Headstart

This is an old book
We are now at SP2
this is written for RC2!

Syngress Media, Inc.

Osborne McGraw-Hill

Berkeley New York St. Louis San Francisco Auckland Bogotá Hamburg London Madrid Mexico City Milan Montreal New Delhi Panama City Paris São Paulo Singapore Sydney Tokyo Toronto

Osborne McGraw-Hill
2600 Tenth Street
Berkeley, California 94710
U.S.A.

For information on translations or book distributors outside the U.S.A.,
or to arrange bulk purchase discounts for sales promotions, premiums, or fund-raisers,
please contact Osborne/**McGraw-Hill** at the above address.

MCSE Windows® 2000 Certification Headstart

234567890 AGM AGM 019876543210

ISBN 0-07-212250-1

Publisher
Brandon A. Nordin

**Associate Publisher and
Editor-in-Chief**
Scott Rogers

Acquisitions Editor
Gareth Hancock

Editorial Management
Syngress Media, Inc.

Project Editors
Cynthia Douglas
Carolyn Welch

Acquisitions Coordinator
Tara Davis

Series Editors
Thomas W. Shinder, MD
Debra Littlejohn Shinder

Copy Editor
Beth A. Roberts

Proofreaders
Mike McGee
Linda Medoff
Paul Medoff

Indexer
Irv Hershman

Computer Designers
Jim Kussow
Michelle Galicia
Jani Beckwith

Illustrators
Brian Wells
Beth Young
Robert Hansen

Series Design
Roberta Steele

This book was published with Corel VENTURA™ Publisher.

From Global Knowledge

At Global Knowledge we strive to support the multiplicity of learning styles required by our students to achieve success as technical professionals. In this book, it is our intention to offer the reader a valuable tool for developing and applying Microsoft Windows 2000 skills.

As the world's largest IT training company, Global Knowledge is uniquely positioned to offer these books. The expertise gained each year from providing instructor-led training to hundreds of thousands of students worldwide has been captured in book form to enhance your learning experience. We hope that the quality of these books demonstrates our commitment to your lifelong learning success. Whether you choose to learn through the written word, computer-based training, Web delivery, or instructor-led training, Global Knowledge is committed to providing you the very best in each of those categories. For those of you who know Global Knowledge, or those of you who have just found us for the first time, our goal is to be your lifelong competency partner.

Thank you for the opportunity to serve you. We look forward to serving your needs again in the future.

Warmest regards,

Duncan Anderson
President and Chief Executive Officer, Global Knowledge

The Global Knowledge Advantage

Global Knowledge has a global delivery system for its products and services. The company has 28 subsidiaries, and offers its programs through a total of 60+ locations. No other vendor can provide consistent services across a geographic area this large. Global Knowledge is the largest independent information technology education provider, offering programs on a variety of platforms. This enables our multi-platform and multi-national customers to obtain all of their programs from a single vendor. The company has developed the unique CompetusTM Framework software tool and methodology which can quickly reconfigure courseware to the proficiency level of a student on an interactive basis. Combined with self-paced and on-line programs, this technology can reduce the time required for training by prescribing content in only the deficient skills areas. The company has fully automated every aspect of the education process, from registration and follow-up, to "just-in-time" production of courseware. Global Knowledge, through its Enterprise Services Consultancy, can customize programs and products to suit the needs of an individual customer.

Global Knowledge Classroom Education Programs

The backbone of our delivery options is classroom-based education. Our modern, well-equipped facilities staffed with the finest instructors offer programs in a wide variety of information technology topics, many of which lead to professional certifications.

Custom Learning Solutions

This delivery option has been created for companies and governments that value customized learning solutions. For them, our consultancy-based approach of developing targeted education solutions is most effective at helping them meet specific objectives.

Self-Paced and Multimedia Products

This delivery option offers self-paced program titles in interactive CD-ROM, videotape and audio tape programs. In addition, we offer custom development of interactive multimedia courseware to customers and partners. Call us at 1 (888) 427-4228.

Electronic Delivery of Training

Our network-based training service delivers efficient competency-based, interactive training via the World Wide Web and organizational intranets. This leading-edge delivery option provides a custom learning path and "just-in-time" training for maximum convenience to students.

ARG

American Research Group (ARG), a wholly-owned subsidiary of Global Knowledge, one of the largest worldwide training partners of Cisco Systems, offers a wide range of internetworking, LAN/WAN, Bay Networks, FORE Systems, IBM, and UNIX courses. ARG offers hands on network training in both instructor-led classes and self-paced PC-based training.

Global Knowledge Courses Available

Network Fundamentals
- Understanding Computer Networks
- Telecommunications Fundamentals I
- Telecommunications Fundamentals II
- Understanding Networking Fundamentals
- Implementing Computer Telephony Integration
- Introduction to Voice Over IP
- Introduction to Wide Area Networking
- Cabling Voice and Data Networks
- Introduction to LAN/WAN protocols
- Virtual Private Networks
- ATM Essentials

Network Security & Management
- Troubleshooting TCP/IP Networks
- Network Management
- Network Troubleshooting
- IP Address Management
- Network Security Administration
- Web Security
- Implementing UNIX Security
- Managing Cisco Network Security
- Windows NT 4.0 Security

IT Professional Skills
- Project Management for IT Professionals
- Advanced Project Management for IT Professionals
- Survival Skills for the New IT Manager
- Making IT Teams Work

LAN/WAN Internetworking
- Frame Relay Internetworking
- Implementing T1/T3 Services
- Understanding Digital Subscriber Line (xDSL)
- Internetworking with Routers and Switches
- Advanced Routing and Switching
- Multi-Layer Switching and Wire-Speed Routing
- Internetworking with TCP/IP
- ATM Internetworking
- OSPF Design and Configuration
- Border Gateway Protocol (BGP) Configuration

Authorized Vendor Training
Cisco Systems
- Introduction to Cisco Router Configuration
- Advanced Cisco Router Configuration
- Installation and Maintenance of Cisco Routers
- Cisco Internetwork Troubleshooting
- Cisco Internetwork Design
- Cisco Routers and LAN Switches
- Catalyst 5000 Series Configuration
- Cisco LAN Switch Configuration
- Managing Cisco Switched Internetworks
- Configuring, Monitoring, and Troubleshooting Dial-Up Services
- Cisco AS5200 Installation and Configuration
- Cisco Campus ATM Solutions

Bay Networks
- Bay Networks Accelerated Router Configuration
- Bay Networks Advanced IP Routing
- Bay Networks Hub Connectivity
- Bay Networks Accelar 1xxx Installation and Basic Configuration
- Bay Networks Centillion Switching

FORE Systems
- FORE ATM Enterprise Core Products
- FORE ATM Enterprise Edge Products
- FORE ATM Theory
- FORE LAN Certification

Operating Systems & Programming
Microsoft
- Introduction to Windows NT
- Microsoft Networking Essentials
- Windows NT 4.0 Workstation
- Windows NT 4.0 Server
- Advanced Windows NT 4.0 Server
- Windows NT Networking with TCP/IP
- Introduction to Microsoft Web Tools
- Windows NT Troubleshooting
- Windows Registry Configuration

UNIX
- UNIX Level I
- UNIX Level II
- Essentials of UNIX and NT Integration

Programming
- Introduction to JavaScript
- Java Programming
- PERL Programming
- Advanced PERL with CGI for the Web

Web Site Management & Development
- Building a Web Site
- Web Site Management and Performance
- Web Development Fundamentals

High Speed Networking
- Essentials of Wide Area Networking
- Integrating ISDN
- Fiber Optic Network Design
- Fiber Optic Network Installation
- Migrating to High Performance Ethernet

DIGITAL UNIX
- UNIX Utilities and Commands
- DIGITAL UNIX v4.0 System Administration
- DIGITAL UNIX v4.0 (TCP/IP) Network Management
- AdvFS, LSM, and RAID Configuration and Management
- DIGITAL UNIX TruCluster Software Configuration and Management
- UNIX Shell Programming Featuring Kornshell
- DIGITAL UNIX v4.0 Security Management
- DIGITAL UNIX v4.0 Performance Management
- DIGITAL UNIX v4.0 Intervals Overview

DIGITAL OpenVMS
- OpenVMS Skills for Users
- OpenVMS System and Network Node Management I
- OpenVMS System and Network Node Management II
- OpenVMS System and Network Node Management III
- OpenVMS System and Network Node Operations
- OpenVMS for Programmers
- OpenVMS System Troubleshooting for Systems Managers
- Configuring and Managing Complex VMScluster Systems
- Utilizing OpenVMS Features from C
- OpenVMS Performance Management
- Managing DEC TCP/IP Services for OpenVMS
- Programming in C

Hardware Courses
- AlphaServer 1000/1000A Installation, Configuration and Maintenance
- AlphaServer 2100 Server Maintenance
- AlphaServer 4100, Troubleshooting Techniques and Problem Solving

About Syngress Media

Syngress Media creates books and software for Information Technology professionals seeking skill enhancement and career advancement. Its products are designed to comply with vendor and industry standard course curricula, and are optimized for certification exam preparation. Visit the Syngress Web site at www.syngress.com.

Contributors

Debra Littlejohn Shinder (MCSE, MCP+I, MCT) is an instructor in the AATP program at Eastfield College, Dallas County Community College District, where she has taught since 1992. She is Webmaster for the cities of Seagoville and Sunnyvale, Texas, as well as the family Web site at www.shinder.net. She and her husband, Dr. Thomas W. Shinder, provide consulting and technical support services to Dallas area organizations. She is also the proud mom of a daughter, Kristen, who is currently serving in the U.S. Navy in Italy, and a son, Kris, who is a high school chess champion. Deb has been a writer for most her life, and has published numerous articles in both technical and nontechnical fields. She can be contacted at deb@shinder.net.

Stuart Cartin (MCSE, CNE) is a full-time IT consultant in Atlanta, Georgia focused on the design and implementation of Microsoft BackOffice technologies, with current emphasis on systems management and scripting technologies. As a firm believer in constant learning and professional growth, he is also pursuing the MCDBA and CCNA certification paths to broaden his technical knowledge. Aside from his hours spent working and studying, Stuart enjoys paintball, scuba diving, and working toward his private pilot's license.

Melissa Craft (MCSE, CCNA, MCNE, CCP) is a senior consulting engineer for MicroAge. MicroAge is a global systems integrator headquartered in Tempe, Arizona. MicroAge provides IT design, project management, and support for distributed computing systems. Melissa develops enterprise-wide technology solutions and methodologies for client organizations. These technology solutions touch every part of a system's lifecycle—from network design, testing and implementation, to operational management and strategic planning. Aside from earning a bachelor's degree from the University of Michigan, Melissa has several technical certifications, including Microsoft's MCSE, Cisco's CCNA, Novell's Master CNE, and Citrix's CCP. Melissa is a member of the IEEE, the Society of Women Engineers, and American MENSA, Ltd. Melissa Craft currently resides in Phoenix, Arizona with her family, Dan, Justine, and Taylor, and her two dogs, Marmaduke and Pooka. She can be contacted at mmcraft@compuserve.com.

Derrick Woo (MCSD, MCSE, MCP+I, CCNA, A+) is a networking and solution development specialist. He is currently the technical director of ecandy.com, where he is architecting and designing the specifications for their e-business solution. Prior to ecandy.com, Derrick was the chief technology officer of LA.com/Hawaii.com. LA.com and Hawaii.com are portal sites that cater to both locals and tourists. He founded Obelisk Software, worked as a network engineer at IBM, consulted for numerous Southern California firms, and was part of the support team for the world's largest fully switched Ethernet network. He works primarily with Windows NT and BackOffice solutions. In his spare time (if he has any), he enjoys investing, online chatting, weight training, and, of course, writing.

Ralph Crump (MCSE, CNE, MCNE) is an architecture and design engineer in Atlanta, Georgia with a major telecommunications company. He specializes in Windows NT and BackOffice applications, including Exchange and SMS and Novell NetWare solutions. He is certified as an MCSE and a CNE 3.x, 4.x, and 5.x with a Master CNE in Integrating Windows NT. He has been working in the IT industry for five-plus years and is currently working toward the Cisco certifications.

Brian Frederick (MCSE, ASE, MCNE, Network+) is a systems engineer with over seven years of technical background. Brian started working with computers with an Apple II+. Brian attended the University of Northern

Iowa, and is married with two adorable children. Brian's hobbies include his kids, family, and golfing. Brian is a systems engineer for Entre Information Systems, a leading Midwest Novell Platinum Partner and Microsoft Certified Solution Provider. Entre is a sister company with New Horizons Computer Learning Company, a premier Microsoft ATEC and Novell Authorized Training Partner. Brian owes his success to his parents and brother for their support and backing during his Apple days and in college, and to his wife and children for their support and understanding when Dad spends many hours in front of their computer.

Tony Hinkle (MCSE+Internet, MCP+Internet, CNE) resides in Indianapolis, Indiana and works as a systems consultant specializing in Microsoft Exchange. He started his career in 1995 repairing PC hardware and quickly moved on to Novell and Microsoft networking. His interests include the future of humankind in space, great mathematicians, Frisbee, cycling, and the outdoors in general.

Amy Thomson (A+ certified technician) is a software and A+ instructor in Halifax, Nova Scotia, and she has over 10 years of experience in dealing with computer hardware and applications. Amy has taught computer classes from one end of Canada to the other and back again. She holds an Honours B.Sc. in Psychology and is currently preparing for certification as an MCP in Windows 95 and as a Network+ certified technician.

Shane Clawson (MCSE, MCT) is a principal in Virtual Engineering, a consulting and engineering firm specializing in network consulting and technology process reengineering. Shane has over 20 years' experience as an instructor and in the networking field. He is a Microsoft Certified System Engineer (MCSE) and a Microsoft Certified Trainer (MCT) who has been working with NT since its inception. He specializes in Microsoft networking and BackOffice products. Shane may be reached at ShaneCSE@msn.com.

Steve Linthicum (MCSE, MCT, ICT) is an assistant professor with Sierra College's Computer Science Department in Rocklin, California. Mr. Linthicum has a B.S. from Arizona State University's College of Engineering and a J.D. from University of Pacific. He is an MCT, MCSE, and an Intel Certified Instructor. He can be reached at slinthi@ns.net.

Series Editor

Thomas W. Shinder, M.D. (MCSE, MCP+I, MCT) is a technology trainer and consultant in the Dallas-Ft. Worth metroplex. Dr. Shinder has consulted with major firms, including Xerox, Lucent Technologies, and FINA Oil, assisting in the development and implementation of IP-based communications strategies. Dr. Shinder attended medical school at the University of Illinois in Chicago, and trained in neurology at the Oregon Health Sciences Center in Portland, Oregon. His fascination with interneuronal communication ultimately melded with his interest in internetworking and led him to take down his shingle and focus on systems engineering. Tom works passionately with his beloved wife, Deb Shinder, to design elegant and cost-efficient solutions for small and medium-sized businesses based on Windows NT/2000 platforms.

Technical Reviewers

Cameron Brandon (MCSE, CNE, CNA, MCSE+Internet, A+, Network+) is a network engineer/administrator in the greater Portland, Oregon area. His specialty is Windows NT with BackOffice Integration.

Cameron participated in the Intel migration to Windows NT in Oregon, the largest migration of its kind in history. He completed his MCSE, CNE, CNA, MCPS:Internet Systems, and A+ certifications in five months' time, which shows what you can do if you set your mind to it.

Brian M. Collins (MCNE, CNI, MCSE, MCT, CTT) is a technical trainer for Network Appliance Inc. (NASDAQ: NTAP), a premier provider of Network Attached Storage, and a consultant and trainer through his own company, Collins Network Engineering. Brian is an 18-year veteran of technology industries and has worked as a network engineer, trainer, software developer, and consultant for government, Fortune 500 companies, and small business. His hobbies include hiking, golf, and operating systems. Brian lives in the redwood forest of Boulder Creek, California, 30 miles from California's Silicon Valley.

Erik Sojka is a system administrator and trainer currently working for a major software company. He is an MCSE and has a BS in Information Science and Technology from Drexel University.

ACKNOWLEDGMENTS

We would like to thank the following people:

- Richard Kristof of Global Knowledge for championing the series and providing us access to some great people and information.

- To all the incredibly hard-working folks at Osborne/McGraw-Hill: Brandon Nordin, Scott Rogers, and Gareth Hancock for their help in launching a great series and being solid team players. In addition, Tara Davis, Cynthia Douglas, and Carolyn Welch for their help in fine-tuning the book.

- To Monica Kilwine at Microsoft Corp., for being patient and diligent in answering all our questions.

CONTENTS AT A GLANCE

CONTENTS

Contents

Contents

PREFACE

This book's primary objective is to help you prepare for the required MCP/MCSE exams under the new Windows 2000 certification track. As the Microsoft program transitions from Windows NT 4.0, it will become increasingly important that current and aspiring IT professionals have multiple resources available to assist in increasing knowledge and building skills.

At the time of publication, Microsoft has not finalized and released all of the exam objectives for the Windows 2000 track, and the examinations themselves are still in development. What Microsoft has announced is its commitment to measuring real-world skills. This book was designed with that premise in mind; its authors have practical experience in the field, using the Windows 2000 operating systems in hands-on situations, and have followed the development of the product since early beta versions.

Because of the exams' anticipated focus on application and understanding, as opposed to memorization of facts, no book by itself can fully prepare you to obtain a passing score. It is essential that you work with the software. Toward that end, this book includes practical step-by-step exercises in each chapter that are designed to guide you in truly learning Windows 2000, not just learning about it.

In This Book

This book is organized in such a way as to serve as an in-depth introduction to Windows 2000 for both experienced Windows NT professionals and newcomers to Microsoft networking technologies. Each chapter covers a major component of the operating system, with an emphasis on the "why" as well as the "how to" of working with and supporting Windows 2000 as a network administrator or engineer.

In Every Chapter

We've created a set of chapter components that call your attention to important items, reinforce important points, and provide helpful exam-taking hints. Take a look at what you'll find in every chapter:

- Every chapter begins with the **Headstart Objectives**—what you need to know in order to prepare for the section on the exam dealing with the chapter topic. The Headstart Objective headings identify the objectives within the chapter, so you'll always know an objective when you see it!

- **Heads Up** notes call attention to topics that may be a somewhat tricky. These helpful hints are written by authors who are MCSE certified and who know all of the ins and outs of Windows 2000 —who better to tell you what to worry about? They know what you're about to go through in your quest for certification!

- **Headstart Exercises** are interspersed throughout the chapters. These are step-by-step exercises that mirror vendor-recommended labs. They help you master skills that are likely to be an area of focus on the exam. Don't just read through the exercises; they are hands-on practice that you should be comfortable completing. Learning by doing is an effective way to increase your competency with a product.

- **Accelerating to Windows 2000** sidebars describe the issues that come up most often in real-world settings. These sidebars give you a valuable perspective into Windows-related topics. In these sidebars, authors who are experts in Windows NT, as well as Windows 2000, highlight some of the important differences between the two. They provide useful knowledge for you as you prepare for a transition from an NT environment to a Windows 2000 environment.

- **Q & A** sections lay out problems and solutions in a quick-read format:

- The **Chapter Summary** is a succinct review of the chapter and a re-statement of salient points regarding the exam.

- The **Two-Minute Drill** at the end of every chapter is a check list of the main points of the chapter. It can be used for last-minute review.

QUESTIONS AND ANSWERS

Is Active Directory scalable?	Yes! Unlike the Windows NT security database, which is limited to approximately 40,000 objects, Active Directory supports literally millions of objects.
Is Active Directory compatible with other LDAP directory services?	Yes! Active Directory can share information with other directory services that support LDAP versions 2 and 3, such as Novell's NDS.

■ The **Self Test** offers you a unique opportunity to test your knowledge of the subject matter covered throughout each chapter. The answers to these questions, as well as explanations of the answers, can be found in Appendix A. By taking the Self Test after completing each chapter, you'll reinforce what you've learned from that chapter.

The Global Knowledge Web Site

Check out the Web site. Global Knowledge invites you to become an active member of the Access Global Web site. This site is an online mall and an information repository that you'll find invaluable. You can access many types of products to assist you in your preparation for the exams, and you'll be able to participate in forums, online discussions, and threaded discussions. No other book brings you unlimited access to such a resource. You'll find more information about this site in Appendix B.

Some Pointers

Once you've finished reading this book, set aside some time to do a thorough review. You might want to return to the book several times and make use of all the methods it offers for reviewing the material.

1. *Re-read all the Two-Minute Drills*, or have someone quiz you. You also can use the drills as a way to do a quick cram before the exam.

2. *Re-read all the Heads-Up notes.* Remember that these are written by authors who have taken the exam and passed. They know what you should expect—and what you should be careful about.

3. *Review all the Q & A scenarios* for quick problem solving.

4. *Re-take the Self Tests.* Taking the tests right after you've read the chapter is a good idea, because it helps reinforce what you've just learned. However, it's an even better idea to go back later and do all the questions in the book in one sitting. Pretend you're taking the exam. (For this reason, you should mark your answers on a separate piece of paper when you go through the questions the first time.)

5. *Complete the exercises.* Did you do the exercises when you read through each chapter? If not, do them! These exercises are designed to cover exam topics, and there's no better way to get to know this material than by practicing.

6. *Check out the Web site.* Global Knowledge invites you to become an active member of the Access Global Web site. This site is an online mall and an information repository that you'll find invaluable. You can access many types of products to assist you in your preparation for the exams, and you'll be able to participate in forums, online discussions, and threaded discussions. No other book brings you unlimited access to such a resource. You'll find more information about this site in Appendix B.

MCSE Certification

This book is designed to be your Certification Headstart. At the time this book was written, no exam objectives had been officially published. We wrote this book to give you a complete and incisive introduction to the functions and services available in Windows 2000. The information contained here will provide you with the required foundation of knowledge to become a success at attaining the new and improved Windows 2000 Microsoft Certified Systems Engineer certification.

The nature of the Information Technology industry is change. The requirements and specifications for certification can change without notice. Microsoft expects you to regularly visit their Web site at `http://www.microsoft.com/mcp/certstep/mcse.htm` to get the most up-to-date information on the entire MCSE program.

The Windows 2000 core certification exams are listed here.

TABLE fm-1 Windows 2000 Certification Track

Core Exams		
Candidates who have <u>not</u> already passed Windows NT 4.0 exams. All four of the following core exams required:	**OR**	**Candidates who have passed three Windows NT 4.0 exams (Exams 70-067, 70-068, and 70-073). Instead of the four core exams at the left, you may take:**
Exam 70-210: Installing, Configuring, and Administering Microsoft® Windows® 2000 Professional		**Exam 70-240**: Microsoft® Windows® 2000 Accelerated Exam for MCPs Certified on Microsoft® Windows NT® 4.0. The accelerated exam will be available until December 31, 2001. It covers the core competencies of exams **70-210, 70-215, 70-216, and 70-217**.

TABLE fm-1	Windows 2000 Certification Track *(continued)*

Core Exams
Exam 70-215: Installing, Configuring and Administering Microsoft® Windows® 2000 Server
Exam 70-216: Implementing and Administering a Microsoft® Windows® 2000 Network Infrastructure
Exam 70-217: Implementing and Administering a Microsoft® Windows® 2000 Directory Services Infrastructure

PLUS—All Candidates—*One of the Following Core Exams Required:*
***Exam 70-219**: Designing a Microsoft® Windows® 2000 Directory Services Infrastructure
***Exam 70-220**: Designing Security for a Microsoft® Windows® 2000 Network
***Exam 70-221**: Designing a Microsoft® Windows® 2000 Network Infrastructure

PLUS—All Candidates—*Two Elective Exams Required:*
Any current MCSE electives when the Windows 2000 exams listed above are released in their live versions. **Electives scheduled for retirement will not be considered current.** Selected third-party certifications that focus on interoperability will be accepted as an alternative to one elective exam.
***Exam 70-219**: Designing a Microsoft® Windows® 2000 Directory Services Infrastructure
***Exam 70-220**: Designing Security for a Microsoft® Windows® 2000 Network
***Exam 70-221**: Designing a Microsoft® Windows® 2000 Network Infrastructure
Exam 70-222: Upgrading from Microsoft® Windows® NT 4.0 to Microsoft® Windows® 2000

*Note that some of the Windows 2000 core exams can be used as elective exams as well. An exam that is used to meet the design requirement cannot also count as an elective. Each exam can only be counted once in the Windows 2000 Certification.

Let's look at two scenarios. The first applies to the person who has already taken the Windows NT 4.0 Server (70-067), Windows NT 4.0 Workstation (70-073), and Windows NT 4.0 Server in the Enterprise (70-068) exams. The second scenario covers the situation of the person who has not completed those Windows NT 4.0 exams, and would like to concentrate *only* on Windows 2000.

In the first scenario, you have the option of taking all four Windows 2000 core exams, or you can take the Windows 2000 Accelerated Exam for MCPs if you have already passed exams 70-067, 70-068, and 70-073. (Note that you must have passed those specific exams to qualify for the Accelerated Exam. If you fulfilled your NT 4.0 MCSE requirements by passing the Windows 95 or Windows 98 exam as your client operating system option, and did not take the NT Workstation Exam, you don't qualify).

After completing the core requirements, either by passing the four core exams or the one Accelerated exam, you must pass a "design" exam. The design exams include Designing A Microsoft Windows 2000 Directory Services Infrastructure (70-219), Designing Security for Microsoft Windows 2000 Network (70-220) and Designing a Microsoft Windows 2000 Network Infrastructure. One design exam is REQUIRED.

You also must pass two exams from the list of electives. However, you cannot use the design exam that you took as an elective. Each exam can only count once toward certification. This includes any of the MCSE electives that are current when the Windows 2000 exams are released. In summary, you would take a total of at least two more exams, the upgrade exam and the design exam. Any additional exams would be dependent on which electives the candidate may have already completed.

In the second scenario, if you have not completed, and do not plan to complete, the Core Windows NT 4.0 exams, you must complete the four core Windows 2000 exams, one design exam, and two elective exams. Again, no exam can be counted twice. In this case, you must pass a total of seven exams to obtain the Windows 2000 MCSE certification.

How to Take a Microsoft Certification Examination

If you have taken a Microsoft Certification exam before, we have some good news and some bad news. The good news is that the new testing formats will be a true measure of your ability and knowledge. Microsoft has "raised the bar" for its Windows 2000 certification exams. If you are an expert in the Windows 2000 operating system, and can troubleshoot and engineer efficient, cost-effective solutions using Windows 2000, you will have no difficulty with the new exams.

The bad news is that if you have used resources such as "brain-dumps," boot-camps, or exam-specific practice tests as your only method of test preparation, you will undoubtedly fail your Windows 2000 exams. The new Windows 2000 MCSE exams will test your knowledge, and your ability to apply that knowledge in more sophisticated and accurate ways than was offered for the MCSE exams for Windows NT 4.0.

In the Windows 2000 exams, Microsoft will use a variety of testing formats that include product simulations, adaptive testing, and possibly even "fill in the blanks" questions (also called "free response" questions). The test-taking process will measure the examinee's fundamental knowledge of the Windows 2000 operating system rather than the ability to memorize a few facts and then answer a few multiple-choice questions.

In addition, the "pool" of questions for each exam will significantly increase. The greater number of questions combined with the adaptive testing techniques will enhance the validity and security of the certification process.

We will begin by looking at the purpose, focus, and structure of Microsoft certification tests, and examine the effect these factors have on the kinds of questions you will face on your certification exams. We will define the structure of examination questions and investigate some common formats. Next, we will present a strategy for answering these questions. Finally, we will give some specific guidelines on what you should do on the day of your test.

Why Vendor Certification?

The Microsoft Certified Professional program, like the certification programs from Lotus, Novell, Oracle, and other software vendors, is maintained for the ultimate purpose of increasing the corporation's profits. A successful vendor certification program accomplishes this goal by helping to create a pool of experts in a company's software and by "branding" these experts so that companies using the software can identify them.

We know that vendor certification has become increasingly popular in the last few years because it helps employers find qualified workers, and because it helps software vendors like Microsoft sell their products. But why vendor certification rather than a more traditional approach like a college degree in computer science? A college education is a broadening and enriching experience, but a degree in computer science does not prepare students for most jobs in the IT industry.

A common truism in our business states, "If you are out of the IT industry for three years and want to return, you have to start over." The problem, of course, is *timeliness*; if a first-year student learns about a specific computer program, it probably will no longer be in wide use when he or she graduates. Although some colleges are trying to integrate Microsoft certification into their curriculum, the problem is not really a flaw in higher education, but a characteristic of the IT industry. Computer software is changing so rapidly that a four-year college just can't keep up.

A marked characteristic of the Microsoft certification program is an emphasis on performing specific job tasks rather than merely gathering knowledge. It may come as a shock, but most potential employers do not care how much you know about the theory of operating systems, networking, or database design. As one IT manager put it, "I don't really care what my employees know about the theory of our network. We don't need someone to sit at a desk and think about it. We need people who can actually do something to make it work better."

You should not think that this attitude is some kind of anti-intellectual revolt against "book learning." Knowledge is a necessary prerequisite, but it is not enough. More than one company has hired a computer science graduate as a network administrator, only to learn that the new employee has no idea how to add users, assign permissions, or perform the other day-to-day tasks necessary to maintain a network. This brings us to the second major characteristic of Microsoft certification that affects the questions you must be prepared to answer. In addition to timeliness, Microsoft certification is also job task oriented.

The timeliness of Microsoft's certification program is obvious, and is inherent in the fact that you will be tested on current versions of software in wide use today. The job task orientation of Microsoft certification is almost as obvious, but testing real-world job skills using a computer-based test is not easy.

Computerized Testing

Considering the popularity of Microsoft certification, and the fact that certification candidates are spread around the world, the only practical way to administer tests for the certification program is through Sylvan Prometric or

Vue testing centers, which operate internationally. Sylvan Prometric and Vue provide proctor testing services for Microsoft, Oracle, Novell, Lotus, and the A+ computer technician certification. Although the IT industry accounts for much of Sylvan's revenue, the company provides services for a number of other businesses and organizations, such as FAA pre-flight pilot tests.

Historically, several hundred questions were developed for a new Microsoft certification examination. The Windows 2000 MCSE exam pool is expected to contain thousands of new questions. Microsoft is aware that many new MCSE candidates have been able to access information on test questions via the Internet or other resources. The company is very concerned about maintaining the MCSE as a "premium" certification. The significant increase in the number of test questions, together with stronger enforcement of the NDA (Non-disclosure agreement) will ensure that a higher standard for certification is attained.

Microsoft treats the test-building process very seriously. Test questions are first reviewed by a number of subject matter experts for technical accuracy, and then are presented in a beta test. Taking the beta test may require several hours, due to the large number of questions. After a few weeks, Microsoft Certification uses the statistical feedback from Sylvan to check the performance of the beta questions.

Questions are discarded if most test takers get them right (too easy) or wrong (too difficult), and a number of other statistical measures are taken of each question. Although the scope of our discussion precludes a rigorous treatment of question analysis, you should be aware that Microsoft and other vendors spend a great deal of time and effort making sure their examination questions are valid. In addition to the obvious desire for quality, vendors strive for fairness to all candidates in developing their exams.

The questions that survive statistical analysis form the pool of questions for the final certification examination.

Test Structure

The questions in a Microsoft form test are equally weighted; this means they all count the same when the test is scored. An interesting and useful characteristic of a form test is that you can mark a question you have doubts about as you take the test. Assuming you have time left when you finish all the questions, you can return and spend more time on the questions you have marked as doubtful.

Microsoft has implemented *adaptive* testing. To use this interactive technique, a form test is first created and administered to several thousand certification candidates. The statistics generated are used to assign a weight, or difficulty level, for each question. For example, the questions in a form might be divided into levels one through five, with level-one questions being the easiest and level five the most difficult.

When an adaptive test begins, the candidate is first given a level-three question. If it is answered correctly, a question from the next higher level is presented, and an incorrect response results in a question from the next lower level. When 15–20 questions have been answered in this manner, the scoring algorithm is able to predict, with a high degree of statistical certainty, whether the candidate would pass or fail if all the questions in the form were answered. When the required degree of certainty is attained, the test ends and the candidate receives a pass/fail grade.

Adaptive testing has some definite advantages for everyone involved in the certification process. Adaptive tests allow Sylvan Prometric or Vue to deliver more tests with the same resources, as certification candidates often are in and out in 30 minutes or less. For candidates, the "fatigue factor" is reduced because of the shortened testing time. For Microsoft, adaptive testing means that fewer test questions are exposed to each candidate, and this can enhance the security, and therefore the overall validity, of certification tests.

One possible problem you may have with adaptive testing is that you are not allowed to mark and revisit questions. Since the adaptive algorithm is interactive, and all questions but the first are selected on the basis of your response to the previous question, it is not possible to skip a particular question or change an answer.

Question Types

Computerized test questions can be presented in a number of ways. Some of the possible formats are used on Microsoft certification examinations, and some are not.

True/False

We are all familiar with True/False questions, but because of the inherent 50-percent chance of guessing the correct answer, you will not see questions of this type on Microsoft certification exams.

Multiple Choice

The majority of Microsoft certification questions are in the multiple-choice format, with either a single correct answer or multiple correct answers. One interesting variation on multiple-choice questions with multiple correct answers is whether or not the candidate is told how many answers are correct.

EXAMPLE:

Which two files can be altered to configure the MS-DOS environment? (Choose two.)

Or

Which files can be altered to configure the MS-DOS environment? (Choose all that apply.)

You may see both variations on Microsoft certification examinations, but the trend seems to be toward the first type, where candidates are told explicitly how many answers are correct. Questions of the "choose all that apply" variety are more difficult, and can be merely confusing.

Graphical Questions

One or more graphical elements are sometimes used as exhibits to help present or clarify an exam question. These elements may take the form of a network diagram, pictures of networking components, or screen shots from the software on which you are being tested. It is often easier to present the concepts required for a complex performance-based scenario with a graphic than with words.

Test questions known as *hotspots* actually incorporate graphics as part of the answer. These questions ask the certification candidate to click on a location or graphical element to answer the question. As an example, you might be shown the diagram of a network and asked to click on an appropriate location for a router. The answer is correct if the candidate clicks within the *hotspot* that defines the correct location.

Free Response Questions

Another kind of question you sometimes see on Microsoft certification examinations requires a *free response* or type-in answer. An example of this type of question might present a TCP/IP network scenario and ask the candidate to calculate and enter the correct subnet mask in dotted decimal notation.

Knowledge-Based and Performance-Based Questions

Microsoft Certification develops a blueprint for each Microsoft certification examination with input from subject matter experts. This blueprint defines the content areas and objectives for each test, and each test question is created to test a specific objective. The basic information from the examination blueprint can be found on Microsoft's Web site in the Exam Prep Guide for each test.

Psychometricians (psychologists who specialize in designing and analyzing tests) categorize test questions as knowledge based or performance based. As the names imply, knowledge-based questions are designed to test knowledge, while performance-based questions are designed to test performance.

Some objectives demand a knowledge-based question. For example, objectives that use verbs like *list* and *identify* tend to test only what you know, not what you can do.

EXAMPLE:

Objective: Identify the MS-DOS configuration files.

Which two files can be altered to configure the MS-DOS environment? (Choose two.)

    A. COMMAND.COM

    B. AUTOEXEC.BAT

    C. IO.SYS

    D. CONFIG.SYS
      Correct answers: B, D

Other objectives use action verbs like *install, configure*, and *troubleshoot* to define job tasks. These objectives can often be tested with either a knowledge-based question or a performance-based question.
EXAMPLE:

Objective: Configure an MS-DOS installation appropriately using the

PATH statement in AUTOEXEX.BAT.

Knowledge-based question:

What is the correct syntax to set a path to the D: directory in AUTOEXEC.BAT?

   A. SET PATH EQUAL TO D:

   B. PATH D:

   C. SETPATH D:

   D. D:EQUALS PATH
   Correct answer: B

Performance-based question:

Your company uses several DOS accounting applications that access a group of common utility programs. What is the best strategy for configuring the computers in the accounting department so that the accounting applications will always be able to access the utility programs?

   A. Store all the utilities on a single floppy disk, and make a copy of the disk for each computer in the accounting department.

   B. Copy all the utilities to a directory on the C: drive of each computer in the accounting department, and add a PATH statement pointing to this directory in the AUTOEXEC.BAT files.

   C. Copy all the utilities to all application directories on each computer in the accounting department.

   D. Place all the utilities in the C: directory on each computer, because the C: directory is automatically included in the PATH statement when AUTOEXEC.BAT is executed.
   Correct answer: B

Even in this simple example, the superiority of the performance-based question is obvious. Whereas the knowledge-based question asks for a single fact, the performance-based question presents a real-life situation and requires that you make a decision based on this scenario.

Testing Job Performance

We have said that Microsoft certification focuses on timeliness and the ability to perform job tasks. We have also introduced the concept of performance-based questions, but even performance-based, multiple-choice questions do not really measure performance. Another strategy is needed to test job skills.

Given unlimited resources, it is not difficult to test job skills. In an ideal world, Microsoft would fly MCP candidates to Redmond, place them in a controlled environment with a team of experts, and ask them to plan, install, maintain, and troubleshoot a Windows network. In a few days at most, the experts could reach a valid decision as to whether each candidate should or should not be granted MCDBA or MCSE status. Needless to say, this is not likely to happen.

Closer to reality, another way to test performance is by using the actual software, and creating a testing program to present tasks and automatically grade a candidate's performance when the tasks are completed. This *cooperative* approach would be practical in some testing situations, but the same test that is presented to MCP candidates in Boston must also be available in Bahrain and Botswana. Many Sylvan Prometric testing locations around the world cannot run 32-bit applications, much less provide the complex networked solutions required by cooperative testing applications.

The most workable solution for measuring performance in today's testing environment is a *simulation* program. When the program is launched during a test, the candidate sees a simulation of the actual software that looks, and behaves, just like the real thing. When the testing software presents a task, the simulation program is launched and the candidate performs the required task. The testing software then grades the candidate's performance on the required task and moves to the next question. In this way, a 16-bit simulation program can mimic the look and feel of 32-bit operating systems, a complicated network, or even the entire Internet.

Microsoft has introduced simulation questions on the certification examination for Internet Information Server 4.0. Simulation questions provide many advantages over other testing methodologies, and simulations are expected to become increasingly important in the Microsoft certification program. For example, studies have shown that there is a very high correlation between the ability to perform simulated tasks on a computer-based test and the ability to perform the actual job tasks. Thus, simulations enhance the validity of the certification process.

Another truly wonderful benefit of simulations is in the area of test security. It is just not possible to cheat on a simulation question. In fact, you will be told exactly what tasks you are expected to perform on the test. How can a certification candidate cheat? By learning to perform the tasks? What a concept!

Study Strategies

There are appropriate ways to study for the different types of questions you will see on a Microsoft certification examination.

Knowledge-Based Questions

Knowledge-based questions require that you memorize facts. There are hundreds of facts inherent in every content area of every Microsoft certification examination. There are several keys to memorizing facts:

- **Repetition** The more times your brain is exposed to a fact, the more likely you are to remember it.

- **Association** Connecting facts within a logical framework makes them easier to remember.

- **Motor Association** It is often easier to remember something if you write it down or perform some other physical act, like clicking on a practice test answer.

We have said that the emphasis of Microsoft certification is job performance, and that there are very few knowledge-based questions on Microsoft certification exams. Why should you waste a lot of time learning filenames, IP address formulas, and other minutiae? Read on.

Performance-Based Questions

Most of the questions you will face on a Microsoft certification exam are performance-based scenario questions. We have discussed the superiority of these questions over simple knowledge-based questions, but you should remember that the job task orientation of Microsoft certification extends the knowledge you need to pass the exams; it does not replace this knowledge. Therefore, the first step in preparing for scenario questions is to absorb as many facts relating to the exam content areas as you can. In other words, go back to the previous section and follow the steps to prepare for an exam composed of knowledge-based questions.

The second step is to familiarize yourself with the format of the questions you are likely to see on the exam. You can do this by answering the questions in this study guide, by using Microsoft assessment tests, or by using practice tests. The day of your test is not the time to be surprised by the construction of Microsoft exam questions.

For example, look at the following question:

Scenario: You have a network with…

Primary Objective: You want to…

Secondary Objective: You also want to…

Proposed Solution: Do this…

What does the proposed solution accomplish?

    A. Satisfies the primary and the secondary objective

    B. Satisfies the primary but not the secondary objective

    C. Satisfies the secondary but not the primary objective

    D. Satisfies neither the primary nor the secondary objective

This kind of question, with some variation, is seen on many Microsoft Certification examinations.

At best, these performance-based scenario questions really do test certification candidates at a higher cognitive level than knowledge-based questions. At worst, these questions can test your reading comprehension and test-taking ability rather than your ability to use Microsoft products. Be sure to get in the habit of reading the question carefully to determine what is being asked.

The third step in preparing for Microsoft scenario questions is to adopt the following attitude: Multiple-choice questions aren't really performance based. It is all a cruel lie. These scenario questions are just knowledge-based questions with a little story wrapped around them.

To answer a scenario question, you have to sift through the story to the underlying facts of the situation, and apply your knowledge to determine the correct answer. This may sound silly at first, but the process we go through in solving real-life problems is quite similar. The key concept is that every scenario question (and every real-life problem) has a fact at its center, and if we can identify that fact, we can answer the question.

Simulations

Simulation questions really do measure your ability to perform job tasks. You must be able to perform the specified tasks. There are three ways to prepare for simulation questions:

1 Visit the Syngress and Osborne McGraw-Hill Web sites (**www.syngress.com/www.osborne.com**) to take advantage of free Personal Testing Centers. Available immediately are self-paced and self-guided question-and-answer banks designed to help you review the material covered throughout this book. Check these Web sites regularly, as realistic exam simulations, complete with in-depth score reporting, will be made available as Microsoft officially releases its MCSE certification objectives. These exam simulations will not only help you identify your areas of expertise and weakness, but will also guide you through the actual test-taking experience, as they will utilize the various testing methods employed by Microsoft.

2. Get experience with the actual software. If you have the resources, this is a great way to prepare for simulation questions.

3. Use official Microsoft practice tests. Practice tests are available that provide practice with the same simulation engine used on Microsoft certification exams. This approach has the added advantage of grading your efforts.

Signing Up

Signing up to take a Microsoft certification examination is easy. Sylvan or Vue operators in each country can schedule tests at any testing center. There are, however, a few things you should know:

1. If you call Sylvan or Vue during a busy time, get a cup of coffee first, because you may be in for a long wait. The exam providers do an excellent job, but everyone in the world seems to want to sign up for a test on Monday morning.

2. You will need your social security number or some other unique identifier to sign up for a test, so have it at hand.

3. Pay for your test by credit card if at all possible. This makes things easier, and you can even schedule tests for the same day you call, if space is available at your local testing center.

4. Know the number and title of the test you want to take before you call. This is not essential, and the Sylvan operators will help you if they can. Having this information in advance, however, speeds up and improves the accuracy of the registration process.

Taking the Test

Teachers have always told you not to try to cram for examinations because it does no good. Sometimes they lied. If you are faced with a knowledge-based test requiring only that you regurgitate facts, cramming can mean the difference between passing and failing. This is not the case, however, with Microsoft certification exams. If you don't know it the night before, don't bother to stay up and cram.

Instead, create a schedule and stick to it. Plan your study time carefully, and do not schedule your test until you think you are ready to succeed. Follow these guidelines on the day of your exam:

1. Get a good night's sleep. The scenario questions you will face on a Microsoft certification examination require a clear head.

2. Remember to take two forms of identification—at least one with a picture. A driver's license with your picture, and social security or credit card are acceptable.

3. Leave home in time to arrive at your testing center a few minutes early. It is not a good idea to feel rushed as you begin your exam.

4. Do not spend too much time on any one question. If you are taking a form test, take your best guess and mark the question so you can come back to it if you have time. You cannot mark and revisit questions on an adaptive test, so you must do your best on each question as you go.

5. If you do not know the answer to a question, try to eliminate the obviously wrong answers and guess from the rest. If you can eliminate two out of four options, you have a 50-percent chance of guessing the correct answer.

6. For scenario questions, follow the steps we outlined earlier. Read the question carefully and try to identify the facts at the center of the story.

Finally, we would advise anyone attempting to earn Microsoft MCDBA and MCSE certification to adopt a philosophical attitude. The Windows 2000 MCSE will be the most difficult MCSE ever to be offered. The questions will be at a higher cognitive level than seen on all previous MCSE exams. Therefore, even if you are the kind of person who never fails a test, you are likely to fail at least one Windows 2000 certification test somewhere along the way. Do not get discouraged. Microsoft wants to insure the value of your certification. Moreover, it will attempt to so by keeping the standard as high as possible. If Microsoft certification were easy to obtain, more people would have it, and it would not be so respected and so valuable to your future in the IT industry.

MICROSOFT CERTIFIED SYSTEMS ENGINEER

Part I

Installing and Configuring Microsoft Windows 2000

Part 1

Installing and
Configuring Microsoft
Windows 2000

MICROSOFT CERTIFIED SYSTEMS ENGINEER

Introduction to Microsoft Windows 2000

Computers continue to be an ever-growing and essential part of businesses today, and there is an increasing demand for powerful, secure, and user-friendly systems. Microsoft is charging into the new millenium with a tool to meet these challenges. The Windows 2000 operating systems are designed to provide ease of use, high administrative control, and low total cost of ownership.

This chapter provides you with an introduction to the Windows 2000 platform and an overview of the major technology that separates Windows 2000 from its predecessors. We also examine the four operating systems within the Windows 2000 platform and the function of each within a Windows 2000 network. We wrap up by discussing the powerful new Active Directory and take a brief look at domain, tree, and forest structure within a multidomain network.

HEADSTART OBJECTIVE 1.01

History of the NT Technology

Windows 2000 is a network operating system, and thus has its roots in the Microsoft Windows NT (New Technology) platform. The story begins in the late 1980s when Microsoft paired up with IBM to create a network operating system called OS/2, designed to run on Intel computers. Following the relative success of OS/2, plans were made to create a more advanced version of OS/2, called OS/2 NT.

Meanwhile, Microsoft and IBM were producing another line of operating system software called Windows, designed to run on stand-alone computers. Several versions of this operating system were released, but due to problems with the program and users' unwillingness to make the switch from DOS, Windows went largely unnoticed.

However, in 1990, Windows 3.0 was released and enjoyed great success and popularity. Microsoft wanted to create a version of Windows that would allow it to compete with OS/2, and IBM wanted the two operating systems to remain separate. In the end, the partnership broke up. IBM kept the rights to existing OS/2 software, and Microsoft kept the rights to existing and future Windows developments. Microsoft changed the name of the OS/2 NT project to Windows NT 3.1 and released it in 1993.

Microsoft Windows NT 3.1 had the same interface as Windows 3.0, and was a 32-bit operating system. Windows NT was not restricted to the same memory boundaries and hardware access as Windows 3.0 and DOS, and could run 16-bit programs in a special environment that would not disrupt 32-bit operations (these features were later incorporated in Windows 95 and Windows 98).

Microsoft has since released version 4.0 of Windows NT, in workstation, server, and enterprise models. With the release of Windows 2000, Microsoft intended to put an end to the parallel progression of the Windows NT and Windows 9x platforms. However, the latest decision by Microsoft is to continue the Windows 9x platform in a new platform codenamed "millenium," and the Windows NT lineup has been renamed Windows 2000. Because the core of the Windows 2000 architecture is based on Windows NT technology, some of the similarities and differences between the two platforms are discussed throughout this chapter.

HEADSTART OBJECTIVE 1.02

The Windows 2000 Platform

The Microsoft Windows 2000 operating system is designed to combine and improve on the ease of use of Windows 95 and 98 with the security and administrative control of Windows NT.

The Windows 2000 Family of Operating Systems

To meet the demands of both end users and network administrators, Microsoft has developed four operating systems within the Windows 2000 platform:

- **Windows 2000 Professional** This operating system is designed for stand-alone users, and for workstations on a network.

- **Windows 2000 Server** Also referred to as Windows 2000 Server Standard Edition, it is designed to provide the security and resources to workstations in a network.

- **Windows 2000 Advanced Server** Formerly known as Enterprise Edition in earlier NT platforms, this OS is a more powerful version of Windows 2000 Server, designed for larger networks.

- **Windows 2000 Datacenter Server** At the high end of the Windows 2000 platform, it includes more advanced features than Windows 2000 Advanced Server, and can support over 10,000 users simultaneously.

QUESTIONS AND ANSWERS

Which operating system should I use if my machine will be a workstation on the network?	Windows 2000 Professional
Which operating system should I use if my machine will act as a server on a small to medium-sized network?	Windows 2000 Server
Which operating system should I use if my machine will act as a server on a medium to large, scalable network?	Windows 2000 Advanced Server
Which operating system should I use if my machine will act as a server to over 10,000 simultaneous users?	Windows 2000 Datacenter Server

New Features in the Windows 2000 Platform

This section describes some of the new features common to all four operating systems, and later sections in this chapter describe the differentiating characteristics and capabilities of each.

Plug and Play

Plug and Play (PnP) allows the operating system to automatically load device drivers and dynamically assign system resources (IRQs, I/O addresses) to computer components and peripherals. Plug and Play was first introduced in Windows 95 through the use of the Configuration Manager and Resource Arbitrator, but was never available in the Windows NT platform. Windows 2000 moves away from this older technology with its use of Kernel-mode and User-mode PnP architecture.

- **Kernel mode** The Kernel-mode Manager is responsible for assigning resources, providing device drivers, and controlling I/O communications and Power Management.
- **User mode** The User-mode Manager is responsible for providing interfaces with PnP components such as Setup and Control Panel windows.

on the job

Microsoft plans to use code signing for third-party device drivers not included in Windows 2000 Plug and Play library. Device drivers that have been tested and approved by Microsoft will be given an electronic signature. Windows 2000 will recognize signed devices, and can be configured to give a warning, or completely block the installation of unsigned devices.

Power Management

Windows 2000 has enhanced power management, due to the use of Advanced Configuration and Power Interface (ACPI) technology. ACPI combines PnP capability with Power Management, and places these functions under complete control of the operating system. This is an improvement over Windows 95, which treated PnP and Power Management as separate functions that relied on their own separate BIOS interfaces to work.

heads ①P *Advanced Configuration and Power Interface (ACPI) combines PnP and Power Management and places them under complete control of the OS.*

Hardware Support

Windows 2000 is breaking the NT mold with its support for hardware such as Accelerated Graphics Ports (AGP), Digital Versatile Disks (DVD), FireWire, Universal Serial Bus (USB), and multiple monitors. In addition, Windows 2000 uses a new driver technology called Windows Driver Model (WDM). This model is compatible with that used in Windows NT, but will not support the VxD (virtual device) driver model used in Windows 9*x*, so many older 16-bit drivers will not run on Windows 2000 at all.

heads ①P *Windows 2000 uses a new driver technology called WDM. Windows 2000 does not support the Windows 9x VxD driver model.*

on the ①ob *Recall that Windows NT 4.0 drivers are supported by Windows 2000. However, drivers also require an associated .inf file for installing the driver and supplying the operating system with information about the device. The Windows NT 4.0 .inf file format is not supported by Windows 2000, although the actual drivers are. This means you may have to update .inf files in order to get some devices working.*

File Systems

Windows 2000 improves on the NTFS 4.0 file system of Windows NT with a new technology: NTFS 5.0. The version 5 improvements include

- **Sparse File Support** Allocates the minimum required hard disk space necessary for very large files. A sparse file is one that contains a large number of null or 0 values, such as a large database. Only parts of the file with non-null values are saved to disk, thus reducing the size needed to store them.

- **Distributed Link Tracking** Preserves and updates shortcuts when files are moved or renamed by the user.

■ **Encrypted File System (EFS) volume support** All data stored on an EFS drive is encrypted, and user access permissions are required for all read and write activities.

Windows 2000 also provides support for the FAT16, FAT32, and NTFS 4.0 file systems. Users have the option of converting FAT16 and FAT32 file systems to NTFS 5.0 using a conversion utility similar to that seen in NT 4.0.

exam
ⓦatch

Windows 2000 supports the FAT16, FAT32, and NTFS 4.0 file systems, in addition to its new NTFS 5.0 file system.

Intellimirror

Intellimirror is a new technology that provides more availability and security to users' data, applications, and settings, and allows for roaming access. Here's how it works: A *mirrored* copy of a user's work is always kept on both the workstation and the server. As the user works, the local copy of his or her files is edited, and the server copy is updated using a write-through cache. This mirrored copy on the server also provides a place for users to store reliable backups of their files

Because there is a mirrored copy on the workstation, users can access their files and settings, even if the network is down or the server is unavailable. The mirrored copy on the server allows users to retrieve their information and settings from any workstation on the network (roaming access).

Kerberos Security System

This new security technology is designed to speed up network processes by integrating security and rights across network domains. It also eliminates the need for workstations to repeatedly authenticate themselves at every domain they access (a *domain* is a group of objects on a network that share the same security rights). Kerberos security also makes it easier to maneuver around networks using multiple platforms such as UNIX or NetWare. This is because Kerberos requires a single authentication for the entire network instead of one for each platform.

When a workstation logs on to the network, it authenticates itself with the Key Distribution Center (KDC) located on the server. The KDC provides the workstation with a Ticket Granting Ticket (TGT). This indicates to other resources on the network that the workstation has been authenticated and that it should be granted access to certain resources. When the workstation needs to access a network resource, it presents its TGT to the appropriate Domain controller and requests a Service Ticket for the specific resource it is trying to access. The workstation then presents its Service Ticket to the appropriate resource, and is allowed access to it. The workstation will then hold onto the Service Ticket for future access within the same session.

To illustrate this concept, imagine that a workstation on the CLOSE domain needs access to a printer on the FAR domain. When the workstation first joins the network, the CLOSE KDC server verifies the password, and gives that workstation an all-purpose ticket (the TGT) that tells the rest of the network, "It's okay, this guy checks out." Before the workstation can send a print job to the FAR printer, it hands its TGT to the controller of the FAR domain and states its purpose there (to use the printer). The FAR domain controller gives the workstation a Service Ticket (in this case, for the printer). The workstation presents the printer with the Service Ticket, and is allowed to proceed with its print job.

HEADSTART OBJECTIVE 1.03

Windows 2000 Professional

The Windows 2000 Professional Operating System is the workstation model in the Windows 2000 platform, and it is designed to accommodate users upgrading from both the NT 4.0 and Windows 9x platforms. It is being marketed by Microsoft as the easiest-to-use Windows yet, and is designed for inexperienced users.

Windows 2000 Professional Enhancements

Professional includes a number of enhancements to make end users less dependent on administrators. Improvements include an easy-to-use Setup program, improved Help and Wizards, and an Active Desktop designed to conform to the way the user accesses desktop features.

Professional in a Stand-Alone Configuration

Stand-Alone users (those upgrading from Windows 9*x*) will probably notice some differences in Windows 2000 Professional, but these are mostly cosmetic. See the "What's New" sidebar for more details about the 2000 Professional desktop and user enhancements.

Professional in a Network Configuration

Workstation users will also notice the cosmetic changes, but the real differences lie in the networking capabilities of the new OS. Windows 2000 Professional shares many core architectures with its predecessor, Windows NT workstation 4.0, such as the registry database, file system architecture, security architecture, system kernel architecture, and device driver model. However, Windows 2000 Professional improves upon many of these core features to provide an overall enhanced operating system. Some of the improvements and new features in Windows 2000 Professional are described here.

When installed on a networked computer, Windows 2000 Professional will automatically seek out a DHCP (Dynamic Host Configuration Protocol) Server. If a DHCP server is not available, Professional will broadcast itself to the network so that other Windows 2000 Professional computers can find and communicate with it. New Windows 2000 Professional computers added to the network will automatically join the in-place workgroup.

Windows 2000 Professional also includes a more powerful Find feature for locating files, folders, people, and hardware resources on the network. The new Active Directory technology (described later in the chapter) allows users to search for hardware based on its characteristics. For example, a workstation with Windows 2000 Professional is able to search the network for printers with specific capabilities (e.g., color, paper size, or resolution).

Windows 2000 Professional can take advantage of the Intellimirror technology provided by network servers. Users on busy networks will notice considerable speed improvements when working with network documents because Intellimirror uses a write-through cache to save users' files on the server. This means that files are edited locally on the workstation, and the server copy of the file is updated only occasionally. Fewer writes to the server means less network traffic, which leads to faster network access.

Another feature that Intellimirror provides to workstations is on-demand application installation. Because users can have roaming profiles, network traffic increases as users' preferences, files, and applications are downloaded to a new workstation every time the user moves. Intellimirror is able to provide application shortcuts to the user, but installations are initiated only when the user invokes that application, not automatically at login time.

Other features of Windows 2000 Professional are that it is able to support up to two CPUs in a single machine, and up to 4GB of memory. It is able to take advantage of server-provided Active Directory (described later in the chapter) and Kerberos security features.

ACCELERATING TO WINDOWS 2000

Sure, But How Does It Look?

Recall that one goal of Windows 2000 is to improve ease of use. In keeping with this strategy, Microsoft conducted thousands of hours of usability testing procedures, designed to determine the way in which desktop features are accessed by the average computer user (nonpower users in most cases). The resulting design of the Windows 2000 desktop is shown in Figure 1-1. Note its similarity to the Windows 9x and NT desktops.

Some ease-of-use features incorporated into the Windows 2000 desktop are described here:

- **Personalized menus**   Because Start menus can become cluttered, Windows 2000 continually monitors applications that are used frequently and displays them in the Start menu. Each menu and submenu includes a double-arrow icon. When the mouse pointer is held over the double arrow, less frequently used applications are displayed.

- **AutoComplete**   Helps with the entry of long Internet and network locations by automatically completing entries with previously used ones. For example, if a user commonly visits the Web site www.syngress.com, he or she only needs to type **www.sy**, and AutoComplete will automatically generate the rest of the URL. The user can then decide to accept the completed name or continue typing.

- **Balloon Help**   This is a variation on ToolTips from previous versions of Windows that offers more extensive help on selected items. Instead of one- or two-word names of a screen feature, Balloon Help offers descriptions of the selected feature, and the options that the user can perform with it.

- **Helpful error messages**   Most error messages provide the user with helpful advice on what action to take to remove the error condition.

FIGURE I-I   The Windows 2000 desktop looks similar to the desktop in Windows NT 4.0 and
Windows 95/98

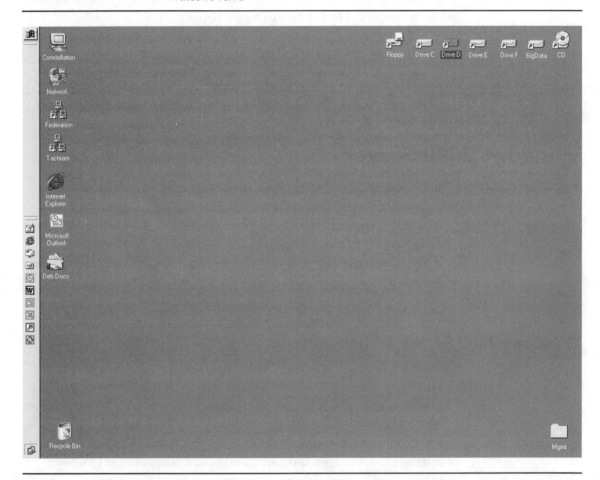

Windows 2000 Professional and NT Workstation 4.0

Although Windows 2000 Professional introduces many new technologies,
keep in mind that it is essentially an improved version of Windows NT
Workstation 4.0. Because of this, migrating to Professional from Workstation
4.0 is easier than from any other Windows operating system. Most device
drivers and applications that run on Windows NT Workstation 4.0 will run
on Windows 2000 Professional. This is because the same Executive service

structure used in Windows NT is supported by the Windows 2000 platform. In addition, Windows 2000 Professional supports system policy and security systems employed by NT Workstation 4.0.

Windows 2000 Server

The Windows 2000 Server OS is designed to provide network security and resources to workgroups. It provides file and print services, as well as application, communication, and Web services. Microsoft expects Windows 2000 Server to be the most popular Server OS in the Windows 2000 platform, as it provides services designed to support small to medium-sized businesses.

Windows 2000 Server Enhancements

Microsoft designed Windows 2000 Server with enhanced reliability and availability in mind. The reliability and availability of a server is a measure of how consistently it can perform its intended functions, and how easily it can be accessed for its resources. To improve on these features, Microsoft analyzed the causes and results of server failures in the NT 4.0 platform, and designed Windows 2000 Server to avoid these pitfalls, or to recover from them, all the while causing little or no network interruption. With these goals in mind, Microsoft added and enhanced many features in the Windows 2000 Server OS, some of which are described next.

Rebooting

One new feature of Windows 2000 is fewer reboots. Network administrators can configure server network addresses, install or remove external PnP devices, and make a host of other changes to the server without having to interrupt the availability of the system with a reboot.

Crashes

Windows 2000 Server is also designed to experience fewer crashes, due to enhanced safety features such as Kernel-mode Write Protection. When kernel-mode applications are loaded into memory, they can sometimes overwrite or corrupt each other's information. The Windows 2000 Memory Manager is designed to protect kernel-level information and device drivers by marking it as write-protected.

To aid in preventing crashes, Microsoft has also included enhanced System File Protection in Windows 2000 Server. Sometimes upon installation, new applications can change the contents of shared files (such as .DLL files) to suit their needs. This can render these shared files unreadable to other applications that rely on them to operate. System File Protection prevents applications from overwriting shared files upon installation, thus preserving their integrity for other programs.

Server Storage Space

Windows 2000 Server also includes enhancements for managing and allocating storage space. Administrators can use Disk Quotas to limit the amount of space that each user can access on the server's hard disk. Another new feature is the Remote Storage Server (RSS), which constantly monitors the amount of storage space on the server's hard disk. When this space dips below the specified level, the RSS removes from the hard drive any data that has also been saved to a remote location.

COM+ Component Services

The Component Object Model (COM) technology that was first available in Windows NT Server 4.0 has been enhanced and modified in Windows 2000 Server. COM+ component services allow applications to access objects across a network, much the way that OLE technology allows applications to access objects from other applications within a computer.

Repair Features

Windows 2000 Server is designed to help administrators fix operating system errors before they lead to system shutdown. Previous versions of Windows (NT Server 4.0, specifically) allowed users to end whole tasks or individual processes using the Task Manager feature. Ending an entire task is usually quite safe, but when a single process is ended, other processes that it has spawned can continue to run. A new feature of Windows 2000 Server is its ability to end all processes related to the one being terminated by the administrator. This utility is called Kill Process Tree.

Another enhanced repair feature is the Windows 2000 Server Recovery Console. This text-based utility can be used to diagnose and resolve boot-up problems with the OS.

Another feature of Windows 2000 Server is that it can support up to 4GB of memory and four CPUs. It is also able to provide Active Directory, Kerberos authentication security, and Intellimirror services to workstations on the network.

Terminal Server

Windows 2000 Server includes the option to run as a Terminal Server, designed to provide resources for "thin clients" on a network. Terminal service client computers contain only the minimum software necessary for making a network connection and providing the Windows interface. All client preferences, screen customizations, files, and applications are processed and provided by the terminal server.

Once a terminal service client has established a connection to the terminal server, every command made at the client computer is processed remotely, by the server. Using Windows 2000 terminal services allows for tight security and control of resources and applications on a network, and it means that all clients have access to the same software. When software needs to be upgraded, it needs to be changed only on the terminal server, rather than at each workstation.

Windows 2000 Server and NT Server 4.0

Windows 2000 Server is based on the registry, security, and architecture technology used in Windows NT Server 4.0. While improving on many of these features, Windows 2000 Server remains compatible with NT Server 4.0, and provides an easy upgrade transition.

HEADSTART OBJECTIVE 1.05

Windows 2000 Advanced Server

As stated earlier, Windows 2000 Advanced Server is built on the technology formerly used in Windows NT Server 4.0, Enterprise Edition. Advanced Server is a more powerful operating system than Windows 2000 Server, and is designed to provide the high availability and scalability required by large networks.

Windows 2000 Advanced Server Enhancements

One key feature of Windows 2000 Advanced Server is that it can support up to eight CPUs (8-way SMP) and 64GB of memory. Windows 2000 Advanced Server also includes all of the features of Windows 2000 Server, plus several features that allow it to maintain an enterprise network.

Server Clustering

Perhaps the most powerful feature of Windows 2000 Advanced Server is its enhanced *clustering* infrastructure. Clustering involves consolidating the functions of multiple servers so that they behave as a solitary unit. On a network with server clustering, there is a higher availability of resources, because the servers can each contribute objects just as easily as any other server.

Windows 2000 Advanced Server clustering also provides *load balancing* among the servers. Because clustered servers behave as a single unit, client requests can be divided equally among the servers within the cluster.

Finally, server clustering provides *fail-over protection* in the event of a server failure. That is, when a server in a cluster goes offline, or is otherwise unavailable to the network, other servers in the cluster take over the responsibilities of that server until it is functional.

Clustering is available in Windows NT Server 4.0, Enterprise Edition, using a technology called Windows NT Load Balancing Service (WLBS).

Windows 2000 Advanced Server improves on clustering technology with the COM+ clustering services. Recall that COM+ also provides object sharing across the network using COM+ component services.

heads !up

COM+ allows for component sharing and server clustering services.

Windows 2000 Advanced Server and Windows NT Server 4.0, Enterprise Edition

Because Advanced Server is an upgrade version of NT Server 4.0, Enterprise, it is expected to be employed in the same types of networks—medium- to large-sized networks that require fault tolerance, load balancing, and high availability.

Enterprise will support up to 8-way SMP, and although the 4-way SMP found in Advanced Server seems like a downgrade, Microsoft states that users upgrading from Enterprise will retain the ability to support up to eight CPUs. The 4-CPU restriction is limited to those performing a clean install of Advanced Server.

HEADSTART OBJECTIVE 1.06

Windows 2000 Datacenter Server

Windows 2000 Datacenter Server is the high-end operating system in the Windows 2000 platform. Microsoft markets it as the most powerful and functional server they have ever offered. It is designed for large-scale enterprise networks that will host large ISPs, very large databases, and perform large-scale engineering simulations, to name a few. Windows 2000 Datacenter Server can support 10,000 users at once.

Windows 2000 Datacenter Server includes all of the features of Windows 2000 Server and Advanced Server, and through enhanced clustering technology is able to focus on projects too large to be handled by Advanced Server. Datacenter Server supports 64GB memory access and up to 16–32-way SMP! Essentially, any off-the-shelf Windows 2000 Datacenter Server will support up to 16 processors, while a Datacenter Server with a customized HAL from the OEM will support up to 32 processors.

Windows 2000 Datacenter Server and Windows NT

Windows 2000 Datacenter Server is a "new" operating system; that is, it has no predecessor in the Windows NT platform. The Windows 2000 Datacenter Server market is expected to be comprised of those administrators who previously used Windows NT Server 4.0, Enterprise, but found it too restrictive in large-scale operations.

HEADSTART OBJECTIVE 1.07

Brief Overview of the Active Directory

Active Directory is probably the most talked-about new feature of the Windows 2000 platform. It is a directory service that is designed to help administrators organize network resources and allow users easy access to those resources, while providing tight security within the network. To better understand Active Directory and how it works, let's first look at the role of a directory service on a network.

The Role of a Directory Service

When a network is created, users and administrators need to be able to find all of the available resources on the network, including things such as printers, files, applications, and other people. A directory service is a database that contains information about who and what is on the network, their attributes, and what their relationship is to each other.

When a user needs a network resource, the directory service is used to locate and access it. Directory services also allow administrators to create security within the system and manage the way network resources are used by particular individuals or groups. Once configured by the administrator, the directory service controls which resources can be accessed by users, and under which conditions, depending on the users' individual or group security authorizations.

As more resources are added to a network, the directory service becomes more important for managing the users on them. A good directory service is structured to provide information about resources in multidomain networks, without making the user remember exact resource names, paths, and locations.

Active Directory Services

The Windows 2000 Active Directory provides the features described next.

A Logical Organization of Network Objects

Resources (people, equipment, files, or applications) on an Active Directory network are all viewed as *objects*. Objects on the network all have certain attributes, and can be grouped into *containers* according to the similarities of these attributes, or their relationships to each other. For example, all people, resources, and files belonging to the Sales department of a company can be grouped together in the SALES container. All objects in the Advertising department belong to the ADVERTISING container. All of these containers may actually be sublevels of a larger MARKETING container or domain. This organization provides users and administrators with a logical and intuitive view of who and what is on each domain in a network. Figure 1-2 demonstrates the concept of using containers on a network.

Recall that Intellimirror registers objects, as well as their attributes. When an object joins an Active Directory network, it automatically registers its attributes with its domain controller. This provides users with the ability to locate objects based on their characteristics; for example, all of the color printers on the first floor.

FIGURE 1-2   Objects within a domain are easier to find when they are organized into containers

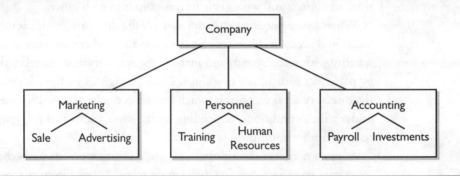

Networkwide Catalog of Objects

The Active Directory is a single networkwide catalog of all objects in all domains. Each domain on the network receives its own copy of the portions of the AD catalog that it needs to use. That is, each domain only receives information about the objects to which it has access. This is called *multimaster replication*. All domain replications of the global directory are synchronized, so when new objects are added or configured in the global catalog, each domain directory is automatically updated. This means that new or changed objects need to be configured only once for the entire network, not for each domain that references that object.

Suppose, for example, that in our previous example, users in the ACCOUNTING domain have access to users in the PERSONNEL domain, but not vice versa. Both the ACCOUNTING and PERSONNEL domains have access to the MARKETING domain. Figure 1-3 shows how multimaster replication works in this relationship.

| FIGURE 1-3 | Multimaster replication places a copy of relevant information in each domain's copy of the directory |

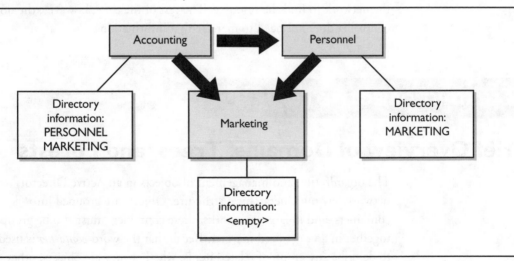

If a new color printer is added to the MARKETING container in the example shown, the directories in the ACCOUNTING and PERSONNEL containers are automatically updated. If a user's configuration is changed in the PERSONNEL container, all directories that reference the PERSONNEL container are updated; in this case, the ACCOUNTING directory only. The result is that network administrators need to configure objects only once for the entire network, not for each domain.

Scalability

Active Directory makes networks highly scalable—over 1 million users in a single domain! Even more users can be added when the domain is part of a tree or forest in the network (trees, forests, and domains are described in the next section).

Active Directory allows for these large networks using the multimaster replication method described earlier. Each domain gets a copy of the information about the objects that pertain to that domain, and the objects that users in that domain use the most. This reduces the size of the directory database within each domain.

Also in each domain's directory is information about how to find other less-often used directories on the network. When the time comes to access an infrequently used resource, the domain controller knows where to go on the network to find the resource. The rest of the time, however, the domain controller does not need to manage that information.

HEADSTART OBJECTIVE 1.08

Brief Overview of Domains, Trees, and Forests

The organization and management of objects in an Active Directory network rely on a hierarchical structure. Objects are grouped into containers, and in larger networks, these containers must also be grouped together in an organized manner. Recall that the word *container* is used to describe any group of related items, whether they are objects, other containers, domains, or an entire network. (Refer to back to Figure 1-2.) Each user and printer is an object. SALES and ADVERTISING are both containers that hold objects, and belong to a larger MARKETING container. The entire MARKETING container is part of a larger COMPANY container.

Domains

A network domain is a group of objects on a network that belong together logically and share common security rights. Each domain on a Windows 2000 network is actually a partition of the Active Directory. (Refer again to Figure 1-2.) All objects in the MARKETING domain share the same security rights, which are different from the security rights of the ACCOUNTING or PERSONNEL domains. Organizing a network into domains prevents administrators from having to set network access rights to every individual object on the network. As you have seen, one domain can contain smaller domains. In our example, COMPANY is a *parent domain*, and MARKETING, ACCOUNTING, and PERSONNEL are *child domains*.

Trees

A Windows 2000 network can be further organized into trees. A domain *tree* is a hierarchical collection of the child and parent domains within a network. Domains in a tree share a common configuration and must have contiguous domain names. Our previous example of domains can be used to illustrate a domain tree (see Figure 1-4). As you can see, the top level of the network is West Computers and has the domain name westcomp.com. The three branches of the tree also contain the root domain name westcomp.com.

The domains in a domain tree share *transitive trust* relationships, based on the Kerberos security model. This means that all domains within a tree automatically and implicitly trust other domains in that tree. This greatly reduces the number of trust relationships that must be configured by administrators of the network. However, administrators can, when necessary, disable transitive trust within a domain tree, and instead create one-way trust relationships.

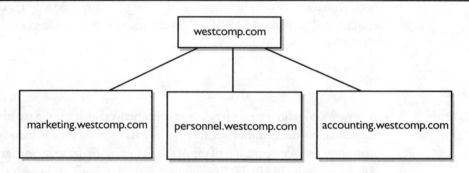

FIGURE 1-4 The domains in a domain tree have contiguous namespaces. In this example, each child domain shares the root of the parent domain name, westcomp.com

Forests

As described previously, all domains in a tree share a contiguous namespace and automatically trust each other. However, a domain tree itself may belong to a larger network or have access to the resources of an altogether unrelated network. Figure 1-5 shows that the PERSONNEL department of the West Computers company has access to the PERSONNEL department of the North Computers company. The configuration and namespace of the two domain trees are different, and they are separate from each other except in their ability to access one or more resources on each other's networks.

Domain trees in a domain forest do not share common security rights, but can access one another through the global catalog. Like domains in a tree, the trees in a forest also have a transitive trust relationship. This means that all domains in a tree share the same trust relationship with domains from another tree in the forest. For example, suppose that accounting.westcomp.com has a trust relationship with accounting.northcomp.com. All other westcomp domains will automatically trust accounting.northcomp.com. Remember though, that specific one-way trust relationships can be created when necessary.

Because the domains in different trees of a forest can access each other's resources, they share a portion of the Active Directory. This allows for massive scalability because changes to one domain or tree can be automatically updated across all domains in a forest. Keep in mind that Figure 1-5 represents a very small network. Large networks can be comprised of hundreds or thousands of forests, each having many trees within them!

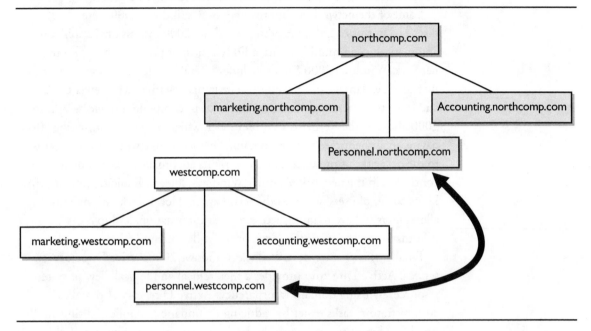

FIGURE 1-5 A domain forest consists of domain trees that have access to each other, but do not share intrinsic trust relationships and do not share domain names

CHAPTER SUMMARY

This chapter provided a brief overview of the new Windows 2000 platform and the four operating systems within it. Windows 2000 Professional is used for workstations in a network, and Windows 2000 Server provides network services and security. Windows 2000 Advanced Server and Windows 2000 Datacenter Server are both designed for larger enterprise networks that use server clustering. Datacenter Server is able to support up to 10,000 users at a time.

Some of the new features in the Windows 2000 platform include an active desktop and less-cluttered Start Menu. Windows 2000 also has enhanced Plug and Play (PnP) capabilities and power management, which use Microsoft's new Advanced Configuration and Power Interface (ACPI) technology. Other features include enhanced hardware support and a more versatile file system. NTFS 5.0 enables features such as Sparse File Support,

Distributed Link Tracking, and Encrypted File System support. Windows 2000 is also able to support FAT16, FAT32, and NTFS 4.0.

Some of the networking improvements of Windows 2000 were discussed in this chapter, including Windows 2000 Professional's ability to automatically communicate with a DHCP host or peer computers on the network. Windows 2000 Server includes several new features that provide increased availability and reliability. The items described were fewer crashes and reboots, better repair features, and COM+ component services. Windows 2000 also uses the Kerberos security model, which prevents workstations from having to authenticate at each domain. That is, when a workstation logs on to the network, its presence and access rights are broadcast to all domain controllers in the network. Another Windows 2000 technology, Intellimirror, keeps copies of users' work on the server and the local workstation. This allows users to have roaming access to their information, and to access that information in the event the server or network is unavailable.

Finally, this chapter described the Windows 2000 Active Directory service. Active Directory provides a hierarchical and logical view of system resources by using domain transparency. Active Directory also makes administrators' tasks easier by reducing redundancy in policy editing and by providing better security with the Kerberos system. The division of objects into domains, forests, and trees allows for an organized view of the network, enables transitive trust, and can simplify the task of setting security rights.

 TWO-MINUTE DRILL

❑ Plug and Play (PnP) allows the operating system to automatically load device drivers and dynamically assign system resources (IRQs, I/O addresses) to computer components and peripherals.

❑ Windows 2000 has enhanced power management, due to the use of Advanced Configuration and Power Interface (ACPI) technology. ACPI combines PnP capability with Power Management, and places these functions under complete control of the operating system.

❑ Windows 2000 is breaking the NT mold with its support for hardware such as Accelerated Graphics Ports (AGP), Digital Versatile Disks (DVD), FireWire, Universal Serial Bus (USB), and multiple monitors.

❏ Windows 2000 improves on the NTFS 4.0 file system of Windows NT with a new technology, NTFS 5.0.

❏ Windows 2000 also provides support for the FAT16, FAT32, and NTFS 4.0 file systems.

❏ Intellimirror is a new technology that provides more availability and security to users' data, applications, and settings, and allows for roaming access.

❏ The Windows 2000 Professional Operating System is the workstation model in the Windows 2000 platform, and it is designed to accommodate users upgrading from both the NT 4.0 and Windows 9x platforms.

❏ The Windows 2000 Server OS is designed to provide network security and resources to workgroups. It provides file and print services, as well as application, communication, and Web services.

❏ Windows 2000 Server is also designed to experience fewer crashes, due to enhanced safety features such as Kernel-mode Write Protection.

❏ The Component Object Model (COM) technology that was first available in Windows NT Server 4.0 has been enhanced and modified in Windows 2000 Server.

❏ Advanced Server is a more powerful operating system than Windows 2000 Server, and is designed to provide the high availability and scalability required by large networks.

❏ One key feature of Windows 2000 Advanced Server is that it can support up to eight CPUs (8-way SMP) and 64GB of memory.

❏ Windows 2000 Datacenter Server is the high-end operating system in the Windows 2000 platform.

SELF TEST

The following questions help you measure your understanding of the material presented in this chapter. Read all of the choices carefully, as there may be more than one correct answer. Choose all correct answers for each question.

1. Which platform is Windows 2000 architecture most similar to?

   A. Windows 3.x

   B. Windows NT

   C. Windows 95

   D. Windows 98

2. Which operating system is the Windows 2000 version of Windows NT Server 4.0, Enterprise Edition?

   A. Windows 2000 Professional

   B. Windows 2000 Server

   C. Windows 2000 Advanced Server

   D. Windows 2000 Datacenter Server

3. Which operating system in the Windows 2000 platform can support up to 10,000 simultaneous users?

   A. Windows 2000 Professional

   B. Windows 2000 Server

   C. Windows 2000 Advanced Server

   D. Windows 2000 Datacenter Server

4. Which operating systems include Plug and Play (PnP) support? (Choose all that apply.)

   A. Windows 95

   B. Windows 98

   C. Windows NT 4.0

   D. Windows 2000

5. Which component in Windows 2000 is responsible for assigning PnP resources to devices?

   A. Resource Arbitrator

   B. Configuration Manager

   C. Kernel-mode Manager

   D. User-mode Manager

6. What is the name of the Windows 2000 technology that places PnP capability and Power Management under complete control of the operating system?

   A. Advanced Configuration and Power Interface

   B. Advanced Power Management

   C. Windows Driver Model

   D. Code Signing

7. Which of the following file systems does Windows 2000 support? (Choose all that apply.)

   A. FAT16

   B. FAT32

   C. NTFS 4.0

   D. NTFS 5.0

8. What is the name of the new Windows 2000 technology that provides roaming access capabilities and allows users to access their files, even when the network or server is down?

   A. Kerberos

   B. Intellimirror

   C. Distributed Link Tracking

   D. None of the above

9. How much memory can be addressed by the Windows 2000 Professional operating system?

   A. 64MB

   B. 2GB

   C. 4GB

   D. 64GB

10. Which *new* Windows 2000 Server feature allows administrators to end all processes related to a process that is causing a problem?

    A. Task Manager

    B. Process Manager

    C. Kill Process Tree

    D. Server Recovery Console

11. Which of the following are improvements in the Windows 2000 Advanced Server operating system? (Choose all that apply.)

    A. Enhanced Server clustering

    B. COM+ services

    C. Improved fail-over protection

    D. Increased SMP support

12. Active Directory focuses on objects in terms of their

    A. Containers

    B. Namespace

    C. Attributes

    D. Forests

13. Which Active Directory feature provides each domain controller with portions of the directory that pertain only to that domain's accessible objects?

    A. Transitive trust

    B. Redundant replication

    C. Mirroring

    D. Multimaster replication

14. A single hierarchical path of domains within a network is called a

    A. Container

    B. Tree

    C. Forest

    D. Domain path

15. What is the name given to domain trees that can access each other's resources, but do not share domain names or security configurations?

    A. Container

    B. Tree

    C. Forest

    D. Parent Domain Path

MICROSOFT CERTIFIED SYSTEMS ENGINEER

2

Installing Microsoft Windows 2000

I nstalling Windows 2000 is much easier than installing Windows NT 4.0. Microsoft improved much of the operating system as well as the setup program, which removes a lot of the administration overhead associated with installing Windows NT. These features incorporate those found in Windows 98 as well as new ones only found in Windows 2000, which eases the lives of administrators everywhere. A few of these enhancements are the Plug and Play (PnP) capabilities of Windows 2000 and the ability to upgrade from all versions of Windows (3.x, 9x, NT). This chapter discusses the differences and improvements of Windows 2000 compared to Windows NT.

HEADSTART OBJECTIVE 2.01

Preparing for Installation

Before you start the Windows 2000 installation, you must do some preparation. A few things you should think about beforehand are the hardware requirements, compatibility issues, partitioning, the networking issues, the type of file system to install Windows 2000, and multiboot configurations.

Hardware Requirements

Before you prepare to install Windows 2000, make sure your computer fulfills the minimum hardware requirements (see Table 2-1).

When your PC fulfills the Windows 2000 hardware requirements, you must also verify that your hardware is on the Windows 2000 Hardware Compatibility List (HCL). An updated version of the HCL exists at the Microsoft Web site. Please note that if your hardware is not in the HCL, you have to contract the hardware manufacturer to determine if the component is Windows 2000 ready. The HCL can be found in the SUPPORT directory on the Windows 2000 CD-ROM or at http://www.microsoft.com/hcl/default.asp.

TABLE 2-1		Windows 2000 Hardware Requirements

Components	Windows 2000 Server Requirements	Windows 2000 Professional Requirements
CPU	Pentium 166+ for an Intel-based system or any Digital Alpha	Pentium for an Intel-based system or any Digital Alpha
Memory	64MB+ for Intel-based systems, 96MB+ for Alpha	32MB+ for Intel-based systems, 48MB+ for Alpha
Hard drive space	685MB+ on the system partition for Intel-based systems, 367MB+ for Alpha	500MB+ on the system partition for Intel-based systems, 351MB+ for Alpha
Networking	One or more network interface cards	One network interface card
Display	VGA graphics adapter and monitor	VGA graphics adapter and monitor
CD-ROM	12X speed+ for normal install, not needed for network install	12X speed+ for normal install, not needed for network install
Accessories	Keyboard and pointing device, such as a trackpad or mouse	Keyboard and pointing device, such as a trackpad or mouse

Network Setup

Windows 2000, like its predecessor, revolves around networking. A crucial part of the Windows 2000 setup is setting up the networking elements such as the domain/workgroup membership and client licensing.

Domain Versus Workgroup Membership

During installation, you need to specify the type of network security group to join: a workgroup or a domain. A workgroup is used mainly for peer-to-peer networking. If you are adding a Windows 2000 Server, it is called a *stand-alone* server. If this is a new workgroup, you need to specify the name of the workgroup. If you want a computer to join an existing workgroup, you assign the name of an existing workgroup. You can also add a computer to a new or existing domain. If you are adding a Windows 2000 Server, you can add it as a *member server* or as a domain controller. A member server is a member that does not have a copy of the Active Directory. When joining a domain, you must specify the domain name and a computer account or an administrator login/password with privileges to create an account.

heads
①P

You can decide to join a domain during or after the Windows 2000 installation as shown in Figure 2-1.

Licensing

In addition to needing a license for each operating system installed, you need to license each client connection to the server.

CLIENT ACCESS LICENSE   When you are installing Windows 2000 Server, you are prompted for a Client Access License (CAL) mode. The CAL allows clients to access the Windows 2000's network services, shared folders, and printers. There are two types of CAL modes: Per Seat and Per Server.

heads
①P

Access to IIS, telnet, and FTP resources do not require client access licenses.

FIGURE 2-1

Changing workgroup membership

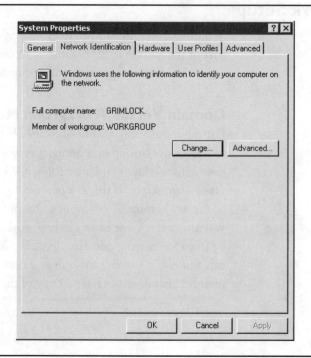

PER SEAT LICENSING   Per Seat Licensing requires one CAL for each client computer that is accessing Windows 2000 Server. This is the best type of licensing when clients need to access more than one server.

PER SERVER LICENSING   Per Server Licensing requires licenses for the maximum number of concurrent connections that is expected to access the Windows 2000 Server. This is the best type of licensing when there are only a few Windows 2000 servers, or for Internet/RAS computers where clients don't need to be licensed. Once the number of concurrent connections reaches the maximum set, Windows 2000 will reject further access attempts until the number of concurrent connections goes down.

If you are unsure of the type of licensing to use, choose Per Server. When you choose Per Server, you can covert to Per Seat at any time. It is not possible to convert from Per Seat to Per Server. Remember, Per Server licensing is sensitive to the number of concurrent connections.

Advanced Setup Options

Once you have evaluated the different setup options, it is time to consider the more advanced setup options, such as the type of file system to install Windows 2000 on and multiboot configuration.

Partitioning

Before you start the Windows 2000 setup, it's important that you decide whether Windows 2000 will exist on a new partition or on an existing partition. During the Windows 2000 setup, you can add, delete, and create new partitions. Keep in mind that when you delete an existing partition, all data on that partition will be lost. During the installation, you must create and size the partition in which Windows 2000 will be installed. Make sure the size of the partition meets the minimum requirements listed in Table 2-1. Also, be aware that you will need more space depending on the applications to be installed on that partition. You can install applications in another partition if you wish. Once Windows 2000 is installed, you can create and size the remaining unpartitioned space on the hard disk as shown in Figure 2-2.

FIGURE 2-2

Partition management with
Computer Management

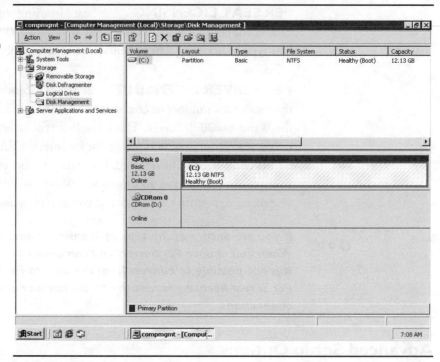

FAT Versus NTFS

When you are installing Windows 2000, you are prompted on which file system you want the partitioned formatted in. Windows 2000 supports three file systems: NT file system (NTFS5), File Allocation Table (FAT), and FAT32. NTFS5 includes features that were available in the previous version of the NTFS, as well as some new enhancements. The features are

- **File and Folder security** NTFS allows you to have different security levels set for files and folders.

- **Disk compression** NTFS can compress folders, subfolders, and files. This can save space, but it slows down access to the file since Windows 2000 must decompress and compress the files on the fly during use.

- **Disk quotas** NTFS can control the amount of disk usage allocated to a user on a volume basis. This is a new Windows 2000 feature.

- **Encryption** NTFS allows encryption to folders, subfolders, and files. This is a new Windows 2000 feature.

Windows 2000 includes compatibility with FAT and FAT32 to ensure compatibility with other operating systems, since Windows NT and Windows 2000 are the only operating systems able to read NTFS. Since FAT and FAT32 do not offer the same features as NTFS, use it only when you need to run a multiboot system with other operating systems. Setup will decide to format in FAT or FAT32 based on the size of the partition. If the partition is less than 2GB, setup will format the partition in FAT. If it is greater than 2GB, setup will format the partition in FAT32.

Multiboot Configurations

With the many operating systems available, many users have opted to have two or more on one system. When a system starts in a multiboot environment, the user is prompted for the operating system to be used in that session. Although Windows 2000 can upgrade from all versions of Windows, the user may still want to have the older version of Windows available as well as the new Windows 2000. Having more than one operating system is mostly seamless; however, there are some things you must aware of:

- When you install Windows 2000 in the same directory as Windows NT, you are upgrading to Windows 2000. When you install Windows 2000 in a different directory, you have access to both operating systems.

- To dual boot with MS-DOS or Windows 95, Windows 2000 must be installed last so the boot sector won't be overwritten. The drive must also be formatted in FAT or FAT32.

- You cannot install Windows 2000 in a non-NTFS compressed drive.

- All applications must be reinstalled for each operating system.

- Since Windows 2000 uses a newer version of NTFS, Windows NT's Chkdsk and Defrag won't work.

- With Windows NT Service Pack 4 and earlier, NT4 is able to read data on NTFS partitions, but it might have problems reading files encrypted in Windows 2000.

- You can't dual boot between Windows NT 3.51 and Windows 2000.

The following questions and answers will help you review the different file systems required for various dual-booting configurations.

QUESTIONS AND ANSWERS

What type of file system should I use if I am dual booting between MS-DOS and Windows 2000?	FAT is the obvious answer. MS-DOS does not run in any other type of file systems but those.
What type of file system should I use if I am dual booting between Windows 98 and Windows 2000?	FAT or FAT32 are the only file systems that you can use with Windows 98. FAT32 is a better choice if your partition is greater than 2GB.
What type of file system should I use if I am dual booting between Windows NT4 and Windows 2000?	FAT or NTFS. Both OS will work with FAT. Windows NT 4 won't work with FAT32. You should be concerned about the new NTFS 5, since some features in the new version of NTFS won't function correctly in version 4, such as file and folder encryption.
What types of file system should I use if I am dual booting between Windows 95 and Windows 2000?	FAT or FAT32 are the only file systems that you can use with Windows 95. FAT32 is only available on Windows 95 OSR2. FAT32 is a better choice if you are running OSR2.x and your partition is greater than 2GB.

HEADSTART OBJECTIVE 2.02

Installing Windows 2000 from a Compact Disc

Installing Windows 2000 from a compact disc is the most common method of installation. The setup consists of four stages: the setup program, the Setup Wizard, Windows networking components, and completing the setup.

Setup Program

This is the first stage of the Windows 2000 setup, when you either boot off the Setup Disk 1 or you start the installation from the CD-ROM. The steps are

1. A minimal version of Windows 2000 is loaded into memory and the setup program starts.

2. The computer restarts and the text-based part of the setup begins. You are prompted to accept the licensing agreement.

3. You are prompted to determine the partitioning configuration on which to install Windows 2000.

4. You are prompted to select the type of file system and then Setup will format the partition in the desired file system.

5. Setup copies the system files to your hard drive in the default C:\WINNT directory, and all configuration data are saved.

6. The computer restarts and the Windows 2000 Setup Wizard begins.

Setup Wizard

The Setup Wizard phase is the graphical aspect of the install. After you set security and the devices are configured and installed, the Windows 2000 Setup Wizard prompts you for the following:

■ **Regional Settings**   Languages, locale, and keyboard settings.

■ **Name and Organization**   Person and organization this copy of Windows 2000 is licensed to.

■ **Licensing Mode**   Per Server or Per Seat Licensing, as discussed earlier in the chapter.

■ **Computer Name**   The name of the computer. Limited to 63 characters and must be different from all the other names on the network.

■ **Password**   The password for the administrator account.

■ **Windows 2000 Optional Components**   Components such as Certificate Services, Internet Information Services, Message Queuing Services, Microsoft Indexing Service, Networking Options, Remote Installation Services, Terminal Services, and Transaction Server.

■ **Display Settings**   Size of desktop, number of colors, and refresh frequency.

■ **Time and Date**   Time zone, time, and date settings.

Once all the sections are completed, the Windows 2000 Setup Wizard installs the Windows networking components.

Windows Networking Components

The following describes what occurs when the Windows 2000 Setup Wizard installs the Windows networking components.

1. The first step is the detection and configuration of your network interface card.

2. Once the network card is configured, you are prompted to select the networking components. The default installation includes the Client for Microsoft Networks, File and Print Sharing for Microsoft Networks, and TCP/IP.

3. After the components are chosen, you are prompted to join a workgroup or domain. If you join a domain, your computer must already have an account in the domain, or you must log on as an administrator.

4. After you join the workgroup or domain, you networking components will be installed.

Completing the Setup

Once the Windows Networking Components are installed, the final step in the setup process occurs. In this phase, the following events occur:

1. Files are copied.
2. Computer is configured.
3. Configuration settings are saved.
4. Temporary files are removed.
5. Computer is restarted.

EXERCISE 2-1

Installing Windows 2000

1. Create the boot disks. Insert a blank floppy disk into the 3.5-inch floppy drive, and the Windows 2000 CD-ROM into the CD-ROM drive. Run <cd-rom drive>:\bootdisk\makeboot a:. Follow the screen instructions.

2. Boot with the Windows 2000 Server Setup Disk 1.

3. When asked, insert Setup Disks 1, 2, and 3. ＆ 4

4. When the Welcome to Setup message appears, press ENTER, and place the Windows 2000 CD into the CD-ROM drive. Press ENTER.

5. Read the License Agreement. Accept the agreement by pressing F8.

6. Setup displays the Windows 2000 Setup screen and prompts you to specify the area of free space/partition in which to install Windows 2000. Delete all partitions. This deletes all data in the previous existing partitions. Select the C: Unpartitioned Space and type **C** to create a partition in that space. Press ENTER.

7. Select the partition and press ENTER when it states the new partition is unformatted.

8. You are prompted for the type of file system to format the partition in. Select NTFS. Press ENTER. Setup will format the partition in NTFS. After the format, Setup checks the volume for physical errors and then copies files to the partition. After all files are copied, Setup restarts the computer.

9. Take out the Windows 2000 CD-ROM and floppy disk. After the computer reboots, Setup starts again and prompts you to insert the Windows 2000 CD-ROM. Setup then copies additional files and reboots the computer.

10. After the computer reboots, the Welcome to the Windows 2000 Setup Wizard page will show. Click Next. Setup will then configure all folder and file permissions, detect the hardware devices, and install all the necessary drivers.

11. The next screen prompts you for your name and organization. After you have typed in the information, click Next.

12. The next screen prompts you for the Licensing mode. By default, Per Server is selected. Click Next.

13. The next screen asks for the computer name and the administrator password. The computer name will be based from the organization name you entered earlier. Change the computer name if you desire and type in the administrator password. Click Next.

14. Setup then displays the Windows 2000 Component page. The system components will be checked to show which components will be installed. You can change this after you install Windows 2000 in the Add/Remove Programs in the Control Panel. Click Next.

15. The next screen prompts you to select the display settings for your video card and monitor. You can change the default settings if you desire. Click Next.

16. The next screen prompts you for the Data and Time settings. Confirm the settings are correct, and click Next.

17. Setup then starts the Windows Network Components stage of the Windows 2000 setup. The default settings are set (DHCP). You can choose whether to join a workgroup or a domain, as well as the name. Click Next.

18. Remove the Windows CD-ROM and click Finish to continue the setup for Windows 2000. The computer will restart and start Windows 2000 for the first time.

19. When you see the login screen for the first time, press CTRL+ALT+DELETE.

20. In the Enter Password box, type **Administrator** and the password for your administrator account. Click OK.

21. Once Windows 2000 is logged on, it automatically detects all the necessary hardware and installs the necessary drivers. If the Found New Hardware Wizard appears, ensure that "Restart the Computer When I Click Finish" is not checked and click Finish.

Congratulations! Windows 2000 is fully installed.

Installing Windows 2000 Over a Network

Installing Windows 2000 is similar to installing it from a CD, except the location of the source files is different.

Preparations

First, you need to set up the distribution server. This can be any computer on the network that clients are able to access. Copy the contents of the i386 folder if it's an Intel-based network installation, or the Alpha folder if it's a Digital Alpha–based installation. Share the folder the installation files are in. Next, create a FAT 850MB+ partition on the target computer. Once the partition is set, install a network client on the client computer. If the client does not have an operating system, you need to have it boot from a disk that includes the network client, which enables it to connect to the distribution server.

Installation Process

The following steps describe the networking installation process:

1. Boot from the network client on the target computer. The process of creating a network client disk is described in the next chapter.

2. Connect to the shared folder on the distribution server.

3. Run winnt.exe. Setup starts and creates four boot disks, the Win_nt.~ls temporary folder on the target computer, and copies the installation files from the distribution folder to the Win_nt.~ls temporary folder.

4. Restart the target computer with the first setup boot disk.

5. Windows 2000 setup starts.

TABLE 2-2	Switch	Description
winnt.exe Switches	/a	Enables the accessibility option.
	/e	The command that is executed at the end of the GUI setup.
	/l:[:]inffile	The filename of the setup information file. Default is DOSNET.INF.
	/r	Option directory to be installed.
	/rx	Optional directory to be copied.
	/s[:]sourcepath	The full path of the source location of the Windows 2000 files.
	/t[:]tempdrive	The drive that contains the temporary setup files. If you do not use this switch, Setup will decide for you.
	/u	Requires the /s switch. Unattended operation.

Modifying Process

You can modify the network install process for Windows 2000 by changing how winnt.exe runs. Table 2-2 lists the available options for running Winnt.exe.

HEADSTART OBJECTIVE 2.04

Automating Installations Using the Windows 2000 Setup Manager Wizard

Windows 2000 is a huge upgrade, and it can be very costly for organizations to upgrade the operating systems on all existing computers. Windows 2000 minimizes the cost of doing mass migrations by automating the deployment process. One way of automating installation is through the Windows 2000 Setup Manager Wizard. The Setup Manager Wizard allows administrators to easily generate Answer files. Answer files are text files that allow an administrator to describe the installation requirements and answer questions that the setup program will prompt the user. The Setup Manager Wizard creates two files: an answer file called Unattend.txt, and a batch file that runs the setup program with the answer file as the command-line argument.

Answer Files

The answer file is a text file, usually called Unattend.txt, that answers questions the setup program asks. The following is an example of an answer file:

```
[Unattended]
Unattendmode = FullUnattended
OemPreinstall = NO
TargetPath = WINNT
Filesystem = LeaveAlone

[UserData]
FullName = "Derrick Woo"
OrgName = "Derrick Woo"
ComputerName = "GRIMLOCK"

[GuiUnattended]
TimeZone = "004"
AdminPassword =passwd
AutoLogon = Yes
AutoLogonCount = 1

[LicenseFilePrintData]
AutoMode = "PerServer"
AutoUsers = "5"

[GuiRunOnce]

[Display]
BitsPerPel = 8
XResolution = 800
YResolution = 600

VRefresh = 70

[Networking]
InstallDefaultComponents = YES

[Identification]
JoinWorkgroup = Workgroup
```

Distribution Folders

Along with the answer file, the Windows 2000 Setup Manager Wizard needs the Windows 2000 distribution files. There are different ways to distribute these files, the two main methods being on a shared folder on the network or a shared CD-ROM. With a shared folder, you can automate the process by having it automatically run as a part of a login script or by e-mailing instructions to users. With the network share, you can have many installations running at once, and it's less cumbersome than providing each user with a copy of the Windows 2000 CD. Another option is to provide each user with his or her own Windows 2000 CD, and e-mail or place the answer file in a bootable floppy. When you make your own customizable CD or when you make a network share, be sure to copy the i386 folder if you are running an x86 machine, or the Alpha folder if you are running a Digital Alpha.

Deployment

The Windows 2000 Setup Manager Wizard creates a batch file that runs Setup with the answer file as the command-line argument. The command line is

```
Winnt[32] /unattend:answerfile /s:source
[/syspart:targetdrive]
```

This is very different from the previous versions of NT. In Windows NT 4.0, you used winnt32.exe only with Windows NT. In other versions of DOS or Windows, you had to use winnt.exe. In Windows 2000, winnt.exe is only used in DOS and Win 3.x. Other versions of Windows use winnt32.exe. The /unattend switch passes the path of the answer file. The /s switch passes the path of the source files. The paths can be standard local computer paths or UNC paths. The /syspart switch copies temporary and boot files to a specified target drive and marks it active. This is used so the drive can be placed in another computer. If there is only one drive, Setup by default ensures that the drive with the boot and temporary files are marked active.

Automating Installations Using Disk Duplication

Another way to speed mass installations is with *disk image replication*. Disk image replication copies the contents of the entire partition onto an image and replicates it on another machine. This is one of the best ways to do mass installs because it's extremely powerful and comprehensive. With disk image replication, the contents of the entire hard partition are replicated. Unlike the other methods discussed earlier, disk duplication is the only way you can duplicate the entire computer. The operating system, all its options, service packs, applications, and files on the disk are put into the image. There is no need to install the service packs and applications, or copy separate files after the operating system is installed. Another reason to use disk duplication is its ease and speed. Once the disk image is created, all transfers of the image can be done via network or local CD-ROM. This is extremely quick and requires very little interaction with the user.

Disk duplication does have numerous downsides to it. Since the exact image of the hard disk is made, the hardware configurations must be very similar. Different hardware configurations can had adverse effects when the image has one piece of hardware configured a certain way, and set a different way in the target computer. Another downside to disk replication is that it duplicates user-specific settings on the source computer onto the target computer. The way to prevent this is to limit the user-specific settings, such as the e-mail address of the user.

System Preparation Tool

A tool that administrators can use to replicate their disks is called the System Preparation Tool. This is a new tool by Microsoft but it is not made available unless your organization has a volume licensing agreement. The free utility is available to the following types of customers:

- Enterprise Agreement
- Microsoft Open License Program (MOLP)
- Microsoft Select
- Microsoft Solution Providers

Before you use the System Preparation Tool, you must prepare the reference system. Install the operating system, service packs, necessary applications, and individual files. Once the reference system is configured, you are ready to run the System Preparation Tool. The tool has the following syntax:

```
Sysprep.exe [/quiet] [/nosidgen] [/pnp]
```

- **/quiet**   Runs sysprep in the silent mode where no messages are displayed.

- **/nosidgen**   Runs sysprep.exe without generating a SID. Normally, each computer must have an individual SID, or security identifier. Use this option only to make a clone of the computer as a backup or to allow the end user to customize the computer.

- **/pnp**   Forces Plug and Play to refresh when the computer reboots to redetect all the hardware devices in the computer.

- **/reboot**   Reboots the computer after sysprep.exe runs.

Once the disk image is made, you can have the image on a network share or a CD-ROM and have it distributed similar to the Windows 2000 Setup Manager Wizard.

Disk Duplication Utilities

Besides Microsoft's System Preparation Tool, a number of third-party vendors provide similar disk duplication utilities. The popular ones are from Symantec, PowerQuest, and Micro House International.

Performing Remote Installations of Windows 2000

Remote installations of Windows 2000 are done with the Remote Installation Service (RIS), which is part of Windows 2000 Server. It allows client computers to install Windows 2000 Professional from a Windows 2000 Server with the service installed.

Remote Installation Service

Before you decide to use this service, you should be aware of how it works. An RIS client, which has a boot ROM on the network interface card or an RIS boot floppy, gets an IP address through DHCP and it then downloads the Client Installation Wizard. The Client Wizard then prompts the user to log on and then provides the user with a menu that includes a variety of options for Windows 2000 Professional.

To create the image used by RIS, administrators use the Remote Installation Preparation Wizard. This is similar to the System Preparation Tool, where a reference computer is created and an image is made from it. The Remote Installation Preparation Wizard goes one step further by removing anything unique to that client, such as the SID, computer name, and hardware settings. This allows computers with multiple hardware configurations to use the same image.

Client Installation Wizard

The Client Installation Wizard starts when the computer boots. The user is then presented with four options:

- **Automatic Setup**   This is the easiest way to install Windows 2000 Professional through the RIS. The user only decides which image or answer file to install. No other questions are prompted.

- **Custom Setup**   This allows the administrator to customize every aspect of the install. This is used to override the automatic and default naming process within Active Directory.

- **Restart a Previous Setup Attempt** This option restarts a failed previous setup attempt.

- **Maintenance and Troubleshooting** This option is used to access third-party maintenance and troubleshooting tools. This is not provided by the RIS.

HEADSTART OBJECTIVE 2.07

Troubleshooting Windows 2000 Setup

There may be some instances where the installation of Windows 2000 may have some problems. Table 2-3 lists some common problems and their solutions.

TABLE 2-3

Common Problems with Windows 2000 Installation

Installation Problem	Solution
Unsupported CD-ROM/DVD drive	Replace it with one that is supported, or install over the network.
Insufficient disk space	Create a larger partition. Reformat an existing partition to free up disk space.
Media errors	Replace the Windows 2000 CD-ROM.
Dependency service can't start	Ensure the network interface card is working and is configured properly. Ensure the network protocols are set up correctly.
Windows 2000 can't install or start	Ensure all of the computer's hardware is Windows 2000 compatible.
Can't connect to the domain controller	Make sure the domain name is correct. Make sure that both the domain controller and the DNS service are running. Ensure the network card is working and the protocols are set correctly. If the computer name exists in the server manager, delete and re-create the computer name.

ACCELERATING TO WINDOWS 2000

Plug and Play

Windows 2000 includes many new features that aid the installation as well as the deployment of Windows 2000 in the enterprise. One of these is Plug and Play (PnP). PnP was previously available in Windows 95 and 98. It autodetects, configures, and installs the necessary drivers in order to minimize user interaction with hardware configuration. Users no longer have to tinker with IRQ and I/O settings.

FAT32/NTFS One important feature that is new with Windows 2000 is support for FAT32 and NTFS5. Support for FAT32, which is the default file system for Windows 95 OSR2 and Windows 98, enables peaceful coexistence with Windows 95/98. This can enable users to dual boot between the two operating systems, which was not possible in the previous version of Windows NT. Another major benefit of support for FAT32 is that Windows 2000 can upgrade from Windows 95/98. This enables Windows 2000 to be a viable upgrade option for shops running Windows 95/98. With Windows 2000, Microsoft upgraded its own NT File System (NTFS). The new incarnation, version 5, includes new features that were previously found in other network operating systems.

This helps support Microsoft's strategy of pushing Windows 2000 to effectively compete with the higher-end network operating system.

DISK QUOTAS/ENCRYPTION Two new features that catch the attention of many IT specialists are disk quotas and disk encryption. With disk quotas, you can limit the use of the hard disk by the user. This eases administration worries of certain users using more than their fair share of space. With disk encryption, folders, subfolders, and files can be encrypted. This makes Windows 2000 a more secure operating system.

ZERO-ADMINISTRATION TOOLS
A major concern of IT planners is the growing total cost of ownership. With every new operating system and application suite, Microsoft touts its role in decreasing the total cost of ownership for each client. Previously, mass deployment caused much confusion and lost productivity. Three new features included with Windows 2000 that make it easy to deploy are the Setup Manager, Disk Image Preparation, and Remote Windows Installation. Setup Manager is a Wizard that helps you create unattended installation files. With the new Setup Manager, you can minimize the amount of user interaction

ACCELERATING TO WINDOWS 2000

during setup. Disk Image Preparation was previously available in third-party applications. Windows 2000 includes its own Disk Image Preparation tool to organizations that have the Microsoft sysprep volume licensing agreement. Sysprep duplicates the contents of computers running Windows 2000 to other computers so the target computer does not need to have the operating system as well as all the applications installed. Sysprep automatically regenerates Security IDs (SID) to ensure each machine is not an exact duplicate. Remote Windows Installation is a tool in Windows 2000 Server that enables remote boot clients to remotely install Windows 2000. With the new Remote Windows Installation, many remote installations can run simultaneously, which lowers administrative overhead.

CHAPTER SUMMARY

In adherence to the zero-administration initiative, Windows is now easier to install and deploy than ever. Before you start the Windows 2000 installation, you must do some preparation. A few things you should think about beforehand are the hardware requirements, compatibility issues, partitioning, the networking issues, the type of file system to install Windows 2000, and multiboot configurations.

Installing Windows 2000 from a CD-ROM is the most common way to install Windows 2000. The setup consists of four stages: the Setup program, the Setup Wizard, Windows Networking Components, and completing the setup. Installing Windows 2000 is similar to installing it from a CD except the location of the source files is different.

Windows 2000 is a huge upgrade, and can be very costly for organizations to upgrade the operating systems on all existing computers. Windows 2000 minimizes the cost of doing mass migrations by automating the deployment process. One method of automating installation is through the Windows 2000 Setup Manager Wizard. The Setup Manager Wizard allows administrators to easily generate answer files. Answer files are text files that allow the administrator to describe the installation requirements and answer questions that the setup program prompts the user. The Setup Manager Wizard creates two files: an answer file called Unattend.txt, and a batch file that runs the setup program with the answer file as the command-line argument. Another way of speeding mass installations is with disk image replication. Disk image replication is copying the contents of the entire disk onto an image and replicating it on another machine. This is one of the best methods to use for mass installs because it's extremely powerful and comprehensive.

Remote installations of Windows 2000 are accomplished with the Remote Installation Service (RIS), which is part of Windows 2000 Server. It allows client computers to install Windows 2000 Professional from a Windows 2000 Server with the service installed.

TWO-MINUTE DRILL

- ❑ Before you start the Windows 2000 installation, you must do some preparation. A few things you should think about beforehand are the hardware requirements, compatibility issues, partitioning, the networking issues, the type of file system to install Windows 2000, and multiboot configurations.

- ❑ When your PC fulfills the Windows 2000 hardware requirements, you must also verify that your hardware is on the Windows 2000 Hardware Compatibility List (HCL).

- ❑ A crucial part of the Windows 2000 setup is setting up the networking elements such as the domain/workgroup membership and client licensing.

- ❑ Per Server Licensing requires licenses for the maximum number of concurrent connections that is expected to access the Windows 2000 Server.

- ❑ Before you start the Windows 2000 setup, it's important that you decide whether Windows 2000 will exist on a new partition or on an existing partition.

- ❑ Windows 2000 minimizes the cost of doing mass migrations by automating the deployment process.

- ❑ Remote installations of Windows 2000 are done with the Remote Installation Service (RIS), which is part of Windows 2000 Server. It allows client computers to install Windows 2000 Professional from a Windows 2000 Server with the service installed.

SELF TEST

The following questions help you measure your understanding of the material presented in this chapter. Read all of the choices carefully, as there may be more than one correct answer. Choose all correct answers for each question.

1. Lucille plans to install Windows 2000 but the video card she just got is nowhere to be found on the Hardware Compatibility List. What can she do?

    A. Nothing. If it's not on the HCL, it won't work.

    B. Get another video card.

    C. Check the hardware manufacturer for updated drivers for the video card.

    D. Use the Windows 95 drivers that came with the card.

2. Marty, an administrator, is in the middle of a Windows 2000 installation and just remembered that he forgot to add the computer to the domain. The nearest Windows 2000 machine is very faraway and he would prefer to not walk so far. What should he do?

    A. Stretch his legs for a few minutes. He's got a long walk ahead of him.

    B. Enter his login/password when prompted.

    C. Nothing. Windows 2000 is automatically added to the domain in every installation.

    D. Add the computer to a workgroup with the same name as the domain.

3. There are 50 Windows 2000 Professional Clients accessing a Windows 2000 Server's print services. There are 40 clients accessing the same server's FTP services. How many Per Seat Client Access Licenses should the Windows 2000 Server have?

    A. 10

    B. 40

    C. 50

4. When can you partition the space on your hard disk?

    A. During the install

    B. Right after the installation

    C. Anytime after the installation

    D. Before the installation

5. What type of file systems does Windows 2000 support?

    A. FAT

    B. FAT32

    C. NTFS

    D. HPFS

6. David is installing a dual-boot system with Windows 2000 and Windows 95. After installing Windows 2000, he realizes all the applications he installed on Windows 95 are not available in Windows 2000. What can he do?

    A. Make shortcuts to the application's executables.

    B. Import Windows 95 registry to Windows 2000.

C. Reinstall all applications.

D. Export the Windows 2000 registry to Windows 95.

7. Billy wants to install Windows 2000 over the network for a workstation that currently has no operating system on it. How can he install Windows 2000 if he can't access the distribution server?

A. Boot off a network client disk.

B. Install a network card with a BOOT ROM.

C. Do a push installation.

D. Do a pull installation.

8. Ryan is doing a Windows 2000 network installation. What switch does he use to specify the source of the distribution files?

A. /a

B. /r

C. /rx

D. /s

9. What is the name of the answer file that the Setup Manager Wizard uses?

A. Unattend.txt

B. Attend.txt

C. Answer.txt

D. Autoanswer.txt

10. What folder do you copy from the Windows 2000 CD when you need to do network installations for Digital Alpha computers?

A. i386

B. x386

C. iAlpha

D. Alpha

11. Felix is setting up Windows 2000 so it can be set up on multiple computers. He is installing boot and temporary files on multiple drives. What switch should he use with winnt32.exe to ensure the proper files are copied to each drive and set as active?

A. /unattend

B. /source

C. /s

D. /syspart

12. Oscar decided to use disk duplication to do mass installation of Windows 2000. His computer is working fine, so he decides to use it as the reference computer. After he installs a few computers, he discovers that all the workstations can access his e-mail. How can he fix this?

A. Change his password.

B. Reconfigure all the workstations.

C. Reinstall the computers with files from a different reference computer.

D. Deny e-mail access from all the workstations.

13. Louis decides to use the System Preparation Tool. However, he wants to ensure that he is never prompted for any messages. Which switch should he use?

A. /quiet

B. /nosidgen

C. /pnp

D. /reboot

14. How is the Remote Installation Preparation Wizard different from the System Preparation Tool?

    A. The Remote Installation Preparation Wizard is for remote installations only.

    B. The System Preparation Tool is for remote installations only.

    C. The Remote Installation Preparation Wizard removes user-specific settings.

    D. The System Preparation Tool removes user-specific settings.

15. When Windows 2000 won't start or install, what is the first thing you should do?

    A. Reinstall Windows 2000.

    B. Ensure all hardware is Windows 2000 compatible.

    C. Reboot the computer.

    D. Reseat the hardware and reboot.

MICROSOFT CERTIFIED SYSTEMS ENGINEER

3

Deploying Windows 2000 Professional Using Remote Installation

HEADSTART OBJECTIVES

A s a part of Microsoft's focus toward a lower total cost of ownership with Windows 2000, time spent on supporting and administrating clients is greatly reduced in Windows 2000. Since Windows 2000 encompasses both the servers and clients, migrations, particularly for large organizations, require much planning and site support. With Windows 2000's new Remote Windows Installation Tool, and syspart and sysprep, onsite installs are minimized. This chapter introduces these new tools and discusses their roles in migrating to Windows 2000.

HEADSTART OBJECTIVE 3.01

Overview of the Remote Installation Service

Total Cost of Ownership, or TCO, is a major issue in evaluating whether to upgrade from older versions of Windows. Initial costs play a big part in the total costs. Windows 2000 includes many new tools to enable more installations with less resources. Sysprep is used to prepare a source computer prior to the disk being imaged. Syspart is similar to sysprep, except it is used for dissimilar computers. Both of these tools are used with an answer file to specify unique settings to the computer, such as user data and network identification. The most exciting remote installation tool for Windows 2000 is the Remote Installation Service (RIS).

Windows 2000 Server ships with the RIS. This tool can dramatically lower the TCO of Windows 2000. It leverages the availability of DHCP and Active Directory to minimize both the need to physically visit each workstation, and the number of calls to help desk support staff. RIS is a pull-type customizable installation service. It is extremely powerful and flexible because it has an array of installation options by using custom answer files, various operating system images, and maintenance and troubleshooting tools for the IT staff.

Before you consider using RIS, you should be aware of how it works. An RIS client, which has an RIS-compatible boot ROM on the network interface card or an RIS boot floppy, gets an IP address through DHCP and it will download the Client Installation Wizard. The Client Wizard will then prompt the user to log on and then present the user with a menu containing a variety of options for Windows 2000 Professional. These images allow the user flexibility in that he or she can choose from an assortment of images. In a network environment, rarely is there a single image that serves the needs of all its users. There might be one image for the help desk staff, one for the marketing staff, and one for the management staff—you can have as many images as you need. This allows computers all over the site to access the different images. This increased flexibility helps to reduce first-time cost of moving to Windows 2000.

To create the image used by RIS, administrators use the Remote Installation Preparation Wizard. This is similar to the System Preparation Tool where a reference computer is created and an image is made from it. The Remote Installation Preparation Wizard goes one step forward by removing anything unique to that client such as the Security Identifier (SID), computer name, and hardware settings. This allows computers with multiple hardware configurations to use the same image; you only need to prepare one image for one type of user. Prior to RIS, third-party disk preparation tools required the clients to be similar. Various computers for one type of user would require the IT staff to make one image for each type of hardware configuration.

Single Instance Store

Single Instance Store is a new feature in Windows 2000 that enables only one copy of a file to exist in an RIS server. Often, an RIS server may contain more than one copy of an operating system for remote boot. When there are many copies of the operating system, there are many overlapping files. This can quickly consume the hard disk space on the RIS server. Single Instance Store fixes this by having a *groveler agent* scan the hard disk regularly and link redundant file. All the redundant files are deleted and they all link to one master file. The links are updated every time the operating system is moved. This allows for seamless activity between the RIS server and the administrator—the administrator does not even have to know it is working. Since the Windows 2000 remote boot install files are mostly the same, this can help conserve the space on the RIS server by 90 percent.

Setting Up a Remote Installation Server

To ensure the RIS, your network must have the following components:

- DHCP Servers
- DNS Servers
- Active Directory Servers
- RIS Servers

The DHCP Server is required for remote clients to get an IP address. DNS servers are used to ensure the clients are able to contact the Active Directory servers. The Active Directory servers must be used to get the boot information for the client. When an RIS-compatible client boots up, it contacts the DHCP server, which has the Boot Information Negotiation Layer (BINL) extensions, to get an IP address. If the DHCP server is prestaged, BINL will direct the client to an RIS server. Once the client is able to contract the RIS server, it downloads the Client Installation Wizard. The Client Installation Wizard logs the user in and gives him or her various operating system installation options. The RIS server will ask the Active Directory server what boot image should be sent to the client. Once it is determined, Active Directory will use TFTP, a lightweight version of FTP that uses UDP, to transfer the first few files needed for the remote installation, such as NTLdr, OSChooser, and SetupLdr. Once the initial install files are transferred, the RIS uploads the boot image to the client. Once the boot image is downloaded, the setup files are run and the remote installation begins. Exercise 3-1 shows you how to install the RIS.

Heads Up: The test might ask you a question with a scenario where RIS should work, but it doesn't. In such a situation, the administrator usually has all the networking options in place, but has forgotten to authorize the RIS server.

Installing the Remote Installation Service

1. Choose Start | Programs | Administrative Tools | Configure Your Server.

2. Click Advanced and then click Optional Components. Click Start The Windows Components Wizard.

3. Once the Windows Components Wizard starts, choose Remote Installation Services. Once the files are installed, go to the Start menu, select Run, and type **RISetup.exe**. The Remote Installation Services Setup Wizard will start. When it does, click Next.

4. The screen shown next prompts you to specify the location for the remote installation folders that will store the remote installation images. The location you specify cannot be on the same drive as your system files. Type in the path, and click Next.

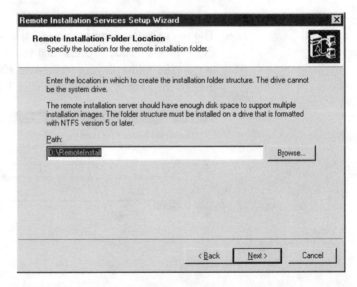

5. The next screen asks you to specify how the RIS server is going to respond to clients. You can choose to have the server respond to client computer requesting service, and not to respond to unknown clients' requests. After you choose, click Next.

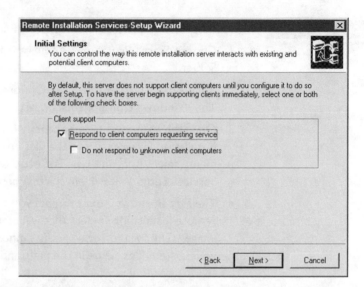

6. The next screen prompts you to specify the location of the files to the Windows 2000 Professional source files. These files are located in the i386 folder in your Windows 2000 Professional CD-ROM. Ensure the path is current, and click Next.

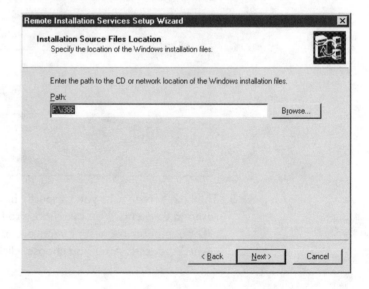

7. The next screen prompts you for the name of the folder where the Windows 2000 Professional images are stored. The default is win2000.pro. Change it if you prefer, and click Next.

8. The next screen, as shown in the following illustration, allows you to set the Friendly Description and Help Text. These are used to identify the images in the Client Installation Wizard. The default friendly description is "Microsoft Windows 2000 Professional." The default help text is "Automatically installs Windows Professional without prompting the user for input." You should change it if you have another image with the default descriptions and texts. Once you type the Friendly Description and Help Text, click Next.

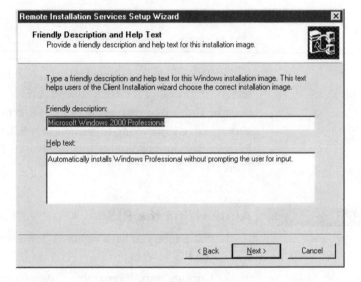

9. The final screen, shown here, shows you your choices and settings. If they are correct, click Finish. If not, you can click Back.

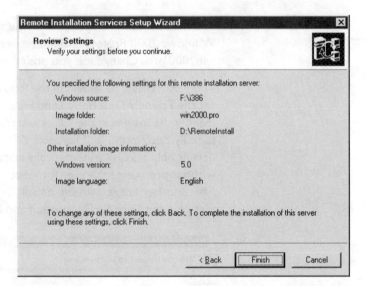

The RIS allows you to control access of the client computers to the RIS servers. In order for the clients to be able to contact a certain RIS server, it must be authorized within the Active Directory. If the RIS server is not authorized, clients trying to request that RIS server will not get a response. Exercise 3-2 shows you how to authorize an RIS server within the Active Directory.

EXERCISE 3-2

Authorizing the RIS

1. Make sure you have rights as domain administrator of the domain the RIS servers are in.

2. Choose Start | Programs | Administrative Tools | DHCP.

3. The DCHP Manager is shown in the following illustration. Right-click DHCP and click Add Server. In the Add Server box, type in the IP address of the RIS server. Click OK.

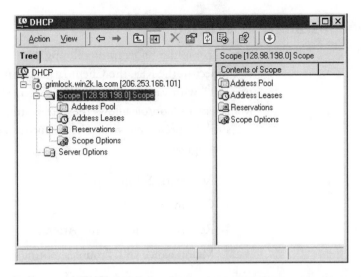

4. Right-click again on DHCP and click Manage Authorized Servers. Select the computer and click Authorize. Click OK.

Distribution Point Management

The distribution point is the place on the RIS server where the operating system source files are held. Remote installations require that these files and their configuration files be stored on the Intellimirror servers. The distribution point can be created through the Windows Remote Installation Services Setup Wizard. After you created it, you can manage it using the Active Directory Users and Computers.

Administrators can set access to the distribution point so only select individuals can manage it. In the Active Directory Users and Computers, you can change many properties of the distribution point, such as installation choices and troubleshooting tools.

on the
Job *Be sure to set the correct permissions in the distribution point folder.*

Client Installation Wizard

After a computer boots from a floppy drive or a boot ROM and is able to connect to the RIS, the Client Installation Wizard starts. The user is presented with various options. The Group Policy snap-in within the Management Console allows the administrator to control the options the users will be presented with. The Client Installation Wizard has four running options:

- Automatic Setup
- Custom Setup
- Restart a Previous Setup Attempt
- Maintenance and Troubleshooting

Automatic Setup Option

This is the default setup option. It is the easiest way to install Windows 2000 Professional through the RIS. The user only decides which image or answer file to install; no other questions will be prompted. The administrator has already provided all information. This setup minimizes user error and minimizes the number of help desk calls. This setup is the ideal choice when the workstations are all the same.

Custom Setup Option

This option allows the greatest flexibility. It should only be used when a member of the IT staff is in front of the machine to be set up. This is extremely costly and timely, but it allows the administrator to customize every aspect of the install. This option is usually used to override the automatic and default naming process within Active Directory.

Restart a Previous Setup Attempt Option

This option restarts a failed previous setup attempt. It is used so the user is not prompted for questions that were answered in the previous setup attempt. When the setup starts again, it will read answers that were written to a text file before the setup failed. This is an option to use. It should be noted, however, that support should be notified any time a remote installation setup fails.

Maintenance and Troubleshooting

Use this option to access third-party maintenance and troubleshooting tools. This is not provided by the RIS. An example of this is if the administrator wants to update the BIOS to make it Y2K compliant. It would run the BIOS update file in the menu option. You can restrict access to this by setting the permissions on the installation setup answer file (SIF). In order to be able to do that, the tool has to be written to be compatible with the installation setup answer file.

Configuring the Remote Installation Service

Once you set up the RIS, you can still go back and change some of the settings. Exercise 3-3 walks you through how to configure the RIS.

EXERCISE 3-3

Configuring the Remote Installation Service

1. Choose Start | Programs | Administrative Tools | Active Directory Users and Computers.

2. Locate your server. Your server has a computer icon with the computer name on it. Right-click on the server object and click Properties. The Properties page shows six tabs: Location, General, Operating System, Managed By, Member Of, and Remote Install as shown next.

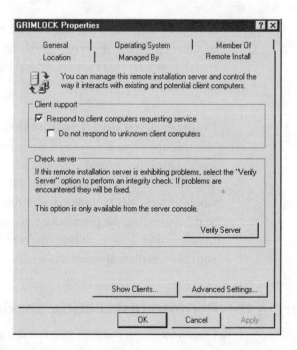

3. The client support options are the same as with the installation of the RIS. Verify Server allows the administrator to ensure the integrity of the RIS server. This starts a wizard that checks all the settings and configurations to make sure they are properly set up and running correctly. Show Clients lists the clients that had their operating systems set up by this RIS server. Advanced Settings displays some more tabs for more advanced settings. Click Advanced Settings.

4. This takes you to the advanced screen. There are three tabs on this screen: New Clients, Images, and Tools. In New Clients, shown next, you can set the client computer-naming format. This option allows the administrator to set a unique way of naming a computer during the remote Windows 2000 installation. You can set the name as the username plus a number (e.g., JOHNSMITH01), or the user's first and last name (e.g., JOHNSMITH). If you want to change the default computer format, click Customize. Another setting is the computer account location. This is used to set the locations for the machine account creation. The three options are (1) default directory service location, (2) same location as the user setting up the computer,

and (3) a specific directory service location. The default directory service location lets you specify the computer account object for the client computer to be created in the Active Directory location where all computer accounts are creating during the domain join by default. The default location is the Computer container within the Active Directory, and the client becomes a member of the same domain as the RIS server. The same location as the user setting up the computer sets up the client computer object in the same Active Directory location as the installing user. A specific directory service location allows the administrator to set a container in which all the client computer account objects will be created.

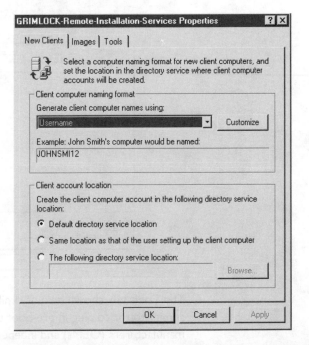

5. Click on the Images tab, shown next. The Images section is for managing the imaged client operating systems installed on the RIS server. The Images tab displays two types of images: CD-based and RIPrep images. The CD-based images are the copy of the Windows 2000 Professional CD. The RIPrep, or the Remote Installation Preparation images, are the customized images made from the base operating system, local installation of applications such as Microsoft

Office, and customized configurations. Three options are available on the Images tab: Add, Remove, and Properties. The Add option allows you to add a new CD image or an unattended setup answer file (*.sif) to an existing CD image. You can associate many unattended setup answer files to the same CD image. The Remove option removes the unattended setup answer file associated with the CD image. The Properties option allows you to view and edit the Friendly Description and Help Text associated with the CD image.

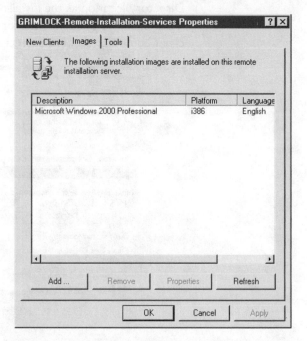

6. The Tools tab, shown next, is similar to the Options tab. It allows the administrator to plug-in pre-boot tools from original equipment manufacturers (OEMs) and independent software vendors (ISVs). In order to add a tool to the RIS, the ISVs and OEMs must provide a setup program that adds the tool in the \RemoteInstall directory. There are two options available on the Tool tab: Remove and Properties. The Remove option removes the SIF file associated with the highlighted tool. Properties allows you to view and edit the Friendly Description and the HelpText about the tool.

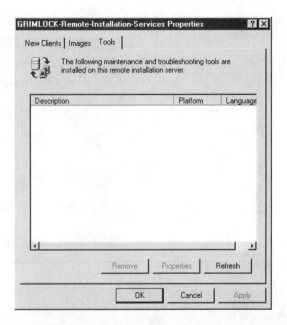

Remote Installation Boot Floppy

There are two ways to access the RIS server from a client: from a PXE Boot ROM on the network interface card, or a remote installation boot floppy. To create the remote installation boot floppy, ensure the RIS is running properly and run the RBFG.exe from the RIS server, on a client connected to the RIS server, or on a computer with the administration tools installed. You can access RGFG.exe by typing the UNC path from the Run command. The default path is\\server_name\RemoteInstall\Admin\ I386\RBFG.exe. The Windows 2000 Remote Boot Disk Generator is shown in Figure 3-1.

To create the remote boot disk, click Adapter List to ensure your network adapter is on the list. If it is, click Create Disk and the disk will be created for you.

heads
①P   *If you try to boot off the remote book disk and it doesn't work, make sure your adapter is supported.*

FIGURE 3-1

Windows 2000 Remote
Boot Disk Generator

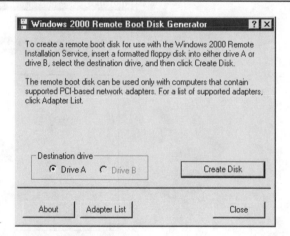

Introduction to Scripting Installation

The answer file is very important in configuring a Windows 2000
Professional CD install. It contains settings where you can set the username,
computer name, domain name, workgroup name, whether it's a domain
controller or a stand-alone server or a workstation, network configuration,
password, and time zones.

The answer file has a default name of unattend.txt. It is included in the
Windows 2000 CD-ROM where you can copy, edit, and rename it. The
answer file in a Windows 2000 installation answers questions that the install
normally asks the user. Since the questions are automatically answered, user
interaction can be minimized. To use an answer file in a scripted installation,
you specify it in the winnt or winn32 command with the /u switch, which
means it's an unattended and scripted installation. A typical unattended setup
command looks like:

```
Winnt32 /b /s:d:\i386 /u:d:\i386\unattend.txt
```

Creating the Answer File

The unattend.txt, or whatever name you want to call your answer file, can be created in three ways: create the file yourself, use Setup Manager, or modify the unattend.txt that comes with Windows 2000. If the parameters are not predefined in the answer file, users will have to interact with the installation. Table 3-1 lists the parameters the Setup Manager will prompt you for. The Setup Manager Wizard is a graphical tool that allows you to make an answer file easily, without the headache associated with writing the answer file yourself. The Windows 2000 Setup Manager Wizard is available on the Windows 2000 Professional CD-ROM as setupmgr.exe.

Windows 2000 Setup Manager creates two files that allow an unattended installation: the unattended answer file, called unattend.txt, and a batch file

TABLE 3-1		
Windows 2000 Setup Manager Parameters	**Parameter**	**Description**
	Installation Path	The path to where Windows 2000 will be installed.
	Upgrade option	This parameter specifies what type of installation this is. This installation can be a fresh installation, a non-Windows NT/2000 upgrade, or a Windows NT/2000 upgrade.
	Target computer name	This parameter specifies the computer name, the name of the user, and the organization name.
	Product ID	The Product ID of Windows 2000. This ID is found in the Windows 2000 documentation.
	Role of the computer	The role of the computer is whether the computer is a workstation within a domain or workgroup, a stand-alone server, or a domain controller.
	Workgroup or domain	Name of the workgroup or domain to which the computer belongs.
	Time Zone	The time zone in the location of the user.
	Network Configuration information	This parameter defines the type of network adapter and the network protocol configuration information.

that launches the Windows 2000 setup program with the answer file as the command-line argument.

Another way to create an unattend.txt file is to simply write it yourself. You can write it from scratch with a text editor, such as Notepad, or you can edit the sample answer files found on the Windows 2000 CD-ROM. The unattend.txt files on the CD-ROM are samples that also have documentation included. By looking at the unattend.txt files, you can create more thorough answer files than you would if you use the Windows 2000 Setup Manager Wizard. The following is a sample script that allows an unattended installation.

```
[Unattended]
Unattendmode = FullUnattended
OemPreinstall = NO
TargetPath = WINNT
Filesystem = LeaveAlone

[UserData]
FullName = "Derrick Woo"
OrgName = "Derrick Woo"
ComputerName = "Win2k "

[GuiUnattended]
TimeZone = "004"
AdminPassword = password
AutoLogon = No
AutoLogonCount = 20

[Display]
BitsPerPel = 8
XResolution = 800
YResolution = 600
VRefresh = 70

[LicenseFilePrintData]
[TapiLocation]
    AreaCode=818
[Networking]
InstallDefaultComponents = YES
[Identification]
JoinDomain = Domain
CreateComputerAccountInDomain=Yes
DomainAdmin=Administrator
DomainAdminPassword=AdminPass
```

Designing and Automating the Remote Installation Service

The chief tools for designing and automating the RIS are sysprep and syspart. Sysprep is used to duplicate entire configurations of one computer on other computers. The configuration includes the entire operating system, applications, and other miscellaneous files. To use sysprep, you must ensure sysprep.exe, setupcl.exe, and the optional sysprep.inf are in the sysprep folder on the local hard drive. Sysprep.exe has four optional switches that are used during execution:

- /quiet
- /nosidgen
- /pnp
- –reboot

The /quiet switch runs sysprep without showing onscreen messages. The /nosidgen switch runs sysprep without generating the security identifier. The /pnp switch forces a plug-and-play scan of all the hardware. The –reboot switch forces a reboot once the disk duplication is completed.

The sysprep.inf is an answer file that uses the same syntax and key names as the setup answer file. Setupcl.exe does many things that allow the duplication of Windows 2000 images on the network. It changes the SID to eliminate duplicate SIDs in the organization. It writes an entry into the registry to mark the fact that the computer was cloned. It processes the sysprep.inf and launches the mini-setup wizard.

Since sysprep is for identical computers, Microsoft has included syspart for computers with different hardware. The syntax for the sysprep switch of winn32 is:

```
Winnt32 /unattend:unattend.txt /s:install_source
/syspart:drive_letter
/tempdrive:drive_letter.
```

The /syspart:drive_letter copies the files from the install source to the drive specified, and marks the drive as active. Once the computer is restarted, the next setup phase starts. The /syspart switch in winnt32 speeds up the deployment time of Windows 2000 because the file-copy phase of the setup is eliminated.

In terms of planning for remote installation for the RIS, you must ensure your computers meet or exceed their minimum requirements. RIS hardware requirements are:

- Pentium 166 or greater
- 64MB of RAM or greater
- 2GB partition for the RIS directory tree
- 10 mb/s or greater network adapter card

The client hardware requirements are:

- Pentium 166 or greater NetPC client computer
- 32MB of RAM or greater
- 1.2GB or greater driver
- PXE DHCP-based boot ROM version .99c or greater, or a network adapter card supported by the RIS boot floppy

HEADSTART OBJECTIVE 3.05

Introduction to Imaging Windows 2000 Professional for Remote Installations

Besides using the standard Windows 2000 Professional default images, you can also create images from normal client computers. The advantage of using a "personalized" Windows 2000 Professional image is that you can replicate entire systems, such as the operating system, as well as applications, configuration settings, and files. This reduces management overhead in rolling out many machines, especially for a major upgrade such as Windows 2000. A good feature about the Windows 2000 images is that they are not hardware dependent. The Remote Installation Preparation uses Plug-and-Play to detect the hardware differences between the image and the target computer.

HEADSTART OBJECTIVE 3.06

Setting Up a Reference Computer

You must have administrator rights to set up the reference computer; only administrators can run the Remote Installation Preparation Wizard. The Wizard can only make an image of a single partition, so you must ensure that all the operating system files, applications, and miscellaneous files are on one partition. You cannot replicate encrypted files. The destination computer must have more hard drive space than the source computer partition. Once the image is written, it cannot be changed. If you want to make changes, you must make another image.

HEADSTART OBJECTIVE 3.07

Designing Remote Installation Images

You can configure your source computer to a set standard. You can set screen colors, background, install applications, or set bookmarks. Exercise 3-4 walks you through setting up a remote installation image.

EXERCISE 3-4

Setting Up a Remote Installation Image

1. Install the base Windows 2000 Professional image from an RIS server onto a client computer.

2. Install Office 2000. Change the background to Solar Eclipse. Connect to the RIS server by selecting Start | Run. In the open box, type **\\RISServer\RemoteInstallShare\Admin\RIPrep.exe**. The RISServer is the name of the RIS server. The RemoteInstallShare is the name of the Remote Installation Share. Admin is the name of the directory that contains RIPrep.exe.

3. The Remote Installation Preparation Wizard will start. Click Next.

4. You are prompted for the name of the RIS server to replicate the client's image to. Type it in, and click Next.

5. You are prompted for the name of the directory in which the image will be copied. Specify the path, and click Next.

6. You are prompted for the Friendly Description and Help Text describing it. Type in the information so users can identify the image, and click Next.

7. The next screen allows you to review your choices. If you need to make changes, click Back and make the necessary changes. Click Next. The image is now being prepared and replicated to the IRS server. Once the replication is completed, remote boot clients are able to access the images of this customized client.

HEADSTART OBJECTIVE 3.08

Troubleshooting

Many factors can cause the RIS to stop functioning. It's fairly easy to diagnose the problem depending on where you are in the process. In the beginning, when the BOOTP message shows up on the client, but the computer cannot get past this part, there are several things that you can do. During this step, the client is requesting an IP address. If it does not pass this step, it means the client is unable to receive the IP. The main thing to look at is the DHCP server. Ensure the following:

- The server is available and the service has started.
- The DHCP server is authorized in the Active Directory.
- There is an active IP address scope.
- The router between the client and the DHCP server is allowing DHCP packets to go through.

After the client gets past the BOOTP screen and shows DHCP, it has successfully obtained an IP address. If it does not pass this step, it means the client cannot contact the remote installation server. Ensure that:

- The remote installation server is available and the RIS has started.
- The RIS server is authorized in the Active Directory.
- If you have a remote boot client, the client is supported by checking the PXE ROM version on the client computer.
- The router between the client and the RIS is allowing the DHCP request and response to go through.

After the client changes to BINL or prompts the user to press F2, it means the client has contacted the RIS server and is waiting for the first image file. If you are unable to get a response from the RIS server, or the client times out, stop and restart the RIS. If this still doesn't fix it, check the event log for errors relating to the DHCP, DNS, and RIS.

ACCELERATING TO WINDOWS 2000

The RIS is entirely new to the Windows NT family. With it, staff members no longer have to be onsite to deploy a configured workstation. In previous generations of Windows NT, the IT staff had to use third-party software to replicate the image of the hard drive with the configured operating system as well as the applications. To use the RIS, you must have a DHCP server, DNS servers, RIS server, and the new Active Directory Server.

Once the service is set up, you can set up the images on the server by using the Remote Installation Preparation Wizard. An important feature of the Remote Installation Preparation Wizard is that it eliminates unique client settings such as the SID, computer name, and hardware settings. This is different from the System Preparation Tool and third-party tools because it's smarter than just making an exact image of the hard drive. This allows computers with multiple hardware configurations to use the same image.

One innovative new feature of the RIS is the Single Instance Store. The Single Instance Store uses the groveler agent to scan the distribution point of the remote installation images. It ensures that only one master copy of a file exists. With many images, many files are duplicated in each. The Single Instance Store minimizes the space needed to store the images.

To ease client access to the RIS server, RIS includes support for a PXE boot ROM, as well as a bootable floppy. By using the boot ROM, the IT staff does not have to be burdened with making a bootable floppy. When the workstation is using a supported PXE boot ROM, remote installation becomes true "plug and play."

QUESTIONS AND ANSWERS

What type of automated installation should I use if I want to duplicate exact replicas of machines as quickly as I can?	Sysprep is the way to go. The sysprep tool allows you to make images of hard drives with computers of exact configurations so you don't need to reinstall applications or add miscellaneous files.
What type of automated installation should I use if I want to duplicate machines with different hardware?	Use winnt32 with the /syspart switch. The /syspart switch allows for duplication of the machine without reliance on its hardware.
I want to roll out many machines with a vanilla-type setup of Windows 2000 Professional that eliminates all user-based customization. What should I do?	Use the RIS. It allows for customizable images, but eliminates all user-specific settings.
I want to have a scripted installation. What should I use?	If you need to have a scripted installation similar to Windows NT 4, use unattend.txt with winnt32.

CHAPTER SUMMARY

Windows 2000 Server ships with many tools to do remote automated installations. One of them is the RIS, or the Remote Installation Service. It leverages the availability of DHCP to minimize both the need to physically visit each workstation and the number of calls to help desk support staff. Another tool is sysprep, which is used to clone and duplicate disks to another computer. The /syspart switch for winnt32 used in conjunction with answer files is used to copy images to another computer with different hardware.

Similar to Windows NT 4.0, Windows 2000 still uses an unattend.txt file. This file answers questions that are asked normally to a user during installation. With the unattend.txt, installations are scripted and can be done with minimal user interaction. New with Windows 2000 is the Windows 2000 Setup Manager. It allows easy generation of the unattend.txt file by making the process GUI based. Instead of reading the file on the CD-ROM, the administrator can just run setupmgr.exe and answer the questions.

In older versions of Windows NT, disk duplication was usually done with third-party software. In Windows 2000, Microsoft includes sysprep.

Sysprep is a tool that prepares the hardware for cloning, images it, and then copies it to another computer. The configuration includes the entire operating system, applications, and other miscellaneous files. Users can quickly have an entire desktop waiting for them in less time than a normal install, and IT can do it for less money because the utility is now included in Windows 2000.

Winnt32 uses a /syspart switch that allows for automated installations of Windows 2000 on heterogeneous hardware. This utility is perfect for environments in which there is a combination of new and old equipment from different vendors. This is used in conjunction with an unattend.txt to further streamline the installation. By installing Windows 2000 this way, the file copy phase is eliminated, thus reducing deployment time.

Administrators use the Remote Installation Preparation Wizard to create a standard image or a customized image. The Remote Installation Preparation Wizard differs from the System Preparation Tool by allowing the elimination of unique client settings, such as the SID, computer name, and hardware settings. This allows computers with multiple hardware configurations to use the same image.

TWO-MINUTE DRILL

❑ Total Cost of Ownership, or TCO, is a major issue in evaluating whether to upgrade from older versions of Windows. Initial costs play a big part in the total costs.

❑ Sysprep is used to prepare a source computer prior to the disk being imaged. Syspart is similar to sysprep, except it is used for dissimilar computers.

❑ To create the image used by RIS, administrators use the Remote Installation Preparation Wizard. This is similar to the System Preparation Tool where a reference computer is created and an image is made from it.

❑ Single Instance Store is a new feature in Windows 2000 that enables only one copy of a file to exist in an RIS server.

❑ The DHCP Server is required for remote clients to get an IP address. DNS servers are used to ensure the clients are able to contact the Active Directory servers. The Active Directory servers must be used to get the boot information for the client.

❑ The distribution point is the place on the RIS server where the operating system source files are held.

❑ After a computer boots from a floppy drive or a boot ROM and is able to connect to the RIS, the Client Installation Wizard starts.

❑ There are two ways to access the RIS server from a client: from a PXE Boot ROM on the network interface card, or a remote installation boot floppy.

❑ The answer file is very important in configuring a Windows 2000 Professional CD install. It contains settings where you can set the username, computer name, domain name, workgroup name, whether it's a domain controller or a stand-alone server or a workstation, network configuration, password, and time zones.

❑ The answer file Windows 2000 Setup Manager creates two files that allow an unattended installation: the unattended answer file, called unattend.txt, and a batch file that launches the Windows 2000 setup program with the answer file as the command-line argument can be created in three ways: create the file yourself, use Setup Manager, or modify the unattend.txt that comes with Windows 2000.

❑ To use sysprep, you must ensure sysprep.exe, setupcl.exe, and the optional sysprep.inf are in the sysprep folder on the local hard drive.

❑ The advantage of using a "personalized" Windows 2000 Professional image is that you can replicate entire systems, such as the operating system, as well as applications, configuration settings, and files.

❑ You must have administrator rights to set up the reference computer; only administrators can run the Remote Installation Preparation Wizard.

❑ You can configure your source computer to a set standard. You can set screen colors, background, install applications, or set bookmarks.

❑ Many factors can cause the RIS to stop functioning. It's fairly easy to diagnose the problem depending on where you are in the process.

SELF TEST

The following questions will help you measure your understanding of the material presented in this chapter. Read all of the choices carefully, as there may be more than one correct answer. Choose all correct answers for each question.

1. What is the difference between the System Preparation Tool and the Remote Installation Preparation Wizard?

   A. Nothing.

   B. The Remote Installation Preparation Wizard removes anything unique to the client.

   C. The System Preparation Tool removes anything unique to the client.

   D. The Remote Installation Preparation Wizard adds unique items to the client.

2. You have just copied many installed images on to the RIS server. Why do the remote boot images not add up?

   A. Windows 2000 is incorrectly reporting the space for the RIS image.

   B. The images you have uploaded are incomplete.

   C. Windows 2000 uses the groveler agent to eliminate redundant files across many images.

   D. You may have an incomplete image.

3. What components must your network have to ensure the RIS will function correctly?

   A. DHCP Servers

   B. DNS Servers

   C. Active Directory Servers

   D. RIS Servers

4. Unlike Windows NT, services such as the RIS server must be authorized. How do you authorize the RIS server?

   A. Type in your login/password when prompted.

   B. Proper permission is given when the RIS is installed.

   C. Ensure client accessing service has permission to access the RIS service.

   D. You must authorize it within the Active Directory.

5. Where can you change the properties of the distribution point?

   A. Component Services

   B. Data Sources

   C. Active Directory Users and Computers

   D. Computer Management

6. Which option in the Client Installation Wizard do you set if you want the most streamlined and painless client installation?

   A. Automatic Setup

   B. Custom Setup

   C. Restart a Previous Setup Attempt

   D. Maintenance and Troubleshooting

7. Which option in the Client Installation Wizard do you set if you want to restart a client installation that has been prematurely aborted?

   A. Automatic Setup

   B. Custom Setup

   C. Restart a Previous Setup Attempt

   D. Maintenance and Troubleshooting

8. Which option in the Client Installation Wizard do you use to access third-party tools?

   A. Automatic Setup

   B. Custom Setup

   C. Restart a Previous Setup Attempt

   D. Maintenance and Troubleshooting

9. You want to create an unattend.txt file for an automated installation of Windows 2000. Your colleague is new to Windows 2000. He wants to create the unattend.txt by hand. What new feature should you tell him about in Windows 2000 that allows for easier generation of an unattend.txt file?

   A. None. Create the file yourself.

   B. Copy the file from the CD-ROM and modify it yourself.

   C. Use the Windows 2000 Setup Manager.

   D. Use the Windows 2000 winnt32 tool.

10. After your colleague decides to use the Windows 2000 Setup Manager, he is mildly surprised that the Setup Manager does more than just generate an unattend.txt file. What other file does Windows 2000 Setup Manager generate that allows for an unattended installation?

   A. A new setup.exe

   B. A new winnt32.exe

   C. A batch file that runs the Windows 2000 setup program

   D. A new winnt.exe

11. You are running sysprep to clone hard drives to another computer. Unfortunately, each computer has hardware that is usually not detected during the Windows 2000 installation. What switch should you use to ensure all hardware is detected?

   A. /nosidgen

   B. /pnp

   C. /nopnp

   D. /sidgen

12. You do not have a PXE boot ROM and you need to enable remote client installation. How do you create a remote installation boot floppy?

   A. Run the RBFG.exe from the RIS server.

   B. Run the RBFG.exe from a client connected to the RIS.

   C. Run the RBFG.exe on a computer with administration tools installed.

   D. Run the RBFG.exe on a Windows 2000 Server.

13. When you boot up using the RIS and the BOOTP message shows up on the client, but the computer cannot get past this part, what can you do to troubleshoot it?

    A. Ensure the server is available and the service has started.

    B. Ensure the DHCP server is authorized in the Active Directory.

    C. Ensure there is an active IP address scope.

    D. Ensure the router between the client and DHCP server is allowing DHCP packets to go through.

14. When you boot up using the RIS and the DHCP message shows up on the client, but the computer cannot get past this part, what can you do to troubleshoot it?

    A. Ensure the remote installation server is available and the RIS has started.

    B. Ensure the RIS server is authorized in the Active Directory.

    C. If you have a remote boot client, ensure the client is supported by checking the PXE ROM version on the client computer.

    D. Ensure the router between the client and the RIS is allowing the DHCP request and response to go through.

15. After the client changes to BINL or prompts the user to press F2, it means the client has contacted the RIS server and is waiting for the first image file. If you are unable to get a response from the RIS server, or the client times out, what should you do?

    A. Restart the RIS server.

    B. Ensure DHCP is working.

    C. Ensure Domain Controller is up.

    D. Reboot the computer.

MICROSOFT CERTIFIED SYSTEMS ENGINEER

4

Managing File Resources

HEADSTART OBJECTIVES

T his chapter introduces the various file systems supported in Windows 2000, and discusses the features unique to the NT File System (NTFS). The chapter also presents new technologies implemented in Windows 2000 that assist with the management of file resources. These technologies include NTFS security, the Distributed File System (DFS), the Encrypting File System (EFS), disk quota management, file sharing, and compression.

HEADSTART OBJECTIVE 4.01

File Systems Available/Supported in Windows 2000

This section provides an overview of the file systems supported by the Windows 2000 operating system. For those readers who have worked with previous versions of Windows NT or 9x, many of these file systems will likely already be familiar. Windows 2000 supports all file systems implemented in Windows NT 4.0, as well as some additional file systems. Those supported by Windows 2000 include:

- FAT16/FAT32
- NTFS
- CDFS
- UDF

Note that the OS/2 High Performance File System (HPFS) has not been supported since Windows NT 3.51, and is not supported in Windows 2000.

The File Allocation Table (FAT) File System

The FAT file system is the oldest of the file systems supported by Windows 2000, and has been implemented in Microsoft operating systems since the earliest versions of MS-DOS.

What gives the FAT file system its name is the method in which files and directory structures are stored and accessed, the File Allocation Table. On a partition using the FAT file system, the structure of the hard disk is broken down into areas of space known as *clusters*. A cluster can vary in size, depending primarily on the size of the partition, and are usually anywhere from 8K to 32K. These clusters are chained together to form files.

Information about files including, the name, extension, size, modification date, and the cluster details are stored in the FAT. Information about a file is retrieved from the FAT any time a file is accessed, and serves as the map of the partition to allow the operating system to locate a file quickly without the need for physically scanning the disk.

Comparison of FAT16 and FAT32

The earlier version of the FAT file system implemented in MS-DOS is known as FAT16, to differentiate it from the improved FAT32. The FAT32 file system was first implemented in Windows 95 OSR2, and was supported by Windows 98 and now Windows 2000.

While FAT16 cannot support partitions larger than 4GB in Windows 2000, FAT32 can support partitions up to 2TB (Terabytes) in size. However, for performance reasons, the creation of FAT32 partitions is limited to 32GB in Windows 2000.

The second major benefit of FAT32 in comparison to FAT16 is that it supports a significantly smaller cluster size—as low as 4K for partitions up to 8GB. This results in more efficient use of disk space, with a 15–30% utilization improvement in comparison to FAT16.

Both FAT16 and FAT32 support the use of Long File Names (LFNs) in Windows 2000.

NTFS

NTFS has been implemented since the initial version of Windows NT, and continues to be the most commonly used file system in Windows NT/2000 enterprise environments. While Windows 2000 introduces some added features of NTFS that were not found in earlier versions of Windows NT, all of the original features from previous versions are still implemented, including:

- File/directory-level security
- Native file compression
- POSIX compliancy
- Support for large partitions

Some of the new features of NTFS 5.0 introduced in Windows 2000 that are discussed in later sections include:

- Quota management
- EFS

NTFS stores information about files in the Master File Table, or MFT. Each file is assigned a record number, and each record in the MFT includes most information about the file, including size and attributes.

ACCELERATING TO WINDOWS 2000

NTFS Enhancements in Windows 2000

Windows 2000 introduces several enhancements to the NTFS. Now known as NTFS version 5, the following functionality has been added to the file system since NTFS version 4 in Windows NT 4.0:

- Quotas can be assigned to a partition for individual users, enabling an administrator to control disk utilization and log events on a per-user basis when utilization is high.

- Files can be encrypted using EFS, complementing NTFS permissions to provide for ultimate file-level security.

- Physically remote data can be represented to users in a single logical directory structure using DFS.

- Aliasing of local directories using Directory Junctions enable

greater flexibility in directory management.

- Volume mount points, which enable partitions to be mounted anywhere in the file system, result in fewer drive letters to manage.

- Sparse file support is a new method that minimizes the disk utilization overhead when storing data containing large areas of consecutive binary zeros. These files can be marked as sparse, resulting in a higher efficiency of storage for meaningless data.

All of these enhancements are restricted to file systems running NTFS, and cannot be enabled on volumes running the FAT16 or FAT32 file systems.

File/Directory Security

One of the major advantages of NTFS over FAT is the ability to set Security permissions on files and directories. File and Directory permissions are discussed in greater detail later in this chapter. NTFS is the only file system implemented in Windows 2000 that supports file/directory-level security.

Native File Compression

NTFS natively supports the ability to compress files on an individual basis by enabling the Compress property on the General tab of a file or directory's properties. Compressed files can be easily recognized when browsing the hard drive by enabling the "Display compressed files in alternate color" option in Windows Explorer Properties.

Note that enabling file compression can have an overall negative performance impact on the server, due to the need for the CPU to process decompression algorithms whenever the file is accessed. The larger the cluster size used on the partition, the less effective compression will become. At cluster sizes greater than 4K, the negative performance impact of compression typically outweighs the minor savings in disk space. Therefore, all compression options are disabled on volumes configured to use clusters of 4K or greater. For this reason, file compression can only be enabled on volumes running NTFS.

POSIX Compliancy

NTFS is POSIX.1 compliant in its ability to differentiate between similarly named files based on the case of the name. For example, the files MyDoc1.doc, MYDOC1.doc, and mydoc1.doc can all be different files in a single NTFS directory.

NTFS also includes other POSIX-compliant features, including the ability to use LFNs and the implementation of an extended Date/Time attribute called "Last Accessed." The Last Accessed attribute records the last time a file was accessed, and can be viewed through File Properties in Windows Explorer. When viewing properties for a file located on a non-NTFS partition, the "Last Accessed" property will display (unknown).

Support for Large Partitions

NTFS allows for partitions larger than any other file systems supported by Windows 2000. The architecture of NTFS theoretically supports partition sizes of up to 16 *exabytes*—that's 17,592,186,044,416 Megabytes! However, limiting factors such as current hardware designs limit partition sizes to 2TB.

The CD-ROM File System (CDFS)

CDFS is a Read-Only file system that enables Windows 2000 to access data on CD-ROMs. The CDFS file implemented in Windows 2000 is fully ISO 9660 compliant. The ISO 9660 standard defines a method for storing data on a CD that can be accessed by various hardware platforms and operating systems, including UNIX and MacOS.

The Universal Disk Format File System (UDF)

UDF is the successor of CDFS, described in the preceding section. UDF is compliant with ISO 13346, and was first implemented by Microsoft in the Windows 98 operating system. UDF is currently used in Windows 2000 for accessing Digital Versatile Disc (DVD) media, but may possibly be used in the future to provide a common storage area between Windows 2000 and other operating systems such as UNIX. Currently, however, Windows 2000 implements a Read-Only version of UDF.

HEADSTART OBJECTIVE 4.02

Sharing and Publishing File Resources

File sharing in Windows 2000 is the method in which users are allowed to access data on a server computer. A directory created on a server is of no use to end users until they are able to access the data from their client, and this client-server connection must be made to a server share point. A share can be created on either NTFS or the FAT file system. There are several ways to enable file sharing on a directory, and several options that can be configured. These are all presented in this section.

How to Share a Directory in Windows 2000

In Windows 2000 there are several ways to enable a directory for sharing, some of which are

- The Create Shared Folder Wizard
- The Directory Properties Window
- The Shared Folders node in the Computer Management Console
- The Command Prompt

It is important to recognize what is required when sharing a directory in Windows 2000. The local directory path and the share name are both required fields. Optionally, the administrator can also add a description for the share, customize Share permissions, and enable caching for offline access to the share. Note that Share permissions are not the same as NTFS permissions, which are discussed later in this chapter. Share permissions can, however, work in conjunction with NTFS permissions, and must be considered when calculating a user's Effective permissions to shared resources.

The Create Shared Folder Wizard

The Create Shared Folder Wizard is designed so that an administrator can easily configure a directory on a server for sharing. Like all wizards in Windows 2000 Server, the Create Shared Folder Wizard walks the administrator through every step involved, with advice available along the way. The first screen of the Create Shared Folder Wizard presents fields to choose the directory to be shared, the name of the share, and optionally, a comment to describe the share. The wizard also suggests three basic configurations of Share permissions:

- All users have full control.
- Administrators have full control; other users have read-only access.
- Administrators have full control; other users have no access.

Custom permissions can be defined for specific users and groups by clicking ADVANCED.

The Create Shared Folder Wizard can be launched through either the Computer Management Console, or from the "Configure Your Server Wizard." In the "Configure Your Server Wizard," you can select File Server to create shares. In the Computer Management Console, navigate to the path outlined in Figure 4-1, and select New Share from a right-click context menu.

The Directory Properties Window

Directories on NTFS or FAT partitions in Windows 2000 can be shared by using the Sharing tab in My Folder Properties in Windows Explorer. Simply click Share this Folder and enter a share name. From this same screen, security on the share can also be configured using the PERMISSIONS button. The completed information in the My Folder Properties window shown in Figure 4-2 will enable sharing for the My Folder directory as My Share with a description of My Shared Folder.

Sharing Files from the Command Prompt

File sharing can also be configured from the Windows 2000 Command Interpreter. For the full syntax of the *net share* command, type **net help share** from a command prompt. The following syntax presents the command in its most simplistic form, and can be used to share a directory with no options:

    net share <sharename>=<full path to directory>

FIGURE 4-1

Navigating to the
Shares component
in the Computer
Management Console

```
Computer Management (Local)
         ┊┈┈┈┈┈┈ System Tools
                      ┊┈┈┈┈┈┈ Shared Folders
                                    ┊┈┈┈┈┈┈ Shares
```

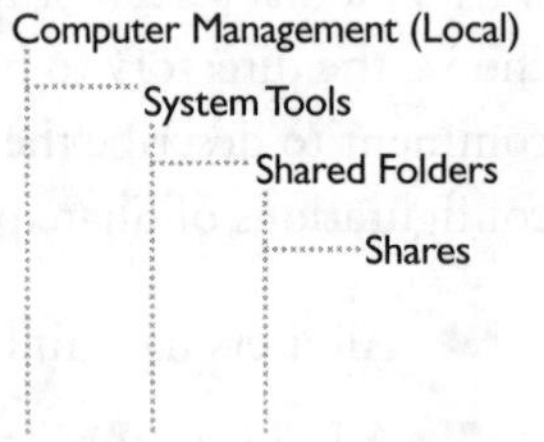

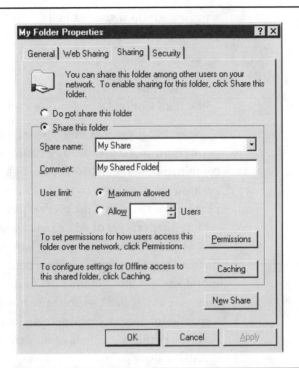

FIGURE 4-2

Sharing a folder using the
My Folder Properties
Sharing tab

Defining Share Permissions

Share permissions are Security permissions assigned to specific users or
groups to allow access to a share. Share permissions are separate from NTFS
permissions. Share permissions can be used in conjunction with
File/Directory permissions on NTFS volumes. On FAT partitions, Share
permissions are the only means of locking down directory access, as FAT
does not support File/Directory-level permission assignments.

Share permissions include only limited options for restricting access, and
any permission applied to the share will play a role in calculating the user's
Effective permissions (discussed later in this chapter). By default, the

Everyone group is granted Full Control to a share. The following permissions can be applied to a share in Windows 2000:

- Read
- Change
- Full Control

Note that if a user is a member of one or more groups that are assigned permissions to a share, the user's effective Share permissions become a combination of the rights. For example, if a user is assigned Read permissions to a share, and is a member of a group with Change permissions to a share, the user's effective permissions are Change.

The disadvantage of relying solely on Share permissions is the inherent lack of granularity. When using Share permissions to control access to file/directory resources, the Share permissions govern the access to all subfolders and files. Another disadvantage of using Share permissions is that they only are in effect when the resources are being accessed remotely. Users logged in interactively who access a local folder will not be restricted based on Share permissions at all, as they are accessing the data directly and not through a share point.

Administrative and Hidden Shares

For the exam, you should have knowledge of the default administrative shares. These are listed in Table 4-1.

Notice that all of the default administrator shares have a dollar sign ($) appended to the end of the Share Name. Appending this character to the end of any share causes it to be "hidden"; that is, the share does not appear

TABLE 4-1   Default Administrative Shares

Share Name	Default Path	Description / Purpose
C$, D$, etc.	C:\, D:\, etc.	Administrative share for each partition installed
ADMIN$	%SystemRoot%	Administrative share for Windows 2000 installation directory
Print$	%SystemRoot%\System32\Spool\Drivers	Provides clients access to retrieve drivers when configuring a printer

in the list when browsing a computer. Hidden shares are most commonly used to keep the browse list size minimal (for example, when hundreds of shared user home directories exist on a single server), or to provide a means of security through obscurity.

on the **job**

You should never rely solely on hidden shares for security. Names and paths of hidden shares are stored in clear text in the registry along with the regular shares, and Authenticated Users have Read permission to these values. Most standard software will not display hidden shares when browsing, but a user with the right tools (or a lucky guess) can always potentially find and access your hidden shares.

Connecting to a Shared Directory

Once a directory has been shared on a Windows 2000 server, a drive letter can then be mapped from a client computer to access data on the share. Drive mappings are performed on a client by specifying a drive letter and the Universal Naming Convention (UNC) path for the share. The UNC path for a share consists of the server name and the share name, and is referenced in the format \\servername\sharename.

The Map Network Drive interface can be initiated from the right-click context menu on the My Network Places icon. The window shown in Figure 4-3 will appear.

FIGURE 4-3

The Map Network
Drive window

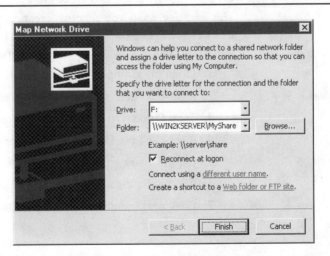

The next available drive letter will be selected automatically; however, you can select any available drive letter to use for the network connection. The shared folder to which you want to connect can be selected by clicking BROWSE, or can be manually entered in UNC format. Note that hidden shares must be manually entered, as they will not appear in the browse list.

You can also connect to a share in the context of a different user by selecting Connect using a different user name. If you select this option and select Reconnect at logon, you will be prompted for the second user's password on each logon in order to reauthenticate to the computer as the specified user.

Drive letters can also be mapped by executing the *net use* command from a command prompt. Run *net help use* for detailed information on the syntax of the *net use* command.

Mapping a drive is just one way that information on a share can be accessed. Assuming the share is not hidden, the contents of a share can be accessed directly through My Network Places when browsing. If the share is hidden, or you know what you are looking for and don't want to browse, you can simply enter the UNC path from a Start | Run dialog box to bring up the contents of the share in Windows Explorer.

A share can also be accessed through a DFS, discussed in the next section.

EXERCISE 4-1

Creating Shared Directories

This exercise walks you through creating several directories and making them available as Windows 2000 shares. Leave the directories created and shared, as they will be used in other exercises in this chapter.

1. Open My Computer and double-click the C:\ drive.

2. Right-click in an empty area in the right pane, and select New | Folder.

3. Type **Departments** for the directory name and click ENTER.

4. Right-click the Departments folder and click the Sharing option.

5. On the Sharing tab, click Share this folder.

6. Accept the default share name of Departments.

7. Click APPLY and then OK to exit the Properties sheet.

8. Repeat steps 2 through 7 for the following directories. These will be used in the next exercise.

   ■ Finance
   ■ Marketing
   ■ Sales

Administering Shared Folders Using DFS

DFS uses a single root share to facilitate hierarchical management of multiple shares. These shares can be on many different servers, but all appear to the end user as existing in one folder. DFS has the both the advantage of a central file storage location (a single drive mapping) for the end user, as well as a single point of share administration for the network administrator.

There are two options when creating a DFS root in Windows 2000: It can be created as a stand-alone root, in which a single server stores the DFS configuration; or as a Domain DFS root, which is hosted by a domain. A Domain DFS root stores its configuration in Active Directory, and provides for fault tolerance and DNS naming.

To access a DFS share from a Windows 9x workstation, you must install the DFS client. The client is available from the Microsoft Web page (www.microsoft.com).

EXERCISE 4-2

Creating a DFS

1. Launch the Distributed File System console from Start | Programs | Administrative Tools.

2. Right-click the Distributed File System node in the left window, and select New DFS Root.

3. Select NEXT, and choose the Create Stand-alone DFS Root option. Click NEXT again.

4. Leave the default local name in the server field, and click NEXT.

5. Select Use an Existing Share and choose the Departments share from the list. If the Departments share does not exist, verify successful completion of step 1. Click NEXT.

6. Enter a comment of **Central Storage of Department Data**.

7. Click NEXT, and then FINISH to exit the Wizard.

8. Expand Distributed File System and right-click your new DFS root directory.

9. Select New DFS Link.

10. Type **Finance Department** for the link name, and **\\<Your_Server>\Finance** for the path.

11. Repeat step 10 for the Marketing and Sales shares.

12. Map a drive to \\<Your_Server>\Departments and browse the directory structure to verify successful creation of your DFS root and link structure.

13. Create a text file in C:\Sales and verify that it appears in the Sales Department folder when accessed through the DFS root.

Remember that DFS links can, and in most cases do, point to shares that are on remote servers. In a real-world situation, this example could be used to transparently redirect users to separate servers owned by the Marketing, Finance, and Sales departments—perhaps in different offices in different cities. A single standard drive mapping to the DFS root could then be automated through a login script for all users, allowing them to browse the servers as a seamlessly integrated directory structure.

HEADSTART OBJECTIVE 4.04

Exploring NTFS Permissions

NTFS permissions are used to assign users or groups a specific set of permissions to a file or directory resource on an NTFS partition. This section teaches you the core concepts of NTFS permissions, a hotspot on the MCSE exam.

Types of NTFS Permissions

NTFS permissions are used on volumes formatted with NTFS. NTFS permissions allow an administrator or user to define security on a file or directory level. This sounds simple enough, but without a fundamental understanding of how NTFS security operates, it can quickly seem unmanageable. This section helps you effectively understand and manage NTFS permissions.

NTFS File Permissions

NTFS File permissions are those permissions that are assigned to files on an NTFS partition. Table 4-2 presents the standard NTFS File permissions, and provides a brief description of the access provided by each permission type.

NTFS Directory Permissions

NTFS Directory permissions are similar to NTFS File permissions, with the underlying difference residing in Permission Inheritance. A file or directory created on an NTFS partition will inherit the permissions of the parent directory. Permission Inheritance can be managed and filtered in Windows 2000, and is discussed in greater detail later in the chapter.

Table 4-3 lists the standard permissions that can be assigned to an NTFS directory in Windows 2000. These permissions essentially represent a "standard" combination of individual NTFS permissions.

TABLE 4-2	**Permission Name**	**Description of Access Provided**
Standard NTFS File Permissions	Read	Provides a user or group the ability to see a file on the directory list, and access the file contents or copy it to another location.
	Read & Execute	Same as the Read permission, with the added ability to launch binary executables.
	Write	Can overwrite a file and change file attributes only.
	Modify	Grants same permissions as Read & Execute and Write, with the added ability to modify file contents or delete the file altogether.
	Full Control	Combination of all the permissions described, also with the ability to take ownership of the file object.

TABLE 4-3	Permission	Description of Access Provided
Standard NTFS Directory Permissions	List Folder Contents	Grants only the ability to view the files or subdirectories in a given directory, but not to read or copy those files.
	Read	User or group can read or copy files in the directory, and can view security properties and attributes.
	Write	User or group can create files and subdirectories in the directory, and modify attributes of the directory.
	Read & Execute	Provides ability to move through the directory structure, regardless of permissions, and gives Read permission to contents.
	Modify	User or group can perform all rights of the Write and Read & Execute permissions, and can delete the folder.
	Full Control	User or group has all permissions over the directory, including the ability to take ownership of the directory.

Advanced (Special) Permissions

The NTFS File and Directory permissions presented thus far are actually predefined configurations that involve the assignment of several "special" permissions. Special permissions can be assigned on an NTFS file or directory by clicking ADVANCED, and selecting View/Edit. Figure 4-4 displays the configuration window for defining advanced NTFS permissions on a file.

There is some information worth reading about each of the Advanced permission types in the Windows 2000 help file. Execute a search for "special permissions overview."

When assigning permissions on an NTFS directory, the "Apply these permissions to . . ." option seen in Figure 4-4 is enabled, and any of the self-explanatory options can be used to set the level at which the new permissions will take effect. The available options are:

- This folder only
- This folder, subfolders, and files (Default)
- This folder and subfolders

- This folder and files
- Subfolders and files only
- Subfolders only
- Files only

This improves on the method that Directory permissions were assigned in previous versions of NTFS, in which permissions could only be applied in one of two ways: to either the current folder only, or the current folder and all file/subfolder contents.

Advanced Permissions on an NTFS file object

File Ownership and the Take Ownership Permission

Use careful consideration before granting the Take Ownership or Full Control permissions. The Take Ownership permission is usually only ever used by administrators, as users will automatically be granted ownership to the files that they create.

Even if a user has ownership of a file, and an administrator does not have any assigned NTFS permissions (or is denied permissions by the user), the administrator can still take ownership of the file based on the Take Ownership *user right* assigned to administrators by the operating system. This security ownership model is designed to ensure that a user cannot lock an administrator out from accessing server file resources.

An important fact to remember pertaining to file ownership is that ownership is always *taken*, and never *granted*. An administrator or user cannot assign ownership to another user or group. The only time file ownership is set or changed is when a file is created or copied, or when ownership is taken.

Users who are administrators are never individually owners of NTFS resources. Rather, any object created or taken ownership of by an administrator falls under ownership of the Administrators group. This is the only scenario in which an object is owned by a group and not a user.

The Effect of Copying and Moving Files on NTFS Permissions

Now that you have a solid grasp on how NTFS permissions are assigned, let's take a closer look at what happens when these files are moved and copied throughout the file system.

COPYING AN NTFS OBJECT Understanding the impact of copying NTFS objects is as simple as understanding the concept of what takes place during a file copy. When a file is copied on any file system, including NTFS, a new file is created and the data is read from the source file and written to the destination. Since a new file is always created, the standard creation rules apply: the destination file inherits the permissions of the parent directory, and the user copying the file becomes the owner.

When copying a file in Windows 2000, the user copying the file must have at least the Read permission to the source directory and the Write permission to the destination directory.

MOVING AN NTFS OBJECT   The effect of moving an NTFS object depends on the destination of the move; specifically, if the file will be moved to another location on the same partition, or to another partition entirely.

When moving an NTFS object to another location on the same partition as the source, the file retains its original permissions; however, the user moving the file becomes the owner of the new file. When moving the file to another partition, the file inherits the permissions of the destination folder.

When moving an NTFS object to a different partition, the user copying the file must have at least the Modify permission to the source directory, and the Write permission to the destination directory. The Modify permission is required because Windows 2000 deletes the source file after it has been moved successfully to the destination.

heads
⊕p

If you move a file or directory from an NTFS volume to a FAT16 or FAT32 volume, it loses all NTFS permissions that were previously assigned. This is because neither FAT16 nor FAT32 support File/Directory-level permissions.

Now let's examine the following scenarios involving copying or moving files, and the results.

QUESTIONS AND ANSWERS

A file on an NTFS partition is copied to another folder on the same NTFS partition.	The file inherits the permissions of the destination folder, and the user copying the file becomes the owner of the new file.
A file is copied from one NTFS partition to a folder on a different NTFS partition.	The file inherits the permissions of the destination folder, and the user copying the file becomes the owner of the new file.
A file on an NTFS partition is moved to another folder on the same NTFS partition.	The original File permissions are retained, and the user moving the file becomes the owner.
A file is moved from one NTFS partition into a folder on a different NTFS partition.	The file inherits the permissions of the destination folder, and the user moving the file becomes the owner.

Permission Inheritance

Those familiar with NTFS permissions in Windows NT versions 4.0 and earlier will recall that any file or directory, by default, always inherits the permissions of the parent directory. This fundamental concept has not changed in Windows 2000 NTFS; however, it has been further expanded on to allow the blocking of the inheritance flow down the file/directory hierarchy.

Permission Inheritance can be blocked at any level of the directory structure to prevent child directories from inheriting the permissions of the parent. This is useful when you wish to have one set of permissions at the directory level, but a separate set of permissions for the files or subfolders.

In Windows 2000, it is necessary to first disable the Permission Inheritance of an object before custom permissions can be defined. Clearing the "Allow inheritable permissions from parent to propagate to this object" check box on the Security tab of the object's properties disables the inheritance from its parent objects. If you attempt to remove an inherited permission while allowing inherited permissions to be propagated, you will receive an error message similar to that shown in Figure 4-5.

Of course, the permission could also be removed at the parent level (assuming that *it* wasn't an inherited permission), and would then be removed from the child object.

FIGURE 4-5

Attempting to remove an inherited permission

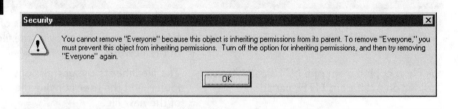

Calculating Effective Permissions

Effective permissions are the permissions that a user actually has on an object, and take into account permissions from both the share and file/directory hierarchy. To calculate the Effective permissions, the Effective File/Directory-level permissions must first be determined, and then the Share permissions factored.

Determining the Effective File/Directory permissions is fairly straightforward, as the inherited permissions are displayed in the security properties along with the explicit permissions assigned to the object.

Determining Effective File/Directory Permissions

When determining Effective File/Directory permissions, the important fact to remember is that permissions are cumulative. For example, if a user is assigned permissions to an object, and a group of which the user is a member is assigned permissions, the user's Effective permissions are the combination of the two. For example, if Joe in the Finance department is assigned the Read permission to a file and the Finance group is assigned the Change permission, Joe's Effective File/Directory permission is Change based on his permissions inherited through the Finance group.

UNDERSTANDING THE DENY PERMISSION   Permissions can be granted or denied to specific users or groups. Being assigned Deny for permission is not the same as not having that permission at all. If a user or group is assigned Deny to a permission, they will never be able to access it, regardless of permissions obtained through group membership. For example, if a user is a member of a group that has been granted the Change permission, but the user has been explicitly denied all permissions, the user has no access to the object. This is because Deny always overrides any other permissions.

Those familiar with NTFS permissions in Windows NT 4.0 and earlier will recall that access was blocked using the No Access permission. This is no longer a permission type in Windows 2000. In Windows NT, the No

Access permission completely prohibited any time of access to the resource, regardless of other permissions set. The new approach in Windows 2000, in which individual permissions can be denied, allows an administrator a greater degree of granularity when restricting permissions.

Considering Share Permissions

Compare:
least restrictive share
least restrictive NTFS
then take
Least restrictive of
the two
BUT:
Deny permission will
override any
combination.

When determining Effective permissions, the share must be considered as a gateway to the directory. As such, a share can only be used to restrict access assigned through the file system, and not to grant additional access.

Perhaps the best way to calculate Effective permissions is to follow this method: Take the *least restrictive* of the *Share* permissions and the *least restrictive* of the *NTFS* permissions, then compare the permissions and take the *more restrictive* of the two.

For example, if a user has Full Control to the file system but only Read access through the share, he or she will only be able to perform the rights of the Read permission as long as the data is accessed through that share point. Conversely, if the user has Read access to the file system and Full Control to the share, the user still only has Read access to the files. On volumes that are not formatted with NTFS, Share permissions are the only method of restricting access to shared data.

Auditing NTFS Resource Access

In security-sensitive environments or for data of a confidential nature, it may be desired to audit access to NTFS files or directory resources. Auditing keeps a log of which users access specific data, and can later be used to trace the exact history of the access of a file.

Enabling NTFS Auditing in Windows 2000

Auditing can be enabled on a file or directory through Windows 2000 by configuring the options shown on the Auditing tab of the Properties window. Like permissions, auditing is configured on an individual basis for users or groups, and the level of auditing is a combination of that configured for the user and any groups of which the user is a member. The auditing configuration window is shown in Figure 4-6.

FIGURE 4-6

Auditing an NTFS object

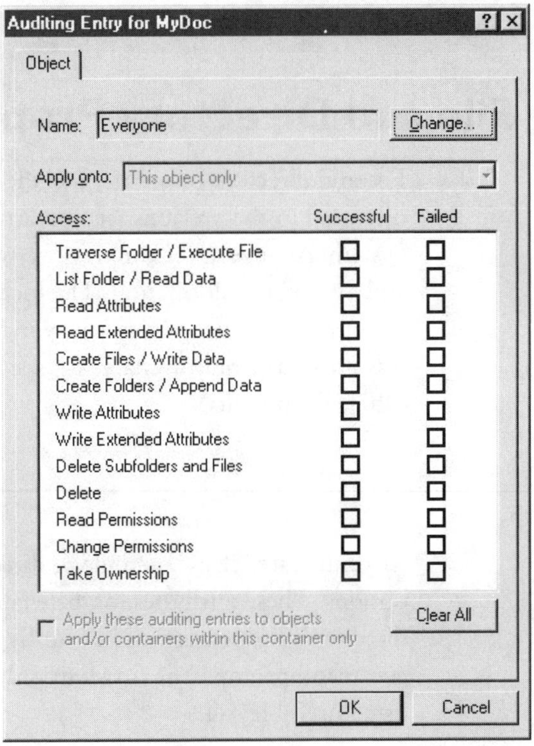

How Audit Results Are Stored and Accessed

Audited information about an object's access is stored in the Security Event Log of the server on which the file resides. It is therefore possible in a DFS hierarchy for audit results to be distributed among multiple servers, depending on where the physical object is located. The audit results stored in the Event Log will be stored for a period of time defined by the properties of the Security Event Log.

Like Security permissions, audit settings flow down the file/directory hierarchy, and inheritance of audit settings can be disabled for an object.

Before you can begin collecting audit information about an object, auditing must be enabled in Local Policy Editor or Group Policy Editor (if the machine receives policy settings from the domain). Policies are discussed in greater detail in Chapter 6.

HEADSTART OBJECTIVE 4.05

Setting File and Directory Properties

File and directory properties include the Security and Auditing options discussed in the previous section; attributes such as Hidden, Read-Only, System, Archive and Compress; version information for some binary files; and Summary information. The inclusion of Summary information in a file or directory properties is new in Windows 2000. Summary information was previously only available for specific types of files, such as Microsoft Office documents.

Attributes

Attributes are "flags" on a file or directory that enable specific system options. These attributes can be enabled on the General tab of a file or directory's Properties window, or by using the *attrib* command from a command prompt (the first four only). Attributes and their functions are listed in Table 4-4.

Version Information

The Version tab displays any information that may have been placed in the header of a binary file by the manufacturer. The information shown in this tab includes:

- Company Name
- Internal Name
- Language
- Original File Name
- Product Name
- Product Version

TABLE 4-4	Attribute Name	Attribute Function
File Attributes	Read-Only	File cannot be changed or deleted, regardless of NTFS permissions.
	Archive	Used by backup programs to determine if the contents of a file have changed since the previous backup. This is automatically set by the operating system when a file changes, or can be manually set by clicking ADVANCED in the file Properties window.
	System	File is used by the Windows 2000 operating system.
	Hidden	File or directory cannot be viewed without enabling the "Show Hidden Files" Folder Option, or by using the /a:h switch for the *dir* command.
	Compress	Enables compression on a file or directory. Accessed through the ADVANCED button on the file Properties window.
	Encrypt	Enables encryption on a file or directory. Accessed through the ADVANCED button on the file Properties window.
	Enable Indexing	Allows the Indexing Service to record catalog information for the file or directory, enabling faster searching of the hard disk. Indexing is enabled by default.

Summary Information

The Summary Information tab includes many of the fields that were previously only available for specific documents, such as those created in Microsoft Office. All fields in the Summary tab are optional, and can be used by the user or administrator to store a description of the file as well as origin information. These options are listed in Table 4-5.

TABLE 4-5	Description	Origin
Summary Properties	Title	Source
	Subject	Author
	Category	Revision Number
	Keywords	
	Comments	

Managing Disk Quotas on NTFS Volumes

Disk quotas are a new feature of NTFS v5 that allows administrators to control the amount of disk space that individual users are able to consume on a server.

Quotas on NTFS volumes in Windows 2000 are configured for a specific user context (either a domain or local user), and are assigned on a per-volume basis. That is, quotas assigned to a user on one volume (e.g., C:) do not affect the user's ability to create data on other volumes (e.g., D:, E:, etc.).

Quotas are based on file ownership. Therefore, if a user takes ownership of a file, the size of the file is assessed against the user's quota regardless of the original owner. You will recall that when an administrator owns a file, ownership is granted to the Administrators group as opposed to the individual user. Files owned by the Administrators group should not be considered when calculating quotas, as quotas cannot be defined for the Administrators group.

Quotas are enabled through the Properties window of a local volume, as shown in Figure 4-7.

The quota properties for a logical disk also enable an administrator to set default quota and warning levels, eliminating the need to manually create quota entries as new users begin to store files on a volume. Other options are also configurable from this window, such as the ability to block a user from writing additional files when the quota limit is reached, and the ability to log specific events relating to quota limits and warning levels.

Quotas for specific users (domain or local) can be configured by clicking QUOTA ENTRIES on the Quota tab in the Properties window. This launches another window that lists the Quota Entries currently in use, and provides the ability to create a new quota entry or modify one that already exists.

Quota definitions can also be exported and imported from the Quota Entries window. A useful example of this feature is needing to save the existing quota definitions prior to server maintenance (e.g., rebuilding a volume), so they can be later imported to avoid loss of the configuration. The backup utility provided with Windows 2000 does allow for a volume's

FIGURE 4-7

The Quota tab in the
Properties window

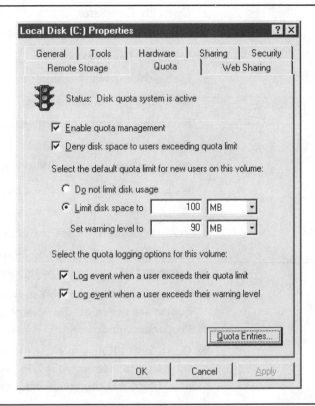

quota entries to be backed up; other third-party backup utilities may not
support this functionality.

EXERCISE 4-3

Configuring Disk Quotas

This exercise walks you through enabling quotas on a volume, and
configuring a user's quota on a directory. This exercise assumes that you
are an administrator, have a C:\ partition formatted with NTFS , and that
you have the directories created in Exercise 4-1.

1. Select Start | Run and enter the following case-sensitive command:

   net user ch3ex3 password /add

   This creates a user named "ch3ex3" with a password of "password"
   on your computer. You will learn more about user management in
   Chapter 14.

2. Open My Computer.

3. Right-click the C:\ drive and select Properties.

4. Select the Quota tab.

5. Enable the following options:

   ■ Enable Quota Management

   ■ Deny disk space to users exceeding quota limit

   ■ Limit disk space to: 10MB

   ■ Set warning level to: 8MB

   ■ Log event when a user exceeds the quota limit

   ■ Log event when a user exceeds the warning level

6. Verify all options are set correctly, and then click APPLY.

7. You will receive a dialog box informing you that the drive will be rescanned to update usage statistics. Click OK.

8. When the traffic light icon shows a green light, indicating that quotas are active on the volume, click OK to exit the drive Properties window.

9. Go to Start | Run, and enter the following command exactly as shown to connect to your DFS root in the context of the ch3ex3 user. Note that the command is case sensitive.

   net use X: \\%computername%\Departments password /user:ch3ex3

10. Launch My Computer and open the C:\ drive.

11. Right-click the Program Files directory, and select Copy.

12. Click BACK to go back to My Computer.

13. Right-click the X: drive that you mapped in step 9, and select Paste. If you do not have an X: drive, verify that steps 1 and 9 were completed correctly, and that the commands were all typed in lowercase as shown.

14. After a few seconds of data transfer, you should receive a message similar to the one shown next.

15. Click OK to close the message box.

16. Right-click the C:\ drive, select Properties, and open the Quota tab.

17. Click QUOTA ENTRIES.

18. You should see that a quota entry for the ch3ex3 user has been automatically created, and that the user has reached the warning threshold with a Percent Used value of somewhere between 90 and 99 percent.

19. Close the Quota Entries window.

20. Disable Quotas by clearing the Enable Quota Management check box, and click OK.

21. Right-click the X: drive connection, and select Disconnect.

HEADSTART OBJECTIVE 4.07

Increasing Security with EFS

EFS is a new technology in NTFS v5, and was not an option in Windows NT 4.0 and earlier without a third-party application.

You may be wondering why file encryption is needed when NTFS security manages access to the files. NTFS security works great as long as the volume is mounted under the operating system on which the security was configured. NTFS files without EFS encryption can, however, be easily accessed by mounting the volume under another instance of Windows 2000 or another operating system that supports mounting of NTFS partitions.

With EFS enabled, the files are actually stored in an encrypted format, eliminating the ability to mount a partition on another system and bypass all security.

EFS uses the Data Encryption Standard-X (DES-X) encryption technology. DES-X uses an XOR (exclusive-or) algorithm, and by default is based on a standard 56-bit encryption level (40-bit for export outside of the U.S. and Canada). For enhanced security, Windows 2000 installations in North America can be upgraded to a 128-bit EFS encryption level by applying the Windows 2000 CryptoPAK, available for download from Microsoft's Web page at www.microsoft.com. However, files encrypted with the CryptoPAK installed cannot be decrypted on a system using a 56-bit encryption level.

Encryption is enabled on a file or folder by clicking ADVANCED on the Properties window. Files that are compressed or marked with the Read-Only or System attributes cannot be encrypted.

If a folder is marked for encryption, files added to that specific folder will be encrypted. However, note that encryption is not inherited. If an encrypted file is moved to a folder that is not marked for encryption, the file still remains encrypted. The only exception to this is if the file is moved to a location on a non-NTFS (FAT or FAT32) volume. In this case, encryption is lost because only NTFS v5 volumes support file encryption.

EXERCISE 4-4

Encrypting Files with EFS

1. Open My Computer and double-click the C:\ drive.

2. Right-click the Finance directory, and select Properties.

3. Click ADVANCED.

4. Select the Encrypt contents to secure data check box.

5. Click OK twice, and then OK at the Confirmation window to enable the encrypt attribute for the current folder only.

6. Create a new text file in the C:\Finance directory and name it "Encryption Test."

7. Right-click the new file and select Properties.

8. Click ADVANCED, and verify that the "Encrypt contents to secure data" check box is selected.

9. Deselect the check box and click OK.

10. Click OK to close the Properties window, and then again to confirm the decrypt action.

HEADSTART OBJECTIVE 4.08

Defragmenting Hard Disks

When Windows 2000 creates or expands files on a disk, the clusters are not necessarily created in areas of contiguous space; that is, they often become fragmented throughout the hard disk. Fragmentation of a volume increases in proportion to time and utilization.

Understanding Defragmentation

Defragmentation refers to the process of organizing the clusters on the hard drive to reduce the time required to read a file. Servers that have a lot of creations and deletions, such as print servers that perform intense spooling, are more prone to fragmentation than others. Defragmentation should be performed:

- At least once a month.
- When disk performance (Read or Write) is below average.
- After massive addition or deletion of data.

Defragmenting a Logical Disk

In Windows 2000, a disk defragmentation tool called "Disk Defragmenter" is included with the operating system. Windows NT versions 4.0 and earlier did not have a defragmentation utility, and administrators were forced to rely on third-party applications to perform this task.

Disk Defragmenter organizes the clusters that make up a file by grouping them, to the extent possible, into one location on the hard disk. Disk Defragmenter also consolidates clusters that are marked as *free space*, which speeds up performance when creating new files. Disk Defragmenter is able to defragment FAT16, FAT32, and NTFS partitions.

on the job

To avoid fragmentation of the Windows 2000 paging file, it is a good idea to set the minimum and maximum sizes of the page file to the same values (a static page file). This prevents the continual size adjustment performed by the operating system, which can lead to a page file fragmentation and cause slower paging performance.

The Disk Defragmenter utility (Figure 4-8) is accessed through the Computer Management Console, and can be used to either analyze or defragment a volume. Analysis of a volume can be performed prior to a defragmentation, and provides a graphical view of the level of fragmentation, along with a recommendation as to whether or not you need to defragment.

The following exercise walks you through defragmenting your C:\ volume. Since disk defragmentation is a processor-intensive operation, you should close all applications and disable any antivirus software that may be running prior to beginning this exercise.

FIGURE 4-8

The Disk Defragmenter

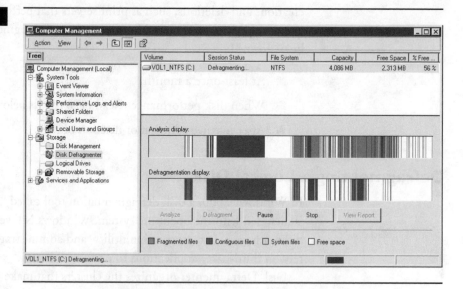

EXERCISE 4-5	**Defragmenting a Logical Disk**

1. Right-click My Computer and select Manage.

2. Expand Storage, and double-click Disk Defragmenter.

3. In the right window, right-click your C:\ drive and select Analyze4.

4. Windows 2000 then analyzes your C:\ volume for fragmentation. This takes a couple of seconds. You then receive a recommendation message telling you whether or not you need to defragment.

5. Click VIEW REPORT to view volume information and a detailed analysis of fragmented files.

6. Click DEFRAGMENT to begin defragmenting your hard disk.

7. Defragmentation may take a while. You can click STOP on the Disk Defragmenter window at any time to stop the defragmentation process.

HEADSTART OBJECTIVE 4.09

Using the Convert Program

At the beginning of this chapter, you learned about the differences between the FAT16/FAT32 file systems and NTFS. To enjoy the benefits of NTFS, you may need to convert your existing FAT16 or FAT32 volumes.

Microsoft provides a tool with Windows 2000, named "CONVERT," that allows an administrator to convert existing FAT file systems to NTFS. The CONVERT utility is executed from a command prompt, and follows the following syntax, where X: is the drive letter of the FAT16/FAT32 volume that you are converting:

```
convert X: /FS:NTFS
```

The CONVERT utility has not changed significantly since earlier versions of Windows NT, with the only exception being that it can now convert FAT32 volumes to NTFS.

Converting a FAT Partition to NTFS

The following exercise assumes that you have a C:\ partition formatted with either FAT or FAT32. If you are already running NTFS, you may skip this exercise.

If you are performing this exercise at work, you should check with your system administrator before converting your partition. Once converted to NTFS, the partition cannot be converted back to FAT.

1. Log on to your server as a local administrator.

2. Launch Command Prompt from Start | Programs | Accessories.

3. Type **CONVERT C: /FS:NTFS** at the command prompt, and click ENTER.

4. You will receive a message stating that the conversion will take place on the next reboot.

5. Click Y to confirm, and type **EXIT** when returned to a prompt.

6. Reboot your Windows 2000 server. Conversion of the file system will take place during the boot sequence.

7. Log on to your server as a local administrator.

8. Launch My Computer.

9. Right-click your C:\ drive and select Properties.

10. Notice that File System reads "NTFS."

11. Exit the drive Properties window.

CHAPTER SUMMARY

Effectively managing file resources is an important task in designing and administering a Windows 2000 environment. Determining the appropriate file system is a critical first step.

NTFS v5 introduces several new technologies to assist an administrator with the management of file resources. EFS adds another layer of security on top of NTFS permissions to protect valuable NTFS files, eliminating the ability to mount an NTFS volume on another local installation of NT or Windows 2000 to bypass Security permissions.

DFS helps organize physically dispersed data into a logical, hierarchical view, while Quota Management enables an administrator to restrict the amount of disk utilization on a per-user basis.

Disk Defragmentation is also introduced in NTFS v5, which provides a method for reorganizing the physical data on a hard disk to increase disk access efficiency and improve server response time.

TWO-MINUTE DRILL

- ❑ Windows 2000 supports all file systems implemented in Windows NT 4.0, as well as some additional file systems. Those supported by Windows 2000 include FAT16/FAT32, NTFS, CDFS, and UDF. *cd-Rom*

- ❑ The FAT file system is the oldest of the file systems supported by Windows 2000, and has been implemented in Microsoft operating systems since the earliest versions of MS-DOS.

- ❑ The earlier version of the FAT file system implemented in MS-DOS is known as FAT16, to differentiate it from the improved FAT32. The FAT32 file system was first implemented in Windows 95 OSR2, and was supported by Windows 98 and now Windows 2000.

- ❑ NTFS has been implemented since the initial version of Windows NT, and continues to be the most commonly used file system in Windows NT/2000 enterprise environments.

- ❑ One of the major advantages of NTFS over FAT is the ability to set Security permissions on files and directories.

- ❑ NTFS natively supports the ability to compress files on an individual basis by enabling the Compress property on the General tab of a file or directory's properties.

- ❑ CDFS is a Read-Only file system that enables Windows 2000 to access data on CD-ROMs.

- ❑ File sharing in Windows 2000 is the method in which users are allowed to access data on a server computer.

- ❑ The Create Shared Folder Wizard is designed so that an administrator can easily configure a directory on a server for sharing.

❑ Share permissions are Security permissions assigned to specific users or groups to allow access to a share.

❑ Once a directory has been shared on a Windows 2000 server, a drive letter can then be mapped from a client computer to access data on the share.

❑ DFS has both the advantage of a central file storage location (a single drive mapping) for the end user, as well as a single point of share administration for the network administrator.

❑ To access a DFS share from a Windows 9x workstation, you must install the DFS client.

❑ NTFS permissions are used to assign users or groups a specific set of permissions to a file or directory resource on an NTFS partition.

❑ NTFS permissions are used on volumes formatted with NTFS. NTFS permissions allow an administrator or user to define security on a file or directory level.

❑ If you move a file or directory from an NTFS volume to a FAT16 or FAT32 volume, it loses all NTFS permissions that were previously assigned.

❑ In Windows 2000, it is necessary to first disable the Permission Inheritance of an object before custom permissions can be defined.

❑ Effective permissions are the permissions that a user actually has on an object, and takes into account permissions from both the share and file/directory hierarchy.

❑ Auditing keeps a log of which users access specific data, and can later be used to trace the exact history of the access of a file.

❑ Like Security permissions, audit settings flow down the file/directory hierarchy, and inheritance of audit settings can be disabled for an object.

❑ The inclusion of Summary information in a file or directory properties is new in Windows 2000. Summary information was previously only available for specific types of files, such as Microsoft Office documents.

❑ Attributes are "flags" on a file or directory that enable specific system options.

❏ The Version tab displays any information that may have been placed in the header of a binary file by the manufacturer.

❏ All fields in the Summary tab are optional, and can be used by the user or administrator to store a description of the file as well as origin information.

❏ Disk quotas on NTFS volumes in Windows 2000 are configured for a specific user context (either a domain or local user), and are assigned on a per-volume basis.

❏ EFS uses the Data Encryption Standard-X (DES-X) encryption technology.

❏ If a folder is marked for encryption, files added to that specific folder will be encrypted. However, note that encryption is not inherited.

❏ Defragmentation refers to the process of organizing the clusters on the hard drive to reduce the time required to read a file.

❏ Disk Defragmenter organizes the clusters that make up a file by grouping them, to the extent possible, into one location on the hard disk.

❏ Microsoft provides a tool with Windows 2000, named "CONVERT," that allows an administrator to convert existing FAT file systems to NTFS.

SELF TEST

The following questions help you measure your understanding of the material presented in this chapter. Read all of the choices carefully, as there may be more than one correct answer. Choose all correct answers for each question.

1. Which of the following file systems are supported by Windows 2000? (Check all that apply.)

   A. NTFS

   B. FAT

   C. HPFS

   D. UDF

2. Which of the following file systems can be used to format a volume in Windows 2000? (Choose all that apply.)

   A. FAT16

   B. FAT32

   C. NTFS

   D. UDF

3. As an administrator of a Windows 2000 server, you have been given the task of selecting a file system for the server's single partition. The partition must be formatted as 6GB, will hold the Windows 2000 system files, must support Long File Names (LFNs), and must allow for file/directory-level security. Which of the following file systems will support this? (Choose all that apply.)

   A. FAT16

   B. FAT32

   C. NTFS

   D. DES

4. You are attempting to compress data stored on a 6GB FAT32 volume; however, the Compression option is disabled. What is most likely the cause of the problem?

   A. Encryption has been enabled on one or more directories on the volume.

   B. The partition size is too large.

   C. You do not have the Compress permission to the root folder.

   D. Compression cannot be used on FAT32 volumes.

5. Which of the following shows the correct UNC name syntax to be specified when connecting to a share?

   A. servername.sharename

   B. \\servername\sharename

   C. \\sharename\servername

   D. sharename.servername

6. As an administrator of several Windows 2000 servers, you want to provide your users with a method to access files from several servers through a single logical directory hierarchy. Which of the following technologies will you implement?

   A. DES

   B. EFS

   C. UDF

   D. DFD

7. The C:\Marketing directory is shared as Marketing on the Departments server. The only permission assigned to the Marketing share is Ray:Change. The C:\ drive is formatted with NTFS , and the Marketing directory has the following Security permissions: Marketing: Full Control, Ray: Read. What are Ray's Effective permissions when accessing the Marketing data through the \\Departments\Marketing share?

   A. Full Control

   B. Read

   C. Change

   D. No Access

8. The Payroll directory has been moved from C:\, an NTFS volume, to D:\, a FAT32 volume on the Departments server. The Payroll share has been reconfigured to point to D:\Payroll, and security is set on the share as Payroll: Full Control. The Payroll Directory permissions were set to Payroll:Change prior to the move. What are the Effective permissions for members of the Payroll group accessing the data through the \\Departments\Payroll share?

   A. Full Control

   B. Change

   C. Read

   D. No Access

9. Betty is a member of the Managers group on the Departments server. The Managers directory has been shared from C:\, an NTFS volume as Managers. The only permission on the share is Managers: Change. On the Managers directory, the following permissions are in effect: Managers: Full Control, Betty: Deny for all permissions. What are Betty's Effective permissions to the Managers data when accessing it through the \\Departments\Managers share?

   A. Change

   B. No Access

   C. Full Control

   D. List Data

10. How can encryption be enabled on a Windows 2000 NTFS directory?

   A. By entering ENCRYPT /FS:NTFS from a command prompt

   B. By using ATTRIB +E <filename>

   C. By adding All Users with the Encrypt permission

   D. By enabling the Encrypt Advanced attribute in the file Properties window

11. You have enabled the Auditing Policy on your local computer, and have enabled auditing for the delete event on the Inventory directory. You suspect that someone has deleted critical data out of this folder. How can you find out which user deleted the file?

   A. View the Security Event Log

   B. View the Auditing Event Log

   C. View the contents of the Master File Table

   D. View the AUDIT.LOG file in the C:\WINNT\Logs directory

12. You plan to bring a new server online with a larger storage capacity than your existing machine. Both servers will be online running Windows 2000, and you plan to copy the data across the network from one server to the other. You have hundreds of customized quota entries on the old Windows 2000 server. What is the best way to ensure that quota entries are populated on the new server?

    A. Export the quota configuration using the Quota Entries console, and import it on the new server.

    B. Export the quota configuration using QEXPORT, and import it on the new server using QIMPORT.

    C. Back up the quota to tape using the Windows 2000 backup program.

    D. You must recreate all quota entries manually.

13. What type of encryption is used on the Encrypting File System (EFS)?

    A. DES+

    B. DES-X

    C. AES

    D. DFS

14. When should you defragment your hard drive? (Choose all that apply.)

    A. At least every month

    B. After deletion of large amounts of data

    C. When disk write performance is slow

    D. When disk read performance is slow

15. You currently have Windows 2000 installed on a FAT32 volume, but you would like to convert to NTFS to allow for the implementation of file/directory level security. Which is the easiest method to convert your FAT32 volume to NTFS?

    A. CHKDSK C: /CONVERT:NTFS

    B. CONVNTFS C:

    C. CONVERT C: /FS:NTFS

    D. FAT32 cannot be converted to NTFS

MICROSOFT CERTIFIED SYSTEMS ENGINEER

5

Using Group Policy to Manage Desktop Environments

HEADSTART OBJECTIVES

This chapter looks at another of Windows 2000's showcase features: Group Policy. Windows NT administrators will be familiar with System Policies and poledit.exe, the System Policy Editor. Although Windows 2000 includes the System Policy Editor for setting policies for down-level clients, and although it is possible to use the poledit utility to set NT 4.0–style policies for Windows 2000 clients, it is preferable when working with Windows 2000 clients to use the new Group Policy feature.

Group Policy might be described as System Policies on steroids; using Group Policy adds functionality, flexibility, and granularity to give an administrator far more control over the users' environment than was ever possible in NT.

Introduction to Group Policy and Microsoft Management Console

A group policy is a set of configuration settings that can be applied to an Active Directory object (or group of objects) to define the behavior of the object and its child objects. Group policies can serve many purposes, from application and file deployment to global configuration of user profile settings and restriction of access.

Those who have worked with NT will discover that many of the administrative settings that were scattered throughout various administrative tools in the old operating system are now combined in one place and easily accessible in the Group Policy Microsoft Management Console (MMC). For instance, setting of audit policies, assignment of user rights, and management of what was formerly referred to as account policies (governing user passwords) are now all accomplished through the Group Policy console.

You can use Group Policy to run scripts at specified times; to fine-tune security settings; and, in short, to control the user environment to whatever degree is desired. Group Policy gives an administrator the power to enhance productivity throughout the organization by completely managing the users' desktop environment.

The Group Policy MMC

Group Policy is a powerful tool that should be used only by designated Group Policy administrators (this may or may not include all domain admins). In fact, Microsoft recognized this and took steps to limit its use. If you go looking for the Group Policy Editor in Windows 2000's Administrative Tools, you won't find it. Group Policy is managed through a custom MMC (which you must create and to which you add the Group Policy snap-in).

The MMC is a key feature in Windows 2000, designed to ease the burden of administration by providing a standardized interface for using administrative tools and utilities. The management applications contained in an MMC are called *snap-ins*, and custom MMCs hold the snap-in(s) required to perform specific tasks. Custom consoles can be saved as files with the .msc file extension. See Figure 5-1, which shows the Group Policy Console for a domain controller.

Creating a custom MMC for administering Group Policy is easy. We will create a Group Policy Console later in this chapter. First, let's look at some of the terminology that you must understand when discussing Group Policy. It's especially important to familiarize yourself with the following terms and their acronyms:

- Group Policy Object (GPO)
- Group Policy Container (GPC)
- Group Policy Template (GPT)

Group Policy Objects

GPOs are where the policies themselves are stored. If you think of the Group Policy snap-in as the application program that creates group policies, just as Microsoft Word is an application that creates documents, the

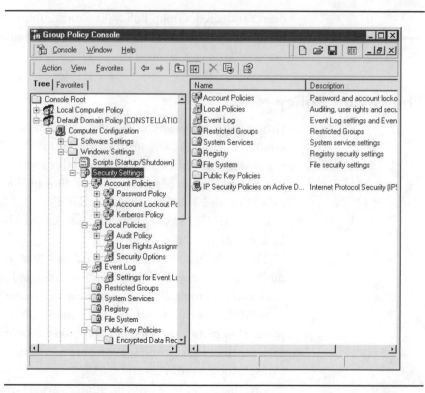

FIGURE 5-1

A custom Group
Policy Console

individual GPOs would be analogous to individual document files, each of
which contains information.

Local Versus Nonlocal GPOs

GPOs can be either local or nonlocal, depending on what type of Windows
2000 computer they are stored on. Nonlocal policies are stored on domain
controllers and are dependent on Active Directory being installed. Nonlocal
policies can be applied to a site, domain, or an Organizational Unit (OU).
Microsoft uses the acronym SDOU to refer to these together.

Local policies exist on Windows 2000 member (stand-alone) servers and
workstations running Windows 2000 Professional. These computers store
one local GPO, which contains a subset of the settings available in a
nonlocal GPO. When these computers belong to a Windows 2000 Active

Directory domain environment, both local and nonlocal GPO settings apply. If there is a conflict, the local settings can be overwritten by nonlocal settings.

Group Policy Container

Nonlocal GPOs consist of two parts, which are stored separately: the Group Policy Container (GPC) and the Group Policy Template (GPT).

The GPC is a Directory Service object that includes subcontainers for Machine and User Group Policy information. The GPC contains the following data:

- **Version information** Used to ensure that the information is synchronized with GPT information.

- **Status information** Indicates whether the GPO is enabled or disabled for this site, domain, or OU (SDOU).

- **List of components** Specifies which extensions to Group Policy have settings in the GPO.

- **The class store** Information for software installation, used when assigning or publishing applications.

heads
①p

Remember that Windows 2000 nondomain controller computers have only one local GPO, and it is stored in %SYSTEMROOT%\System32\ GroupPolicy. GPCs are Active Directory objects, and apply only to nonlocal policies. ("SYSTEMROOT" refers to the directory into which Windows 2000 was installed, typically named WINNT.)

Group Policy Template

A GPT is a folder structure consisting of the GPT folder and a set of subfolders, which together contain all the Group Policy information for that particular GPO. The GPT is located in the system volume folder on the Windows 2000 domain controller(s). The folder name is the GUID

(Globally Unique Identifier) of the GPO to which it applies, which is a hexadecimal number. The path would look like the following:

%systemroot%\Sysvol\sysvol\tacteam.net\Policies\{A432C8532-F089-22d4-78E4-00C8FEd00C43}

The subfolders in the GPT folder depend on what group policies are set, but the following questions and answers show some typical subfolder, and their functions.

QUESTIONS AND ANSWERS

Subfolder Name	Subfolder Function
What is the function of the \ADM subfolder?	It contains the .ADM files (administrative templates) associated with this GPT.

What is the function of the \USER subfolder? What about those sub-subfolders under it?	It contains the Registry.pol file with the Registry settings applied to users. It also contains subfolders of its own:
	\USER\APPLICATIONS
	  Contains .AAS files (Advertisement) used by the installation service.
	\USER\FILES
	  Contains files to be deployed to users.
	\USER\SCRIPTS
	  Contains the scripts and associated files for logon and logoff scripting.

What is the function of the \MACHINE subfolder?	It contains the Registry.pol file with the Registry settings applied to computers. (It also contains subfolders similar to those in the /USER subfolder, with the same functions except that they are applied to computers. For example, \MACHINE\SCRIPTS contains scripts and files for startup and shutdown scripting.

**heads
⊕P**

The Registry.pol files in Windows 2000 are not compatible with the ntconfig.pol and config.pol files created by System Policy Editor in Windows NT or Windows 9x. Files created with SPE cannot be applied to Windows 2000 computers.

Now that you understand what GPOs, GPCs, and GPTs are and what they do, let's walk through the steps involved in creating a Group Policy Console to use for management of our GPO.

Deploying the Group Policy Editor Microsoft Management Console Snap-In

Log on to a Windows 2000 computer with administrative privileges.

1. Click Start │ Run.

2. In the Open box, type **mmc**, and click OK. This will open an empty MMC console (shown in Figure 5-2).

3. The next step is setting the mode for your new console. Saving a console in User mode means those who use it cannot add or remove snap-ins, or save the console. If you save it in Author mode, access will include full functionality, including the ability to modify the console. We will save our Group Policy console in Author mode; to do so, click Console and choose Options.

4. The Options dialog box (shown next) appears, allowing you to select the mode in which the console will be saved (or, if User mode

FIGURE 5-2

A new, empty management console, ready for customization

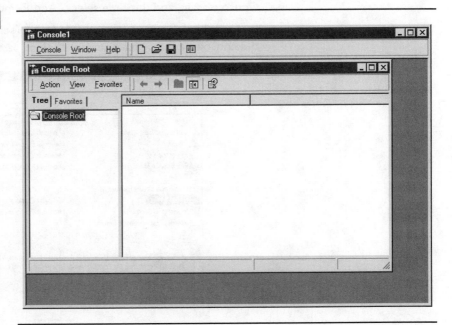

is chosen, further define the level of access). Choose "Author mode" and click OK.

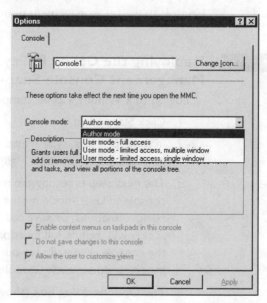

5. Now we will add the Group Policy snap-in to our console. Click Console again, and this time select "Add/Remove snap-in."

6. In the dialog box that appears, click Add to select a snap-in to add to the console. You will have several choices, as shown next.

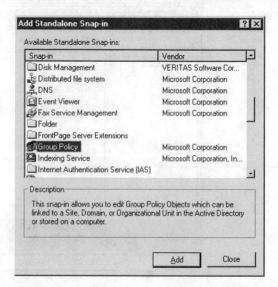

7. Click Add. Now you will be able to select the GPO, as shown in Figure 5-3.

8. By default, the GPO that this snap-in controls is the Local Computer. If you are logged on to a domain controller and wish to use the MMC to manage group policy for the domain, click Browse. You will see a dialog box similar to the one shown next.

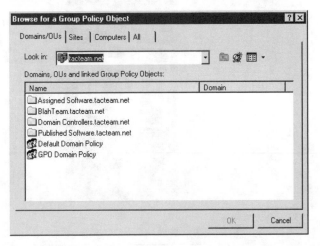

9. Select the GPO that you wish to manage with this Group Policy snap-in. For purposes of this exercise, choose the Default Domain Policy.

10. Click OK, and then click Finish at the next screen. You will now see the selected GPO in the console tree, as shown in Figure 5-4.

11. The last step is giving our Group Policy MMC a descriptive name. One choice is to name it after the GPO it will control. Click Console, then Save As, and type a name (with the .msc extension) as shown next.

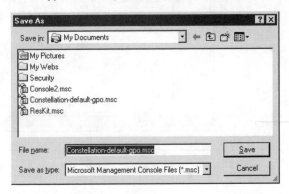

FIGURE 5-3

Selecting the Group
Policy Object

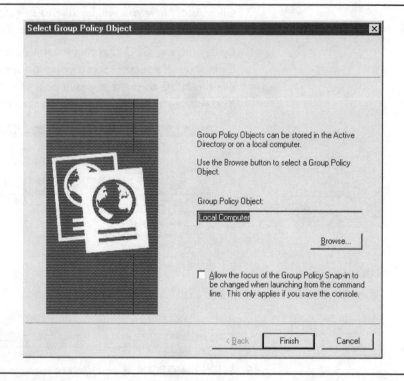

FIGURE 5-4

The Group Policy
Object now appears
in the console tree

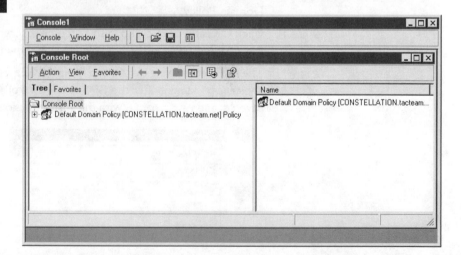

By default, the console file will be saved in the My Documents folder. You can create a shortcut on the desktop for it if you like.

In the next section, we learn how to use our newly created console to apply group policies to users and computers in the domain.

Applying Group Policy

Group policies are applied to two types of Active Directory objects: Users and Computers. Security groups can be used to filter policies, but the policies are not applied to groups.

Computer policies are applied at the time the machine boots into Windows 2000, and User policies are applied at the time that the user logs on.

Order in Which Policies Are Applied

First, NT 4.0–style policies (those created with the System Policy Editor) are applied. Then the Local GPO is applied. Site GPOs are applied next. After that, Domain GPOs are applied, and finally, the OU GPOs are applied, starting with the parent OU and proceeding through child OUs in that order. If there are multiple GPOs for a site, domain, or OU, the administrator can specify the order of application.

The policies applied first are overwritten by those applied later in case of a conflict. If there is no conflict, the effective policy will be an accumulation of all applied policies.

As you can see, the local GPO is the least influential of Windows 2000 group policies in an Active Directory environment because it is overwritten by nonlocal policies that are applied later.

Modifying Default Policy Application Behavior

Windows 2000 provides several ways to modify the default behavior when it comes to the application and inheritance of group policies.

POLICY FILTERING Group Policy can be filtered by security group membership. In Windows 2000, computers can belong to security groups. To define which computers and users a GPO influences, administrators can use security groups.

For any GPO, administrators can filter its effect on computers that are members of specified security groups. To do so, use the standard Access Control List (ACL) editor. (To use the ACL editor, click a GOP's Properties sheet, and then click Security. See Figure 5-5.)

heads ⓤP

The policies in a GPO only apply to the users who have Read permission for that GPO. You can filter the scope of the GPO by creating security groups and assigning Read permissions to those groups (in other words, you can prevent the policy from applying to a particular group by denying the group Read permission to the GPO).

Using the ACL editor to modify the Access Control Entry (ACE) for a security group that contains computers

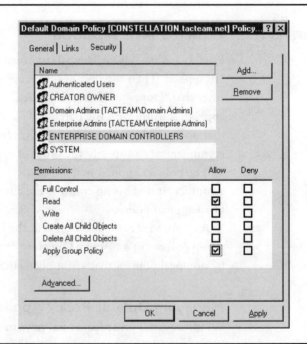

BLOCKING POLICY INHERITANCE   As an administrator, you can block the inheritance of policies, which would by default be propagated from higher site, domain, or OU levels.

To do this, right-click on the SDOU name in the Users and Computers MMC, select Properties, and click on the Group Policy tab (as shown in Figure 5-6).

Check the Block Inheritance check box. If this option is selected for a child-level GPO, the Child object will not inherit any policy from a parent-level GPO.

ENFORCING THE HIGHER-LEVEL POLICIES WITH THE NO OVERRIDE OPTION   You can also force Child containers to inherit policies from their higher-level Container objects, so that the policies in the selected GPO cannot be overridden. To do this, refer back to Figure

FIGURE 5-6

Blocking inheritance via the Group Policy tab of the Properties sheet for the tacteam.net domain

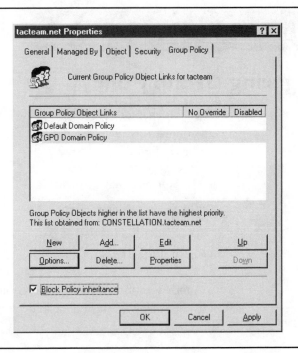

5-6 and this time, click Options. You will see the dialog box shown next. Select "No override."

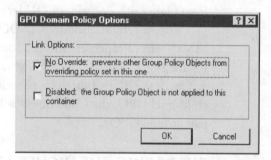

DISABLING THE GROUP POLICY OBJECT FOR A SPECIFIC SDOU If you do not want the selected GPO to be applied to a particular Container object (site, domain, or OU), you can check the Disabled check box shown in the dialog box just shown to accomplish that.

HEADSTART OBJECTIVE 5.03

Configuring Group Policy

Since this chapter's focus is on using Group Policy to manage the user environment, we will be looking at four basic areas in which Group Policy can be configured:

1. Software Management

2. Security Management

3. Folder Redirection

4. Running Scripts

Another important function of Group Policy is the installation of software. Using Group Policy to deploy applications (by assignment or publication) is discussed in Chapter 6, "Using Group Policy to Manage Software."

Let's look now at each of the ways Group Policy can be configured.

Software Management Overview

Administrators can use Group Policy to globally configure many of the software settings in user profiles. This includes the desktop, the Start menu, and applications settings.

Software management applies to applying Group Policy settings to applications, and/or to Windows 2000 components.

on the *Job*

A common problem for network administrators is the "adventurous user," who likes to explore and experiment with the settings on the computer. These users have "just enough knowledge to be dangerous."

With Group Policy, you can now control exactly what these users are able to do on the computer, and reduce or prevent the damage resulting from their explorations. When Group Policy is combined with NTFS permissions, you can go so far as to create a totally locked-down environment. Users will be unable to access programs or data on the computer for which they do not have authorization, and you eliminate such problems as users accidentally (or otherwise) moving or deleting important system files, changing Windows configuration settings, installing unapproved software, or running applications they should not be using.

Software Settings Nodes

There are two Software Settings nodes in Group Policy: Settings for Computers and Settings for Users. Let's briefly examine each.

SOFTWARE SETTINGS FOR COMPUTERS   \Computer Configuration\Software Settings\ is for software settings that apply to all users who log on to the computer.

SOFTWARE SETTINGS FOR USERS   \User Configuration\
Software Settings\ is for software settings that apply to users regardless of
which computer they log on to.

(There is a Software Installation subnode in each of the Software Settings
nodes, and there may be other subnodes as well, which are placed here by
Independent Software Vendors.)

Windows Settings Nodes

Likewise, there are two Windows Settings nodes, one for Computers and
one for Users:

WINDOWS SETTINGS FOR COMPUTERS   \Computer
Configuration\Windows Settings\ is for Windows settings that apply to all
users who log on to the computer. There are two subnodes: Security
Settings and Scripts.

WINDOWS SETTINGS FOR USERS   \User Configuration\
Windows Settings\ is for Windows settings that apply to users regardless of
which computer they log on to. There are three subnodes: Folder
Redirection, Security Settings, and Scripts.

See Figure 5-7, which shows the Software and Windows settings in the
console tree.

Implementing and Modifying Software Policies

The computer settings for Windows 2000 are stored in the Registry in
HKEY_LOCAL_MACHINE, and the user settings are stored in
HKEY_CURRENT_USER. Microsoft has made it easy for administrators
to modify these settings in a Windows 2000 Active Directory environment.
The following exercise walks you through the steps.

FIGURE 5-7

The Group Policy Console, showing the Computer Configuration subfolders for Software and Windows settings

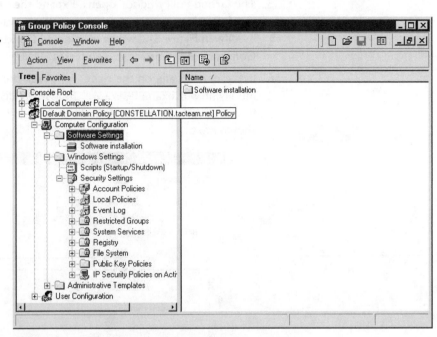

EXERCISE 5-2

Implementing Group Policy

Log on to the Windows 2000 domain controller with administrative privileges.

1. Open the Active Directory Users and Computers: Start | Administrative Tools | Active Directory Users and Computers.

2. Right-click on the object (domain or OU) for which you want to modify the GPO.

3. Click on the Group Policy tab.

4. Select the GPO you want to modify. Click Edit.

5. The Group Policy Editor opens. Expand the item under Computer Configuration that contains the policy you want to implement or modify. In Figure 5-8, we have selected Desktop under User Configure, Administrative Templates.

6. In the details pane on the right, right-click the policy you wish to modify. In our example, we will choose "Hide Internet Explorer icon on desktop." Select Properties. You will see the dialog box shown next.

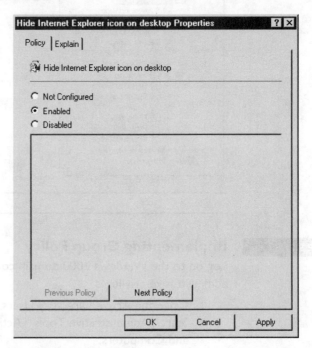

7. Click Enabled to implement the policy.
   You will note that the Explain tabcontains useful information about exactly how this policy works.

Congratulations! You have implemented the software policy.

FIGURE 5-8

Configuring or modifying
the User Configuration
Desktop settings

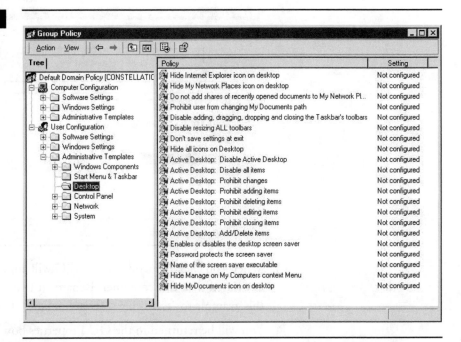

Modifying Software Policies

To modify the software policies for an OU, you open the selected OU in
Active Directory Users and Computers and access the Group Policy tab of
its Properties sheet (following the same steps as in the preceding exercise).
Then do the following:

1. Click Add, and the Add a Group Policy Object Link box appears.

2. Select the All tab, and then click the Create New GPO icon, as
   shown next.

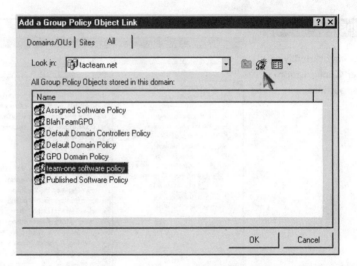

3. When you click the icon, a new GPO will appear in the list of GPOs associated with this container. Rename it (we renamed the one in this example to "team-one software policy"). Click OK.

4. You will be returned to the OU Properties box. Now select the new GPO and click Edit (as shown next).

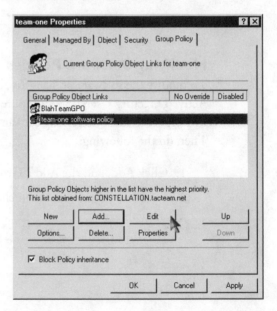

5. You will be returned to the Group Policy console. Expand the tree as shown in Figure 5-9.

6. Select Administrative Templates | Control Panel | Display. In the details pane on the right, choose "No HTML wallpaper" and right-click. Select Properties.

7. Enable the policy (as you did in Exercise 5-2).

8. Close the Group Policy console and the AD Users and Computers MMC.

Congratulations! You have modified a software policy, thereby preventing users in the team-one OU from using anything other than .bmp files as desktop wallpaper.

FIGURE 5-9

Selecting a policy to link to the team-one OU

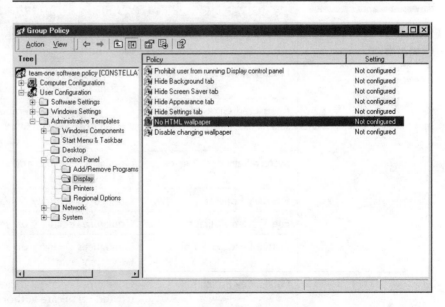

Security Management Overview

In Windows 2000, security configurations can be configured for computers using Group Policy. Table 5-1 shows the security areas that can be set.

There are two Security Settings nodes in Group Policy: Settings for Computers and Settings for Users. Let's look at each.

Security Settings for Computers

\Computer Configuration\Windows Settings\Security Settings\ is for security settings that should apply to all users who log on to the computer. This has two subnodes: IP Security Policies on Active Directory, and Public Key Policies.

Security Settings for Users

\User Configuration\Windows Settings\Security Settings\ is for security settings that should apply to users regardless of which computer they log on to. This has a Public Key Policies subnode.

TABLE 5-1	Security Policy Area	What It's Used For
Security Configuration Areas	Account Policies	Configures policies for passwords, account lockout, and Kerberos.
	Local Policies	Configures auditing, user rights, and security options for the local machine.
	Restricted Group Policies	Configures group membership for groups that are security sensitive (by default, this includes the Administrators group).
	System Services Policies	Configures startup and security settings for services.
	Registry Policies	Configures security on Registry keys.
	File System Policies	Configures security on specific file paths.
	Active Directory Policies	Configures security on specific Directory objects.
	Public Key Policies	Configures encrypted data recovery agents, trusted certificate authorities, etc.
	IP Security Policies	Configures network IP security.

Modifying Security Settings

You use the Group Policy custom MMC that you created earlier to manage security settings. (See Figure 5-10.)

The Security Settings node allows a security administrator to manually configure security levels assigned to a GPO or local computer policy. This can be done after, or instead of, using a security template to set system security.

Using Security Templates

The Security Template snap-in is a tool for defining security templates that can then be applied to a GPO to define system security settings. The Security Templates snap-in is added to the custom MMC in the same way as any other snap-in, via the "Add/Remove snap-in" option (refer to Exercise 5-1).

To define a security template, following these steps:

1. In Security Templates, expand the Security Templates node.

2. Right-click on the node where you want to store the new template, and click New Configuration.

FIGURE 5-10

The Security Settings subfolder in the Group Policy Console tree

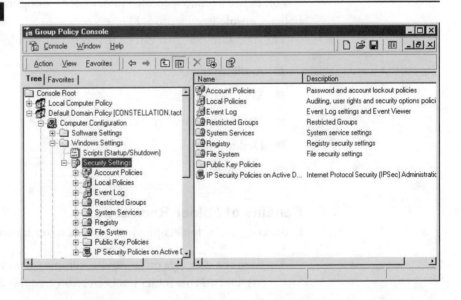

3. Enter the name and description for your new security template.

4. Expand the new security template node to display the security areas.

5. Expand the node for the security area you want to configure.

6. Double-click the security attribute you want to configure.

Now you must import the security template to a GPO. Follow these steps:

1. In a console from which you manage Group Policy settings, click the GPO to which you want to import the security template.

2. In the console tree, right-click Security Settings.

3. Click Import Policy.

4. Click the security template you want to import.

User Document Settings (Folder Redirection)

Folder Redirection is an extension to Group Policy, which you can use to redirect certain Windows 2000 special folders to network locations.

Folder Redirection is located under User Configuration in the Group Policy Console (see Figure 5-11).

The special folders that can be redirected in Windows 2000 include

- Applications Data
- My Documents
- My Documents\My Pictures
- Desktop
- Start Menu

Benefits of Folder Redirection

Redirecting users' folders provides benefits to both users and administrators:

- Even if a user logs on to various computers on the network, if the My Documents folder has been redirected, his or her documents will always be available.

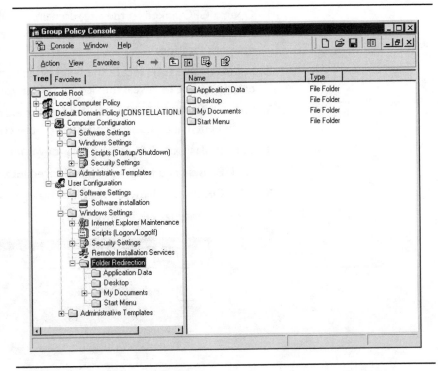

FIGURE 5-11

Using the Group Policy Console to redirect folders

Offline File technology (part of Intellimirror, wherein files stored on the local hard drive and those stored on the server are synchronized) allows users to have access to My Documents even while they are not connected to the network.

Data stored on a shared network server can be backed up as part of routine system administration, requiring no action on the part of the user.

The system administrator can use Group Policy to set disk quotas, limiting the amount of space taken up by user's special folders.

EXERCISE 5-3

Implementing Folder Redirection Policy

To redirect the Windows 2000 special folders to one location for everyone in the site, domain, or OU, follow these steps:

1. Open a GPO linked to the site, domain, or OU containing the users whose Windows 2000 Special Folders you wish to redirect to a network location.

2. In the console tree, locate the Folder Redirection node and double-click it to reveal the Special Folder you want to redirect.

3. Right-click the desired Special Folder (for example, Desktop or My Documents) and choose Properties on the context menu.

4. Choose Basic on the Settings drop-down menu.

5. Click Browse and browse to the desired location.

6. Click OK on the Browse for Folder dialog box.

7. Click the Settings tab (shown next).

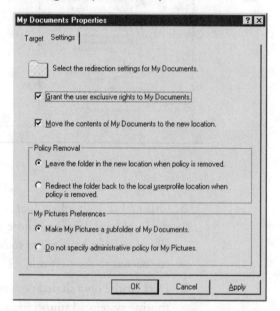

8. Set each of the following options. The defaults are recommended:

A. Grant the user exclusive rights to the Special Folder (enabled by default).

B. Move the contents of the user's current Special Folder to the new location (enabled by default).

9. Choose one of the two options for Policy Removal. The default setting is recommended:

   A. Leave the files in the new location when the policy is removed. This is the default.

   B. Redirect the folder back to the local user profile location when the policy is removed. If you select this option, read the following Heads Up.

heads ⊕p *By default, the user and the local system have full rights to the folder, and no one else, not even administrators, have any rights. If this setting is disabled, no changes are made to the permissions on the folder. Whatever permissions apply by default remain in effect.*

Best Practices for Redirection of Folders

There are several recommended practices for redirection of folders:

1. Enable Client Side caching (an allotted amount of local disk space to be used for temporary offline copies of network files), especially for users with laptops.

2. Incorporate %USERNAME% into fully qualified UNC paths so that users have their own folders. For example, \\server\share\%USERNAME%\My Documents.

3. In general, accept the default Folder Redirection settings.

Scripts

Group policies can also be used to assign and run scripts at prescribed times, such as when a user logs on or when the computer is shut down. Scripts folders are stored in the Scripts subfolder in the GPT.

Scripts assigned to run at logon or logoff are stored in the \USER\SCRIPTS subfolder of the GPT, and those assigned to run when the computer starts up or shuts down are stored in the \MACHINE\SCRIPTS subfolder.

Assigning a Script to Run at User Logon

To assign a user logon script, following these steps:

1. Open the Group Policy snap-in.

2. In the console tree, click the Scripts node.

3. In the details pane, click the Logon icon.

4. In the Logon properties page, click Add.

5. In the Add a Script dialog box, set the options you want to use, and then click OK:

   Script Name: Type the path to the script, or click Browse to search for the script file in the Netlogon share of the domain controller.

   Script Parameters: Type any parameters you want to use as you would type them on the command line.

6. In the Logon properties page, specify any options you want to use:

   A. Logon Scripts for: Lists all scripts currently assigned to the selected GPO. If you assign multiple scripts, the scripts are processed according to the order you specify. To move a script up in the list, click it, and then click Up; to move it down, click Down.

   B. Add: Opens the Add a Script dialog box, where you can specify any additional scripts to use.

   C. Edit: Opens the Edit Script dialog box, where you can modify script information such as name and parameters.

   D. Remove: Removes the selected script from the Logon Scripts list.

   E. Show Files: Use to view the script files stored in the selected Group Policy.

HEADSTART OBJECTIVE 5.04

Guidelines for Implementing Group Policy

The following guidelines will help you implement Group Policy in the most effective and efficient way:

1. Use Group Policy rather than Windows NT 4.0 System Policy whenever possible. (You can override this default precedence by way of a Group Policy setting, but it is not recommended.)

2. Disable the unused parts of a GPO. If a GPO has only settings that are Not Configured, then you can avoid processing those settings by disabling the node. This will speed up the startup and logon for those users and computers subject to this GPO.

3. Use the Block Policy Inheritance feature sparingly, because routine use of this feature makes it difficult to troubleshoot policy. Use the No Override feature sparingly (for the same reason).

4. Minimize the number of GPOs associated with users in domains or OUs. The more GPOs are applied to a user, the longer it takes for the user to log on.

5. Filter policy based on Security Group membership. Users who do not have an ACE directing that a particular GPO be applied to them can avoid the associated logon delay, because the GPO will not be processed for those users. Filtering can only be done using membership in Security Groups.

6. Override user-based Group Policy with computer-based Group Policy only when absolutely necessary. This should be done only if you need the desktop configuration to be the same regardless of which user logs on.

7. Avoid using cross-domain GPO assignments, because the processing of GPOs will take much longer.

ACCELERATING TO WINDOWS 2000

Accelerating to Windows 2000

Group Policy is a brand new feature in Windows 2000. Although it is based on NT 4.0's System Policy, the improvements and added features make it an entirely different "animal."

- Administrative templates give you granular control in managing users' desktop environments through Registry-based policies.

- Folder Redirection is an exciting new concept that can provide more fault tolerance for users' data, as well as greater convenience for those who work at different computers or sometimes log on from laptops.

- Startup, shutdown, logon, and logoff scripts are now much easier to specify and run using Group Policy.

- Control of security settings allows greater fine-tuning, and is accomplished from one place instead of being scattered among several different administrative tools.

- The ability to filter policies by group membership further enhances the granularity of control.

- It's easy to alter the default behavior of policy inheritance by simply checking a check box to prevent or force inheritance of a Parent object's policies by its Child objects.

CHAPTER SUMMARY

This chapter introduced the concept of Group Policy and led you through a series of exercises designed to show you the basics of putting those concepts into practice.

You learned that Group policies can be used to define various components of the user's desktop environment that a system administrator wants to manage; for example, the programs that are available to users, the programs that appear on the user's desktop, and Start menu options.

You learned how to create a specific desktop configuration for a particular group of users, using the Group Policy snap-in.

You also learned the terminology associated with Group Policy. The settings you specify are contained in a Group Policy Object (GPO), which is in turn associated with selected Active Directory objects—sites, domains, or Organizational Units (OUs). You learned when and how to use Group Policy Templates, and where they are stored in the directory tree.

We discussed the differences between Group Policy settings for User Configuration, which affect users, and those for Computer Configuration, which affect computers.

Finally, we examined some guidelines, or best practices, for applying and modifying Group Policy in the enterprise environment.

Group Policy is a large and complex topic, and the limited scope of this chapter prevents an in-depth treatment. The best way to learn about Group Policy is by working with it. If you can, set up some test OUs containing unused computer and user accounts, create some test security groups, and practice implementing your group policies with them before applying them to mission-critical Directory objects.

Windows 2000's Group Policy is a tremendous aid to the network administrator, allowing him or her to make decisions regarding user environment, then "set it and forget it," relying on the system to enforce those decisions.

 # TWO-MINUTE DRILL

❑ A group policy is a set of configuration settings that can be applied to an Active Directory object (or group of objects) to define the behavior of the object and its child objects.

❑ Group Policy is a powerful tool that should be used only by designated Group Policy administrators (this may or may not include all domain admins).

❑ Group Policy is managed through a custom Microsoft Management Console (MMC), which you must create and to which you add the Group Policy snap-in.

❑ Group Policy Objects (GPOs) are where the policies themselves are stored.

❑ Nonlocal GPOs consist of two parts, which are stored separately: the Group Policy Container (GPC) and the Group Policy Template (GPT).

❑ A GPT is a folder structure consisting of the GPT folder and a set of subfolders, which together contain all the Group Policy information for that particular GPO.

❑ Saving a console in User mode means those who use it cannot add or remove snap-ins, or save the console. If you save it in Author mode, access will include full functionality, including the ability to modify the console.

❑ Group policies are applied to two types of Active Directory objects: Users and Computers. Security groups can be used to filter policies, but the policies are not applied to groups.

❑ The local GPO is the least influential of Windows 2000 group policies in an Active Directory environment because it is overwritten by nonlocal policies that are applied later.

❑ Administrators can use Group Policy to globally configure many of the software settings in user profiles. This includes the desktop, the Start menu, and applications settings.

❑ The computer settings for Windows 2000 are stored in the Registry in HKEY_LOCAL_MACHINE, and the user settings are stored in HKEY_CURRENT_USER.

❑ In Windows 2000, security configurations can be configured for computers using Group Policy.

❑ There are two Security Settings nodes in Group Policy: Settings for Computers and Settings for Users.

❑ Folder Redirection is an extension to Group Policy, which you can use to redirect certain Windows 2000 special folders to network locations.

❑ Group policies can also be used to assign and run scripts at prescribed times, such as when a user logs on or when the computer is shut down.

SELF TEST

The following questions will help you measure your understanding of the material presented in this chapter. Read all of the choices carefully, as there may be more than one correct answer. Choose all correct answers for each question.

1. Which of the following is included with Windows 2000?

    A. System Policy Editor

    B. Group Policy

    C. Both of the above

    D. Neither of the above

2. Which of the following purposes can be served by Group Policy? (Choose all that apply.)

    A. Control of a user's desktop environment

    B. Redirection of special folders to a network location

    C. Management of security settings

    D. Assignment of scripts to run at computer startup

3. Who should apply and configure Group Policy?

    A. All administrators.

    B. Designated Group Policy administrators only.

    C. All domain users should configure their own policies.

    D. None of the above.

4. What is the term used to refer to the Group Policy management application that is added to your custom MMC for managing Group Policy?

    A. Plug-in

    B. Applet

    C. Snap-in

    D. Tool

5. Group policies themselves are stored in which of the following, in much the same way word processing data is stored in an individual document?

    A. GTPs

    B. GPCs

    C. GPFs

    D. GPOs

6. What type of GPO resides on Windows 2000 member servers and workstations running Windows 2000 Professional?

    A. Nonlocal policies

    B. Local policies

    C. Domain policies

    D. Active Directory policies

7. What is the folder name for the Group Policy Template folder as it appears in the Sysvol directory?

A. An eight-character name designated by the administrator

B. "GPT," followed by a 32-bit binary number, which is randomly assigned by the system

C. A hexadecimal number that represents the GUID for the GPO to which it applies

D. Poltemp, followed by a decimal number assigned to each GPT in sequence (e.g., Poltemp1, Poltemp2, etc.)

8. Which of the following is true of the \USER subfolder in the GPT? (Choose all that apply.)

A. It contains the Registry.pol file with the Registry settings applied to users.

B. It contains the .ADM files.

C. It contains several subfolders.

D. It contains the scripts and related files for startup and shutdown scripting.

9. Which of the following are modes in which an MMC console can be saved? (Choose all that apply.)

A. User mode

B. Editor mode

C. Control mode

D. Author mode

10. When you add the Group Policy snap-in to a console, the GPO that the snap-in will control by default is which of the following?

A. The default domain GPO

B. The local computer GPO

C. The site GPO

D. The organizational unit GPO

11. Which of the following check boxes must be checked in order to force Child containers to inherit policies from their higher-level objects?

A. Force Inheritance

B. Prevent Inheritance

C. No Override

D. High-Level Container Priority

12. Which of the following security areas should be modified to control password configuration policies?

A. User rights

B. Account policies

C. Password policies

D. NTFS permissions

13. Which of the following is a special folder that can be redirected to a network location via Group Policy folder redirection? (Choose all that apply.)

A. My Documents

B. Winnt (system root folder)

C. Sysvol

D. Start menu

14. If you assign multiple logon scripts, in what order are they processed?

A. Alphabetical order based on the script's file name.

B. The order in which you assigned them.

C. The order in which you specify by moving them up or down in the dialog box.

D. All are run simultaneously.

15. Disabling the unused parts of a GPO will have what effect?

A. It will speed up the startup and logon process for all users.

B. It will speed up the startup and logon process for the users and computers subject to that GPO.

C. It will slow the startup and logon process for the users and computers subject to that GPO.

D. It will have no effect on performance.

MICROSOFT CERTIFIED SYSTEMS ENGINEER

6

Using Group Policy to Manage Software

HEADSTART OBJECTIVES

T his chapter discusses Windows 2000's use of Group Policy for software management throughout the entire software life cycle. Using Group Policy, an administrator can remotely manage the complete distribution and maintenance of software applications throughout the Windows 2000 network.

HEADSTART OBJECTIVE 6.01

Examining the Software Life Cycle

The distribution of software using Group Policy in Windows 2000 must be managed at various different stages. This management can be divided into four distinct phases that comprise the software life cycle.

■ Preparation

■ Deployment

■ Maintenance

■ Removal

The Preparation Phase

Before you can begin deploying software using Group Policy, a few items must be checked. First, it must be packaged correctly. Windows 2000 implements a new technology, Windows Installer, to accomplish this.

ACCELERATING TO WINDOWS 2000

Windows Installer

Windows Installer is one of the major improvements in Windows 2000. In earlier versions of Windows, there were multiple methods by which an application could be installed. Even software applications made available by Microsoft did not implement a standard installation routine. Software manufacturers often used third-party installer programs, and then corporations would often repackage the software in their standard packaging software. What a mess!

Windows Installer addresses the issue of not having a standard installation routine by providing a standard technology that software developers can use to package an application for installation. Administrators can also customize these packages for individual users or departments.

Besides a common installation interface, Windows Installer also provides a cleaner method for software removal. This technology provides a more efficient and more standardized process for uninstalling software, resulting in a lesser chance of a software removal leaving undesired files, or affecting other applications by removing shared .DLL components.

Another benefit of Windows Installer is its ability, under certain circumstances, to repair an application if it detects a problem. For example, if a critical file in an application becomes corrupt or is deleted, Windows Installer has the intelligence to reload the affected file when you next attempt to launch the application.

Windows 2000 compliant applications provide a Windows Installer, or .MSI file, for software installation. However, as an administrator, you may need to install applications for which the manufacturer has not provided an .MSI file. For these applications, a .ZAP file can be created to allow for installation using Group Policy. ZAP files are discussed later in this chapter.

The Deployment Phase

Once an application has been packaged correctly, a Group Policy Object (GPO) can be created and the software can be deployed. A GPO can be assigned to any of the following:

- Domain
- Site
- Organizational Unit (OU)

There are two methods to deploy software using Group Policy. An application can either be *assigned* or *published*. Only computers running a Windows 2000 operating system are capable of receiving software using Group Policy.

heads ⏻P

Group Policy cannot be used to deploy software to non-Windows 2000 workstations (such as Windows NT). However, the .MSI files can be manually launched or deployed using Systems Management Server if the Windows Installer client components are installed.

Assigning Applications

When an application is assigned to a *user*, an icon for that application is created in the user's Programs listed in the Start menu. This shortcut, when launched by the user, launches Windows Installer to install the assigned application. Assigning an application to a *computer* automatically installs the application on the computer, regardless of the user logged on.

Publishing Applications

Another method for software to be deployed is to publish the application to a user. When an application is published, the "friendly name" for the application appears in the Add/Remove Programs window. The user can check this location for published applications, and manually install programs by simply clicking Add on the application he or she wishes to install. Published applications can also be categorized, for easier browsing by the user.

Another method for installing published or assigned applications is when a user clicks an unknown file type related to an application. For example, if Microsoft Word 2000 is published to a user and that user attempts to launch a .DOC file, the package can be configured to automatically install the application and launch the .DOC file.

The Maintenance Phase

The maintenance phase of the software life cycle refers to the ongoing process of keeping applications on the latest version, by applying the appropriate upgrades and fixes as they become available by the developer.

If you assign an upgrade to an application using Group Policy, the application can be automatically upgraded using Windows Installer the next time the user launches it.

The Removal Phase

The final phase of the software life cycle is the removal phase. This phase is needed to effectively manage applications that are no longer needed by the business, or applications that have been retired for other reasons. In Windows 2000, a software object can be removed from a Group Policy in two ways: forced and optional.

With a forced removal, the application is automatically removed on the workstations to which the specific Group Policy applies. This is accomplished by the operating system running a Windows Installer uninstall routine.

When you specify an optional removal, the application is no longer available for other clients to install. An optional removal essentially just removes the application from the Group Policy. Using this method leaves the application on any workstations on which it may have been installed in the past.

Deploying Software

The deployment phase is perhaps the most involved phase of the software life cycle. Software deployment through Group Policy can be accomplished in many ways. Software can be *assigned* or *published*, and can be advertised to a *user* or to a *computer*.

When configuring the Software Settings of a Group Policy, you will notice that a package can either be published or assigned to a user; however, it can only be assigned to a computer. The two rules for publishing and assigning applications are

- Software cannot be *published* to a *computer*. It must be *assigned*.
- Software can be either *published* or *assigned* to a *user*.

When software is published or assigned to a user, it is installed after the user logs on to the workstation. When software is assigned to a computer, the software is installed the next time the computer reboots.

Software is published or assigned by creating a package in the Group Policy Editor. To do this, a new group policy must be created or an existing policy modified on a domain, site, or organizational unit must be edited. Using the Group Policy Editor, software packages are created either under Computer Configuration | Software Settings or User Configuration | Software Settings, depending on the type of application deployment desired.

Benefits of Deploying Software Using Group Policy

When managed effectively, using Group Policy for software distribution in Windows 2000 can save time and resources, contributing to a lower Total Cost of Ownership (TCO) for your Windows 2000 workstations.

Windows 2000 is the first Microsoft operating system to natively support a centralized software distribution technology. Previously, administrators were forced to either visit the desks of all users when installing, upgrading, or removing an application, or to purchase expensive third-party software distribution applications.

Using Group Policy allows an administrator to centrally administer and manage an application throughout all phases of the software life cycle.

Understanding the Difference Between Assigning and Publishing

As mentioned earlier, software applications can either be published or assigned (see the following illustration). Whether the application should be published or assigned is based on how the installation should take place on the client, as well as the expected use of the application. Remember, the same package can be added to multiple GPOs, so it is possible to assign an application to some users while publishing it to others.

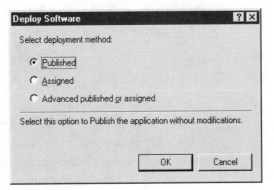

Assigning a Software Package

Group Policy software packages can be assigned to a computer or user. When assigning a package to a user, an icon is added in the Start menu. It is important to note that this does not mean the application has been installed. The icon in the Start menu is simply a link the Windows Installer package that will install the application. When a package assignment is made to a computer, the application is actually installed, and does not require the user launching a shortcut on the Start menu to initiate the installation.

When software is assigned to a user, the application will be available the next time the user logs on to a Windows 2000 workstation. When software is assigned to a computer, the software will become available the next time the computer is restarted. Once an application has been assigned to a computer, only only an administrator can remove it. However, applications assigned to a user can be removed by using the Add/Remove Programs applet in the Control Panel.

As an administrator, you will typically want to assign an application when it is pertinent to the user's job. If you know that the majority of users will use a package that has been created in a GPO, it is best to assign it.

heads

⊕p *Make sure you understand the differences between assigning an application to a user and assigning it to a computer. Also know when to assign an application, and when it is better to publish it.*

Publishing a Software Package

When publishing a software package, the software appears in the Add/Remove Programs applet and does not show up in the Start menu. Installation can be initiated either through Add/Remove Programs, or by attempting to launch an associated file type. Software can be published only to users, never to computers. One disadvantage of publishing software, as opposed to assigning it, is that the software does not have the same level of resiliency built in. Once an application is deleted, it will not be automatically reinstalled the next time the user logs on or when the computer is rebooted as it would if it were assigned. It can, however, be manually reinstalled using the Add/Remove Programs applet. By design, publishing an application places more of the responsibility of software management on the user than does assigning.

Published software is typically used when you want to make an application available for users to install, but it is not required for the targeted users to do their job. Remember, you can publish software to some users while assigning it to others by implementing different GPOs for different containers.

Types of Packages Deployed Using Group Policy

Several types of packages can be deployed using Group Policy. The primary method of deploying software is by using a Windows Installer application installation package. There are other types of Windows Installer packages, though, including modifications and patch files. There are also ways to manage the distribution of software that has not been packaged in Windows Installer. This chapter discusses the features and limitations of each type of package.

Windows Installer Packages

Windows Installer packages are stored as files with an .MSI extension, and are essentially a relational database of the various configuration changes that should be made to a workstation. The .MSI database for an application includes information about the following:

- Components to be added
- Registry changes to be modified
- Shortcut modifications
- Services to be installed
- File types to be associated

Windows Installer Package Transforms

When deploying an application, you may want to customize the installable components for different OUs. For example, if you were to deploy Microsoft Access, your Software Development department may require the advanced tools and wizards, whereas a user may require simply the basic functionality.

Transforms, also referred to as *Modifications*, are stored in .MST files in a similar format to .MSI files. One or more modification packages can be added to a software package in a GPO, and are applied in list order.

Non-Windows Installer Applications

You may find that you need to deploy an application for which an .MSI file has not been provided by the vendor. For these situations, a .ZAP file can be created to enable software deployment using Group Policy.

You may also have packages that were previously compiled in other third-party applications. In some circumstances, these can be converted to .MSI files using a utility provided by the third-party application vendor. At the least, they can usually be installed using a .ZAP file.

USING .ZAP FILES When an application must be deployed using Group Policy for which a Windows Installer package does not exist, the administrator must create a .ZAP file. A .ZAP file is a text-based file that follows a similar format to the unattended text files used in Windows NT for installation of the operating system.

A .ZAP file is not actually a software package; it simply initiates another setup program. If the setup program supports unattended installation, it is a good idea to include the necessary switches in the .ZAP file so that no user intervention is required.

The primary limitation of .ZAP files is that they can only be published, and not assigned. Another limitation is that .ZAP packages do not run with elevated privileges, so the user installing the application must have the appropriate rights to the file system and registry as required by the application installation process.

The following shows an example of the layout of a basic .ZAP file, with comments explaining what each section means. This example shows the .ZAP file that was used for the beta version of the "Hello World!" application, before an .MSI file was released.

```
[Application]                          ; Required section
FriendlyName =                         ; Displayed in Add/Remove Programs
    "Hello World Beta v1.0"            (Required)
SetupCommand = setup.exe /auto         ; Command to launch automated install (Required)
DisplayVersion = Beta 1                ; Version information (optional)
Publisher = Syngress Media             ; Publisher information (optional)
URL = http://www.syngress.com          ; URL for support Web site (optional)
LCID = 1033                            ; Language code (optional)
Architecture = Intel                   ; Platform Architecture (optional)
[Ext]                                  ; Optional auto-install extensions
HLO=                                   ; Auto-installs when user launches .HLO file
HW=
```

Application Patches and Fixes

Like software installation programs, patches and fixes to applications have been provided in a range of different formats in previous versions of Windows. Windows Installer answers this with another type of file, an .MSP file, which can be developed by manufacturers specifically for the purpose of applying patches and fixes to their applications.

Deployment Phases

The deployment phase of the software life cycle is actually divided into a few steps. Following these stages of the deployment process provides a greater chance of a smooth rollout that does not interrupt the user by causing unnecessary downtime.

Testing and Development Stage

Before deploying an application to a production environment, it is best to fully test the application and the deployment process in a lab environment. The ideal lab setup has one or more computers with a clean installation of Windows 2000, and one or more computers running your standard business software. A test Active Directory tree is useful for testing completely outside of your production environment, but is not required.

In the test lab, an application should be packaged in Windows Installer if necessary. The installation process should then be fully tested, and when possible should be an automated installation that requires no user intervention. Any modification packages should also be built and tested in the test lab.

Both the application itself and the deployment process should be tested. To the extent possible, the lab should be used to calculate installation times and to determine if any client, server, or network performance issues exist with the installation. Also, at this stage, it should be determined whether an application should be published or assigned.

Pilot Deployment Stage

The next step in the deployment phase is to execute a pilot rollout of the application. A pilot group is a small percentage of your total users that provides an accurate sample of the desktop configuration you have in the field. The pilot deployment should be kept as separate as possible from the production deployment. Allow for some time in between each to analyze pilot results.

The scope of your pilot deployment depends entirely on your environment. In an environment that spans multiple locations, it is best to pilot the deployment on machines at locations linked with slow links, as well as those with fast links. This makes it possible to determine if any WAN bandwidth issues exist at the slower sites.

One step of the pilot phase that is often overlooked is to analyze the results of the pilot. If there are issues encountered during the pilot, they must be addressed before deployment. Depending on the types of problems discovered it might be necessary to continue work in the lab before proceeding to a production rollout.

Production Deployment Stage

Once an application has been fully tested and a successful pilot deployment has been executed, you are ready to roll it out to production. The production deployment involves modifying the appropriate GPOs that will be using the package, and configuring the package properties that you defined in the development stage.

Best Practices for Managing Distribution Points

Before a package can be assigned or published using Group Policy, it must first be copied to a server, and the source directory must be shared. In large enterprise environments, it is impractical for all users to use a single source for application installations. If your environment spans multiple locations, each containing at least one server, you may consider assigning the package to a GPO for each site, and specify a local Distribution Point for each.

on the
job

To better manage multiple application source shares on multiple servers, you may consider creating a Distributed File System (DFS) containing the various distribution points. You will learn more about managing DFS in Chapter 30, "Managing File Resources." If you are currently using Microsoft Systems Management Server 2.0, you may consider using it to manage your distribution points and keep them updated with the latest package versions.

Since users will be executing the installation application directly from the Distribution Point, make sure that they have at least Read permissions to both the share and the folder. The best practice is to restrict Authenticated Users to read-only permissions, while allowing administrators full control over the source files.

HEADSTART OBJECTIVE 6.03

Using Software Management to Control Registry Settings

As well as building custom Administrative Templates (.ADM files) to control registry settings using Group Policy, you can also use Software Management. In order to do this, you must create an .MSI database that will apply the desired registry changes to a computer on which it is installed. Remember, if you do decide to use .ADM files to perform registry changes, the Windows 2000 .ADM files cannot be used in a Windows NT 4.0 environment.

Custom registry settings can be used to control desktop environments outside of the options available in the default Administrative Templates. They can also be used to customize software for which Transform (.MST) files are not available. The three ways to make customizations to application preferences through registry settings are

- Custom .ADM files
- Custom .MSI files
- .MST files provided by the manufacturer

HEADSTART OBJECTIVE 6.04

Upgrading Software

After an application has been deployed using Group Policy, there will likely be a future need to upgrade the version of the software when the software manufacturer makes enhancements or fixes.

When upgrading an application, the upgrade package is first added to the policy as any other package. In the Properties window for that package, the Upgrade tab is then used to define the configuration for the upgrade settings.

When making a package an upgrade package, you must specify an existing package that is to be upgraded. The existing package is typically in the same GPO; however, it may be located in any GPO in your Active Directory forest. If the package is designed for an upgrade, you can select the "Package can upgrade over the existing package" option. Otherwise, the default setting of "Uninstall the existing package, then install the upgrade package" can be left enabled. The Add Upgrade Package window is shown in Figure 6-1.

FIGURE 6-1

Adding an upgrade package

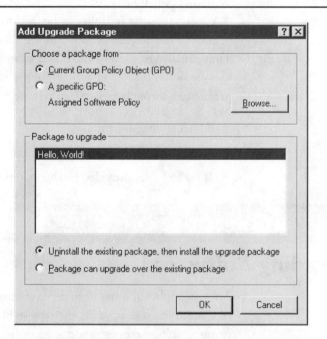

Removing Software

In the past, an administrator often overlooked the removal of software . This was typically due to the fact that removal of older software was not worth the time and effort; it was often easier to just leave it there (or simply remove the icons).

Windows Installer, packaged in Windows 2000 Group Policy, can be removed on all clients using the Group Policy Editor. When deleting a software package using the Group Policy console, an administrator has the option of removing it on all workstations that previously installed it from the policy, or simply removing it from the GPO without affecting current installations. The following illustration shows the options presented when removing a software package.

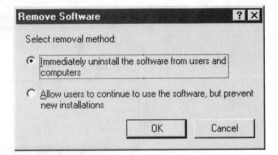

Managing Software

Windows Installer and Group Policy provide administrators with some appreciable features to manage software installations. Some of the items that can be managed using software policies include

- Software categories
- File type associations
- Deployment settings

Managing Software Categories

When applications are published to a user, they appear in the Add/Remove Programs applet in the Control Panel. When multiple applications are published, this list can potentially become large and unmanageable. As an administrator, you can create various software categories for your applications and assign each package to one or more categories. By default, there are no categories, and all applications appear only in All Categories to the user.

Categories are created through the Group Policy Editor console, by right-clicking Software Installation under Software Settings, and selecting Properties. In the Properties window, categories can be added and removed on the Categories tab (Figure 6-2).

FIGURE 6-2

Creating software
categories

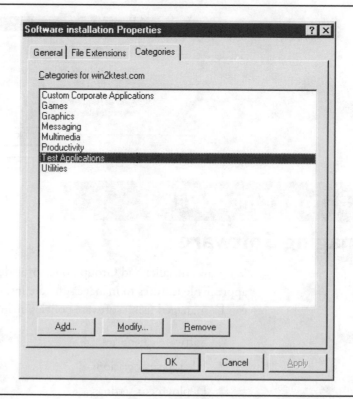

Once created in a Group Policy, applications can be assigned to one or more categories. To assign a package to a category, right-click the package in the Group Policy Editor console and select Properties. A package is assigned to categories through the Categories tab, as shown in Figure 6-3.

Managing File Type Associations

When publishing or assigning an application to a user, the application can be installed when the user attempts to launch a file with the associated file type. For this to function, the file types to associate with the installation must have been specified in the Windows Installer package or .ZAP file.

The reason that file types need to be managed is that more than one application may be made available to a user that uses the same file types. For example, you may be advertising two different graphics applications

FIGURE 6-3

Assigning software
categories to an application

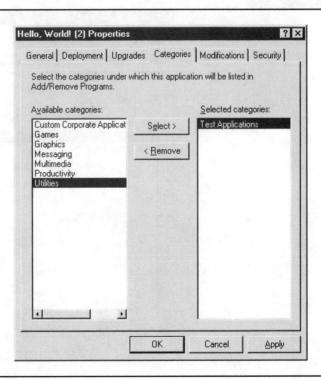

that both will install when a user attempts to open a .TIF file. As an administrator, you have the capability of managing the order of precedence of each application based on each individual file type. This is accomplished through the File Extensions tab of the Software Installation Properties, as shown in Figure 6-4.

Managing Deployment Settings

Deployment properties are managed by right-clicking a package in the Group Policy Editor, and selecting Properties. Figure 6-5 shows the options available on the Deployment tab. These options include

■ Deployment type

FIGURE 6-4

Managing precedence of file types

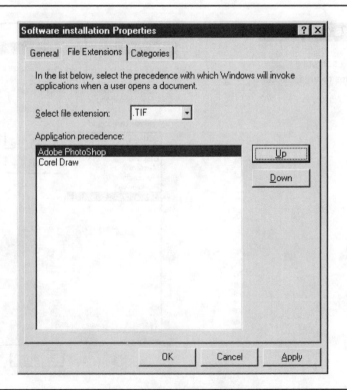

- Deployment options
- User interface options

Deployment Type

In the deployment type frame, there are two options: Published and Assigned. After creating a package, you can change the installation type. If the package is created in the Computer Configuration section, however, the Published option will be grayed out.

Deployment Options

In the deployment options section, you can specify whether an application should be installed when a user launches a file type that has been associated

---

Deployment properties

in the .MSI file. This option will be grayed out if there are no associated file types.

In this section, you can also specify to uninstall an application when the GPO no longer applies to the user or computer, as well as configure whether the application will appear in the user's Add/Remove Programs window.

User Interface Options

There are two available user interface options when configuring a package. The default value, Basic, is used for automated installations that do not require user intervention. The Maximum options setting allows users to enter custom parameters for the installation, as defined in the software package.

HEADSTART OBJECTIVE 6.07

Troubleshooting Software Deployment

In order to successfully deploy an application, the package properties and Group Policy settings must be configured correctly. There are several reasons why problems may occur during the deployment process. The following matrix shows some of the problems, and provides possible resolutions.

QUESTIONS AND ANSWERS

The software application does not appear in the user's Start menu.	The application has been published instead of assigned. Check the deployment type option in the Deployment Properties tab.
The software application does not appear in the user's Add/Remove Programs window.	The application has been assigned instead of published. Check the deployment type in the Deployment Properties tab. The application has been configured to not display in Add/Remove programs. Check the deployment options in the Deployment Properties tab.
Applications are not being installed on the computer.	Verify that the user has at least read access to the package Distribution Point (DP) share and folder. Verify that there are no other conflicting Group Policies with a higher precedence. Check that the GPO is applied to the appropriate group, if the GPO security permissions have been modified from the default.
Applications deployed using .ZAP files fail to install.	Verify that the user has the appropriate permissions to install software. Obtain or package an .MSI file for the application, so it may run with elevated privileges.
Application upgrades are not taking place automatically.	Verify that the "Required upgrade for existing packages" option has been set, and that the correct package has been specified to upgrade.
Launching unknown file types does not install the appropriate application.	The package may not contain file type association information. Verify that the "Auto-install this application by file extension activation" deployment option is enabled.
Launching an unknown file type installs the incorrect application.	Check the list of file extensions in the Software Installation Properties window, and make sure that all applications for the given extension are sorted as desired.

CHAPTER SUMMARY

Windows Installer and Windows 2000 Group Policy enable administrators to effectively manage software through the entire life cycle. Software preparation, deployment, maintenance, and removal can all be administered using Windows Installer in conjunction with Group Policy. Windows Installer also provides many enhancements to the ongoing management of software with its self-repair and improved removal technologies.

When creating a package in a Windows 2000 Group Policy, an application can either be assigned or published. When assigning an application to users, it will become available for installation under the Start menu. When publishing the application, it can be installed through the Add/Remove Programs Wizard. Using either method, software can be installed when a user attempts to launch a file with a specific extension. At any time, the software can be removed from all workstations on which it was installed simply by deleting the package in the Group Policy Editor.

Several deployment options are available to administrators to allow for greater flexibility in the deployment of applications. These options enable the Administrator to define how a package should be deployed and upgraded, and how the user can install the application.

TWO-MINUTE DRILL

❑ Windows Installer addresses the issue of not having a standard installation routine by providing a standard technology that software developers can use to package an application for installation.

❑ Windows 2000 compliant applications provide a Windows Installer, or .MSI file, for software installation.

❑ There are two methods to deploy software using Group Policy. An application can either be *assigned* or *published*.

❑ When an application is assigned to a *user*, an icon for that application is created in the user's Programs listed in the Start menu.

❑ If you assign an upgrade to an application using Group Policy, the application can be automatically upgraded using Windows Installer the next time the user launches it.

❑ Windows 2000 is the first Microsoft operating system to natively support a centralized software distribution technology.

❑ Transforms, also referred to as *Modifications*, are stored in .MST files in a similar format to .MSI files.

❑ Custom registry settings can be used to control desktop environments outside of the options available in the default Administrative Templates.

❑ When applications are published to a user, they appear in the Add/Remove Programs applet in the Control Panel.

❑ In the deployment options section, you can specify whether an application should be installed when a user launches a file type that has been associated in the .MSI file. This option will be grayed out if there are no associated file types.

SELF TEST

The following questions help you measure your understanding of the material presented in this chapter. Read all of the choices carefully, as there may be more than one correct answer. Choose all correct answers for each question.

1. Identify the first phase of the software life cycle.

   A. Deployment

   B. Preparation

   C. test lab and development

   D. Pilot

2. Which of the following file types relate to applications package in Windows Installer?

   A. .IPF

   B. .MWI

   C. .MSI

   D. .ZAP

3. A Group Policy Object (GPO) *cannot* be assigned to which of the following? (Choose all that apply.)

   A. Domain

   B. Site

   C. Organizational Unit (OU)

   D. User

4. When assigning an application to a computer, which of the following is true?

   A. The application is automatically installed when the user logs on.

   B. The application is automatically installed when the computer starts.

   C. The application is added to the Start menu in preparation for installation.

   D. The application is added to Add/Remove Programs in preparation for installation.

5. When publishing an application to a user, which of the following is true?

   A. The application is automatically installed when the user logs on.

   B. The application is automatically installed when the computer starts.

   C. The application is added to the Start menu in preparation for installation.

   D. The application is added to Add/Remove Programs in preparation for installation.

6. As an administrator, you must decide how Microsoft Excel should be deployed to your enterprise. Every user in the Finance department requires the application for day-to-day operations. Some users in Information Technology also need the application. Both departments are in the same tree and domain, but each its own OU. What is the best way to deploy the application using Group Policy?

   A. Assign the application to the domain using a single GPO.

   B. Publish the application to the domain using a single GPO.

C. Create a GPO for both OUs. Assign the package to the Finance OU, and publish it to the Information Technology OU.

D. Create a GPO for both OUs. Publish the package to the Finance OU, and assign it to the Information Technology OU.

7. How is deployment of a non-Windows Installer application managed using Group Policy?

A. A .ZAP file must be created.

B. An .MST file must be created.

C. It can be deployed in the same method as any other application.

D. A non-Windows Installer application cannot be deployed using Group Policy.

8. Users at remote sites are complaining of slow performance when installing required applications across the WAN. You are currently using a single GPO to assign software to all users at the domain level. What should you do to increase performance?

A. Assign the software to computers instead of users.

B. Assign software at the site level, using individual Distribution Points for each site.

C. Stagger user logon hours, to reduce concurrent WAN traffic.

D. Publish the application instead of assigning it.

9. What is the easiest way to remove an application that was previously assigned using Group Policy?

A. Create an Uninstall package in Windows Installer, and make it assigned.

B. Delete the package in the Group Policy console, and select the Uninstall option.

C. Send a memo to the users requesting that they remove the application using Add/Remove Programs.

D. Manually remove the application from each workstation while logged on as a local administrator.

10. Which of the following sections of a .ZAP file is required?

A. [Application]

B. [Ext]

C. [CLSIDs]

D. [ProgIDs]

11. You have assigned an application to the users at your site. However, when users attempt to launch the installer from the Start menu, they receive an "Access Denied" message. What is the probable cause of the problem?

A. Users are not local administrators.

B. Users do not have access to the Distribution Point share.

C. The policy does not apply to the user.

D. The application was created using a .ZAP file.

12. Which of the following are limitations of deploying software using .ZAP files? (Choose all that apply.)

    A. Applications can only be published.

    B. Applications can only be assigned.

    C. Users must have local permissions to install software.

    D. GPOs can only be created at the OU level.

13. A published application will open three types of files; however, when users attempt to launch any one of the file types, the application is not being automatically installed. Which of the following are potential causes of the problem? (Choose all that apply.)

    A. The package does not have any associated file types defined.

    B. The administrator has not specified file types in package properties.

    C. The "Auto-install this application by file extension activation" option is disabled.

    D. The file type is already assigned to another published application that uses the same extension with a higher precedence.

14. To assign a category to a software package, you must first:

    A. Define the categories internally in the package.

    B. Define the categories in Software Settings properties.

    C. Create the categories on all client workstations.

    D. Create the categories in the package properties.

15. Group Policy can be used to deploy software to which of the following clients? (Choose all that apply.)

    A. Windows 95/98

    B. Windows NT 4.0 Workstation

    C. Windows 2000 Professional

    D. Windows 2000 Server

MICROSOFT CERTIFIED SYSTEMS ENGINEER

7

Installing and Configuring Terminal Services

There has been a lot of talk in the computer networking community recently about "thin clients." This refers not to those lean and mean folks who hire us to troubleshoot their systems, but to the low-powered desktop machines they buy to save the company money. These inexpensive network PCs don't have the memory, processor speed, or hard disk space of a true workstation, but we consultants and administrators will be expected to make them perform as if they do.

The Thin Client Concept

With Microsoft's Terminal Services, now included in all the Windows 2000 Server family operating systems, we can almost accomplish the impossible. The users of those "skinny" computer systems can now use the Windows 2000 operating system even though their hardware may not be up to par, and run applications on their desktops that require more resources than those systems have. And they can do all this without losing the functionality of their old operating systems or the ability to run their old applications from the local machine.

Hand Over the Remote Control

Terminal Services also provides systems administrators the ability to run the server from any location on the network, including a remote connection. Administrators can take complete control of the server, and can even shut down or reboot it from the remote location.

All This and Add-Ons, Too

For even more flexibility and functionality, Citrix Metaframe software can be used along with the Windows 2000 Terminal Services to extend its features to such a degree that the thin client solution becomes not just a feasible alternative, but a superior option for networks of all sizes. We will be looking at how you can make Microsoft's Terminal Server even better by using the Citrix add-ons.

With Windows NT, gaining the advantages of Terminal Services meant buying the special (and expensive) Terminal Server version of NT Server. Consequently, this useful piece of software was unrecognized and underutilized, as many companies that could benefit from it were not even aware of its existence. Microsoft's decision to include Terminal Server in all "flavors" of Windows 2000 Server changes that, and we can expect more and more organizations to investigate the thin client solution in the future.

In this chapter, we look at Microsoft's implementation of Terminal Services in Windows 2000 Server and the ways in which it can bring exciting new functionality to the networks in which it is deployed.

HEADSTART OBJECTIVE 7.01

Describe the Purpose and Use of Terminal Services

Windows 2000's built-in Terminal Services software transforms a PC into a thin client, giving desktop machines remote access to a server desktop by functioning as a terminal emulator. Terminal Server transmits the user interface to the client, and the client returns input (via keyboard and mouse) back to be processed by the server.

When a user logs on, he sees only his own individual session, which is managed transparently by the server operating system. It is independent of any other client sessions that may be going on at the same time. The user's desktop can be configured as desired, and different users can have different desktop configurations.

The client software can be installed on personal computers and/or Windows-based Terminals. Macintosh computers or UNIX-based workstations can also connect to a Terminal server (with third-party software such as Citrix Metaframe, discussed later in this chapter). The Terminal Services Client window is shown in Figure 7-1.

FIGURE 7-1

The Terminal Services
Client window, showing the
server desktop

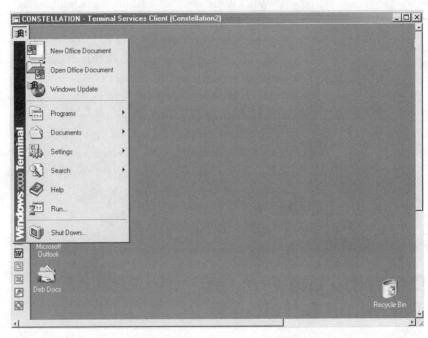

Terminal Services can be installed on the server in two modes: application server mode, or remote administration mode. Although you can change modes, Terminal Services cannot run in both modes simultaneously.

As an application server, Terminal Services provides net administrators with an effective and reliable way to distribute Windows-based programs with a network server and fully utilize older, less powerful hardware. Terminal Services application server delivers the Windows 2000 desktop and the most current Windows-based applications to computers that might not normally be able to run Windows 2000 at all.

In the remote administration mode, which is shown in Figure 7-2, Terminal Services can be used to administer the server from anywhere within the network. Administrators can connect from a remote location and perform the same administrative tasks they would be able to do while sitting at the server machine.

FIGURE 7-2

Using Terminal Services in remote administration mode

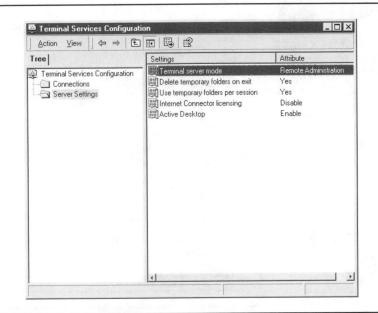

Difference between Remote Control and Remote Node

Terminal Services allows you to connect to the server as a remote node, or to actually remotely control another user's session. There is a big difference between the two, and it's important that you understand that difference.

Remote control allows you to monitor the other user's session, and when you are in a remote control session, you share every input and output with the session that you are monitoring. Before the monitoring begins, the server will warn the user that the session is about to be remotely controlled (unless this warning has been disabled).

To remotely control a session, you use the Terminal Services Manager on the server machine. Simply click on the name of the user whose session you wish to monitor or control, and choose Remote Control from the Action menu, as shown in Figure 7-3.

You must have Full Control permission to remotely control another session, and your session must be capable of supporting the video resolution

To remote Control:
★ Use Terminal Services Manager on server.
★ need Full control perm★
★ Same Video resolution as the Client you are trying to remote control.

FIGURE 7-3

Establishing remote control
of a user's session

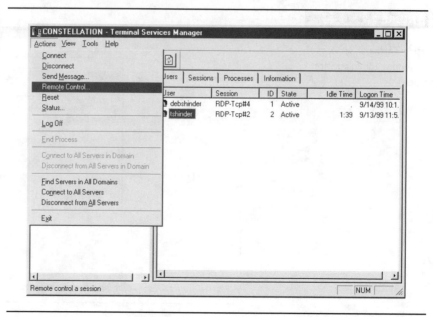

used at the session you are remotely controlling, or the remote control
operation will fail.

To end the remote control session, press CTRL+asterisk (*). If desired,
you can define another hot key to perform this function.

Before we go too deeply into discussing what you can do with Terminal
Services, let's take a look at some factors to consider when planning the
installation and deployment of this exciting feature that is now included
free with Microsoft's server software.

HEADSTART OBJECTIVE 7.02

Plan a Terminal Services Installation

There are several considerations to keep in mind when planning to install
and deploy Terminal Services on your Windows 2000 network. These
include hardware factors, software requirements, and user needs.

Hardware Considerations

To give acceptable performance, a Terminal server requires a Pentium or higher processor, 64MB of RAM, and an additional 4 to 8MB RAM for each user to support running each user's programs on the server.

In general, you can support double the number of users on a multiprocessor Pentium system by doubling the number of processors and doubling the amount of memory. This means it may be worth the investment to buy a system that supports multiple processors, even if you only plan to purchase one processor at the outset. This will let you increase capacity easily as your network's requirements increase.

Hard disk performance will affect the Terminal server's performance as well. If possible, a SCSI RAID array, although relatively expensive, will offer the best throughput.

Software Requirements

Some application types are more suited for deployment on a Terminal server than others. Because the Terminal application server is used by multiple users simultaneously, programs that require large amounts of system resources should be limited. Luckily, it's easy to restrict user or group access to certain program types, and you can also disable unnecessary features that require the most resources. If you have several programs of this type, one solution is to install them on separate servers.

Remember that the RAM and CPU requirements will increase according to the number of sessions that will be running at any given time. There is not a true one-to-one correlation, but this gives you a basis for projecting program performance.

User Needs

To determine just how powerful your servers need to be, consider the types of users who will be using them. Task-based users place the lightest load on the server's resources. By "task-based user," we mean one who typically runs a single program used for data entry in which he or she enters data.

A typical user, on the other hand, runs one or two programs, but usually only one at a time. These are generally programs that do not place great demands on the system, such as word processors or Web browsers.

Advanced users place the heaviest load on the server. We define an "advanced user" as a more sophisticated user—someone who runs multiple programs at the same time. These programs are more likely to be the kind that place heavy demands on computing power, such as database queries or processor- and memory-intensive 3D rendering programs.

Best Practices in Planning Your Terminal Services Deployment

Microsoft recommends the following when planning to deploy the Windows 2000 Terminal Services:

- Install Terminal Services on a stand-alone server, not on a domain controller. When enabled on a domain controller, a Terminal server's performance will suffer because of the additional memory, network traffic, and processor time required to perform the duties of a domain controller in a Windows 2000 domain.

- Use Terminal Services on a server that has an NTFS file system partition. NTFS provides greater security for users in a multisession environment when those users access the same data structures.

- Install the programs you want to use with Terminal Services after you have enabled Terminal Services. This will make the programs available for multisession access, because they are installed in the centrally located \Win2000 directory rather than in a user's home directory.

HEADSTART OBJECTIVE 7.03

Install Terminal Services

The first step in deploying Terminal Services, once you've completed the planning stage, is to enable the service on the Windows 2000 server, and then install the client software on the client machines.

Enabling Terminal Services on the server is a straightforward process. The following exercise walks you through the steps.

Installing Terminal Services on a Windows 2000 Server

Be sure you are logged on to the server with administrative privileges.

1. Open the Control Panel and click on the Add/Remove Programs applet. Click Add/Remove Windows Components. This opens the Windows Components Wizard.

2. Select Terminal Services and Terminal Services Licensing, and then click Next. (Terminal Services Licensing is a required component that licenses clients on a Terminal server if you are running in Application Server mode. The licenses are not required to run Terminal Services in remote administration mode. For purposes of this exercise, we will install Terminal Services in Application Server mode.)

3. If you have any programs already installed that will not work properly when Terminal Services is enabled, you will see them listed on the Terminal Services Setup page. You will have to reinstall these programs for multisession access if you want them available to Terminal clients. To do this, use Add/Remove Programs after Terminal Services is enabled.

4. On the Terminal Services Licensing Setup page, specify whether you want the license server to serve your entire enterprise or your domain/workgroup, and then provide the directory location for the database. Click Next, and then click Finish.

The required files will be copied to your hard disk. After you restart the system, the server software will be ready to use.

Creating the Client Disks and Installing the Client Software

To create client disks, follow these steps:

1. Open the Terminal Services Client Creator:

   Start | Programs | Administrative Tools | Terminal Services Client Creator

2. You will see the Network Client Administrator dialog box, shown next, which allows you to make the installation disks.

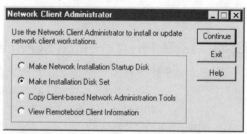

3. Click the Terminal Server Client you want to create, as shown next.

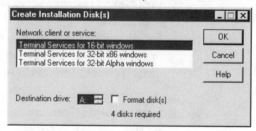

4. Insert a disk and click OK.

Now that you have the client installation disks, simply install the client software on each client computer by running the setup.exe program on the first disk.

Before installing Terminal Server Client, the client computer must be properly configured and connected to the network. If you are installing the 16-bit client on a computer running Windows for Workgroups 3.11, you might also need to install TCP/IP-32 if it is not already installed.

HEADSTART OBJECTIVE 7.04

Configure Terminal Services

There are two parts to configuring Terminal Services. First we look at how to configure the server, and then we walk you through the steps involved in configuring the client and creating a new connection.

FIGURE 7-4

Configuration options for the Terminal Server settings

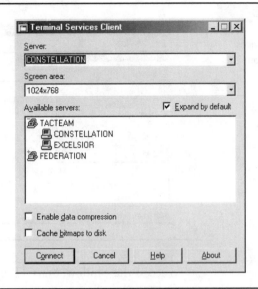

Configuring the Server

The Terminal server is configured through the Terminal Services Configuration MMC, shown in Figure 7-4. To access this tool:

Start | Programs | Administrative Tools | Terminal Services Configuration

From this window, you can change the server mode from remote administration to application server or vice versa. You can also specify whether temporary folders should be deleted upon exit, specify whether to use temporary folders per session, enable or disable Internet Connector licensing, and enable or disable the Active Desktop on the terminal screens.

Configuring the Client

To configure the client to connect to the Terminal server, first open the Terminal Services Client dialog box, shown in Figure 7-5.

FIGURE 7-5

The Terminal Services
Client configuration
window

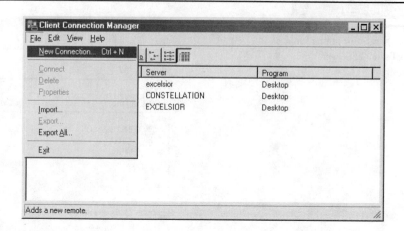

To access the window: Start │ Programs │ Terminal Services
Client │ TS Client

You can use this window to change the configuration information that
you put in when you installed the client software, and view available
Terminal servers.

HEADSTART OBJECTIVE 7.05

Establish a Terminal Session

Once you have the services configured on the client and server, establishing
a terminal session is easy. The first step, if you haven't already done so, is to
create a new connection. Windows 2000 includes a wizard to take you
through the process step by step.

EXERCISE 7-3

Making a New Connection with the Connection Manager

1. Open the TS Connection Manager, shown next:

   Start │ Programs │ Terminal Services Client │ Connection Manager

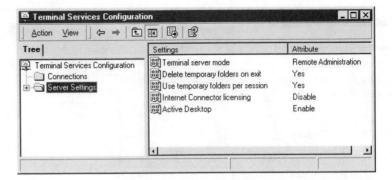

2. Click on the File menu and choose New Connection.

The New Connection Wizard will walk you through the steps. Be sure you have the following information ready:

1. A descriptive name for the connection.

2. The name or IP address of the Terminal server.

3. The username and password with which you will log on.

4. The screen resolution at which you wish to run the terminal screen.

You will be given the option to enable data compression and caching of bitmaps, and to automatically start a program when you open this connection. After inputting this information (if desired), click Finish and the Wizard will display your new connection. You can create a shortcut to it on your desktop by right-dragging the icon.

Connecting to the Server

After you've set up the new connection, there are two ways to connect to the server from the client machine:

1. Double-click on the shortcut icon you've made on your desktop or toolbar.

2. Start | Programs | Terminal Services Client | Client Connection Manager

Highlight the name of the connection you wish to use, and click on the File menu, then choose Connect (see Figure 7-6).

Using the Client
Connection Manager
to connect to a
Terminal server

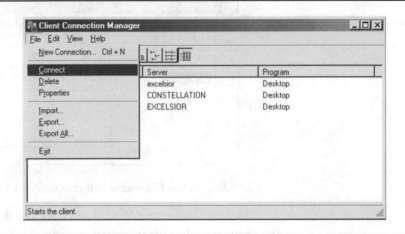

If you have configured the Terminal Services client to always log on to this connection with a specific username and password, you need do nothing. If not, you will be prompted for a username and password. The settings for your account will be loaded and then you're ready to work on the terminal screen.

heads
①P

When the connection to the server is broken for any reason (including a request, a connection error, or because an idle or active limit is reached), the administrator can either place a client's session into the disconnected state or reset the session. A session that is reset can no longer be activated by a user and is closed.

Reset = Closed. by Admin
user conf reconnect
x must use new
session

HEADSTART OBJECTIVE 7.06

Install Applications on a Server Running Terminal Services

Since Terminal Services provides the capability for multiple sessions simultaneously, applications must be installed according to Microsoft's directions so that each session will be able to run a program on the server without disrupting the server or other sessions.

Preparing to Install Programs

Microsoft recommends that you install programs before you provide client access to the server. This is so that you can test the program before it is accessed, and make any necessary adjustments.

If you do install a program after clients have been granted access, check to be sure that there are no users logged on to the server during the installation process. (You can use the server's Terminal Services Manager to send clients a message regarding time and duration of the installation.) Disable all connections before starting the installation.

To disable a connection, open the Terminal Services Configuration tool from the Administrative Tools menu (Start | Programs | Administrative Tools | Terminal Services Configuration). Click Connections in the left pane. In the Details pane, right-click the connection you want to disable, point to All Tasks, and then click Disable Connection (see Figure 7-7).

Now you're ready to start installing the application program(s).

FIGURE 7-7

Disabling a connection with the Terminal Services Configuration tool

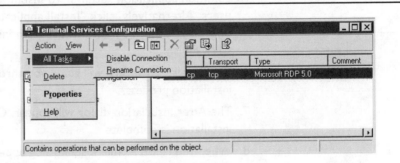

Program Installation Methods

Programs can be installed in one of two ways: through the Add/Remove Programs applet in Control Panel, or by using the Change User command. We look at both procedures and a step-by-step account of how to use each method.

Installing a Program through the Control Panel Add/Remove Programs Applet

It's easy to install a new application program with the Add/Remove Programs applet in Control Panel. The process is similar to using the applet to install an application on a Windows 2000 computer that is not a Terminal server, with a few differences. The following exercise walks you through the steps.

EXERCISE 7-4

Installing a Program with Add/Remove Programs

1. Log on to the Terminal server as administrator and close all programs.

2. Open Control Panel and click Add/Remove Programs.

3. In the Add/Remove Programs dialog, click Add New Programs.

4. Select the method to install the program and follow the instructions in the wizard.

5. In the Change User Option dialog, click "All users begin with common application settings" to install the application for all users. Alternatively, click "Install applications setting for this user only" if you do not want this program installed for multiple users. Click Finish.

6. The installation wizard will guide you through the rest of the installation process.

7. The After Installation dialog will appear. Click Next when the installation is complete.

8. When the Finish Admin Install dialog appears, click Finish.

9. If you are prompted to restart the computer to finish the installation, click Finish in Add/Remove Programs before accepting the prompt to restart the computer.

Some application programs will need to finish their installation process after you reboot. Microsoft Internet Explorer is one; after rebooting, it configures a variety of settings. In these cases, you will have to log on as the same user once the server has been rebooted in order to finish the application installation properly. Be careful not to allow any other users to log on before this step has been completed.

Installing a Program Using the Change User Command

The second way to install a program to be used with Terminal Services is by using the Change User command. Some administrators will be more comfortable with the command-line interface, and others prefer the graphical interface offered by the Add/Remove Programs applet. You should be familiar with both methods.

The following exercise walks you through the steps:

EXERCISE 7-5

Installing a Program with the Change User Command

1. Log on to the Terminal server as an administrator and close all applications.

2. Click Start, point to Programs, point to Accessories and then click Command Prompt. The Command Prompt window appears.

3. Type **change user /install**. Press ENTER (see the following illustration).

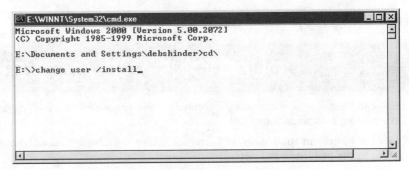

```
E:\WINNT\System32\cmd.exe
Microsoft Windows 2000 [Version 5.00.2072]
(C) Copyright 1985-1999 Microsoft Corp.

E:\Documents and Settings\debshinder>cd\

E:\>change user /install_
```

4. Install the program on a local NTFS formatted drive (for security purposes) as directed by the installation program.

5. At the command prompt, type **change user /execute** when installation is complete.

Verifying that the Installation Was Successful

Regardless of which method you use to install new application programs, you should always test to verify that the application was successful before making it available to network users.

There are several reasons that your application may not work as anticipated. Some programs installed using the Change User command won't work at first because of the locked-down state of the system. Some 16-bit programs must be able to write to the directory where the program .ini file is stored. Some 32-bit programs create registry entries that are needed for proper operation.

You should enable event logging and then log on to the server using a temporary user account created with the same permissions as the user or users who will be accessing the program. Launch the program and go through the basic procedures for using it. Then, use Event Viewer to determine which files or directories need Write access and which registry keys require Read access by the user in order for the program to operate properly.

heads UP

Many programs, particularly older ones, were not designed for multisession use. As a result, some programs need to be tuned before they can run on the Terminal server. Microsoft provides installation scripts for some programs with known installation issues. Scripts should be run after the application installation process is complete and before running the application for the first time.

Installing Applications

QUESTIONS AND ANSWERS

How can I install an application on Terminal Server using a graphical interface?	Use the Add/Remove Programs applet in Control Panel.
How can I install an application on Terminal Server at the command prompt?	Use the Change User command.
Why doesn't my application work properly when I use the Change User command?	The locked-down state of the system prevents the application from working properly at first.
I have an older application that wasn't designed for multisession use. Can I still run it on Terminal Server?	Check with Microsoft to see if they have an installation script to be used with your program. Scripts are available for many popular applications with known issues.

Running Applications

To run an application, the user must first establish a connection to the Terminal server. To do so, the user need only double-click the icon for the connection if a shortcut was created on the desktop during configuration, or perform the following steps:

Start | Programs | Terminal Services Client | [name of connection]

Once the user is logged on, either with the preset information input during configuration of the connection or by typing in a username and password, the Terminal screen desktop appears. Applications can be run from the Start menu on the terminal in the same way programs are run on the local computer.

heads
UP

Windows 2000 Terminal Services provides seamless clipboard sharing, making clipboard contents available to applications locally on a user computer and within a Terminal Services session. You can copy text from a document within a session, and paste it into a document on your local machine. (Clipboard sharing can be disabled on a per-connection basis using Terminal Services Configuration).

Disconnecting without Ending the Session

A client can disconnect from the Terminal server without ending the session, via a simple two-step procedure:

1. In the Terminal Server Client window, click Start and then click Disconnect. The Disconnect Windows 2000 Session dialog box appears.

2. Click OK.

The Terminal Server Client will then automatically reconnect to this session the next time you connect to this Terminal server (if the connection is configured for reconnection of disconnected sessions).

Starting a Program Automatically When the User Logs On

Administrators can configure the Terminal Services to automatically start a specified program when a user logs on. In a Windows 2000 domain environment, this is done using the Active Directory Users and Computers MMC. Follow these steps:

1. Double-click the username for which you want to change the Starting program.

2. Click the Environment tab.

3. In "Starting program," select "Start the following program at logon:."

4. In "Program file name," type the name of the program to start when the user logs on. You can also specify a working directory by typing the path in "Start in."

5. Click Apply, and then click OK.

Terminal Services Profiles

Using the Terminal Services User Profile, administrators can assign a profile to a user that applies to Terminal sessions. The Terminal Services profile can be used to restrict access to applications by removing those programs from the user's Start menu. Administrators can also create and store network connections to printers and other resources.

Configuring Client Settings

You can configure client settings to gain more control over users' sessions; for instance, you can cause the clients' mapped drives and printers to be automatically restored when they log on to the Terminal server. You can also prevent users from mapping specific drives or other devices if you wish.

Connecting Client Drives and Printers at Logon

Follow these steps to cause client drive and printer mappings to be automatically restored when a user logs on:

You should be logged on to the Terminal server with administrative privileges.

1. Open the Terminal Services Configuration tool. In the console tree, click Connections.

2. In the details pane, right-click the name of the connection you want to modify, and then click Properties.

3. Click the Client Settings tab.

4. In Connection, select the "Connect client drives at logon" and the "Connect client printers at logon" check boxes.

5. If you want the users' applications to default to the main client printer when they print, check the "Default to main client printer" check box.

Now the mapped drives and printer mappings for all users will be automatically restored when the user logs on to the Terminal server.

Preventing the Client from Mapping Specific Devices

To prevent the client from mapping specific devices when connected to the Terminal server, follow these steps:

1. Open the Terminal Services Configuration tool.

2. In the console tree, click Connections.

3. In the details pane, right-click the connection for which you want to prevent clients from mapping devices, and then click Properties.

4. Click the Client Settings tab, and check the check boxes for the devices you do not want a user to be able to map (see Figure 7-8).

5. Click OK to save your settings.

Using the Client
Settings tab to prevent
mapping of devices

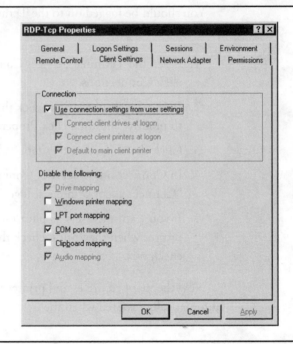

HEADSTART OBJECTIVE 7.07

Using Terminal Services for Remote Control Administration

Even if your network has no need for Terminal Server as an application server and your organization is not interested in implementing the thin client concept at this time, the Windows 2000 Terminal Server can still be used to provide network administrators with a way to control and administer the server from any desktop on the network, including one that is using a remote (dial-up) connection.

Connecting to One or More Terminal Servers

To connect to one or more Terminal servers for remote administration, follow these steps:

- Open the Terminal Services Manager.
- In the console pane, expand the domain containing the servers to which you want to connect.
- To connect to a specific Terminal server, right-click the server and then click Connect.
- To connect to all Terminal servers in the domain, right-click the domain and then click Connect to All Servers in Domain. (Note: It's recommended that you only connect to one Terminal server at a time, since connecting to multiple servers simultaneously can overload the system's resources.)

Connecting to a Terminal Server Over a Dial-Up Connection

If the administrator has remote access to a network that contains Terminal servers, he or she can use the connection to access a Terminal server from a remote location over a dial-up connection, and administer the server from virtually anywhere in the world.

To use remote access to connect to a Terminal server, you must first install dial-up networking on your computer. You will then be able to connect to the network where the Terminal server resides, start the Terminal Server Client on your remote machine, and log on to the Terminal server normally.

You can also modify connection, disconnection, and idle time-out settings to allow for reconnection if the phone lines are disconnected.

Shutting Down the Computer Remotely Using the tsshutdn Command

An administrator can run the tsshutdn command from the command line to shut down or reboot the Terminal server computer, using the following syntax:

At the command line, type: tsshutdn [wait time]

The tsshutdn command sends a notice to users that their Terminal sessions are going to be disconnected. "Wait time" specifies how long, in seconds, the Terminal server will wait after the notification before ending the user sessions and beginning the shutdown process.

Use the /reboot switch to reboot the Terminal server computer after shutdown, or the /powerdown switch to power off the server if the computer supports software control of AC power.

Citrix MetaFrame Additions to Terminal Server

Citrix MetaFrame is server-based software designed to work with Microsoft's Windows 2000 Server with Terminal Services installed. The purpose of MetaFrame is to extend the Windows Terminal Services by providing additional client and server functionality. This includes support for heterogeneous computing environments, enterprise-scale management, and seamless desktop integration. Using MetaFrame with Terminal Services provides improved application manageability, access, performance, and security. Citrix MetaFrame system software, which incorporates Citrix's Independent Computing Architecture (ICA), provides a complete Server-based computing solution for multiuser Windows 2000 environments.

Some areas in which MetaFrame software extends the Windows 2000 Terminal Services are discussed in the following sections.

Heterogeneous Computing Environment

Microsoft Terminal Services supports Windows-based devices and IP-based connections. With MetaFrame, you can deliver access to those Windows-based applications to almost every type of client hardware, operating platform, network connection, and LAN protocol.

Support for Both Windows and Non-Windows Clients

MetaFrame provides additional functionality for all types of Windows clients including Windows 9x, Windows CE, Windows NT Workstation, Windows for Workgroups, and Windows 3.x systems. MetaFrame also supports non-Windows clients including DOS, UNIX, Mac OS, Java, and OS/2 Warp, and a broad range of client hardware including legacy PCs, Pentium PCs, Windows-based terminals, network computers, wireless devices, and information appliances.

Network Connectivity

MetaFrame can connect users to the network through standard telephone lines, WAN links (T1, T3, 56Kb, X.25), broadband connections (ISDN, Frame Relay, ATM), wireless connections, corporate intranets, and the Internet.

Popular LAN and WAN Protocol Support

MetaFrame supports popular LAN and WAN protocols, including TCP/IP, IPX/SPX, NetBIOS, and direct asynchronous connections.

Enterprise-Level Management Tools

MetaFrame provides enterprise organizations with robust management tools that simplify the support of multiple applications and thousands of users throughout the large network. Servers can be added easily and transparently without touching user desktops. You can administer applications across multiple servers from one location. With MetaFrame software, organizations can cost-effectively manage and support large enterprises as they grow in size and complexity.

Improved Tools for Systems Management

Administrators can reduce the computing costs and resources needed to support users and systems with the management tools provided by Citrix. The Load Balancing Services allow multiple MetaFrame servers to be grouped into a unified "server farm" to meet the needs of a growing user base. SecureICA Services offer end-to-end RSA RC5 encryption for the ICA data stream to ensure security of data.

Tools for Better Management of Applications

The Citrix application management tools simplify and speed the initial deployment and later updates of applications across the enterprise network. Application Publishing utilities make it easy for administrators to deploy applications across multiple MetaFrame servers. Application Launching & Embedding (ALE) makes it easy to integrate Windows- and Web-based applications without rewriting the code, thereby saving time and money. You can define the ReadyConnect Client with published applications, phone numbers, IP addresses, server names, and connection options prior to first-time installation. This decreases the time required to deploy applications throughout the network.

Tools for Managing User Sessions and Installing Client Software

To improve the productivity of end users and IT professionals, MetaFrame includes Session Shadowing. This feature allows administrators to take control of one user's or multiple users' sessions for support, diagnosis, and training. With the Automatic Client Update utility, the Citrix ICA client software can be updated automatically from the server.

Desktop Integration Features

The MetaFrame software provides complete access to all local system resources, including full 16-bit stereo audio, local drives, COM ports, and local printers. Although applications run remotely from the server, they look, feel, and perform as though they are running locally. This reduces the need for training of users and increases user productivity.

For more information about the Metaframe product, visit the Citrix Web site at http://www.citrix.com.

ACCELERATING TO WINDOWS 2000

Windows 2000 Terminal Services provides all the features of Windows NT 4.0's Terminal Server, and delivers them more conveniently and to a wider audience. With the new third-party add-ons designed specifically for Windows 2000 Server (with Terminal Services enabled), the financial department's dream of fully functional inexpensive thin clients can become a reality.

- In Windows 2000, Terminal Services is included with all versions of the Server operating system (Server, Advanced Server, and Datacenter Server). No longer must you buy a special version of the Server software in order to get the Terminal Server and Terminal Services client software.

- Terminal Services user accounts in a domain environment are now managed through the Active Directory's Users and Computers MMC, giving you the same flexibility in terms of administrative control that you have with other Active Directory objects.

- Citrix has developed a version of its popular Metaframe's add-on specifically for the Windows 2000 Terminal Services, designed to provide seamless desktop integration, a myriad of management tools, and support for both Windows and non-Windows client operating systems.

There will be few surprises in store for those who have deployed the Windows NT 4.0 Terminal Server Edition. However, the most exciting new feature of the Windows 2000 Terminal Services software is its availability to all organizations that run the Windows 2000 Server software, regardless of which class of server operating system is purchased.

CHAPTER SUMMARY

In today's enterprise environment, where computing power must be provided to thousands or even tens of thousands of users in an organization at the lowest cost and highest productivity return possible, "thin" is in.

When users must rely on their desktop machines alone to run their programs, hardware quickly becomes obsolete as faster and more powerful systems are required to run the latest and greatest applications. The ability to continue using older equipment with less memory and slower processors saves money for large companies with many users. Windows 2000 Terminal Services allows organizations to do just that by providing a solution in which processing is performed on the more powerful server computer, and multiple users can connect to and run sessions on that machine from low-powered desktop systems.

The "thin client" concept is not just for huge conglomerates, however. Small companies with tight budgets will appreciate the advantages of running certain applications from the Terminal Server and the convenience of remote administration. Terminal Services offers administrators flexibility and control over users' sessions, including the ability to monitor or disconnect them, and the capability of administering the server (including shutdown and reboot) from a remote machine anywhere on the network.

The Windows 2000 Terminal Server's already impressive usefulness can be extended even further by the addition of the Citrix Metaframe's add-on components.

In this chapter, we discussed some of the features included in the Windows 2000 implementation of Microsoft's Terminal Services. We examined some factors that should be taken into account in planning a Terminal Services installation. You learned how to enable the Terminal Services on the server, how to install the client software, and two methods of installing user applications on the server for multisession use. Finally, we pointed out the benefits of using Citrix Metaframe's in conjunction with Terminal Services to make a good thing even better.

TWO-MINUTE DRILL

- ❏ Windows 2000's built-in Terminal Services software transforms a PC into a thin client, giving desktop machines remote access to a server desktop by functioning as a terminal emulator.

- ❏ Terminal Services can be installed on the server in two modes: application server mode, or remote administration mode.

- ❏ Terminal Services allows you to connect to the server as a remote node, or to actually remotely control another user's session.

- ❏ To give acceptable performance, a Terminal server requires a Pentium or higher processor, 64MB of RAM, and an additional 4 to 8MB RAM for each user to support running each user's programs on the server.

❑ The first step in deploying Terminal Services, once you've completed the planning stage, is to enable the service on the Windows 2000 server, and then install the client software on the client machines.

❑ The Terminal server is configured through the Terminal Services Configuration MMC.

❑ Since Terminal Services provides the capability for multiple sessions simultaneously, applications must be installed according to Microsoft's directions so that each session will be able to run a program on the server without disrupting the server or other sessions.

❑ Citrix MetaFrame is server-based software designed to work with Microsoft's Windows 2000 Server with Terminal Services installed.

❑ MetaFrame can connect users to the network through standard telephone lines, WAN links (T1, T3, 56Kb, X.25), broadband connections (ISDN, Frame Relay, ATM), wireless connections, corporate intranets, and the Internet.

❑ The MetaFrame software provides complete access to all local system resources, including full 16-bit stereo audio, local drives, COM ports, and local printers.

SELF TEST

The following questions will help you measure your understanding of the material presented in this chapter. Read all of the choices carefully, as there may be more than one correct answer. Choose all correct answers for each question.

1. Which of the following is one of the two modes in which Terminal Services can be installed on the server?

   A. Remote control

   B. Remote access

   C. Remote administration

   D. Remote logon

2. What tool is used to remotely control a user's terminal session?

   A. Terminal Services Client Connection Manager on the client machine

   B. Terminal Services Manager on the server machine

   C. Terminal Services Configuration tool on the server machine

   D. Terminal Services Remote Manager on the client machine

3. If your attempt to remotely control a user session fails, which of the following would be a likely explanation for the failure? (Choose all that apply.)

   A. The video card on the client machine does not support the resolution used at the session you are trying to remotely control.

   B. Your processor is incompatible with the processor in the machine on which

the session is running that you are trying to remotely control.

   C. You do not have Full Control permissions required to remotely control the session.

   D. You do not have the "remotely control terminal sessions" user right.

4. Which of the following is the minimum recommended hardware configuration for acceptable performance from a Terminal server?

   A. 64MB of RAM, and an additional 4 to 8MB RAM for each user, and a Pentium processor

   B. 32MB of RAM, and an additional 1 to 2MB RAM for each user, and an X486 processor

   C. 128MB of RAM, and an additional 4MB RAM for each user, and a Pentium II or higher processor

   D. 256MB of RAM, and an additional 2 to 4MB RAM for each user, and a Pentium processor

5. Which of the following is recommended for increased performance if you have several application programs that use a great deal of resources? (Choose all that apply.)

   A. Install them all on the same Terminal server.

   B. Disable unnecessary features.

   C. Install them on separate Terminal servers.

D. Restrict access to only certain users and groups.

6. Which type of user places the lightest load on the server's resources?

A. Typical users

B. Task-based users

C. Advanced users

D. Power users

7. Which of the following is considered a best practice when deploying Terminal Services as an application server in the typical network environment?

A. Install the applications you want to use with Terminal Services first, before you enable the Terminal Services on the server.

B. Put the Terminal Services applications on a FAT16 partition, not on a partition formatted with NTFS.

C. Install the Terminal Services on a domain controller, not on a member or stand-alone server.

D. None of the above.

8. The Terminal Services Licensing is a required component that licenses clients on a Terminal server if you are running in which mode?

A. Licensed mode

B. Remote administration mode

C. Application server mode

D. Terminal user mode

9. Which of the following is NOT one of the choices you are given in the Network Client Administrator dialog box?

A. Make installation disk set.

B. Make emergency repair disk.

C. Copy client-based network administration tools.

D. View remoteboot client information.

10. Which of the following can be done from the Terminal Services Configuration MMC? (Choose all that apply.)

A. You can choose whether to delete temporary folders on exit.

B. You can enable or disable Active Desktop.

C. You can send a message to Terminal Services users.

D. You can change Terminal server mode from remote administration to application server.

11. Which of the following pieces of information do you need to have at hand when you create a new connection in Terminal Services Client Connection Manager? (Choose all that apply.)

A. The name or IP address of the Terminal server.

B. The username and password with which you will log on.

C. The IP address of the client machine.

D. The screen resolution at which you wish to run the terminal screen.

12. When an administrator resets a client's session, what happens?

    A. The session continues as before, and the client is unaware that the session was reset.

    B. The session is disconnected, but can be reactivated by the user.

    C. The session is not disconnected, but a message is sent to the user notifying him that the session was reset, and all unsaved data at the time of the reset is lost.

    D. The session is closed and can no longer be activated by the user.

13. Which of the following are ways to install an application on the Terminal server so as to run in the multisession environment? (Choose all that apply.)

    A. Use the Install Programs tab on the Terminal Services Manager properties sheet.

    B. Use the Add/Remove Programs applet in Control Panel.

    C. Use the Change User command at the command line.

    D. Use the Multi-session Applications button on the toolbar of the Terminal Services Configuration tool.

14. What is the command-line command that an administrator can use to shut down the computer remotely?

    A. shutdown

    B. srvshtdn

    C. tsshutdn

    D. termserv powerdwn

15. Which of the following is true regarding connecting an OS/2 client to the Microsoft Terminal Server?

    A. It is impossible to use OS/2 clients with Terminal Server.

    B. Terminal Server supports OS/2 clients with no necessity for third-party software or special configuration.

    C. OS/2 clients can connect to Terminal Server by installing the OS/2 Client services software included on the Windows 2000 CD.

    D. OS/2 clients can connect to Terminal Server by using Citrix Metaframe software with Microsoft Terminal Server.

MICROSOFT CERTIFIED SYSTEMS ENGINEER

8

Supporting DHCP and WINS

I n the course of reading this book, you will be introduced to a number of new services and capabilities made available in Windows 2000. In this chapter, we visit two old friends, WINS (the Windows Internet Naming Service) and DHCP (Dynamic Host Configuration Protocol). We have entire chapters devoted to these services and how to install and configure them in Windows 2000. In this chapter, our primary focus is the enhanced functionality of these familiar services in Windows 2000.

HEADSTART OBJECTIVE 8.01

New DHCP Functionality

DHCP provides network administrators a method to easily and reliably assign IP addressing information to all TCP/IP hosts on their networks. Prior to the introduction of DHCP, network administrators would have to visit each machine and manually enter IP addressing information, such as IP address, subnet mask, and default gateway. This manual approach had several disadvantages, including

- The likelihood of human error when entering the IP address and other TCP/IP configuration options.

- The need to manually track those IP addresses already in use in order to prevent inadvertent reuse of previously assigned IP addresses.

- An increased likelihood that a user would "experiment" with the numbers entered in the IP addressing information dialog box.

- The need to visit each machine whose IP addressing information was incorrect, in order to correct configuration errors.

In addition to DHCP's traditional role of providing IP addressing information to hosts on a TCP/IP-based network, Microsoft has delivered enhanced functionality to the DHCP server included in Windows 2000. These features include the following:

- The Windows 2000 DHCP server is now able to dynamically update Address (A) records and Pointer (PTR) records in a Windows 2000 DNS server. This aids in the dynamic updating of DNS records, which are the core of the Dynamic Domain Name System (DDNS) server included in Windows 2000.

- More counters in Performance, which allows for more detailed monitoring of a DHCP server's status and network performance.

- Enhanced DHCP logging capabilities and improved checks to prevent loss of logging information in the event of a potential "disk full" condition.

- The ability to create Multicast Scopes to allocate multicast addresses to servers and applications when required.

- Detection of unauthorized or "rogue" DHCP servers on the network, and the ability to automatically shut down these servers.

- Support for Automatic Client Configuration. This allows DHCP clients to automatically configure their own basic IP addressing information in the event that a DHCP server is not available.

- The ability of a DHCP client to detect when it has been disconnected and reconnected to another network via "media sensing." This is a boon to Notebook users who may disconnect and then reconnect to another network without turning off the computer. The computer automatically reconfigures itself with TCP/IP parameters received from a DHCP server on the new network.

- Support for Superscope configuration. This feature was initially introduced in Windows NT 4.0 after the application of Service Pack 2, and has been carried forward into Windows 2000.

- The ability to offer dynamic IP addressing information to BOOTP clients. Formerly, Client Reservations were required for BOOTP clients. The Windows 2000 DHCP server is able to dynamically allocate IP addressing information to BOOTP clients.

We will look at some of these capabilities in greater depth soon. First, let's look at the role of DHCP in network planning and infrastructure.

How DHCP Fits with TCP/IP and UDP

A DHCP server is used to automatically assign IP addressing information to TCP/IP host computers on a TCP/IP network. There are several components to consider when assessing DHCP functionality: the process of assigning IP addressing information, the building of Scopes and Scope Options, DHCP client configuration, and special considerations for DHCP clients and servers that are located on different subnets.

The DHCP Lease Assignment Process

IP addressing information is leased to clients who request this information from a DHCP server. By default, the client may keep the IP address and other information leased to it for eight days. At 50 percent of the lease period, the client requests to renew its lease. If the DHCP server that issued the lease is available, it renews the lease. If the issuing DHCP server is not available, the client continues to use the leased information because it still has 50 percent of its lease period remaining.

At 87.5 percent of the lease period, the client again attempts to renew its lease. If the DHCP server that issued the lease is available, the client is allowed to renew its lease. If the DHCP server that issued the lease is still not available, the client attempts to renew its lease with any available DHCP server on the network. If no DHCP server is able to renew the client's leased IP address and other IP addressing information, the client goes through the process of obtaining an entirely new lease from any available DHCP server.

HOW A CLIENT OBTAINS A LEASED IP ADDRESS   It is helpful to think of our aunt "DORA" when remembering the order of the IP lease assignment process to DHCP clients. DORA is the process or dialog that the DHCP client and server participate in to grant a client a lease: Discover, Offer, Request, and Acknowledgement.

- DHCP<u>D</u>ISCOVER (D)—The DHCP client issues a DHCPDISCOVER message if the client has never obtained a lease before, or if the client must obtain an entirely new lease because it was not able to renew a previous one. The DHCPDISCOVER message is broadcast to the entire subnet. All DHCP servers on the subnet respond to the DHCPDISCOVER message.

- DHCP<u>O</u>FFER (O)—All DHCP servers respond to the client's DHCPDISCOVER message with a DHCPOFFER message. The DHCPOFFER message includes the IP address that the DHCP server offered to lease to the host. The client accepts the first offer it receives, and rejects any additional offers. The DHCP servers whose offers were rejected retract their offers.

- DHCP<u>R</u>EQUEST (R)—After the DHCP client receives a DHCPOFFER message, it returns a DHCPREQUEST message to the issuing DHCP server. The message contains a request to the issuing DHCP server that the client would like to accept the offer and keep the IP address assigned to it.

- DHCP<u>A</u>CKNOWLEDGEMENT (A)—The DHCP server sends the client a DHCPACKNOWLEDGEMENT message after the DHCP server receives the DHCPREQUEST message from the client. A positive DHCPACKNOWLEDGEMENT message (DHCPACK) is sent to the client to confirm that the client has successfully leased an IP address.

heads
①P

If for some reason the DHCP client is not allowed to keep the IP address it received in the DHCPOFFER message, a DHCPNACK (negative DHCPACKNOWLEDGEMENT message) is sent. If a DHCPNACK is sent, the client has to start over and issue another DHCPDISCOVER message. This starts the entire lease request process over again.

DHCP Servers and Scopes

How does the DHCP server know which IP addresses to give out? You tell it! You do this by creating *scopes*. Each Scope contains IP addressing information for a particular subnet. A single DHCP server can contain several Scopes. Therefore, a single DHCP server has the potential to service multiple subnets.

After you install the DHCP server software on a DHCP server, you must "populate" that server with Scopes. For example, let's say that we have a group of computers on network ID 192.168.1.0. We would create a single Scope for this network ID. This DHCP server would now be able to hand out IP addresses for computers on network ID 192.168.1.0. If we had another network ID 192.168.2.0, we would create a second Scope for that Network ID. Now the server can also hand out IP addresses for network ID 192.168.2.0.

EXCLUDED IP ADDRESSES   You can choose to "exclude" IP addresses if you don't want the DHCP server to hand out all the IP addresses in a particular Scope. For example, you have a UNIX server that always has the same IP address, 192.168.1.5. You do not want the DHCP server to hand out this IP address, since the UNIX server needs to use it all the time. In this case, you would exclude 192.168.1.5 from the IP address pool. You might also exclude the IP addresses of your domain controllers, DHCP servers, WINS servers, DNS servers, and router interfaces.

RESERVED CLIENTS   A *reserved client* is a computer that is always assigned the same IP addressing information by the DHCP server. This reserved client always obtains the same IP address that you configure in the DHCP manager.

How does the DHCP server know that a specific computer is a reserved client that should always get the same IP address? It can do this because when the DHCP client issues a DHCPDISCOVER message, it includes in this message its MAC addresses (media access control or "hardware" address). When you create a Client Reservation on the DHCP server, you include the MAC address of the reserved client. Whenever a computer with that MAC address issues a DHCPDISCOVER message to the DHCP server, the DHCP server knows to hand out only the IP address that you have configured for that computer's MAC address.

You might consider creating Client Reservations for computers that have IP addresses that never change, such as UNIX computers on your Windows 2000 network.

DHCP OPTIONS When you first configure the Scope, you include the first and last IP address included in that Scope, as well as the subnet mask. This provides basic IP addressing information to clients requesting an IP address from your DHCP server. However, a DHCP server can provide much more than just IP addresses.

DHCP Options can inform the DHCP client computer of the IP address of its Default Gateway, the IP address of its DNS server, the IP address of its WINS server, and its NetBIOS node type. There are other options in addition to these that you can configure to meet your special needs. By configuring these options on the DHCP server, you automatically inform DHCP clients of this vital information.

DHCP Options come in several different groupings:

- Server Options (formerly known as Global Options)
- Scope Options
- Client Options (for reserved clients only)
- Class Options (see the Class Options sections for more details)

Server Options apply to all Scopes maintained on a particular DHCP server. If you configure a Server Option for a DNS server address of 192.168.1.2, then all Scopes maintained on that server inform their DHCP clients that they use 192.168.1.2 as their DNS server.

Scope Options apply to a single Scope. For example, if I have three Scopes on the DHCP server—192.168.1.0, 192.168.2.0, and 192.168.30—I can configure the 192.168.1.0 Scope to use the DNS server at 192.168.1.4. If I leave the Server Option set as before, the other two Scopes use the DNS server at 192.168.1.2. Scope Options give us more granular control over assignment of DHCP Options. If there is a conflict between a Scope Option and a Server Option, the Scope Option overrides the Server Option.

Client Options are created for reserved clients. This gives you more granular control over IP addressing information. If you want a specific DHCP client to have customized DHCP Options, you first configure that client with a Client Reservation. Then you configure options for that Client Reservation. These are referred to as Client Options. If there is a conflict between the Scope Options for the reserved clients network ID, the Client Options override any Scope Options.

Class Options are something entirely new with Windows 2000. Class Options come in two types: Vendor Classes and User Classes. Check the section on Class Options for more details on the uses and functionality of these new DHCP Options.

CLIENT OPERATING SYSTEMS AND CLIENT SETUP

Microsoft operating systems that support DHCP include

- Windows 2000

- Windows NT

- Windows 9x

- Windows 3.x (with TCP/IP-32 installed)

- Microsoft Network Client 3.0 for MS-DOS (with real-mode TCP/IP driver)

- LAN Manager version 2.2c

All operating systems that support DHCP client functionality can use the Windows 2000 DHCP server to provide them with IP addressing information. Examples include Linux and OS/2 machines that are set up as DHCP clients.

Configuring a Windows 2000 machine to be a DHCP client is simple. The machine can be configured to be a DHCP client during the installation of the operating system, or after installation has been completed. For Windows 2000 clients, all you need to do is select an option button for "obtain IP address automatically."

Authorizing a **DHCP** Server in Active Directory

DHCP clients obtain their IP addresses from a DHCP server via a DHCPDISCOVER message. This message is a broadcast issued to every computer on the segment, and to DHCP servers on other segments if there is a local DHCP Relay Agent (or if an RFC-compliant router separates the client from the DHCP Server).

The broadcast nature of the DHCPDISCOVER message causes it to be indiscriminate. This can lead to problems when a "rogue" DHCP server shows up on the network. A rogue DHCP server is defined as a DHCP server that has not been approved by the IT department, and therefore will likely contain invalid Scopes and DHCP Options. DHCP clients can unknowingly obtain inaccurate IP addressing information from these rogue DHCP servers. This can lead to disruption of network communications for these hapless clients, and calls to the IT department to sort out the matter will ensue.

Windows 2000 networks running only Windows 2000 DHCP servers have the capability to recognize and shut down such rogue DHCP servers. This is accomplished by keeping a list of "authorized" DHCP servers in the Active Directory. Any DHCP server that starts up and is not included in the authorized list IS shut down automatically.

heads **UP**

Rogue DHCP server detection is only available on Windows 2000 DHCP servers. If someone were to introduce a Windows NT DHCP server on the network, rogue NT DHCP server detection would not detect it.

How Rogue DHCP Servers Are Detected

When a Windows 2000 DHCP server starts up on a network, it broadcasts a DHCPINFORM message to all computers on its segment. This DHCPINFORM message is part of a new and evolving DHCP specification. The DHCPINFORM message contains vendor-specific option types that can be interpreted by Microsoft DHCP servers. These included option types allow the new DHCP server to obtain information about the network from other DHCP servers extant on the segment. The DHCPINFORM message can submit queries to other DHCP servers.

When existing DHCP servers on the segment receive the DHCPINFORM message, they respond to a query asking for information about the Enterprise root name and location. The queried DHCP servers respond by sending back to the new DHCP server a DHCPACK message that includes Directory Services Enterprise Root information. The new DHCP server receives DHCPACK messages from all the DHCP servers on its segment. This allows the new DHCP server to collect information about all the DHCP servers on its segment, and about all identified Directory Service Enterprise Roots that the extant DHCP servers are presently aware.

If the new DHCP server receives information about an existing Directory Services Enterprise Root, it queries the Active Directory to assess whether its IP address is included in the list of authorized DHCP servers. If the machine's IP address is included on the list, it successfully initializes DHCP server services. If its IP address is absent from the list, DHCP-related services do not initialize and are shut down.

The new DHCP server can only start DHCP server services if:

- There are other DHCP servers on the segment that are authorized DHCP servers listed in the Active Directory, and the new DHCP server is listed in the Active Directory's list of authorized DHCP servers.

- The new DHCP server is the only DHCP server on the segment. Since it is the only DHCP server on the segment, there are no other DHCP servers to respond to the DHCPINFORM message. Without a response to the DHCPINFORM message query, the new DHCP server cannot be made aware of existing Directory Services Enterprise Roots.

In the second instance, the new DHCP server is not able to contact another DHCP server that might have information about a Directory Services Enterprise Root. However, the "lone" DHCP server continues to send DHCPINFORM messages every five minutes in an attempt to contact authorized DHCP servers. Should the new DHCP server receive a DHCPACK from a DHCP server later that contains information about the Enterprise Root, the new DHCP server seeks its IP address listing on the

Active Directory's list of Authorized DHCP servers. If the new DCHP server is not on that list, DHCP server services are disabled.

Authorizing a DHCP Server

After installing the DHCP server software, you must first authorize it in the Active Directory. This exercise walks you through the steps necessary to authorize your DHCP server.

1. Click Start | Programs | Administrative Tools | DHCP. This opens the DHCP Management Console.

2. Right-click on your computer name and click Authorize on the menu that appears.

3. Your DHCP server is now authorized.

Confirming Authorization of a DHCP Server

In this exercise, we confirm that our server has been authorized in the Active Directory.

1. Log on as administrator at a domain controller in the domain in which the DHCP server was authorized.

2. Select Start | Programs | Administrative Tools | Active Directory Sites and Services.

3. You should see something like the screen shown next.

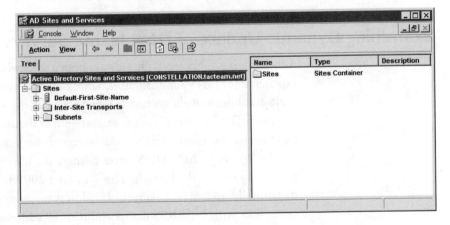

4. Right-click Active Directory Sites and Service and point to the View menu. Click Show Services Node. You should now see a services node in the left pane.

5. Expand the services node and click on the Net Services folder. In the right pane, you should see the Fully Qualified Domain Name (FQDN) of your newly authorized DHCP server with the type DHCPClass. In the screen shown next, you see that exeter.tacteam.net has now been authorized.

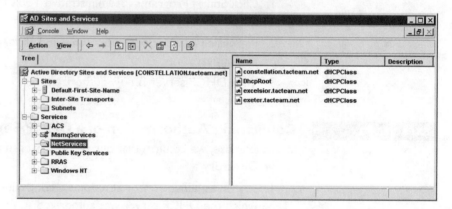

6. Close the Active Directory Sites and Services console.

Congratulations! You have confirmed that your DHCP server is successfully authorized in the Active Directory.

Examining Dynamic Update of DNS Name Servers

Administering DNS servers has always been a somewhat harrowing experience for DNS administrators. Unlike WINS server administrators, the DNS administrator always had to manually enter the address records into a Microsoft DNS server. If your organization had thousands of computers, you had to enter thousands of DNS address records for your hosts.

The Windows 2000 DNS server changes the life of the DNS administrator (for the better!). The Windows 2000 DNS server is able to dynamically update host name to IP address mappings, just like a WINS server does with NetBIOS names and their IP addresses. Unfortunately, only Windows 2000 host computers can natively update their own address records in the DNS server. But, as we shall see, even down-level clients get to register their names in the DNS.

Let's look at a couple of scenarios and see how they affect Dynamic Name Registration on a Windows 2000 Dynamic DNS server.

Using Only Windows 2000 DDNS Servers and Windows 2000 DHCP Servers

The Windows 2000 DHCP server supports Option Code 81, which allows the client to return to the DHCP server its FQDN. After the DHCP server receives the FQDN from the client, it can report this information to a Windows 2000 Dynamic DNS (DDNS) server. The DHCP server can then update the client's A Record and PTR Record on the DDNS server. How this works depends on whether the host is a Windows 2000 machine or a down-level client:

- A Windows 2000 DHCP client updates its A record on the DDNS server itself. The DHCP server updates the client's PTR record on the DDNS server.

- A down-level client updates neither the A record nor the PTR record itself. The DHCP server updates both on the DDNS server.

Legacy DNS Servers

If you have legacy (non-Windows 2000) DNS servers on your network, no client is able to dynamically update its A Address Records on the server. Even if you use a Windows 2000 DHCP server, you are not able to dynamically update A Records on a legacy DNS server. This presents a special problem when you are using DHCP to assign IP addresses, and WinSock programs need to locate computers by their IP addresses on the network.

Your options are limited in this kind of situation. You essentially have two choices:

- Install a WINS server, and allow your legacy DNS servers to perform a WINS lookup.

- Upgrade your legacy DNS servers to Windows 2000 DDNS servers.

Advantages of Using Dynamic DNS Servers

The DDNS server provided by Windows 2000 allows computers to automatically register their host names and IP addresses in the form of an A record. Assigning hosts their IP addresses via DHCP was problematic, because each time a host machine received a new IP address via DHCP, its A record had to be manually updated on the DNS server. The new functionality afforded by DDNS allows the widespread use of DHCP, and allows for the dynamic update of host names in the same fashion as WINS provided dynamic updates of NetBIOS name to IP address mappings.

WINS servers should be decommissioned as NetBIOS functionality is phased out of network applications. DDNS allows administrators to utilize the strengths of DHCP without the drawbacks.

Configuring DHCP Scopes in Windows 2000

You must create and configure Scopes in order to make your DHCP server functional. In this section, we examine the procedures involved in creating and configuring DHCP Scopes and Options.

You create a single DCHP Scope for each network ID. You are ready to create Scopes for each network ID after you identify which networks you want to assign IP addresses. After identifying the network IDs you want to create Scopes for, you are then ready to create each Scope using the DHCP Manager MMC snap-in.

A Wizard guides you in the creation of a Scope in Windows 2000. This is a nice usability improvement over the process used in Windows NT 4.0.

Select the Range of the Scope

After deciding on the network ID, you choose which host IDs will be available in the Scope. You choose the first and last IP addresses in the pool of IP addresses that you want the DHCP server to deliver. The subnet mask is also entered when defining the Scope.

Decide on Ranges of IP Addresses to Exclude

Typically, you include all the IP addresses in a particular network ID in your Scope. Then you "exclude" or remove those IP addresses from the Scope that you do not want the DHCP server to "hand out." Examples of such IP addresses would be for those computers or devices that must have static IP addresses, such as UNIX hosts, domain controllers, WINS/DNS/DHCP servers, and router interfaces.

It is a good idea to think about the IP numbering scheme you will use for your devices that require static IP addresses in advance. This is because you define these excluded IP addresses as *ranges* (consecutively numbered IP addresses). Administration will be easier if you define your static IP addresses as consecutive numbers. Typically, the lowest and highest numbers in the Scope are excluded.

Basic DHCP Options

Decide in advance which DHCP Options you want to assign to the Scope. The Scope Wizard will ask you if you want to configure basic DHCP Options. These basic DHCP Options include WINS server address, DNS server address, and Default Gateway address. You can define DHCP Options later if you choose not to assign DHCP Options during the creation of the Scope.

EXERCISE 8-3

Installing and Configuring DHCP in Windows 2000

In this exercise, we install DHCP and then proceed to create a Scope with basic DHCP Options included.

Part I: Installing the DHCP Server Software

1. Log in as administrator.
2. Select Start | Settings | Control Panel.
3. Open the Add/Remove Programs applet.
4. Click the Add/Remove Windows Components icon.

5. In the Windows Components Wizard dialog box, scroll down so that you can see the Networking Services option. Click on that to highlight it, as shown next.

6. Click Details in the Windows Components Wizard dialog box. Place a check in the box next to Dynamic Host Configuration Protocol, as shown next. Click OK.

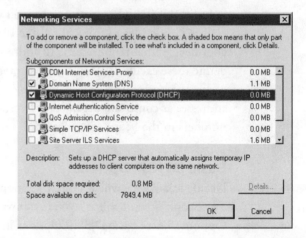

7. After clicking OK, you are returned to the Windows Components Wizard dialog box. Now click Next.

8. It will appear as if other components are being installed at the same time. When the installation of the DHCP server software is complete, you will be notified of a successful installation. Click Finish.

9. Close the Add/Remove Programs dialog box.

Congratulations! You have just installed the DHCP server software.

Part 2: Configuring a DHCP Scope

In this part of the exercise, we configure a Scope on our DHCP server using the Scope Wizard.

1. Select Start | Programs | Administrative Tools | DHCP.
   This opens the DHCP MMC snap-in, which you use to manage the DHCP server.

FIGURE 8-1

Preparing to configure
the DHCP Scope on
your server

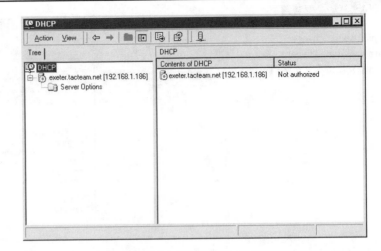

2. Expand all levels in the left pane. You should see your server name
   and a folder for Server Options as they appear in Figure 8-1.

3. If you have other DHCP servers on your network that are
   authorized in the Active Directory, you need to authorize your
   server first. If you do not authorize your server, it will be shut down
   as a rogue DHCP server. Follow the procedure discussed earlier to
   authorize your server. After authorization, your server status will be
   labeled "running."

4. Click on your computer's name. In this case, I will click on
   exeter.tacteam.net. Notice that the toolbar changes its appearance.
   Compare the appearance of the toolbars in Figures 8-1 and 8-2.

5. Now we will create a new Scope. The Scope will be for network ID
   192.168.2.0 with a subnet mask of 255.255.255.0 (the default Class
   C subnet mask, which uses 24 bits). To begin creating a new Scope,
   either right-click on your computer's name and select New Scope,
   or click the icon in the toolbar that looks like a video screen.

FIGURE 8-2

Dynamic toolbar changes
appearance when different
nodes are selected

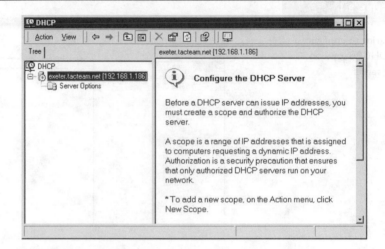

6. This opens the New Scope Wizard. You see the Welcome Screen
   now. Click Next.

7. Enter the name of your Scope and a Description that will help you
   remember some characteristics of the machines using that Scope, as
   shown next. After entering this information, click Next.

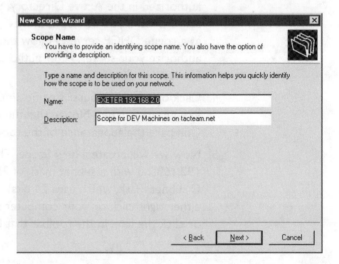

8. Now enter the first and last IP addresses that encompass the range of addresses this Scope will be able to "hand out." If you plan to subnet your network, be sure to enter the appropriate Subnet Mask. Enter **192.168.2.1** as the Start IP address and **192.168.2.254** as the End IP address. Click Next.

9. The Wizard now asks if we want to exclude some IP addresses from the range we defined. In this example, let's exclude the bottom 5 and top 10 IP addresses. We want to use these addresses in the future for clients that require static IP addresses. First, enter the Start IP address **192.168.2.1** and the End IP address **192.168.2.5**, and click Add. Then, enter the Start IP address **192.168.2.245** and the End IP address **192.168.2.254**, and click Add. Your screen should look like the one shown next. Click Next.

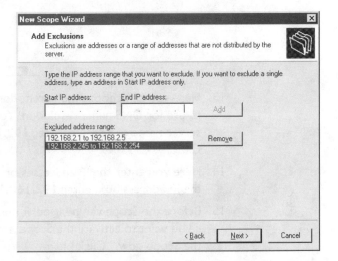

10. This next screen allows you to set the lease duration for IP addresses delivered by this Scope. This is a relatively stable network; so let's change the lease duration to 14 days. Click Next.

11. Now you are asked if you want to configure some of the common DHCP Options. Select "Yes, I want to configure these options now." Click Next.

12. The first option is for the Router (Default Gateway). Enter **192.168.1.16** in the IP address space, and then click Add. You should now see this in the list as shown next. Click Next.

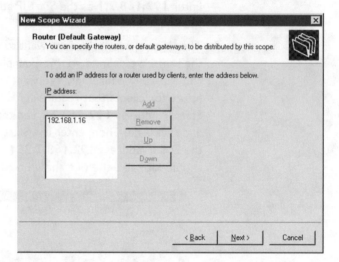

13. Here you can choose the parent domain you want your DNS clients to use for DNS name resolution. You can also configure your DNS server name or address. Enter **192.168.1.185** in the IP address box. Click Next.

14. Here you enter the IP addresses or names of your WINS servers. In the IP address box, enter **192.168.1.185**, and click Add. Click Next.

15. Before the Scope can be used, it must be activated. The Wizard asks if you want to activate the Scope now. Select "Yes, I want to activate the Scope now." Click Next.

16. The Wizard tells you that you are finished. Click Finish.

Congratulations! You have successfully created a Scope. Return to the DHCP Management Console. You should see something that looks like Figure 8-3.

FIGURE 8-3

Viewing the newly created
Scope in the DHCP MMC

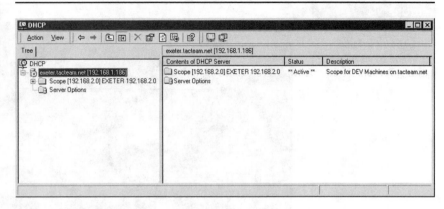

EXERCISE 8-4

Testing DHCP Functionality

In this exercise, we examine the changes that take place when a client
moves from manually set IP addressing information to automatically
assigned information via DHCP.

1. Log on as administrator at a Windows 2000 computer that is not a
   domain controller and is not a DHCP, DNS, or WINS server. This
   computer should already have manually configured IP addressing
   information.

2. Open a command prompt. At the command prompt, type

   ipconfig /all

   You should see a screen showing information similar to that in
   Figure 8-4.

3. Close the command prompt window.

4. Right-click on My Network Places and click Properties.

5. You should now see the Network and Dial-Up Connections
   window. Inside this window, there should be an entry for Local
   Connection. Right-click the local connection icon and click
   Properties.

FIGURE 8-4

Using the ipconfig /all
command to view DHCP
information

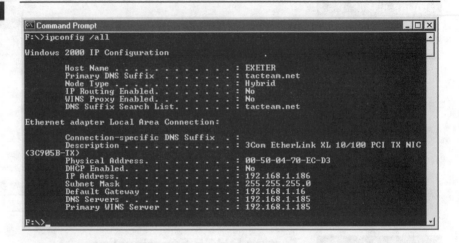

6. This opens the Local Area Connection Properties dialog box. Click
   Internet Protocol (TCP/IP), and click Properties.

7. You now see the Internet Protocol TCP/IP Properties sheet similar
   to the one shown next. Note the IP address, subnet mask, default
   gateway, and the preferred and alternate DNS servers. Click
   Advanced.

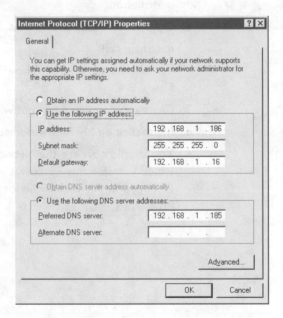

8. You now see the Advanced TCP/IP Settings Properties sheet. Note that there are four tabs. Click on each of the tabs and note the entries made for DNS, WINS, and Options. You will see the IP addresses for the DNS and WINS servers.

9. Now close the TCP/IP Properties sheets.

10. Move to the computer that is your DHCP server. Log in as administrator. Select Start | Programs | Administrative Tools | DHCP.

11. The DHCP administrative console is now open. Expand all nodes in the left pane. Click the Scope Options node and notice the settings for the different options. Make special note of settings that are different from those you saw in the ipconfig /all screen print. The options should look similar to those seen in Figure 8-5.

12. Click the Address Leases node. Note that your non-DHCP client is not listed in the right pane.

13. Close the DHCP console.

14. Select Start | Programs | Administrative Tools | DNS. Expand all nodes in the left pane. Click on the node that bears your domain name. If your computer is listed there, right-click the computer's name and click Delete. (Important: Do not remove the domain controller!) After the computer is made a DCHP client, it will register itself again automatically in the DNS.

FIGURE 8-5

Viewing the settings for the Scope Options node in the DHCP MMC

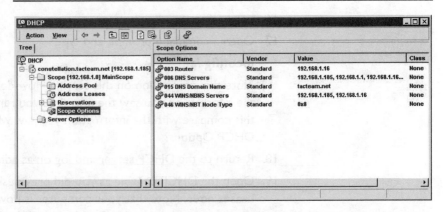

15. Return to the computer that had the manually configured IP addressing information. Return to the TCP/IP Properties sheet. On the General tab, select "Obtain an IP address automatically." Also select "Obtain DNS server address automatically." The screen should now appear like the one shown next. Click OK. Restart the computer. (The machine will immediately obtain its new settings from the DHCP server, but may not reliably register itself in the Active Directory unless you reboot.)

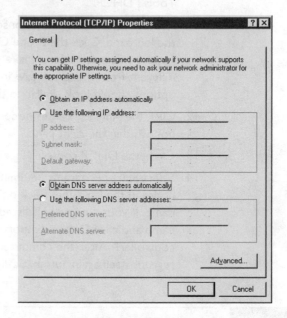

16. Log in again as administrator.

17. Open a command prompt, and type

    ipconfig /all

    Note the information on this screen. How does this compare with the information you saw the first time you ran ipconfig? How does this compare with the information you saw when perusing the DHCP Options?

18. Return to the DHCP server and log on as administrator.

19. Open the DHCP console as you did previously. Click the Address Leases node. Note that your computer is now listed in the right pane along with its leased IP address and the date of its lease expiration, as shown in Figure 8-6.

FIGURE 8-6

Viewing the DHCP lease
address information in the
DHCP MMC

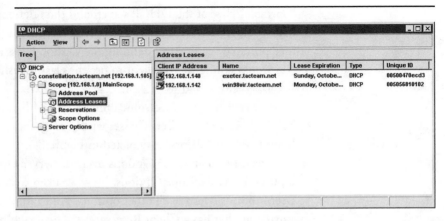

20. Close the DHCP console and open the DNS console as you did
previously. Click on your domain name. Note that your computer
has reregistered its A Address record. Close the DHCP console.

Examining Option Classes

Option Classes represent a new feature available only in the Windows 2000
DHCP server. Option Classes allow you to classify your DHCP clients
based on either User Class or Vendor Class. Option Classes allow the
DHCP client computer to send information about itself during the IP
address acquisition process. This allows the DHCP server to return to the
client a specialized group of DHCP Options in return. Let's look at each
type of Option Class in more detail.

User Classes

User Classes are part of a proposed Internet standard that is being
considered by the Internet Engineer Task Force (IETF). The purpose of
User Classes is to identify a DHCP client to a DHCP server, so that the
DHCP server can return to the client a specific set of options relevant to the
"class" the client had identified itself as a member of.

In order to implement User Classes, you must first define them at the
DHCP server. You could classify a group of computers as "portable."
Suppose that you would like your portable computers to use a specific IP
address, subnet mask, or default gateway. First, you would define the

"portable" class at the DHCP server, and then define DHCP Options that would be returned to any client that identifies itself as a member of the "portable" class. After defining the Option Class at the server, you would configure the client to use the class by using the ipconfig /setclassid command

Microsoft has included some built-in classes that are available "out of the box." These include Users Classes with special options for BOOTP and Remote Access Clients, as depicted in Figure 8-7.

Remember that Scope Options override Server Options, and Client Options override Scope Options. Now we need to add one more factor: User Options override all other options. For example, imagine that we have a machine that has a Client Reservation. This machine's Client Reservation Options override any other options that might be set for the server or for the Scope. However, if the reserved client identifies itself as a member of a certain User Class, the User Class Options override any reserved Client Options that it finds in conflict.

FIGURE 8-7

Server Options dialog box demonstrating built-in User Classes.

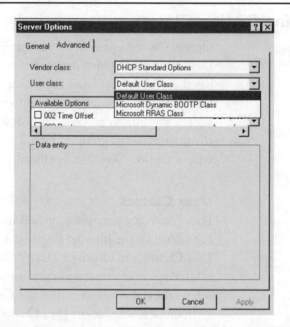

User Options allow us a greater level of granularity in the assignment of DHCP Options. This improved granularity gives the administrator greater control over the TCP/IP parameters configured on the DHCP clients in his network.

Vendor Classes

Vendor Classes are included in accepted DHCP drafts (RFCs 2131 and 2132). Vendor Classes allow hardware and software vendors to identify their components to the DHCP server. If the manufacturer of a particular operating system wants to have specialized DHCP Options sent to their DHCP client, they can choose to include this information when their DHCP client initializes and requests IP addressing information from the DHCP server. The DHCP server will recognize the Vendor Class identifier and forward to the client the options that the vendor has configured.

Before these vendor-specific DHCP Options are returned to the client, the DHCP server must be made aware of their existence. You configure Vendor Class Options at the DHCP server. Microsoft has included Vendor Class Options for Windows 2000 and Windows 98 clients. Microsoft has also included a generic Microsoft operating system Vendor Class that can be used to deliver DHCP Options to any Microsoft operating systems that include MSFT as a client identifier during the client initialization. You can see these Microsoft Options in Figure 8-8.

Microsoft Vendor-Specific Options include

- **Disable NetBIOS over TCP/IP (NetBT)**—This option allows you to configure the DHCP server to instruct the client whether NetBT should be enabled or disabled.

- **Release DHCP lease on shutdown**—This option informs the client that it should release its lease when the machine is shut down. You might use this with laptop computers that move on and off the network frequently. This will free up more IP addresses in the Scope.

- **Default router metric base**—This option is used to set the default base metric for the DHCP client. This value is used to calculate the fastest and least-expensive routes.

FIGURE 8-8

Server Options dialog
box showing built-in
Vendor Classes

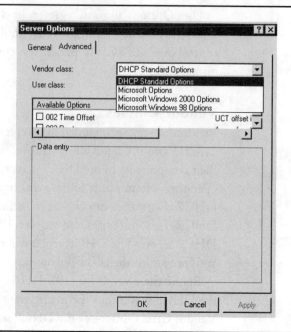

- **Proxy autodiscovery**—This option is used by clients that have Internet Explorer 5.0 only. This option informs the client of the location of the Internet Explorer 5.0 automatic configuration file.

Vendor Class Options are provided by the hardware or software vendor, and are not options that the administrator would configure himself.

Examining Automatic Private IP Addressing

Automatic Client Configuration, or APIPA (Automatic Private IP Addressing), is a new feature that was initially available in Windows 98. The feature has been extended to Windows 2000 and allows DHCP client computers to self-configure their IP addressing information in the event a DHCP server is not available when the computer issues a DHCPDISCOVER message, or when it senses that it has been moved from a previous network via Windows 2000 *media sensing* capabilities. (Media sense refers to the capability of the operating system to detect when it has been disconnected and reconnected to a network. This functionality was provided with NDIS 4.0 and works with network interface cards that support this capability.)

heads
⑪p

APIPA is only useful when clients are connected as workgroups or domains that consist of a single segment, and all the machines on that segment utilize automatic client IP address configuration.

Should a Windows 2000 computer discover that it cannot contact a DHCP server either to obtain an IP address or to renew an IP address, the client self-configures its IP addressing information so that it can continue to participate in network activities.

If a DHCP server cannot be found, the DHCP client attempts to auto-configure its IP addressing information. The IP address is drawn from a Microsoft Private Class B network ID, 169.254.0.0 with the default Class B subnet mask of 255.255.0.0.

In order to prevent auto-configuring clients from assigning themselves duplicate IP addresses, the client first selects an IP address and then issues an ARP request for that IP address. The ARP broadcast requests the MAC address of the computer that presently holds that IP address. If there is no response to the ARP broadcast, the auto-configuring client keeps the IP address it selected. If there is a response, the auto-configuring client chooses another IP address. This continues for up to ten addresses.

The client continues to use the auto-configured IP address until it can contact a DHCP server. The DHCP client continues to search for a DHCP server by issuing DHCPDISCOVER messages every five minutes. Once a DHCP server is located, the DHCP client abandons its auto-configured settings and assumes the settings delivered to it by the DHCP server.

Autoconfiguration (APIPA) and the Lease Renewal Process

When a client already has a lease, the sequence of events is a little different. If the lease is still valid, the client attempts to renew its lease with the DHCP server that issued the lease. If the DHCP client is not able to contact the issuing DHCP server, it PINGs the default gateway that was included in its lease.

If the PING is successful, the DHCP client assumes that it is still on the same network, and that there is a problem with the DHCP server itself. The client continues with the normal lease renewal process at 50 percent and 87.5 percent of the client's lease period.

If the PING of the default gateway listed in the client's lease is unsuccessful, the client assumes that it has been moved to another network. In this event, the client gives up its lease and auto-configures via the process described earlier.

QUESTIONS AND ANSWERS

What is APIPA?	Automatic Private IP Addressing, also called automatic client configuration.
What does it do?	Allows a DHCP client that is unable to obtain an IP address from a DHCP server to configure itself to temporarily use an IP address from a preassigned range.
What operating systems use APIPA?	Windows 98 and Windows 2000.
Is there a way to disable auto-configuration?	Yes. You must edit the following Registry key: HKEY_LOCAL_MACHINE\SYSTEM\CurrentControlSet\Services\Tcpip\Parameters\Interfaces\adapter_name to add a value key of: IPAutoconfigurationEnabled: REG_DWORD and then set the value to 0. WARNING: Always use caution when editing the Registry.

New WINS Functionality

WINS was first introduced in Windows NT 3.5x. The purpose of WINS remains the same today as it was when it was first introduced: to resolve IP addresses from NetBIOS names.

NetBIOS applications require knowledge of the NetBIOS name of a destination host before creating a session. However, TCP/IP is only concerned with destination IP addresses and is oblivious to NetBIOS names. We must, therefore, have some mechanism to resolve NetBIOS names to IP addresses in order for NetBIOS-based applications to function properly on a TCP/IP-based network. This is the primary function of WINS.

WINS maintains a database of NetBIOS names and IP address mappings. A computer that is configured to be a WINS client automatically registers its name and IP address with a WINS server. A Host computer that is configured as a WINS client queries the WINS database when it needs to establish a NetBIOS connection with a destination computer.

Without WINS, a host computer must broadcast a NAMEQUERYREQUEST in order to resolve the NetBIOS name to an IP address. Such broadcasts have two inherent limitations:

- They introduce excessive network traffic that can impede the smooth flow of information exchange.
- Broadcasts typically do not cross routers.

WINS client computers are configured with the IP address of the WINS server that they register with and query. WINS clients, therefore, can issue a directed datagram to the WINS server itself and avoid broadcasts. Resolving IP addresses of computers on other subnets is no longer a problem because of the directed nature of a WINS client's communication with the WINS server.

New Features Included in the Windows 2000 WINS Server

The Windows 2000 implementation of the WINS server introduces new features and functionality, including

- Persistent connections
- Manual tombstoning
- WINS Manager integrated into the MMC
- Improved record searching and filtering capabilities
- Record verification and version number checking
- The ability to export WINS records in a delimited text file
- Increased fault tolerance for clients

Let's look at these features in more detail.

The Ability to Maintain Persistent Connections with Replication Partners

Former implementations of WINS required replication partners to open and close network connections when performing either a push or pull operation. This opening and closing of connections required a modest number of processor cycles, and decreased the overall performance of the servers during this process. This overhead is avoided by using persistent connections.

WINS servers are also able to immediately update each other on changes to the WINS database if persistent connections are enabled. By setting update counts to 0 for push operations, updates are immediately sent to replication partners.

Manual Tombstoning

Tombstoning refers to marking records as "extinct" in the WINS database. When a record is marked as extinct, it is no longer considered a valid record by the WINS database. A question that many have is, "why doesn't the WINS server just delete the record?" The reason that WINS doesn't delete the record rather than tombstone it is related to issues involved in the replication process.

Let's say that we have a computer whose NetBIOS name is JOE1. JOE1 has been removed from the network. After JOE1 releases its NetBIOS name, the WINS server waits the period of time as configured in the "extinction interval" before marking it as extinct (and will tombstone the record). This tombstoned record is no longer valid, and when the WINS database is replicated to its replication partners, the tombstoned state of JOE1 is also replicated. After the extinction time-out period has passed, the tombstoned records are removed from the WINS database.

Since JOE1 has been tombstoned, when push/pull partners share data with each other, JOE1 is not returned to the original owner of JOE1's WINS record. This is because there is already a record in its WINS database noting that JOE1 is tombstoned. After the "extinction time-out" period, JOE1's record entirely disappears from all WINS servers that have JOE1's tombstoned record in their database.

Now consider what happens with manual deletion. Rather than tombstoning JOE1, let's just delete his record from the WINS server that owns his record. When this WINS server replicates with its partners, it does not include any information about JOE1, so nothing takes place regarding JOE1 on the WINS server's replication partners.

However, when the WINS server that is the owner of JOE1's record receives a replication from its partners that *still have* JOE1 in their databases, what do you think happens? JOE1 reappears in the original WINS server, and it appears as an active record!

It is much better to tombstone records rather than deleting them. Take advantage of this new capability to manually tombstone in the Windows 2000 WINS server.

Add More Than Just a Primary and Secondary WINS Server on Windows 2000 Clients

You can configure Windows 2000 clients with up to 12 secondary WINS servers. This is a great improvement over the single secondary WINS server that could be configured on WINS clients in Windows NT 4.0. This ability to designate additional secondary WINS servers adds fault tolerance to name resolution.

A WINS client contacts its primary WINS server when it attempts to register its NetBIOS name or resolve a NetBIOS name to an IP address. If the primary WINS server does not respond after three attempts to contact it, a secondary WINS server is contacted. If there are multiple secondary WINS servers, each of these are tried three times before the client moves to the next one on the list.

The ability to assign many more secondary WINS servers sounds like a no-lose situation at first blush. However, Microsoft warns that there is a balance between fault tolerance and speed of name resolution. Here's why:

The normal NetBIOS name resolution process for H-node machines includes

1. *Searching the NetBIOS name cache*
2. *Querying configured WINS server(s)*

3. Issuing a local broadcast

4. Searching the LMHOSTS file

5. Searching the HOSTS file

6. Querying the preferred DNS server

It can take an excessive amount of time to move through a list of 12 secondary WINS servers versus moving through the normal NetBIOS name-resolution process. Consider this when configuring your clients with secondary WINS server addresses.

Improved Records Verification and Version Number Validation

WINS server records verification allows the WINS administrator to verify that the NetBIOS name and IP address mappings for each entry in a WINS server exist on all other WINS servers.

You'll have to do a little leg work in advance in order to accomplish the verification process. First, you have to define what NetBIOS names you want checked. Then, you have to define what WINS servers you want these records checked on. There are two ways you can configure these lists of NetBIOS names and WINS servers:

- Create separate text files called names.txt and servers.txt. The names.txt file will contain the NetBIOS names of the computers that you want to verify, and the servers.txt file will contain the names of the WINS server on which these NetBIOS names will be checked.

- Enter the NetBIOS names and WINS server names in the GUI interface provided with the WINS manager MMC snap-in.

After you start the verification process, the names list is used to create a query. Each WINS server on the servers list will be queried for each of the NetBIOS names in the names list. If a WINS server fails to respond to the query, it will be retried three times before moving onto the next server.

Version number validation ensures that all WINS servers on the network have the most recent version of the database entry (NetBIOS name to IP address entry) as included in the WINS server that is the owner of the record.

When you initiate version consistency checking, records are pulled from remote WINS servers' databases and are checked to determine whether the record on the remote WINS server is identical to the one on the local WINS server. If the version ID number is lower on the local database, the pulled record will be added, and the older record will be deleted.

See the WINS chapter for more information on Version ID numbering and how this is involved in WINS database replication.

Export WINS Database Entries to a Delimited Text File

You are now able to export the WINS database entries into either a tab- or a comma-delimited text file. You can take this delimited file and import the information into a Microsoft Excel Workbook or Access Database. You can create impressive and compelling reports by using the sophisticated report-building features included in these two programs.

HEADSTART OBJECTIVE 8.02

The Difference Between WINS and DNS

Students often have difficulty with the distinction between the functions of WINS and DNS. They usually remember that both are responsible for matching up a computer's name and its IP address, but often wonder why two services are needed in order to accomplish the task.

The answer lies in the fact that WINS and DNS track different types of computer names. A WINS server maintains a database of NetBIOS names and their corresponding IP addresses, while a DNS server keeps a list of host names and their matching IP addresses. Why do we need so many different names?

NetBIOS Names and Microsoft Networking

All programs must interact with the Network protocols via the Application layer of the DOD (TCP/IP) model. Within the Application layer there are two Application Programming Interfaces (APIs) that a program can interact with on Microsoft TCP/IP networks: the NetBIOS API, or the WinSock API.

NetBIOS Over TCP/IP

The API that a program uses to access the network depends on whether the program was written to work on a TCP/IP-based network or a NetBIOS network. Microsoft networking programs have historically been written to the NetBIOS Session layer interface. This is because NetBEUI (NetBIOS Enhanced User Interface) was the network transport protocol of choice for Microsoft Networks until TCP/IP took precedence as the networking protocol of modern networks.

NetBIOS programs must know the name of the destination host before establishing a session with that host. Typically, the source computer broadcasts a NetBIOS NAMEQUERYREQUEST to the local segment. If the destination host that owns the name that is being requested is on the local segment, it returns its MAC address to the requestor. This is all a NetBIOS program needs to know. NetBIOS programs are totally oblivious to IP addresses, and they do not care about them a bit.

A problem arises because TCP/IP does not care at all about NetBIOS names. NetBIOS names are not part of the TCP/IP specification, and TCP/IP does not use them. TCP/IP only cares about the destination host's IP address. How can we get NetBIOS-based programs to work on TCP/IP-based networks?

By implementing NetBIOS over TCP/IP (NetBT). When NetBIOS programs interact with the NetBIOS interface, they utilize NetBT in order to work properly on TCP/IP-based networks. However, NetBT adds an "extra step" to the process of session establishment with destination hosts.

When a NetBIOS program attempts to establish a session with a destination host, it interfaces with the network protocols via the NetBIOS interface. This leads the source machine to attempt to resolve the destination host's NetBIOS name to an IP address, rather than just trying to broadcast the destination computer's NetBIOS name and directly receiving the destination host's MAC address. This NetBIOS name to IP address resolution process is the extra step. The last step is to broadcast an ARP request (Address Resolution Protocol), which will then resolve the IP address to a MAC address. After the MAC address is obtained, a session can be established.

NetBIOS Names and WINS Servers

The process of resolving the NetBIOS name to an IP address can be handled in two ways:

- By broadcasting a NAMEQUERYREQUEST to the local segment
- By issuing a query directly to a WINS server

A WINS server maintains a database of NetBIOS names and their associated IP addresses. NetBIOS-based programs can utilize a WINS server in order to obtain the required destination host's IP address. This avoids excessive broadcast traffic and facilitates NetBIOS name resolution across routers.

All of Windows NT basic networking components were dependent on NetBIOS and NetBIOS names. This has changed in Windows 2000, which is not dependent on NetBIOS for network operations. However, a great many applications are dependent on NetBIOS, and therefore WINS servers will remain an important component of a Windows 2000 network until all NetBIOS-based programs are retired.

Host Names and DNS

Programs that are written specifically for TCP/IP networks use the WinSock interface. These programs are native to TCP/IP-based networks and do not need to know the name of the destination host in order to establish a session. All WinSock programs need to know is the destination IP address in order to establish a session. Examples of WinSock programs are Web browsers, FTP client programs, and Internet e-mail client programs.

Host Names Are Not Required

Most people are better able to remember names rather than numbers. Think about all the Web sites you have visited in the last week. What if you wanted to visit a site that you visited last week again? You could type the IP address into the address bar, but it would be difficult to remember all the IP addresses of your favorite Web sites.

We can give computers host names to make it easier for us to remember them. Now all we have to remember is a host name and its domain name, rather than an IP address. Remembering www.microsoft.com is a lot easier to remember than 207.46.131.15. The purpose of host names is to make our lives easier. Host names are *not required* by WinSock programs in order to establish a session; they are a mere convenience.

We must have a method to resolve host names to IP addresses in order to make using them work. This is the job of the DNS server. The DNS server maintains a database of host names and their corresponding IP addresses. WinSock programs contact a DNS server for host name resolution prior to establishing a session with the destination computer. This is because WinSock programs must know the destination host's IP address.

So, now you know the difference between WINS and DNS servers. Both are responsible for resolving computer names to IP addresses. However, the WINS server resolves NetBIOS names, and the DNS server resolves host names. NetBIOS programs require NetBIOS names in order to establish a session with another computer, and they use the NetBIOS interface. WinSock programs are written for TCP/IP networks, and they utilize the WinSock interface. These programs do not require the use of host names. Host names are merely a convenience for people who find remembering names easier than numbers.

ACCELERATING TO WINDOWS 2000

There's much to like about Windows 2000, not the least of which are the new and improved versions of DHCP and WINS, which include the following features:

- APIPA. Automatic Private IP Addressing, previously available only in Windows 98, which allows a DHCP client to function on the network even if it's unable to obtain or renew a lease from a DHCP server.

- Support for media sensing, and dynamic addressing for BOOTP clients. Previously, the only way to assign BOOTP client IP addresses via DHCP was by creating Client Reservations for each BOOTP client.

- Rogue DHCP server detection. Only DHCP servers authorized in the Active Directory are able to initialize their DHCP server service.

- Better integration with the performance-monitoring tool, allowing administrators to collect information about the DHCP server.

- DHCP integration with DDNS, providing for more efficient name registration and resolution.

- Support for Options Classes, allowing more fine-tuning in assigning TCP/IP configuration through DHCP.

- WINS support for persistent connection with replication partners.

- Manual tombstoning of WINS records, better search and filtering capabilities, and support for exporting to delimited text files.

- Improved fault tolerance, and enhanced WINS reliability.

CHAPTER SUMMARY

In this chapter, you learned about many of the new features included in WINS, DNS, and DHCP.

Major improvements in the Windows 2000 WINS server include the ability to maintain persistent connections. Persistent connections allow computers that are configured as replication partners to keep an open channel to each other. This persistently open channel allows immediate push updates to configured replication partners. Manual tombstoning allows the administrator to set the tombstone attribute to any entry in the WINS database. Tombstoning is preferred over deleting WINS database entries, because this prevents outdated entries from returning to the server that owns the entry. WINS clients can now be configured with up to 12 secondary WINS servers.

The Windows 2000 DHCP server introduces new features, including support for user and Vendor Classes, the ability to communicate with a DDNS server, and the capability to detect and disable rogue DHCP servers. Vendor and User Classes allow DHCP clients to send information about themselves to the DHCP servers. The DHCP server can use this information to send custom DHCP Options to the client. The Windows 2000 DHCP server can now communicate with a Windows 2000 DDNS server and automatically update A Address records and PTR records for a DHCP client. Automatic detection of rogue DHCP servers prevents unauthorized DHCP servers from starting up on the network. Windows 2000 DHCP servers use a DHCPINFORM message to obtain information about the Active Directory, and can search for themselves among a list of authorized servers.

The Windows 2000 DNS server supports dynamic updates to the DNS database. Windows 2000 clients can directly update their entries in the DNS. Down-level clients can also have their DNS entries updated automatically if they are configured as Windows 2000 DHCP server clients. The Windows 2000 DDNS server is designed to eventually supplant WINS servers as NetBIOS programs are phased out in favor of programs written to the WinSock interface.

TWO-MINUTE DRILL

- DHCP provides network administrators a method to easily and reliably assign IP addressing information to all TCP/IP hosts on their networks.

❑ A DHCP server is used to automatically assign IP addressing information to TCP/IP host computers on a TCP/IP network.

❑ IP addressing information is leased to clients who request this information from a DHCP server.

❑ A *reserved client* is a computer that is always assigned the same IP addressing information by the DHCP server.

❑ All operating systems that support DHCP client functionality can use the Windows 2000 DHCP server to provide them with IP addressing information.

❑ When a Windows 2000 DHCP server starts up on a network, it broadcasts a DHCPINFORM message to all computers on its segment.

❑ APIPA is only useful when clients are connected as workgroups or domains that consist of a single segment, and all the machines on that segment utilize automatic client IP address configuration.

❑ WINS maintains a database of NetBIOS names and IP address mappings.

❑ *Tombstoning* refers to marking records as "extinct" in the WINS database.

❑ NetBIOS programs must know the name of the destination host before establishing a session with that host.

❑ Programs that are written specifically for TCP/IP networks use the WinSock interface.

SELF TEST

The following questions will help you measure your understanding of the material presented in this chapter. Read all of the choices carefully, as there may be more than one correct answer. Choose all correct answers for each question.

1. Manual assignment of IP addressing information has which disadvantages?

   A. Increased probability of human error when entering the numerical information

   B. Automatic assignment of IP addresses to properly configured clients

   C. Reduction in paperwork required by the network administrator

   D. Allows central administration of IP address assignments

2. New features available in the Windows 2000 DHCP server include (Choose all that apply.)

   A. Enhanced DHCP logging capabilities and improved checks to prevent loss of logging information in the event of a potential "disk full" condition.

   B. The ability to create Multicast Scopes to allocate multicast addresses to servers and applications that require these.

   C. Detection of unauthorized or "rogue" DHCP servers on the network, and the ability to shut down DHCP

servers automatically on these rogue DHCP servers.

   D. The ability to back up the DHCP server database information.

3. The default lease period for IP addressing information from the Windows 2000 DHCP is

   A. 4 days

   B. 6 days

   C. 8 days

   D. 16 days

4. What are the four components in the dialog between a DHCP client and server during the process of IP address assignment?

   A. DISCOVER, OFFER, REQUEST, ACKNOWLEDGEMENT

   B. REQUEST, DISCOVER, OFFER, ACKNOWLEDGEMENT

   C. OFFER, REQUEST, ACKNOWLEDGEMENT, RELEASE

   D. RELEASE, RENEW, ABANDON, DISCOVER

5. Several of your users report to you that they intermittently receive error messages on their screens indicating that a duplicate address has been detected on the network. Your network contains primary Windows

2000 and Windows NT computers, along with three UNIX servers. What is the most likely cause of the problem?

A. The users are in error and there is no problem.

B. The UNIX servers are using static IP addresses, and their IP addresses have not been excluded from the Scope.

C. Duplicate IP addresses on the network are common with DHCP.

D. The Windows 2000 TCP/IP stack has an *autoresolve* mechanism that can allow for duplicate IP addresses on the network, and therefore there will be no problems in this situation.

6. What are the major groupings of DHCP Options?

A. Server Options

B. Scope Options

C. Client Options

D. Class Options

7. After installing a Windows 2000 DHCP server, you find that you get numerous error messages from the service control manager informing you that the DHCP service has been shut down. What can you do that might correct this situation?

A. Increase the number of Scopes on the DHCP server.

B. Remove duplicate Scope Options if they appear in different Scopes on the same DHCP server.

C. Authorize the DHCP server in the Active Directory.

D. Reinstall Windows 2000.

8. You have mostly Windows NT 4.0 Workstations on your network. How can you have these machines dynamically update their Address (A) records and Pointer (PTR) records in a Dynamic DNS (DDNS) Server?

A. Install the Windows 2000 DNS redirector on all the Window NT machines.

B. Make the Windows NT computers clients of a Windows 2000 DHCP server.

C. This cannot be done.

D. Configure the Windows 2000 DDNS server for Windows NT compatibility.

9. User Classes included with Windows 2000 DHCP servers include

A. Default User Class

B. Microsoft Dynamic BOOTP Class

C. Microsoft RRAS Class

D. Microsoft Linux Class

10. Vendor Classes included with Windows 2000 DHCP servers include

A. DHCP Standard Options

B. Microsoft Options

C. Microsoft Windows 2000 Options

D. Microsoft Windows 98 Options

11. Microsoft Vendor-Specific Options include

    A. Disable BOOTP dynamic assignment
    B. Disable NetBIOS over TCP/IP (NetBT)
    C. Release DHCP lease on shutdown
    D. Default router metric base

12. You have moved your Windows 2000 Professional computer that is configured as a DHCP client to another subnet. The computer has been turned off for three months. There is no DHCP server on the new subnet. When the computer tries to communicate with other computers on the new subnet, you find that it is unable to establish a session. What is the most likely cause of the problem?

    A. The other computers are down-level machines, and therefore cannot connect to Windows 2000 computers.
    B. The Windows 2000 computer cannot communicate with its domain controller, and therefore will not initialize its networking protocols.
    C. The Windows 2000 Professional computer has auto-configured its IP address with a network ID different from the network ID that it is now located on.
    D. The Windows 2000 computer requires a DHCP server on its segment in order to start its networking protocols.

13. What are some of the advantages of WINS servers maintaining persistent connections?

    A. Replication partners are able to immediately perform push updates.
    B. Fewer processor cycles are committed to establishing and tearing down sessions.
    C. Re-replication of deleted objects is eliminated.
    D. Tombstoned objects reactivate spontaneously.

14. How many secondary WINS servers can you configure for a Windows 2000 WINS client?

    A. 1
    B. 4
    C. 12
    D. 256

15. What is the difference between WINS and DNS?

    A. A WINS server maps IP addresses to NetBIOS names, and a DNS server maps host names to IP addresses.
    B. WINS servers can dynamically update their databases, and Windows 2000 DNS servers have static databases.
    C. WINS has been eliminated in Windows 2000.
    D. DNS maintains a list of NetBIOS names, and WINS confirms host MAC addresses.

9

Performing Disk Management

Windows 2000 offers easier management of hard drives and more powerful utilities for administrators. The new Disk Manager, which replaces Disk Administrator, allows for some new features not previously available in Windows NT 4.0. There is now support for partitions, logical drives, and new dynamic volumes. One of the key focuses of Windows 2000 is less downtime, and online disk management is one of the results of this focus. Online disk management allows changes to be made without requiring a server reboot. Another feature important to disk management with Windows 2000 is the ability to remotely manage hard drive configuration. This makes centralized management of the network servers and workstations possible.

HEADSTART OBJECTIVE 9.01

Windows 2000 Disk Storage Types

Windows 2000 supports the same file system types that Windows NT 4.0 supports, along with other file system types not previously supported. With Windows 2000, you are able to at least read and write FAT32 volumes. FAT32 was introduced with the OEM Service Release 2 of Windows 95 to address the need for supporting larger hard drives with Windows 95.

NTFS 5

The NT File System (NTFS) is still going to be the file system of choice. NTFS 5 offers some new features not previously available. The first major improvement is the per-volume, per-disk, per-user disk quota. This is based on the user Security Identifier (SID), and will help administrators better handle volume space management.

Other new features of NTFS 5 include better *transactional tracking* and better support for *sparse files*. Transactional tracking is a method of tracking changes in the system. The better transactional tracking will make recovery from a long period of changes easier. Previous versions of transactional tracking only kept transactional tracking logs until the next server reboot. Support for sparse files will help in managing space on the hard drive better. Sparse files are those that are small, and after a period of time are only taking up a minute amount of space on the volume.

Defragmentation

Another new feature implemented into the file system with NTFS 5 is defragmentation of the hard drive. With Windows NT 4.0, you had to use third-party utilities to defragment a hard drive. Windows 2000 incorporates this support in its core operating system features. Figure 9-1 shows the Management Console where you take care of defragmentation of the hard drives.

The Disk Defragmentation is actually a manual version of Diskeeper. The retail version of Diskeeper will still be available for automated defragmentation of NTFS volumes.

Other File Systems

Windows 2000 has enhanced support for Digital Versatile Disc (DVD). This was not previously supported in Windows NT 4.0. Windows 2000 also supports the Universal Disk Format (UDF). UDF allows for cross-platform data interchange and is based on the ISO 13346 standard.

FIGURE 9-1

Windows 2000 defragmentation

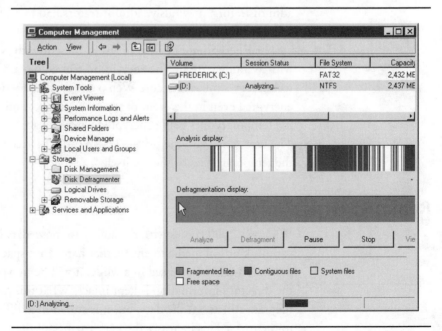

CDFS (ISO 9660)
NTFS (4×5*)
* UDF (ISO 13346)
* DFS
* NTMS
FAT (16×32*)
* EFS (needs NTFS)

UDF is the newer CD file system that will replace the ISO 9660 standard. line? UDF will be used mainly with DVDs. UDF also has a packet writing route that is used in CD-R and CD-RW technology.

Distributed File Services (DFS) is also a feature included in Windows 2000. DFS allows administrators to take multiple servers and incorporate them into one directory. This helps centralize files and data for users so they will no longer have to connect to multiple shares or keep track of server and share names. This feature is available for Windows NT 4.0 with an add-on download. DFS allows you to make it appear that resources reside on a single server. Users don't have to browse multiple servers on the network in order to find what they are looking for. They still need to access those resources via shares. The servers themselves are not placed in a single directory, just the shared resources.

Removable media is becoming more widely used with the increasing need for other forms of storage. Windows 2000 has a file system known as NT Media Services (NTMS). This file system works with various types of removable storage devices such as optical drives, tape libraries, CD-ROM, and robotic loaders. NTMS will help with disaster recovery situations for administrators; previously, administrators had to rely on third-party solutions for disaster recovery.

The Encrypting File System (EFS) present with NTFS is more secure with Windows 2000. The encryption technology uses public-key technology similar to secure Web pages on the Internet. The file remains encrypted even in the event of system or application failure. This is due to the temporary files being encrypted when the application has them in use. The user must have the private key in order to access the files, whether it is the temporary files or the file itself.

Remote Storage Services

Windows 2000 comes with the ability to move data back and forth from various kinds of media to ensure that hard drive space is utilized properly. If data has not been accessed in a while, it will be moved to offline storage, but the directory information is kept intact. What this means for users is that they can still access the data, but it is stored in a different location unknown to the users. This increases the performance of the local disk and ensures the volume does not run out of space or come close to doing so. There are thresholds that are set by the administrator so the operating system knows when it needs to take action.

Remote Storage Services is not a default installation option and must be installed and configured in order to work. Remote Storage has its own utility and is not included in the Computer Management utility. It is a snap-in that is integrated into the Microsoft Management Console.

Clustering

Windows 2000 supports the Microsoft Cluster Server (MSCS). With this functionality, you will be able to use multiple servers for fault tolerance. Cluster Server can also be used for workload management and load balancing. Figure 9-2 shows an example of a 2-node cluster server where server B picks up where server A fails.

You can have two servers running the same SQL database, and if one of them goes down, you can just fire up the other one after you've restored the database from tape to the replacement server.

FIGURE 9-2

Server clustering

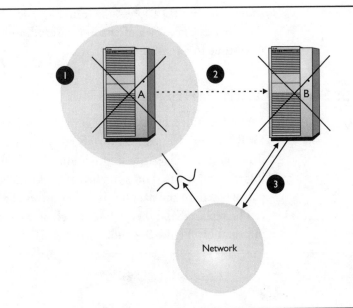

RAID Explanation

Fault tolerance is very important to organizations of any size. To keep from losing data, a network has to have more than just a tape backup. This is where Redundant Array of Inexpensive Disks, or RAID, comes in. Almost all servers today have more than one hard drive. There are different levels of RAID. The three that Windows NT and Windows 2000 support are RAID 0, RAID 1, and RAID 5. Two of these offer fault tolerance, the other does not. In order for RAID 5 and RAID 1 to be available, the drives have to be dynamic. There is one exception to this when you are upgrading from Windows NT 4.0.

RAID 1: Mirroring

Q Do you need to boot from A Disk with Win 2k?

RAID 1 is called *mirroring*. RAID 1 consists of two drives that are identical matches, or mirrors, of each other. If one drive fails, you have another drive to boot up and keep the server going. Of course, with Windows NT you have to create a boot disk to get you to boot from the other drive. Figure 9-3 shows what RAID 1 looks like from a physical perspective. If one drive fails, the other can take over after some basic administration. This keeps server downtime to a minimum.

RAID 5: Striping with Parity

RAID 5 is called Disk Striping with Parity. There must be three hard drives for RAID 5 to be possible. *Striping* is when the data is striped across the drives and there is parity information along with the data. The parity information is based on a mathematical formula that comes up with the parity based on the data on the other drives. This way, if one drive fails, it can be replaced and then rebuilt based on the existing data and the parity information. Figure 9-4 shows what RAID 5 looks like in physical terms.

| FIGURE 9-3 | RAID 1: Mirroring |

 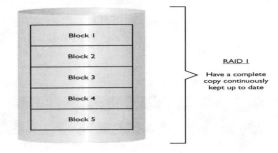

| FIGURE 9-4 | RAID 5: Disk Striping with Parity |

RAID 0: Disk Striping

RAID 0 is also supported by Windows NT and Windows 2000, but offers no fault tolerance. RAID 0 is many disks with the data striped across them. I know it sounds similar to RAID 5, but in this case, there is not a parity drive. Therefore, if one drive fails, the only way to restore the data is to break the Stripe set and restore from tape. Even though this RAID level is not fault tolerant, it does offer performance improvements in terms of speed. About the only time you would use RAID 0 is to increase performance in read and write when you cannot have RAID 1 or RAID 5.

HEADSTART OBJECTIVE 9.03

Difference Between Hardware- and Software-Based RAID

With RAID and fault tolerance comes the decision of whether it will be software-level RAID or hardware-level RAID. In order to have hardware-based RAID, you must install an *array controller.* An array controller is a SCSI controller that has software routines built into the chipset that allows it to mirror, or stripe drives automatically so the operating system does not have to worry about it.

There are two issues to keep in mind when considering if hardware-based RAID or software-based RAID is the right solution. The first is cost, which can be the overall deciding factor. Hardware-based RAID configurations are more expensive than software-based RAID. This is due to the additional hardware that is required that is relatively expensive to acquire. The second piece to this, though, is performance. Performance takes a big hit when you use software-based RAID. The reason for this is that the CPU is handling not only normal processing tasks, but also all the RAID tasks. Sometimes the expense incurred for a bigger processor and more memory can outweigh the cost of an array controller.

for Sw Based RAID

on the job

Downtime is generally more from a cost perspective than hardware-based RAID due to downtime being longer. A client of mine had one of their hard drives crash, and it was using software-level mirroring. Unfortunately, the configuration was not correct on the second drive. When the first drive failed, they could not boot from the second drive, which resulted in three days of downtime. We had to rebuild the server and restore the data from the last good backup. If there had been an array controller managing the mirroring, the server would have only been down from the time the call was made for support to the time that the technician arrived onsite. This would have been all of an hour or two. This was a mistake on the part of the individual who installed and configured the server.

HEADSTART OBJECTIVE 9.04

Using Disk Management

As mentioned earlier in this chapter, the Disk Administrator utility we were all familiar with from Windows NT 4.0 has been updated and replaced by the Computer Management utility. This utility allows for administering many different areas. One of these is the Disk Management function that administrators have to go through. Figure 9-5 shows a screen shot from the Computer Management utility.

To get to the Computer Management Utility, you can either go through the shortcut under Administrative Tools or get there through the Control Panel. To take care of Disk Management, you have to select the Storage item in the left window frame and you will see the contents of the right window frame change. The drives and disks in the server or workstation will appear in the right window frame.

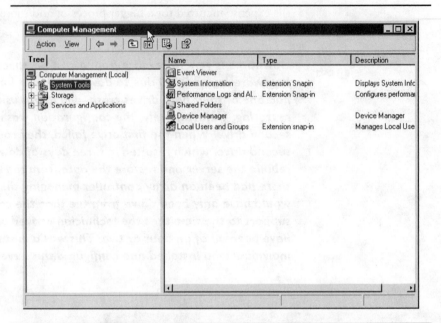

FIGURE 9-5

Computer Management Utility

Basic Disks Versus Dynamic Disks

Windows 2000 has two types of disks that you can have. The first is called Basic. A Basic Disk is what Windows NT 4.0 users are familiar with. There can be various volumes and file system types. The big difference is that you cannot resize volumes on the fly. Windows 2000 now comes with a powerful tool for dynamically configuring the volumes on your server. The key point to remember, though, is that these partitions are not compatible with Windows NT 4.0. Basic Disks are using the previous configuration information that other Windows operating systems use. The newer Dynamic Disks are not accessible by other operating systems if you have a multiboot machine.

The new Dynamic Disk, or Dynamic Volume, with Windows 2000 is a feature that is not backward compatible. On the surface, you would think there is no difference in terms of a Basic Disk versus a Dynamic Disk. The availability of Dynamic Disk management without server downtime is a nice feature for network administrators. Being able to dynamically change the size, span, stripe, or mirror on the fly without creating server downtime adds to the value of the operating system.

There are some pieces that may be confusing to Windows NT 4.0 administrators. With Windows 2000, we have to think in terms of volumes versus partitions. For NetWare administrators, this is probably easy. A volume is managed by the Logical Disk Manager, which is controlled by the Disk Management snap-in of the Microsoft Management Console. A quick way to break the difference down is shown in Table 9-1.

Figure 9-6 shows what the Disk Management section of the Management Console would look like with a Dynamic Disk. Within the Dynamic Disk is the Dynamic Volume information. There is another term to become familiar with in regard to Dynamic Volumes: Simple Volume. A Simple Volume acts as though it IS a physically separate part of the hard disk than other volumes.

Another point about Basic and Dynamic Disks is that you can convert between the two. This is also done within the Management Console. Figure 9-7 shows how to upgrade a Basic Disk to a Dynamic Disk by right-clicking on the drive. We examine this more closely later in this chapter.

TABLE 9-1	Basic Storage	Dynamic Storage
Basic Versus Dynamic Storage	Partition	Volume
	System or Boot Partition	System or Boot Volume
	Active Partition	Active Volume
	Extended Partition	Volume or unallocated space
	Logical Drive	Simple Volume
	Volume, Stripe, Mirror Set	Volume, Stripe, Mirrored Volumes

FIGURE 9-6

Dynamic Disk Properties

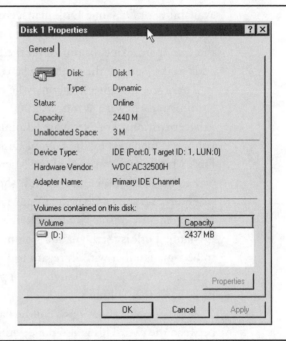

FIGURE 9-7

Upgrading Basic to
Dynamic Disk

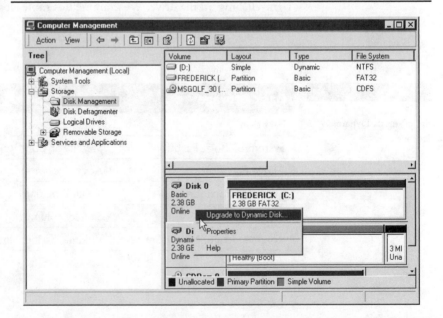

Dynamic Disk Requirements

In order to be able to upgrade or configure a Dynamic Disk, you have to know the requirements to have a Dynamic Disk. There are certain types of drives and media that cannot be upgraded, and there are some that have a certain stipulation in order to configure them successfully. Figure 9-8 shows the management of Dynamic Disks with the Management Console.

First of all, a Dynamic Disk must have 1MB of unallocated space at the end of the drive. This is for administrative information that the disk management routines use. Another key point to remember is that removable storage cannot be configured as a Dynamic Volume. Removable media can only have primary partitions, which would be a Basic Disk configuration. Even though they are primary partitions, they cannot be set to Active to make them bootable. Drives such as Jaz drives cannot be a boot device.

If a disk is part of a stripe set with or without parity, all drives in the set must be Dynamic Disks. If they are not, the configuration change will fail.

FIGURE 9-8

Management Console with Dynamic Volumes

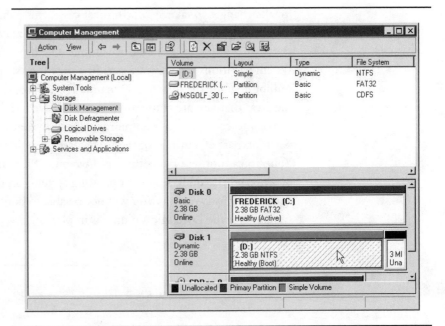

Each drive must have 1MB of space at the end to be changed to Dynamic Volumes. Another factor that can be a hindrance if you are not careful is the sector size of your drive. If the sectors are larger than 512 bytes, the disk must remain a Basic Disk; it cannot be upgraded to a Dynamic Disk. A note here is that IDE are low-level formatted at the factory so changing the sector size will not happen. You can low-level format SCSI disks. If you do, be sure you use a sector size of 512 bytes.

A Dynamic Volume is the same as a primary partition on a Basic Disk. Simple Volumes can only exist on a Dynamic Disk, and cannot contain partitions or logical drives. Simple Volumes can be configured as FAT 16, FAT32, or NTFS. To have multiple file systems, you must have multiple volumes.

Any other operating system besides Windows 2000 cannot access the disk locally. Therefore, if you try to boot to a DOS boot disk, you cannot get to the Simple Volume even if it is configured as a FAT16 file system. This is because the Dynamic Volume is only accessible locally from the Windows 2000 operating system.

There are some exceptions to the no reboot rule. If the volume you are making a change to is the boot or system volume, you will have to reboot for the changes to take affect. In most cases, this volume, once configured, will not require any changes. Hopefully, all the data and applications will reside on a different disk and/or volume. The flip side to the boot and system partitions is if they are part of a mirror or stripe set. If they are, you cannot upgrade the disk to a Dynamic Disk. Also, if any files are in use in the areas that you are converting, you will have to reboot.

Now to confuse you even more, you can make the boot or system partition part of a mirror or stripe set after the volume is set up as Dynamic. You just cannot set up a volume as Dynamic if it is already part of a mirror or stripe set. If you have other operating systems on the drive you are configuring as Dynamic, you will not be able to boot from that operating system after the Dynamic Volume is in place.

QUESTIONS AND ANSWERS

You have removable media you want to upgrade to Dynamic Volumes.	This cannot be done.
You have existing volumes that span various drives.	You can do this as long as you upgrade all disks in the set.
You want to upgrade your boot partition.	You can do this as long as you can reboot the server.
Your boot partition is part of a mirror set.	You cannot upgrade this disk to Dynamic.
You have a drive that has sectors larger than 512K.	This drive cannot be upgraded because of the sector size.

HEADSTART OBJECTIVE 9.05

Creating Dynamic Volumes

To create a Dynamic Volume, you have to have a Dynamic Disk. To upgrade a Basic Disk to a Dynamic Disk, you can select the disk and then right-click to choose Upgrade. This process does not require a reboot unless the disk being upgraded is the system or boot disk.

Once you have a Dynamic Disk, you add a Simple Volume, boot or system volume, or a fault-tolerant volume to the free space. To do this, simply select the free space and right-click to add a volume. Figure 9-9 shows what adding a Simple Volume would be like.

Simple Volumes are shown with a different color in the Disk Management utility. When resizing a volume, you can only extend the volume; shrinking a volume is not possible. When working with Simple Volumes, you can also add a mirror. If you refer back to Figure 9-6, you see the option for adding the mirror.

FIGURE 9-9

Adding a Simple Volume

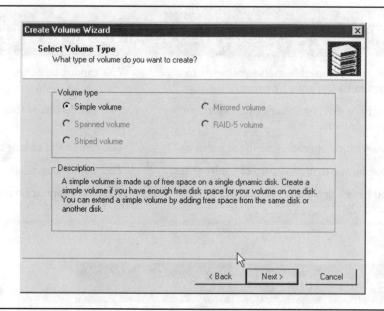

Working with Dynamic Storage

Working with dynamic storage is a process that will be new for many Windows NT 4.0 users. In this exercise, we go through some of the basics of dynamic storage. For this exercise, you will set up a server with two drives with similar amounts of unallocated space.

1. Open the Computer Management utility by selecting Start | Programs | Administrative Tools | Computer Management.

2. If both of your drives are still Basic, upgrade them to Dynamic by right-clicking the Disk 0 or Disk 1 box (see Figure 9-7) and selecting Upgrade to Dynamic.

3. Once both of your drives are Dynamic, you can now set them up as mirrored drives. To do this, select the unallocated space by right-clicking, and select Create Volume.

4. The Create Volume Wizard starts, and you can select Mirrored Volume and follow the remaining prompts.

5. Once the mirrored volumes are created, copy some data to one of them.

6. Now select the Simple Volume by right-clicking, and select Add Mirror. This will mirror your system volume.

7. Once your mirrors are created, you should be able to disconnect the main drive and connect the mirrored drive as the main drive.

8. The server should boot normally. Reconnect the main drive and mirrored drive, and bring the server up again.

9. Once the server is up and running, open the Computer Management utility again, and right-click to select one of the mirrored volumes.

10. There should be an option to Resynchronize Mirror. It may be grayed out if everything is up to date; if not, select the option to resynchronize the mirrors.

11. Follow any prompts on the screen.

This exercise is just an introduction to managing Dynamic Volumes. Be sure to spend some time acquainting yourself with the Computer Management utility and Disk Management snap-in.

HEADSTART OBJECTIVE 9.06

Performing Common Disk Management Tasks

Administering servers means taking care of the hard drives that are on them. This includes checking for errors, defragmenting, and managing volumes. The properties of the disks have changed considerably with Windows 2000. Figure 9-10 shows what this screen looks like.

The General tab allows you to see the used and free space on the drive, along with the drive label. The Disk Cleanup option allows an administrator to compress old files, delete temporary files and other items to ensure disks are performing at their peak. The bottom of the General tab has the Compress option that was previously available in NT, but also has a new option for indexing the disk for faster file searching.

The Tools tab has the same options we are used to seeing in the Windows $9x$ operating systems. This includes a scan disk utility for checking for errors.

FIGURE 9-10

Local Disk Properties

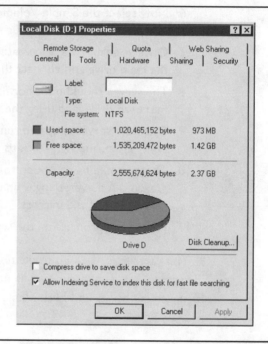

Along with the error checking are the backup and defragmentation options. The Hardware tab allows you to troubleshoot and look at the properties of the various drives, including removable storage. The Sharing tab is pretty much the same as it was, with some new additions. The one change that stands out is the Caching option, which allows for caching of share information for offline access. The Security tab has changed with Windows 2000 and is something to become more familiar with.

There are three tabs in Windows 2000 that didn't exist previously in Windows NT: Remote Storage, Quota, and Web Sharing. The Remote Storage tab allows for configuring the remote storage administration feature available in Windows 2000. The Quota tab allows for the configuration of the Quota management, which allows an administrator to limit the space on the hard drive for users. Web Sharing allows for sharing of folders and files in a Web fashion for access. These three tabs are not available with all file system types. For example, the FAT32 tabs are only General, Tools, Hardware, Sharing, and Web Sharing.

ACCELERATING TO WINDOWS 2000

There are many new features with Windows 2000 that were not previously available with Windows NT and Windows 9x operating systems. The biggest change administrators will see is the integration of features into single tools.

- Included in these tools is the Disk Administration component that is different from the old Disk Administrator.

- The Computer Management tool includes the Disk Management applet that allows administrators to make changes to their drive and volumes. This version of Windows still supports software-level RAID levels 1 and 5, but new to this version is the Dynamic Disk. The Dynamic Disk is a new feature that allows for more online disk management and administration. This has some limitations, however. Certain types of drives and media are not capable of being Dynamic Volumes. There is support for plug-and-play hardware, so adding devices in terms of drives will be easier. The Dynamic Volume allows for online configuration changes in the form of resizing, creating and breaking stripe sets and mirrors,

and renaming and making volumes active or inactive.

- The Logical Disk Manager is what the operating system uses to dynamically manage the disk. There is a partition created at the end of the drive that stores information needed for Dynamic Disk management.

- Windows 2000 supports FAT32.

- Along with support for FAT32 is the support for the Distributed File System (DFS) that allows users to access data easier using a common naming scheme.

- There is also support for the Encrypting File System (EFS), which uses public-key encryption to encrypt local NTFS data.

- Remote Storage Management is another tool now available with Windows 2000. This allows the operating system to automatically move data to other storage devices if it is not used often. Optical disks are popular for this type of storage.

- New to Windows 2000 is the ability to set Disk Quotas so users will not use up all the available disk space. This is done from the properties of the disk or

ACCELERATING TO WINDOWS 2000

volume. This can be accessed by the Disk Management utility or within My Computer. This information is based on Security ID (SID), so each user has a set amount of space available.

■ Also new as a native part of the operating system is the ability to defragment the drives on Windows

2000 machines. Previous versions of Windows NT required third-party utilities. This technology is built into Windows 2000. The one drawback is that it has to be manually launched. For automation, you still have to buy the third-party utility.

CHAPTER SUMMARY

Disk management in Windows 2000 has gone through some serious changes since the days of Windows NT 4.0. Centralizing different facets of administration was one of the goals of Windows 2000 designers. The new Computer Management utility brings different administrative functions together. One of these is disk management. Online and maximum uptime are what the new disk management features bring to Windows 2000.

Windows 2000 supports some file systems that were not supported in previous versions of Windows NT or the Windows 9x operating systems. FAT32 that was central to the Windows 9x operating systems is now compatible with Windows 2000. Windows 2000 has support for DVD as well as UDF. DFS that was introduced late in the NT days is a base part of Windows 2000. Also, there is a file system known as NTMS that has support for various removable media. Encryption is stronger in Windows 2000 than NT, so EFS is more secure. Support for clustering is an integral part of Windows 2000.

Also with this release of Windows is the support for disk quotas, which NT did not have. Disk quotas allow an administrator to determine how much disk space a user may consume. This was unlimited in Windows NT. Another new feature of NTFS 5 is the built-in ability to defragment the hard drive. This required third-party utilities with Windows NT, but there is built-in support with Windows 2000. This is actually a built-in version of Diskeeper, which was previously a third-party utility. The built-in version is manual only, so if automation of defragmentation is what you are looking for, you still need to get the third-party version.

Fault tolerance still exists and hasn't changed much. The same levels of RAID are supported with Windows 2000. RAID levels 0, 1, and 5 are supported as they were in Windows NT. RAID 0, though, is not actually a fault-tolerant RAID level. RAID 1 is Mirroring and requires two or more drives. RAID 5 is Disk Striping with Parity, which requires three or more drives. Fault-tolerant drives are only possible with Dynamic Disks.

Another new feature of Windows 2000 is the Dynamic Disk. Dynamic Disks are changeable on the fly and offer online disk management with minimal downtime. The Basic Disk only offers the normal disk management options that were available with Windows NT. With Basic Disks, you cannot span, stripe, mirror, or change the size without rebooting the server. With Dynamic Disks, you can do these disk management tasks and keep the server up and running. There are some compatibility items to know about Dynamic Disks. They must have 1MB of unallocated space at the end of the drive for configuration information. If the drive is part of a stripe set with or without parity, all disks in the set must be upgraded to Dynamic. If the sectors are larger than 512 bytes, the disk cannot be upgraded to a Dynamic Disk. There are exceptions to changing to a Dynamic Volume and not having to reboot. If the drive is the boot or system drive, the server will need to come down and be rebooted. Also, if files are in use, a reboot will be required. Along with Dynamic Disks are Simple Volumes that you should become familiar with. The Simple Volume is what you can do the Dynamic Disk configuration functions with. The Simple Volume is a nonfault-tolerant volume, whereas a striped volume or mirrored volume can be fault tolerant.

Remote Storage Services allows for moving data from the hard drives to offline storage, yet keeping the original directory information intact. This means users see no difference in regard to where their data is stored. This can be stored on optical disk or other storage formats. This is managed by a snap-in to the Microsoft Management Console.

TWO-MINUTE DRILL

❑ Online disk management allows changes to be made without requiring a server reboot.

❑ With Windows 2000, you are able to at least read and write FAT32 volumes.

❑ Transactional tracking is a method of tracking changes in the system. The better transactional tracking will make recovery from a long period of changes easier.

❑ Windows 2000 has enhanced support for Digital Versatile Disc (DVD). This was not previously supported in Windows NT 4.0.

❑ Windows 2000 comes with the ability to move data back and forth from various kinds of media to ensure that hard drive space is utilized properly.

❑ Remote Storage has its own utility and is not included in the Computer Management utility.

❑ Windows 2000 supports the Microsoft Cluster Server (MSCS). With this functionality, you will be able to use multiple servers for fault tolerance.

❑ The three levels of RAID that Windows NT and Windows 2000 support are RAID 0, RAID 1, and RAID 5.

❑ RAID 1 is called *mirroring*. RAID 1 consists of two drives that are identical matches, or mirrors, of each other.

❑ RAID 5 is called Drive Striping with Parity. There must be three hard drives for RAID 5 to be possible.

❑ RAID 0 is also supported by Windows NT and Windows 2000, but offers no fault tolerance. RAID 0 is many disks with the data striped across them.

❑ In order to have hardware-based RAID, you must install an *array controller*. An array controller is a SCSI controller that has software routines built into the chipset that allows it to mirror, or stripe drives automatically so the operating system does not have to worry about it.

❑ The Disk Administrator utility from Windows NT 4.0 has been updated and replaced by the Computer Management utility.

❑ The new Dynamic Disk, or Dynamic Volume, with Windows 2000 is a feature that is not backward compatible.

❑ A Dynamic Disk must have 1MB of unallocated space at the end of the drive. This is for administrative information that the disk management routines use.

❑ To create a Dynamic Volume, you have to have a Dynamic Disk. To upgrade a Basic Disk to a Dynamic Disk, you can select the disk and then right-click to choose Upgrade.

❑ There are three tabs in Windows 2000 that didn't exist previously in Windows NT: Remote Storage, Quota, and Web Sharing.

SELF TEST

The following questions will help you measure your understanding of the material presented in this chapter. Read all of the choices carefully, as there may be more than one correct answer. Choose all correct answers for each question.

1. Which of the following is NOT a new feature of disk management with Windows 2000?

   A. Dynamic Volumes

   B. Disk Administration Utility

   C. Less Downtime

   D. Remote Disk Management

2. Which of the following file system types are supported with Windows 2000? (Choose all that apply.)

   A. FAT

   B. NTFS

   C. HPFS

   D. FAT32

3. Which of the following is a new benefit of NTFS 5?

   A. Per-disk, per-user disk quota

   B. Permissions assignments on folders

   C. Unreadable by a FAT boot disk

   D. Transactional tracking

4. In order to configure automated defragmentation with Windows 2000, what do you have to do?

   A. Use the Computer Management Utility.

   B. It is not possible at all, even with a third-party utility.

   C. A third-party utility must be acquired.

   D. None of the above.

5. What service, introduced with Windows NT 4.0, allows an administrator to take shares from diverse locations and incorporate them into one directory?

   A. UDF

   B. DFS

   C. MSCS

   D. EFS

6. Which RAID level has a parity block for fault tolerance and requires at least three drives to function?

   A. RAID 0

   B. RAID 1

   C. RAID 2

   D. RAID 5

7. What two ways can you open the Computer Management utility? (Choose two.)

   A. Through the Control Panel.

   B. It starts automatically.

   C. Shortcut on desktop.

   D. Shortcut under Administrative Tools.

8. What is the new type of disk in Windows 2000 that is not backward compatible?

   A. Basic Disk.

   B. RAID Configuration.

   C. Dynamic Disk.

   D. All formats are backward compatible.

9. What steps need to be taken to upgrade a Basic Disk to a Dynamic Disk?

   A. Right-click on any volume on the disk and choose Upgrade to Dynamic.

   B. Right-click on the disk and choose Upgrade to Dynamic Disk.

   C. Right click on the Storage folder and choose Dynamic Upgrade from the Tools pull-down menu.

   D. This is not possible. Dynamic Disks must be made dynamic at installation.

10. You try to upgrade to a Dynamic Disk and receive an error. The drive you are trying to upgrade is a 4.3GB hard disk and has a 4.3GB partition on it that is almost full. Why can't you upgrade this disk to a Dynamic Disk?

    A. 4.3GB drives cannot be upgraded to Dynamic Disks.

    B. There needs to be 1MB of unallocated space at the end of the drive.

    C. The drive needs to have 1MB available at the beginning of the drive.

    D. You cannot upgrade Basic Disks to Dynamic Disks.

11. You are trying to upgrade a Basic Disk to a Dynamic Disk and have the following information on the disk: 9.1GB, 16MB unallocated at end of drive, sector size is 1024KB. Why can't you upgrade this disk?

    A. 9.1GB drives cannot be dynamic.

    B. There is not enough space at the end of the drive.

    C. The sector size is wrong.

    D. You should be able to upgrade this drive.

12. How do you access the Quota configuration for a drive?

    A. Use the Control Panel.

    B. Right-click on the drive and choose Properties, and then the Quota tab.

    C. Right-click on a drive and choose Quota.

    D. Through the Disk Administrator utility.

13. Which RAID level has two drives that are identical copies of each other?

    A. RAID 0

    B. RAID 1

    C. RAID 2

    D. RAID 5

14. What services allow for fault tolerance by having two servers share the same storage, so if one fails, the other can pick up and keep the network running?

    A. MCS

    B. MSCS

    C. EFS

    D. NTFS

15. What type of disk has partitions and not volumes, is not resizable without server reboot, and does not allow configuration of mirrors or stripe sets without server reboot?

    A. Dynamic.

    B. Simple.

    C. Basic.

    D. With Windows 2000, all disk types are configurable without server reboot.

10

Implementing Disaster Protection

HEADSTART OBJECTIVES

The word "disaster" can mean many things, depending upon the context. In computer networking terms, a disaster is defined as a catastrophic event that results in loss of the system's capability to function. Some examples are loss or corruption of critical system files, destruction of the hard drive's master boot record or boot sector, hardware failure of the hard disk(s) on which the operating system's files are stored, or even a fire or flood that physically damages the computer so it is unable to boot up and load the operating system.

Disaster protection consists of two parts:

- Planning and implementation of measures to prevent catastrophic events
- Planning for a fast and efficient recovery process if a disaster does occur

In this chapter, we look at both preventative measures and the steps we can take to minimize the damage done if those preventative measures fail.

HEADSTART OBJECTIVE 10.01

Importance of Disaster Protection

Ask yourself this: How important is it that you are able to log on to your system and access resources? The roles the computer and the network play in your company's daily activities and functionality determine how important it is for you to develop a disaster protection plan. Loss of access to important data may cripple your operation completely, or it may be a mere inconvenience that forces you to spend precious time duplicating previous efforts or taking the long way around to accomplish necessary tasks.

A good disaster protection plan considers cost/benefit ratios, and focuses on the most cost-effective prevention and recovery methods. Windows 2000 Server was designed with *fault tolerance* in mind. Fault tolerance is defined as the computer's (or the operating system's) capability to recover from a catastrophic event without a loss of data.

Windows 2000 incorporates several mechanisms for surviving disastrous events with critical data intact, including support for software implementation of RAID (Redundant Array of Independent Disks), advanced startup options, and the Recovery Console. All these fault tolerance features do not, however, negate the need for a well-planned backup program. In this chapter, we look at Windows 2000's backup utility, and discuss some basic guidelines for developing a backup strategy that will serve as an "insurance policy" if other recovery options fail.

heads
UP

Only Windows 2000 Server supports Disk fault tolerance; Windows 2000 Professional does not allow for the creation of fault-tolerant volumes.

Implemented software only — Hw will work.

HEADSTART OBJECTIVE 10.02

Disaster Protection Features in Windows 2000

Disastrous events most common in today's computer networking environments include:

- Hard disk failure due to defect or physical damage
- Damage to operating system or Registry files due to configuration changes
- Complete loss of data and/or operating system and program files, which necessitates reinstallation and restoration from backup tapes or other media

Microsoft includes features in Windows 2000 that make it easier to prevent or recover from these and other disasters and protect the integrity of your data.

Protection from Hard Disk Failure

A major feature included in Windows NT 4.0, which is carried over to Windows 2000, is the ability to create fault-tolerant volumes. This is also known as software RAID, and it provides for redundancy in writing data to disk. In fact, Windows 2000 allows you to retain fault-tolerant volumes created in Windows NT when you upgrade the operating system, although you are not able to take advantage of all the features of Windows 2000 fault tolerance.

In Windows 2000 Server, fault-tolerant volumes are created on dynamic disks. Dynamic storage is a new feature in Windows 2000 that overcomes some of the limitations of basic storage (the industry standard supported by previous Windows operating systems).

In the section entitled "Using Fault-Tolerant Volumes," we discuss how dynamic disk features work, and demonstrate the procedure used to create RAID volumes with Windows 2000's disk management utility.

Protection from Configuration Errors

Administrators who have worked with Windows operating systems will recognize the "familiar faces" of the Advanced Startup Options. A Safe Mode option, previously a part of the Windows 95/98 boot process, is now included with Windows 2000, along with the VGA Mode and Last Known Good configuration that Windows NT users had available.

Windows 2000 Server also offers the Directory Services Restoration Mode and the Debugging Mode. These startup options, in many cases, let you load the operating system when there are problems with the normal boot process.

Another new and powerful feature included in Windows 2000 is the Recovery Console, a tool that allows administrators to reconfigure or repair a system from the command line, when unable to boot the operating system.

We look at each of these options in detail in the sections entitled "Examining Advanced Startup Options" and "Examining the Recovery Console."

The Windows Backup Utility

Finally, Windows 2000 provides a new and improved version of Windows Backup, a built-in utility that can be used to back up and restore data quickly and efficiently. The Windows NT backup utility supported backing up to SCSI tape devices only. Windows 2000's backup program lets you back up to files, which can be stored on hard disks, writable CDs, or removable media such as those components made by Iomega and Syquest.

In "Using the Backup Utility," we look at how you can use Windows Backup to back up and restore data, including backup and restoration of the Active Directory.

Emergency Repair Process

In this chapter's final section, we take a look at how to create and use the Emergency Repair Disk (ERD) to fix problems with the Registry, boot sector, startup environment, or system files that might prevent Windows 2000 from starting.

Implementing a Comprehensive Disaster Protection Plan

All of the Windows 2000 disaster protection features work together as part of your disaster prevention and recovery plan, along with other preventive/protective measures such as use of a UPS (Uninterruptible Power Supply) to guard against data loss due to electrical surges or outages, and a security plan to prevent malicious destruction of data by outside forces, or accidental data loss due to user error or experimentation.

Table 10-1 summarizes the disaster protection features discussed in this chapter, along with the specific function of each.

TABLE 10-1   Windows 2000 Disaster Protection Features at a Glance

Feature	Function
Disk Fault Tolerance	Recovery from failure of a hard drive that is part of a RAID set.
Advanced Startup Options	Provides ability to load the operating system when files used in the normal boot process have been damaged or corrupted.
Recovery Console	Perform administrative tasks from a command-line utility that can be started from the Windows 2000 setup floppies or installed on your computer.
Windows Backup	Provide for manual or scheduled backup to tape or file, and quick-and-easy restoration of backup sets, files, and folders.
Emergency Repair Process	Repair problems with the Registry, startup environment, system files, and boot sector that prevent the computer from starting.

on the
ĵob

In today's fast-paced business environment, we often have more good intentions than we have time. Many network administrators know that they need a better, more comprehensive disaster prevention and recovery plan, but have so many other pressing duties that they put it off as something to be addressed later, "when things slow down."

Unfortunately, disaster has a way of striking during the busiest times, not when it's most convenient for us. Humans tend to be reactive creatures, so we wait for something to happen and then look for ways to deal with it. It's important to counteract that tendency by forcing yourself to be proactive, making the development of your plan a top priority.

When it comes to computer networking, experienced administrators know the question is not whether the server will crash, but when it will crash. Despite the increasing stability of computer operating systems, it's inevitable that you will eventually find yourself with a system that won't boot, a hard drive that can't be read, an entire network destroyed by fire, tornado, earthquake, or other act of nature, or some other situation that causes a loss of your computer's functionality and/or data. If you are prepared, this may mean some extra work, some loss of productivity, and perhaps a cut into your company's profit margin. If you aren't prepared, it could truly mean disaster.

Creating a Windows 2000 Boot Floppy

Before we examine each of the more sophisticated disaster prevention and recovery features built into Windows 2000, we need to take steps to ensure that we will be able to start the computer and boot into the operating system to make repairs. Therefore, the first step in our disaster preparedness plan should be to create a Windows 2000 boot floppy that can be used to load the operating system in the event of corrupt or missing system files that prevent Windows 2000 from starting.

Making a boot floppy is easy and takes only a few minutes, and can save you much time and trouble if and when a disaster does occur.

1. Format a floppy on a computer running Windows 2000. (This is important: Do not use a floppy formatted under another operating system. Information is written to the boot sector of the floppy disk, which causes it to look for the loader file when you boot from the floppy.)

2. Copy the following files from the Windows 2000 computer's system partition (usually the C: drive):

   ■ Ntldr

   ■ ntdetect.com

   ■ boot.ini

   ■ ntbootdd.sys (only if using a SCSI controller with no SCSI BIOS or BIOS disabled)

   If you don't see these files in Windows Explorer, you may need to change your View options to display hidden and system files. To do this, select the Tools menu in Explorer, choose Folder Options, select the View tab, and uncheck the "Hide protected operating system files" check box (see Figure 10-1).

| FIGURE 10-1 | Using Tools | Folder Options | View to make Windows Explorer display hidden system files |

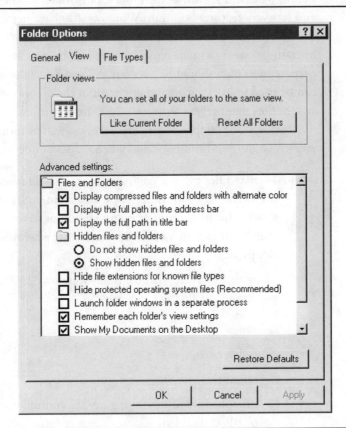

Using Fault-Tolerant Volumes

Earlier, we defined *fault tolerance* as the ability of the computer to recover from a catastrophe, such as a disk failure, without losing critical data. A key concept in the construction of a fault-tolerant system is *redundancy*. Your dictionary may define the word as "unnecessary repetition," but in the world of electronics, "redundancy" means duplication or repetition of elements in equipment to provide alternative functional channels in case of failure.

A fault-tolerant system will have more than one of as many critical components as possible. This could include backup power supplies, multiple disk controllers, and disks on which data is duplicated via mirroring, striping with parity, or other fail-safe mechanisms. Extending this redundancy concept to its limits, we can duplicate entire servers, a practice known as *clustering* and implemented in Microsoft's Cluster Server software or similar third-party solutions.

Clustering is beyond the scope of this chapter, but in this section, we examine ways in which we can use the concept of redundancy to protect our servers in case of failure of a hard disk that holds important data.

Fault-Tolerant Disk Arrays (RAID)

RAID (Redundant Array of Independent—or Inexpensive, depending on the source—Disks) is a disk structuring method recognized throughout the industry as a means of providing fault tolerance at the disk level. RAID implementations are both hardware- and software-based. Hardware RAID requires that the hardware manufacturer incorporate an interface that controls creation and regeneration of redundant data. Hardware solutions have several advantages; for example, most vendors support "hot swapping," or the replacement of a hard disk without shutting down the system. Hardware solutions may also offer faster disk performance. However, hardware RAID is significantly more expensive than software solutions.

With Windows 2000's software implementation of RAID, no extra equipment expense is required, and it's easy to set up and use. Support for fault-tolerant volumes is built into Windows 2000's new Disk Management system, and administered through the Computer Management Console.

Supported RAID Levels

RAID options are categorized into levels 1 through 10, depending on implementation factors, performance, cost, and reliability. The following questions and answers summarize the levels of software RAID supported by Windows 2000 Server. (Remember that Windows 2000 Professional does not support disk fault tolerance, although it does support RAID Level 0.)

QUESTIONS AND ANSWERS

What is RAID Level 0 (disk striping with no parity)? How does it work?	Data is divided into 64KB blocks and written in stripes across two or more disks in an array. Note: RAID Level 0 is used for performance enhancement and is *not* fault tolerant.
What is RAID Level 1 (disk mirroring and duplexing)? How does it work?	Mirroring creates an exact duplicate of a partition on a second disk. Duplexing does the same, but the second disk uses a separate disk controller. RAID Level 1 provides fault tolerance in case of disk failure.
What is RAID Level 5 (disk striping with parity)? How does it work?	Data is written in blocks across three or more disks, with a parity block added for each stripe, which can be used to reconstruct data in case of failure of one disk.

Other RAID levels, such as Level 2 (disk striping with error correction code, or ECC), Level 3 (ECC stored as parity), and Level 4 (disk striping with large blocks) are not supported by Windows 2000.

Let's take a closer look at RAID Levels 0, 1, and 5.

[handwritten: Mirroring: same controller. Duplexing - separate controllers.]

RAID 0: Disk Striping (No Parity) *[handwritten: Not Fault Tolerant.]*

RAID Level 0 can be used to turn several small partitions on different disks into one large logical partition for more efficient storage. When multiple SCSI controllers are used, it also speeds performance, since data can be written to and read from more than one disk simultaneously.

It is important to note that RAID Level 0 does not offer any fault tolerance whatsoever. It is mentioned here because its inclusion as a RAID level may lead administrators to believe it can be used for disaster protection. In fact, a RAID Level 0 array is actually less fault tolerant than individual volumes, because when partitions are combined in a stripe set with no parity information, if one partition fails, you lose the entire set.

RAID 1: Disk Mirroring and Duplexing

Disk mirroring and duplexing are simple and effective ways to protect a disk through redundancy of data. These methods simply create an exact copy, or mirror, of one disk on another disk. Windows 2000 Server uses ftdisk.sys (a fault tolerance driver) to write the data to both physical disks at the same time.

MIRRORING   If the two disks are on the same controller, they are called a *mirror set* (on basic disks) or a *mirrored volume* (on dynamic disks). If one fails, the remaining disk will still have all the data intact and the system will continue to operate; the bad disk can be replaced and a new mirror set created.

Disk mirroring, like other disk fault-tolerance methods, can only be created on dynamic disks in Windows 2000, but if you upgrade from NT 4.0, mirror sets created there are retained on basic disks. A mirror set can contain any partition desired, including the boot partition (where the operating system files are stored) and/or the system partition (where boot.ini, ntldr, ntdetect.com, and other boot files are stored). This is worth noting because stripe sets cannot contain the boot or system partition.

The biggest disadvantage of disk mirroring is the cost. It requires double the amount of storage space for a given amount of data, so it requires more hard disk space than striping.

DUPLEXING   When the data is written to two disks that are on different controllers, we call it *disk duplexing*. This works identically to disk mirroring as far as the software is concerned, but provides an extra layer of protection at the hardware level in case of controller failure. Cost, of course, is even higher than with disk mirroring, since a second controller must be purchased.

See Figure 10-2 for an illustration of both disk mirroring and disk duplexing.

FIGURE 10-2

Disk mirroring creates an exact copy of the selected partition on a second physical hard disk. Duplexing does the same, except that the second disk is attached to a second disk controller

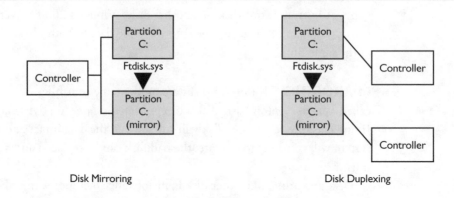

Disk Mirroring   Disk Duplexing

RAID 5: Disk Striping with Parity

Disk striping with parity is known as RAID Level 5, and is a fault-tolerance implementation that uses disk space more efficiently than mirroring/ duplexing. As in RAID Level 0, data is written across the entire array of disks in stripes. The important difference is that in addition to the data itself, each stripe includes parity information, which provides the means to recover data in case of a disk failure.

Parity may sound mysterious, but it's really just a mathematical formula used to check the integrity of data by comparing the number of odd or even bits in a series of numbers. If one hard disk in a striped array fails, the operating system can use the remaining data along with the parity information to reconstruct the missing data on the bad disk. (Unfortunately, this won't work if you have multiple simultaneous disk failures; then your only option is to restore from backup.)

Because of the parity stripe, RAID 5 requires a minimum of 3 physical disks (RAID 0 only requires 2), and Windows 2000 supports a maximum of 32 disks in a RAID 5 array. Like the other disk fault-tolerance methods, a striped volume with parity can only be created in Windows 2000 on disks that use dynamic storage.

Do RAID 5 vols upgraded from NT remain?

Unlike a mirrored volume, a RAID 5 volume does not double the amount of hard disk space required. The space needed for the parity information is equal to the space on one volume (this can be expressed as follows: space used for parity information equals 1/n of total disk space in the array, where n equals the number of partitions in the stripe set). You can see, then, that as you add more disks to the set, the percentage of total disk space used up by the parity information decreases.

With mirroring, 50 percent of the total disk space is always used for the redundant data. With a RAID 5 implementation using 10 disks of 2GB each, your total amount of disk space is 20GB, and the space used for the parity information is only 2GB, or 10 percent. This leaves 90 percent of the total space free for the storage of data.

It's obvious that a major advantage of disk striping with parity is cost; you don't have to purchase nearly as much hard disk space to get the same amount of data storage. Striping with parity does have a few disadvantages when compared to RAID 1, however. First, performance during write operations is slower, because of the calculations involved in formulating the parity information. This is balanced, though, by the fact that RAID 5 with multiple controllers will show faster performance on read operations.

For low-cost, easily implemented fault-tolerant storage of data files, striping with parity is a viable solution. Figure 10-3 illustrates how data and parity information are written across an array of disks when you create a RAID 5 volume in Windows 2000.

| FIGURE 10-3 | In a RAID 5 volume, data and parity information are "striped" across the disks in rows, arranged so that the data and its parity information are always on different disks |

Creating Fault-Tolerant Volumes in Windows 2000

Fault-tolerant volumes are created using the Disk Management tool in the Computer Management Console. Before you can create a RAID 1 or RAID 5 volume, however, you must upgrade your basic storage disks to dynamic storage if you haven't already done so.

To upgrade a disk to dynamic storage, expand the Storage object in the Computer Management tree, and click Disk Management. (You can access the Computer Management Console by right-clicking the My Computer icon and choosing Manage). A graphical view of your disks will be displayed as shown in Figure 10-4 (it may take a few moments for disk configuration information to be loaded, so be patient).

FIGURE 10-4

The first step in creating fault-tolerant volumes in Windows 2000 using the Disk Management tool to upgrade those disks that will be part of the set to dynamic storage

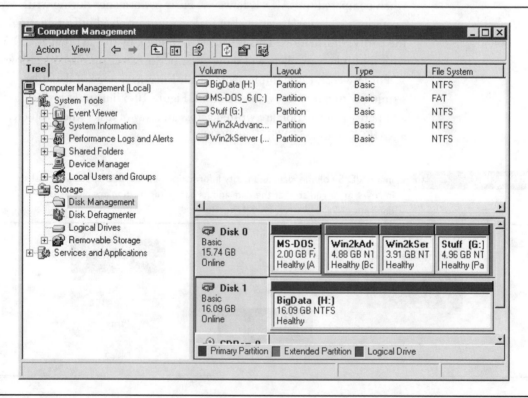

1. Right-click the disk you wish to upgrade (be sure you are clicking on the disk, not on a partition).

2. Choose Upgrade to dynamic disk.

After you have converted your disks from basic to dynamic, right-click on the unallocated space on a dynamic disk and choose Create Volume to invoke the Create Volume Wizard (see Figure 10-4). The Wizard will walk you through the steps of creating a fault-tolerant volume:

■ Selecting the disks that will be included in the fault tolerant volume (exactly 2 disks for a mirror set, or 3 to 32 for a stripe set with parity)

■ Setting the size of the volume by specifying the amount of space on each disk that will be used in the set

■ Assigning a drive letter to the fault-tolerant volume

■ Formatting the new fault-tolerant volume

heads
⊕p

Remember that fault-tolerant volumes can be created only on Windows 2000 Server (Windows 2000 Professional does not support disk fault tolerance), and only on disks that have been upgraded to dynamic storage. Windows 2000 disks are configured for basic storage by default, and must be upgraded using the Disk Management utility in the Computer Management Console.

EXERCISE 10-1

Implementing Fault-Tolerant Volumes

Make sure you are working with disks that have been converted to dynamic storage, on a Windows 2000 Server computer. Log on with administrative privileges.

1. Right-click the My Computer icon and choose Manage.

2. Expand the Storage icon, and select Disk Management.

3. In the graphical representation of a dynamic disk, right-click on an area of the disk that has unallocated space. Select Create Volume.

4. The Create Volume Wizard appears. Click Next.

5. The Select Volume Type page appears. Select the two disks that will be part of a RAID Level 1 mirror set.

6. Specify the amount of disk space to use on each disk.

7. Choose a drive letter to assign to the new mirror set.

8. Set formatting options for the volume.

Disaster Recovery when a Member of a Mirrored Volume Fails

The purpose of mirroring is to create an exact duplicate of the mirrored volume. The data is written to each disk at the same time, so if one member of the set fails at any given time, the same data is intact on the other member.

Recovery after the failure of a member of a mirrored volume is relatively simple. Exact procedure depends on whether it is the mirrored disk (first member of the set) or the mirroring disk (second member) that goes bad. If the second disk fails, only a few simple steps are required:

1. Take the failed disk out of the computer.

2. Remove the disk from the RAID 1 volume in the Disk Management Console in Computer Manager by right-clicking the graphic representation of the functional disk under Failed Redundancy. Then select Remove Mirror.

3. Add the new physical disk.

4. Add the new disk to the RAID 1 volume in the Disk Management Console to recreate the mirror set.

If the first disk of the set fails, and your boot partition is on it, recovery is a bit more complicated. You will need to use a boot floppy to be able to boot the computer. Be sure you have previously made an NT boot disk as part of your disaster recovery plan.

You may also need to edit your boot.ini file and change the ARC (Advanced RISC Computing) path to point to the second (still functional) partition. Figure 10-5 shows a typical boot.ini file on a multiboot system.

Remember that the boot.ini file is a read-only file; you will need to change this attribute before you can edit it. To do so, find the file on your system partition (usually the C: partition) in Windows Explorer and right-click on it. Deselect the Read-only check box. Now you can make changes in any text editor, such as Notepad.

[handwritten margin note:]
Mirrored Disk = FIRST DISK IN SET

Mirroring Disk = SECOND DISK IN SET

**heads
ⓤp**

Remember that in Microsoft's terminology, the system partition is where the boot files (ntldr, ntdetect.com, and boot.ini) are stored, and the boot partition is the one on which the operating system files (typically the winnt directory) are located.

Note that boot.ini is a system file. It may not show up in Explorer if you have View options set to Hide system files. See the previous section, "Creating a Windows 2000 Boot Floppy" for instructions on viewing hidden system files.

Editing boot.ini to Change the ARC Path

Ntldr uses the boot.ini file during the boot process to locate the operating system files (the system root directory, usually named "winnt"). You should be familiar with the syntax used to designate the path to the boot partition, called the ARC path.

Example: multi(0) disk(0) rdisk(1) partition(2)

"Multi" indicates the controller type; in this case, any controller except a SCSI disk controller with the SCSI BIOS disabled. For the latter, the ARC path begins with "SCSI" instead of "Multi" as shown in Figure 10-5.

The number following "Multi" or "SCSI" indicates the controller number (determined by the order in which the adapters load and initialize). Numbering begins with 0, so in this case we are pointing to the first controller.

FIGURE 10-5

A typical boot.ini file showing the ARC paths to the operating systems installed on the computer

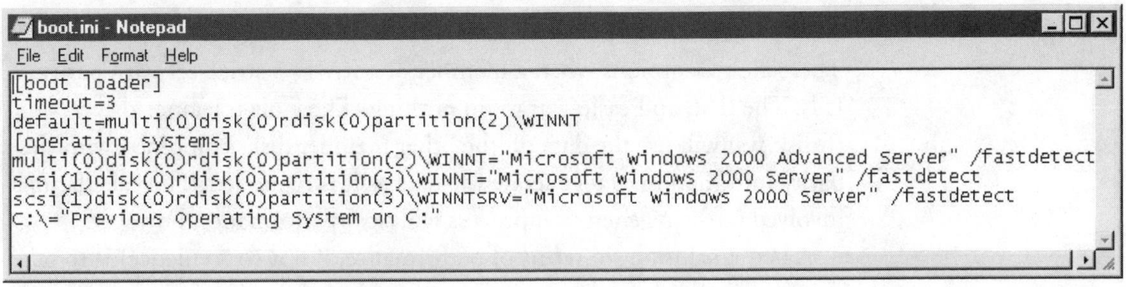

```
boot.ini - Notepad                                                    _ □ ✕
File  Edit  Format  Help
[[boot loader]
timeout=3
default=multi(0)disk(0)rdisk(0)partition(2)\WINNT
[operating systems]
multi(0)disk(0)rdisk(0)partition(2)\WINNT="Microsoft Windows 2000 Advanced Server" /fastdetect
scsi(1)disk(0)rdisk(0)partition(3)\WINNT="Microsoft Windows 2000 Server" /fastdetect
scsi(1)disk(0)rdisk(0)partition(3)\WINNTSRV="Microsoft Windows 2000 Server" /fastdetect
C:\="Previous Operating System on C:"
```

The number following "Disk" indicates the SCSI identification number. If the path starts with "Multi," this number will always be 0.

The number following "Rdisk" indicates the disk number when the path begins with "Multi." Again, numbering begins with 0, so in this case we are pointing to the second disk. If the path begins with "SCSI," this number will always be 0.

Finally, the number following "Partition" indicates the partition number on the previously indicated disk. Unlike the other parameters, the numbering begins with 1, so our example points to the second partition on the disk.

h e a d s
⚊ p

The Microsoft exams presume a thorough knowledge of ARC path syntax, so it is important to understand what each section of the path means and how it is numbered. Given a scenario describing the location of the boot partition, you should be able to properly construct the ARC path that would be used to point to that partition in the boot.ini file.

After you finish making the appropriate changes to the boot.ini file, don't forget to change it back to Read-Only to prevent further inadvertent changes, which could render the operating system unloadable.

o n t h e
⚊ o b

If one member of your mirror set stops functioning, you will still be able to use the system—until you shut down and restart. That's when you may find that your operating system files are now "lost" and you must edit boot.ini.

Disaster Recovery when a Member of a RAID 5 Striped Volume Fails

What tosh!

There are two options when a member of a RAID 5 stripe set with parity fails. The first, and easiest, is to do nothing. The fault-tolerance driver (ftdisk.sys) will use the data on the other member disks combined with the parity information to regenerate the data as it is requested. The calculations involved in the regeneration process will slow performance, however.

A better solution (in terms of performance, if not convenience) is to take out the failed disk, replace it with a new one, and then perform a repair operation on the RAID 5 stripe set. In this case, the information on the remaining members will be used to recreate the failed member of the set.

Repairing a RAID 5 set is a relatively simple procedure:

1. Right-click My Computer, and choose Manage. Click Disk Management.

2. Under Failed Redundancy, right-click the graphic representation of a volume in the stripe set with parity. Choose Repair Volume.

3. A dialog box will open that offers a list of hard disks available to be used to replace the failed member. Choose a disk, and click OK.

4. The data and parity information from the failed disk will be recreated and written to the new member. Performance will return to normal.

Unfortunately, regardless of how many disks are in the array, regeneration will only work with a single disk failure. If multiple disks fail, your only recovery option is to restore the data from backup.

HEADSTART OBJECTIVE 10.04

Examining Advanced Startup Options

Windows 2000 provides you with several options at startup that are designed to help troubleshoot and/or recover from boot problems. Choices include VGA Mode, Safe Mode, Directory Services Restore Mode, Debugging Mode, and Last Known Good Configuration. Let's look at each of these advanced startup options, and discuss when to use each.

VGA Mode

This option is familiar to Windows NT 4.0 users. Selecting the boot menu item designated as VGA Mode will load Windows 2000 with only a basic generic VGA video driver. This option can be a lifesaver if you make changes to your display settings that render the video unusable upon rebooting. A common example is setting too high a refresh rate; if your hardware doesn't support it, when you boot back into Windows, you won't be able to see anything on the screen, which makes it difficult or impossible to change the settings back.

You can, however, select the VGA Mode choice when presented with the operating system menu, boot into Windows in (admittedly not pretty, but functional) 640 x 480 16 colors with a generic driver, and correct the display settings.

Safe Mode

Although it may be new to NT users, the Safe Mode option is familiar to those who have worked with Windows 95/98. Pressing F8 during the display of the operating system menu brings up a screen with more boot option choices. Choosing Safe Mode from this second menu attempts to load Windows 2000 using only basic drivers. If Windows is not starting because of a bad driver or configuration, Safe Mode may allow you to boot the operating system and make changes to the appropriate settings.

Safe Mode with Networking is the same, except that in addition to the drivers for keyboard, mouse, VGA, hard drive controller and system services, the operating system networking components and NIC adapter driver are also loaded. This is useful if the files necessary to make repairs are located on a network drive.

Safe Mode with Command Prompt also loads the basic drivers, but displays the command line instead of the GUI interface.

Directory Services Restore Mode — *Server only*

This option is brand new to Windows 2000, and is available only in the Server version of the operating system. The purpose of the Directory Services Restore Mode is to allow restoration of the Active Directory on domain controllers.

The specifics of backing up and restoring the Active Directory are addressed later in this chapter, in the "Using the Backup Utility" section.

Debugging Mode *— Server Only*

Debugging Mode is another option that is only available for Windows 2000 Server, not Professional. You can select this option to enable debugging.

Last Known Good Configuration

An old friend from Windows NT 4.0, the Last Known Good Configuration option is still alive and well in Windows 2000. Many network administrators have recovered an ostensibly unbootable operating system by using this "secret trick." Last Known Good is used when the loading of a driver changes the Registry configuration, and the system doesn't like the change. The Last Known Good option allows you to revert to a previous configuration that did work.

Here's how it works: During the boot process, the operating system kernel copies the Current Control Set data in the Registry to a control set called the Clone Control Set. (A control set is just a collection of configuration information used to control the system). When a user is able to successfully log on, the data in the Clone Control Set is assumed to be good, and the system copies it to the Last Known Good Control Set.

This is the configuration data that is used when you invoke the Last Known Good configuration at startup. Configuration changes you made during the last session will be bypassed, and you will be logged on using the previous control set. Be aware that changes you made will be overwritten and the Last Known Good configuration will become the Current configuration.

heads
①p

In some cases the system will automatically revert to the Last Known Good control set without your intervention, such as when a critical device driver has been disabled.

Last Known Good is an important recovery tool, but remember that if you do successfully log on after making configuration changes, the Last Known Good configuration will be updated and you will no longer be able to boot to the previous Last Known Good. If you make changes that you believe may cause startup problems, be sure to invoke Last Known Good *before* logging on.

Boot Logging

Using the advanced startup options (except the Last Known Good configuration) automatically causes a log file to be written to the systemroot folder. The log file is a text file named ntbtlog.txt. You can also manually enable boot logging by selecting the Enable Boot Logging option in the advanced startup options menu.

Using the Advanced Startup Options

Microsoft has provided several advanced startup selections in the Windows 2000 boot process that can often be used to boot into an operating system that has been damaged to the point of being unbootable. Determining which is appropriate depends on the cause (or suspected cause) of the startup problem. The advanced startup options and their uses are summarized in Table 10-2.

TABLE 10-2   The Advanced Startup Options Available in Windows 2000

Startup Option	Description
VGA Mode (Available in both Server and Professional)	Used to boot into a system when the video display has been corrupted by improper display settings.
Safe Mode (Available in both Server and Professional)	Used to load the operating system with only the minimal drivers and files necessary to start Windows 2000. Variations include Safe Mode with Networking and Safe Mode Command Prompt.
Directory Services Restore Mode (Available only in Server)	Used to restore the Active Directory on domain controllers.
Debugging Mode (Available only in Server)	Used to enable debugging.
Last Known Good Configuration (Available in both Server and Professional)	Used to revert to the configuration information used in the most recent successful logon.

HEADSTART OBJECTIVE 10.05

Examining the Recovery Console

The Recovery Console is a brand new feature in Windows 2000. It's a command-line utility that you start from the Windows 2000 Setup program. Using the Recovery Console, you can start and stop format drives, read and write data on a local drive (including drives formatted to use NTFS), and perform other administrative tasks. You must be an administrator to use the Recovery Console.

You can start the Recovery Console in one of two ways:

- If your computer won't start, you can run the Recovery Console from the Windows 2000 Setup disks or from the Windows 2000 Professional CD if your CD drive is bootable.

- You can also install the Recovery Console on your computer so it will be available if you need it to restart Windows 2000 at a later time. If you install it, you will be able to select the Recovery Console option from the list of available operating systems in the boot menu.

Installing the Recovery Console on Your Computer

With Windows 2000 running, insert your Windows 2000 Professional CD into your CD-ROM drive and follow these steps:

1. Click No when asked if you want to upgrade to Windows 2000.

2. At the command prompt, switch to your CD-ROM drive, and type the following:

   \i386\winnt32.exe /cmdcons

   You will see the message shown in Figure 10-6. Click Yes and Recovery Console will be installed.

FIGURE 10-6   The Recovery Console setup dialog box

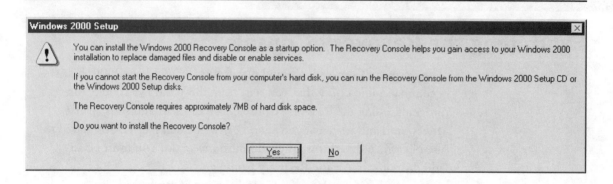

Using the Recovery Console

You can use the Recovery Console to enable and disable services, repair a corrupted master boot record, or copy system files from a floppy disk or CD-ROM.

Using Recovery Console to Repair a System that Won't Start

1. Restart your computer, and then choose Windows 2000 Recovery Console from the list of operating systems in the boot menu.

2. Follow the instructions that appear.

   The Recovery Console should then display a command prompt.

3. Now you can make the required changes to your system, using the available commands. For a list of commands available for use on the Recovery Console, type **help** at the command prompt.

Using the Backup Utility

The single most important part of your disaster prevention and recovery preparation is to make certain you have a strategic plan in place for regular, complete backup of all critical data. Then, if the worst does happen and all your front lines of defense fail, you will still be able to replace damaged or destroyed systems, format, restore your data, and go forward with nothing lost except some time. None of the mechanisms discussed previously negates the need to back up your files—especially data that is original, and thus irreplaceable.

Using Windows 2000 Backup

Recognizing the importance of backing up critical data, Microsoft has built a backup utility into all of its modern operating systems. The Windows 2000 backup program has incorporated several improvements that make it easier to use and more effective than its NT 4.0 counterpart. Perhaps the most significant of these is the new ability to back up data to files that can be stored on all types of removable media (the NT backup supported only SCSI tape drives, and only a limited number of the brands and models available).

Backup and restoration policies should be developed and documented; your organization should have clear, written instructions regarding procedures to follow in backing up and recovering critical data.

If you are using the Distributed File System (DFS) features, you should incorporate your DFS topology into your backup plan. You can build a volume with DFS that includes all the storage on the network, and then you will be able to back up all your data using a single namespace.

The DFS tree can include all your servers, allowing you to easily back up this one tree in a single backup operation.

Planning Issues

Before developing and implementing your backup plan, consider the following questions:

1. **Who will have permission to back up data?** By default, all users can back up their own files and folders, and those for which they have Read, Read and Execute, Modify, or Full Control permissions. In addition, Administrators, Backup Operators and Server Operators can back up all files and folders, including those for which they have no assigned permissions.

2. **Will backups be done manually or unattended?** Unattended backups can be scheduled to take place on a regular basis.

3. **Where will backup data be stored?** Data can be backed up to tape or to file. The latter can be stored on zip or jaz disks or other removable media, or written to compact disks or optical media.

4. **Which files and folders will be backed up?** This will depend on the importance and uniqueness of the data, and how difficult it is to recover or recreate it.

5. **How often will data be backed up?** You must determine whether to back up daily, weekly, or on some other schedule. You may find that some data should be backed up more often than other data.

Once you have answered all these questions, you can begin to develop a strategic backup plan. To implement your plan, you need to become familiar with the Windows Backup utility. Let's take a look at this handy software component.

The Backup and Restore Wizard and Configuration Tabs

To start Windows Backup, go to the Accessories submenu in the Programs menu, and choose Backup (or alternatively, run ntbackup from the command line). This starts the Backup and Restore Wizards Welcome Screen. Select the Backup tab (see Figure 10-7).

FIGURE 10-7   The Backup tab in the Windows 2000 Backup screen

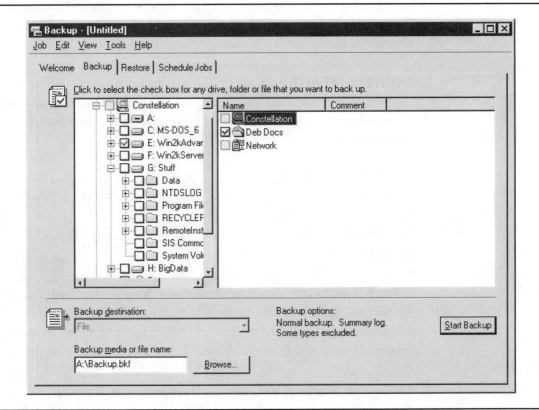

Backup Choices

The Backup utility supports the same five backup types that were used in the Windows NT 4.0 backup program, so that you can choose what data to back up and how to do so. The five options are Normal, Differential, Incremental, Copy, and Daily Backup. Let's briefly look at each.

NORMAL BACKUP   This is a straightforward backup procedure in which all the files and folders you have selected are backed up. No markers are used to determine which files to back up, and any markers that exist are cleared by the backup program, which then marks each file as having been backed up. Normal backup gives you a complete backup set that is easy to restore. However, it uses more tape (or other media) than some of the other methods.

DIFFERENTIAL BACKUP   Files that have previously been marked are backed up in a differential backup. Markers are not cleared so there is no flag indicating that those files have been backed up. This means the same files will be backed up in subsequent differential backups.

INCREMENTAL BACKUP   The incremental backup is similar to the differential in that marked files are backed up, but in this case, the markers are then cleared so that a subsequent incremental backup does not back up those same files again.

COPY BACKUP   All the selected files and folders are backed up when you do a Copy. Markers are not used to determine which files and folders to back up, and existing markers are not cleared. This type of backup can be done between other types without affecting the regular scheduled backups.

DAILY BACKUP   As the name implies, this type of backup backs up the selected files and folders that have been changed during that day. It does not use the archive markers to determine which files and folders to back up (instead, it looks to the date marker), and it does not clear existing markers.

Using the Backup Wizard to Perform the Backup

When you have determined what files and folders to back up and what type of backup you wish to perform, click Backup Wizard on the Welcome screen. The wizard will walk you through the process, which includes the following steps:

1. **Specify what to back up.** You have three choices:
   - Back up everything on the computer.
   - Back up Selected files, drives, or network data.
   - Only back up the System State Data.

   The backup options page of the Backup Wizard are shown in Figure 10-8.

Specifying what to back up with the Backup Wizard

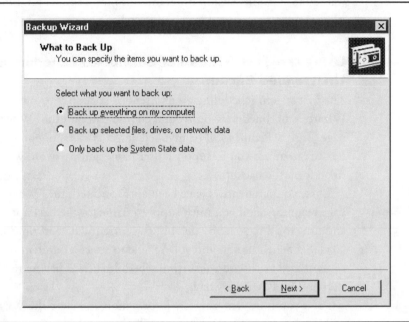

Note: The last option includes Active Directory services database and SYSVOL if you are performing the backup on a Windows 2000 domain controller. On all Windows 2000 systems, the System State Data includes the Registry, the COM+ Class Registration database, and system boot files.

2. Specify what to back up to (the backup media type). Choose to back up the data to tape or to file.

3. Click Finish to start the backup process.

A backup log will be saved as a text file on your hard drive, and you can read it for more information about the backup operation.

Scheduled Unattended Backups

Another improvement in the Windows 2000 backup utility is the ability to use the Task Scheduler to schedule a backup to run at a specific time. In

NT 4.0, it was necessary to use the AT command to run a batch file if you wanted to start the backup program, but now a simple GUI interface makes it easy to run unattended backup jobs whenever you want.

Using the Task Scheduler Service to Schedule an Unattended Backup

The first step in scheduling an unattended backup is to run the Backup Wizard as outlined previously, and choose Later on the "When to back up" page. Task Scheduler will be invoked automatically, popping up a dialog box that requires you to supply a user name and password with permissions to perform the backup.

Once your credentials have been authenticated, the "When to back up" page reappears, and you must supply a name for the backup, and the date and time for it to start. By default, the current date and time are entered. Click Set Schedule and you will be able to select a different date and/or time, as well as choose a recurring schedule such as having the backup start at 7:00 P.M. every day.

After you finish entering the information and close the Wizard, the job will be placed in the schedule and will begin and run automatically when that date/time arrives.

Restoring Data from Backups

The first rule, when it comes to restoring data from backups: Test the restoration process before you actually need it. Occasionally do a trial run of restoring data from your backup tapes or other media to be sure the process works as you expect it to.

Steps in Restoring Data from Backups

First you must select the data to restore. Then open the Restore Wizard (selected from the welcome screen we worked with previously).

1. Select the media type on which your data to be restored is located (tape or file).

2. Expand the media set, making all the data you want to restore visible in the tree.

3. Select the data you want to restore. Click Next.

4. Review the default settings for the restoration, and click Finish to perform the restoration.

Next, we will complete an exercise to give you some hands-on practice in using the Windows 2000 backup utility.

Restoring the System State Data (Authoritative Restore)

In Backup, the Active Directory service and other distributed services are contained in the System State data. When you back up the System State data on a domain controller, you are backing up all Active Directory data on that server (along with other system components such as the SYSVOL directory and the Registry). In order to restore these distributed services to the server, you must restore the System State data.

If you have more than one domain controller in your organization, and your Active Directory is replicated to any of these other servers, you may want to perform what is called an authoritative restore in order to ensure that your restored data gets replicated to all of your servers.

To authoritatively restore Active Directory data, you need to run the Ntdsutil utility after you have restored the System State data but before you restart the server. The Ntdsutil utility lets you mark Active Directory objects for authoritative restore. This will ensure that any replicated or distributed data that you restore is properly replicated throughout your organization.

The default method of restoring the System State data to a domain controller is *nonauthoritative*. In this mode, any component of the System State that is replicated with another domain controller, such as the Active Directory directory service or the File Replication service (including the SYSVOL directory), will be brought up to date by replication after you restore the data.

In order to restore the System State data on a domain controller, you must first start your computer in Restore Directory Services Mode. This will allow you to restore the SYSVOL directory and the Active Directory.

The Ntdsutil utility and accompanying documentation are located in the \Support\Reskit\Netmgmt folder on the Windows 2000 installation CD.

[handwritten margin note: NTDSUTIL used to restore AD.]

[handwritten margin note: Non authoritative restore – default – uses replication to update restored data.]

Using the Backup Utility to Restore Active Directory

You must be using a Windows 2000 domain controller to restore the Active Directory. You must have previously backed up the System State data. Note that you can only restore the System State data on a local computer; you cannot restore it on a remote computer.

1. Start the computer in Restore Directory Services Mode (see advanced startup options). Log on as an administrator.

2. Run ntbackup.exe or open the Backup utility in the Accessories submenu in the Programs menu.

3. Click the Restore tab, and then in "Click to select the check box for any drive, folder, or file that you want to restore," click the box labeled System State.

4. Choose whether you want to perform an authoritative restore or a nonauthoritative restore.

5. If you choose authoritative restore, run the Ntdsutil utility.

6. Restart the computer.

Creating and Using the ERD

You can use the Backup Wizard to create an ERD in Windows 2000. You will need a blank 1.44MB floppy disk.

Creating the ERD with the Backup and Restore Wizard

The Welcome screen of the Wizard is shown in Figure 10-9, along with the option to create an ERD.

1. Open the Backup Wizard by choosing Start | Programs | Accessories | Backup or run ntbackup.exe.

2. Click Create an Emergency Repair Disk.

3. Follow the instructions that appear on your screen.

Choosing "Also back up the registry to the repair directory" will save your current registry files in a folder within your systemroot/repair folder. This is useful if you need to recover your system in the event your hard disk fails.

FIGURE 10-9   Using Windows 2000 Backup and Recovery tools to create an ERD

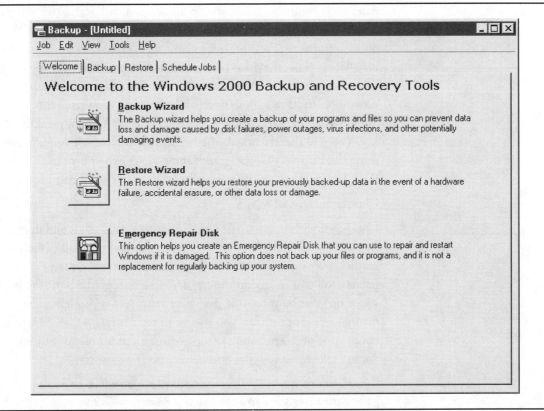

Unfortunately, floppy disks are small and easily lost. You should keep your (up-to-date!) ERD in a safe place. If you lose it anyway, the repair directory can be your salvation. More than one administrator has found that having the ERD information "magically" available on the hard drive was the only thing that saved the system from disaster.

Using the ERD to Repair a System that Will Not Start

The following steps provide a general overview of the emergency repair process:

1. Start your computer from the Windows 2000 setup disks or CD.

2. Choose the Repair option during setup.

    After your computer starts, the Setup program will start. You will be asked whether you want to continue installing the Windows 2000 operating system. Press ENTER to continue. This starts the installation process, which allows you to repair your system. During this process, you can choose whether you want to install a fresh version of Windows 2000, or repair an existing installation of Windows 2000. To repair a damaged or corrupt system, press the R key. You will then be asked whether you want to repair your system using the Recovery Console or the emergency repair process. Press the R key to repair your system using the emergency repair process

3. Choose the type of repair.

    Choose either the fast repair option (which is the easiest and doesn't require any user interaction), or the manual repair option (which requires user interaction). The fast repair option will attempt to repair problems related to the registry, system files, the partition boot sector on your boot volume, and your startup environment. The manual repair option lets you choose to repair system files, partition boot sector problems, and startup environment problems, but it doesn't allow you to repair problems with the Registry.

    If you want to manually repair individual registry files or replace your entire Registry, you can use the Recovery Console.

4. Start the repair process.

    To start the repair process, you should have the ERD that you created in the Backup utility, and the original Windows 2000 installation CD. If you do not have an ERD, the emergency repair process will try to find your Windows 2000 installation and search the repair folder for the information needed to repair your system, but it may not be able to do so. Remember that this data is only as current as the last time you updated the repair information.

5. Restart the computer.

If the emergency repair process isn't successful, you should try using the Recovery Console or reinstalling Windows 2000.

Backup Considerations for Mission-Critical Data

The more important and/or irreplaceable your data is, the more essential it is that you not only back it up on a regular basis, but that you make more than one copy of the backup tapes or other media. Remember that redundancy is the key element in any fault-tolerance strategy, and this applies to backups, too.

Store copies of mission-critical data in several different locations, including at least one copy stored completely offsite.

on the

Job

It is important that you always attempt to see the "big picture" when planning your disaster protection program, and anticipate every eventuality, not just the most common ones. Many network administrators are diligent about making certain that data gets backed up every night, and they carefully label and organize the backup tapes—and then store them in a drawer next to the server.

If the server's data is lost due to a hard drive crash or computer virus, the administrator may congratulate him/herself on the care that was taken to protect the data. However, if disaster strikes in a different form, it will become apparent that the backup plan was not as well thought-out as it seemed. If the server's data should be lost because of a fire or flood, it's very likely that those backup tapes or disks will be destroyed right along with the system they were designed to protect.

Always store copies of important backups offsite, or at the very least in another part of the building, away from the machine(s) whose hard drives you back up. If data is both important and sensitive or confidential, many organizations store copies of their backup tapes in a safety deposit box or other secured location.

ACCELERATING TO WINDOWS 2000

In Windows 2000, the disaster prevention and recovery components built into the operating system have been improved and added to, making it easier for the network administrator to develop and implement a comprehensive data protection program.

- Dynamic disks, new to Windows 2000, provide an environment in which fault-tolerant volumes can be created and managed within storage space that is easily reconfigured without destruction of data.

- The Disk Management tool in the Computer Management Console offers a user-friendly interface for creation and management of RAID Level 1 and 5 volumes that is more intuitive and easier to use than the NT 4.0 Disk Administrator.

- Windows 2000 has retained NT's VGA Boot Mode and the Last Known Good configuration for troubleshooting startup problems, and has added additional advanced startup options, including Safe Mode, Safe Mode with Networking, Safe Mode Command Prompt, Directory Restore Mode, and Debugging Mode.

- The new Windows Backup utility uses Wizards and easy-to-navigate dialog screens to walk you through the process of selecting backup options and restoring data from backup.

- Windows Backup can now back data up to files that can be stored and restored from zip or jaz disks or other removable media, as well as the tape drives that were the only backup devices supported by NT 4.0.

It is now easy to schedule unattended backup jobs with the Task Scheduler, using a friendly graphical interface. In NT 4.0, scheduling backups had to be done through the command line or with third-party add-on utilities.

CHAPTER SUMMARY

In this chapter, we discussed just a few of the elements involved in designing and putting into practice a good disaster protection plan for our Windows 2000 Server and network. The purpose of our computers and our networks is the creation, manipulation, and preservation of information, so keeping that information safe is one of our most important duties as network administrators.

As we discussed, Windows 2000 provides us with several components to help us accomplish that task, including disk fault tolerance, advanced startup options, the Recovery Console, and the Windows Backup utility.

We examined Windows 2000 Server's support for the creation of fault-tolerant volumes using software RAID implementations to make mirrored or duplexed sets (RAID Level 1) and stripe sets with parity (RAID Level 5). We practiced creating fault-tolerant volumes using Windows 2000's Disk Management tool in the Computer Management Console, and discussed the procedure for restoring data in the event of a disk failure.

We then took a look at the advanced startup options in Windows 2000 to help us boot into the operating system even when key files are corrupted, Registry information is overwritten, or configuration changes cause the system to fail to start. Specifically, we learned the functions of VGA Mode, Safe Mode, and its variations, and the Last Known Good configuration. We also examined two modes supported in Windows 2000 Server only: the Directory Services Restore Mode and the Debugging Mode. We noted that we can review the text file ntbtlog.txt for more information about the boot process when we enable boot logging in advanced options, or when it is enabled automatically because we've chosen one of the advanced boot modes.

Next, we familiarized ourselves with the new Windows 2000 Recovery Console, a powerful command-line utility that lets us perform administrative tasks from outside the Windows 2000 graphical interface, to repair or reconfigure a system that won't start. We explored the new features in the Windows 2000 Backup utility and the types of backup jobs that it can perform. We met the Backup and Restore Wizard, and walked through the steps involved in making a backup of data and restoring that data from tape or file.

Finally, we discussed the special considerations to keep in mind when backing up especially sensitive, confidential, or mission-critical data, remembering that the key to disaster protection is redundancy, and the best plan is one that addresses both prevention of data loss and recovery of data that is lost in spite of our precautions.

TWO-MINUTE DRILL

❑ In computer networking terms, a disaster is defined as a catastrophic event that results in loss of the system's capability to function.

❑ Disaster protection consists of two parts: planning and implementation of measures to prevent catastrophic events, and planning for a fast and efficient recovery process if a disaster does occur.

❑ A good disaster protection plan considers cost/benefit ratios, and focuses on the most cost-effective prevention and recovery methods.

❑ Windows 2000 incorporates several mechanisms for surviving disastrous events with critical data intact, including support for software implementation of RAID (Redundant Array of Independent Disks), advanced startup options, and the Recovery Console.

❑ Only Windows 2000 Server supports Disk fault tolerance; Windows 2000 Professional does not allow for the creation of fault-tolerant volumes.

❑ A major feature included in Windows NT 4.0, which is carried over to Windows 2000, is the ability to create fault-tolerant volumes. This is also known as software RAID, and it provides for redundancy in writing data to disk.

❑ The first step in your disaster preparedness plan should be to create a Windows 2000 boot floppy that can be used to load the operating system in the event of corrupt or missing system files that prevent Windows 2000 from starting.

❑ A key concept in the construction of a fault-tolerant system is *redundancy*.

❑ A fault-tolerant system will have more than one of as many critical components as possible. This could include backup power supplies, multiple disk controllers, and disks on which data is duplicated via mirroring, striping with parity, or other fail-safe mechanisms.

❑ RAID (Redundant Array of Independent—or Inexpensive, depending on the source—Disks) is a disk structuring method recognized throughout the industry as a means of providing fault tolerance at the disk level.

❑ With Windows 2000's software implementation of RAID, no extra equipment expense is required, and it's easy to set up and use.

❑ Remember that Windows 2000 Professional does not support disk fault tolerance, although it does support RAID Level 0.

❑ RAID Level 0 can be used to turn several small partitions on different disks into one large logical partition for more efficient storage. It is important to note that RAID Level 0 does not offer any fault tolerance whatsoever.

❑ Windows 2000 Server uses ftdisk.sys (a fault tolerance driver) to write the data to both physical disks at the same time.

❑ Disk striping with parity is known as RAID Level 5, and is a fault-tolerance implementation that uses disk space more efficiently than mirroring/duplexing.

❑ Fault-tolerant volumes are created using the Disk Management tool in the Computer Management Console. Before you can create a RAID 1 or RAID 5 volume, however, you must upgrade your basic storage disks to dynamic storage if you haven't already done so.

❑ Windows 2000 disks are configured for basic storage by default, and must be upgraded using the Disk Management utility in the Computer Management Console.

❑ The purpose of mirroring is to create an exact duplicate of the mirrored volume. The data is written to each disk at the same time, so if one member of the set fails at any given time, the same data is intact on the other member.

❑ Remember that in Microsoft's terminology, the system partition is where the boot files (ntldr, ntdetect.com, and boot.ini) are stored, and the boot partition is the one on which the operating system files (typically the winnt directory) are located.

❏ The Microsoft exams presume a thorough knowledge of ARC path syntax, so it is important to understand what each section of the path means and how it is numbered.

❏ If one member of your mirror set stops functioning, you will still be able to use the system—until you shut down and restart. That's when you may find that your operating system files are now "lost" and you must edit boot.ini.

❏ Windows 2000 provides you with several options at startup that are designed to help troubleshoot and/or recover from boot problems. Choices include VGA Mode, Safe Mode, Directory Services Restore Mode, Debugging Mode, and Last Known Good Configuration.

❏ In some cases the system will automatically revert to the Last Known Good control set without your intervention, such as when a critical device driver has been disabled.

❏ Using the Recovery Console, you can start and stop services, format drives, read and write data on a local drive (including drives formatted to use NTFS), and perform other administrative tasks. You must be an administrator to use the Recovery Console.

❏ You can use the Recovery Console to enable and disable services, repair a corrupted master boot record, or copy system files from a floppy disk or CD-ROM.

❏ The single most important part of your disaster prevention and recovery preparation is to make certain you have a strategic plan in place for regular, complete backup of all critical data.

❏ The Windows 2000 backup program has incorporated several improvements that make it easier to use and more effective than its NT 4.0 counterpart. Perhaps the most significant of these is the new ability to back up data to files that can be stored on all types of removable media (the NT backup supported only SCSI tape drives, and only a limited number of the brands and models available).

❑ Another improvement in the Windows 2000 backup utility is the ability to use the Task Scheduler to schedule a backup to run at a specific time.

❑ The first rule, when it comes to restoring data from backups: Test the restoration process before you actually need it.

❑ You can use the Backup Wizard to create an ERD in Windows 2000. You will need a blank 1.44MB floppy disk.

❑ The more important and/or irreplaceable your data is, the more essential it is that you not only back it up on a regular basis, but that you make more than one copy of the backup tapes or other media. Remember that redundancy is the key element in any fault-tolerance strategy, and this applies to backups, too.

SELF TEST

The following Self Test questions will help you measure your understanding of the material presented in this chapter. Read all the choices carefully, as there may be more than one correct answer. Choose all correct answers for each question.

1. Which of the following is a form of disk fault tolerance supported by Windows 2000 Server? (Choose all that apply.)

    A. RAID Level 0

    B. RAID Level 1

    C. RAID Level 4

    D. RAID Level 5

2. Which of the following is true of disk fault tolerance in Windows 2000?

    A. Fault-tolerant volumes can be created in both Windows 2000 Professional and Windows 2000 Server.

    B. Fault-tolerant drives can only be created on dynamic disks.

    C. Implementing disk fault tolerance removes the need to do regular backups.

    D. Fault-tolerant volumes are created using the Device Manager component of the Computer Management Console.

3. What is the minimum and maximum number of disks used in a stripe set with parity?

    A. Minimum of 1, maximum of 3

    B. Minimum of 2, maximum of 10

    C. Minimum of 3, maximum of 32

    D. Minimum of 4, no limit on maximum

4. Which of the following files will need to be edited to point to the second disk in a mirror set if the first disk fails and the operating system files are stored on the mirrored partition?

    A. ARC.dll

    B. config.sys

    C. w2000os.com

    D. boot.ini

5. Which of the following is the Windows 2000 fault-tolerance driver?

    A. ftdisk.sys

    B. ftolerant.dll

    C. ftdriver.com

    D. ntdetect.com

6. Which of the following advanced startup options is available only in Windows 2000 Server?

    A. VGA Mode

    B. Safe Mode with Networking

    C. Debugging Mode

    D. Safe Mode with Command Prompt

7. In which of the following cases might the Last Known Good configuration allow

you to load an operating system that has been rendered unbootable?

A. You have changed the refresh rate in your display adapter settings to an unsupported rate.

B. You have installed a new device driver that is incompatible or corrupt and have not been able to log on since the installation.

C. You have accidentally deleted the winnt system root directory.

D. You have changed the location of the operating system files to a different partition.

8. Which of the following statements is true of the Windows 2000 Recovery Console? (Check all that apply.)

A. The Recovery Console can only be run by administrators.

B. The Recovery Console is run by selecting Administrative Tools from the Start menu.

C. The Recovery Console can be installed on your computer and will thereafter show up as a choice in the boot menu.

D. The Recovery console can be used to repair a faulty master boot record.

9. Which of the following commands can be used to open the Backup and Restore Wizard?

A. runbackup.exe

B. backup.exe

C. ntbackup.exe

D. w2000backup.exe

10. In which of the following backup methods are all marked files backed up, but the markers not cleared?

A. Incremental

B. Differential

C. Daily

D. Copy

(Raise this)

11. Which of the following options is/are available in the Backup Wizard when asked to specify what to back up? (Choose all that apply.)

A. Back up everything on the computer

B. Only back up System State data

C. Back up device driver files only

D. Back up selected files, drives, or network data

12. What happens next when you choose Later on the "when to back up" page of Backup Wizard?

A. The Wizard closes, and you can reopen it later and start where you left off.

B. The Task Scheduler starts, and you are asked for a user name and password.

C. The Wizard pops up a dialog box asking you for a time and date to do the backup.

D. The Backup automatically starts one hour later.

13. How do you restore data from backup tapes or files?

    A. Run the Recovery Console and choose Restore.

    B. Open the Disk Management tool and choose Regenerate Data.

    C. Select the files to be restored in Windows Explorer, right-click on them, and select Restore to Original Location.

    D. Select the data to be restored and open the Restore Wizard.

14. Which of the advanced startup options attempts to load Windows 2000 Professional or Server with only basic drivers?

    A. VGA Mode

    B. Debugging Mode

    C. Safe Mode

    D. Basic Driver Mode

15. Which of the following is true of an ARC path in the boot.ini file that begins with SCSI(1)?

    A. The winnt directory is located on a drive that uses the first SCSI controller with the SCSI BIOS enabled.

    B. The winnt directory is located on a drive that uses the first SCSI controller with the SCSI BIOS disabled.

    C. The winnt directory is located on a drive that uses the second SCSI controller with the SCSI BIOS enabled.

    D. The winnt directory is located on a drive that uses the second SCSI controller with the SCSI BIOS disabled.

MICROSOFT CERTIFIED SYSTEMS ENGINEER

11

Upgrading a Network to Windows 2000

HEADSTART OBJECTIVES

Upgrading to Windows 2000 requires very serious planning and preparation to ensure success. The domain has changed with the introduction of Active Directory, so configuration is going to be vastly different after the upgrade. We will look at each type of machine in a Windows 2000 network, from the Domain Controller to the Workstation.

The first stage of any upgrade or major change on your network is the planning and preparation. You have to review your existing network infrastructure, file print and Web servers, applications, and other items that will be directly affected.

With Windows 2000, there is a new term you need to become familiar with: Root Domain. The Root Domain is the centerpiece to your new Windows 2000 network. The Domain Naming System (DNS) hierarchy is another area to become comfortable with when administering a Windows 2000 network. We will look at these terms later in this chapter.

Along with servers comes the workstation upgrade. Windows 2000 Professional is the workstation equivalent. We will discuss the upgrade process and take a brief look at what is new and different with this workstation operating system. The Windows 2000 family has different features that are distinct to each level of the operating system. This chapter provides a brief overview of those.

EXERCISE 11-1

Upgrading Your Windows NT 4.0 Network to Windows 2000

In this exercise, we look at the steps to upgrade from Windows NT 4.0 to Windows 2000. This process can be done with many variables in mind, but here we want to give the basics on the upgrade path. There are three phases to the setup process: WINNT32,.TEXT, and GUI.

WINNT32 Phase:

1. When inserting the CD into an existing server, you will be prompted to upgrade. If you agree to this, the WINNT32.EXE will start.

2. Dosnet.inf is loaded, and the compatibility check is run.

3. Files are copied to a temporary directory, $win-nt$.~bt. A boot.ini file is created in the temporary directory and the system reboots.

TEXT Phase:

4. Once the computer reboots, the text phase starts, which copies the core components of Windows 2000 to the selected directory.

5. The Windows 2000 you are installing will default to the existing operating system's directory for installation.

6. The NTLDR is copied to the root and the system is prepared for the GUI portion of the setup.

GUI Phase:

7. The GUI phase starts by detecting the hardware on the machine and enumerating plug-and-play (PnP)devices.

8. All of the prompts you see during this phase default to the existing settings of the current operating system. Therefore, in most cases, there will not be much input during the upgrade—more verification than anything.

9. The temporary files and directories are deleted and the system is ready for the first logon.

This is just a basic overview of the upgrade process. There are many planning stages before proceeding with the upgrade. One very important point is that you cannot upgrade by booting from the CD or boot disks for Windows 2000. You must install from within the operating system from which you are upgrading.

HEADSTART OBJECTIVE 11.01

Planning a Network Upgrade

Planning a network upgrade is the most important piece to ensuring a successful upgrade. Considerations include

- Network infrastructure
- Security

- File servers
- Print servers
- Web servers
- Server applications
- Network standards

We will look at each of these areas to assist you in establishing a baseline for upgrading your network. The basic point of planning a network upgrade is to know where you start and what each step is to reach the end result.

Network Infrastructure

When you hear about network infrastructure, you may simply think that you need to look at the hubs, switches, cabling, and servers on the network. The truth is, you need to look at many more areas as well. The key word to remember when doing an audit on your existing network is *details*. What I mean is, you cannot forget about name resolution configuration, remote access, network addressing and protocols, and many more. One key component that many administrators are using more and more is a diagram of the physical devices and layout of the network. This should include bandwidth, especially in a WAN environment.

Along with diagramming the network comes documenting other areas, including name resolution services, IP addressing schemes, and remote access. In today's environments, the necessity of name resolution means that configuration and documentation are a must. Name resolution will include DNS servers, WINS servers, or possibly even other NetBIOS naming conventions. NetBIOS naming uses the computer name.

With the Internet being as huge as it is, more and more networks are moving to TCP/IP as their main protocol. With this in mind, you have to know if your network is using DHCP, or if the addresses are static. Diagramming your network with layouts of subnets or supernets will come in handy for troubleshooting and expansion.

Many organizations have a need for remote access to their network. In order to configure and maintain a remote access configuration, you have to know how the configuration works currently so you can adapt it for future upgrades and changes. Remote access can include dial-up access, such as a RAS in Windows NT. Nowadays, the new remote access method is the Virtual Private Network (VPN). Giving access to your network across the Internet in a secure fashion takes considerable configuration steps to ensure that the security and integrity of the network stay intact. When upgrading or changing the network, you have to ensure you will maintain the access with the security in mind.

Security

Securing your network and protecting your data are vital to successful administration. Many networks are connected to the Internet, which opens them up for external intrusion. A firewall will protect your network. When you are considering upgrading your network, you have to develop a list of security concerns or risks if major changes are made on the network.

Along with the firewall configuration and a list of security concerns, document items such as

- Offsite backups
- Desktop configuration for security
- Server configuration for security
- Mobile configuration for security
- Internal network security versus public network security

Another item often overlooked is what happens in the event of a disaster and you have to rebuild the network from the ground up.

If you are upgrading the network, you have to ensure your disaster recovery plan will still work after the changes. With the new Active

Directory, and the other new features in Windows 2000, you have to ensure that the steps you have in place for recovering your network will still work. Things to keep in mind are

- Security differences
- Terminal services
- COM+ services
- Internet and Web services
- File system compatibility

Do plenty of research with various types of software vendors to ensure that your backup solution supports the newer Windows 2000 file systems and security.

File, Print, and Web Servers

When designing the plan for the network upgrade, you have to consider what is in place for various server responsibilities, along with what you are going to have when the network is completed. Microsoft breaks the server platforms into three distinct areas based on size: Enterprise, Divisional, and Departmental. Enterprise is a large WAN environment; Divisional is pretty specific to the task performed; and Departmental is more application-specific servers on a smaller basis than Divisional.

Enterprise Servers

Enterprise servers are usually located in the corporate data center. They serve the users by providing user home directories, print queues, or simple communication services. They may also be Web servers that serve the corporate intranet or extranet. These types of servers are backed up daily or at least weekly in most cases.

In an Enterprise environment, there are usually many servers spread out among many locations. Figure 11-1 shows what an Enterprise WAN may look like.

FIGURE 11-1	Enterprise WAN

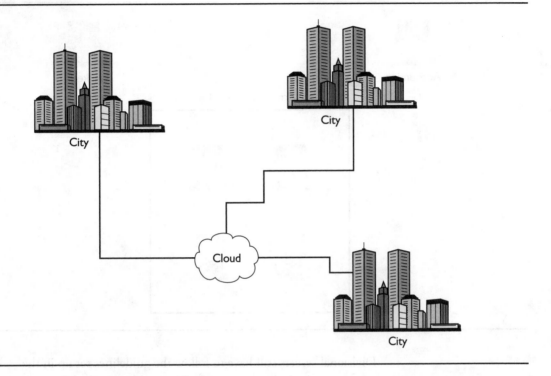

Enterprise servers include file and print servers, along with Web servers. These types of servers are usually the more powerful servers available.

Divisional Servers

The same people who support the Enterprise servers support the Divisional servers. The cost of these servers in usually incurred by the division that requires them. They have no file services for user storage, and are for specialized and specific applications or projects. The benefit is that the entire Enterprise or organization as a whole does not incur the cost of the specially needed servers. Figure 11-2 shows some examples of what a breakdown of Divisional servers might look like.

FIGURE 11-2	Divisional servers

Accounting

Marketing

Information Technology

Divisional servers still have to follow the guidelines set up in the corporate standards documentation. This includes both software and hardware standards. Divisional servers are considered differently when it comes to the financial aspect of purchasing, installation, and continued support.

Departmental Servers

Departmental servers are the ones that stand out the most. There are not handled by the Enterprise support team like the other two types of servers. Departmental servers are usually for storage of larger items, such as graphics or special projects. Sometimes these servers are kept separate for reasons of security or privacy. They may hold confidential corporate information and, in some people's minds, if the server is in their control, the more they feel it is more secure.

Departmental servers are usually not as robust as Divisional or Enterprise servers, and do not have large quantities of users accessing them. The

Departmental server may have a large amount of drive space, but usually processor and RAM specifications are lower than in an Enterprise or Divisional server.

Categorizing the Data

As you gather data, you will need to organize it for review. This will make the planning and design stage much easier. Not only do you want to classify them as one of the three areas discussed already, you also need to look at

- Hardware details
- Network services (e.g., print, Internet, backup)
- Maximum downtime
- Software installed
- Protocols
- Operating system
- Patches and updates

Once the data is organized, you can determine which servers may not meet specifications. Whether it is hardware or software, you have to be prepared to make appropriate adjustments. Some applications may have to be modified to work with the changes in Windows 2000. Some applications or hardware just may not make the cut and major changes have to be made.

The key is getting the details to make the appropriate planning decisions. In all of the audits and design plans I've seen, the biggest component (and I think the most important component) is the planning stage. If this stage isn't handled properly, the remaining part of the design and upgrade will not go as smoothly as you want it to.

Server Applications

Server applications are vital to the function of everyday business. If an upgrade takes place and one of your mission-critical applications does not work, you could lose money because of productivity slowing or sometimes coming to a complete halt. Organizing the application information will help when doing the research necessary to ensure that the application will work, or in determining what needs to be done to get the application to work.

Some examples of what to document and have ready when you do your research include

- Version number
- Patch level/Service Pack level
- Number of servers
- Maximum downtime
- Windows 2000 compatible?
- Active Directory support?
- Drives the business?
- Contact for support by phone
- Web site for research
- Other contacts

Once you compile the necessary information, you can make the contacts and do the research. Don't forget to leave room for making notes. Some applications may take a simple update, while others may require a complete upgrade. Windows 2000 compatibility information can be found on Microsoft's Web site. As of this writing, the URL to reach this is ftp://ftp.microsoft.com/services/whql/win2000hcl.txt, or you can go to http://www.microsoft.com/hcl.

There are many types of server applications on which to focus, including Microsoft Exchange, backup software, virus software, and management software. The most important consideration is Active Directory compatibility.

Network Standards

After everything is compiled and researched, and your design and plan is prepared, you have to meet with the financial people in your organization to determine if the proposal is adequate. Before this happens, though, we should review the design to ensure it adheres to corporate standards.

Some standards are as simple as naming servers in a certain fashion. Others include where applications are stored, or where data is stored. Other items may have to do with backup rotation and plan, virus protection configuration, or even server location and WAN layout.

Standards may not be present in all organizations; however, as a network grows, the need for standards will become evident. Administration can become cumbersome within large organizations. Having standards in place ensures that everyone maintaining and using the network is on the same page. More documentation will need to be reviewed, updated, or possibly even implemented before upgrading to Windows 2000. If this isn't done, the total cost of ownership goes up. Some of the standards will include

- Server configuration
- Workstation configuration
- Laptop configuration
- Router/Switch/Hub configuration

The preceding list covers the physical network components. Along with this are the standards of the logical pieces of the network. This includes machine naming, IP addressing, Remote Access, and DNS configuration, among others. If these items are not well documented, and the network layout does not hold up to the standards, productivity will suffer, especially from a support perspective. Table 15-1 lists the recommended documentation for each planning and design stage.

TABLE 11-1   Network Upgrade Planning

Planning and Design Stage	What to Document
Network infrastructure	Cabling, physical devices, name resolution
Security	Desktop, server, mobile, offsite backups
File, Print, Web servers	Departmental, Divisional, Enterprise
Server applications	Version number, number of servers, patches
Network standards	Corporate standards, naming standards, data locations

There are some critical areas in the planning and design stage that, if not handled properly, can adversely affect the actual network upgrade. As network integrator and solution provider for various clients, we service many types of environments. When going into an organization and looking at its existing network, we have found it is better for the client if we do an audit and design on the network. This usually can take anywhere from two to three days, or as many as four weeks. Larger enterprise environments, of course, take the most time. The following items can affect the amount of time the audit and design stage of a network upgrade takes:

> *Number of servers*
> *Number of users*
> *Number of applications*
> *Number of locations*
> *Number of workstations*
> *Topology/infrastructure*

Failing to take the time up front to consider the crucial factors in implementing a network design can result in future support costs and delayed rollouts. This can make for an unhappy customer. Even if you are a network administrator for a company, you can see that not preparing properly and not letting your users know what to expect can result in unhappy "customers" in the form of users. This can mean that money is lost from a productivity standpoint. With this in mind, make sure you have all your bases covered to make the transition to the new network a positive one for your "customers."

HEADSTART OBJECTIVE 11.02

Establishing the Root Domain

Domain management is vastly different with Windows 2000. Prior to Windows 2000, there was a domain, and if multiple domains were present, there were trusts. There were different trust models with Windows NT 4.0. These included single domain, master domain, multiple-master domain, and the infamous complete trust. Upgrading from each of these takes some different configuration. When there is one domain to upgrade, the process is straightforward: when the domain is upgraded, there is an Active Directory database with one domain in it.

The process becomes a little different with the other domain models. The reason for this is the fact that a root domain has to be established. Active Directory uses DNS, which uses the hierarchical structure starting from a root. Active Directory is going to be hierarchical, so a root domain has to be established.

The design goal for most networks will be a single domain with various Organizational Units (OUs). OUs can be based on location, job function, or other logical groupings of network objects. The Active Directory structure will be based on the same type of structure for DNS. This means that large corporations will need to have their DNS group and their network design group cooperate on managing the layout and design of the network.

HEADSTART OBJECTIVE 11.03

Configuring Domain Controllers

Domain Controllers in Windows 2000 are much more advanced; therefore, there is much more to configure. The biggest change is the use of Active Directory. Domain Controllers are still the central component to security and authentication and any domain interaction with users; however, how the data is stored and managed is different from Windows NT 4.0. A domain can still have more than one Domain Controller. Most of the time, the single Domain Controller scenario is all you see on a small network. As the network grows, you may see Domain Controllers added. Multiple Domain Controllers are possible and are not a bad idea for fault tolerance of directory information. With Windows 2000, there are no longer any Primary and Backup Domain Controllers. All the servers now are simply Domain Controllers.

There can be multiple Domain Controllers, but with Active Directory and the new method of the directory, there can only be one *Operations Master*. The Domain Operation Master is the main place for updates and changes to the security and permissions in the domain. This is similar to how Novell has one master replica, and other servers are read-and-write replicas. The one difference is the fact that there are different roles that can be served:

- Domain Naming Master
- Schema Master
- Primary Domain Controller Emulator
- Relative Identifier Master
- Infrastructure Master

Domain Naming Master

The Domain Naming Master is what handles the responsibility of adding and removing domains in the Forest. The Forest is similar to the Tree in NetWare. There are trees within a Windows 2000 network as well, so be sure to understand that the tree in NetWare is the Directory just as the forest in Windows 2000 is the directory. As in the past with Primary Domain Controllers, there can only be one Domain Naming Master in the forest.

Schema Master

The Schema Master is what controls the schema in the forest. From time to time, the schema will be updated. There can only be one Schema Master in the forest.

PDC Emulator

There will be networks where not every workstation is running the Windows 2000 client software. In this case, you need to have something to process the older style logons. This is where the Primary Domain Controller emulator comes into play. It takes information on changes in the domain and replicates this information out to the Backup Domain Controllers, if they exist.

Relative Identifier Master

The Relative Identifier Master is the one server that handles the database and allocation of Relative IDs (RIDs). When each workstation is added, it has a Security Identifier, or SID. This was evident in Windows NT 4.0. The SID consists of the domain security ID and the relative ID. The domain security ID is the same on each workstation. The relative ID is specific to that workstation.

Infrastructure Master

The Infrastructure Manager handles changes and configuration of groups and group-to-user relations. There must be one of these in your domain.

Another concept to become familiar with is *multimaster* replication. This is the replacement for the Backup Domain Controller of Windows NT 4.0. Multimaster replication keeps the information synchronized across all Domain Controllers. This ensures that there is fault tolerance in the event of server failure.

Planning the Domain

When it comes to planning your domain layout, you have to make more considerations than you did with Windows NT 4.0. If the network you are implementing is a small LAN, a single domain will serve your purpose. When you find that the single domain no longer works for your organization, you can expand the network and add more.

The new part to the domain with which NetWare administrators are already familiar is the OU. These exist within a domain and can be used to organize your network. With domains, you can have hundreds and hundreds of network objects, and you can use the OU to separate different locations. Depending on the size of the network, you can use different domains for different geographic locations. Figure 11-3 is a graphic that represents the OU versus the Domain separation.

Now that you have an idea of what the OU looks like, you are starting to formulate in your mind what Active Directory is, if you haven't already.

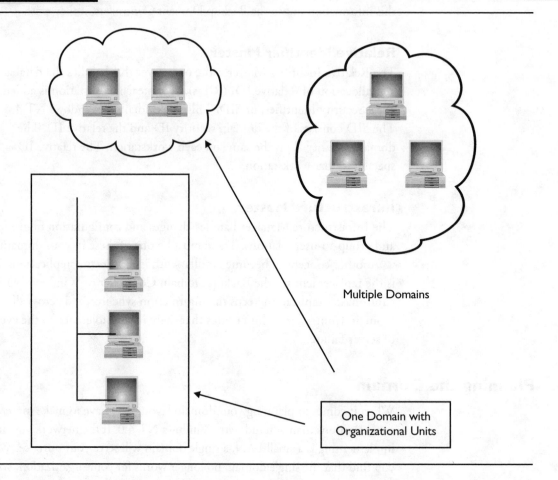

FIGURE 11-3

OUs versus multiple domains

Organizational Units

If you are familiar with Novell Directory Services, the following will seem very familiar to you. OUs in Windows 2000 are objects that are containers for other objects, such as users, groups, or other organizational units. Objects cannot be placed in another domain's OUs. The whole purpose of an OU is to have a hierarchical structure to organize your network objects. You can assign a group policy to an OU. Generally, the OU will follow a structure from your company. It may be a location, if you have multiple locations.

It can even be a department-level organization. In some cases, you can use OUs to reduce the number of domains on your network; instead of having multiple domains to manage, you would have multiple OUs. Having multiple domains versus OUs will make synchronization more difficult. One domain and multiple OUs will make the synchronization of the directory information much more efficient.

With OUs, you can also delegate administrative authority. With this in mind, you can create an administrative model and it can be scaled appropriately. You can give administrative authority to multiple units or one. Being able to assign permissions/rights this way is much easier in 2000.

Upgrading and Promoting Member Servers

With Windows NT 4.0, we had member servers. These servers were basically servers that had nothing to do with authentication and security in the domain. They were usually application, storage, or database servers. These are just some examples. With Windows 2000, these are known as *servers* and not *domain controllers*. Due to the Active Directory content, the domain controllers should really be the ones you upgrade first. Once Active Directory is in place, the application servers can be implemented, as well as other nondomain controller servers.

Upgrading Client Computer Operating Systems

Within the Windows 2000 product line is Windows 2000 Professional, which is the workstation version similar to Windows NT Workstation 4.0. The workstation or client computer does not have to be running Windows 2000 to be in a Windows 2000 domain.

One focus of Windows 2000 Professional is ease of installation. Installation scripts are more powerful and make administrators' jobs even easier. The new Setup Manager allows an administrator to configure settings for a user. All the user has to do is log on the first time with Windows 2000, and a customized profile is automatically updated on the workstation. Windows 2000 is ready out of the box for networking, as were previous Windows 9x operating systems.

Workstations are not required to have Windows 2000 Professional as their operating system. The one key component, though, is the network client software.

ACCELERATING TO WINDOWS 2000

There are many factors to consider when upgrading to Windows 2000. We've touched on a few, and there will be more that you will discover as you make the migration to Windows 2000. One difference is how Windows 2000 deals with the term *domain controller*. There were Primary Domain Controllers and Backup Domain Controllers in Windows NT 4.0; Windows 2000 simply has Domain Controllers and servers. The domain is now similar to Internet Domain with Active Directory; previous versions simply had a domain independent of any real directory standard.

Domain Controllers can have five different roles: Domain Naming Master, Schema Master, PDC Emulator; Relative Identifier Master, and Infrastructure Master. Previous versions had PDC, BDC, or Member Server.

Now within Domains are Forests, Trees, Organizational Units (OUs), Users, and other network objects arranged in a hierarchical structure. Previous Windows NT versions had separate utilities for user management, workstations management, and so forth.

OUs can be used to group similar network entities in Windows 2000. Windows NT 4.0 simply had local or global groups to match logical groupings of network objects. Windows 2000 can group together other types of network objects.

Client operating systems came with necessary client software with Windows NT 4.0. Windows 2000 will require a client upgrade for the Windows 9x systems and Windows NT Workstation. Windows 2000 Professional is the replacement workstation-level operating system.

CHAPTER SUMMARY

Upgrading your network seems simple on the surface, but planning is critical. Proper planning and design can make or break the upgrade process. If design considerations are not made, the network could fail all together.

The considerations that have to be made include network infrastructure, security, file servers, print servers, Web server, server applications, and network standards. Documenting every possible detail about the network and its configuration will make moving to Windows 2000 much easier and result in a lot less problems.

The domain environment is different with Windows 2000. The domain is much more like the Domain Naming System used on the Internet. Active Directory is a new piece to Windows 2000. The Domain models that we were familiar with in Windows NT are now built around Active Directory and the hierarchical structure. A term you will hear often is *Organizational Units*. These are logical groupings based on location, job function, department, or whatever is pertinent to your organization.

With the domain, a server can perform five different roles:

- Domain Naming Master
- Schema Master
- Primary Domain Controller Emulator
- Relative Identifier Master
- Infrastructure Master

Along with Domain Controllers are the member servers that are not involved in authentication or directory management. These servers are simply just that, servers. Also, there is the client-side. Windows 2000 Professional is the workstation version, or replacement for Windows NT Workstation. Windows 9*x* operating systems will function as well; however, a client should be installed with these.

TWO-MINUTE DRILL

❑ With Windows 2000, there is a new term you need to become familiar with: Root Domain. The Root Domain is the centerpiece to your new Windows 2000 network.

❑ Planning a network upgrade is the most important piece to ensuring a successful upgrade.

❑ One key component that many administrators are using more and more is a diagram of the physical devices and layout of the network. This should include bandwidth, especially in a WAN environment.

❑ Diagramming your network with layouts of subnets or supernets will come in handy for troubleshooting and expansion.

❑ With the new Active Directory, and the other new features in Windows 2000, you have to ensure that the steps you have in place for recovering your network will still work.

❑ Microsoft breaks the server platforms into three distinct areas based on size: Enterprise, Divisional, and Departmental.

❑ Organizing the application information will help when doing the research necessary to ensure that the application will work, or in determining what needs to be done to get the application to work.

❑ There are many types of server applications on which to focus, including Microsoft Exchange, backup software, virus software, and management software. The most important consideration is Active Directory compatibility.

❑ Some standards are as simple as naming servers in a certain fashion. Others include where applications are stored, or where data is stored. Other items may have to do with backup rotation and plan, virus protection configuration, or even server location and WAN layout.

❑ Active Directory uses DNS, which uses the hierarchical structure starting from a root. Active Directory is going to be hierarchical, so a root domain has to be established.

❑ The design goal for most networks will be a single domain with various organizational units (OUs).

❑ With Windows 2000, there are no longer any Primary and Backup Domain Controllers. All the servers now are simply Domain Controllers.

❑ With domains, you can have hundreds and hundreds of network objects, and you can use the OU to separate different locations. Depending on the size of the network, you can use different domains for different geographic locations.

❑ OUs in Windows 2000 are objects that are containers for other objects, such as users, groups, or other organizational units.

❑ Once Active Directory is in place, the application servers can be implemented, as well as other nondomain controller servers.

❑ The new Setup Manager allows an administrator to configure settings for a user. All the user has to do is log on the first time with Windows 2000, and a customized profile is automatically updated on the workstation.

SELF TEST

The following questions will help you measure your understanding of the material presented in this chapter. Read all of the choices carefully, as there may be more than one correct answer. Choose all correct answers for each question.

1. Which of the following is the most important piece to ensuring a successful upgrade?

   A. Network infrastructure

   B. Planning

   C. Security

   D. Installation

2. What is one component when planning an upgrade that could be documented and would include hubs, routers, switches, and multiple locations?

   A. Network infrastructure

   B. Protocol plan

   C. Device database

   D. None of the above

3. If you want to make sure you can build the network from the ground up, what should you have in place?

   A. Active Directory Services

   B. Floppy backup of network

   C. Disaster Recovery Plan

   D. Workstations and Servers

4. What are the three areas that Microsoft breaks its servers into?

   A. Enterprise

   B. Small Business

   C. Divisional

   D. Departmental

5. Which of the three server models is the one the corporate IT people do not administer and take responsibility for?

   A. Enterprise

   B. Small Business

   C. Divisional

   D. Departmental

6. What is one key component to plan for when upgrading that would include the backup software, possibly virus protection, or others.

   A. Server Farms

   B. Server Domain Controller

   C. Server Applications

   D. Third-Party Suites

7. In order to keep consistency across the network and ensure that corporate needs are met, what should you have documented before upgrading?

   A. Hard drive sizes

   B. Machine types

    C. Network Standards

    D. Amount of RAM

8. If your users dial in to your network from home, you should already have this documented. How are they accessing the network, what are they using?

    A. DNS

    B. Remote Access

    C. IP Addressing

    D. WINS

9. What is the new service that allows for a large database of network objects, including users, printers, server, etc.?

    A. Active Directory

    B. Windows Directory Services

    C. Windows ZAK

    D. NSD

10. Which of the following is not one of the five roles a Domain Controller can fill?

    A. Domain Naming Master

    B. Schema Master

    C. PDC Emulator

    D. Backup Domain Controller

11. How many total Schema Masters can there be in any Active Directory Forest?

    A. 1

    B. 2

    C. 3

    D. 10

12. What Domain Controller role handles changes and configuration of groups and group-to-user relations?

    A. Infrastructure Manager

    B. Primary Domain Controller

    C. Schema Master

    D. Domain Naming Master

13. In order to have redundancy in the network, what does Windows 2000 use for a replacement to the Backup Domain Controller?

    A. Multimaster replication

    B. Multidomain replication

    C. Multidomain Controller replication

    D. Multisite replication

14. How will Windows 2000 organize network objects in the forest into a hierarchical structure?

    A. With Organizational Pieces

    B. With Organizational Units (OUs)

    C. With Organizational Groups

    D. With Organizational Roles

15. What new utility can administrators use to preconfigure user settings for client workstations?

    A. Setup Configurator

    B. Setup Scripts

    C. Setup Manager

    D. Installation Manager

Part II

Directory Services

12

Planning the Active Directory Namespace

A directory service stores information about users and groups, computers, printers, security data, and other network objects. One of the biggest and most exciting changes in Microsoft's Windows 2000 operating system is the Active Directory (AD), which provides both users and administrators with a whole new way of locating and managing resources. While the NT directory services were flat and self-limiting, the Active Directory supports millions of objects and is built on a hierarchical structure like the Internet. In fact, the familiar Domain Naming System (DNS) of the Internet is the basis for the Active Directory namespace. Windows 2000 domain names are DNS names, and the Active Directory is compatible with Novell Directory Services (NDS) and other directory services that conform to LDAP (Lightweight Directory Access Protocol) standards, as defined in Requests for Comments (RFC) 1777. RFCs are readily available on the World Wide Web.

This chapter addresses the concepts involved in creating the Active Directory namespace in both single and multiple domain environments, with an emphasis on development of a strategic plan prior to implementation.

HEADSTART OBJECTIVE 12.01

Describing the Active Directory Namespace

In this section, we look at the inverted tree structure that makes up the DNS namespace, and how it is incorporated in Windows 2000's Active Directory. We define the two types of namespaces, and discuss the relationships between objects within each type of namespace.

What Is a Namespace?

A *namespace* is a characteristic of directory services representing a space in which a name is resolved, or translated into the information represented by that name. Consider a familiar example, the telephone directory. You use it to resolve names of people to their street addresses or telephone numbers. The Active Directory namespace is used to resolve the name or attributes of an object to the object itself. *Attributes* are data that describe or identify the object. For example, some attributes of a user object would include the user's name and e-mail address. Attributes of a printer object would include its brand, model, and whether it prints in color.

Because the domain structure of Windows 2000's Active Directory is based on the DNS name system, the namespace is hierarchical, representing different levels in the structure: domains, subdomains, and hosts. An example of a hierarchical name is www.mydomain.com, in which "com" represents the top-level domain, "mydomain" refers to the second-level domain, and "www" designates a Web server in that domain. The levels are separated by dots. An example of a flat namespace is the NetBIOS name of a computer in an NT network, such as "Server1."

What Are the Two Types of Namespaces?

Active directory namespaces fall into two categories: *contiguous* and *disjointed*. The distinction is based on how the names of parent objects and their child objects relate to one another.

Contiguous Namespace

A contiguous namespace is one in which the child object contains the name of the parent domain. A contiguous namespace in Windows 2000 is called a *tree*. A domain tree is comprised of a parent domain and subdomains called *child* domains, which reside under the parent, and the objects within them. The Fully Qualified Domain Name (FQDN) of each child domain is made up of the combination of its own name and the FQDN of the parent domain. For example, if the parent domain is named yourdomain.com, you could create two child domains within the tree called dallas.yourdomain.com and houston.yourdomain.com. Child domains can have their own "children," as well (see Figure 12-1).

The tree represents the entire hierarchy of objects. Domains contain other objects; within domains reside deeper level containers, and within those containers are the "endpoint" objects (those of you familiar with some other directory services will recognize these as "leaf" objects).

FIGURE 12-1   The parent domain (also called the root domain) is at the top of the tree, with its "children" and "grandchildren" at lower (and deeper) levels beneath it.

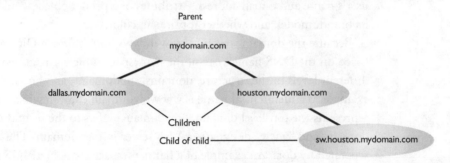

Disjointed (Noncontiguous) Namespace

When more than one tree is created in a Windows 2000 Active Directory, the collection of trees is called a *forest*. Each tree will have its own distinct namespace. For example, you could have two trees named mydomain.com and yourdomain.com, each with its respective child domains, forming two separate contiguous namespaces. In this case, the Active Directory namespace is said to be *disjointed* (see Figure 12-2).

Relationships of Objects within Contiguous and Noncontiguous Namespaces

The objects within a tree (contiguous namespace) have a parent-child relationship in which the child inherits some of its parent's attributes. There

FIGURE 12-2   When you create a forest of trees in Active Directory, each has a distinct namespace, but all trees share a common global catalog, and there is a two-way trust relationship between the parent (root) domains of the trees

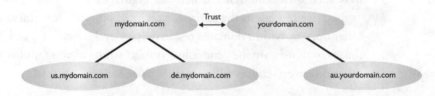

automatically exists a two-way transitive trust relationship between a parent domain and each of its "children." This means users will, with the proper permissions, be able to access resources anywhere in the tree.

However, each domain has its own security configuration, and the administrator of a parent domain does not automatically have administrative privileges over the child domain(s). Active Directory offers a great deal of flexibility in establishing administrative authority, and it is easy to implement either a centralized or decentralized administrative structure, whichever best fits your company's needs.

When trees are grouped into a forest (creating a disjointed namespace), a trust relationship automatically exists between the parent domains of the trees. This trust relationship, like that between parent and child within the same tree (and unlike Windows NT trusts), is two-way and *transitive*, which means every domain in the forest can share resources.

All trees in a forest share the same schema, configuration, and Global Catalog (these concepts will be defined and discussed in the section entitled "Planning the Naming of Objects in Active Directory.") A forest does not require a unique name, as a tree does. The forest is the set of trees within it, and the relationships of those trees to one another.

Naming Domains within the Namespace

Before you can create trees and/or forests within your organization's namespace, you must consider a scheme for naming the domains and subdomains that will inhabit them. It is important to plan carefully, since changing domain names—especially the name of the internal root domain—will cause many headaches later on.

heads
①P

Because Active Directory names are DNS names, the DNS service must be installed and configured in order for Active Directory to work properly.

The first step in planning and defining the namespace is to decide on the scope of your namespace, by evaluating the types of objects you will be describing, determining whether you expect the requirements to change later on, and considering whether you will need more than one Active Directory.

Choosing a Name for the Internal Root Domain

The starting point for your Active Directory namespace is your Active Directory's root domain. The first domain you create in Windows 2000 will become the root domain in the Active Directory. It is important that you choose a name that will remain the same, regardless of company reorganization and other organizational changes. Short, simple names are better than long, complex ones. After all, which do you find easier to remember: mydomain.com or thislittledomainofmine.com?

If your organization already has a registered domain on the Internet, it may seem logical to use the same root domain name internally. Before doing so, however, determine whether this meets your needs. There are many good reasons to use separate names for the internal and external domains. These will be discussed in the section entitled, "Planning the Integration of a Namespace with the Internet."

Your organization's root domain will be a child domain of one of the top-level domains: .com, .org, .net, etc. These are the same as those used on the Internet, and their names are based on the type of organization or, if outside the United States, on the country in which the company operates or originated.

For an example of the most often used top-level domains, and the types of organizations that fit into each category, see Table 12-1.

Choosing Names for Subdomains

The names you choose for subdomains will depend on several factors:

- Size of the organization
- Administrative structure of the organization
- Physical layout of the network

In a large organization, names of subdomains (child domains) might be based on geographic factors. For example, if the company has branch offices

TABLE 12-1

Common Top-
Level Domains

Domain	Organization
.com	Commercial businesses
.net	Networks
.org	Nonprofit organizations
.edu	Educational institutions
.mil	U.S. military entities
.gov	U.S. governmental bodies
.uk	Great Britain
.au	Australia
.ca	Canada

on each coast with a central headquarters, logical choices for subdomain names would be sandiego.ourdomain.com, newyork.ourdomain.com, and dallas.ourdomain.com. Alternately, you might choose west.ourdomain.com, east.ourdomain.com, and hq.ourdomain.com.

Smaller organizations may want to name subdomains after departments or divisions (finance.ourdomain.com and personnel.ourdomain.com), although this may be less desirable since a company reorganization often merges, abolishes, or renames such business units within the organization.

heads
P

There are two ways to locate basic information about Active Directory. You can use RootDSE (the Root Directory Specific Entry) to locate objects, or RootDSE can be used to access standard information about Active Directory. RootDSE is a special node that can be queried by LDAP clients (LDAP version 4 and later) to discover the schema and Directory Information Tree (DIT). Typically, the client isn't able to change the properties of the RootDSE, but it is able to read what the directory schema contains and how it is structured.

Checklist for Defining the Active Directory Root Domain

Following are the primary points to keep in mind when defining the root domain name for your organization:

- Choose your organization's top-level domain name based on the common DNS top-level domains used on the Internet.

- Choose a second-level domain name that is short, simple, and readily identifies your organization, and that has not already been registered by someone else with the Internet name registration authorities.

- Choose subdomain names that are based on logical structural divisions within your organizations, preferably those that are not subject to frequent change.

EXERCISE 12-1

Planning a Namespace for a Single Domain

You are setting up a Windows 2000 network for a small company, Stanford-Beckett Consulting, Inc., which operates out of a single location. Administration is centralized, although the firm has two distinct operational divisions: the Web Development Group and the Network Support Group. Sales, Marketing, and Finance Departments handle those roles for both divisions.

1. Choose an appropriate name for your root domain in accordance with suggested guidelines.

HEADSTART OBJECTIVE 12.02

Planning the Naming of Objects in Active Directory

Objects in the Directory represent network resources, and can be grouped in *classes*. A class is a group of objects with the same types of attributes, or characteristics. Users, groups, and domains are examples of object classes.

Objects that can contain other objects are known as *container objects*. A special type of container object that you can create in the Active Directory is the Organizational Unit (OU). You can put users, groups, computers, shares, and even other OUs into an Organizational Unit. You can then delegate administration of an OU to a person without giving that person administrative authority over the rest of the domain. This allows for much more specificity in assigning administrative tasks than is possible with the NT domain models.

In computer programming, a schema (pronounced SKEE-mah) is the organization or structure for a database. The *schema* is the part of the Active Directory that defines what attributes objects of a particular class can have and which of those attributes are required (see Figure 12-3). You can create new classes and define them with the Schema Manager snap-in. (See Chapter 19, "Controlling Schema Modifications," for more information about schema definition and modification).

The *global catalog* (GC) contains information about all of the objects in a tree or an entire forest. The global catalog is used to find objects within the network. By default, the first domain controller on which the Active Directory is stored is the global catalog server, but you can specify additional GC servers with the Sites and Servers Management snap-in for the Microsoft Management Console.

FIGURE 12-3   Representation of how the schema defines the contents and structure of Active Directory

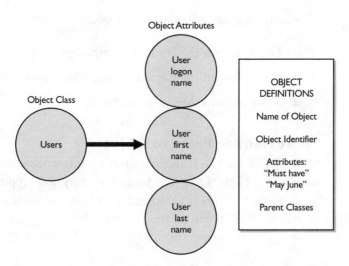

Naming Conventions

Each Active Directory object must have a name, to identify it to users on the network. Several different naming conventions are supported, making it possible to search the Directory in different ways. For example, you can query by name, or by object attributes if you don't know the exact name of the object. Four naming conventions are used to identify objects:

- Distinguished Names
- Relative Distinguished Names
- User Principal Names
- Globally Unique Identifiers

LDAP Distinguished Naming Paths

The Distinguished Name (DN) must uniquely identify the object. The LDAP DN includes the domain name in which the object resides and the complete path to the object. The DN must be unique in the Directory. An example of a DN:

   /DC=COM/DC=mydomain/OU=finance/CN=Users/CN=John Smith

Note the following attributes for DNs:

- DC represents the Domain Component Name
- OU represents the Organizational Unit Name
- CN represents the Common Name

Short Naming Paths to Objects

It is easier for users to remember short naming paths instead of the complicated LDAP DN. The Active Directory also supports use of Relative Distinguished Names (RDNs) and User Principal Names (UPNs), to give users more flexibility in locating objects.

RELATIVE DISTINGUISHED NAMES   The RDN represents part of a DN that is an attribute of the object. In the previous example, the RDN of the child object is John Smith.

As an analogy, think of how we use names in everyday life. The master of ceremonies at a seminar might introduce a guest speaker as "Dr. John Wayne Smith III, with the Acme Company out of Houston, Texas." This is comparative to the DN, as it specifically identifies the person (object), where he is from (Houston representing the subdomain and Texas representing the top-level domain), and his organizational unit (Acme Company). However, if you were trying to find him in the crowded reception area after the seminar, you would merely ask if anyone had seen "John Smith"—his RDN (which is part of the more complete identification label used by the MC).

RDNs must be unique within the OU.

USER PRINCIPAL NAMES   The UPN is a "friendly" name for a user account, which consists of a shortened version of the user name and domain tree name where that account resides. An example of a UPN is jsmith@mydomain.com.

The GUID

The Globally Unique Identifier (GUID) is a unique numerical identification created at the time the object is created. An analogy would be a person's social security number, which is assigned once and never changes, even if the person changes his or her name, or moves.

Other Identifiers

Other names that can be used to uniquely identify an object include:

- Security Account Manager names
- NetBIOS names

The Active Directory also supports name formats familiar to users, such as:

- UNC names. *Example:* \\mydomain.com\finance\budget.xls

■ HTTP names. *Example:*
http://mydomain.com/finance/99budget.html

Naming Guidelines

DNS is the distributed namespace of the Internet, used to resolve Fully Qualified Domain Names to IP addresses. You should follow standard DNS naming criteria when you create your domain names. This is especially important in the case of your root domain.

■ Use characters a–z and 0–9.

■ You can use a hyphen (-) to separate/connect words.

■ Use simple and precise names, which are easy to remember.

Domain names can be up to 63 characters, and the entire FQDN can be up to 255 characters (including the periods). Although DNS supports Unicode, you should use Unicode characters only if all DNS servers support it.

It is best to limit the number of domain levels to simplify administration. However, in some cases you will need to create a tree consisting of multiple levels of domains. In the next section, we look at how to plan the namespace in such a hierarchy.

Checklist for Naming Objects in the Active Directory

There are many factors to consider when planning your object names in the Active Directory, including:

■ Name objects based on object classes into which they fit.

■ Modify the schema to create new classes of objects if necessary.

■ Specify additional global catalog servers if needed.

■ Consider the concepts of DNs, RDNs, and UPNs when creating objects.

■ Use standard DNS naming conventions for naming Active Directory objects.

■ Limit the number of domain levels to simplify administration.

HEADSTART OBJECTIVE 12.03

Planning a Namespace in a Hierarchy of Domains

One hierarchical group of domains and subdomains (one Domain tree) may be sufficient for the organization and administration of the objects in your network. The Active Directory offers a great deal of flexibility and control within the tree structure. The domains in the tree all share the same Directory, and administration can be centralized if desired. Network resources can be easily located throughout the entire tree.

On the other hand, security and administration can be decentralized if this better fits your organization's needs. Administrative functions can be confined to individual domains or even OUs. This makes for easy adaptation to changes within the company.

The steps in planning a namespace in a hierarchy of domains are:

1. Ensure that all domain names are unique.

2. Ensure that object names are unique in the multiple domain environment.

Considering the Need for Multiple Domains

All domains in a tree share the same Active Directory, and parent and child domains enjoy automatic two-way transitive trust relationships. This allows users to access resources for which they have permissions, regardless of the domain in which the resource resides. By default, administrative privileges do not flow down the tree; each domain is administered separately. However, you can easily create a centralized security structure if you wish, or delegate administrative authority on the basis of OUs. Because the domain is no longer the lowest level of administrative authority, as it was in Windows NT networks, it may not be necessary to create multiple domains for administrative purposes.

Microsoft recommends that, if possible, you should build your network as a single domain. This simplifies administration and may be appropriate for most small and medium-sized networks. Larger networks, and those with special considerations as listed next, will usually need to structure the network as a tree of domains.

Some reasons you might find it desirable to create multiple domains, joined in a hierarchical tree:

■ The organization spans international borders, and administration should be done in each country's own language.

■ Due to internal organizational or management considerations, managers wish to separate and distinguish between resources of different divisions or offices.

■ You want to reduce replication traffic due to slow links between locations.

Creating the Multiple Domain Namespace

Since multiple domains are often used because of geographic separation of company divisions, one logical domain-naming scheme would reflect the physical locations of the divisions. For example, in Figure 12-4 the parent domain, mydomain.com, has child domains whose names indicate the regional scope of each division (e.g., na.mydomain.com for North American offices and sa.mydomain.com for those in South America).

Each of those subdomains has its own "children" as well, further designating individual office sites within those broader regions. This allows each location to have administrative control over all the resources physically located there (the decentralized administrative model).

Checklist for Creating a Multiple Domain Namespace

Planning a multiple domain namespace can become extremely complex. Be certain you take into consideration all of the following issues:

■ Evaluate your need to create more than one domain, based on geographic separation, administrative decentralization, internal political considerations, and reduction of replication traffic.

FIGURE 12-4

The parent domain represents company headquarters, while the child domains are based on the physical location of the offices where the resources are located

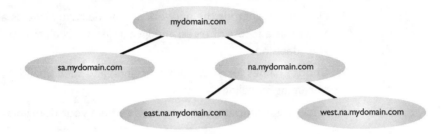

- Create names for your domains that will, insofar as possible, remain static.

- Create OUs within domains to further fine-tune the delegation of administrative authority.

- Consider the trust relationships between parent and child domains when planning the tree of domains.

on the **job**

If your previous experience has been in implementing Windows NT networks, you must "unlearn" much of what you know about domain models and structures. The Active Directory changes everything! It is very important that, prior to installing Active Directory on your domain controllers and setting up your domain(s), you develop a tactical deployment plan. Step One should be to carefully evaluate the physical and administrative structure of the company itself. Step Two involves deciding on an administrative model. Only after completing both these steps can you effectively determine what your domain structure and an appropriate naming scheme should be.

EXERCISE 12-2

Planning a Namespace for Multiple Domains

Your company, Accelerated Access, Inc., is a nationwide company with offices in Texas (Dallas, Austin, and Corpus Christi), California (Sacramento and Los Angeles), and Seattle, Washington. Because of differences in state laws under which the sites must operate and the physical separation of the network resources, you have determined that a multiple domain model with decentralized administration is appropriate. Each branch has its own sales force and manages its own finances.

1. Determine whether the network should be structured as a domain tree or as a forest of trees, and give at least three reasons for your decision.

2. Choose names for your root domain(s) and subdomain(s) according to naming guidelines.

3. Choose appropriate names for OUs within your domain(s).

HEADSTART OBJECTIVE 12.04

Planning the Integration of a Namespace with the Internet

Many organizations will already have an Internet presence prior to implementing the Active Directory services on their internal networks. Those that don't will probably want to develop a Web presence at some point in the future, and may have already registered a second-level domain name. An important consideration in planning your Active Directory namespace is whether to use the same domain name internally as the one you present to users outside your network, on the Internet. There are advantages and disadvantages to both choices. We'll look at factors to take into account, and best practices for implementing each.

Using a Single Namespace for the Internal Network and the Internet

The biggest advantage of using the same domain name internally and on the Internet is consistency. Tree names and user account names will be the same for both internal and external resources. There is also a (very) small savings in cost, since you only have to register one domain name with name registration authorities.

However, there are security issues that must be addressed when using one DNS namespace for both purposes. You certainly don't want to expose all of your internal resources to the entire Internet. One way to solve this problem is to set up separate DNS zones and servers for resolution of internal and external names. External resources may need to be mirrored inside a firewall so internal users are able to resolve both internal and external DNS names, while your internal resources are still protected from outsiders.

You may find it less complicated to establish separate and distinct namespaces for your internal resources and your web site, ftp site, and other external resources.

Using Separate Namespaces for the Internal Network and the Internet

Although this option requires you to register two domain names, it makes for easier implementation when security is a concern. When using this method, your Internet domain might be atlanticpublishing.com and your internal root domain might be atpub.com. This avoids the problem of having to mirror the external servers inside the firewall. You simply set up one zone outside the firewall with a server that will resolve atlanticpublishing.com names, and another inside that will resolve all atpub.com names.

You may wonder why atpub.com needs to be registered at all, since you're only using it internally. Although it would be possible to implement this option without registering the internal domain name, if another person or company did later register it, your DNS servers would not be able to distinguish between internal and external servers unless you established two separate zones to handle internal and external requests. Otherwise, they might return the "foreign" Web site when internal users try to access www.atpub.com.

Although the problem would seem to be solved by establishing two zones using internal and external servers, there could still be problems if someone else on the "outside" registers the name. Your company's clients and potential clients (and perhaps its managers and stockholders as well) would find themselves at the "wrong" www.atpub.com site anytime they tried to access it from home or anywhere else outside the company network. This could cause confusion, embarrassment, or even lost business. Remember that you would have no control over the type of material displayed on the "outside" site. Imagine your straight-laced boss giving out the "atpub.com" URL to his friends and family members, only to discover that when he types in that address from home, it brings up a Web page designed for the downloading of pornographic pictures. The small expense and effort required to register the internal name is well spent to prevent such incidents.

Registering the name of your internal site would not mean the IP address of the internal servers was registered or exposed to those on the Internet, it would merely reserve that domain name so that it couldn't be used by anyone else "out there."

Checklist for Planning Integration with the Internet

Depending upon your organization's needs, choose one of the following options in integrating your internal namespace with your Internet presence:

- Use the same namespace for external and internal resources if your primary concern is consistency and you don't want to register a second domain name.

- Use different namespaces for external and internal resources if your primary consideration is security and you want to avoid confusion over the two types of resources.

EXERCISE 12-3

Integrating a Namespace with the Internet

1. Your company, FastLink Corp., already has an established Internet presence using the registered domain name fastlink.com. You now want to implement an Active Directory namespace within the organization. You want to maintain consistency in naming of external and internal resources, but you also wish to protect the company's internal resources from the view of those outside. How can you accomplish both of these objectives?

2. You are designing the Active Directory namespace for a small firm that does not yet have an Internet presence, but plans to establish one in the near future. Of primary concern is high security and making a clear distinction between internal and external resources. What is the best way to plan the namespace to accomplish this?

HEADSTART OBJECTIVE 12.05

Planning DNS Support for Active Directory

DNS is the traditional name resolution method for the Internet, but in networks employing Microsoft operating systems prior to Windows 2000, WINS (Windows Internet Naming System) was the name resolution method of choice because of the reliance on NetBIOS. WINS resolves flat NetBIOS names to IP addresses, while DNS was designed to resolve hierarchical FQDNs to IP addresses. One advantage of WINS was its dynamic nature; while the DNS database was typically updated manually, the WINS database was updated without administrator intervention through NetBIOS broadcasts.

With the introduction of Windows 2000 and Microsoft's Dynamic DNS server, the role of DNS in Microsoft networks has undergone a drastic change. The Active Directory is dependent on DNS to function properly, and it will be the primary name resolution method in Windows 2000 networks.

DNS Structure and Management

DNS is based on the inverted tree structure, with the "root" of the tree at the top, and those domains residing just below the unnamed root being called *top-level* domains. As we discussed earlier, in the DNS tree of the Internet, the top-level domains are the commonly known .com, .net, .edu, .mil, .gov, and so forth. The domains that reside just below the top-level domains are called *second-level* domains. These are the domain names that are registered by organizations and individuals with the Internet registration authorities. All lower-level domains are called *subdomains*. Subdomains are not registered, and are managed by the owners of their parent (second-level) domains.

In NT, the domain name did not really relate to the DNS name, but in Windows 2000 networks, the Active Directory namespace is the same as the DNS namespace. Every domain in the Active Directory appears as a domain in DNS. Each domain is a partition in the Active Directory, and becomes a zone in DNS.

This means that the same criteria that apply to naming your Active Directory domains will apply when you create domains in DNS. The Active Directory and DNS namespace should be the same. As with Active Directory domains, separate DNS domains can be created to designate separate physical locations of company sites, or separate divisions or units within the organization.

DNS Service Resource Records

Active Directory uses DNS Service Resource Records, referred to as SVR RRs, to publish the addresses of servers so they can be located even if all you know is the domain name. The format for the name of a SRV RR is <service>.<protocol>.<domain>.

Newly installed servers can use Dynamic DNS (DDNS) to publish their addresses in the Directory upon installation.

Options for Choosing a DNS Server

It is not required that you use Microsoft's implementation of DNS for Active Directory, as long as the DNS server you use is RFC compliant. However, there are advantages to using Microsoft's DNS server. For example, it will store the zones for which it is authoritative in the Active Directory, and replicate DNS information to other Microsoft DNS servers as a part of Active Directory replication instead of the zone transfer process.

Dynamic DNS is also not required, but is highly recommended, so the necessary records will be automatically entered in the DNS database. If a static DNS server is used, records will have to be entered manually, which is time-consuming and more prone to error.

How DNS Information Is Stored in Active Directory

There are standard object classes for DNS information in the base schema included in Windows 2000. The DNS database information is stored in a subtree beneath each Windows 2000 server domain database tree. The root is in the System container object at the root of each Active Directory domain.

Advantages of Storing the DNS Namespace in Active Directory

You can store the DNS and Active Directory namespaces separately, but this offers few advantages. Administration will be more complex, and you will not derive the many benefits of Windows 2000's tight integration of Active Directory and DNS.

Integrating DNS storage into the Active Directory allows you to manage the storage and replication of both DNS and Active Directory information as one unified administrative entity. Active Directory's performance in directory replication is faster and more efficient because processing is done on a per-property basis. Using standard zone transfer/update methods, as you must do if you separate DNS and Active Directory storage, may require the transfer of the entire zone.

This directory-integrated zone storage also provides for enhanced security, since you can use the Access Control List editing feature to secure a dnsZone object container in a directory tree. Thus, you can grant granular access to the zone, or to a specific resource record within the zone.

Checklist for Integrating Active Directory and DNS Domains

- Define your DNS namespace.
- Identify your DNS resource records.
- Develop an integration plan.
- Create a DNS zone for each Active Directory Domain.

Planning and Identifying DNS Requirements to Support Single and Multiple Domains

1. Your small, nonprofit organization, Save The Flowers, operates out of one geographic location and administrative control is centralized. You have no Internet presence at the current time and no plans for developing one in the near future. You wish to set up your internal network using Active Directory. Based on this scenario, provide answers to the following questions:

    A. Should your DNS namespace be planned as a single or multiple domain environment?

    B. What is the best way to provide DNS name resolution within your internal network?

    C. Should your DNS and Active Directory namespaces be maintained separately or combined?

2. Your company has recently expanded from its original headquarters to open two branch offices in other states. Each office has control over its own administrative tasks. You are upgrading the existing Windows NT 4.0 network to Windows 2000 and implementing the Active Directory. Based on this scenario, provide answers to the following questions:

    A. Should your DNS namespace be created as a single domain or would multiple domains be more appropriate?

    B. Should you continue to use your existing DNS servers with standard zone storage and transfer methods, or integrate your DNS zone storage with the Active Directory? Why or why not?

    C. What are the advantages and disadvantages of using a Microsoft DNS server? What are the advantages and disadvantages of implementing Dynamic DNS?

Planning a Namespace for International Deployment

In one respect, planning the namespace for an organization that operates across national boundaries is easier, in that the geographic separation may provide you with logical divisions for the creation of separate domains. However, in most ways, the complexity of an international network will require more forethought and planning, and careful consideration of a multitude of factors.

Creating the Domain Structure for an International Organization

While Microsoft recommends setting up your Windows 2000 network as a single domain whenever possible, when a network crosses national boundaries, there are many good reasons to consider creating multiple domains. These include local control of resources, language differences, and policy differences.

Local Control of Resources (Decentralization of Administration)

Due to geographic separation, cultural differences, and disparities in laws and business practices, it is likely that administration of company business will be decentralized, at least to some extent. Creating separate domains will give local corporate managers more control of their own resources.

Language Differences

Separate domains may be necessary to address differences in language between offices located in different countries. Related reasons would be the use of different currency standards in different countries.

Policy Differences

If your company wishes or needs to address domain policy issues differently in different offices due to distinct management philosophies or other factors, you will need to establish separate domains, since Windows 2000 domain policies affect every user in a particular domain.

heads
① p

Remember that domain policies (which are different from group policies) apply to all the users in a particular domain.

Domain Replication Traffic

You can reduce the amount of network traffic due to replication by setting up separate domains. This becomes especially important in an international organization since the geographically separate locations may be connected via slow WAN links.

However, if creating domains that span geographic locations is desirable for other reasons, another way to reduce replication traffic is by configuring subnets within the same domain to belong to different *sites*.

Subnets and Sites

When a network, such as that of an international organization, is made up of subnets located in different geographic areas, the concept of Active Directory sites comes into play. Sites define the physical structure of the network—they do not show up in the Active Directory as part of the namespace. Sites are used in configuring replication.

Domain structure is entirely independent of site structure; a site can contain more than one domain, or a domain can span more than one physical site. A site can consist of more than one IP subnet, but they should be connected by high-speed links. Microsoft recommends that the connection be a minimum of 512 Kbps in bandwidth. In general, sites would cover about the same area as a typical local area network.

Establishing sites will allow you to define replication schedules for the Active Directory partitions. Replication between the domain controllers within the same site will be configured differently than replication between domain controllers that reside on different sites, since the latter will most likely be connected by slower links.

heads
⏻p

Remember that sites and domains are maintained separately in the Active Directory, and sites are not part of the namespace. Domains define the network's logical structure, while sites define its physical structure. When configuring sites, a primary consideration is the available bandwidth for replication traffic.

When to Create Site Objects

Sites can be used for several purposes, such as a means of exercising greater control over user logons, to help users find resources that are physically close to their area, and to reduce replication traffic within a domain.

Controlling Where Users Log On

If a domain spans geographic areas, and you wish to separate logons in one area from those in the other, you can create and configure two sites (such as Paris and London) for the domain. Then if a user logs on at the Paris site, the Active Directory will be searched for a domain controller that is local to that site.

Providing Information about the Physical Location of Resources

Sites can be used to provide users with a way to locate a global catalog server or a node in a DFS tree that is close to the user. Microsoft's upcoming release of Exchange Server is expected to use sites, and it is likely that more applications will be written to take advantage of the concept in the future.

Reducing Replication Traffic within a Domain

Perhaps the most important reason for dividing physically separated subnets into sites is to control the network traffic produced by replication of the Active Directory within a domain. Replication between different sites is "compressed"; in other words, the replication topology is configured with fewer replication paths between domain controllers. In addition, replication can be scheduled to occur at a time when there is less traffic on the network. (See Chapter 21, "Maintaining and Optimizing Active Directory," for more details regarding site replication.)

Checklist for Creating an International Namespace

Although at first glance, it may seem that the logical geographic divisions of the organization simplify creating an international namespace, several guidelines should be followed:

- Ensure that all domain names meet DNS standards.
- Use the same character set for network logon and Active Directory names.
- Customize the language for the user interface.

QUESTIONS AND ANSWERS

Is Active Directory scalable?	Yes! Unlike the Windows NT security database, which is limited to approximately 40,000 objects, Active Directory supports literally millions of objects.
Is Active Directory compatible with other LDAP directory services?	Yes! Active Directory can share information with other directory services that support LDAP versions 2 and 3, such as Novell's NDS.
Must the Active Directory's logical structure mirror the physical structure of the organization?	No! Active Directory allows you to arrange resources in logical groupings and locate them by name regardless of where they may be physically located, making the physical structure transparent to users.
If my company already has a registered domain name on the Internet, can we use that for our Active Directory namespace?	Yes! The existing namespace can be extended so that you are able to use the same namespace for both internal and external resources, and can use the same logon and user names internally and externally.
If my company already has a registered domain name on the Internet, do we have to use that for our Active Directory namespace?	No! You can have two different namespaces to separate your internal and external resources, in order to provide for a more defined separation of the two, and to simplify the configuration of your browser and/or proxy client.

Applying Guidelines when Planning an Active Directory Namespace

Careful planning of the Active Directory namespace prior to implementation will save you many headaches later, and ensure that your organization reaps all the benefits of Microsoft's new and exciting directory services.

Basic guidelines to apply when planning your namespace include:

1. Determine the scope of your Active Directory based on the size, structure, and physical environment of your organization.

2. Define your Active Directory's top-level domain name based on the type of business or organization or country of origin.

3. Organize your Active Directory information, and locate basic information about Active Directory before defining your Active Directory domains.

4. Consider the types of objects you want the Active Directory to define.

5. Consider whether you will need more than one Active Directory.

6. Consider whether the administration of Active Directory resources will be centralized or decentralized.

7. Plan the naming of objects in the Active Directory by constructing LDAP naming paths and short naming paths, as well as naming paths for down-level clients (SAM names and NetBIOS names).

8. Plan unique domain names within the domain tree.

9. Plan the naming of trees within the forest to reflect the organizational structure.

10. Plan the integration of Active Directory with DNS by using the same criteria to create your Active Directory and DNS namespaces.

11. Consider special needs when planning for an international organization, such as differences in language, currency, local laws, and business practices.

Remember: planning is important. Creating the right tree structure for your organization is a highly individual matter. It is possible to reshape the tree by moving domains within it, but taking the time to create the domain structure that will most effectively work within the parameters of your company's physical and administrative organization will save you a lot of time and effort later on.

ACCELERATING TO WINDOWS 2000

The Active Directory itself is a whole new way of doing things for Administrators who worked with Windows NT. The new, hierarchical structure of the directory services allows for easier management and location of resources across the network, regardless of their physical location.

Domain Objects

While the number of user, group, and computer accounts in an NT domain was limited by the size of the SAM database (to approximately 40Mb, or 40,000 accounts), Active Directory domains are not subject to such limitations. Millions of objects can be stored in one Active Directory.

Domain Controllers

In a Windows NT network, a single Primary Domain Controller holds the security database for the domain. Although Backup Domain Controllers can be added for fault tolerance to authenticate user logons when the PDC is down, changes cannot be made to the security database until the PDC comes back online. There is no PDC in Windows 2000. Instead, the Active Directory is replicated to all Domain Controllers in a domain; they act as peers and all are capable of managing changes and fully performing all functions of a DC.

Namespace

The Active Directory namespace, unlike the flat NetBIOS-based namespace of NT

ACCELERATING TO WINDOWS 2000

domains, is arranged in a hierarchical manner in which the names of child objects include the names of their parent objects. This mirrors the DNS namespace used on the Internet, and offers much more naming flexibility.

Role of DNS

In Windows NT networks, DNS was an optional name resolution method, used primarily for accessing external resources (on the Internet) and compatibility with UNIX systems. WINS was the preferred method for resolving names within the internal network. Windows 2000 requires that you implement DNS (or its new and improved version, Dynamic DNS) in order for the Active Directory to work correctly.

Organizational Units

In the Windows NT networking model, the domain was the smallest level of administrative

authority. Windows 2000 allows you to create OUs within domains and delegate the administration of those OUs, providing much more specificity in assigning administrative tasks and responsibilities.

Multiple Domains and Trusts

When designing a multidomain Enterprise network using Windows NT, you are typically limited to a few domain masters: the master domain model, the multiple master model, and the complete trust model. In all of these models, in order for users to access resources across domains, explicit trust relationships must be established. With the Active Directory, trusts are already in place between parent domains and their "children," and unlike Windows NT trust relationships, these trusts are two-way and transitive, allowing a user with the appropriate permissions to access resources in any domain in the tree.

CHAPTER SUMMARY

Planning the namespace for your Active Directory can be more complicated than it might appear at first. There are many issues to be considered, including both the physical and the logical structure of your organization. It is also important to evaluate the possibilities relating to anticipated growth and/or restructuring in the future.

The Windows NT domain model is not a good guideline for developing your Active Directory structure. The NT namespace is flat, while the hierarchical nature of the Active Directory namespace and its integration with DNS require rethinking your domain naming scheme. If you already have a presence on the Internet, you will need to determine the best way in which to integrate your internal and external resources, either by creating a new namespace for the internal network, or by extending the existing namespace.

If your company's operations extend beyond the borders of one country, you will have additional considerations in planning the Active Directory domain tree or forest of trees. Creation of additional domains or trees may be based on language and cultural differences, differences in local law, management philosophy, and business practices, as well as bandwidth considerations if geographically separated sites are linked by low-bandwidth connections.

The Active Directory gives Administrators a great deal of flexibility in delegating responsibilities, and proper planning of the namespace and naming of the objects within it will allow you to take full advantage of Windows 2000's new administration, security, and resource location features.

 TWO-MINUTE DRILL

- ❏ A directory service stores information about users and groups, computers, printers, security data, and other network objects.

- ❏ While the NT directory services were flat and self-limiting, the Active Directory supports millions of objects and is built on a hierarchical structure like the Internet.

- ❏ Windows 2000 domain names are DNS names, and the Active Directory is compatible with Novell Directory Services (NDS) and other directory services that conform to LDAP (Lightweight Directory Access Protocol) standards.

❏ A *namespace* is a characteristic of directory services representing a space in which a name is resolved, or translated into the information represented by that name.

❏ The Active Directory namespace is used to resolve the name or attributes of an object to the object itself. *Attributes* are data that describe or identify the object.

❏ Active directory namespaces fall into two categories: *contiguous* and *disjointed*.

❏ A contiguous namespace is one in which the child object contains the name of the parent domain. A contiguous namespace in Windows 2000 is called a *tree*.

❏ The tree represents the entire hierarchy of objects. Domains contain other objects; within domains reside deeper level containers, and within those containers are the "endpoint" objects.

❏ When more than one tree is created in a Windows 2000 Active Directory, the collection of trees is called a *forest*. Each tree will have its own distinct namespace.

❏ When trees are grouped into a forest (creating a disjointed namespace), a trust relationship automatically exists between the parent domains of the trees. This trust relationship, like that between parent and child within the same tree (and unlike Windows NT trusts), is two-way and *transitive*, which means every domain in the forest can share resources.

❏ Before you can create trees and/or forests within your organization's namespace, you must consider a scheme for naming the domains and subdomains that will inhabit them.

❏ Because Active Directory names are DNS names, the DNS service must be installed and configured in order for Active Directory to work properly.

❏ The first domain you create in Windows 2000 will become the root domain in the Active Directory. It is important that you choose a name that will remain the same, regardless of company reorganization and other organizational changes.

❑ There are two ways to locate basic information about Active Directory. You can use RootDSE (the Root Directory Specific Entry) to locate objects, or RootDSE can be used to access standard information about Active Directory.

❑ *Objects* in the Directory represent network resources, and can be grouped in *classes*. A class is a group of objects with the same types of attributes, or characteristics.

❑ Objects that can contain other objects are known as *container objects*. A special type of container object that you can create in the Active Directory is the Organizational Unit (OU).

❑ The *global catalog* (GC) contains information about all of the objects in a tree or an entire forest.

❑ Each Active Directory object must have a name, to identify it to users on the network.

❑ DNS is the distributed namespace of the Internet, used to resolve Fully Qualified Domain Names to IP addresses.

❑ Domain names can be up to 63 characters, and the entire FQDN can be up to 255 characters (including the periods).

❑ The Active Directory offers a great deal of flexibility and control within the tree structure. The domains in the tree all share the same Directory, and administration can be centralized if desired.

❑ Because the domain is no longer the lowest level of administrative authority, as it was in Windows NT networks, it may not be necessary to create multiple domains for administrative purposes.

❑ Since multiple domains are often used because of geographic separation of company divisions, one logical domain-naming scheme would reflect the physical locations of the divisions.

❑ The biggest advantage of using the same domain name internally and on the Internet is consistency. Tree names and user account names will be the same for both internal and external resources.

❑ You may find it less complicated to establish separate and distinct namespaces for your internal resources and your web site, ftp site, and other external resources.

❑ Registering the name of your internal site would not mean the IP address of the internal servers was registered or exposed to those on the Internet, it would merely reserve that domain name so that it couldn't be used by anyone else "out there."

❑ DNS is the traditional name resolution method for the Internet, but in networks employing Microsoft operating systems prior to Windows 2000, WINS (Windows Internet Naming System) was the name resolution method of choice because of the reliance on NetBIOS.

❑ DNS is based on the inverted tree structure, with the "root" of the tree at the top, and those domains residing just below the unnamed root being called *top-level* domains.

❑ Active Directory uses DNS Service Resource Records, referred to as SVR RRs, to publish the addresses of servers so they can be located even if all you know is the domain name.

❑ The DNS database information is stored in a subtree beneath each Windows 2000 server domain database tree. The root is in the System container object at the root of each Active Directory domain.

❑ While Microsoft recommends setting up your Windows 2000 network as a single domain whenever possible, when a network crosses national boundaries, there are many good reasons to consider creating multiple domains, including local control of resources, language differences, and policy differences.

❑ Remember that domain policies (which are different from group policies) apply to all the users in a particular domain.

❑ Sites define the physical structure of the network—they do not show up in the Active Directory as part of the namespace. Sites are used in configuring replication.

❑ Domains define the network's logical structure, while sites define its physical structure. When configuring sites, a primary consideration is the available bandwidth for replication traffic.

❑ Creating the right tree structure for your organization is a highly individual matter. It is possible to reshape the tree by moving domains within it, but taking the time to create the domain structure that will most effectively work within the parameters of your company's physical and administrative organization will save you a lot of time and effort later on.

SELF TEST

The following questions will help you measure your understanding of the material presented in this chapter. Read all of the choices carefully, as there may be more than one correct answer. Choose all correct answers for each question.

1. The name resolution and location service used by Active Directory is:

    A. WINS

    B. HOSTS file

    C. DNS

    D. HTTP

2. The term that best describes an object into which you can put other objects is:

    A. Hierarchy

    B. Container

    C. Site

    D. Schema

3. What is the type of namespace in which the name of the child object in the hierarchy always includes the parent domain's name?

    A. Disjointed namespace

    B. Distinguished namespace

    C. Conventional namespace

    D. Contiguous namespace

4. The trust relationship between a parent and child object in a contiguous namespace is:

    A. One-way: parent domain trusts child domain.

    B. One-way: child domain trusts parent domain.

    C. Two-way: parent and child domains trust each other.

    D. By default, there is no trust relationship between the parent and child domains.

5. The .com, .net, and .org domains commonly seen on the Internet are known as:

    A. Domain extensions

    B. Top-level domains

    C. Root domains

    D. Second-level domains

6. A group of objects in the Active Directory with the same types of attributes or characteristics is called a:

    A. Class

    B. Container

    C. Distribution group

    D. Global catalog

7. A "friendly" name for a user account that consists of a shortened version of the user name and the domain tree where that account resides is called the:

    A. Globally Unique Identifier (GUID)

    B. Relative Distinguished Name (RDN)

    C. Distinguished Name (DN)

    D. User Principal Name (UPN)

8. Which of the following is a DNS naming convention (Choose all that apply)?

   A. Characters A–Z and a–z are allowed.

   B. Numerical characters 0–9 are allowed.

   C. Names should be long and complex to ensure their uniqueness.

   D. Underscores should be used to connect words.

9. Which of the following is *not* a good reason to create multiple domains?

   A. The organization spans international borders, and the office in each country wishes to conduct administrative tasks in its native language.

   B. You wish administration to be centralized.

   C. You want to reduce the amount of replication traffic.

   D. Managers wish to separate resources due to internal political considerations.

10. Which of the following is true of the practice of using the same namespace for external (Internet) resources and the internal network (Choose all that apply)?

   A. You will only have to register one domain name.

   B. There will be no need for separate DNS zones to resolve internal and external names.

   C. You will have to address security issues to keep external users from accessing the internal network.

   D. It often proves to be more complicated to administer than establishing separate and distinct namespaces for internal and external resources.

11. The purpose of DNS is to:

   A. Resolve NetBIOS names to IP addresses

   B. Resolve Fully Qualified Domain Names (FDQNs) to IP addresses

   C. Resolve computer hardware addresses to IP addresses

   D. Automatically assign names to newly created objects

12. Which of the following is used by Active Directory to publish the addresses of servers?

   A. RFCs

   B. Zone transfers

   C. SRV RRs

   D. NetBIOS names

13. Which of the following is true of DNS when used with Active Directory (Choose all that apply)?

   A. Microsoft's DNS server is the only one that works with Active Directory.

   B. Dynamic DNS is required if you wish to use Active Directory.

   C. If a static DNS server is used, records must be entered manually.

   D. There are no advantages to using Microsoft's DNS server.

14. One or more IP subnets, connected by fast links, make up a:

   A. Site
   B. Directory
   C. Domain
   D. Forest

15. Which of the following is true of sites (Choose all that apply)?

   A. Sites can be used to control user logon location.
   B. Each site requires a Primary Domain Controller.
   C. Sites are the smallest unit of administrative authority.
   D. Creating sites can help reduce replication traffic.

13

Planning the Organization of a Domain

HEADSTART OBJECTIVES

When it comes to organizing objects in a domain, planning is key to success. With Active Directory, we now have the opportunity to lay out our domain in a hierarchical structure. This can make administration much easier. It can also, however, if not done properly, make administration much more difficult. The most important part is organizing objects and network resources so that you, as the administrator, can find them, and users can get to the information they need.

The issue of security is important in the object and organization layout of a network. If you don't have your domain planned and set up so you can easily administer it, and your users can't get to the resources they need, then you are failing as an administrator. In this chapter, we look at the basic practices that make up the planning and design stage of laying out the domain. There are, of course, many different scenarios that can come up in terms of how the network objects can be organized. In this chapter, we look at several examples based on network size. Object-oriented networking is one of the most important topics discussed in this chapter. What this means is that each network component will have one or more objects in the domain associated with it. This will be familiar to you if you understand how Domain Naming System (DNS) structures are organized. Active Directory was built off of this, and considerations must be made between DNS naming and Active Directory Naming. The reason for this is for expansion. Even if the Internet isn't a factor in your business today, it may very well be an integral part of your organization in the future. Planning ahead will prevent having to redo the entire object naming and planning stage.

HEADSTART OBJECTIVE 13.01

How the Organization of Objects in a Domain Affects Network Administration

In order to make administration as efficient as possible, the organization of the network objects in a domain has to be planned out. This involves establishing a namespace plan. This is going to be new for many people, but will seem somewhat familiar to network administrators who have dealt with NetWare's Directory Services. There are many variables that determine the organization of objects in the domain, including:

- Number of servers
- Number of sites
- Number of Organizational Units (OUs) needed
- Number of users
- WAN connectivity

The biggest variable in the preceding list is probably the number of sites or locations. This is because, in most cases, the network objects will be organized based on location and break down from there. Figure 13-1 shows an example of a company with locations in different countries.

| FIGURE 13-1 | Multiple-site network |

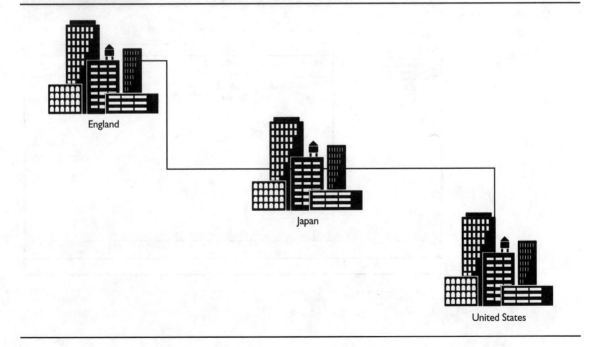

When you are planning your domain structure, you have to consider if you will have multiple domains, or one domain with OUs that group similar objects. This is where the hierarchical structure comes into play. Figure 13-2 shows the Active Directory utility for managing users.

By default, there are various built-in containers for keeping information organized. As shown in Figure 13-2, you see a Users container and a Built-In container. From the root of the domain, you can create OUs and name them whatever you wish. Figure 13-3 shows what a domain layout would look like in a DNS environment. Windows 2000's Directory should be laid out in the same hierarchical fashion, starting at the root and going down through the tree.

FIGURE 13-2

Active Directory User and Group Manager

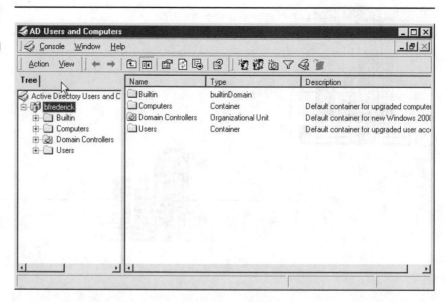

FIGURE 13-3   DNS layout

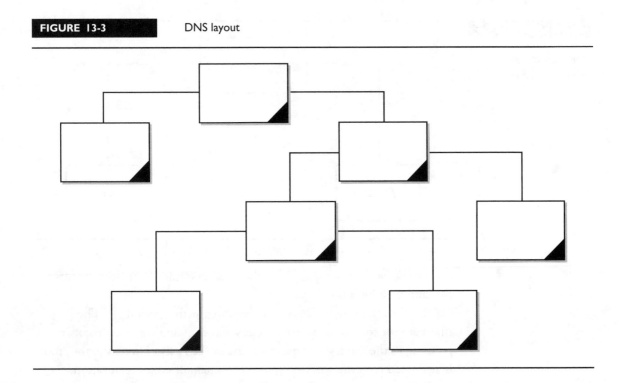

Different Network Layouts

When designing your directory structure, you have to take into consideration how you want to divide the company structure. The size of your organization can make a difference in how you want the general layout to be. Larger company structures may require that you start your layout with locations from the root, and then branch out by department. Other designs may include country first and then location if there are multiple locations in the countries, as shown in Figure 13-4.

To make it even more confusing, you can have the department branches first, and then break down each department by its location. This may make for tougher administration. If you have too many branches, finding network objects can be more confusing. The key factor is always to lower

FIGURE 13-4

Directory structure
based on country

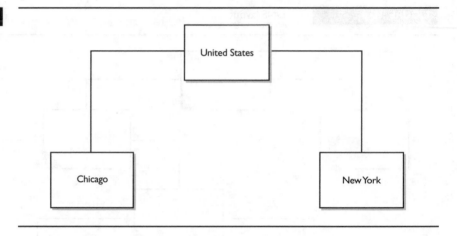

administrative duties. Figure 13-5 shows an example of the departments first and then location.

"Root" in the Internet sense is represented with a period ".". The Internet root consists of 13 root servers that contain delegation records pointing to the top-level domain servers. In the Active Directory, the "root" is associated typically with the top-level domain of your organization.

Multiple Network Operating Systems

In many environments today, there is a mix of NetWare and Microsoft networking products. With this in mind, you have to consider the interaction of the different directory services. NetWare and Microsoft have similar Directory Service methods, but they are vastly different at the core. This means you have to decide how they will interact with each other, or if one will be the primary directory controlling the other.

Once the decisions are made, you have to decide what tools you will use. There are different tools available for migrating from NetWare to working together with NetWare. These include services for NetWare to connect to the NetWare directory and use both Windows NT and NetWare servers and networks simultaneously. The migration tools allow for moving from

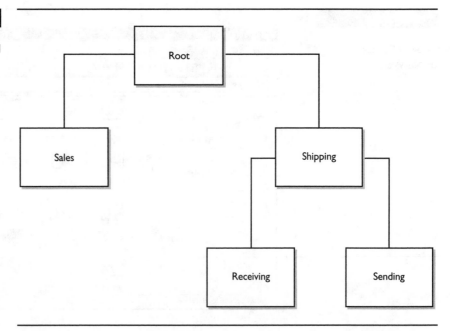

NetWare Directory Services to Microsoft's Directory Services. One such
utility is the Directory Service Migration tool, which is used to migrate
from NetWare to Windows 2000. Another is the Gateway Service for
NetWare. This allows for access to NetWare servers from a Windows 2000
network. Figure 13-6 shows the Control Panel applet for the Gateway
Service for NetWare.

In some cases, you will have both NetWare and Windows 2000. With
this in mind, you have to decide what directory will be the primary
directory. Windows 2000 has the tools to manage NetWare directory
objects. NetWare also has tools to manage directory objects. The goal is to
have only one directory to administer. If you have to administer multiple
directories, your administration is not very affective. The point to
remember is to make administration productive to accomplish the goals you
have set for your network.

Gateway Service
for NetWare

Load Balancing

A massive number of users can make for a challenging decision when it
comes to laying out your network design in terms of directory. You don't
want to have a directory that isn't laid out in a fashion of equilibrium. What
I mean is, you don't want a lopsided tree. This can make administration
harder, but the biggest factor is replication of information. Having a
lopsided tree can mean lengthy synchronization time. You want to avoid
having the sort of layout shown in Figure 13-7. This type of network layout
would be harder to maintain and harder on your servers. As we said before,
when you have too many OUs, or too many objects within a container, the

FIGURE 13-7

Lopsided layout

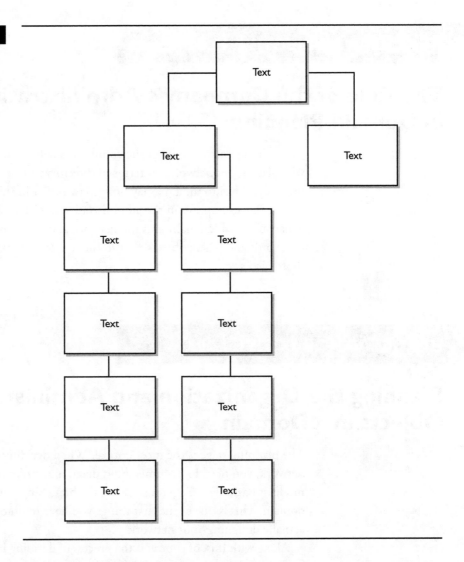

domain is harder to administer. A nicely structured organization makes administration and routine network directory maintenance much easier.

The Role of the Company's Administrative Model in Domain Planning

The administrative model of the company is commonly used as a guideline when laying out networks in terms of directory services. This is very similar in look and feel to the DNS layout we saw earlier in this chapter.

The one exemption in the administrative model example is the IT department, which maintains the network and needs information such as passwords and where objects exist in the tree so they can administer those pieces.

Planning the Organization and Administration of Objects in a Domain

The planning stage is the most critical. When deciding how to lay out your network, you need to document and diagram the object model. The object model is basically a diagram showing the branching out of each OU or domain. This is one of the first things you have to do before you start actually designing your network.

Along with this, of course, is the process of deciding how the network will be divided. What I mean is, dividing the network in a logical sense versus a physical sense. The physical divisions have to be taken into account, but the logical divisions may be different. You may want to make more than one diagram showing your alternatives. Making these diagrams involves not only laying out the different divisions, whether they are the domain or OUs, but also requires knowing where each object will go in the network. Figure 13-8 shows a diagram with more detail than the previous diagrams.

FIGURE 13-8   Network directory design with detail

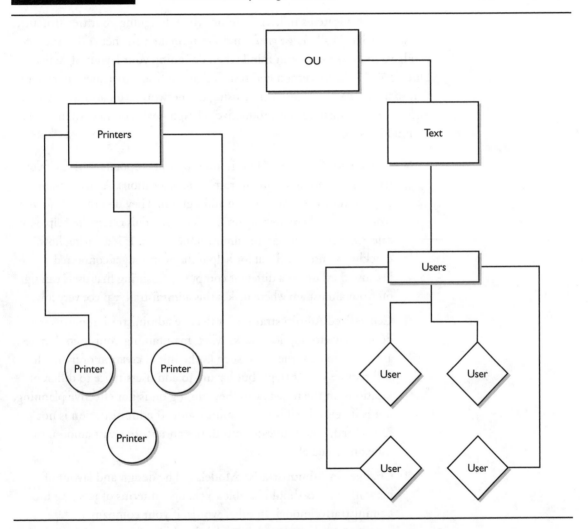

Another factor that can make a difference in the layout of your network is whether you will have container administrators. What I mean is, you can have someone administer a certain portion of the network directory tree, and this can help decide how to organize the objects in your network. This may be based again on location, job function, or other certain terms. Remember, the goal is always to make administration easier and less time consuming.

Design Goals

There are various items to keep in mind when designing your tree structure. These are what I call *design goals*. In order to make your network a success, you have to keep the user in mind when designing your layout of Active Directory. There are certain end results that you want to achieve to ensure that users have a much easier time using the network. You also want to make sure administration is productive. Design goals you may want to keep in mind include:

- **Single User Sign-On** This is important in corporate settings if you have users who may sign on from various locations. All users want to do is sit down at a workstation and sign on. They do not want to worry about where they are on the network. This can make help desk calls regarding user sign-on almost nonexistent. It is amazing how quickly end users will call for help if they cannot get connected because they are on a different computer. Ensuring that users can sign on from almost anywhere makes this administrative piece very low.

- **Centralized Administration** Effective administration means you do not have to duplicate tasks when maintaining your users. There are going to be some tasks, such as the initial creation of users, that will require repeat steps, but having to add users twice to different locations on the network so they can log on is not effective planning, nor is it centralized for an administrator. If administration is not centralized, you duplicate your duties and waste a vast amount of time on remedial tasks.

- **Changes in Administrative Models** The design and layout of network objects should be able to change in terms of meeting the administrative model. In other words, if your company is restructured, your network model should be able to accommodate these changes. Another possibility is if your company merges with another company. Even if the other company is prepared to merge existing networks, having your network ready will make the migration to one network easier. If you have different network directory structures, bringing the directories together can be difficult.

On that same note, if you run them as separate directories with administrators at each location, there has to be the ability to send information back and forth, and security configuration has to be taken care of.

These are only a few of the main areas with which you should be concerned. There are many different variables in any network, and we cannot cover every possible scenario here. If you start with the three basics listed previously to form the foundation to your planning, you can build your focus from there.

While designing the network, you have to look at the design in two facets. One is the detail. You have to view the network piece by piece, detail by detail. Along with this is the flip side, where you have to think outside the box and look at the big picture. Look at how the design will affect the company as a whole, and how each of the detail pieces will affect each other. When adding an office, for example, and adding a container to the directory, how will this affect replication across the wide area network connection?

Building from the Ground Up

When it comes to designing your network, you need to build from the ground up. Just as a tree grows from its roots, so does your network. The network starts at the root and branches out from there. This is important, because once you have your network laid out, you may not be able to make major changes.

As stated earlier, the idea of having more than one diagram worked out ahead of time is important so you can explore all the possibilities and scenarios available. If you start designing by department, for example, and two years later you have multiple locations, you have a mess on your hands. At this point, you then have to Band-Aid your existing network design or start over. In most cases, it is best to start over so everything is done the way you want it, again, from the ground up. This is not true in all cases, but the point to be stressed again and again is that planning is vital to success.

Interoperability

Another piece to organizing and planning your domain involves the interoperability of Windows 2000 Active Directory with other servers such as Windows NT 4.0. Remember that Windows NT 4.0 had a Primary Domain Controller (PDC) with Backup Domain Controllers (BDCs). Windows 2000 does not have these, but does have emulation pieces that will allow for interoperability with these types of servers. One of the roles a Windows 2000 domain controller can assume is the PDC Emulator.

There are two type of domains with Windows 2000. The first, and default, is a mixed domain where you have Windows NT 4.0 domain controllers on the network. The second is the native domain that only has Windows 2000 domain controllers. Once you convert to a native domain, you cannot go back to a mixed environment. This is very important to remember. Figure 13-9 shows an example of a mixed domain.

FIGURE 13-9

Mixed domain environment

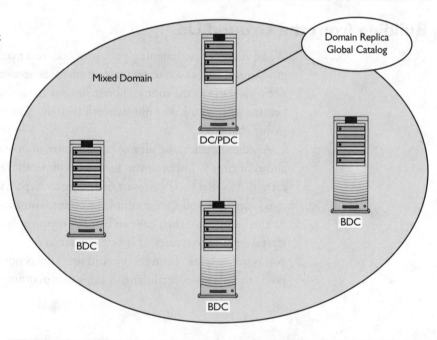

There are different scenarios in which the mixed or native environment is ideal. If you are doing a gradual conversion from a Windows NT 4.0 to a Windows 2000 network, the mixed environment is appropriate. If you know for sure you will not have any Windows NT servers on your network once you convert to the new operating system, then you can have a native environment. You have to look not only at your upgrade path now, but consider the future; you will not be able to go from native to a mixed environment once you choose native.

HEADSTART OBJECTIVE 13.04

Analyzing Various Domain Organizational Models

We have briefly looked at the most common types of organizational models. Now let's get to the detail of each organizational design. The most common one you will be presented with in Microsoft exams is a WAN environment with multiple locations. Also, there is the departmental model for a single, or multiple locations. These are most common examples and the ones we will look at here.

Multilocation WAN Environment

There are some very important factors to consider when designing a network with multiple locations:

- How many locations
- Server locations
- Replication
- User load balancing

These areas are the most important when designing your directory. The reason for this is *replication*. Replication across a domain happens for fault tolerance. Instead of the directory information being stored in one location, it is replicated to other domain controllers in case the master database becomes corrupt or the master database domain controller fails. The master database is known as the Global Catalog (GC). Figure 13-10 illustrates replication.

We can only cover some of the basics of replication here; a whole book will eventually be written on this subject. This is going to be one of the more challenging aspects of Windows 2000 for administrators. Ensuring that your locations have efficient speed over affordable WAN links is vital to network success. If your design is causing delays in logging on and

FIGURE 13-10   Domain directory replication

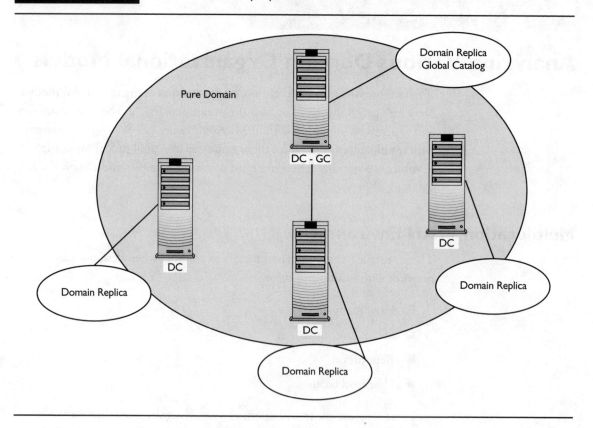

problems for users accessing resources, then your design is flawed. The key to successful WAN environments involves having a domain controller at each location so people are not logging on across WAN links. This is similar to having a BDC in each location with Windows NT 4.0. It is better to replicate the small changes across WAN links versus users authenticating across them. This makes for more efficient use of the WAN bandwidth.

Departmental Environment

When you have an environment with very few multiple locations, you can have a design that is divided by departments versus locations. This makes more sense for a small network. The Enterprise environment is much larger and requires a different configuration as stated earlier. Figure 13-11 shows what different departmental OUs would look like in Windows 2000.

FIGURE 13-11

Department organizational units

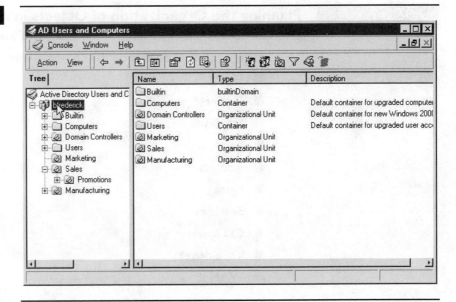

Best Practices for Organizing Objects in a Domain

When deciding what the best design is for your domain, you have to make replication an important part of that decision making. The reason for this is the fact that WAN links are slower than your LAN connectivity. You should have a domain controller at each location so your users are not authenticating for resources across WAN links. This is standard for most operating systems.

It is important that you and your users can easily utilize resources, and that administration is centralized. Keep this in mind when designing your directory. Look at the network from the viewpoint of a user, and consider each type of user when determining your network layout.

EXERCISE 13-1

Planning the Organization of Objects in a Domain

In this exercise, we look at some of the basic steps involved in planning.

1. Make a list of all objects on the network. This includes:

   ■ Users

   ■ Printers

   ■ Workstations

   ■ Servers

   ■ Routers

   ■ Hubs

   ■ Switches

   ■ CD towers

   ■ Tape drives

   ■ WAN links

2. Determine how you want to lay out your network based on the size of your network.

3. Draw up a diagram with your choice of design.

4. Draw up a second diagram based on other possibilities (e.g., location versus department).

5. Compare the design to your administrative model.

6. Evaluate the administration factors of maintaining the users, printers, servers, etc.

7. Now look at your network in terms of applications to which users will have access.

8. Make changes to your existing diagrams based on application and user resource access.

9. If you have multiple sites, evaluate if the WAN links mean moving objects around in the tree.

10. Once you have your design drawn to your satisfaction, start adding items to your domain.

11. Reevaluate your design with some of the basic objects added to see if it works.

heads Up

Active Directory will be a key focus on the exam, and understanding how to lay out your domain will be very important. Be sure to brush up on these areas.

on the Job

When I designed one of my first networks, very little planning and design went into the process. It turned out that we ended up having to redo everything, which meant a lot of overtime hours spent in starting over. This is not much fun, especially if you are on salary. I can't stress enough how I learned not to be quick about the layout without first considering all the options available and the implications if the right decisions are not made. Be sure you don't go through what I did. With proper planning and decision making, you can avoid the extra hours spent reconfiguring something that could have been done right the first time.

ACCELERATING TO WINDOWS 2000

The biggest change with Windows 2000 is the implementation of Active Directory Services. This means that you have to plan properly for your domain to make administration easier and access to user resources efficient. With Windows NT 4.0, the domain existed on more of a flat level versus a hierarchical structure.

With Windows 2000 you now have network objects that represent your users, printers, workstations, servers, and eventually hubs, routers, switches, and other hardware found in networks. With this in mind, the planning stages are even more vital to success. There is context to work about, as well as a true directory of network items.

QUESTIONS AND ANSWERS

If you do not have Windows NT 4.0 Servers on your network, which domain model do you use?	Native
Both Windows NT 4.0 and Windows 2000 will be on your network. Which domain model do you use?	Mixed
A gradual migration to Windows 2000 will take place. Which domain model do you use?	Mixed and then native once everything is converted.
There is a possibility of one Windows NT 4.0 Server on the network indefinitely. Which domain model do you use?	Mixed

CHAPTER SUMMARY

When designing your domain and the structure of your directory, you have to take several steps to plan properly. The goal is to make administration easier once the network is implemented. This requires proper planning and design. The other main goal is to make it as easy as possible for your users to access the resources they need to get their jobs done. Windows 2000 now has Active Directory for organizing the various network objects, including printers, users, workstations, file servers, and volumes.

Planning the domain organization involves determining how you will divide up the network. This can be by location or by department, for example. There are other ways to divide up the network, but these are the most common. Look at all of your options when considering how to organize your network. This is because of replication, user authentication, and other reasons.

Integration with Windows NT 4.0 and possibly NetWare is important when considering how your directory will work. There are different configurations that can be accomplished with either of these two network operating systems on your network. When considering your network layout, plan for the possibility of other network operating systems. This way, if changes occur for whatever reason, you have things in place to plug the other NOS into your existing network.

Having a diagram of the planned layout of your network is a good idea. It is also good to have multiple scenarios drawn up so you can make the appropriate decisions on what to do with your network. The key points to keep in mind are:

- Centralized administration and management
- User access to resources
- WAN links and how they will affect performance
- Number of objects in the domain
- Replication of Directory database

These are just a few of the items you need to consider. Keeping these in mind is important to forming a starting point to successful planning of implementing a Windows 2000 network.

✔ TWO-MINUTE DRILL

❑ In order to make administration as efficient as possible, the organization of the network objects in a domain has to be planned out. This involves establishing a namespace plan.

❑ By default, there are various built-in containers for keeping information organized: a Users container and a Built-In container.

❑ Larger company structures may require that you start your layout with locations from the root, and then branch out by department. Other designs may include country first and then location if there are multiple locations in the countries.

❑ The key factor is always to lower administrative duties.

❑ "Root" in the Internet sense is represented with a period ".". The Internet root consists of 13 root servers that contain delegation records pointing to the top-level domain servers. In the Active Directory, the "root" is associated typically with the top-level domain of your organization.

❑ Having a lopsided tree can mean lengthy synchronization time. When you have too many OUs, or too many objects within a container, the domain is harder to administer.

❑ The administrative model of the company is commonly used as a guideline when laying out networks in terms of directory services.

❑ When deciding how to lay out your network, you need to document and diagram the object model. The object model is basically a diagram showing the branching out of each OU or domain.

❑ Look at how the design will affect the company as a whole, and how each of the detail pieces will affect each other.

❑ One of the roles a Windows 2000 domain controller can assume is the PDC Emulator.

❏ Replication across a domain happens for fault tolerance. Instead of the directory information being stored in one location, it is replicated to other domain controllers in case the master database becomes corrupt or the master database domain controller fails.

❏ The key to successful WAN environments involves having a domain controller at each location so people are not logging on across WAN links.

❏ When you have an environment with very few multiple locations, you can have a design that is divided by departments versus locations.

❏ When deciding what the best design is for your domain, you have to make replication an important part of that decision making. The reason for this is the fact that WAN links are slower than your LAN connectivity.

SELF TEST

The following questions will help you measure your understanding of the material presented in this chapter. Read all of the choices carefully, as there may be more than one correct answer. Choose all correct answers for each question.

1. For a hierarchical structure without multiple domains, what would you use to organize the network?

   A. Organizations

   B. Groups

   C. Organizational Units (OUs)

   D. Units of Organization

2. Which of the following is not a default container with Windows 2000?

   A. Built-In

   B. Users

   C. Computers

   D. Accounting

3. What is the biggest factor in determining your network object layout?

   A. Number of Organizational Units

   B. Overall Size of the Network

   C. Number of Login Scripts

   D. Novell Directory Services

4. When you have a NetWare 4.x and Windows 2000 mixed environment, what is the biggest concern?

   A. Size of the network

   B. Different Types of Directory Services

   C. Bindery Emulation

   D. NetWare Client

5. Which Control Panel applet allows for integration between NetWare and Windows 2000?

   A. Gateway Service for NetWare

   B. Gateway Service for Novell

   C. Gateway Service for NDS

   D. Gateway Service for NOS

6. When there is a large number of objects, what do you want to plan for when designing your network?

   A. Large quantity of users in one container, with a small number of objects in other containers

   B. Lopsided network layout

   C. Equal layout of objects throughout the domain

   D. Duplicate users throughout the network

7. What can be used as a guideline to assist in layout of the network?

   A. Administrative Model

   B. List of users

   C. Physical Diagram of all objects on the network

   D. Department List

8. What can you use when planning to help you visual your network layout in hierarchical fashion?

   A. Diagrams showing the layout

   B. Written documents with user information

   C. Printer configuration print-outs

D. BIOS configuration pages from Workstations

9. If you want to have a person at each location help you administer the network, what would you do?

   A. Make that person an administrator on the network

   B. Make that person an administrator of his or her location container

   C. Keep that person as a general user and have him or her contact IS for help

   D. Give that person multiple user accounts for administering the network, and one for each location

10. Select the design goals discussed in this chapter. (Choose all that apply.)

    A. Single User Sign-On

    B. Changes in the Administrative Model

    C. Centralized Locations

    D. Centralized Adminstration

11. If you are only going to have Windows 2000 domain controllers on your network, what type of network do you have?

    A. Mixed

    B. Native

    C. Multi

    D. Master

12. If you have an environment that will contain both Windows NT 4.0 and Windows 2000 servers as domain controllers, what domain model would you use?

    A. Native

    B. Native Mixed

    C. Mixed

    D. Mixed Native

13. What is the master database copy of the directory called?

    A. Master Database

    B. Global Catalog

    C. Global Database

    D. Master Catalog

14. If you have a mixed environment domain model, what role must one of your Windows 2000 domain controllers assume?

    A. Primary Domain Controller

    B. Backup Domain Controller

    C. Domain Controller Master

    D. Primary Domain Controller Emulator

15. If you have both NetWare and Windows 2000 servers on your network, what is the main consideration with this scenario?

    A. Determining which Network Operating System directory you will use

    B. Making sure all NetWare boxes are on Token Ring

    C. Native versus Mixed domain model

    D. Gateway Services for NetWare

14

Implementing a Domain and Planning and Implementing a Multiple Domain Directory

HEADSTART OBJECTIVES

14.01	Creating a New Domain
14.02	Creating Organizational Units within a Domain
14.03	Creating Objects in a Domain
14.04	Managing Objects within a Domain
14.05	Determining the Need for Multiple Domains
14.06	Implementing a Tree of Domains

The Active Directory is the directory service for Windows 2000. It is implemented through incorporating multiple domains into a forest structure. The multidomain structure can use multiple Domain Naming System (DNS) namespaces. The forest structure enables multiple namespaces to cohesively function in the same distributed Active Directory database.

HEADSTART OBJECTIVE 14.01

Creating a New Domain

Creating a new domain is as simple as installing a single domain controller. The installation process is identical for a domain controller as it is for a member server. This process was discussed in Chapter 2, "Installing Windows 2000 Professional."

What makes a domain controller installation different from that of a member server is the process of installing the Active Directory. This process is executed with the DCPROMO.EXE command, better known as the Active Directory Wizard.

When Windows 2000 Server is installed on a new computer, it automatically becomes a member server, or stand-alone mode. If Windows 2000 Server is upgraded from a Windows NT Primary (PDC) or Backup Domain Controller (BDC), it will start the Active Directory Wizard immediately after installation. Otherwise, the installer will need to start the Active Directory Wizard.

Before a member server can be upgraded to a domain controller, it must first run NTFS as its file system. NTFS is absolutely required for the Active Directory to perform its multimaster replication. If the server is not already using NTFS, you can type **CONVERT /FS:NTFS** at a command prompt, which is most easily executed by clicking Start | Run, typing **CMD** in the box, and then clicking OK. This is one of the few configuration changes in Windows 2000 that requires a reboot. The server will only convert the file system to NTFS after it is rebooted.

When installing Windows 2000 domain controllers, you must use NTFS, or convert the hard drive to NTFS before running the Active Directory Wizard.

EXERCISE 14-1

Creating a New Domain

There are two ways of executing the Active Directory Wizard:

1. Click Start | Run, type **DCPROMO,** then click OK.

   Or,

2. From the Navigation bar of the Configure Windows 2000 screen, click Active Directory. You will then be taken to the screen shown in Figure 14-1. In this dialog box, scroll down until you see the item to start the Active Directory Wizard, and click it.

3. The Active Directory Wizard begins with a Welcome dialog box. Just click Next to continue.

FIGURE 14-1

Active Directory

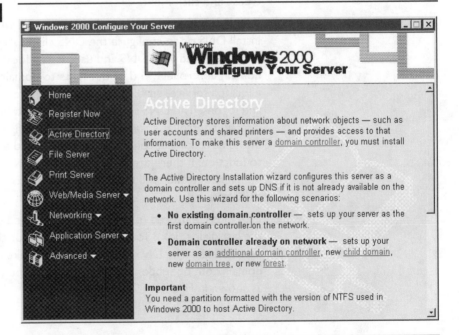

4. After that, you are prompted to explain what type of domain controller you are creating. Is this a domain controller for a new domain, or is it a domain controller for an existing domain? Select the first option for a new domain and then click Next to continue with the Wizard.

5. The following dialog screen asks whether this domain will be the root of a new domain tree, or if it will be a subdomain of an existing domain tree. Domain trees are linked by their DNS namespace, which is further explained in a later section of this chapter. If a domain will be the first one in the forest, it will have to be a new domain tree. Therefore, click on the first option "Create a new domain tree." Click Next to continue.

6. Now the Active Directory Wizard knows that this is a domain controller for a new domain, which is the root of a domain tree. Next, a screen prompts you to either create your new domain tree in a new forest, or in an existing forest. Since this is going to be a root domain for a forest, select "Create a new forest of domain trees" and click Next.

7. If DNS is not configured on this server, you will be prompted to install DNS or to configure the DNS client. Active Directory is fully integrated with DNS and uses it as a locator service between domain controllers, and from clients to domain controllers. DNS, as a locator service, enables communications for replication, queries, and logons. The DNS server that is authoritative for the new domain controller's zone should be preconfigured with the name of the new domain controller, in order for the Active Directory to function. If there are problems with a DNS configuration, the domain controller will typically exhibit Remote Procedure Call (RPC) errors.

8. If DNS is configured (or after DNS is installed or configured from the last dialog box), you will be prompted for the DNS name of the new domain. The DNS domain name will take the form of domain.com or subdomain.domain.com. Type the name in the box as shown in Figure 14-2, then click Next.

FIGURE 14-2

A new DNS domain name

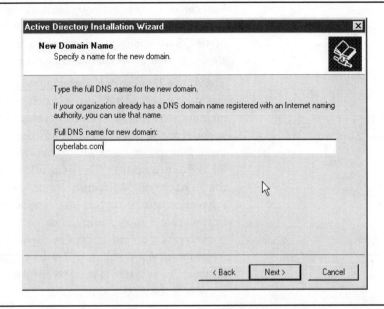

heads

⓵p

DNS is required for Active Directory to be installed. If the Active Directory Wizard does not detect a DNS server on the network, it will prompt for DNS to be installed on the server, or for the DNS client to be configured.

9. For backward compatibility with clients and servers that use the legacy Windows NT domain structure, the Active Directory Wizard will request a NetBIOS name. Not only will it request the name, but it will suggest one that is a shortened version of the DNS domain name. If the name of the domain is the same as any NetBIOS entity on the network, then the Wizard will append a digit to the end of the name to ensure that it is unique. For example, if the NetBIOS name of a server somewhere on the network was CYBERLABS, and the DNS name of the domain was CYBERLABS.COM, then the Wizard would suggest CYBERLABS0 as the NetBIOS name. Even though the Wizard will suggest a name, you do not have to use it.

You can use any name you please as the NetBIOS name, as long as there are no NetBIOS conflicts on the network. Either accept the NetBIOS name suggested, or type a new one in the dialog box shown in Figure 14-3. Then click Next.

10. The Active Directory is a distributed database that is contained in files on the server hard drive. Additionally, to be able to execute multimaster replication and to enable better disaster recovery, updates to the directory are recorded in log files. The placement of these files should be carefully considered and should enable growth for the entire domain. The default location—C:\WINNT\NTDS—in the %systemroot% directory is not ideal. Best practices for installation usually suggest placing system files on a separate partition from data and applications. Since system files have a much smaller growth rate than either data or applications, this partition is usually limited in size. If possible, place the database files on a separate partition from system files, and ensure that it has enough space for growth of the directory.

11. Log files are also suggested by the Active Directory Wizard to be placed in the C:\WINNT\NTDS directory. This, again, is not ideal. To optimize performance, it is best to place log files on a separate

NetBIOS Domain Name

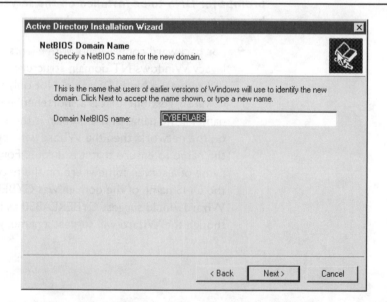

physical disk from the database files. This optimizes performance, since both physical disks can write the changes and write the logs at the same time. The separate disks also enable disaster recovery, since log files are used to recover the database. If the log files are kept with the database files on a single disk that is damaged, they will not be of any use. When using a large RAID 5 array, separate physical disks may not be available. In that case, create separate partitions, and place the log files and the database files away from each other and away from the system files. The Active Directory Wizard prompts for file locations. Click Next after entering your information.

12. In the dialog box shown in Figure 14-4, you are prompted to decide the location of SYSVOL, or the system volume. SYSVOL is a directory structure that is replicated to every domain controller. It contains the information required by the Active Directory for replication purposes, and also contains group policy information, scripts, and the NETLOGON folder. The default folder location is C:\WINNT\SYSVOL. Placing this directory with the system files is not recommended. Where possible, place these files in a partition that has enough room for growth. After typing in the appropriate information, click Next.

FIGURE 14-4

Shared System Volume

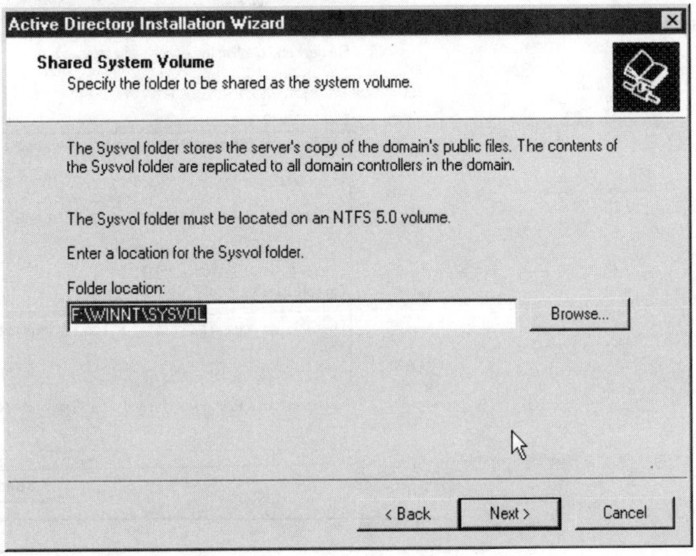

13. The Wizard will attempt to contact the DNS server, and if not found or if no dynamic updates are found, you will be prompted to install and configure DNS on the domain controller. Permissions are the dialog subsequent to any DNS notification. This dialog is meant specifically for backward compatibility with legacy Windows NT Remote Access servers. If no legacy servers will be used for Remote Access, then select the option for Permissions compatible only with Windows 2000 servers, and click Next.

14. The next security-related item is the Directory Services Restore Mode Administrator Password. This will be a different password than the server's current local Administrator account, and likely a different password from the Domain Administrator's account. Type in a password in the Password box and then retype it in the Confirm password box. Whatever password is selected here, make sure to write it down and place it aside in case you need to restore the Active Directory on this domain. Then, click Next.

15. There will be a Summary dialog as illustrated in Figure 14-5. You should review this page and be certain that the intended

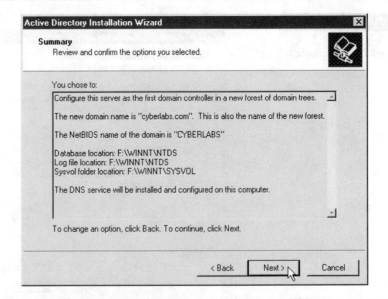

FIGURE 14-5

Summary dialog

configuration for the new domain controller is what is listed on this page. You have your last chance here to click Back and change your answers to the various dialog screens. If the configuration is correct, click Next.

16. The Active Directory will begin installing with the dialog shown next and configuring the new domain controller. This process is rather lengthy—it certainly is not instantaneous—but the time it takes to install and configure will vary depending on your selected configuration.

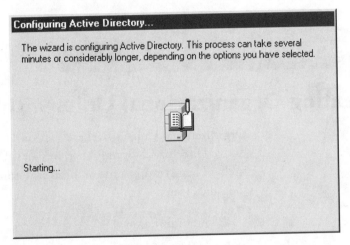

17. When the Active Directory configuration is complete, you will see the Completion screen. Click Finish and you will then be prompted to restart the domain controller so that the changes can take effect.

Whenever you configure the Active Directory Wizard, it will branch out into various screens depending upon your answers to the previous screens. For example, a member server that is going to be promoted to an additional domain controller in an existing domain will skip many of the screens that you needed to answer in order to create the first domain controller in a new domain that is the root of a new forest. There is no need to select anything beyond which domain this domain controller will be added to, the DNS configuration, locations for the files on the server itself, and a restore mode password. All the other information would be known by the existing domain, and replicated to the new domain controller once it had completed its configuration.

DCPROMO is not simply for promoting a server; it is also used to demote a domain controller into a member server or stand-alone server. If, for example, you wish to demote a domain controller to a member server, you would run DCPROMO, check whether the domain controller is the last in its domain, type in the administrator's name and password, give the new local administrator account a password, and then finish.

Creating Organizational Units within a Domain

Organizational Units (OUs) are the containers for objects within the Active Directory. Not only that, but an OU is an Active Directory object itself. When creating a hierarchical structure, there are several items you should consider:

- Administration
- Hidden objects
- Group Policies
- Organizational structure

If an organization is planning on decentralizing its administration, it can use OUs to reach its goal. This is ideal for many reasons, not the least being the reduction in the incremental costs caused by having multiple domains. If an organization does implement OUs for delegation of administrative duties, then those OUs should be placed at the top of the structure. The top-level administrators can then further delegate administrative duties to lower-level OUs.

Hidden objects are those user accounts, computers, printers, or other Active Directory objects that an organization may not want to have browsed by users. These should be placed in an OU, literally off to the side of the structure below their designated administrator's OU. Then, permissions can be placed on the OU so that no one else can see the objects.

Group Policies are used to manage the environment for users and computers. A Group Policy can be applied separately to users from their computers, so that designated computers have their specific environment, and so that designated users are granted the appropriate environment and access regardless of which computer they log on to. These OUs should be placed below their designated administrator's area. The OUs should be created to group computers together that require a specific environment, and to group users together that require a specific environment. The users and computers do not need to be grouped directly together.

The lowest level of OUs can be created to organize users or computers in a logical manner. Typically, this is a method that duplicates the organizational chart of a company. When creating OUs, remember the following:

- OUs are easily created, moved, and deleted.

- OU changes do not affect network traffic to any great degree.

- Objects in one OU can be easily moved to other OUs.

<table>
<tr><td>EXERCISE 14-2</td></tr>
</table>

Create an Organizational Unit

To create an OU, click Start | Programs | Administrative Tools

1. Select the Active Directory Users and Computer. You will see a screen similar to that in Figure 14-6.

2. For a top-level OU, you do not need to expand the domain hierarchy. However, if you will be creating OUs below other existing OUs, you will want to click the plus (+) sign to the left of the domain name in the left pane to expand it. Navigate to the container where you wish to place a new OU in the left pane.

3. Right-click on the container. Then, from the pop-up menu, select New. From that menu, select Organizational Unit. Or, you may select the container, click the Action menu, and choose New.

4. The dialog for creating a new OU will appear, as shown next. Type in the appropriate name and click OK. The OU should appear in the

FIGURE 14-6

Active Directory Users and Computers

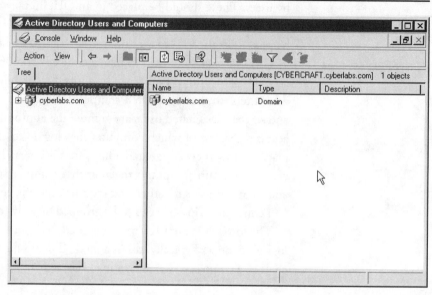

Active Directory Users and Computers screen below the container in which you placed it.

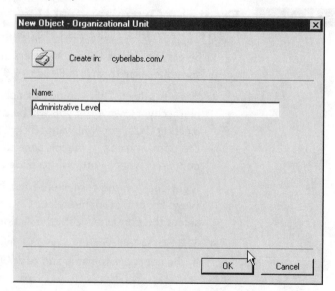

Creating Objects in a Domain

The Active Directory is a storage space for user accounts, computers, printers, and other network resource information. These network resources are stored as objects in the Active Directory database.

Most Active Directory objects are created in the same way that an OU is created. The exceptions to this rule are only for those items that are created using a special application that is Active Directory aware, or for those items created using other utilities, such as the Resource Kit utility ADSIEdit.

Most of the day-to-day administration of user accounts and resource information will occur in the Active Directory Users and Computers console. To create any object, you can right-click on the container for that object, select New, and then select the type of object that it will be. Alternatively, you can click on the container so that it is highlighted, then click the Action menu, choose New, and then select the type of object that you are creating.

For example, the process for creating a new logon account begins with selecting User from the New dialog. A New Object—User dialog box will appear. In it, complete the user's name and logon ID, as shown next. Then, click Next.

The second user dialog prompts for the password, password confirmation, and some basic password settings, as shown next.

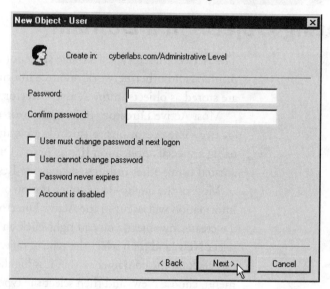

A final summary screen appears. Click Finish, and the user is created. There are two categories for groups in Active Directory:

- **Security**   The group can be used for the assignment of permissions.
- **Distribution**   The group can cross over into other domains to "distribute" it.

There are three types of groups available, and they can be one or both categories:

- **Domain Local**   Both a security and distribution group that can contain users, Global groups, and Universal groups. This type of group stays within a single domain
- **Global**   Both a security and distribution group that can contain users and other Global groups. This type of group stays within a single DNS namespace, or domain tree.
- **Universal**   Only a distribution group that can contain users, Global groups, and other Universal groups. This type of group can be used anywhere within a forest.

When you create a group, by selecting Action menu, New, and Group item, you will be prompted for the group's name, scope, and type. Once this group's scope and type are selected, they cannot be changed.

Creating a computer in the Active Directory uses the same method as any other object. When creating each computer, the administrator can select the user or group account within the Active Directory who can have permission to join that computer to the domain. This is an important feature when rolling out Windows 2000 where different individuals are expected to join their own workstations to the new Active Directory.

Even though a printer is an object within the Active Directory, it is not a Windows 2000 printer. The object is simply a printer for pre-Windows 2000 computers. Windows 2000 printers are made available to users through the Printers folder on the Windows 2000 servers.

on the Job

When upgrading Windows 9x computers to Windows 2000 Professional, the new Windows 2000 machines will need to be able to join domains. Users can be granted the authority to join their own computers to the Active Directory domain. This permission is granted through the computer object properties, which an administrator should create in advance of the upgrade.

HEADSTART OBJECTIVE 14.04

Managing Objects within a Domain

When you created a user in the previous section, you did not see all the attributes that are available to a user account. As an administrator, there are many more things that you will want to manage simply from an information perspective, much less a security perspective.

To edit information about any object in the Active Directory, you can open up the Active Directory Users and Computers console, navigate to the object's location in the hierarchy, and double-click it. A user account's properties are shown in Figure 14-7.

Note the many tabs at the top of this dialog screen. The user account has many variables that apply to its environment simply by changing its properties. Table 14-1 guides you in deciding which property set to select and edit when establishing a user's properties.

FIGURE 14-7

User properties

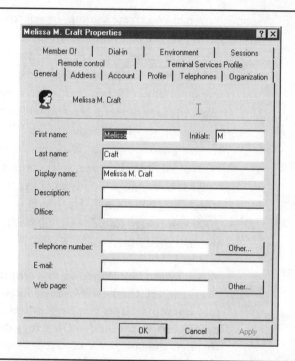

TABLE 14-1

User Properties
Information

Tab	Function
General	Name, e-mail address, and general information about the user
Address	Street address, state, zip code, and country
Account	Account name, password and security information such as Kerberos requirements, Smart Cards, and DES, etc. required for logon
Profile	Desktop profile location
Telephones	The user's phone numbers for home, mobile, pager, office, and IP phone, plus a space for comments
Organization	Title, department, company, and links to the manager's user account and direct reports
Member Of	Groups in which this user is a member, ability to add and remove groups

TABLE 14-1	**Tab**	**Function**
User Properties Information *(continued)*	Dial-In	Remote access information, granting permission to dial in, and whether callback is enabled.
	Environment	Terminal Services startup environment information
	Sessions	Terminal Services session timeout and disconnection information
	Remote Control	Terminal Services remote control settings
	Terminal Services Profile	The profile to use when entering a Terminal Services session

The properties of groups are shown in Figure 14-8. They are identical for each type of group, except that the scope and type of group is designated and cannot be changed. The most important changes that you can make are to the Membership tab and the Members Of tab. The Membership tab lists the users and groups who are members of this particular group.

FIGURE 14-8

Group properties

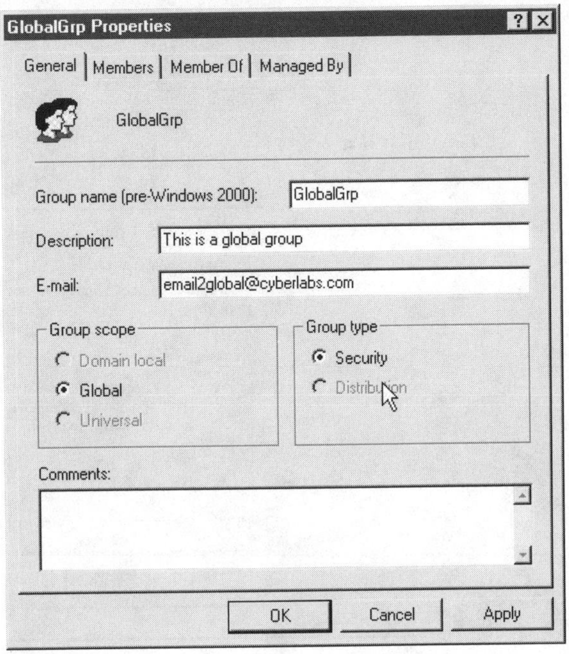

New in the Active Directory are *nested groups*. This is done by making groups members of other groups. When one group is nested within another, the child group automatically inherits the permissions of the parent group. The child group can be granted additional permissions as well. Nesting groups is especially recommended for Universal groups. Universal groups publish their user list within the Global Catalog (GC). To avoid an excessively large GC, use Global groups nested within Universal groups.

Nested groups are used in domains that are running in Native mode. Domains are automatically in Mixed mode and must be changed to Native mode. To change a domain to Native mode, first make sure that no more legacy Windows NT domain controllers exist in the domain. Then, in the Active Directory Users and Computers console, right-click on the domain and select Properties, as is shown in Figure 14-9. Click Change Mode and

---

FIGURE 14-9

Changing a domain to
Native mode

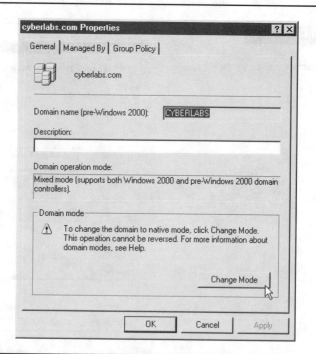

the domain will be changed to Native mode. Once changed to Native mode, the domain cannot be changed back.

Moves and deletions of Active Directory objects are a standard part of an Active Directory administrator's job. Moving involves right-clicking on the object that you wish to move to another OU, and then navigating and selecting the destination container in the dialog. To delete an object, you can click once on an object and then press Delete on your keyboard, or right-click on the object and select Delete. You will be prompted to confirm the deletion before it is actually deleted. Remember that deleted objects exist in the Active Directory as *tombstones* for a period of time before they are actually purged from the directory. Tombstoning, or marking an object for deletion, will remove the item from view, but will enable all replicas to agree to delete the object. If this method was not used, there could be spontaneous reappearances of previously deleted objects.

Manage Computers

When Windows 2000 computers have joined an Active Directory domain, they can be managed. The Computer Management console can be invoked from the computer account within the Active Directory, already connected to the computer. To administer a computer, right-click on the computer object within the Active Directory Users and Computers console, then select Manage from the pop-up menu.

HEADSTART OBJECTIVE 14.05

Determining the Need for Multiple Domains

Each namespace is a different partition of the Active Directory. This means that a domain is, by itself, a single partition of the database. Each domain can contain about a million objects. If an organization has more than a million objects, it should probably implement multiple domains.

The domain is the ultimate administrative division within a forest. An administrative account does not pass to another domain without explicit permissions from that administrator, and without being a member of an enterprise administrative account that has been granted permissions to multiple domains. Whenever a group within an organization wishes to completely maintain a separate administrative model, a new domain can be designated for that group. Use this method sparingly, however, because OUs can offer nearly the same level of administrative delegation of control. The areas of administration that cannot be separated by OUs are the domain-wide password policy, the account lockout policy, and the Kerberos ticket policy.

Domains are a namespace division. If a company has two subsidiaries, each with a separate namespace, then they will require two separate domains to be able to use them. For example, Cybrrr, Inc. is a refrigerator company, and it has a subsidiary called CybrLabs, which is a scientific research firm that investigates cryogenics. It also has a subsidiary called BrrrServices, which is a company that repairs refrigerators. Each of the companies has a separate DNS name: cybrrr.com, cybrlabs.com, and brrrsvc.com. To use each of these names, there must be three domains.

HEADSTART OBJECTIVE 14.06

Implementing a Tree of Domains

A domain tree is a set of domains that share a namespace, as well as a common schema, configuration, and GC. A domain tree is created by several domains sharing the same root domain name. The tree must be implemented by the first domain having the root of the namespace.

For example, Roots Co., a forestry service company, has a domain name of roots.com. Since Roots Co. uses roots.com on the Internet, they decide to use corp.roots.com as the root namespace for their Windows 2000 domain tree. Two other domains are planned: branch.corp.roots.com and leaf.branch.corp.roots.com. When the three domains are installed, they form a domain tree as shown in Figure 14-10.

FIGURE 14-10

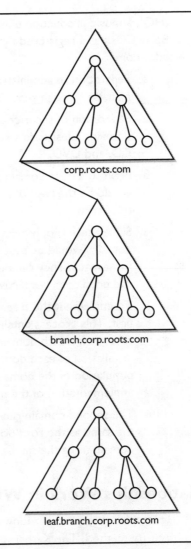

corp.roots.com

branch.corp.roots.com

leaf.branch.corp.roots.com

EXERCISE 14-3

Planning and Implementing a Tree

BeadyCDs is a company that produces compact disc products. They have three business units that have separate administrative groups. Each business unit has a separate security policy. The business units are Headquarters

(HQ), a music production unit (CD), and a video production unit (DVD). BeadyCDs has a registered DNS name: bdcd.com. To begin the design for bdcd.com:

1. Separation of administration can either be provided through an OU plan, or through separate domains.

2. Separation of security policy can only be provided by separate domains. Designate a separate domain for each business unit: HQ, CD, and DVD.

3. Next, the root domain must be decided. Logically, the HQ domain would be the root domain. This can be given the DNS name of bdcd.com.

4. Since there is only a single namespace (bdcd.com), the other two domains would be best served as subdomains of the same namespace. They can be given the names cd.bdcd.com and dvd.bdcd.com, respectively.

5. To implement the tree, always start by installing the root domain first. This process entails the registration of the service resource records for each domain controller and server in the DNS server, installation of each domain controller and member server, population of the domain with users and computers, and implementation of the network services.

6. The second domain can be either of the subdomains. The process is the same as the root domain. Finally, the installation of the third domain using the same process.

How Trust Relationships Work in Windows 2000

Trust relationships in Windows 2000 are based on Kerberos, an Internet security method. The Kerberos trust relationship is *transitive* and *bidirectional*. Bidirectional means that if the Cling_On domain trusts the Federation domain, then the Federation domain will also trust the Cling_On domain. Transitive trusts mean that if the Federation domain further trusts the Volcan domain as well as the Cling_On domain, then the Cling_On and Volcan domains implicitly trust each other.

Within a forest of domain trees, all domains automatically trust each other through the transitive, bidirectional Kerberos trusts. However, outside the forest, there are no automatic trust relationships. When a user within one domain in one forest must access a resource in a domain within another forest, then an explicit trust must be created. This trust, which is unidirectional and nontransitive, is exactly the same as a legacy Windows NT trust relationship. The domain in which the resource resides, known as the *resource domain*, must trust the domain in which the user resides, known as the *account domain.*

Trusts are executed using the Active Directory Domains and Trusts console. To establish an explicit trust in this console, right-click the domain to which you are adding a trust relationship. Choose the Properties option from the pop-up menu. Select the Trusts tab. To make the domain you have right-clicked able to offer resources to other domains, click Add under "Domains trusted by this domain." If you want to make users in this domain able to access another domain's resources, click Add under "Domains that trust this domain." Browse in your resulting dialog and select the appropriate domain, then click OK. Both domains involved in this transaction must establish their side of the trust relationship.

Implementing a Forest with Multiple Domain Trees

In its simplest form, a forest can be a single domain. Each time a domain is installed, the installer is requested to create a new forest or join an existing forest. As the domains grow, the forest grows. Domain trees must always remain wholly within a single forest, since their namespace cannot cross forests. A *forest*, by definition, is a set of domains and domain trees that use multiple DNS namespaces, yet share a single GC, a single schema, and a single configuration.

EXERCISE 14-4	

Planning and Implementing a Forest

Safer Shavers is a company that manufactures razors. It is a subsidiary of Grocer Aisles, Inc. Grocer Aisles also owns Blue Fruits and Red Breads. Both Blue Fruits and Red Breads are completely separate from Grocer

Aisles and Safer Shavers, with their own separate administrative groups and security policies. Two of these companies have different DNS names: safeshave.com and groceraisle.com.

1. There are four domains that need to be created to accommodate the two namespaces and the separate administration and security requirements.

2. Since there are two namespaces, the first decision for the forest concerns what the root namespace for the forest should be. Because Grocer Aisles is the owning company, groceraisles.com should be the root namespace.

3. Safer Shavers namespace is decided, so the placement of Blue Fruits and Red Breads in the forest is required. They can be placed below groceraisle.com or below safeshave.com. Since both of these companies are owned by Grocer Aisles, they should be placed in its namespace. Their names can be bluefruit.groceraisle.com and redbread.groceraisle.com.

4. The implementation of the forest begins with the root of the forest. This will be groceraisle.com.

5. The groceraisle.com subdomains (bluefruit.groceraisle.com and redbread.groceraisle.com) can be implemented second and third.

6. The safeshave.com domain can be implemented last. Note that the order of the implementation of each of these domains can be changed without any drastic consequences.

Querying Active Directory in a Multiple Domain Environment

When there are multiple domains, the Active Directory uses a GC to index its contents. The GC is a partial replica of each resource and account. When a user wants to access users that exist outside the user's domain, the user queries the GC automatically through the Windows 2000 Search utility. Browsing for some resources outside the domain, however, requires that the user is aware of the domain's namespace where the resource resides.

Developing a Plan for a Multiple Domain Directory

When you plan a forest, or multiple domain directory, you need to pay attention to where the user needs to log on. A domain, with a capacity of a million objects, can be quite large and complex, so do not be afraid to select a large portion of the Active Directory to be a single domain. Each user will log on to his or her domain's domain controllers. They cannot log on to another domain, even if the other domain is part of the domain tree or forest. The authentication process, from the user's perspective, is much improved when a domain controller is located near the users rather than several slow hops away.

Other items to remember when planning the domains are:

- Domains cannot be merged.

- Domains cannot be split.

- DNS must exist on the network, and must support service resource records. Dynamic update support is also recommended for DNS.

- Each physical site should be planned with a domain controller, a DNS server, and a GCS.

- Except for the Infrastructure FSMO, any domain controller can also be a GCS. Any domain controller may also be a DNS server.

- Domains are the ultimate administrative and security boundaries within a forest.

Developing a Plan to Delegate Administration in a Multiple Domain Environment

Since each domain is a separate administrative boundary, the delegation of administration among the domains is fairly simple to design. First, make sure that each domain is designated an Administrator or Administrative Group. When the same Administrative group is designated to manage two separate domains, then create a Universal group that is made a member of each domain's Domain Admins and Enterprise Admins groups.

There should also be a designated administrator or group of administrators who are given rights to manage the schema for the entire forest. This group should be a Universal group that is made a member of the Schema Admins group within each domain.

Within each domain, the top-level OUs should be designated as an administrative boundary. Administrators at the top level should be granted the right to delegate rights to other, lower-level OU administrators. When an administrator delegates authority within a domain, there is a simple process: create a group, grant the group the correct authority, and populate the group with users.

You can use a Delegation of Control Wizard to delegate authority over lower-level OUs. First, start the Active Directory Users and Computers console and navigate to the OU that you will be giving a user authority over. Right-click on the OU and select Delegate Control from the pop-up menu. The Wizard walks you through the process:

1. There is a Welcome dialog to bypass and then a screen that displays the OU path. Click Next to go past these screens.

2. In the third screen, click Add. Here you will select the group or user to whom you will grant administrative authority.

3. At the Predefined Delegations screen, you can select either a set of already established authorities, or you can click on "Do customized delegation" to define your own set of rights. Select "Do customized delegation," and click Next.

4. The Active Directory object type screen allows you to select an entire OU, or a set of objects within the OU, such as only users. Select the entire OU and click Next.

5. The Permissions box appears. To delegate all rights to this group, select Full Control and click Next.

6. You will be given a summary dialog last. Click Finish to establish the new authority.

Best Practices for Managing a Multiple Domain Directory

The best practices for managing a multiple domain directory are centered on coordination.

- Make sure that very few administrators are granted authority to manage more than one domain.

- Make sure that there are a few select administrators granted authority to extend the schema for the forest.

- When delegating authority, only delegate the individual rights required. For example, if a help desk will be taking over the task of changing passwords, only grant them the authority to change passwords, and do not grant them authority to change other features of the user objects.

- In designing OUs, make sure to designate authority for the top-level OUs to the top-level administrators in the domain. From there, those administrators can delegate individual rights to other administrators in lower-level OUs.

- Because the Active Directory uses multimaster replication, two administrators can make changes on different domain controllers that are in conflict with each other. Even though the last change will be the one accepted into the Active Directory, a good practice to establish is coordination of the management of Active Directory objects between the administrators.

ACCELERATING TO WINDOWS 2000

The Active Directory is an entirely new concept to Windows networking. Previously, Windows NT servers used a domain concept that enabled a single logon authentication to NetBIOS domains, if those domains were established with the correct trust relationships. Models of these domain configurations and trust relationships were created to enable the single logon. You may recognize some of these:

- Single Domain model
- Master Domain model
- Multiple Master Domain model
- Complete Trust model

Except for the Single Domain model, each of these models involves trust relationships that flow in a single direction from the domain that contains the resources to the domain that contains the user accounts. These trust relationships were nontransitive, so if Domain A trusts Domain B, and Domain B trusts Domain C, then there is no trust relationship between Domains A and C.

The Active Directory does away with the entire legacy Windows NT model system. It uses Kerberos trusts, which are both bidirectional and transitive, and which are always created automatically as domains are added to the forest. As a result, each domain within a forest has the potential of receiving access to the resources and accounts of other domains. Note the word *potential*. Even though the trust relationships exist, the Active Directory only enables a pathway between domains. The administrator must still grant permissions to users to access domains.

ACCELERATING TO WINDOWS 2000

The Active Directory forest contains a single schema for all domains within it to share. The schema is basically a list of the types of objects and their attributes that can exist within that particular forest. For example, the base Active Directory schema contains a user object with an attribute of e-mail address. There can be multiple instances of the user object: Bob with an e-mail address of bob@domain.com, Sandy with an e-mail address of sandy@domain.com, Joe with an e-mail address of joe@domain.com, and so forth. If one department requires a new attribute to the schema, it can be extended. However, what do you do if two departments want two different attributes, and don't want each other's attributes? The only thing that can be done is to implement two separate forests.

Another "forest-only" attribute is the use of User Principal Names, or UPN. The UPN is a name for users that is in the form of an e-mail address. Each forest can support a single UPN namespace. That means that if the UPN namespace is domain.com, then users who want to use cyberdomain.com cannot. They must create another forest with its own UPN. The UPN does not affect the user's e-mail address, however. It is simply in the same format as an e-mail address.

QUESTIONS AND ANSWERS

After changing a domain to native mode, Joe wants to install an NT 4 BDC. Why can't he?	After a domain is changed to Native mode, it cannot be changed back to Mixed mode. A Mixed-mode domain contains a PDC emulator that will serve BDCs. A Native-mode domain does not.
Grace has installed a domain that includes users from two business units. One of the business units will be spun off into another business. Can Grace split the domain?	No. A domain cannot be split. There are utilities such as ClonePrincipal or the Domain Migration Wizard for migrating selected users from one domain to another, however. Grace would not be able to retain the schema, configuration, or GC if the new domain was in a different forest, though.
Dave needs to change the phone numbers for a sales office that was moved to a new building. Where would he go about changing these numbers?	Dave would use the Active Directory Users and Computers console.

CHAPTER SUMMARY

In this chapter, we discussed how to create a domain, and the process of upgrading a Windows NT 4.0 Primary (PDC) or Backup (BDC) domain controller to a Windows 2000 domain controller. We identified the process of creating a new domain, or adding to an existing domain, and also the purpose of domains and subdomains. We also installed and configured the Active Directory on a domain controller.

Next, we discussed the need to create organizational Active Directory objects within our domain to logically group users and computers, and ease administration.

We then discussed the various objects that can be created within a domain, such as users, computers, printers, and other network resource objects. We also learned how to manage the more complex Active Directory objects, such as user accounts that contain large amounts of information on the user, including permissions and group membership.

We then discussed implementing a tree of domains, and the details involved in deciding whether to create a new domain namespace, or have the new domain managed by a parent domain. This included a detailed description of the delegation of administration between managing a multiple domain directory.

TWO-MINUTE DRILL

❏ The Active Directory is the directory service for Windows 2000. It is implemented through incorporating multiple domains into a forest structure.

❏ Creating a new domain is as simple as installing a single domain controller. The installation process is identical for a domain controller as it is for a member server.

❏ When Windows 2000 Server is installed on a new computer, it automatically becomes a member server, or stand-alone mode.

❏ Best practices for installation usually suggest placing system files on a separate partition from data and applications. Since system files have a much smaller growth rate than either data or applications, this partition is usually limited in size.

❑ To optimize performance, it is best to place log files on a separate physical disk from the database files.

❑ DCPROMO is not simply for promoting a server; it is also used to demote a domain controller into a member server or stand-alone server.

❑ Organizational Units (OUs) are the containers for objects within the Active Directory. Not only that, but an OU is an Active Directory object itself

❑ The Active Directory is a storage space for user accounts, computers, printers, and other network resource information. These network resources are stored as objects in the Active Directory database.

❑ Creating a computer in the Active Directory uses the same method as any other object. When creating each computer, the administrator can select the user or group account within the Active Directory who can have permission to join that computer to the domain.

❑ To edit information about any object in the Active Directory, you can open up the Active Directory Users and Computers console, navigate to the object's location in the hierarchy, and double-click it.

❑ New in the Active Directory are *nested groups*. This is done by making groups members of other groups.

❑ Each namespace is a different partition of the Active Directory. This means that a domain is, by itself, a single partition of the database.

❑ A domain tree is a set of domains that share a namespace, as well as a common schema, configuration, and GC. A domain tree is created by several domains sharing the same root domain name.

❑ Trust relationships in Windows 2000 are based on Kerberos, an Internet security method. The Kerberos trust relationship is *transitive* and *bidirectional*.

❑ In its simplest form, a forest can be a single domain. Each time a domain is installed, the installer is requested to create a new forest or join an existing forest.

❏ When there are multiple domains, the Active Directory uses a GC to index its contents.

❏ A domain, with a capacity of a million objects, can be quite large and complex, so do not be afraid to select a large portion of the Active Directory to be a single domain.

❏ Within each domain, the top-level OUs should be designated as an administrative boundary. Administrators at the top level should be granted the right to delegate rights to other, lower-level OU administrators.

SELF TEST

The following questions will help you measure your understanding of the material presented in this chapter. Read all of the choices carefully, as there may be more than one correct answer. Choose all correct answers for each question.

1. Which of the following is the executable that creates a domain controller?

   A. WINNT.EXE

   B. WINNT32.EXE

   C. DCPROMO.EXE

   D. ACTDRWZD.EXE

2. What type of server will a Windows 2000 Server become by default when using a fresh install?

   A. Server

   B. Domain Controller

   C. PDC

   D. BDC

3. Which of the following commands or utilities converts the Windows 2000 Server's file system to NTFS?

   A. NTFS.EXE

   B. CONVERT /FS:NTFS

   C. Disk Administrator

   D. DISK /FS:NTFS

4. When running the Active Directory Wizard on the first Windows 2000 domain controller in your organization, what selection would be made for the Create or Join Forest screen?

   A. Create a new forest

   B. Copy an existing forest

   C. Join an existing forest

   D. Move to a new forest

5. During the Active Directory Wizard, which type of server must be available on the network?

   A. DHCP

   B. NetWare

   C. Web

   D. DNS

6. What is the recommended configuration for the location of log files and database files for the Active Directory?

   A. Log files and database files on two separate servers

   B. Log files with the database files on same partition

   C. Log files and database files on separate physical disks

   D. Do not install Log files, but include database files on system partition

7. What command will demote a domain controller to a member server?

   A. DEMOT.EXE

   B. DCPROMO.EXE

C. WINNT.EXE

D. WINNT32.EXE

8. What type of administration can make use of delegation of administration using Organizational Units (OUs)?

A. Centralized

B. Single Administration

C. Schema Admins

D. Decentralized

9. Which type of group can contain users, Global groups, and Universal groups?

A. Nested groups

B. User groups

C. Domain Local groups

D. Universal groups

10. Which tab on a user's properties will let an administrator change password and security options for that user?

A. Organization

B. Account

C. Profile

D. General

11. If an organization has more than a million users, each with their own assigned computer, should the organization implement more than one domain?

A. Yes

B. No

12. If a company has more than one namespace that it wishes to implement, can it use a single domain?

A. Yes

B. No

13. Which of the following describe Kerberos trusts in the Active Directory? (Choose all that apply.)

A. Bidirectional

B. Unidirectional

C. Transitive

D. Nontransitive

14. Which utility can be used to enable users in one forest to access resources in another forest?

A. TRUSTS.EXE

B. Active Directory Users and Computers

C. Active Directory Domains and Trusts

D. KERBEROS.EXE

15. Trench and Coats are two companies that are planning to merge. Each has a Windows 2000 Active Directory domain, trench.com and coats.com, respectively. Can Trench and Coats merge the domains?

A. Yes

B. No

MICROSOFT CERTIFIED SYSTEMS ENGINEER

15

Delegating and Managing Administrative Authority

Administrative authority, administrative duties, administrative responsibility, and administrative control—sounds like there's a whole lot of administrating going on. In fact, administration of the network is what an NOS (Network Operating System) like Windows 2000 Server is all about. As networks grow larger, it becomes more and more difficult for a network administrator to personally oversee all of the users, computers, and resources on the network. At some point in the growth process, delegation of administrative tasks and responsibilities becomes first desirable, and then essential.

Because Windows 2000 was designed to be scalable all the way up to the Enterprise level, Microsoft has included in the operating system new features that make it easier to assign specific administrative responsibilities to individuals and groups, much more easily than was possible in Windows NT.

Previously, the only practical way administrators of Microsoft networks could assign administrative control was at the domain level. This often forced the division of a network into multiple domains for no reason other than the need for separate administration of resources. This is unnecessary in a Windows 2000 network. Administrative permissions can be assigned with precision, to allow control over specific attributes of an object or, using the sophisticated features of the Active Directory services, can be conveniently assigned on the basis of Organizational Units (OUs), a special type of container object that makes it easy to organize the objects in the directory.

To simplify the assignment of administrative duties even further, Windows 2000 includes the Delegation of Control Wizard, which will walk you through the process in step-by-step fashion. With the Wizard, you can delegate the task of managing an OU, an object, or one or more properties of an object. What was once a time-consuming task now takes only a fraction of the time, and Windows 2000 ultimately gives you, the network administrator, more control by making it easier for you to delegate control to others.

In this chapter, we examine the planning and the procedure for using the Active Directory to customize the administrative duties while maintaining the high level of security required in today's networking environments.

HEADSTART OBJECTIVE 15.01

Customizing Administrative Duties Using the Active Directory Structure

One of Windows 2000 Active Directory's most useful features is the flexibility it gives administrators in delegating their administrative tasks to others on a very granular basis. This ability is further enhanced by new features in the distributed file system and changes to NTFS permissions, and Windows 2000's improved utilization of group policies. In this section, we look at how the design and structure of the Active Directory tree(s) can be used to customize the assignment of administrative duties.

How Administrative Authority Works with Transitive Trusts

As you learned in earlier chapters, the Active Directory supports transitive trusts between domains within a tree. A key point to remember is that although users can access all domains on the network, domains are still security boundaries when it comes to administrative privileges. By default, administrative authority does not flow down the branches of a tree. In other words, the administrator of a parent domain does not automatically have administrative authority over its child domains.

If cross-domain administration is desired, the administrator of Domain A can grant administrative privileges to the administrator(s) of Domain B in one of several ways, depending upon the scope of administrative authority to be given. The Domain B administrator can be assigned administrative permissions over specific objects in Domain A, or over one or more of Domain A's OUs, or his user account can be added to the Domain A administrators group to give him administrative authority within the entire domain.

In this way, centralized authority can be established by adding the user account of the overall network administrator to the domain administrators group of each domain.

A Better Way to Delegate: Using Organizational Units

The OU is a brand new concept in Microsoft networking, and it's likely that some administrators who are used to the NT domain models will fail to take advantage of this handy feature. OUs are a type of container object; that is, an object into which other objects can be placed and organized. OUs can contain

- Users and groups
- Resources (such as printers, shared folders and files, computers, applications)
- Other OUs (nesting)

The Role of OUs in Delegation of Administrative Authority

One of the most important values of using OUs is that each domain can set up the structure of its OUs independently, to meet its own needs. Since administrative authority can be assigned at the OU level rather than the domain level (which is often too broad) or the object level (which can be tedious), proper use and structuring of OUs within a domain gives us a convenient way to delegate administrative control with as much specificity as we need in a given situation.

For instance, if you want one person to have administrative authority over all the printers in the organization, you can put those printer objects into a Printer OU, and then assign administrative permissions for the OU to your printer manager's user account. If you then wanted the printer manager's supervisor, the office manager, to have administrative authority over those printers as well, the Printers OU can be placed inside the Office Management OU, which might contain other OUs over which other subordinates of the office manager are assigned control. See Figure 15-1 for an illustration of how this might work.

The Printer OU would then contain all printer objects, and the Computer OU would contain computer accounts. One person could be assigned administrative permissions over printers, and another given administrative control of the computer accounts.

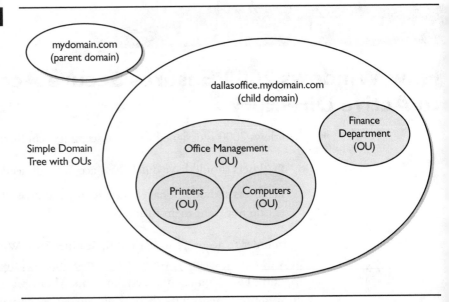

FIGURE 15-1

How Organizational
Units can be nested
within domains

Simple Domain
Tree with OUs

mydomain.com
(parent domain)

dallasoffice.mydomain.com
(child domain)

Finance
Department
(OU)

Office Management
(OU)

Printers
(OU)

Computers
(OU)

Best Practices in Designing an Active Directory Structure for Delegation of Authority

Although the Active Directory places no restrictions on how deep the OU hierarchy can be, Microsoft recommends that you keep the structure as shallow as possible for greater ease of administration.

Microsoft also recommends that administrative authority be assigned at the OU level whenever possible, as this gives you more flexibility than using domains as the primary administrative boundaries. It is also easier and less time-consuming than assigning administrative permissions directly to specific objects.

Your OUs should follow the same naming conventions as other objects within the Active Directory. Names should be short, simple, and unique, and should clearly identify the function of that OU.

Using Custom MMCs in Delegating Administrative Privileges

Windows 2000 conveniently allows you to create custom Microsoft Management Consoles (MMCs) that contain only those snap-ins needed to exercise the particular administrative privileges assigned to a particular user.

In the section on setting group policy, you will create a custom MMC.

How Windows 2000 Ensures Secure Access to Active Directory

Windows 2000 is designed with two seemingly conflicting principles in mind:

- Users should have quick, easy access to all needed resources.
- Users should not have access to any resources that administrators do not want them to access.

In order to accomplish both of these objectives, Windows 2000 must provide strong security, while at the same time making access more user friendly. This is quite an undertaking, but Microsoft has managed to make great improvements in both areas. Ease of access and enhanced security are both integral parts of the Windows 2000 operating system.

To see exactly how this works, we will first look at the Windows 2000 security model, and how object access is controlled. We'll examine both its basis in the NT security model, and how it differs from its predecessor in several subtle but important ways.

The Windows 2000 Security Model

First, let's look at the NT security model, upon which Windows 2000 is based. If you are familiar with NT, you will recall that object access is based on two things: the Access Control List (ACL), which every object has; and an Access Token, which is assigned to each user account at the time of logon. This ACL contains information regarding what users and groups have been assigned permissions to access that object (or specifically denied permission in the case of the No Access permission), and the level of permissions assigned. The Access Token contains information based on that user's account in the security accounts database, defining what groups the user belongs to, and rights and permissions individually assigned to that user.

A user can, of course, belong to more than one group, and those groups may not have the same permissions to a particular resource or other object. Resolving conflicting permissions is an important skill for the Microsoft exams, and we look in detail at how to do this a little later in the chapter.

First, let's turn our attention to Windows 2000 and its new, improved security model.

Windows 2000 Architecture and the Security Subsystem

As you can see in Figure 15-2, the architectural design of Windows 2000 differs slightly from the familiar NT architecture. There is something new in the User Mode layer, the Integral subsystem. The Security subsystem is a part of the Integral subsystem, as are the Workstation and Server services. The two latter subsystems are essential for Windows 2000 to function on a network, as they allow the Windows 2000 computer to access resources on other computers and to share its resources with other computers, respectively.

The third component of the Integral subsystem, the Security subsystem, is the part of the operating system that tracks rights and permissions associated with user accounts, tracks auditing, accepts logon requests, and initiates logon authentication.

FIGURE 15-2

The Windows 2000 Architecture—User and Kernel Modes

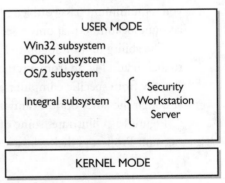

Windows 2000 User Accounts

As with Windows NT, the user account is the basis of the user-level type of security implemented in a Windows 2000 domain. In a domain environment, a user account is necessary to be able to log on to the operating system. This is one important way in which Windows NT and Windows 2000 differ from the $9x$ operating systems. In Windows 95 or 98, it is possible to bypass logon and still use the operating system; a valid user name and password are not required.

A local user account allows logging on to a specific computer to access resources on that system. A domain user account allows logging on to the domain to access network resources. A domain user account is authenticated by a domain controller; in Windows 2000, the domain user account is created in the Active Directory database, and is replicated to all domain controllers in the domain.

As with NT, the user account information is used at log on to create an Access Token, which identifies the user on the network and provides information about that user's security permissions. Also like NT, Windows 2000's Access Token is assigned for the duration of the logon session; changes to those permissions do not take effect until the user logs off and logs back on.

User accounts, especially those with administrative privileges, should be protected with secure passwords. Windows 2000 allows creation of passwords up to 128 characters (the limit in NT was 14 characters), and like NT, lets you set minimum password length, automatic password expiration, and account lockout so that only a set number of bad logon attempts is allowed.

The ability to limit logon to specific days or time ranges, to enable a user to dial in and log on from a remote location, and to restrict users to logging on only from specific computers, are still present in Windows 2000, although the latter option cannot be set if NetBIOS has been disabled.

Figure 15-3 illustrates some of the properties that can be set with the Account Properties dialog box.

FIGURE 15-3

Setting account properties
with the Account
Properties sheet

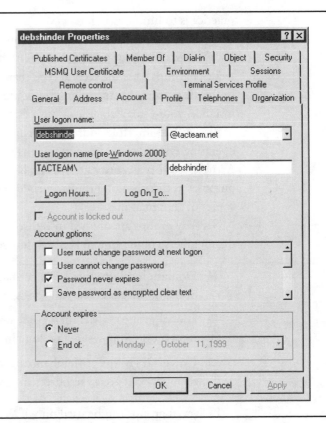

The Role of Security Groups

Another difference between Windows NT and Windows 2000 is an
expansion of group administration functions.

A *group* is simply a container object that can hold one or more user
accounts, and is assigned a unique name to identify it. Groups can be
assigned access permissions and rights just as individual users are. A user
account can be a member of more than one group.

Windows 2000 supports multiple levels of group nesting; that is, placing
groups inside other groups. This was not the case with Windows NT. Best

practice is to limit nesting, however, as the complexity created by deeper levels of nesting can make administration difficult.

Windows 2000 supports two types of groups: distribution groups and security groups. It is the second type that we will concern ourselves with in this discussion. Distribution groups are used by certain applications; for instance, your e-mail client can use a distribution group to simplify sending of messages to multiple addresses. Security groups are those used by the operating system, to which permissions to resources can be assigned. With Active Directory, security groups can be used for the same nonsecurity purposes as distribution groups (such as the example of sending multiple copies of an e-mail message).

Security groups are divided into three types based on their scope (where the members come from and what resources they can access):

- **Domain local groups** Can contain user accounts from any domain, but members can access resources only in the local domain.

- **Global groups** Members come only from the local domain, but can access resources in any domain.

- **Universal groups** Members can come from any domain, and those members can access resources in any domain.

Universal groups can be used only if Windows 2000 is running in native mode, which means all domain controllers have been upgraded to Windows 2000 and there are no down-level domain controllers on the network that require the use of mixed mode.

Microsoft has long recommended that access permissions be assigned to groups rather than to individual users; this makes administration easier, especially as the network grows larger. With Windows 2000, the recommendation is to use a combination of global and local domain groups in a single domain network, and to use global and universal groups when administering a tree of domains.

In Active Directory, groups are created with the Active Directory Users and Computers snap-in. You must have the correct permissions to be able to create groups (by default, administrative privileges or membership in the

Account Operators built-in group). See Figure 15-4, which illustrates the Create New Object dialog box for creating a group.

To create a new group, follow these steps:

1. Open the Active Directory Users and Computers tool (Start | Programs | Administrative Tools | Active Directory Users and Computers). In the console tree, double-click the domain node.

2. Right-click the folder in which you want to add the group, point to New, and then click Group.

3. Type the name of the new group. (By default, the name you type is also entered as the pre-Windows 2000 name of the new group.)

4. Click the Group type you want.

5. Click the Group scope you want. Click OK. (You can also choose a group name, to nest a group inside another group.)

FIGURE 15-4

Creating a new group with the appropriate Create New Object dialog box

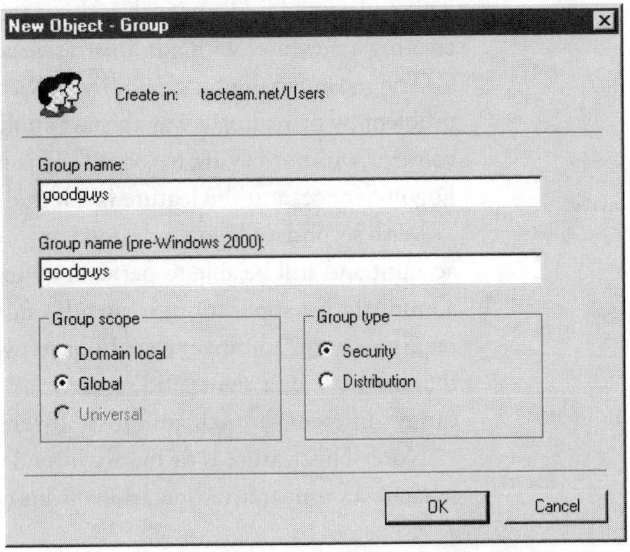

A second way to add members to groups is through the Properties sheet for the user you wish to add. Click the Member of tab to choose a group to which you want to add the user.

Secondary Logon as a Security Tool

Secondary logon is a brand new and highly useful feature in Windows 2000. Previously, a big security problem was the fact that administrators would log on to the administrator account and perform privileged and nonprivileged operations from the same logon session. This is understandable, since it is far more convenient to log on once and complete all of the operations needed than it is to constantly log on and off based on what type of task is being performed. The problem was that this made computers running Windows NT susceptible to Trojan Horse attacks.

The simple act of running Internet Explorer and accessing a nontrusted Web site could be extremely dangerous if done from an administrative account. The Web page might have Trojan Horse code that could be downloaded to the system and then executed in the administrative context. This code could perform such tasks as reformatting a disk, deleting all files, creating a new user with administrative access, and so on.

The secondary logon capability in Windows 2000 takes care of this problem by providing a way to start applications in different security contexts without having to log off. This is done by using the Secondary Logon Service, and the feature is referred to as "Run As."

With secondary logon, administrators can log on to a nonadministrative account and still be able to perform administrative tasks by running administrative applications in an administrative context. Secondary logon requires system administrators to have two user accounts: a regular account that has basic user rights and security, and an administrative account (which can be different for each administrator or shared among administrators).

Note: This feature is primarily intended for system administrators to separate administrative operations from normal operations, but it can be used by any user with multiple accounts to start applications under the different account contexts without needing to log off.

Using Run As to Start a Program as an Administrator

1. In Windows Explorer, click the program, Microsoft Management Console (MMC) tool, or Control Panel item you want to open.

2. Press SHIFT and right-click the program, and then click Run As.

3. Click "Run the program as the following user."

4. Type the user name, password, and domain of the administrator account you want to use.

See Figure 15-5 for an illustration of the Run As Other dialog box.

The Run As Other dialog box

Users, Groups, and Permissions

The whole purpose of creating separate user accounts and groups to put those accounts in is to be able to assign different permissions based on group membership.

Remember what we said earlier: a user can be a member of more than one group. For instance, a user named Jack might have a user account named jacksmith that belongs to three different groups: the Domain Users group, the Finance group, and the New Employees group. Jack's account became a member of Domain Users when the account was created, since by default every new user account created in the domain is added to this group. His account was placed in the Finance group because he is a member of the Finance department; but, since he has just been hired, the administrator also placed his account in the New Employees group, where it will stay until he completes a 90-day probationary period.

Now let's say we have a particular resource, such as a folder named "Budget" that contains files pertaining to the company budget. Domain Users have permission to read the files in this folder, but cannot make changes to them or create or delete files. The Finance group has permission to modify files in this folder, which includes permission to create new files, make changes to files, execute program files, and even the folder. However, the New Employees group has all permissions specifically denied for the Budget folder.

How do we determine what, if anything, Jack can do in relation to this resource? How do we resolve the conflicting permissions?

Before we can do that, it's important to understand the different types of permissions and how they work in Windows 2000. We look at these issues in the next section, apply them to delegating of administrative authority, and discuss how you can use Windows 2000's auditing feature to ensure that users have only the degree of control over resources that you want them to have.

Delegating and Managing Administrative Control Using Permissions and Auditing

Windows NT's user-level security model, coupled with the NTFS file system's file-level security, allowed the administrator to delegate authority over specific resources in a way that was a vast improvement over the Windows 9x workgroup/share-level security model.

Windows 2000 takes it a step further, enhancing and improving on NT's features and incorporating the Active Directory's security features to provide for the most granular and fine-tuned method of delegating administrative control that has ever been possible in a Microsoft operating system.

The first key point to remember is that Windows 2000, like Windows NT, gives you two distinct and separate ways to assign permissions to resources:

- **NTFS permissions**   Apply whether a user is accessing the resource from the local machine or across the network, but can only be used with volumes that are formatted with the NTFS file system.

- **Shared Folder permissions**   Only apply to users accessing the resource across the network, but do not require an NTFS volume to be implemented.

It is not a matter of choosing between these two types of permissions; both can be assigned simultaneously and independently to a given resource, and they work in conjunction with one another to provide added layers of security when resources are accessed from a remote computer.

Let's look at each permission type in turn, and lay out a few guidelines for working with each. Then we'll discuss how they work together.

NTFS Permissions

NTFS permissions work much the same way they did in NT 4.0, but the permissions themselves have been expanded to allow much more specificity, especially in terms of denial of permissions.

NTFS permissions include both folder and file permissions. The folder permissions include

- Read
- Write
- List folder contents
- Read and execute
- Modify
- Full Control

File permissions are almost the same, but do not include the "List folder contents" permission.

What's different in Windows 2000 is that the old familiar No Access permission is missing. Instead, each individual permission can be either granted or denied, which gives administrators far more control than before.

Shared Folder Permissions

Shared folders are used when allowing others to access resources across the network. A shared folder (called just a "share" in Windows NT) can contain any of several types of data: applications (executable files), information (documents, graphics files, sound files), or a user's personal data (in which case it is called a home folder or directory). The type of shared folder permissions that are applicable depends on the type of data in the shared folder.

heads
①p

Remember that shared folder permissions only apply to folders, not to individual files (NTFS permissions can be assigned to both files and folders). Also remember that shared folder permissions apply only when the resource is being accessed across the network, not when a user is accessing the folder from the local machine.

Shared folder permissions are especially useful for protecting resources shared on FAT volumes, since file-level permissions can only be used on volumes formatted in NTFS. It's important to keep in mind, however, that because access is restricted only across the network, and because shared folder permissions apply to folders only, this type of permission is less secure and allows less specificity in assignment of permissions than NTFS permissions.

The default shared folder permission is Full Control for the Everyone group. This means that when you create a new shared folder, unless you specifically change the permissions, anyone on the network will be able to read, write, change, delete, and even change permissions or take ownership.

Keep this in mind, as it may not be what you want when you share a folder. If it's not, you can remove the Everyone group or assign it a more restrictive permission, and/or add other groups to the folder's ACL and assign them the desired access permissions. The shared folder permissions that can be assigned are

- **Read** Allows a user to display folder and file names, and contents and attributes, and allows execution of program files in the folder.

- **Change** Allows a user to create and delete files and folders in the folder, change and save the data/contents, as well as everything included in Read permissions.

- **Full Control** Allows a user to do everything allowed by Read and Change permissions, and also allows the user to change permissions of the files and take ownership.

As with NTFS permissions, the big change in Windows 2000 is that the No Access permission is gone, and you can specifically grant or deny each of the permissions just listed.

Resolving Multiple Permissions

It can be confusing when we try to correctly determine what a given user's permissions to a particular resource would be when that user belongs to more than one group, and/or when that user is attempting to gain access across the network to a shared folder that also resides on an NTFS volume and has file-level permissions assigned. Let's look now at some guidelines for determining what the ultimate permission would be.

The process becomes easier if we take it on a step-by-step basis:

1. To determine the user's Shared Folder permission for the resource, simply combine all user/group permissions for that resource. For example, if a user belongs to two groups, one of which has Read permission and the other Full Control, the user's ultimate Shared Folder permission for the resource will be Full Control, unless a permission is specifically denied.

2. Any specific denial of permission will override other permissions. That is, if the user in the preceding example also belongs to a third group, for which Full Control is denied, the user will not have Full Control despite the fact that Full Control was granted to the second group.

3. NTFS permissions, like Shared Folder permissions, are cumulative. In other words, to determine a user's ultimate NTFS permission for a resource, simply combine the NTFS permissions of all groups to which a user belongs and any individually assigned permissions.

4. The same rule regarding denial of permissions applies to NTFS permissions: Any permission that is specifically denied overrides the granting of that same permission to any other group(s) to which the user belongs.

5. NTFS file permissions override folder permissions. A user who has been assigned permission to access a file can do so even if that user does not have permission to access the folder in which that file resides. However, because resources to which the user does not have permission will not be visible to that user, the only way to access the file is by connecting via the full UNC path.

6. Finally, once the ultimate Shared Folder permission and the ultimate NTFS permission have been determined, a user accessing the resource across the network will be limited to the most restrictive of the two. Remember that if the user is accessing the resource at the local machine, only the NTFS permission applies.

The combination of Shared Folder permissions and NTFS permissions, when taken together with other Windows 2000 security features, provides you with the ability to assign administrative control on an object-by-object basis. This makes delegation of authority easier than it has ever been before.

How Active Directory Permissions Work

NTFS permissions and Shared Folder permissions, although refined for Windows 2000, are familiar to Windows NT administrators. On the other hand, the Active Directory is a brand new concept to many, so we will discuss in some detail just how object access is controlled in the Active Directory security model.

As we learned earlier, the Active Directory is object oriented, and each object has attributes. This includes the object's security attributes. The list of access permissions for the object is stored in the object's ACL.

The nice thing about Active Directory is that it allows you to assign administrative control to a user or group, not only to a single object, but also to an OU or an entire hierarchy of OUs.

What permissions can be assigned for an object is dependent on what type of object it is. A user account object will allow you to set permissions such as "reset password" that do not apply to other types of objects.

Types of Permissions

There are two basic types of Active Directory permissions: Standard and Special. Standard permissions are broader, whereas Special permissions provide for more fine-tuning of control.

Following is a list of standard object permissions for the typical AD object:

- **Read** Allows the user to view the object and its attributes (including the name of the object's owner and its Active Directory permissions).

- **Write** Allows the user to change the object's attributes.

- **Delete All Child Objects** Allows the user to remove objects from an OU.

- **Create All Child Objects** Allows the user to add child objects to an OU.

- **Full Control** Allows the user to change permissions and take ownership of the object, in addition to all actions allowed by the other four permissions.

How to Assign Permissions in Active Directory

Active Directory permissions are assigned using the Security tab in the object's Properties sheet. Follow the steps in Exercise 15-2 to assign standard permissions for an object.

EXERCISE 15-2

Assigning Active Directory Permissions

Be sure you are working with Windows 2000 Server, with Active Directory installed.

1. Select the object to which you wish to assign permissions. On the Action menu, choose Properties, then Security.

2. Click Add, and then click on the user or group to which you want to assign the permissions. Click Add again, and then OK.

3. In the Permissions box, check the appropriate box (Allow or Deny) for each permission you wish to add or deny.

Note: To assign special permissions, click the Advanced button, select the appropriate permission entry, and click View/Edit. This brings up a new dialog box that allows you to see, allow, and deny the more specific special permissions available for that object type.

Once we fully understand how permissions work in Active Directory, we can use them along with the Active Directory structure to delegate administrative control over objects or over all of the objects in an OU or many levels of OUs.

How Permissions Are Inherited

In order to be able to predict a user or group's actual access to an object, we must look not only at how permissions are assigned, but also at how they are inherited, and the effect on permissions of moving or copying an object to another location.

In this area as in many others, Windows 2000 gives you more control than previous Windows operating systems. You can choose to have an object's permissions be inherited by its subobjects, or you can specifically prevent permissions inheritance.

After you set permissions on a parent folder, new files and subfolders you create in the folder inherit these permissions. If you do not want them to inherit permissions, select "This folder only" in Apply when you set up special permissions for the parent folder. If you want to prevent only certain files or subfolders from inheriting permissions, right-click the file or subfolder, click Properties, click the Security tab, and then uncheck the "Allow inheritable permissions from parent to propagate to this object" check box.

If the check boxes appear shaded, the file or folder has inherited permissions from the parent folder. There are three ways to make changes to inherited permissions:

- Make the changes to the parent folder, and then the file or folder will inherit these permissions.

- Select the opposite permission (Allow or Deny) to override the inherited permission.

- Uncheck the "Allow inheritable permissions from parent to propagate to this object" check box. Now you can make changes to the permissions or remove the user or group from the permissions list. However, the file or folder will no longer inherit permissions from the parent folder.

When you move objects to another location in the Active Directory, permissions that are assigned directly to that object will be retained. However, any permissions that were inherited from the former container object will no longer apply; instead, the object will inherit permissions from its new container.

How Auditing Works in Windows 2000

Auditing is used to track specific events that occur on a Windows 2000 computer, including those initiated by users and those performed by the system. There are three basic steps involved in using auditing to control delegated authority:

1. Auditing must be enabled by an administrator, who must also specify which event types to audit (set audit policies). In Windows 2000, this is done through Group Policy (see Chapters 5 and 6 for more information on using Group Policy).

2. When a specified event occurs, the system will record information about it in the security log.

3. An administrator must access and interpret the results of the auditing.

You can track either successful or failed attempts to perform a specified action (such as accessing a file, printing to a printer, or logging onto the system), or both.

heads
①P

Remember that auditing can only be performed on files and folders that are stored on NTFS formatted disks.

The implementation of audit policies differs depending on which version of Windows 2000 you are running and, if the Server version, what role the Server has been assigned. With domain controllers, an audit policy is set to apply to all domain controllers in the domain. For stand-alone (member) servers and Windows 2000 Professional workstations, the audit policy is set for that specific computer.

In order to enable auditing and access the security log, you must be an administrator, or have the user right "manage auditing and security log" (which only administrators have by default). We will look at how to enable and configure auditing in a moment, but first let's discuss planning your audit policies.

Audit Policies

You can audit many different types of events: user access to files and folders, the shutdown and startup of the computer, logons and logoffs, changes being made to user and group accounts, and changes made to Active Directory objects. You can have system log failed attempts as well as successes.

Best Practices in Implementing Auditing

A few guidelines to follow in planning your audit policies:

1. **Don't try to audit everything**   Rarely would it be necessary to track every possible event that can be audited. Auditing uses system resources and thus effects the performance of the computer; uses up hard disk space; and, perhaps most importantly, causes the security log to grow so large and complex that it becomes difficult to find what you're looking for when you review it.

2. **Review the logs on a regular basis**   Decide whether to purge the logs or archive them (you would do the latter if your purpose is to identify trends and patterns over time).

3. **If your purpose is to track access to an object by all persons on the network, be sure you audit the Everyone group instead of the Users group**   The latter will show only those users who have user accounts in your domain.

What Events to Audit

Determining which events to audit will be based on your reasons for auditing. If you suspect that someone is trying to hack into the network, you would want to audit logons, and you would want to audit failures as well as successes. Table 15-1 shows the events that can be audited in Windows 2000.

TABLE 15-1   Windows 2000 Auditable Events

Event	Description
Logon	User logged on or logged off.
Account logon	Domain controller received a request to validate a user.
Object access	User accessed a resource (the specific resources, such as files, folders and printers, must be configured for auditing).
Directory service access	User accessed an Active Directory object (specific objects must be configured for auditing).
Account management	User account or group was created, modified, or deleted, including renaming or disabling accounts and resetting passwords.
Policy change	User security options, audit policies, or user rights were modified.
Privilege use	User exercised a user right.
System	Computer was shut down or restarted, or other system event such as the security log becoming full.
Process tracking	A program performed an action.

Note: Process tracking is generally useful only for programmers who are tracking the specific way in which program code is executed.

How to Set Audit Policies

We will look at the process of implementing auditing, and then at the specific details of how to audit file and folder access and how to audit Active Directory object access.

In either case, there are two steps required:

1. Enable auditing by setting the audit policy.

2. Configure specific objects to be audited.

Setting the Audit Policy

First, you set the type of events to be audited using the Group Policy Editor snap-in. Any or all of the events detailed in Table 15-1 may be audited. You can create a custom MMC console with the Group Policy Editor added (see Figure 15-6) to complete the following exercise.

FIGURE 15-6   Setting audit policies on the local computer

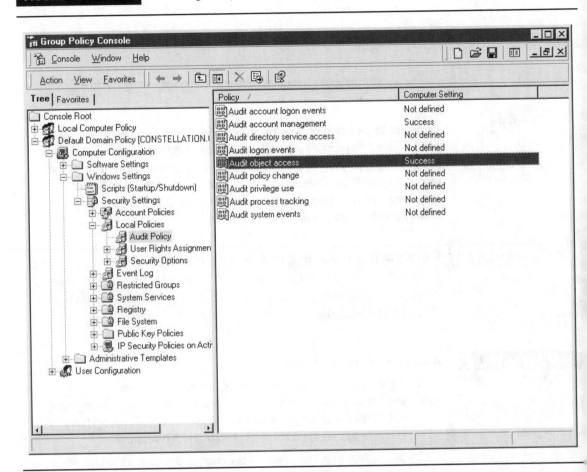

EXERCISE 15-3

Setting Up a Local Audit Policy

The following exercise takes you through the steps of setting a local audit policy on a computer that is not a domain controller (member server or Windows 2000 Professional workstation).

1. Open the MMC console with Group Policy Editor.

2. Expand the Local Policy tree. Double-click "Computer configuration," then "Windows settings," then "Security settings," then "Local policies," then "Audit policy."

3. Select the type(s) of event you want to audit. On the Action menu, choose Security.

4. Choose "Audit successful attempts" and/or "Audit failed attempts." Click OK.

The audit policy has been set, but you still must configure specific objects to be audited.

heads

①P

Changes to policy won't take effect until policy propagation takes place. This happens every eight hours by default, or you can initiate propagation whenever you wish by typing, at the command prompt, secedit /RefreshPolicy /MACHINE_POLICY and then pressing ENTER. Alternatively, you can simply restart the computer and policy changes will be applied.

Configuring Auditing of File and Folder Objects

Audit policy should be set to audit object access (see "Setting the Audit Policy"). The following exercise walks you through the process of enabling file and folder auditing.

EXERCISE 15-4

Auditing Files and Folders

1. Right-click on a file or folder in Explorer, select Properties, and choose the Security tab. (There will be a Security tab on the property sheet only if the file or folder is on an NTFS volume; remember that you cannot audit access to objects stored on FAT volumes.)

2. Select Auditing, then Add. Now choose the user accounts whose access to the file or folder you wish to audit. Click OK.

3. Now on the Object tab of the Auditing Entry dialog box, check Successful or Failed, or both for the events you are auditing. Click OK.

4. If you don't want changes you've made to a parent folder to also apply to child folders and files in the parent and child folders (which is the default), you can uncheck "Allow Inheritable Permissions from Parent to Propagate to this Object." Click OK.

Configuring Auditing of Active Directory Object Access

Enabling auditing of Active Directory objects is done through the Directory Manager. First, the audit policy must be set to audit directory service access. The following exercise takes you through the process of enabling auditing of specific AD objects.

EXERCISE 15-5

Auditing Active Directory Object Access

1. Open the Active Directory Manager; select View, and then Advanced Features.

2. Select the object(s) you wish to audit. On the Action menu, choose Properties. Select the Security tab, and then click Advanced. On the Auditing tab, choose Add, and then choose the users (or groups) whose access to objects you wish to audit. Click OK.

3. Make the appropriate selection in the "Apply onto" box. In this case, choose "this object only." Then check Successful or Failed for each audit event you wish to audit. Click OK.

How to View and Interpret the Log of Audited Events

Now that you know how to set audit policies and enable auditing of access to specific objects, let's look at how to view the results of your auditing. To access the Security Log in which audited events are tracked, you use the Event Viewer. By default, only members of the Administrators group may view the Security Log.

Event Viewer contains three logs: the Application Log, the System Log, and the Security Log. It is this last that we will concern ourselves with here.

Viewing the Security Log

You will find the Event Viewer in the Administrative Tools, which can be accessed through the Control Panel in Windows 2000. Click on Event Viewer, and you will see a console resembling Figure 15-7.

FIGURE 15-7 The Windows 2000 Event Viewer console

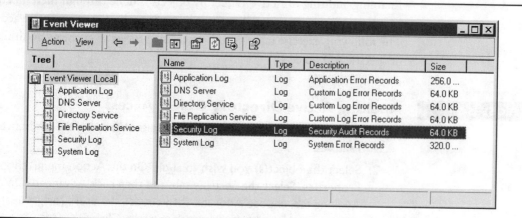

Now choose Security Log. You will be able to see the log recording those events that you selected to audit.

You can use the Filter command to help you locate selected events in the log (select Find on the View menu).

The following scenarios answer some questions about Windows 2000 audit policies.

QUESTIONS AND ANSWERS

What is the first step in configuring auditing?	Set audit policies in the Group Policy Editor snap-in.
What is the second step in configuring auditing?	Enable auditing of the specific resources you want to audit.
How can you initiate policy propagation without restarting the computer?	At a command prompt, type secedit/RefreshPolicy/MACHINE_POLICY

Enforcing Security Policies by Using Group Policies

Another thing that is new to Windows 2000 is the expanded functionality of Group Policies. As you learned earlier, Group Policy is used to enable auditing, but it does much more. Group Policy also allows administrators to control users' desktops and restrict what they can do with the computer. Active Directory enables Group Policy, and Group Policy Objects (GPOs) store policy information. The GPOs are linked to Active Directory containers such as sites, domains, and OUs.

You can use a GPO to sort and filter objects based on security group membership. This makes it easier to manage computers and users in either a centralized or a decentralized environment. Filtering based on security groups helps you customize the Group Policy management scope, so that a Group Policy can be applied at the domain level or at the OU level, then filtered once again by security groups.

You use the Group Policy snap-in and its extensions to define Group Policy options.

With the Group Policy snap-in, you can configure the following settings:

- Registry-based policy settings (using the Administrative Templates node)
- Security settings for local computer, domain, and network security settings
- Software installation
- Scripts
- Folder redirection (which allows you to redirect special designated folders to the network)

You can use the Group Policy snap-in to manage policy. Group Policy has built-in features for setting policy. The data created by Group Policy is stored in a GPO, which is replicated in all domain controllers within the domain.

How Group Policies Work in Windows 2000

Group Policies are typically set at the site or domain level, or they can be set for a specific OU. Group Policy is the network administrator's primary tool for defining and controlling how programs, network resources, and the operating system behave for users and computers in an organization.

When you implement Active Directory, Group Policy is applied to users or computers based on their membership in sites, domains, or OUs.

Several types of group policies affect various network components and Active Directory objects. These include application and file deployment, scripts, software, and security. For more information about the first four, see Chapter 5. In this chapter, we look at security policies and how they can be used to restrict user access and to delegate control over specific objects.

Elements of Group Policies

The elements of Group Policies include Group Policy Objects (GPOs), Group Policy Containers (GPCs), and Group Policy Templates (GPTs).

Group Policy Objects

A GPO contains the configuration settings for the Group Policy. A GPO can then be applied to a site, domain, or OU.

Group Policy information for the GPO is stored in Group Policy containers and in Group Policy templates. Let's take a look at each of these.

Group Policy Containers

The group policy container, or GPC, is an Active Directory object. It contains GPO properties, which can be divided into two categories: version information (the version number is changed each time you modify a GPO) and status information (which indicates whether the GPO is enabled). Group policy information that does not change often is stored in GPCs.

Group Policy Templates

A Group Policy Template, or GPT, resides in the Sysvol folder in the systemroot directory on domain controllers. All group policy information that is subject to frequent change is stored in the GPT. A corresponding GPT is created by the system when you create a GPO. The GPT's folder name will be the GUID of the GPO.

How to Design a Group Policy Object

In order to create a Group Policy, open a GPO, and then configure its settings using the Group Policy Editor.

Creating a New GPO

1. Right-click the Active Directory object (site, domain, or OU) for which you want to create a new GPO. Select Properties, then Group Policy. Click Add (see Figure 15-8).
2. Select All under "Group Policy Objects Linked to this Container."
3. Click Create New Group Policy.
4. Put in a name for the new GPO. Click OK.

Using the Group Policy Editor

The Group Policy Editor is used to configure settings. To use it, first create a custom MMC and add the Group Policy snap-in to it. You can use the Group Policy Editor to edit GPOs for domains and OUs. To edit GPOs for sites, you use the Active Directory Sites and Services Manager.

The following exercise walks you through the steps involved in changing security settings with the Group Policy Editor. We will give the Everyone group the right to back up files and directories.

Creating a new Group
Policy object

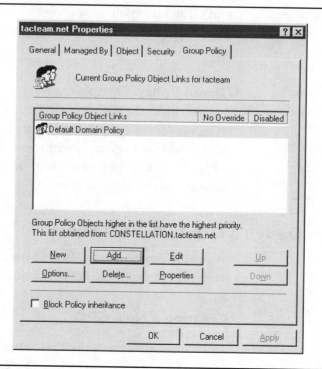

Using the Group Policy Editor
to Change Security Settings

To complete this exercise, you must log on as an administrator with Read
and Write permissions for the GPO being modified.

1. Open the Active Directory Manager. Double-click the name of
   your domain.

2. Now right-click Domain Controllers, then Properties, then Group
   Policy.

3. Next, select Default Domain Controllers Policy in the Group Policy
   Object Links list. Click Edit.

4. Now, in the gpedit window, double-click on Computer Configuration.
   Double-click Windows Settings, then Security Settings, then Local
   Policies.

5. Select User Rights Assignment. In the details window, a list of User Rights Assignments appears (see Figure 15-9).

6. Select "Back up files and directories." Double-click, and the box shown next appears. You will notice that, by default, Administrators and Backup Operators have the right to back up files and directories. Click Add.

FIGURE 15-9   The Group Policy Editor console, showing User Rights Assignments options in the details window on the right

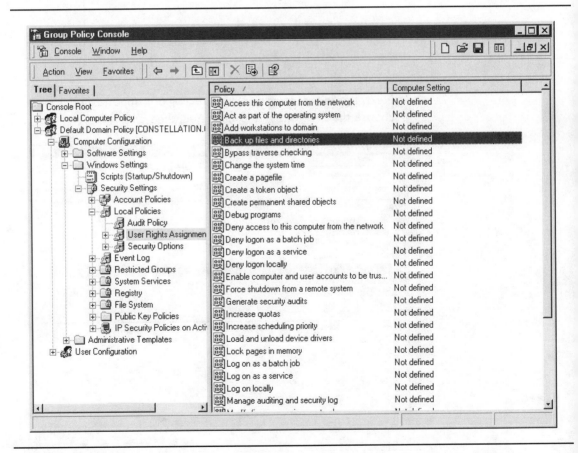

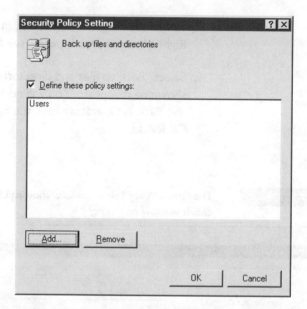

7. Next, the Select Users or Groups dialog box appears. In this case, choose the Everyone group; click Add, then OK.

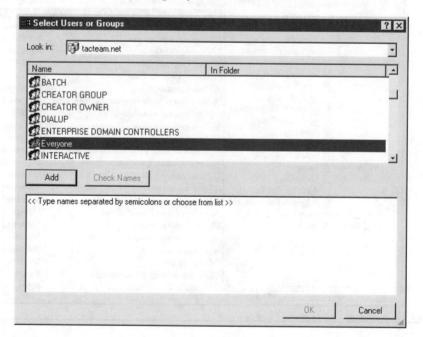

8. Click OK again when the Everyone group appears in the list of those with the right to back up files and directories. Close the Group Policy Editor. Click OK to close the Domain Controllers Properties dialog box. Close the Active Directory Manager window.

HEADSTART OBJECTIVE 15.05

Developing a Plan to Delegate Administrative Authority

Remember that with Windows 2000, it's easy to delegate administrative control to any level of a domain tree by creating OUs in the domain and delegating administrative control for specific OUs to specific users or groups.

Delegating administrative responsibilities lets you do away with the necessity for multiple administrative accounts that have broad authority (over an entire domain).

You can use the Delegation of Control Wizard to give administrative authority to a user or group. The Wizard allows you to choose a user or group to which you want to delegate administrative control, and the OUs and objects you want to give those users the right to control, and assigns the permissions to access and modify objects.

Guidelines to Follow in Delegating Administrative Authority

Here are a few basic guidelines to follow in delegating administrative authority:

- Use a combination of OUs, groups, and permissions to define the most appropriate administrative scope for a particular person. This could be an entire domain, all of the OUs within a domain, or only a single OU.

- Consider the structure of your organization. For example, you might create an OU that enables you to grant to a particular user the administrative authority for all of the user and computer accounts in all branches of an organizational department.

■ You will probably still use the built-in Domain Administrators group for administration of the entire domain, but limit the accounts that are members of Domain Admins to highly trusted administrative users. Authority over smaller units can be handled as discussed previously.

Establishing Policies for Delegation of Administrative Authority

It is important that a policy be established regarding the delegation of administrative authority, and that policy should be known and applied throughout the organization and the network.

If your organization is large, you will need to coordinate the structuring of the Active Directory with other administrators.

Don't neglect the very important issue of proper training for those to whom administrative authority is delegated. Written policies and guidelines will ensure that users who have administrative control will know their responsibilities and how to meet them. Once users have been trained in using their administrative authority, hold them accountable.

HEADSTART OBJECTIVE 15.06

Best Practices for Assigning Permissions on Directory Objects

Consider the following suggestions to make the assignment of permissions and delegation of administrative authority easier:

■ Keep records of permissions assignments by tracking them.

■ Be careful about using the Deny permission. Microsoft recommends that you use this option sparingly; it is better to plan the granting of permissions and assignment of members to groups in such a way that you don't need to specifically deny permissions.

■ Be sure that for every Active Directory object, there is at least one user who has Full Control. This will ensure that the object will not be inaccessible.

■ If possible, grant administrative privileges at the OU level. This limits the scope of a user's administrative control, yet is much easier to plan and implement than assignment of permissions.

The following exercise takes you through the simple steps involved in delegating administrative authority over an OU.

EXERCISE 15-7

Delegating Control Over an OU

1. Start | Programs | Administrative Tools | Active Directory Users and Computers.

2. In the console tree, expand the domain node.

3. In the details pane, right-click the organizational unit, and then click Delegate Control.

Using OUs to delegate administrative authority can actually provide network administrators with a way to sidestep the sometimes sticky issues of internal politics that has often adversely affected the efficiency and security of the network. Now each department head or other middle manager can have his or her own little "empire," and rule over it without having administrative privileges to the rest of the domain. This may be useful in creating a less competitive, more cooperative working environment, at least insofar as computer resources are concerned.

ACCELERATING TO WINDOWS 2000

Windows 2000 is full of new features that allow you to more precisely and more effectively delegate administrative authority, such as these:

- The tree structure of the Active Directory, which allows you to assign administrative control over an entire domain, subdomain(s), nests of OUs, or single OUs.

- In native mode, Windows 2000 now includes three types of security groups: the familiar Local and Global, and the new Universal group. This gives the administrator more flexibility in assignment of permissions and delegation of authority.

- Both NTFS permissions and shared folder permissions can now be assigned with significantly more specificity and granularity, letting administrators

fine-tune the amount of control granted.

- Windows 2000's auditing feature has been expanded and made easier to use, thus making it easier for administrators to keep tabs on when and how users are exercising their delegated authority.

- The use of Group Policies to restrict or expand user rights and authority simplifies the administrator's task of giving each user exactly the amount of control needed to accomplish his or her job duties.

- Numerous Wizards walk administrators and users through the steps of common tasks, including the Delegation of Control Wizard that leads you step by step through the process of assigning administrative authority to those who need it.

 TWO-MINUTE DRILL

- ❑ As networks grow larger, it becomes more and more difficult for a network administrator to personally oversee all of the users, computers, and resources on the network.

- ❑ To simplify the assignment of administrative duties even further, Windows 2000 includes the Delegation of Control Wizard, which will walk you through the process in step-by-step fashion.

❑ One of Windows 2000 Active Directory's most useful features is the flexibility it gives administrators in delegating their administrative tasks to others on a very granular basis.

❑ A key point to remember is that although users can access all domains on the network, domains are still security boundaries when it comes to administrative privileges. By default, administrative authority does not flow down the branches of a tree.

❑ OUs are a type of container object; that is, an object into which other objects can be placed and organized.

❑ One of the most important values of using OUs is that each domain can set up the structure of its OUs independently, to meet its own needs.

❑ Although the Active Directory places no restrictions on how deep the OU hierarchy can be, Microsoft recommends that you keep the structure as shallow as possible for greater ease of administration.

❑ The ACL contains information regarding what users and groups have been assigned permissions to access that object (or specifically denied permission in the case of the No Access permission), and the level of permissions assigned.

❑ The secondary logon capability in Windows provides a way to start applications in different security contexts without having to log off. This is done by using the Secondary Logon Service, and the feature is referred to as "Run As."

❑ The whole purpose of creating separate user accounts and groups to put those accounts in is to be able to assign different permissions based on group membership.

❑ NTFS permissions work much the same way they did in NT 4.0, but the permissions themselves have been expanded to allow much more specificity, especially in terms of denial of permissions.

❑ What permissions can be assigned for an object is dependent on what type of object it is. A user account object will allow you to set permissions such as "reset password" that do not apply to other types of objects.

❑ Active Directory permissions are assigned using the Security tab in the object's Properties sheet.

❑ In order to be able to predict a user or group's actual access to an object, we must look not only at how permissions are assigned, but also at how they are inherited, and the effect on permissions of moving or copying an object to another location.

❑ Auditing is used to track specific events that occur on a Windows 2000 computer, including those initiated by users and those performed by the system.

❑ Remember that auditing can only be performed on files and folders that are stored on NTFS formatted disks.

❑ You can audit many different types of events: user access to files and folders, the shutdown and startup of the computer, logons and logoffs, changes being made to user and group accounts, and changes made to Active Directory objects.

❑ To access the Security Log in which audited events are tracked, you use the Event Viewer. By default, only members of the Administrators group may view the Security Log.

❑ Active Directory enables Group Policy, and Group Policy Objects (GPOs) store policy information. The GPOs are linked to Active Directory containers such as sites, domains, and OUs.

❑ Group Policies are typically set at the site or domain level, or they can be set for a specific OU. Group Policy is the network administrator's primary tool for defining and controlling how programs, network resources, and the operating system behave for users and computers in an organization.

❑ The elements of Group Policies include Group Policy Objects (GPOs), Group Policy Containers (GPCs), and Group Policy Templates (GPTs).

❑ In order to create a Group Policy, open a GPO, and then configure its settings using the Group Policy Editor.

❑ Delegating administrative responsibilities lets you do away with the necessity for multiple administrative accounts that have broad authority (over an entire domain).

❑ It is important that a policy be established regarding the delegation of administrative authority, and that policy should be known and applied throughout the organization and the network.

SELF TEST

The following questions will help you measure your understanding of the material presented in this chapter. Read all of the choices carefully, as there may be more than one correct answer. Choose all correct answers for each question.

1. Which of the following statements is true of Active Directory transitive trusts?

   A. Administrative authority flows down the tree by default, giving the administrator of a parent domain the authority to control child domains.

   B. Domains are security boundaries, and by default an administrator of one domain has no administrative authority in other domains unless it is specifically granted.

   C. Two-way transitive trust relationships are not supported by Windows 2000.

   D. None of the above.

2. What is the maximum length limit for Windows 2000 passwords?

   A. 14 characters.

   B. 15 characters.

   C. 128 characters.

   D. There is no limit.

3. What is the Microsoft-recommended level at which administrative control should be assigned whenever possible?

   A. Forest level

   B. Object level

   C. Tree level

   D. OU level

4. Which of the following is assigned to a user account at the time of logon, and contains information about that user's group memberships, permissions, and rights?

   A. Access Control List

   B. Access Token

   C. Security Identifier

   D. GPO

5. The Integral subsystem in the Windows 2000 architectural model contains which of the following? (Choose all that apply.)

   A. Server service

   B. Executive services

   C. Security subsystem

   D. Hardware Abstraction Layer

6. Which of the following is true of security groups? (Choose all that apply.)

   A. Security groups cannot be used for such purposes as sending a message to a group; that is exclusively the function of distribution groups.

   B. Security groups are used by the Windows 2000 operating system, while distribution groups are used by applications.

C. Windows 2000 security groups can be nested inside other groups.

D. A group can be designated as both a security group and a distribution group at the same time.

7. Which of the following is a type of security group that can be used only when Windows 2000 runs in native mode, and was not used in Windows NT 4.0?

A. Universal group

B. Domain global group

C. Domain local group

D. None of the above

8. What tool is used to create groups in Active Directory?

A. User Manager for Domains

B. Active Directory Users and Computers

C. Directory Manager

D. Domain Tree Administrator

9. The Windows 2000 feature that allows you to run an administrative application as an administrator although you are logged on to a nonadministrative account, using the Run As command, is known as which of the following?

A. Administrative Emulation.

B. Dual Logon.

C. Secondary Logon.

D. There is no such feature.

10. Which of the following is NOT one of the standard NTFS file permissions?

A. Write

B. List Contents

C. Modify

D. Full Control

11. Which of the following is true of NTFS and shared folder permissions?

A. NTFS permissions apply only when accessing the object through the network share, not when accessing from the local machine.

B. NTFS permissions apply only when accessing the object from the local machine, not when accessing through the network share.

C. Shared folder permissions apply only when accessing the object through the network share, not when accessing from the local machine.

D. Shared folder permissions apply only when accessing the object from the local machine, not when accessing through the network share.

12. Which of the following is used to assign Active Directory permissions in Windows 2000?

A. The Security tab in the object's Properties sheet

B. The Sharing tab in the object's Properties shee.

C. The Active Directory Permissions Assignment snap-in

D. Disk Administrator

13. Which two of the following are the steps required to audit object access in Windows 2000?

A. Enable auditing in the Users and Computers snap-in.

B. Enable auditing using the Group Policy Editor snap-in.

C. Configure auditing for specific objects using the Group Policy Editor snap-in.

D. Configure auditing for specific objects using the Security tab on the object's Properties sheet.

14. Where does the Group Policy Template (GPT) reside on a domain controller?

A. In the root directory of the C: drive

B. In the sysvol directory in the root directory of the system volume

C. In the sysvol subdirectory in the systemroot directory

D. In the systemroot/system32/GPT subdirectory on the boot volume

15. Which of the following is considered a "best practice" in assigning permissions? (Choose all that apply.)

A. The Deny permission should be used liberally to restrict access.

B. For every directory object, there should be at least one user who has Full Control.

C. Administrative permissions should be granted at the OU level if possible.

D. You should track permissions assignments to keep records of what permissions have been assigned.

MICROSOFT CERTIFIED SYSTEMS ENGINEER

16

Using Active Directory Replication

HEADSTART OBJECTIVES

The Active Directory is a database that is spread in pieces across multiple domain controllers. There are copies of some of the pieces of the database on domain controllers that belong to the same domain or are designated as Global Catalog Servers (GCS). This configuration provides redundancy in case of a disaster. It also improves performance for users when the network is designed to place domain controllers close to the users who need to log on or query the directory for resources.

HEADSTART OBJECTIVE 16.01

The Windows 2000 Active Directory Replication Model

Replication is the process of synchronizing the Active Directory partitions. When an administrator makes a change to an object, only the change and enough information to locate where that change occurred within the Active Directory partition is replicated. There are several partitions in the Active Directory. Some partitions are replicated across an entire forest, while others are replicated completely within a domain.

- **Active Directory domains**   Each domain is a separate partition of the Active Directory database. All of the domain controllers within that domain contain a complete, identical copy of its partition.

- **Global Catalog**   The Global Catalog (GC) is a partial replica of every object within a forest. It is an index for the Active Directory, provided for users to be able to query for resources on the network. Only certain domain controllers are designated as GCSs. GCSs are not required if there is only a single domain.

- **Schema and configuration**   Every domain controller within the Active Directory forest contains a copy of the schema and configuration.

The replication system in the Active Directory consists of several objects:

- Sites
- Site links and site link bridges
- Connection objects
- IP Subnets

A site is a grouping of IP Subnet objects. The definition of a site is that it is a set of well-connected IP subnets. "Well-connected" is generally intended not to include WAN connections. However, some stable WAN connections have amounts of available bandwidth above 512 Kbps, and may then be considered well-connected, too. Figure 16-1 displays the Active Directory Sites and Services console opened to the contents of a site.

FIGURE 16-1 Contents of a site

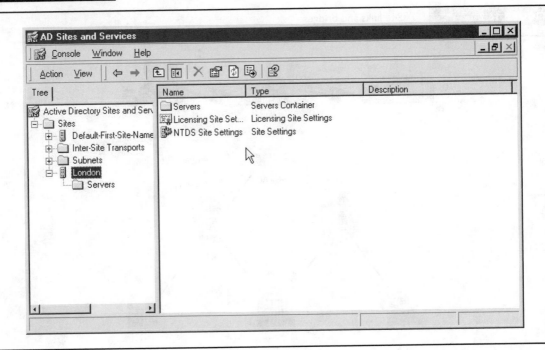

Two objects connect sites together, *site links* and *site link bridges.* A Site Link object provides a path for traffic between two or more sites using a specific protocol, either IP or SMTP. Many sites are connected in point-to-point WAN connections, and a site link that represents it would only contain the two endpoints, or sites, that are connected. Some sites are connected in a multipoint WAN connection, such as a frame relay cloud. A site link that represents this type of connection would include all the sites that are attached to the frame relay cloud.

Site link bridges provide multihop routing through site links that have at least one site in common. For example, if site A is connected to site B, and site B is connected to site C as illustrated in Figure 16-2, a site link AB and a site link BC would enable site B to communicate with A and with C. This does not enable sites A and C to communicate with each other. In order to enable that, a site link bridge would be created with both site links AB and BC within it. With the site link bridge, A and C can communicate.

FIGURE 16-2   Site links and bridges

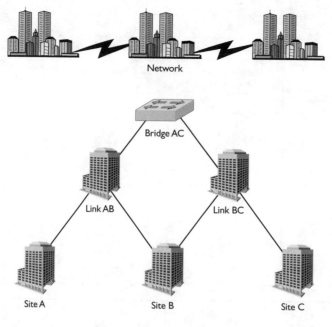

Active Directory Site configuration

Connection objects are enclosed within a domain and exist as unidirectional linkages between domain controllers. If there are two domain controllers that replicate between each other, a Connection object will exist beneath each of the domain controllers and will point at the other domain controller. This creates a replication ring topology within the domain.

IP subnets are created as objects within the Active Directory Sites and Services console. They are assigned to a site. Once an IP subnet is assigned to a site, all workstations and servers that are on that subnet will prefer contacting servers within that site for all queries, authentication, and replication communications.

HEADSTART OBJECTIVE 16.02

How Data Integrity Is Maintained through Replication

The Windows 2000 Active Directory is a database of information about users and network resources. This database is the central traffic cop for security of user accounts and access to resources. A forest creates a single Active Directory database to contain all users and resources. The database is not stored into a single file, nor is any single server the manager of that database.

Instead, the database is split up into multiple partitions. Each namespace context, such as a domain or GC or schema, exists as a separate partition of the whole conglomerate. All domain controllers in a forest hold the schema information. Designated GCSs carry the GC. All domain controllers for a particular domain contain that domain's partition of the database.

How does this affect the network? If there is more than one domain controller in a forest, there will be more than one copy of the schema. If there is more than one domain controller in any particular domain, there will be more than one copy of that domain's partition. If there is more than one GCS, there will be more than one replica of the GC.

Further complicating this setup, each domain controller is a master of its own replica. If an administrator or application connects to that domain controller and makes changes to the Active Directory, the changes are made to the local copy of that Active Directory partition. The challenge, then, is to ensure that the changes made to one partition copy are also made to other replicas. This is the process of *replication.*

When two different administrators make opposing changes to the same resource on different copies of the Active Directory database, there is a conflict when replication occurs. Each replica presents its own update to the other replicas of that partition. The Active Directory handles conflicts by rejecting all the earliest changes and accepting the one with the latest timestamp. That means that if Admin A changes the phone number for Judy to 555-1234 at 2:01 P.M., and Admin B changes the phone number for Judy to 555-2345 at 2:04 P.M., then during replication at 2:30 P.M., Admin B's change wins. The rest of the directory will be updated with Judy's phone number of 555-2345.

heads
⊕p

Active Directory replication always selects the last change when there are conflicting changes to the same attribute or object in the database.

HEADSTART OBJECTIVE 16.03

When to Modify a Network Replication Model

The way that sites are designed is intended to reduce traffic and increase performance. Traffic within a site is not compressed, but it is compressed when replication traffic is sent between sites. Replication can be scheduled for times of day, as well as how frequently per hour during those times. When logging on to the network, workstations try to contact their site's domain controllers. They locate their site through their IP subnet location. All in all, sites provide a method of optimizing performance when they are designed to encompass users, computers, and domain controllers in a well-connected location.

One of the defining factors for network replication is the number and size of domains. When there are fewer, larger domains, or even a single domain, objects are replicated to a great many more domain controllers than they would otherwise be if there were more, smaller domains. That means that many objects would probably be replicated to domain controllers that the users of those objects never access. A remedy would be to create smaller domains that correspond to geographic locations.

When a site spans more than one domain, there is an incremental increase in traffic within that site and between other sites. A site that contains more than one domain will handle replication traffic for multiple domains within it. The remedy is to realign domains and sites so sites do not span domains.

Replication path, or site topology, within a site is automatically managed by a service called the Knowledge Consistency Checker (KCC). This service is installed on every domain controller. The site topology between different sites must be created by a network administrator through the generation of sites, site links, site link bridges, and assignment of IP subnets.

HEADSTART OBJECTIVE 16.04

Creating Connection Objects to Reduce the Time It Takes to Update the Directory

The KCC is a service that runs on each domain controller. It automatically creates Connection objects within the same site between domain controllers in that site, regardless of whether those domain controllers belong to the same domain. The KCC creates a bidirectional ring of Connection objects between the domain controllers in the site. Each domain controller shares its schema, configuration, and domain partition traffic within the ring, as illustrated in Figure 16-3.

FIGURE 16-3

Bidirectional ring
site topology

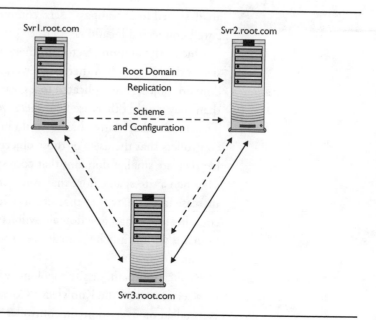

A Connection object represents the flow of traffic between the domain controllers, but only inside a site's boundaries. Each Connection object is found below the NTDS Settings of the domain controller that is the target, or receiving end, of the replication traffic. Figure 16-4 displays a Connection object that was created by the KCC.

Since each Connection object is a single direction, there must be a second Connection object under the other domain controller to send information in the other direction. In Figure 16-3, Svr1 will have a Connection object pointing to Svr2 and a Connection object pointing to Svr3. Both Svr2 and Svr3 will have Connection objects pointing to Svr1, as well as to each other, to complete the ring.

Administrators can manually generate a Connection object. The KCC-generated connections should be sufficient for replication. The only time that an administrator should generate a Connection object is to reduce latency. The KCC does not delete or otherwise change any Connection objects that it did not generate, so if an object is manually created, it must be manually administered thereafter.

FIGURE 16-4

Connection object

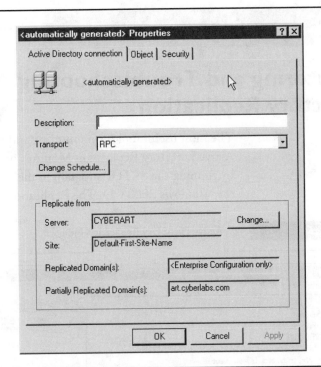

Creating a Connection Object

1. Select Start | Programs | Administrative Tools | Active Directory Sites and Services.

2. Navigate to the server that will be the target of the replication traffic.

3. Expand the server by clicking the plus (+) sign to the right of it.

4. Right-click on the NTDS Settings container below the server.

5. Select New Active Directory Connection.

6. The domain controllers that are within the same site will be displayed in the resulting dialog. Select the source domain controller from this list, and click OK.

7. Type the name for the Connection object in the dialog. The name of the source server will be given automatically, but you may change this.

8. Click OK.

9. If you select the NTDS Settings, the new Connection object appears in the contents pane.

Monitoring and Troubleshooting Active Directory Replication

The most useful tool for monitoring and troubleshooting replication is the Active Directory Replication Monitor, or REPLMON. This tool is installed by running the SETUP program in the SUPPORT\TOOLS directory on the Windows 2000 CD. The Replication Monitor is shown in Figure 16-5.

FIGURE 16-5   Active Directory Replication Monitor

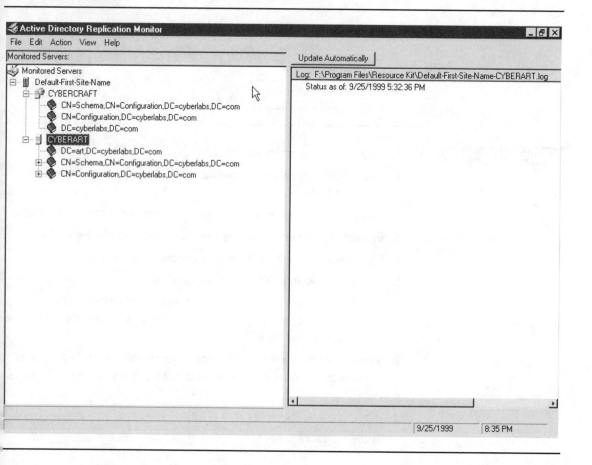

| EXERCISE 16-2 | **Monitoring Active Directory Replication** |

1. Select Start | Programs | Windows 2000 Support Tools | Tools | Active Directory Replication Monitor.

2. Select the Edit menu.

3. Choose Add Monitored Server.

4. In the resulting dialog, select "Search the directory for the server to add," and type in the DNS name of the domain to which the server you are adding belongs.

5. Click Next.

6. Click the plus (+) sign to the right of the site where the server belongs to expand it and select a server, as shown next.

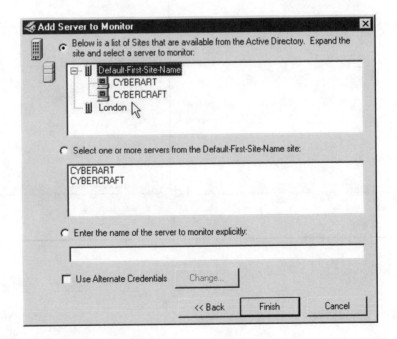

7. Click Finish, and the server will show up in the screen of monitored servers.

8. Below each server, there will be a list of the namespace contexts that are replicated for that domain controller. Expand a namespace context and view the contents as shown in Figure 16-6.

FIGURE 16-6

FIGURE 16-6   Monitored results

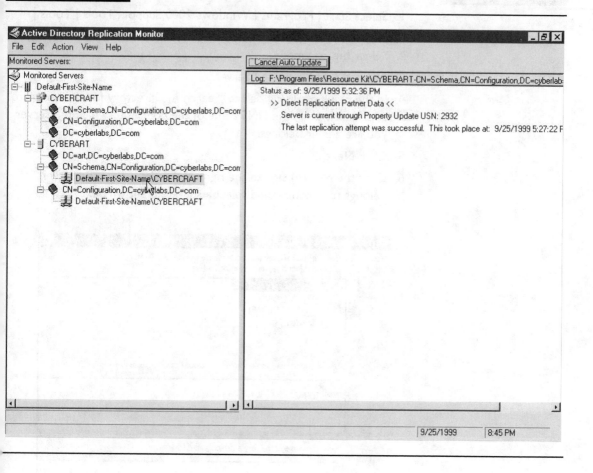

Troubleshooting Active Directory Replication

1. In the Active Directory Replication Monitor, right-click on a monitored server. You should see a dialog similar to the one shown next.

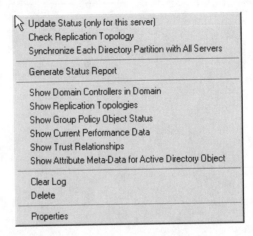

2. You can trigger the KCC to reconfigure the replication topology by selecting Check Replication Topology.

3. If replication has not occurred, you can manually trigger replication by selecting Synchronize Each Directory Partition with All Servers.

4. Select Show Replication Topologies. You should see a graphic view of the replication topology similar to the example shown next.

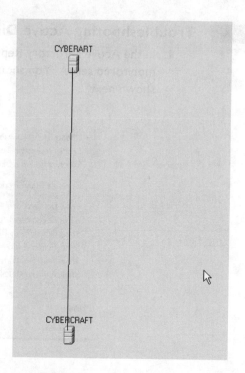

5. Right-click on a server and select Properties. The Server Properties dialog box shown in Figure 16-7 will appear.

6. Click the FSMO Roles tab. Note that if the server is performing the Flexible Single Master of Operations for any of the options, you will be able to click Query to determine whether that replication can occur. If communication is occurring correctly, you will see the notice shown next.

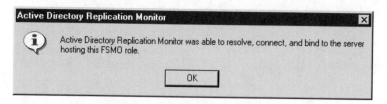

FIGURE 16-7   Server Replication properties

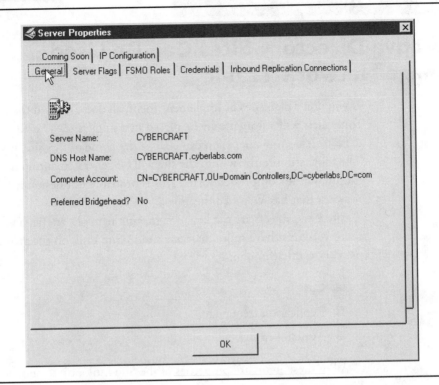

Once a site topology has been created, it probably will remain fairly static unless your organization undergoes significant growth or change. The tool that you will use the most with replication will be the Active Directory Replication Monitor.

How Active Directory Sites Can Be Used to Manage Network Traffic

If you don't plan sites or implement them, all domains and their domain controllers will automatically be placed in a single site. This site is called the default-first-site-name. (You can change the name of this site, if you like.) The replication traffic within the site will be generated automatically and executed in uncompressed form. This is probably not desirable for any network that has WAN connections.

Site Link objects are the key to managing network traffic. To have site links, you must have more than one site. A Site Link object manages network traffic through:

- Cost
- Replication frequency
- Availability

All of these items are properties of the Site Link object, shown in Figure 16-8.

Cost is a logical expense for sending traffic on that particular site link. The higher a cost number, the more likely that the WAN link it represents is slow or highly utilized. When there are two links between the same sites, Active Directory selects the lowest-cost site.

Cost should be designated in inverse proportion to replication frequency. That is, the higher the cost, the less often replication should be executed; the lower the cost, the more often replication should be executed. The replication frequency value can be anything from 15 to 10,080 minutes (a week).

FIGURE 16-8

Site link properties

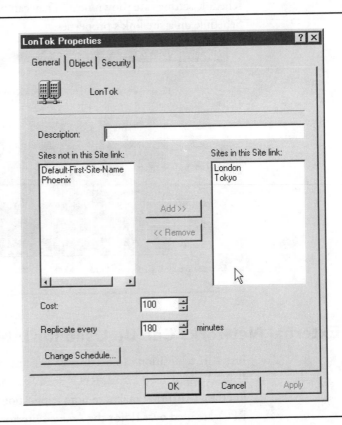

Availability of the link can interrupt replication from occurring during certain time periods. For example, if a company has a weekly videoconference using the network infrastructure, replication can be stopped from occurring during that time to provide more bandwidth to the videoconference. The schedule settings are shown next. They can be accessed by clicking Change Schedule on a site link's properties.

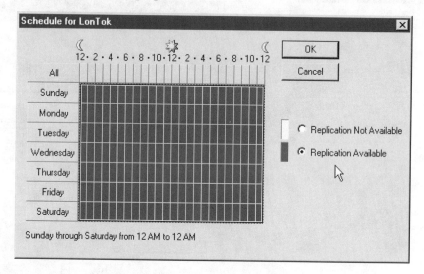

How External Networks Can Be Used for Inter-Site Replication

Inter-site replication can occur over any link that Remote Procedure Calls (RPCs) can be used across. RPCs are a Session-layer application programming interface (API) that makes remote applications appear to be executing locally. RPCs are used over IP for the Active Directory, but are capable of executing over other protocol stacks.

Simple Mail Transfer Protocol, or SMTP, is used for slow WAN links. This transport is an asynchronous mechanism that ensures accurate replication because of the protocol's characteristics. Although SMTP is available as a transport, RPC over IP should be the preferred transport for most links.

The Differences between Inter-Site and Intra-Site Replication

The replication that occurs within a site (intra-site) has several characteristics that differ from the replication that occurs between sites (inter-site). Sites are typically created to represent parts of the internetwork that can communicate easily with each other. Their boundaries are usually WAN links.

Intra-site replication, then, is not compressed to save the time it takes to replicate. Latency is reduced because domain controllers will notify each other with the latest changes made. Intra-site replication only uses RPC transport. Intra-site replication topology is generated automatically by the KCC.

heads
①p

The replication traffic within a site always uses RPCs over IP. The replication traffic between two sites can use either RPC or SMTP. SMTP is used for asynchronous WAN links.

Inter-site replication traffic is compressed, to increase bandwidth availability on the link between the sites. The domain controllers do not notify those in another site when updates have been made. Instead, replication is scheduled. Inter-site replication can use RPC or SMTP transports. The inter-site replication topology must be generated by the network administrator.

Creating Sites and Configuring Inter-Site Replication

Sites are created within the Active Directory Sites and Services console. To create a site, right-click the Sites container, and select New Site. In the resulting dialog box, shown next, type in the name of the site, select a Site Link object (you can change this later), and click OK.

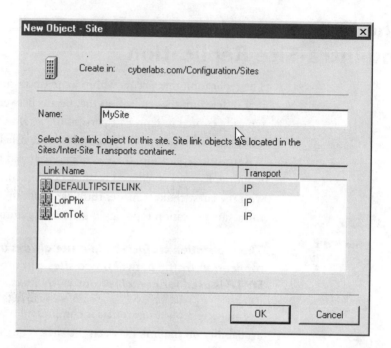

Click OK to close the next dialog box, and the new site will appear in the console.

To create a Site Link object, navigate below the Sites container to the Inter-Site Transports container. Below this, select the inter-site transport, either IP or SMTP. Right-click on it and select New Site Link. In the dialog box shown next, type in a name for the new site link, and then add the sites that this link connects. When you click OK, the link shows up in the console.

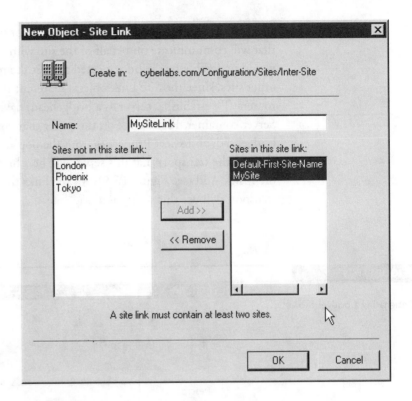

The configuration of inter-site replication is performed through the configuration of the site link properties. Right-click on a site link and select Properties. The default cost of a site is 100. Change the cost to 5. This will allow Active Directory to select this link over others that include the same sites. Change the replication frequency from the default 180 minutes to 35 minutes. Click Change Schedule and remove the hours of 8 A.M. to 12 P.M. on the Monday slot. This will stop any replication from occurring during those hours.

The other task to complete is the selection of the bridgehead servers that will communicate on behalf of the site with other sites. These servers would preferably be the ones located nearest the routers leading to the other sites, since the Site Link objects represent the connections from those routers. To establish a server as a bridgehead, navigate below the site to its Server container. Right-click on the server that you want to designate as a bridgehead, and select Properties from the pop-up menu. In the left pane, click on the transport that this server will be a bridgehead server for, and then click Add (see Figure 16-9). All site links that this site has using that transport will use this server as a bridgehead.

FIGURE 16-9

Designating a bridgehead

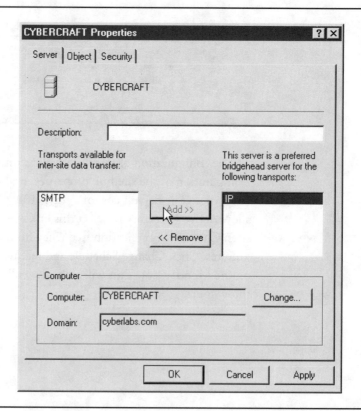

Planning the Active Directory Site Topology for an Enterprise Network Environment

Sites are designated for a single forest. If there are two forests within an enterprise, each will need to have a set of sites created to represent the IP subnets and WAN links on the network. Use the following tips when planning a site topology:

- The IP subnets within sites should be well connected, with fast and reliable communications. A general rule is to avoid spanning WAN links with a site.

- Workstations will attempt to log on to the domain controllers within their own sites before looking elsewhere. Place domain controllers for the users' domains within the same site as the users.

- The Configuration container, which itself is replicated to all domain controllers within a forest, contains the site topology. If changes are made to the site topology, those changes are replicated to all domain controllers, causing some traffic on the wire. A good policy to undertake is not to make changes to sites until a time that users are not as active, such as weekends and evenings.

- Create sites for network sections that are not directly connected to the network, such as those that use dial-up connections or that communicate across IP tunnels. For those sites, use SMTP as the transport of the site links.

- Use standard DNS naming conventions for site names: the characters a through z (both upper and lowercase), the dash (-), and the numbers 0 through 9.

- When there is a redundant backup network connection to a remote site, create two site links, one with a lower cost for the standard network connection, and one with a very high cost to represent the backup connection. Active Directory will select the link with the lowest cost unless it is unavailable.

■ Always place at least two domain controllers within a site and within a domain for redundancy.

■ Add more domain controllers within a site when the workload caused by the number of users within the site increases.

■ Place at least one GCS within each site to handle the queries by end users.

■ Place at least one DNS server within each site to ensure that DNS is available to the Active Directory to serve logon requests and Active Directory communications.

■ Small branch offices may not require a separate site, even though they exist across a WAN link.

EXERCISE 16-4

Planning and Implementing Sites

1. When designing your site topology, you should first already have the forest and domains designed. The second prerequisite is to have knowledge of the WAN links that exist within the internetwork.

2. Create a site for each location that is bounded on all sides by WAN links.

3. Examine each location and determine whether there are at least two domain controllers already designated for that location.

4. For each site that does not have two domain controllers designated for it, review whether there are enough users within the site in order for it to remain separate. If there are few users (roughly less than 50), select the fastest link to the next site, if it is connected to more than one site, and make it part of that site.

5. For any networks that are not directly connected, create a separate site, and use SMTP as the site link transport.

6. Create a site link for each WAN link that exists between sites, and use IP as the transport.

7. For sites that are not able to communicate directly with each other through site links, create a site link bridge.

8. Create IP Subnet objects for each IP subnet, and assign it to the appropriate sites.

ACCELERATING TO WINDOWS 2000

Replication itself is not new to Windows NT. The legacy Primary Domain Controller (PDC) had a read-write copy of a domain's database, called a SAM, or Security Account Manager. All of the Backup Domain Controllers (BDCs) held a read-only copy of the domain database. When an administrator made a change to the network security, it was made to the PDC only. Then the PDC would update all of the BDCs with the change. There were no possibilities of conflicts because there was only one place that a change could be made.

Multimaster replication adds a wrinkle to how you manage the network. Unlike the Windows NT single master model using PDCs, a change can be made to any possible domain controller anywhere within the domain or forest, after which it must be copied to all the other relevant domain controllers. Because of this, administrators who make significant changes to the Active Directory database by adding, moving, or deleting objects can cause so much replication traffic that domain controllers are too busy to allow logons.

Rapid changes may be required when migrating a large set of users to the Active Directory, but the changes should only be made during times when the network is less busy, or in smaller sets of changes.

When a user is logging on to the Active Directory, he or she must be able to contact the domain to which he or she belongs in order to complete the logon. If the domain is not available to the user, then the logon will be denied. This is done for security purposes. If the Active Directory had allowed the logon, the user may have been able to access resources that would normally have been denied to the user.

Take note of where administration occurs within the network, and how replication flows from that site to others. If an administrator is located in one site, and makes changes that affect users in another site, then those changes may not be available to those users until after inter-site replication takes place.

The Active Directory engine is based on the one used by the Exchange Server software. This is a proven multimaster replication system. Exchange Server network designers are taught that a one-to-one correspondence of sites to domains is a viable configuration for the database. This also applies to the Active Directory. By keeping domains and sites from spanning each other, the domain partition of the Active Directory is maintained within the same site replication topology, which optimizes replication traffic.

So, replication itself may not be new, but replication from different master domain controllers is. The multimaster aspects of it will influence how you manage your Windows 2000 network.

QUESTIONS AND ANSWERS

Do you have to depend on the KCC to create your intra-site replication topology?	No. An administrator can delete any Connection objects that the KCC creates, and then create any Connection objects needed. The next time the KCC runs, it will not change the objects made by the administrator, but will attempt to optimize traffic where there are no Connection objects by creating them.
Does the KCC check the inter-site replication topology?	No. The inter-site replication topology must be manually created by an administrator through the generation of sites, site links, site link bridges, and IP subnets.
If you have a small branch office connected by a WAN link to a large internetwork, and you don't want to put a domain controller there, should you create a site?	No. Creating a site would optimize traffic for the branch office only if there were domain controllers placed within it.
Once you create a site, can you delete it later?	Yes. Sites can be changed around at any point in time. They can be deleted, renamed, and assigned different IP subnets as needed. This will let your sites grow with your network.

CHAPTER SUMMARY

Domain controllers in Windows 2000 have a copy of their own domain database, schema, and configuration, and some have copies of the Global Catalog (GC) database. Administrators can make changes to the Active Directory on any domain controller. Replication ensures that the updates made on one domain controller are synchronized with all other domain controllers and their changes. This system is optimized to replicate only the changed information and its location within the Active Directory.

Replication within a site, called *intra-site* replication, is generated automatically by the KCC, or Knowledge Consistency Checker. It creates Connection objects between all the domain controllers within the site in a bidirectional ring topology. Each Connection object is placed below the NTDS Settings object for that server, and points at the source domain controller for the replication traffic.

Replication from outside a site, called *inter-site* replication, must be created by an administrator. The topology consists of Site objects, Site Link objects, Site Link Bridge objects, and IP subnets. The administrator can designate certain servers to communicate with servers in other sites by adding them as bridgehead servers for a certain transport. The transports available for inter-site replication are IP and SMTP. However, only IP—more specifically, RPCs over IP—is available as a transport within a site.

To manage the replication topology, the administrator can use the Active Directory Sites and Services console. To monitor and troubleshoot replication, the administrator can use the Active Directory Replication Monitor.

TWO-MINUTE DRILL

- ❏ The Active Directory is a database that is spread in pieces across multiple domain controllers.
- ❏ *Replication* is the process of synchronizing the Active Directory partitions.
- ❏ There are several partitions in the Active Directory. Some partitions are replicated across an entire forest, while others are replicated completely within a domain.
- ❏ A site is a grouping of IP Subnet objects.
- ❏ A forest creates a single Active Directory database to contain all users and resources. The database is split up into multiple partitions.
- ❏ One of the defining factors for network replication is the number and size of domains. When there are fewer, larger domains, or even a single domain, objects are replicated to a great many more domain controllers than they would otherwise be if there were more, smaller domains.
- ❏ Replication path, or site topology, within a site is automatically managed by a service called the Knowledge Consistency Checker (KCC).
- ❏ The KCC creates a bidirectional ring of Connection objects between the domain controllers in the site.

❑ The most useful tool for monitoring and troubleshooting replication is the Active Directory Replication Monitor, or REPLMON.

❑ Site Link objects are the key to managing network traffic. To have site links, you must have more than one site.

❑ Cost is a logical expense for sending traffic on that particular site link. The higher a cost number, the more likely that the WAN link it represents is slow or highly utilized. When there are two links between the same sites, Active Directory selects the lowest-cost site.

❑ Inter-site replication can occur over any link that Remote Procedure Calls (RPCs) can be used across.

❑ Intra-site replication is not compressed to save the time it takes to replicate. Latency is reduced because domain controllers will notify each other with the latest changes made.

❑ Inter-site replication traffic is compressed to increase bandwidth availability on the link between the sites.

❑ Sites are created within the Active Directory Sites and Services console. To create a site, right-click the Sites container, and select New Site.

❑ Sites are designated for a single forest. If there are two forests within an enterprise, each will need to have a set of sites created to represent the IP subnets and WAN links on the network.

SELF TEST

The following questions will help you measure your understanding of the material presented in this chapter. Read all of the choices carefully, as there may be more than one correct answer. Choose all correct answers for each question.

1. What are the benefits of using multimaster replication? (Choose two.)

   A. Single point of failure

   B. Redundancy

   C. Optimizes performance

   D. Immediate synchronization

2. Which of the following represent partitions of the Active Directory database?

   A. Domains

   B. Global Catalog

   C. Schema and configuration

   D. All of the above

3. What is a grouping of IP subnets called?

   A. Site

   B. Site link

   C. Connection

   D. Site link bridge

4. What are Connection objects used for?

   A. Inter-site replication

   B. Bridging two links together

   C. Establishing the IP subnet

   D. Intra-site replication

5. What characteristics represent intra-site replication? (Choose all that apply.)

   A. Uses SMTP transport

   B. Uses RPCs over IP transport

   C. Automatically generated via Connection objects

   D. Relies on site links and site link bridges

6. Which of the following is used to generate the replication topology?

   A. KCC

   B. RPC

   C. IP

   D. SMTP

7. Which of the following tools can help troubleshoot replication?

   A. The Active Directory Replication Troubleshooter

   B. Active Directory Sites and Services

   C. Knowledge Consistency Checker

   D. Active Directory Replication Monitor

8. What happens to a domain controller if the administrator never creates a site topology?

   A. It cannot be installed.

   B. It is automatically demoted to a member server.

   C. It is placed into a site called "default-first-site-name."

   D. It is placed into a "waiting" container.

9. Which of the following is compressed?

   A. Inter-site replication

   B. Intra-site replication

   C. Connection objects

   D. Sites

10. How can inter-site replication be prevented from occurring across a site link?

    A. It can't

    B. Change the cost of a site link to 0

    C. Change the frequency of replication to 10,080

    D. Change the schedule of availability

11. Which object's properties enable the selection of bridgehead servers?

    A. Server

    B. Site

    C. Site link

    D. Site link bridge

12. True or False: If an organization has two forests, it can use the same sites to handle both forests' replication traffic.

    A. True

    B. False

13. Where do workstations attempt logon first?

    A. Within the site of the user who is logging on

    B. Within the workstation's site, indicated by its IP subnet

    C. Anywhere within the forest

    D. Anywhere within its own domain

14. What is the minimum recommended number of domain controllers to place within a site?

    A. Zero

    B. One

    C. Two

    D. Three

15. If a site is not directly connected to the rest of the forest's network, what transport should it use?

    A. IP

    B. SMTP

    C. RPC

    D. KCC

MICROSOFT CERTIFIED SYSTEMS ENGINEER

17

Maintaining and Optimizing Active Directory

Y ou have already learned about the advantages of Windows 2000's Active Directory and how it makes life easier for both administrators and users in a large, complex network. As discussed in previous chapters, however, planning and implementing the Active Directory is not a simple matter. Once installed, there is still a certain amount of ongoing maintenance involved.

As the network grows and changes, the structure of your Active Directory will necessarily change as well. As administrator, it will be your responsibility to oversee its evolution and ensure that it continues to serve the purposes of your organization.

In order to reap all the benefits of this exciting new feature, it is important that you learn how to practice preventative medicine by periodically performing "housekeeping" tasks, such as reorganization and backup. This chapter addresses the necessary maintenance duties, and looks at ways to optimize the performance of the Directory services to maximize its functionality and ease of use.

HEADSTART OBJECTIVE 17.01

Performing Periodic Database Maintenance Tasks

There are a number of tasks that should be performed on a regular basis, to ensure that the Active Directory structure is up to date and accurately addresses the needs of its users. Of course, all actions performed on Active Directory objects are, in fact, part of maintaining the database. We discuss a few common tasks in this section, including defragmentation of the database, other "housekeeping" duties, using Windows 2000 resource kit utilities, monitoring replication, and publishing printers to the directory.

The ntdsutil.exe Tool

This is a command-line utility provided in the Windows 2000 Server resource kit that can be used to perform several administrative tasks related to database management. It allows you to compact, repair, and check the integrity of the Active Directory database, and clean up directory metadata. (*Meta* is a prefix that in most information technology usages means "an underlying definition or description." Thus, *metadata* is a definition or description of data.)

The ntdsutil tool can analyze and clean up core directory structures, for example, when you have removed a domain controller from the network.

The ntdsutil help screen describes some of the available commands (see Figure 17-1).

As you can see, ntdsutil can be used to perform an authoritative restore (for more information on authoritative restore, see the section entitled "Developing a Plan to Back Up and Restore Active Directory in a Multimaster Environment," later in this chapter). ntdsutil allows you to manage NTDS database files, clean up the objects left behind by decommissioned servers, clean up duplicate SIDs, and check the database for correct syntax.

Active Directory Cleanup and Database Defragmentation

The Active Directory database is stored in a file named ntds.dit. Objects that are no longer being used clutter the database. Active Directory also

FIGURE 17-1   Some of the ntdsutil functions

```
E:\WINNT\System32\ntdsutil.exe                                       _ □ ×
E:\WINNT\System32\ntdsutil.exe: help

?                              - Print this help information
Authoritative restore          - Authoritatively restore the DIT database
Domain management              - Prepare for new domain creation
Files                          - Manage NTDS database files
Help                           - Print this help information
IPDeny List                    - Manage LDAP IP Deny List
LDAP policies                  - Manage LDAP protocol policies
Metadata cleanup               - Clean up objects of decommissioned servers
Popups %s                      - <en/dis>able popups with "on" or "off"
Quit                           - Quit the utility
Roles                          - Manage NTDS role owner tokens
Security account management    - Manage Security Account Database - Duplicate SI
D Cleanup
Semantic database analysis     - Semantic Checker

E:\WINNT\System32\ntdsutil.exe: _
```

produces numerous log files, which are not needed after changes are written to the database. If not removed, all these extraneous files and objects consume hard disk space and slow performance.

Self-Cleaning Operations

Active Directory performs regular cleanup tasks automatically, at which time unnecessary log files are deleted, tombstoned objects (those unused objects tagged to be deleted after a specified time period) are removed, and online defragmentation is performed.

HOW ONLINE DEFRAGMENTATION WORKS   When the database file is updated, the fastest method is to write to the first available database pages. Online defragmentation, performed by the Active Directory as part of its automatic maintenance feature, rearranges the order of data in the database to optimize the layout of the database. However, online defragmentation does not reduce the size of the database file. In order to do that, you have to use offline defragmentation, which we next discuss in some detail.

Offline Defragmentation

Offline defragmentation should rarely be necessary; but, if the content of the database is significantly reduced, you could free a lot of space by performing this action. Offline defragmentation is also used when you test the database size as part of the Active Directory optimization process (discussed later in this chapter).

   To perform offline defragmentation, you must first—as the name implies—take the domain controller to be defragmented offline. Then use the ntdsutil.exe tool from the resource kit in Directory Services Repair mode. The command to use is "compact to <target_directory>." This defragments the database file, and then writes the new compacted file to the directory named. Now you can replace the old ntds.dit file with the new defragmented version (but move the old one to another location, instead of deleting it immediately, and be sure the new file works properly before deleting the old file).

Points to remember:

- When the directory is loaded with objects, the database will be in a fragmented state, and this makes it impossible to tell how much space the objects really consume in the database file.

- Online defragmentation makes space available, but does not shrink the database file.

- Only offline defragmentation gives you a clear picture of the space consumption.

Other Active Directory Housekeeping Duties

As an example of the type of "cleanup" that may be required from time to time, the file replication service may occasionally be unable to determine where an object should be placed when performing replication. The designers of Active Directory anticipated this possibility and included the LostAndFound container object as a "holding place" for these objects. If an object has been created in, or moved to, a location that is missing after replication, the "lost" object is added to the LostAndFound container.

The administrator should periodically check this folder to decide whether objects that have been parked there need to be moved or deleted.

Examining the LostAndFound Container

To examine the contents of the LostAndFound container on your Windows 2000 server, first open the Active Directory Users and Computers MMC (Start | Administrative Tools | Active Directory Users and Computers). Expand the domain tree.

Select LostAndFound (see Figure 17-2).

Now you can move any lost objects to the desired location in the directory (see details on how to move objects in the section "Reorganizing Objects in Active Directory," later in this chapter).

Monitoring Replication Status

The Windows 2000 resource kit includes many handy utilities that can be used in maintaining Active Directory. DSASTAT, for example, allows you

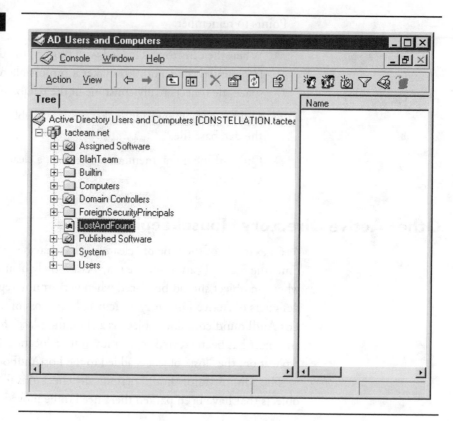

to monitor the status of replication by comparing the directories on
Windows 2000 domain controllers. This is useful for monitoring
replication status; in fact, it includes the option to perform a comparison of
full attributes between the replicated objects. DSASTAT can provide you
with detailed statistics. You can also use it to obtain such information as
how many objects exist in Active Directory for each object class.

You can force replication events using one of two other resource kit tools.
REPADMIN is a command-line utility, and REPLMON is a graphical
interface tool that allows you to do the same thing. Both utilities also allow
you to display replication metadata and determine whether replication is up
to date.

Publishing Printers in Active Directory

Publishing new printers to the directory is another task that will be necessary as part of your routine administrative duties. You can publish a printer shared by a computer running Windows 2000 by using the Sharing tab of the printer property dialog. By default, the "listed in *directory name*" option is enabled. (This means that the shared printer will be published by default.) The printer is published in the corresponding computer container in the directory as <server>-<Printer name>.

The print subsystem automatically propagates changes made to the printer attributes (location, description, loaded paper, and so forth) to the directory.

EXERCISE 17-1

Sharing and Publishing a Printer

1. To create a new printer: Start | Settings | Printers | Add Printer. Follow the instructions on your screen.

2. Once you have created the printer, select the Listed in Directory check box, as shown in Figure 17-3.

The Printer object will be published under the Computer object to which it is attached.

Publishing Non-Windows 2000 Printers

You can publish printers shared by systems other than Windows 2000 in the directory. The simplest way to do this is to use the pubprn script. This script publishes all the shared printers on a given server. It is located in the system32 directory.

Alternatively, you can use the DS MMC snap-in to publish printers on non-Windows 2000 servers.

To use the DS MMC snap-in to publish printers:

1. Right-click the name of the organizational unit (such as "Marketing"), click New, and click Printer.

2. In the Name field, type the name of the printer.

3. In the UNC path name, type the path to the printer, such as \\qonos\prprint.

FIGURE 17-3

Publishing a new printer by checking the List in the Directory check box

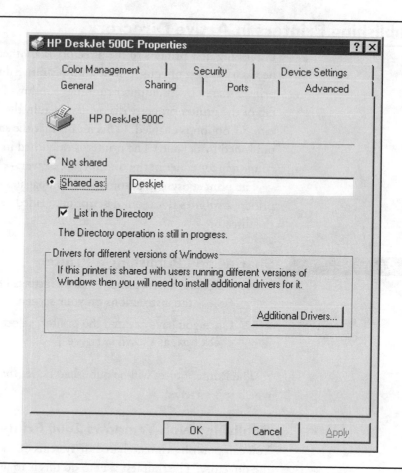

HEADSTART OBJECTIVE 17.02

Reorganizing Objects in Active Directory

It is inevitable that, no matter how carefully you plan your Active Directory structure prior to implementation, you will at some point have to reorganize the Active Directory objects to accommodate changes within the organization.

Windows 2000 eases the burden of this administrative task.

Moving Active Directory Objects

There are many reasons why you may need to move objects within the Active Directory; for example, if an employee is transferred from one department to another, or a computer is moved to a different function. Most Active Directory objects can be easily moved from one OU to another.

It's very easy to move a user or computer account to a new location. Just select the object you want to move, right-click it, choose Move, and select the new location. In the following exercise, we go through the steps of moving a computer account to a new container object.

Moving a Computer Account

1. Open Active Directory Users and Computers (Start | Programs | Administrative Tools | Active Directory Users and Computers).

2. In the console tree, click Computers or click the container that contains the computer that you want to move.

3. In the Details pane, right-click the computer, and then click Move.

4. In the Move pane, click the domain node.

5. Click the container to which you want to move the computer, and then click OK.

How Moving an Object Affects Permissions

When you move an object from one OU to a different OU, any permissions directly assigned to that specific object are retained. However, permissions inherited by the object from the old OU will cease to apply to that object.

Be sure that you consider this when moving objects, and ensure that the object's permissions in the new container are as you want them to be.

Pruning and Grafting

Pruning and *grafting*—in keeping with the "forest" and "tree" concepts describing Active Directory structure—are one way in which many objects can be moved simultaneously. The MOVETREE command-line utility can now be used to move a subtree of objects (OUs, leaf objects) from one domain within a tree/forest to another domain. Machine objects are then rejoined to the new domain using the NETDOM tool. (Later in this chapter, we discuss updating the Access Control List after moving computers, using the sidwalk.exe utility.)

Using the MOVETREE Utility to Prune and Graft Directory Objects

The resource kit utility MOVETREE gives you a way to move Active Directory objects across domains within a forest. The objects you move can be specified as a domain, or they can be specified as a subtree in a domain. Passwords are replicated to the new domain, and if duplicate names are encountered, the new objects are relegated to the LostAndFound container, which we discussed earlier.

Associated data that is not moved during a MOVETREE operation includes policies, profiles, logon scripts, and user's personal data.

Computer objects will not function in the new domain until you join them using the NETDOM utility. You may also need to use SIDWALKER to update the Access Control Entries.

heads
① p

Remember that domain local and global groups cannot be moved across domains with the MOVETREE utility.

EXERCISE 17-3

Using MOVETREE to Move an OU from One Domain to Another

In this example, you may substitute the names of domains and OUs present in your own Active Directory.

In the Marketing domain there is an organizational unit, Promotions, and a server, Server1.

In the Sales organizational unit is a server, Server2. The desired operation is to move the Promotions organizational unit from Marketing to Sales and rename the new OU "Sales Promotions."

1. At the command prompt, type

MOVETREE /TEST /START

/s:Server1.Marketing.Acme.Com

/d:Server2.Sales.Acme.Com

/sdn:OU=Promotions,DC=Marketing,DC=Acme,DC=Com

/ddn:OU=Sales Promotions,C=Sales,DC=Acme,DC=Com

The preceding command performs a test run, and if no errors are encountered, performs the move operation.

See Figure 17-4 for the syntax of the MOVETREE command.

Walking the SID

The Windows 2000 resource kit includes a utility, Sidwalker, which is useful when you move computers and local groups and need to update the Access Control List. The Sidwalker and Security Migration Editor tool allows you to delete or replace each instance of an old Security ID with a new SID on all ACLs.

The following Questions and Answers section will answer some of your questions about Windows 2000 Directory Services Utilities.

FIGURE 17-4   The MOVETREE utility syntax

```
E:\WINNT\System32\cmd.exe                                                _ □ ×

THE SYNTAX OF THIS COMMAND IS:

MoveTree [/start ¦ /continue ¦ /check] [/s SrcDSA] [/d DstDSA]
         [/sdn SrcDN] [/ddn DstDN] [/u Domain\Username] [/p Password] [/quiet]

   /start        : Start a move tree operation with /check option by default.
                 : Instead, you could be able to use /startnocheck to start a mov
e
                 : tree operation without any check.
   /continue     : Continue a failed move tree operation.
   /check        : Check the whole tree before actually move any object.
   /s <SrcDSA>   : Source server's fully qualified primary DNS name. Required
   /d <DstDSA>   : Destination server's fully qualified primary DNS name. Require
d
   /sdn <SrcDN>  : Source sub-tree's root DN.
                 : Required in Start and Check case. Optional in Continue case
   /ddn <DstDN>  : Destination sub-tree's root DN. RDN plus Destinaton Parent DN.
   Required
   /u <Domain\UserName>  : Domain Name and User Account Name. Optional
   /p <Password> : Password. Optional
   /quiet        : Quiet Mode. Without Any Screen Output. Optional
```

QUESTIONS AND ANSWERS

Which tool would I use if I wanted to move user and group objects from one domain to another within the same forest?	MOVETREE
Which tool would I use to move computer accounts between domains?	NETDOM
Which tool would I use to clean up directory metadata?	NTDSUTIL
Which tool would I use to update SIDs?	SIDWALKER

HEADSTART OBJECTIVE 17.03

Developing a Plan to Back Up and Restore Active Directory in a Multimaster Environment

Active Directory uses multimaster replication. Practically speaking, what this means is that there is a copy, or replica, on each domain controller of the partition containing Active Directory info for that domain. All of these copies are writable. This differs from Windows NT, where changes can be made only on the Primary domain controller, which then replicates those changes to its Backup domain controlers. In Windows 2000, all domain controllers are created equal; changes made to any replica are replicated to those on the other domain controllers.

Because of this, backing up and restoring the Active Directory requires some way to ensure that all DCs have the same information after the restoration. Microsoft addressed this by providing *authoritative restore*. Before we look at how to do an authoritative restore, let's examine the features of the new backup utility and discuss the steps involved in backing up a Windows 2000 Server domain controller.

The backup utility in Windows 2000 has been improved and enhanced over the NT 4.0 version, although it is still called ntbackup.exe. These improvements are welcome, as they make it much easier for administrators to perform necessary disaster prevention and recovery tasks. When operating in a multimaster environment, with more than one Windows 2000 domain controller, it becomes especially important that you be able to back up and restore the Active Directory database.

The Active Directory database is a distributed service; thus, you only have to back up one Active Directory database from each domain. Just be sure changes made at other domain controllers have been replicated to the server being backed up.

Backing Up the Server

The new Windows 2000 ntbackup utility has three Wizards that simplify backup and restore operations:

■ The Backup Wizard takes you through the steps to perform a system backup.

■ The Disaster Recovery Preparation Wizard allows you to prepare a set of Disaster Recovery disks that can be used to fully recover a failed system.

■ The Recovery Wizard takes you through the steps to recover a system.

In the following exercise, we use the Backup Wizard to back up the entire server. You can then manually restore the system without using the Restore Wizard.

EXERCISE 17-4

Backing Up a Windows 2000 Domain Controller with Active Directory

First, be sure you are logged on to the Windows 2000 Server Domain Controller using an account that has Administrator or Backup Operator privileges. If you log on using an account that does not have these privileges, you cannot back up the Active Directory.

1. Start the Backup Wizard. There are two ways to do so:
Start | Programs | Accessories | System Tools | Backup,
or run ntbackup.exe, using the Run command on the Start menu or at the command line in a DOS window.

2. Click Backup Wizard to start the backup process.

3. Click Next.

4. Select "Back up everything on my computer."

5. Select the destination media. If you have a tape backup unit installed, you can select the tape drive. In this example, we use a backup file on the disk system (see Figure 17-5).

6. Create a backup file. In this example, the file name is backup.bkf.

7. Specify your media options. This example creates a new backup and overwrites any data that is present on the backup media.

8. Complete the remaining Wizard screens, and begin the backup operation. A progress indicator shows the status of the backup operation.

Restoring the Server

You can use your system backup media to restore the server. The restore process recovers the Windows 2000 Server operating system configuration,

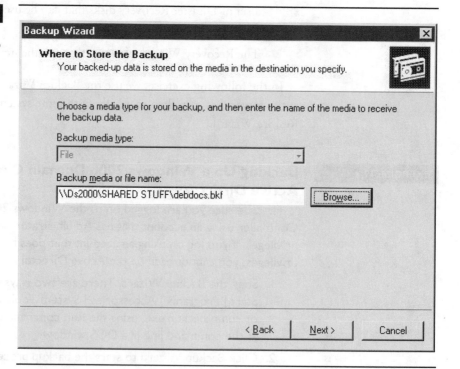

the Active Directory (including database and registry settings), the Certificate Server database files, and the File Replication Service.

When the restoration process is finished, you can optionally restart in Directory Service Repair mode and verify that the Active Directory database has been restored. Let's discuss this process and walk through the steps involved.

When you restart the server in Normal operational mode, the system automatically performs a series of steps to ensure data integrity. The Active Directory database files undergo an automatic consistency check, and they are re-indexed. Both the Active Directory and File Replication Service is brought up to date from their replication partners using the standard replication protocols for each of those services.

Finally, you can verify the success of the restore process by checking that the Active Directory, Certificate Server, and File Replication Services are all operational.

EXERCISE 17-5

Using Windows NT Backup to Restore the Server

1. Start Windows NT Backup: from the Start menu, point to Programs | Accessories, and then click Backup.

2. Click Restore Wizard on the Welcome page.

3. Create a catalog. To build the catalog, right-click the File icon, and then select Catalog File.

4. Use the browse dialog to locate the backup set that you created previously. In this example, the file is backup.bkf.

5. Ensure that all of the volumes and System State options are selected. The System State refers to the distributed services components—the Active Directory, Certificate Server, and File Replication Service.

6. Select the backup media name for the restore operation. In this example, where the backup media was a disk file, the backup file backup.bkf created during the previous backup operation is selected.

7. Click OK and continue the restore process. A visual progress indicator is displayed.

Verifying Active Directory Restoration

After the restore is completed, you can either restart the server in Normal operational mode and perform basic verification, or continue with the advanced verification. Both processes are explained next.

BASIC VERIFICATION

1. Once the restore operation has completed, restart the computer in Normal operational mode. The Active Directory and Certificate Server automatically detect that they have been recovered from a backup. They perform an integrity check and re-index the database.

2. After you can log on to the system, browse the directory. All of the user and group objects that were present in the directory before backup should be restored. Similarly, files that were members of a File Replication Service replica set and certificates that were issued by the Certificate Server should be present.

ADVANCED VERIFICATION The following procedure introduces an advanced option, which is not normally required for normal recovery operations. Incorrect usage of the utility described in this section can corrupt the Active Directory database, requiring you to restore the database from backup to ensure reliable operation.

1. Immediately after performing the restore operation, restart the server and select Directory Service Repair mode from the boot menu.

2. Once the system has started, log on using the administrator account for the server machine.

3. Verify that the Active Directory is in a state consistent with having been recovered from a backup. To do this, check for a specific registry key. Start Registry Editor: from the Start menu, click Run, and then type

   Regedit

4. Click OK.

5. Select the registry key:
   HKEY_LOCAL_MACHINE\SYSTEM\CurrentControlSet\
   Services\NTDS

6. Check that there is a subkey Restore In Progress. This key is automatically generated by Windows NT Backup, and indicates to the Active Directory Service that the database files have been restored and that Active Directory Service should perform a consistency check and re-index the next time the directory is started. This key is automatically removed upon completion of this check. DO NOT ADD or DELETE this key.

7. Close the Regdt32 utility.

8. Use the ntdsutil.exe utility to check for the recovered Active Directory database files. From the Start menu, point to Programs, and click Command Prompt. At the command prompt, type **NTDSUTIL**.

9. At the NTDSUTIL prompt, type **Files**.

10. At the file maintenance prompt, type **Info**.
    If the Active Directory files have been recovered successfully, you should see list information.

11. Once you have confirmed that the Active Directory has been restored from the backup and that the registry keys are present, restart the server in Normal mode.

When the computer is restarted in Normal mode, the Active Directory automatically detects that it has been recovered from a backup and performs an integrity check and re-indexes the database. Once you can log on to the system, you should be able to browse the directory. All user and group objects that were present in the directory before backup should be restored.

Authoritative Restore

In the Windows Backup utility, distributed services such as the directory service are in a collection known as the System State data. When you back up the System State data on a domain controller, you are backing up all Active Directory data that exists on that server. To restore these distributed services to that server, you must restore the System State data. However, if you have more than one domain controller in your organization, and your Active Directory is replicated to any of these other servers, you need to perform an authoritative restore to ensure that your restored data gets replicated to all of your servers.

Performing authoritative restore of Active Directory data requires that you run the ntdsutil utility after you have restored the System State data but before you restart the server. This utility lets you mark Active Directory objects for authoritative restore. When an object is marked for authoritative restore, its update sequence number is changed so it is higher than any other update sequence number in the Active Directory replication system. This ensures that replicated or distributed data that you restore is properly replicated or distributed to all of the domain controllers.

To restore the System State data on a domain controller, you have to start your computer in Directory Services Restore mode. This allows you to restore the SYSVOL directory and the Active Directory.

heads
①p   *You can only restore the System State data on a local computer. You cannot restore the System State data on a remote computer.*

Restoring the System State Data

To restore System State data, use the follow steps:

STARTING THE COMPUTER IN DIRECTORY SERVICES RESTORE MODE

1. Click Start, and then click Shut Down.

2. Click Restart, and then click OK.

3. When you see the message "Please select the operating system to start," press F8.

4. Use the arrow keys to highlight the appropriate Safe mode option, and then press ENTER.

   NUM LOCK must be off before the arrow keys on the numeric keypad will function.

5. Use the arrow keys to highlight an operating system, and then press ENTER.

USING NTBACKUP TO RESTORE THE SYSTEM STATE DATA IN DIRECTORY SERVICES RESTORE MODE

1. Open the Backup utility.

2. Click the Restore tab, and then in "Click to select the check box for any drive, folder, or file that you want to restore," click the box next to System State. This restores the System State data along with any other data you have selected for the current restore operation.

HEADSTART OBJECTIVE 17.04

Optimizing Active Directory Performance

In this section, we look at some ways to enhance the performance of the Active Directory, and provide access to more of its advanced features.

Changing to Native Mode

A Windows 2000 domain can operate in one of two modes:

- Mixed mode, which supports coexistence of Windows 2000 domain controllers and NT Server DCs. This is the default mode, and most organizations find it advantageous to set up their domains this way in the beginning and continue to use their old servers.

- Native mode, which does not support NT 4.0 domain controllers.

As your Windows 2000 network grows and old hardware is replaced, it is likely that eventually you will replace old down-level (NT 4.0) domain controllers with Windows 2000 servers. When this transition is complete, you will want to upgrade from a Mixed-mode environment to Native mode.

Running your Windows 2000 domain in Native mode lets you take advantage of new features such as universal groups, which cannot be used in Mixed mode.

Do not change to Native mode until you are sure you wish to abandon support for the down-level BDCs, as you cannot reverse the action.

Switching to Native mode is accomplished via the following steps:

1. Select Start | Programs | Administrative Tools | Active Directory Domains and Trusts.

2. Right-click on the domain whose mode you wish to change.

3. Click Properties.

4. Select the General tab, and click Change Mode (see Figure 17-6).

Remember to ensure that all domain controllers are running Windows 2000 Server before changing from Mixed to Native mode.

FIGURE 17-6

Changing to Native mode with the domain properties dialog box

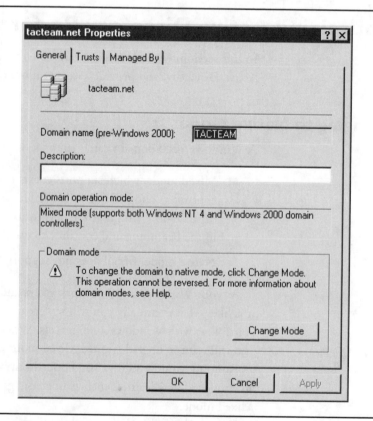

Active Directory Database Sizing

The Active Directory database has been tested for up to 1.5 million objects. Performance tests show logon performance for a single LDAP client to be the same with 10,000 objects, 100,000 objects, and 1.1 MM objects—the directory service does not slow measurably when the size of the database increases.

However, in a Mixed-mode environment in which backup DCs are running Windows NT 4.0, the recommended limit for number of security-principal objects per domain is 40,000 (the sum of users, groups, and computers). This limit is based on SAM (Security Account Manager) database storage capacity.

Be sure you have enough space for the ntds.dit file on your disk, and that you plan for future growth.

Best practices include

- Provide at least twice the disk space estimated for the database itself, to allow for defragmentation, tombstoning, and future growth.

- Estimate the size of the database, allocating 3.6 k per user object or other security principal, 1.1 k per nonsecurity principal, and 75 bytes per Access Control Entry per object. (A security principal is a user or security group account or a computer account, i.e., an object to which a SID would be assigned.)

- Allocate additional space for domain controllers serving as Global Catalogs.

You may wish to determine the size of your database more precisely. Recall that the Active Directory database is stored in a file named ntds.dit. If you want to do database-sizing tests, you need a way to determine the size of the ntds.dit file. If you monitor the size of the ntds.dit file while an Active Directory domain controller performs many write operations, it will seem that the database file size doesn't change. This is because NTFS records the size of a file when the file is opened and does not refresh before the file is closed again.

The Active Directory opens the database file when the DC boots up and does not close it again until the computer shuts down. This means you cannot use the size of the ntds.dit file reported by Windows Explorer or a command prompt to find out how big the file actually is.

You can, however, use one of the two following methods to determine the size of the ntds.dit file:

■ Reboot the DC, which closes the file. Then it will be reopened when the directory service restarts, and NTFS will report the correct file size (see Figure 17-7).

■ Use the Windows Explorer Properties dialog on the partition where the ntds.dit file is located. This always reports the correct amount of available space. You should make a record of the amount of available space both before and after the test to compute the correct file size.

Placement of Database and Log Files for Enhanced Performance

To enhance performance on domain controllers that must handle high request rates, place the Windows 2000 operating system on one hard disk, the Active Directory database file on a second, and the log files on a third.

FIGURE 17-7   Checking the size of ntds.dit after rebooting

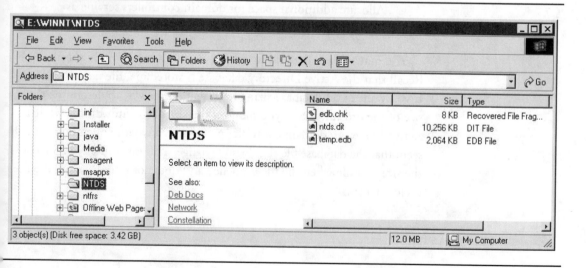

For a Windows 2000 network administrator, a large part of what you do each day can be defined, in some way, as maintaining and optimizing the Active Directory. Because the Active Directory is truly the foundation of the new operating system, it is imperative that you become familiar with managing it, backing it up, and repairing or restoring it. Learning to use the tools built into Windows 2000 and those included in the resource kit will make your job and your life easier as the world of Windows expands in scope and functionality.

ACCELERATING TO WINDOWS 2000

The Active Directory itself is a whole new world for the Microsoft network administrator, and brings you a whole new way to do old, familiar tasks. The following is just a few of the new features in Windows 2000 designed to help you maintain and optimize this exciting implementation of directory services.

- Active Directory Users and Computers MMC snap-in allows you to easily manage AD objects, their properties, and attributes. Many housekeeping duties, such as monitoring the LostAndFound container for objects "lost" during replication, can be performed here.

- A variety of resource kit utilities are included to provide an administrator with the means to move and manipulate Active Directory objects.

  - NTDSUTIL allows you to compact, move, repair, and check the integrity of the directory database.

  - MOVETREE allows you to move directory objects across domains within a forest.

  - NETDOM allows you to move computer accounts across domains without altering local groups.

  - SIDWALKER allows you to update the security identifier on Access Control Entries and create SID profile files.

  - REPADMIN and REPLMON allow you to monitor and force replication events.

- A new, improved version of ntbackup that supports backup and restoration of the Active Directory information as part of the System State data.

- The ability to do an authoritative restore of the Active Directory information to ensure that it is updated properly to all domain controllers.

CHAPTER SUMMARY

This chapter addressed the issues of maintaining and optimizing the performance of your Active Directory, and introduced you to some tips, tricks, and tools that can be used to accomplish that dual purpose. Many network administrators focus only on the short-term goal of implementing Active Directory in their organization's network, but we must not forget the long-range objective: keeping the directory services performing in such a way as to make the jobs of the users (and, we hope, the administrators) easier.

Toward that end, we discussed defragmentation of the database, both the automatic defragmentation process that Active Directory imposes upon itself at set intervals while the server is up and running, and the ability of an administrator to do an offline compacting of the database using the command-line utility ntdsutil.

We examined other housekeeping duties and the tools we can use to perform them, and worked through exercises in moving Active Directory objects, and backing up and restoring the Active Directory database.

Finally, we addressed Active Directory performance issues, and things that we can do to enhance it.

TWO-MINUTE DRILL

- [ ] The Active Directory database is stored in a file named ntds.dit. Objects that are no longer being used clutter the database. Active Directory also produces numerous log files, which are not needed after changes are written to the database.

- [ ] Active Directory performs regular cleanup tasks automatically, at which time unnecessary log files are deleted, tombstoned objects (those unused objects tagged to be deleted after a specified time period) are removed, and online defragmentation is performed.

❑ You can only restore the System State data on a local computer. You cannot restore the System State data on a remote computer.

❑ The Active Directory database has been tested for up to 1.5 million objects. Performance tests show logon performance for a single LDAP client to be the same with 10,000 objects, 100,000 objects, and 1.1 MM objects—the directory service does not slow measurably when the size of the database increases.

❑ DSASTAT allows you to monitor the status of replication by comparing the directories on Windows 2000 domain controllers.

❑ Running your Windows 2000 domain in Native mode lets you take advantage of new features such as universal groups, which cannot be used in Mixed mode.

SELF TEST

The following questions help you measure your understanding of the material presented in this chapter. Read all of the choices carefully, as there may be more than one correct answer. Choose all correct answers for each question.

1. Which of the following tools can analyze and clean up core directory structures?

    A. Disk Management snap-in

    B. ntdsutil.exe

    C. dirclean.exe

    D. replmon

2. What is the purpose of the LostAndFound container?

    A. It is a desktop folder in which you can deposit miscellaneous files.

    B. It is part of the Recycle Bin.

    C. It is used by the directory replication process as a "holding" place for objects when the service cannot determine where the object should be placed.

    D. It is used by the administrator as a shared folder where users can look for objects when they have forgotten the object's location.

3. Which of the following resource kit utilities can be used to monitor the replication process? (Check all that apply.)

    A. REPADMIN

    B. DSASTAT

    C. NETDOM

    D. NTDS.DIT

4. How can you publish printers shared by non-Windows 2000 computers in the Active Directory? (Check all that apply.)

    A. Use the pubprn script.

    B. Use the PMON utility.

    C. Use the DS MMC.

    D.

5. Which of the following is used to move a subtree of objects from one domain to a different domain in the same forest?

    A. MOVEDOM

    B. TREEMOVE

    C. MOVETREE

    D. NETDOM

6. When the database file is updated, the fastest method is to write to the first available database pages. However, this causes which of the following problems?

    A. Fragmentation of the database

    B. Deletion of some of the data

    C. Inability to find the data, which is placed in the LostAndFound container

    D. None of the above

7. What happens to an object's permissions when you move it to a different OU?

   A. It retains all permissions it had in the original OU.

   B. It loses the permissions specifically assigned to it in the original OU but retains those that were inherited.

   C. It retains the permissions that were specifically assigned to it in the original OU but does not retain those it inherited.

   D. It loses all permissions it had in the original OU.

8. Which resource kit tool is used to replace instances of a SID on ACLs when you move accounts and need to update the ACL?

   A. ACLUPDATE.EXE

   B. SIDUPDATE.EXE

   C. SIDWALK.EXE

   D. SYSDIFF.EXE

9. What is the Windows 2000 backup program called?

   A. W2000bu.exe

   B. ntbackup.exe

   C. backw2k.exe

   D. nt5backup.exe

10. Which of the following would you back up in order to back up the Active Directory information?

    A. Replication data

    B. LDAP data

    C. System State data

    D. Directory data

11. Which of the following is true of authoritative restore? (Check all that apply.)

    A. To restore System State data on a domain controller, you must start the computer in Directory Services Restore mode.

    B. An authoritative restore can be done only on a Primary domain controller.

    C. You use the ntdsutil.exe tool to do an authoritative restore.

    D. You use the adrestore.exe tool to an authoritative restore.

12. In which domain mode would your Windows 2000 server operate if there are still Windows NT domain controllers on your network?

    A. NT emulation

    B. Native

    C. Hybrid

    D. Mixed

13. Which of the following allows you to accurately see the size of the ntds.dit file?

    A. Refresh the Explorer window.

    B. Reboot the computer.

    C. Use the Windows Explorer Properties dialog on the partition where the ntds.dit file is located.

    D. Right-click the file name and select "update file size."

14. What is the recommended limit for number of security-principal objects per domain in a Mixed-mode environment?

    A. 10,000

    B. 40,000

    C. 75,000

    D. Approximately 1.3 million

15. Which of the following enhances performance on domain controllers that must handle high request rates?

    A. Place the Active Directory database file and log files on the same hard disk.

    B. Place the database file and operating system files on the same hard disk, but place the log files on a separate disk.

    C. Place the database, operating system, and log files on three separate hard disks.

    D. The placement of the files has no effect on performance.

MCSE
MICROSOFT CERTIFIED SYSTEMS ENGINEER

18

Deploying Windows 2000 Directory Services

HEADSTART OBJECTIVES

D irectory services, such as Windows 2000 Active Directory, can support a huge scope of features and capabilities in an enterprise environment. Microsoft designed Windows 2000 and Active Directory with the enterprise network in mind. Their goal in developing the new operating system and directory service was scalability that would extend to large and complex network configurations.

Toward that end, Active Directory includes the following features:

- A *data store* (another term for the directory), which stores information about Active Directory objects. Active Directory objects include shared resources such as servers, files, printers, and user and computer accounts.

- A set of rules, called the *schema*, which defines the classes of objects and attributes contained in the directory, the constraints and limits on instances of these objects, and the format of their names.

- The *global catalog* (GC) that contains information about all the objects in the directory. The GC allows users and administrators to find directory information without having to know which server or domain actually contains the data.

- A means of querying and indexing this information, so that objects and their properties can be published and found by network users (or by applications that need to access them).

- A replication service, which distributes directory data across the enterprise network. All domain controllers in a domain participate in replication and contain a complete copy of all directory information for their domain. Changes to directory data are automatically replicated to all domain controllers in the domain.

- A security subsystem that provides for a secure logon process to the network, as well as access control on both directory data queries and data modifications.

- The ability to join domains into a domain tree, and join trees in a forest, creating a trust relationship that allows for easy access by all users in the multidomain network to all resources for which their accounts have the appropriate access permissions.

- The means to exert granular control over entire sites, domains, or organizational units (OUs) through the use of Group Policy, making management of an enterprise-level network easier for the administrator.

As attractive as its features are, deploying the Active Directory Services in an enterprise network is a major undertaking. Before you attempt to do so, it is important that you have a plan, one that takes into consideration not only your goals and the steps you must take to accomplish them, but also a contingency plan in case all doesn't go completely smoothly.

In this chapter, we look closely at how you can make this transition as painlessly as possible.

HEADSTART OBJECTIVE 18.01

The Steps Required to Deploy Windows 2000 Directory Services in an Enterprise

Any big project can seem overwhelming when taken as a whole, but it becomes manageable if you break it down into logical steps. So, let's forget for a moment what a daunting prospect it is to think about making such a drastic change to a network that services thousands or even tens of thousands of users, and perhaps even spans national boundaries. Instead let's individually consider each step involved in the deployment of a brand new directory service.

A Step-by-Step Guideline

There are different ways in which you could approach the deployment of Active Directory in an existing enterprise network. The following sequence of events shows a typical planning check list:

- Assess the current network directory services.
- Assess the organization's administrative model.

- Formulate an IT mission statement and goals.
- Identify current and needed resources.
- Develop a multiphase action plan for deployment.
- Develop a contingency plan.

Assessing the Current Network Directory Services and Domain Structure

Identify existing directory services being used in your network. This includes NT Directory Services, Microsoft Exchange directory service extensions, and those of other vendors, such as Novell bindery and/or NDS. This is done to develop a plan for either migrating other directory services, or synchronizing them across the enterprise.

The assessment of an existing NT enterprise network should include diagramming of the domain model, showing trust relationships between domains. See Figure 18-1 for a typical domain architecture diagram.

Remember that NT domain models include

- **Single domain**   There is only one domain for the entire network.
- **Single master domain**   There is one "master" domain where user accounts reside, and resource domains that trust the master domain.

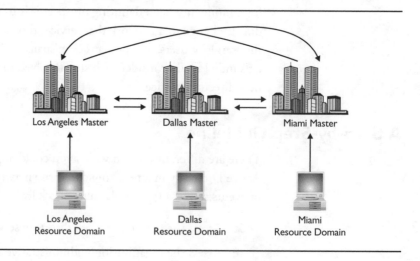

FIGURE 18-1

A Simple diagram of trust relationships in an enterprise network that utilizes the multiple master domain model, created with Visio

Los Angeles Master   Dallas Master   Miami Master

Los Angeles
Resource Domain

Dallas
Resource Domain

Miami
Resource Domain

- **Multiple master domain** Similar to the single master, except that due to the number of user accounts, more than one master domain exists. All master domains trust one another.
- **Complete trust model** All domains trust all other domains.

Your upgrade plan will be influenced by which NT domain model is currently being used in your enterprise network.

The diagram can be drawn by hand, or created using diagramming software such as Visio Professional for Windows.

As part of this step, you should also attempt to identify where users have multiple accounts, with an eye toward reducing the total number of user accounts per user throughout the enterprise.

Assess the Organization's Administrative Model

In conjunction with assessing the domain structure, you should assess the administrative model or models for the organization itself and for the existing directory services.

The purpose of defining the organization's overall administrative model is to help in planning the structure of your Active Directory and Domain Naming System (DNS) namespaces. You will want to know the administrative models for other directory services in order to combine, integrate, or automate them insofar as possible to increase efficiency of the administration of Active Directory.

The deployment of the new directory services is also an excellent time to implement some standardization of administrative procedures if there are none already in place.

Formulate an IT Mission Statement and Goals

Identify exactly what you wish to accomplish, in terms of increased efficiency and effectiveness of IT services, by deploying Active Directory throughout the enterprise.

Look at whether the organization has a centralized IT department, or IT services are decentralized and spread over various locations. Either way, it will be important for key IT personnel to define objectives and set priorities concerning the implementation and administration of the directory services.

on the
!
job

In many large organizations, divisions that operate in different geographic locations may be used to working independently, with little standardization or sense of teamwork throughout the enterprise.

For instance, you may have IT personnel in the Dallas office who are eager to move ahead and migrate their NT domain to Windows 2000, upgrade their Exchange 5.5 server to Platinum, and integrate all existing directory services into Active Directory. Within the same company, you might have IT personnel in Miami who have been running NetWare file servers and using NDS, and are perfectly happy with the status quo and reluctant to make a change.

A very real challenge, in planning the deployment of any new technology on an enterprise-wide scale, lies in bringing together differing points of view and developing a strategy that will, if it is not possible to please everyone, at least incorporate some of the ideas and address some of the concerns of each key member of the team. This can be accomplished through meetings, memos, training sessions, and, in general, by disseminating as much information as possible along each step of the way. People are more cooperative (even when they aren't enthusiastic about the changes) if they have a solid sense of what is happening, why, and how it will impact them.

Identify Current and Needed Resources

Deployment of Active Directory will require that you have sufficient resources, both in terms of hardware and personnel, to accomplish the upgrade itself and to administer and maintain the new directory services.

HARDWARE RESOURCES   There is no denying that Windows 2000 machines require more processor and memory resources than machines running NT. This is particularly true of Windows 2000 domain controllers running the Active Directory services.

Part of your planning will involve determining how many domain controllers you will need at each location, and whether you will need to upgrade hardware in order to deploy them.

A domain can have one or more domain controllers. An enterprise network with many network locations will need one or more domain controllers in each location to provide high availability and fault tolerance.

Microsoft's recommendation for NT Server minimum hardware configuration is shown in Table 18-1. Realistically, this should be considered a bare minimum, and for adequate performance in an enterprise environment, you should plan to exceed these requirements, especially in the area of physical memory (RAM).

It is recommended that you consult the HCL (Hardware Compatibility List) published by Microsoft and available on their Web site, to ensure that your hardware has been tested with Windows 2000.

PERSONNEL RESOURCES   You will need to assess the available IT personnel, and their qualifications to roll out and administer Active Directory across the enterprise.

It is highly recommended that persons responsible for the deployment attend training courses to learn to work with the new directory service, prior to undertaking the job of transforming your enterprise domain model into a Windows 2000 Active Directory domain, tree, or forest.

Also, be certain that you plan the timing of the deployment so that the key persons who need to be involved will be free to participate fully in the deployment process. As always, coordination is a key factor.

DEVELOP A MULTIPHASE ACTION PLAN FOR DEPLOYMENT.   The deployment plan should be constructed and conducted in distinct phases that flow in a logical order (so that those components on which others depend, such as DNS, are put in place first). The steps could be broken down further, but a general guideline would be

1. Evaluation

2. Testing

3. Support training

4. Pilot program

5. User training

6. Deployment

7. Production support

8. Analysis/Review

TABLE 18-1

Minimum Hardware
Requirements for
Windows 2000 Servers

Component	Microsoft Recommended Minimum
Processor	Pentium 133 or higher
Memory (RAM)	64MB required, 256MB recommended
Hard disk space	850MB + 100MB per each 64MB of RAM

Deployment itself will be divided into projects. Projects might be grouped together to create the phases. For instance, in phase one, you might upgrade the server hardware that requires it. Phase two might include deploying the DNS server. Phase three could include deployment of the Windows 2000 domain controller(s), while Phase four would involve configuring the Active Directory. Later phases would address configuration of Group Policy, deployment of the DNS servers within the Active Directory site model, and application publication and assignment.

heads
①p

In an enterprise environment, it will be critical to plan your deployment around the organization's own calendar. Not only should you establish tentative deadlines for completion of specific phases, you should also be particularly aware of dates that must be "frozen." This refers to time periods during which the network cannot be down, and no upgrading or changes should be made. Examples would include early spring for an income tax preparation firm, or the Christmas season for a company engaged in retail toy sales.

DEVELOP A CONTINGENCY PLAN   Although your upgrade to Windows 2000 and deployment of Active Directory services may very well go off without a hitch, it is vital that before you begin any phase of actual deployment, you develop a sound contingency plan for recovery in case you do encounter serious problems.

If you are upgrading an NT 4.0 domain, the recovery plan could be as simple as taking one of the domain's Backup Domain Controllers (BDCs) off the network during the upgrade process, so that it could be brought back online and promoted to Primary Domain Controller (PDC) if necessary. Then the original PDC can be upgraded to Windows 2000 and promoted to domain controller status, thus deploying Active Directory, without endangering the integrity of the network if something goes wrong.

Taking the BDC offline completely is the best tactic, because the PDC replicates its SAM (Security Accounts Manager) database to the BDCs. If the upgrade of the PDC fails, it could corrupt the SAMs of all the BDCs as well, leaving the domain unable to function (see Figure 18-2).

The goal of your contingency plan is to give you a means of restoring your domain to its original state if the upgrade fails.

HEADSTART OBJECTIVE 18.02

Planning the Logical Design of the Active Directory Namespace for an Enterprise

General guidelines for planning an Active Directory namespace are covered in Chapter 12, "Planning the Active Directory Namespace," but planning the namespace for an enterprise network requires even more forethought. Although Microsoft recommends that your Active Directory network be implemented as a single domain if possible, you will find that in the

FIGURE 18-2

Taking one of the domain's Backup Domain Controllers off the network while the Windows 2000 upgrade and Active Directory deployment are being performed

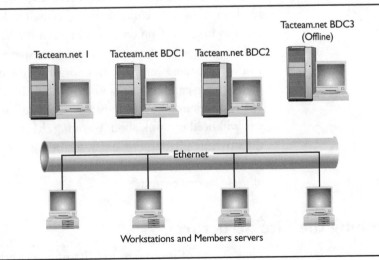

enterprise environment there are usually compelling reasons to ignore this advice and create a domain tree, or even a forest of trees.

It is the hierarchical nature of the Active Directory namespace that makes it so much more scalable than the old flat namespace used by down-level (NT) directory services. Building a large, complex network with NT was difficult, and locating and managing resources within that network was a nightmare, both for users and administrators. Because the Active Directory uses the domain tree concept, it is much easier to organize the network resources logically, and users can access those resources without even being aware of where they are located physically.

The Active Directory, as you learned in previous chapters, uses the following basic units of organization:

- OUs, which exist within domains
- Domains, which form administrative boundaries
- Trees, which are collections of domains arranged hierarchically
- Forests, which are groups of trees with unrelated namespaces, and share a schema and a GC
- Sites, which are connected via a high-speed link

The GC is the repository for information about all of the objects that reside in all of these containers, and is used to locate resources anywhere in the network, based on criteria defined in the object properties.

Designing your Active Directory namespace involves determining how you will use these components to organize the objects (users, computers, files, printers, and other resources) within the structure of your network.

In considering how to most effectively utilize this hierarchical approach, you will need to think about planning the structure of your sites, planning the structure of your domain(s), including trees and/or forests, and planning the structure of OUs within those domains. We will look at each of these factors separately.

Planning the Site Structure

The concept of *sites* is new to Microsoft networking in Windows 2000. Simply, a site is defined as an area where network connectivity is fast (high bandwidth). A site is associated with one or more TCP/IP subnets in the Active Directory. Sites are used to locate the resources that are in closest proximity to the user and to reduce replication traffic, as well as for the isolation of logons so that those requests from one branch office, for example, will always log on at a particular domain controller. This will prevent the problems that occur when a user in Dallas tries to log on to a domain controller in London over a 56K link for authentication, instead of the one in Austin, which is connected via a high-speed T1 line.

In the enterprise network, sites are sure to be a factor, since the network may span a large geographic area, and some connections between locations may be over slow WAN links.

You provide information about the cost of a site link, times when the link is available for use, and how often the link should be used. Active Directory uses this information to determine which site link will be used to replicate information. Customizing replication schedules so replication occurs during specific times, such as when network traffic is low, will make replication more efficient.

You should plan your site structure for highest efficiency. Establish a separate site with its own domain controllers when you feel domain controllers are not responding fast enough to meet the needs of your users. You must assess the performance of the various physical links between locations to determine how best to divide the network into sites. The illustration shown next shows an example of planning sites.

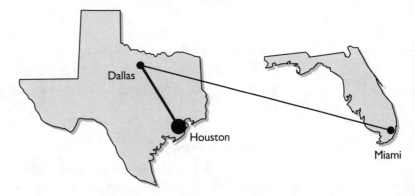

In this situation, the Dallas and Houston offices could comprise one site, with the Miami office being part of a second site. The thick line connecting

Dallas and Houston represents a high-speed link, and the thin line connecting Dallas and Miami represents a slow link.

Remember that the site structure is completely separate from the domain structure, which does not necessarily have to follow geographic boundaries at all (although sometimes there are good reasons for doing so, such as when users in different locations speak different languages).

Planning the Domain Structure

How the Active Directory domain(s) will be structured is dependent on both the organization's size and its operational structure (the latter will usually be influenced by the former).

Microsoft's general recommendation is that you use a single domain model if possible; this simplifies administration in the small or medium-sized network. In the enterprise, however, you will more often be faced with one or more reasons to create additional domains. These could include

- A decentralized administrative model
- Offices in different countries need to use different languages
- Requirement for different domain policies
- Isolate or balance domain replication traffic
- Divisions of the organization that have distinct namespace (requiring a forest)

When you have determined how many domains you will need for your enterprise network, you'll need to decide on the hierarchy into which they will be organized. Remember that the first domain you create in a tree will be the "root" domain, and the first tree in a forest will be the "root" tree of the forest.

Trees and Forests

You may recall from Chapter 12 that Active Directory names will be structured like (and indeed, are) DNS names. When your network has multiple domains, those domains will be arranged in one or more trees and/or forests. A domain tree shares a contiguous namespace. This means the top or "root" domain's name will be included in the name of its "children." For example, if tacteam.net were the root domain, it might have a child domain named east.tacteam.net, and one named west.tacteam.net.

An organization that operates as a single entity will probably use a tree of domains. An enterprise that includes distinct entities (such as separate companies operating as part of a conglomerate) may choose to organize its domains into forests. In a forest, each tree has a contiguous namespace. The namespaces of the root domains of each tree bear no relationship to one another. For example, a forest could consist of domain trees with roots named tacteam.net and federation.net. For more information about how this works, see Chapter 12.

Differences between NT Domains and Windows 2000 Domains

With Windows NT, domains were often created in order to delegate administrative authority; if each department or division within an organization wanted to have control over its resources, separate domains would be set up to accomplish this. The problem with the NT multiple domain models was that, in order for users to access resources in other domains on the network, trust relationships had to be explicitly established between the domains. In a large enterprise-scale network, this not only required a lot of time and effort, it could also get confusing.

With Windows 2000, the domain is still a basic line of demarcation for administrative purposes. That is, administrators of a parent domain do not have administrative privileges in the child domains. However, in Windows 2000 there exists an implicit, two-way transitive trust between all the domains in a tree, and between the root domains in a forest, so that users are able to access network resources in any domain (assuming they have the appropriate permissions to do so).

This makes the Windows 2000 multiple domain models far easier to manage in the enterprise environment than NT multiple domain models.

Planning the Organizational Units Within the Domain(s)

We said that domains form administrative boundaries, but unlike in NT, the domain unit is not the smallest unit of administrative responsibility in

Windows 2000. In many instances, we can avoid creating domains for this purpose, by assigning administrative privileges for OUs. The OU structure resides within the domain structure; although unlike domains, OUs are not part of the namespace. They are visually represented as folders in Active Directory Users and Computers.

An OU is a *container object*. As the name implies, this means other objects can be put inside it. OUs can contain users, groups, computers, printers, and shared folders, as well as other OUs. The benefit of using OUs to delegate administrative authority becomes obvious as you work more with the Active Directory. For example, all user accounts for the Human Resources department could be placed in the HR OU. One person could be assigned full administrative control over that OU (and thus, the accounts inside it), but would not have administrative privileges elsewhere in the domain.

OUs can also be used to organize resources so they can be located more readily. All printer objects could be placed in a Printers OU, making it easy to find and administer them all, regardless of where they are physically located on the network.

The OU structure should be designed in a way that is meaningful for your organization. OUs can be created inside OUs, but take care not to create more levels of OUs than is absolutely necessary. Deep hierarchies (such as OUs inside OUs that are inside other OUs) can negatively affect performance in searching the directory.

If your enterprise contains several domains, you can create OU structures within each domain, independent of the OU structures in the other domains.

**heads
Up**

OUs are also the smallest scope to which you can assign Group Policy settings (the others are sites and domains). This enables you to determine access, configurations, and use of resources for the OU and any or all of its child objects (including other OUs).

QUESTIONS AND ANSWERS

What are some differences between a domain and an OU?	Domains are a part of the namespace, whereas OUs exist inside domains and their names are not part of the namespace. Domains are replication boundaries. Changing domain structure and names is more difficult than changing the structure and naming of OUs.
What is the default relationship between domains within a tree?	There is an implicit two-way transitive trust, so users can access resource in any domain if they have appropriate permissions. Domains are administrative boundaries, however. Administrators of a parent domain do not automatically have administrative privilege in child domains.
What types of objects can be placed inside an OU?	Users, groups, computers, printers, shared folders, and/or other OUs.
What are the scopes to which Group Policy can be assigned?	Sites, domains, and OUs.

EXERCISE 18-1

Creating the Logical Design of a Directory Service

The following step-by-step process should be followed when creating the logical design of your Active Directory namespace:

1. **Determine the number of domains your organization requires** To predict how many domains you will need, Microsoft recommends that you estimate the number of attributes and objects that each domain will maintain for at least a three-year period of time. These numbers will depend on your unique business environment, but make a high-end estimation of objects and attributes.

2. **Determine how you will organize and name your domains** Once you have decided on the number of domains for your organization, arrange them in a logical structure and assign each domain a DNS name. Every Active Directory domain requires a DNS name that reflects its position in the namespace. Microsoft recommends that you avoid naming your domains for divisions, departments, buildings, floors, or groups.

3. **Determine your DNS requirements** If you have an existing DNS server in your environment, determine if it meets the following DNS name requirements:

   A. Provides support for Service Location Resource Records (SRV RRs). SRV RR (Request for Comment (RFC) 2052) is a DNS record that maps to the name of a server offering that service, much like the "service identifier" character (the 16th character) of a NetBIOS name..

   B. Supports the dynamic update protocol IETF RFC 2136, which is strongly recommended.

   If you do not have a DNS server or if you are planning to replace the existing DNS server, use Microsoft DNS server included with Windows 2000 Server.

4. **Create your domain design document, detailing the results of your assessment and decision-making**

HEADSTART OBJECTIVE 18.03

Planning the Implementation of Active Directory Considering the Physical Network Environment

The physical environment of the network will be a factor in planning your Active Directory implementation. This includes geographic separation of network resources and the links between them (see the previous discussion on sites), as well as such physical factors as the layout/topology of the network, the speed of both local and remote links, and how heavily the network segments (and the links between segments) are utilized.

Other physical issues that must be taken into account are the number of users in each geographic local and in each separate business unit, and the company's expectations for growth and expansion in the future.

Although with Active Directory, users can access resources anywhere on the network regardless of physical location, you will want to consider where to physically locate certain resources for best efficiency. If all of the files on a particular file server are used primarily by members of the Accounting department, it makes no sense to locate that machine miles away on the other side of a slow WAN link.

It is especially important to consider where to place domain controllers for best management of logon authentication traffic. To access a network application or resource (unless clustering is being used to create virtual servers), users have to connect to a physical server (a specific computer on the network identified by a unique name and IP address) that is designated as a domain controller, to log on to the network.

If you put a domain controller at each site, all users will have a local computer that can service their requests without having to create slow-link traffic. It may be advantageous to configure domain controllers at smaller sites to receive directory replication updates only during off-hours. This will help optimize traffic flow.

Creating the Physical Design of a Directory Service

1. Determine where to place domain controllers.

   Consider the following guidelines for placing domain controllers in your enterprise:

   ■ A domain controller must be able to respond to client requests in a timely manner.

   ■ The best query performance happens when you place a domain controller (at a small site) with a global catalog server (GCS), enabling that server to fulfill queries about objects in all domains on your network.

2. Determine where to place GCs.

   Consider the following guidelines for placing GCs in your enterprise:

   ■ In a multisite environment, it is a good idea to place one GC in each site for the following reasons:

     ■ To provide a backup resource that will reduce the possibility of disruption in service.

     ■ A client must contact a GC to log on to the network. If no GC is available, the client will not be able to log on.

■ At a minimum, you must have at least one GC in the forest so that your users can log on to the network. That is why the first domain controller you install in a forest is automatically configured as a GCS.

Developing and Testing a Prototype of the New Windows 2000 Directory Services Environment

Before rolling out a Windows 2000 upgrade and implementing Active Directory throughout the enterprise, best practice is to create a prototype directory services environment on which you can test your important applications and with which you can become familiar with administering Active Directory on a nonmission-critical machine.

When testing uncovers problems, the test lab can provide the means for developing and validating alternative solutions, without affecting productivity or endangering the integrity of your network.

Prototype Implementation Check List

Before installing Windows 2000 Server and Active Directory on your prototype machine(s), you will want to consider some of the following factors:

■ Whether to upgrade an existing NT server or servers, or install Windows 2000 in a new installation

■ Whether you will need to upgrade the hardware on your prototype server(s) to run Windows 2000 and Active Directory

■ How complex your prototype network will be

Upgrade Versus New Installation

You may have extra NT Server machines that could be upgraded to Windows 2000 for your prototype network. This is certainly one option;

however, you will probably find it more efficient in the long run to install Windows 2000 fresh on a newly formatted hard disk. This will allow you to evaluate the operating system and implement its features on a "pure" basis, and if you run into problems, you won't have to wonder whether it was something in the original NT installation that caused it.

Hardware Considerations

Be sure the machine(s) used for the prototype network meets the minimum system requirements for installation of Windows 2000 Server. It's tempting to try to utilize old, out-of-service machines for this purpose, but you will only get a realistic assessment of how Windows 2000 is going to perform on the "real" network by emulating the hardware conditions there insofar as possible.

At the very least, check the HCL and ascertain that your equipment is on the list, and don't skimp on RAM. Active Directory is memory intensive, and in order to get a true picture of how it works, you need to work with hardware that is able to support it effectively.

Complexity of the Prototype Network

Some organizations will want to build a fairly complex network on which to test and evaluate the new directory services. The complexity of your prototype network will depend on several factors, including budget, rollout deadlines, and available personnel.

In order for the prototype to provide realistic predictions regarding your Windows 2000 and Active Directory implementation in a multidomain enterprise network, you should also create a multiple domain environment in the prototype network. If your enterprise will be a mixed-mode environment (with down-level domain controllers), it would be beneficial to include at least one NT DC in the prototype network as well.

The Test Lab Environment

A well-designed test lab provides a controlled environment for the range of testing that will take place throughout the project life cycle, including the following:

■ Experimenting with the technology

■ Comparing design solutions

■ Validating compatibility of server and client applications

■ Fine-tuning the rollout process.

A good lab does not have to be a large resource or capital funding investment; it can range from a few pieces of hardware in a small room to a full-scale network in a data center environment.

Installing the First Domain Controller

The first step in implementation of the prototype Active Directory environment is to create an isolated network, and either upgrade an NT 4.0 machine or do a fresh installation of Windows 2000 Server or Advanced Server. This machine will become your first domain controller; however, in Windows 2000 you do not choose to create a domain controller during the installation of the Server software, as you do with NT.

EXERCISE 18-3

Planning for Directory Services Deployment

Once Server (or Advanced Server) has been installed on the machine, the first time you log on with the administrator account created during installation, you will see the Configure Your Server screen shown in Figure 18-3.

As you can see in Figure 18-3, one of the configuration choices in the left-side pane is Active Directory. Selecting it will take you to a scrollable information screen that gives you some basic tips about choices to be made when installing Active Directory, as well as a hyperlink that will start the Active Directory Wizard. If you click on that link, you will then see a screen welcoming you to the Active Directory Setup Wizard.

heads
⑪P

An alternative way to start the Active Directory Wizard is by typing dcpromo *at the command prompt.*

Regardless of which method you used to start the Wizard, when you click Next at the welcome screen, you will see the first of many dialog

FIGURE 18-3

FIGURE 18-3

The Configure Your Server tool, which will be onscreen the first time you start up a newly installed server, and can be accessed later through the Start menu

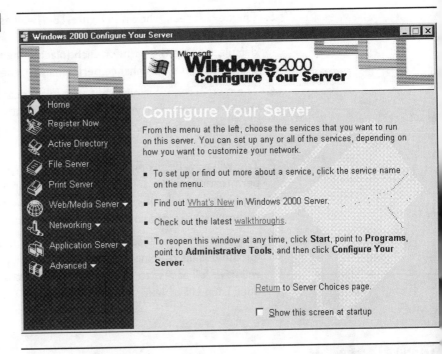

boxes asking you for information to be used to make this server a domain controller.

1. Choose "Create new domain," then click Next, and you will see the screen in which you are given the option of creating a child domain in an existing tree, or creating a whole new domain tree.

   The next screen looks similar, but asks if you want to create a new forest, or put this new domain tree into an existing forest.

2. Choose "Create new forest of trees," then click Next.

3. Now you will be asked to type a name for your new domain. Remember to use the DNS hierarchical naming convention (for example, alphaquadrant.net). Click Next.

4. You'll be shown the name that will be visible to down-level (NT) clients, which will be a flat NetBIOS name without the top-level name extension (in other words, in the preceding example, ALPHAQUADRANT will be the down-level name). Click Next.

5. The next screen (shown in Figure 18-4) will ask for a location where you want to store the Active Directory database and log. Accept the default, or type the path for each (placing them on different physical disks if possible, to enhance performance); then click Next.

6. The next screen is similar, but asks for a location in which to store the system volume (sysvol). This location must be on a partition formatted with NTFS. Type a path or accept the default, and click Next.

7. You will now be prompted to choose the type of default permissions for the server. Make the appropriate selection, depending on whether you will have down-level servers on the network (those running Windows NT). Click Next.

8. The next screen will ask you to type in and then confirm a password for the default Administrator account. Remember that this account will have full access to the server, so make the password a secure one. Then click Next.

Specifying the location for storage of Active Directory database and log

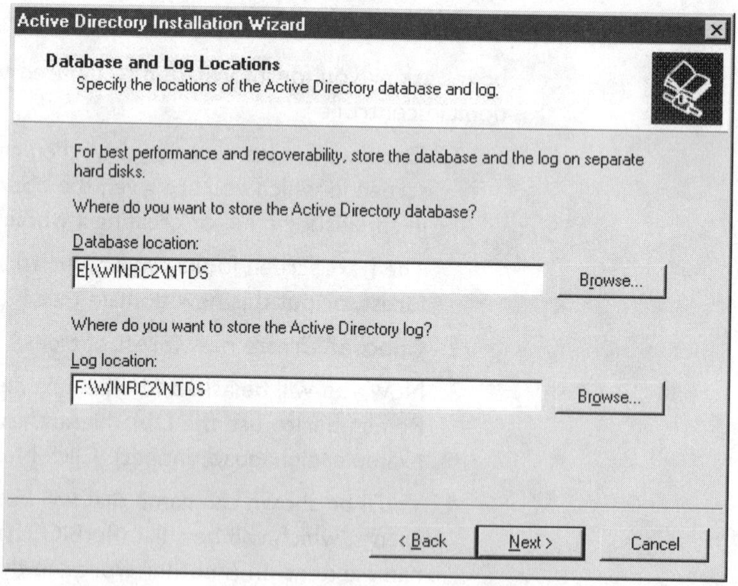

9. At this point, you will be shown an informational screen that summarizes what you have entered for configuring the server. Review it and click Back to make any changes, if necessary. Then click Next. You will see the screen shown next.

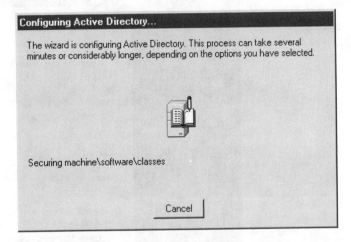

10. Finally, you will receive a message informing you "Active Directory is now installed on this computer for the domain [*domain name you specified*]." Congratulations! You have upgraded the server to domain controller, created a new domain, and installed the Active Directory services! Click Finish.

Configuring Active Directory for the First Time

You must restart the server after running the Active Directory Wizard. Note that when you log back on, if you try to open Active Directory Users and Computers, you will receive an error message telling you the domain cannot be located (even though you can see it in Network Places). This can be confusing the first time you create a domain controller. But don't worry, your Active Directory installation didn't fail. There is one more thing you must do before you can start administering Active Directory.

If the Configure Your Server screen did not appear automatically when you logged on, bring it up by choosing Start | Programs | Administrative Tools | Configure Your Server.

Select Active Directory again in the left-side pane, and click "Manage user accounts and group settings" (as shown in Figure 18-5).

FIGURE 18-5

Setting up user accounts is the first step in using the Active Directory

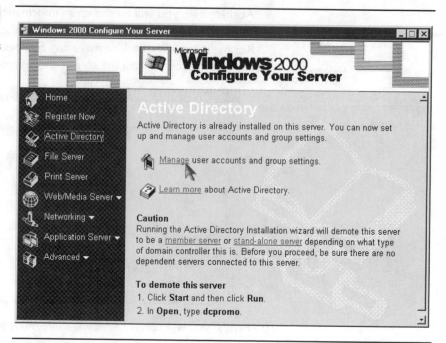

Then you will get a screen similar to the one in Figure 18-6.

This is the Active Directory Users and Computers snap-in. After bringing it up through Configure Your Server the first time, you will now be able to access it via the Administrative Tools in the Start menu.

You can now set up the users and groups as desired for your prototype directory services network.

HEADSTART OBJECTIVE 18.05

Implementing the New Windows 2000 Directory Services in an Enterprise

Remember that the Active Directory directory service is compatible with Windows NT when you operate in the mixed mode, using both Windows

FIGURE 18-6

Active Directory Users and
Computers screen

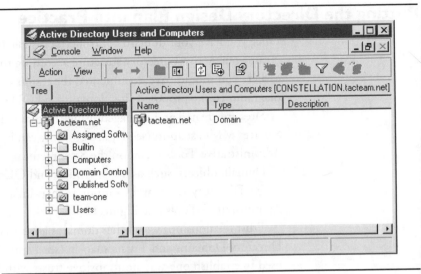

2000 Server domain controllers and Windows NT Server 4.0 domain
controllers. The nice thing about this is that because Active Directory
supports mixed mode, you can upgrade domains and computers at your
own pace, based on your organization's needs.

Active Directory also supports the NTLM protocol used by Windows
NT (in addition to Windows 2000's Kerberos authentication). This enables
the authorized users and computers from a Windows NT domain to log on
and access resources in Windows 2000 domains. To Windows NT clients
and Windows 95 or Windows 98 clients (unless they are running the Active
Directory client software, located on the Windows 2000 Server CD in the
Clients directory), a Windows 2000 domain appears to be a Windows NT
Server 4.0 domain.

Your upgrade to Active Directory can be gradual, and if you plan it
properly, it can be performed without interrupting normal network
operations. If you follow Microsoft's domain upgrade recommendations, it
should never be necessary for you to take an entire domain offline to
upgrade domain controllers, member servers, or workstations.

heads
⑪p

*When upgrading a Windows NT domain, you must upgrade the
primary domain controller first. You can upgrade member servers and
workstations at any time after this.*

Putting the Directory Design Plan into Practice

Once you have your domain controller(s) installed and configured, you can create your Active Directory structure according to the plan you made earlier. You should have documented the results of your assessment and diagrammed the proposed site, domain, and OU structures.

Sites are created and managed using the Active Directory Sites and Services MMC snap-in (see Figure 18-7). It can be accessed through the Administrative Tools menu on the Start menu.

Domain objects, such as users, groups, and OUs, are managed via the Active Directory Users and Computers snap-in, also accessible in Administrative Tools (see Figure 18-8).

Trust relationships with other domains are established via the Active Directory Domains and Trusts snap-in (see Figure 18-9). This tool can be used to establish one-way nontransitive trusts with NT domains. Remember that in a domain tree, there is already an implicit two-way trust relationship between all domains.

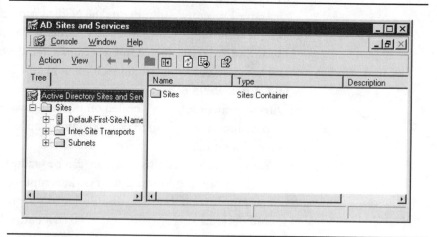

FIGURE 18-7

Active Directory Sites and Services

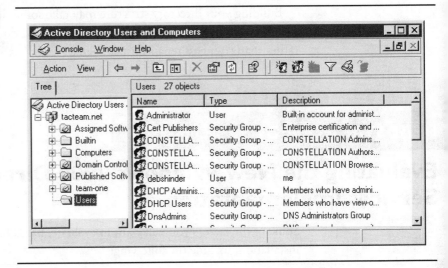

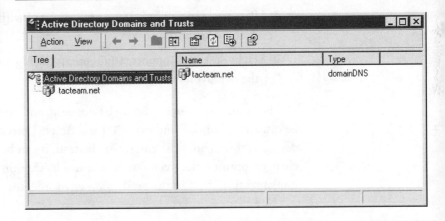

Building your directory structure may take some time. In the long run, it will be much more efficient to proceed slowly and do it right the first time, rather than trying to repair mistakes later.

HEADSTART OBJECTIVE 18.06

Evaluating the New Windows 2000 Directory Services Implementation

Some of the factors you will want to evaluate, based on your prototype installation, include the following:

- Windows 2000 and Active Directory performance and reliability
- A trial run of tasks your administrators commonly perform
- Windows 2000 Server migration from other operating systems
- Windows 2000 Server interoperability with other operating systems
- Potential training requirements associated with the deployment of Active Directory
- Help desk and support requirements during and following the deployment

The evaluation process should be ongoing, and your test lab should not be dismantled once Windows 2000 and Active Directory have been deployed throughout the enterprise. Instead, it can be utilized for testing changes, optimization techniques, and troubleshooting before implementing them in the production environment.

ACCELERATING TO WINDOWS 2000

- Active Directory is a robust LDAP-compliant directory service that brings a host of new administrative and end-user benefits to Microsoft networking in an enterprise environment. Active Directory features that make it especially appropriate for the enterprise include the directory data store, the schema, the GC, directory indexing and querying, security integration, and the replication model.

- Active Directory's support for a mixed-mode environment, in which Windows 2000 domain controllers can coexist with down-level (NT) domain controllers, make it easier for an enterprise network to migrate gradually. Down-level clients (NT Workstation and Windows 9*x*) will be able to utilize limited features of the Active Directory when you install the client software, which is included on the Windows 2000 Server CD.

- The Active Directory Wizard simplifies promotion of a Windows 2000 server to domain controller status, and walks you through the steps of creating a new domain, and setting up your directory services.

- The configuration tools in Windows 2000, such as Active Directory Users and Computers, Active Directory Sites and Services, and Active Directory Domains and Trusts MMC snap-ins, ease the tasks involved in creating your site, domain, and OU structures and putting your Active Directory services into operation.

- Microsoft's Windows 2000 Resource Kit provides extensive documentation to guide you through the planning process, as well as specifications for prototype testing environments and tips on creating the most effective Active Directory structure to fit your organization's needs.

CHAPTER SUMMARY

Windows 2000's Active Directory was designed with enterprise networking in mind. Some of the features that make it especially attractive to administrators of large, multidomain networks that span geographic boundaries include the management infrastructure services in Windows 2000 Server, which provide IT with tools that enable the highest levels of service available and reduce ownership costs.

Implementing Active Directory services in the enterprise environment can be an overwhelming task. For the most time-effective and cost-effect rollout, planning is essential. You should develop a detailed, documented strategy for designing your Active Directory namespace and building your sites, domains, and OUs.

Prior to implementing Windows 2000 and Active Directory throughout the enterprise, you should set up a test lab and build a prototype network on which you can install the directory services, and evaluate performance, security, and other issues of concern.

Active Directory's directory services will add a new dimension to the management of Microsoft enterprise-level network—but only with proper preparation. Your Active Directory should serve you and your users well for a long time, provided you put some thought into planning its structural design and deployment.

 # TWO-MINUTE DRILL

- ❑ Deploying the Active Directory Services in an enterprise network is a major undertaking. Before you attempt to do so, it is important that you have a plan.

- ❑ Identify existing directory services being used in your network. This includes NT Directory Services, Microsoft Exchange directory service extensions, and those of other vendors, such as Novell bindery and/or NDS.

- ❑ In conjunction with assessing the domain structure, you should assess the administrative model or models for the organization itself and for the existing directory services.

❏ Identify exactly what you wish to accomplish, in terms of increased efficiency and effectiveness of IT services, by deploying Active Directory throughout the enterprise.

❏ Deployment of Active Directory will require that you have sufficient resources, both in terms of hardware and personnel, to accomplish the upgrade itself and to administer and maintain the new directory services.

❏ Because the Active Directory uses the domain tree concept, it is much easier to organize the network resources logically, and users can access those resources without even being aware of where they are located physically.

❏ The concept of *sites* is new to Microsoft networking in Windows 2000. Simply, a site is defined as an area where network connectivity is fast (high bandwidth).

❏ Microsoft's general recommendation is that you use a single domain model if possible; this simplifies administration in the small or medium-sized network. In the enterprise, however, you will more often be faced with one or more reasons to create additional domains.

❏ Remember that the first domain you create in a tree will be the "root" domain, and the first tree in a forest will be the "root" tree of the forest.

❏ An OU is a *container object*. As the name implies, this means other objects can be put inside it. OUs can contain users, groups, computers, printers, and shared folders, as well as other OUs.

❏ The physical environment of the network will be a factor in planning your Active Directory implementation. This includes geographic separation of network resources and the links between them, as well as such physical factors as the layout/topology of the network, the speed of both local and remote links, and how heavily the network segments (and the links between segments) are utilized.

❏ Before rolling out a Windows 2000 upgrade and implementing Active Directory throughout the enterprise, best practice is to create a prototype directory services environment on which you can test your important applications and with which you can become familiar with administering Active Directory on a nonmission-critical machine.

❑ The first step in implementation of the prototype Active Directory environment is to create an isolated network, and either upgrade an NT 4.0 machine or do a fresh installation of Windows 2000 Server or Advanced Server.

❑ You must restart the server after running the Active Directory Wizard. Note that when you log back on, if you try to open Active Directory Users and Computers, you will receive an error message telling you the domain cannot be located (even though you can see it in Network Places).

❑ Remember that the Active Directory directory service is compatible with Windows NT when you operate in the mixed mode, using both Windows 2000 Server domain controllers and Windows NT Server 4.0 domain controllers.

❑ Sites are created and managed using the Active Directory Sites and Services MMC snap-In.

❑ Domain objects, such as users, groups, and OUs, are managed via the Active Directory Users and Computers snap-in.

❑ Trust relationships with other domains are established via the Active Directory Domains and Trusts snap-in.

SELF TEST

The following questions will help you measure your understanding of the material presented in this chapter. Read all of the choices carefully, as there may be more than one correct answer. Choose all correct answers for each question.

1. Why should your Active Directory deployment plan include identification of existing directory services being used in your network?

   A. So all existing directory services can be eliminated.

   B. So you can develop a plan for migrating or synchronizing other directory services across the enterprise.

   C. So you will know whether it is possible to implement Active Directory, since it can't be used if other directory services are already in place.

   D. There is no need to identify existing directory services.

2. Which of the following should be included in the assessment phase of your Active Directory deployment plan? (Choose all that apply.)

   A. A diagram of the existing NT network, showing trust relationships between domains

   B. Identification of users who have multiple accounts

   C. The organization's administrative model

   D. The serial numbers of all hardware devices on the network

3. Which of the following is true of Windows 2000 domain controllers?

   A. A domain can have only one domain controller.

   B. A domain must have at least two domain controllers.

   C. A domain can have one or more domain controllers.

   D. One domain controller can control multiple domains.

4. Why might you take one of your NT domain's BDCs off the network prior to upgrading the PDC to Windows 2000?

   A. A PDC cannot be upgraded if there are BDCs on the network.

   B. The BDC taken offline will have the SAM of the original NT domain intact, in case you need to revert to the old domain model.

   C. All BDCs must be demoted to member servers before you can upgrade an NT domain to Windows 2000.

   D. There is no reason to take the BDC offline.

5. Which of the following statements is false? (Choose all that apply.)

A. Building a large, complex network with NT was easier than doing so with Windows 2000, because Active Directory is difficult to configure across the enterprise.

B. Active Directory makes it easier to organize network resources logically, as opposed to NT's directory services.

C. The hierarchical namespace used by Active Directory makes it more scalable than the flat namespace used by NT.

D. NT's directory services used the domain tree concept.

6. Which of the following is one of the basic units of organization in Active Directory? (Choose all that apply.)

A. Domains

B. Forests

C. Schemas

D. Member servers

7. The repository for information about all of the objects that reside in Active Directory containers, used to locate resources on the network, is called the

A. Name server

B. Directory index

C. Global catalog

D. Object log

8. Which of the following is true of sites? (Choose all that apply.)

A. Sites are used to reduce replication traffic across slow links.

B. Sites are used only in small LANs, which are contained in one geographic location.

C. A site is associated with one or more TCP/IP subnet with a high-bandwidth connection.

D. Sites can be used to isolate logon authentication requests.

9. Which of the following is not a reason to create multiple domains?

A. Offices in different countries where users need to use different languages.

B. A requirement for different domain policies.

C. A need to isolate or balance replication traffic.

D. A centralized administrative model.

10. Which domain in a tree is considered that tree's "root" domain?

A. The domain specified by the administrator using the "set root" command.

B. The first domain created in the tree.

C. The domain with the largest number of Active Directory objects.

D. The domain with the name starting with the lowest letter of the alphabet.

11. Which of the following pairs of domains have a contiguous namespace? (Choose all that apply.)

A. tacteam.net, team-one.net

B. tacteam.net, team-one.com

C. tacteam.net, team-one.tacteam.net

D. team-one.tacteam.net, team-one.federation.net

12. Which of the following is true of Windows 2000 domains? (Choose all that apply.)

   A. The administrator of a parent domain also has administrative privileges in all child domains.

   B. There is an implicit, two-way trust between domains within the same tree.

   C. The domain is a basic line of demarcation for administrative purposes.

   D. Windows 2000 multiple domain models are more difficult to manage in an enterprise environment than NT multiple domain models.

13. Which of the following statements is true of organizational units (OUs)? (Choose all that apply.)

   A. OUs can contain users and groups, but cannot contain resources such as printers and shared folders.

   B. OUs can contain other OUs.

   C. Administrative authority can be delegated on the OU level.

   D. Deep OU hierarchies are not recommended because they can negatively impact performance.

14. What is an advantage of placing a domain controller at each Active Directory site?

   A. User logon authentication requests can all be serviced by a local computer.

   B. Users will not be able to access resources outside their sites, thereby enhancing security.

   C. A domain controller at each site is required in order for users at all sites to access Active Directory objects.

   D. IT costs will be lower, because there will be less wear and tear on the server machines.

15. Which of the following is true of a well-designed test lab? (Choose all that apply.)

   A. It can be used for experimenting with the technology without endangering the production network.

   B. It will cost a great deal of money and requires a large amount of dedicated personnel.

   C. It should be dismantled once Windows 2000 directory services have been deployed throughout the enterprise.

   D. It can be used for validating the compatibility of server and client applications.

19

Controlling Schema Modifications

T his chapter delves into the Windows 2000 Active Directory Schema. It discusses the inner workings of the schema, and provides advice pertaining to how and when the schema should be modified.

The Active Directory Schema and Its Structure

The Windows 2000 Active Directory schema is the heart of Active Directory. The schema stores information about the types of objects that can be created in the directory and their location in the hierarchical structure.

There are two subsets of the Active Directory schema: *classes* and *attributes*. Active Directory includes a default schema containing hundreds of classes and attributes. This schema can be modified by an administrator, and can also be extended by software manufacturers for use by an X.500 directory compliant software application. X.500 is a scalable standard that defines a distributed database concept to store information about people or objects, and how that information is made directly available from a local directory replica.

Classes

Every object created in Active Directory is an instance of a class. Classes are defined in the Active Directory schema, and are used to group a set of attributes that can be used by objects created in that class. Objects created in a class are also known as *instances* of that class. The process of creating the object (that is, populating the values for the appropriate attributes), is therefore known as *instantiation*. The concept of *instantiating* an object originates from object-oriented programming; however, understand that instantiation is synonymous with "binding" a new object to a class.

ACCELERATING TO WINDOWS 2000

The concept of a flexible schema is new to Microsoft operating systems with Windows 2000 Active Directory. In the past, a commonly heard complaint from network administrators (especially those who had worked with a directory-based network operating system such as Novell NDS) was that the attributes of an object could not be extended in Windows NT. Not only could they not be extended, even the default objects and attributes were extremely limited.

For example, when creating a user in Windows NT, you could define only the Login Name, Description, and the Full Name of the user. There were some other options that could be configured for account management purposes, such as dial-in capability and login time restriction, but the Full Name and the Description were the extent of the user information that could be defined. There was no built-in support to add other fields, such as phone numbers, street addresses, and other information that may be valuable to your organization.

The default Active Directory schema includes a far greater set of attributes that can be defined for a user and stored in the directory, including phone number, e-mail address, street address—even a thumbnail photo! As an administrator of Active Directory, you now have the capability to extend the default schema to include custom attributes, and even create entirely new classes to enable you to store various different types of objects in the Active Directory.

Common Default Classes

The Windows 2000 Active Directory includes hundreds of default classes. These classes include those used for internal operations (such as Active Directory replication, IP security, and RPC management, etc.), as well as those used to create most of the objects in Active Directory (such as Users or Computers). Some of the default classes are shown in Table 19-1, which includes only some of the attributes that are unique to each class. Each of the classes listed contain many attributes, some of which are used in multiple classes.

TABLE 19-1

Commonly Used Default
Classes

Class Name	Included Attributes	Class Purpose
User	logonHours department	Used for all user objects created in Active Directory
Computer	machineRole networkAddress	Represents all computer objects stored in Active Directory
Organizational Unit (OU)	description ou	Defines the attributes for all OUs created within the Active Directory structure

Class Definition Objects

As you now know, objects in Active Directory are instances of classes, each defined based on the attributes used by the class. So, you may be asking, "How are classes managed in the schema?"

Each class is actually an instance of the classSchema class. Objects in this class are known as *Class Definition Objects.*

Attributes in the classSchema class are used to store information about the class object's position in the namespace, which attributes are mandatory ("must-contain" attributes), and which are optional ("may-contain" attributes) for instances of the class.

Attributes

Attributes are used to store information about objects created in Active Directory. Attributes are grouped to make classes, and multiple classes can use the same attribute. The information that a specific attribute can store is governed by the attribute syntax. There are hundreds of attributes in the default schema, used in the default classes discussed earlier.

Attribute Definition Objects

Similar to Class Definition Objects, *Attribute Definition Objects* are used to store information about the available attributes in the directory. When an attribute is created, a definition object is instantiated in the attributeSchema class.

Attributes of the attributeSchema class are used to store information about an attribute, including the syntax rules, whether the attribute will accept multiple values, and whether the information held in the attribute should be indexed for faster searching.

Attributes Syntaxes

Each attribute created in the Active Directory schema has a *syntax*; that is, a rule that governs the type and range of information that can be entered into objects using that attribute. The following are examples of attribute syntaxes:

- **Boolean**   True or False value
- **Integer**   A 32-bit numerical value
- **Case-Sensitive String**   A text string that is case sensitive (there is a differentiation between upper and lowercase characters)

A minimum and maximum range can be used to further restrict the information that can be entered into a field. For example, you can require that phone numbers contain at least ten numbers, to be sure that the area code is being included.

How the Schema Is Stored and Accessed

There is a single Active Directory schema per forest. A copy of the schema is stored on all domain controllers, and the master copy is stored on the Schema Operations Master. The Schema Operations Master handles changes to the Active Directory schema, as well as the replication of the changes to the domain controllers on the domain.

How the Schema Is Stored

Unlike with some other directory services, the Active Directory schema is not stored in a flat text file that must be read whenever the directory service starts. Rather, the schema is stored as an object within the Active Directory database itself, allowing changes to be replicated to domain controllers using standard Active Directory replication. The schema is stored in the following Active Directory distinguished name:

CN=Schema,CN=Configuration,DC=*Domain*,DC=*RootDomain*

The Active Directory database is stored in the %SystemRoot%\NTDS folder in a file named NTDS.DIT. You may also notice that a SCHEMA.INI file exists in the %SystemRoot%\System32 directory. This file contains information about the default schema, but is only used for the initial configuration of the Active Directory objects and not for ongoing schema operations.

How the Schema Is Accessed

There are always at least two copies of the Active Directory schema on a domain controller at any given time: one that is stored on disk, and a mirror of that information cached (that is, stored in memory) for faster access. When changes are made to the schema, the Schema Operations Master waits for an interval (5 minutes, by default) and then replicates the new schema to all domain controllers. Since clients access the cached copy of the schema, the domain controllers must retain the preexisting copy of the schema in cache until all clients have closed all working threads to the schema. This means that there may be multiple copies of the schema cache in memory at any given time.

Object Identifiers (OIDs)

In an X.500-compliant directory service such as Microsoft's Active Directory, every class and attribute must be assigned an Object Identifier (OID). The OID is used to uniquely identify the object within the schema to prevent potential conflicts that may occur when directories are combined.

Similar to the method in which IP addresses are registered on the Internet, OID number strings must be obtained from an issuing authority. The OID root is controlled by the International Standards Organization (ISO) and is represented by the number 1.

When viewing the schema later in this chapter, you will notice that all of the default schema objects use an OID beginning with 1.2.840.113556.1.*x* (where *x* is 4 for default attributes, or 5 for default classes). These are all valid OID strings that Microsoft has used in its default Active Directory schema.

If we break down and examine this OID, as shown in Table 19-2, we can see where each number originated.

Obtaining an OID

OID strings can be obtained through an issuing authority such as ANSI . OID strings issued by ANSI for use in the United States begin with 1.2.840.

Microsoft also includes a utility, OIDGEN.EXE, with the Windows 2000 Resource Kit that will generate OID strings that appear valid to the Active Directory schema, but are not registered with any issuing authority.

on the job

OIDGEN should be used only in test environments. A production directory for an organization should use a properly issued OID string from a registered naming authority (ANSI). This will prevent conflicts in the event that directories are later merged. If your organization is already using an X.500 directory, you may have an OID that you can extend to include Active Directory objects.

Once an OID has been issued to your organization, it can then be broken down to further subdivide various class or attribute sets. For example, if your organization was issued 1.2.840.12345, you could then

TABLE 19-2	Object ID (OID)	Description
Breaking Down the Default OID Number Strings in Active Directory	1	OID Root—International Standards Organization (ISO)
	1.2	Issued by ISO to the American National Standards Institute (ANSI)
	1.2.840	Designated by ANSI for OID strings issued in the United States
	1.2.840.113556	Issued by ANSI to Microsoft Corporation
	1.2.840.113556.1	Designated by Microsoft for Active Directory

use 1.2.840.12345.1 for your Active Directory tree, and further split the OID into 1.2.840.12345.1.10.*x* for your custom Active Directory classes and 1.2.840.12345.1.20.*x* for your custom Active Directory attributes.

HEADSTART OBJECTIVE 19.02

How and When Schema Modifications Are Made

Modifying the Active Directory schema allows an administrator to extend the types of objects and the information that can be stored for each object in the directory. The schema can also be extended to allow for applications that use an X.500 directory to integrate with Active Directory.

When Schema Modifications Are Made

Understanding when to modify the schema is critical. Before modifying the schema, you should analyze the default classes and attributes to make sure that nothing already in existence will meet your requirements. There are different scenarios in which you may consider making modifications to the default schema.

How Schema Modifications Are Made

Modifications to the Active Directory schema must always be performed on the Schema Operations Master. There may only be a single schema master per forest, which by default is the first domain controller created in the forest.

Schema modifications can be made in a number of ways, including

- The Schema Management MMC snap-in
- A Windows Scripting Host (WSH) script (a default component of Windows 2000)
- A third-party application that uses an X.500 directory service

QUESTIONS AND ANSWERS

When Should I ...	Answer
Add a new class?	When you are sure no existing class meets your needs, or cannot be easily modified to do so.
Modify an existing class?	If you need to modify the attributes used by the class. In order to change the position of the class in the hierarchy. When you must modify the class's Access Control List (ACL).
Add a new attribute?	When you are sure no existing attribute meets your needs.
Modify an existing attribute?	You need to change the syntax rules for the attribute values. To enable replication to the Global Catalog Server (GCS). To index the attribute for faster searching.
Deactivate a class?	When the class is no longer required and any instantiated objects have been removed. Classes cannot be deleted.

By default, the Schema Management MMC snap-in is not available on a Windows 2000 server. Before being able to manage the Active Directory schema using the MMC, a DLL component, SCHMMGMT.DLL, must be registered on the system, and the snap-in must be added to a new or existing console. To modify the schema, you must also be a member of the Schema Admins global security group.

By default, modifications to the schema are not enabled on the Schema Master. Before you can add or modify classes or attributes in the schema, you must change the focus of the console to the current Schema Master, and enable schema modifications as shown in Figure 19-1. It is best practice to change this setting back to the default after the modifications have been made.

Selecting a Schema Master
and enabling schema
modifications

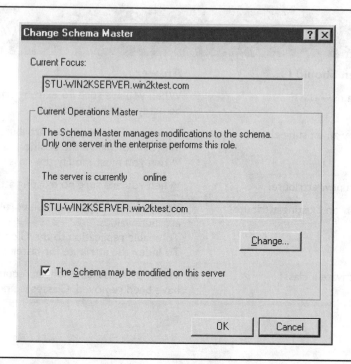

Preparing for Schema Modifications

This exercise walks you through creating a schema management console,
and enabling your domain controller for schema modifications. It is assumed
that you have an account (administrator) that is a member of the Schema
Admins group, and that your domain controller is the Schema Operations
Master for your forest.

1. Log on to your domain as administrator.

2. From Start | Run, enter the following:

   regsvr32 schmmgmt.dll

   This registers the Schema Management snap-in component on your
   system. You should receive a message stating, "DllRegisterServer in
   schmmgmt.dll succeeded."

3. From Start | Run, enter the following:

   mmc /a

   This launches the Microsoft Management Console in author mode.

4. From the Console menu, select Add/Remove Snap-in.

5. Click Add to add a new snap-in.

6. Highlight the Active Directory Schema management snap-in, and click Add, then Close.

7. Click OK to finish adding the new snap-in to your custom console.

8. In the Console Root window, right-click the Active Directory Schema node and select New Window from Here.

9. From the Console menu, select Options.

10. Change the console name from Console1 to AD Schema.

11. Change the console mode to "User Mode – limited access, single window."

12. Click OK.

13. From the Console menu, select Save As.

14. Save the console as Active Directory Schema in the following path:

    C:\Documents and Settings\All Users.WINNT\Start Menu\Programs\Administrative Tools

15. Click Yes on the warning about saving a single-window console.

16. Exit the Microsoft Management Console.

17. From Start | Programs | Administrative Tools, select Active Directory Schema.

18. Right-click Active Directory Schema in the console and select Operations Master.

19. Enable the check box next to "The schema may be modified on this server."

20. Click OK and exit the Active Directory Schema console

Making Schema Modifications

Once you have determined that a schema modification is required, and you have enabled schema modifications on your Schema Operations Master, you are ready to modify the schema.

heads
⓪p

Remember, before extending the Active Directory schema, you must have a globally unique X.500 Object ID (OID) for each schema object you wish to create.

Adding a New Attribute

If you wish to extend the attributes used by an existing class or add an entirely new class, the attributes to be included must first be created in the schema. Attributes are added using the Active Directory schema console you created in Exercise 19-1 by right-clicking Attributes and selecting Create Attribute. The window used to create attributes is shown in Figure 19-2.

When creating a new attribute, all of the fields in Figure 19-2 must be completed, with the exception of the Minimum and Maximum range information.

EXERCISE 19-2

Creating a New Attribute

The following exercise steps you through adding a new attribute to your Active Directory schema. The OID used in this exercise is not a registered OID; therefore, this exercise should only be performed on a test forest.

1. From Start | Programs | Administrative Tools, launch the Active Directory Schema console.

2. Expand Active Directory Schema if necessary.

3. Right-click Attributes and select Create Attribute.

   You will receive a warning message informing you that once an attribute has been added to the schema, it cannot be deleted. Click Continue.

FIGURE 19-2

Creating a new attribute

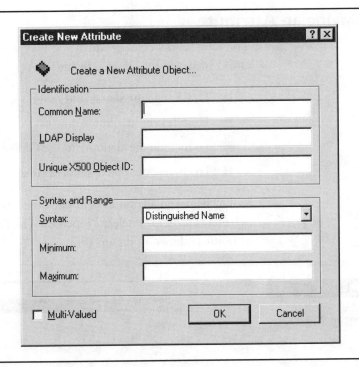

4. Enter the following parameters for the attribute:

Common Name:	chapter19attribute
LDAP Display:	chapter19attribute
Unique X500 Object ID:	1.2.840.12345.1.4.1000
Syntax:	Numerical String
Minimum Range:	0
Maximum Range:	100

5. Click OK.
6. Verify that the chapter19attribute attribute appears in the console.
7. Close the Active Directory Schema console.

Modifying an Attribute

There are several cases in which you may want to modify an attribute that already exists in the schema, including

- To Change the syntax and range
- To index the attribute
- To include the attribute in the Global Catalog (GC)
- To change the object's description

To change an attribute, right-click the attribute in the Active Directory Schema console, and select Properties. The Properties window for an attribute is shown in Figure 19-3.

Modifying an attribute

Attribute Indexing

Similar to indexing in a database, an attribute can be indexed to allow for faster searching. You should index an attribute when frequent searches are performed that need to order information based on the attribute value. Indexed attributes should typically be unique for most objects—there is no use indexing an attribute that maintains consistently identical values for all objects. Also, only single-value attributes should be indexed.

Placing an Attribute in the GC

When the value for an attribute is queried for an object, the client first queries the GCS. The GCS will inform the client of the object's location in the directory, from which it will then retrieve the information. Attributes can, however, be included in the GC for direct responses to directory queries. This is useful when an attribute is frequently accessed from anywhere in the forest, and does not change often.

EXERCISE 19-3

Modifying an Attribute

This exercise walks you through adding a description to the attribute created in Exercise 19-2.

1. From Start | Programs | Administrative Tools, launch the Active Directory Schema console.

2. Expand Active Directory Schema if necessary.

3. Select Attributes in the tree window.

4. Find the chapter19attribute in the description pane.

5. Right-click the attribute and select Properties.

6. Enter a Description of Chapter 19 Attribute.

7. Click OK.

8. Notice the description is displayed in the console.

9. Close the Active Directory Schema console.

Adding a New Class

You may need to add a class to the schema when there is no other class object already in existence that meets your requirements. Remember that you can also *modify* a class, so adding custom attributes to an existing class is preferred if your needs only vary slightly from the default classes.

Right-clicking Classes in the Active Directory Schema console and then selecting Create Class will add a new class to the schema. As is the case with attributes, any classes that are created can never be deleted—only deactivated. The Create New Schema Class window is shown in Figure 19-4. Different types of classes are used in an X.500 directory. These include

- **Structural** Most common. The only class type from which Active Directory objects can be instantiated.

- **Auxiliary** An extended list of attributes that can be added to a Structural or Abstract class.

FIGURE 19-4

Creating a new class

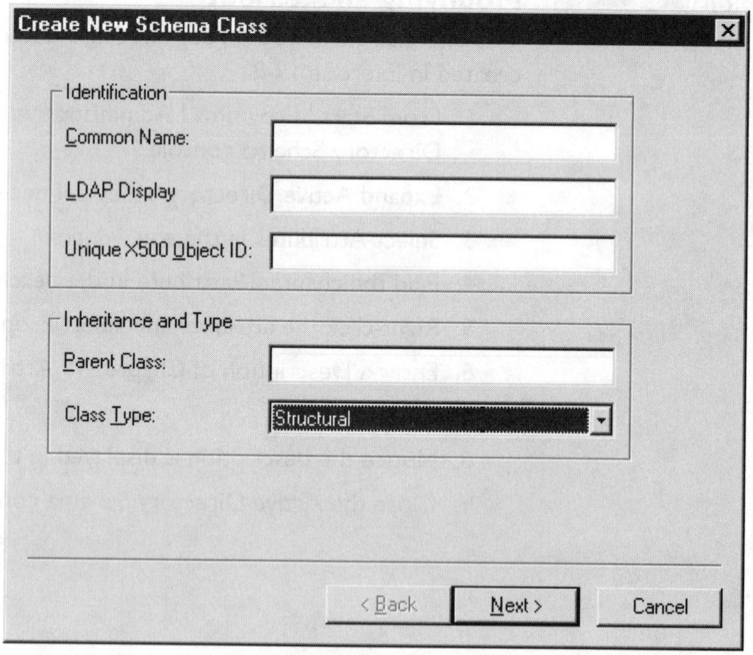

- **Abstract** A "template" or "superclass" used to create other classes.
- **88** Classes defined before 1993, based on the 1988 X.500 specification. A class of this type cannot be created; it is used for backward compatibility only.

Most of the classes that you work with and create will be Structural classes, since these are the only classes from which objects can be created.

EXERCISE 19-4

Creating a New Class

This exercise steps you through adding a class to your Active Directory Schema. You will add the attribute created in Exercise 19-2 as a mandatory attribute.

1. From Start | Programs | Administrative Tools, launch the Active Directory Schema console.
2. Expand Active Directory Schema if necessary.
3. Right-click Classes and select Create Class.
4. Complete the Identification and Inheritance/Type information based on the following:

Common Name:	chapter19class
LDAP Display:	chapter19class
Unique X500 Object ID:	1.2.840.12345.1.5.1000
Parent Class:	<blank>
Class Type:	Structural

5. Click Next to proceed to the Attributes screen.
6. In the Mandatory section, click Add.
7. Highlight chapter19attribute in the list, and click OK.
8. Notice that the OID for chapter19attribute is listed.
9. Click Finish.

Modifying a Class

As an administrator, the reason you would typically want to modify a class is to add one or more mandatory or optional attributes. Any attribute that already exists in the schema (and is not deactivated) may be added to an existing class. You may also remove an existing attribute from a class; however, any objects instantiated after doing so will not be able to contain values for any removed attributes.

Deactivating a Class

Once a class (or attribute) object is created in the schema, it can never be deleted. However, if you are no longer using a class to instantiate new objects, you may deactivate the class.

Deactivating a class results in the discontinuance of the schema object being replicated to the domain controllers in the forest. You do not need to delete existing objects that were instantiated using the deactivated class; however, you cannot create new objects in the class until it is reactivated.

heads
⑪ P
Once a schema object has been created, it can never be deleted—only deactivated. When a class is deactivated, it is no longer replicated, and no new objects can be instantiated in that class. When an attribute is deactivated, it cannot be added to any new classes.

EXERCISE 19-5

Deactivating a Class

In this exercise, you will deactivate the chapter19class schema object that you created in Exercise 19-4.

1. From Start | Programs | Administrative Tools, launch the Active Directory Schema console.

2. Expand Active Directory Schema if necessary.

3. Select Classes in the tree window.

4. Locate and right-click the chapter19class and select Properties.

5. Select "Deactivate this class," as shown in Figure 19-5.

FIGURE 19-5

Deactivating a class

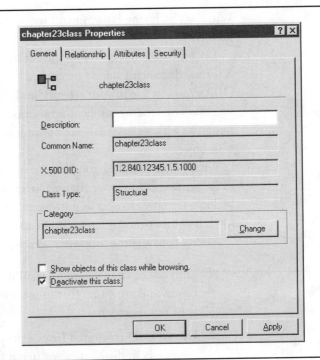

FIGURE 19-5

Deactivating a class

HEADSTART OBJECTIVE 19.04

Developing a Plan for Controlling Schema Modification

The schema is the core of the Active Directory, and modifications must be handled with care. A schema modification policy should be implemented before changes are made, to insure that modifications are thoroughly tested and documented prior to being made to production.

As with all production system changes, it is recommended that changes to the Active Directory schema first be made in a test environment. This is especially true for those changes that are being performed in bulk using

Windows Scripting Host, since a script error may cause unrecoverable problems.

Documentation is critical to the effective control of schema modification. A formal document should be created that includes information about the OID strings in use in your schema, and should also contain a map of your schema. The schema can be diagrammed similar to the directory itself, to recognize which classes are parents and which classes can be instantiated with objects.

Finally, it is usually a good idea to implement as many modifications to the schema before your Active Directory design goes into production. Making as many changes as possible up front will result in fewer worries when it comes time for later modifications.

Always consider the following before modifying the schema:

- **Only make changes when absolutely necessary**   Check existing classes and attributes first to see if the default schema will satisfy your requirements.

- **Use an OID registered from a proper authority**   To avoid potential conflicts, use a registered OID for your schema objects. Carefully document your internal OID structure, and keep it up to date as changes are made.

- **Use standard naming conventions**   Use Common Names and LDAP Display Names that are easily recognized, while following a standard naming convention. Document the naming convention and follow it carefully for future modifications.

- **Carefully control schema access**   Leave the "Schema can be modified" option disabled when changes are not being made. Closely manage and monitor the members of the Schema Admins global security group.

- **Test schema modifications thoroughly**   Make all schema modifications first in a test environment.

- **Be aware of replication traffic**   Only select the "Replicate this attribute to the Global Catalog" option when absolutely required, to eliminate replication overhead.

■ **Deactivate unused classes** When a class is no longer used, deactivate it. This will reduce replication traffic, and it can always be enabled later.

CHAPTER SUMMARY

Windows 2000 Active Directory stores information about available classes and attributes in the schema. This schema is extensible by an administrator, or a third-party application that uses an X.500 directory service. Changes can be made on the Schema Operation Master, and are replicated to all domain controllers in the forest.

Schema modifications must be handled carefully, to avoid conflicts and other problems. An OID is assigned to each schema object to maintain global uniqueness in all directories worldwide. There are hundreds of classes and attributes included with the default schema, so modifications should be made only when absolutely necessary.

TWO-MINUTE DRILL

❑ The Windows 2000 Active Directory schema is the heart of Active Directory. The schema stores information about the types of objects that can be created in the directory and their location in the hierarchical structure.

❑ Every object created in Active Directory is an instance of a class. Classes are defined in the Active Directory schema, and are used to group a set of attributes that can be used by objects created in that class.

❑ The Windows 2000 Active Directory includes hundreds of default classes. These classes include those used for internal operations (such as Active Directory replication, IP security, and RPC management), as well as those used to create most of the objects in Active Directory (such as Users and Computers).

❑ Attributes are used to store information about objects created in Active Directory.

❑ There is a single Active Directory schema per forest. A copy of the schema is stored on all domain controllers, and the master copy is stored on the Schema Operations Master.

❑ In an X.500-compliant directory service such as Microsoft's Active Directory, every class and attribute must be assigned an Object Identifier (OID).

❑ Understanding when to modify the schema is critical. Before modifying the schema, you should analyze the default classes and attributes to make sure that nothing already in existence will meet your requirements.

❑ Modifications to the Active Directory schema must always be performed on the Schema Operations Master.

❑ Once you have determined that a schema modification is required, and you have enabled schema modifications on your Schema Operations Master, you are ready to modify the schema.

❑ If you wish to extend the attributes used by an existing class or add an entirely new class, the attributes to be included must first be created in the schema.

❑ You may need to add a class to the schema when there is no other class object already in existence that meets your requirements. Remember that you can also *modify* a class, so adding custom attributes to an existing class is preferred if your needs only vary slightly from the default classes.

❑ As an administrator, the reason you would typically want to modify a class is to add one or more mandatory or optional attributes.

❑ Once a class (or attribute) object is created in the schema, it can never be deleted. However, if you are no longer using a class to instantiate new objects, you may deactivate the class.

❑ The schema is the core of the Active Directory, and modifications must be handled with care. A schema modification policy should be implemented before changes are made, to insure that modifications are thoroughly tested and documented prior to being made to production.

SELF TEST

The following questions will help you measure your understanding of the material presented in this chapter. Read all of the choices carefully, as there may be more than one correct answer. Choose all correct answers for each question.

1. Every object created in Active Directory is an instance of

   A. An attribute

   B. An object

   C. A schema

   D. A class

2. Class Definition Objects are stored in Active Directories as instances of

   A. The classSchema class

   B. The attributeSchema class

   C. The classSchema attribute

   D. The attributeSchema attribute

3. Attribute Syntaxes are used to

   A. Restrict the range of values that may be entered.

   B. Restrict the type of values that may be entered.

   C. Restrict permissions to the attribute.

   D. Restrict which classes can use the attribute.

4. The schema is stored in which of the following locations?

   A. CN=Schema,CN=Configuration,DC=*Domain*,DC=*Domain*

   B. The %SystemRoot%\SCHEMA. INI file

   C. The Windows NT Registry

   D. The schema is only stored in cache

5. There are always at least how many copies of the schema on a domain controller?

   A. 1

   B. 2

   C. 3

   D. 4

6. Which of the following represents an attribute?

   A. User

   B. Computer

   C. Organizational Unit (OU)

   D. LogonHours

7. In a custom user class, you are currently storing each user's phone number as a 7-number string. You want to require 10 numbers, so that an area code is also assigned to each user. How would you make this change?

   A. Modify the class.

   B. Modify the attribute.

   C. Create a new class and attribute.

   D. Create a new attribute and assign to the existing class.

8. Microsoft Active Directory is based on which standard?

   A. X.5

   B. X.25

   C. X.400

   D. X.500

9. Valid OIDs must be obtained from

    A. An OID naming authority, such as ANSI

    B. The InterNIC

    C. OIDGEN.EXE

    D. Microsoft

10. There is a single Schema Operations Master per

    A. Site

    B. Domain

    C. Tree

    D. Forest

11. Before loading the Active Directory Schema Snap-in component into a new or existing console, what must first be done on the client computer?

    A. The SCHMMGMT.DLL file must be registered using REGEDT32.

    B. The SCHMMGMT.DLL file must be registered using REGSVR32.

    C. The ADSIEDIT.DLL file must be registered using REGEDT32.

    D. The ADSIEDIT.DLL file must be registered using REGSVR32.

12. Which of the following types of classes may be created in the schema? (Choose all that apply.)

    A. Structural

    B. Auxiliary

    C. Abstract

    D. 88

13. What must you do prior to deactivating a class?

    A. Delete all assigned attributes.

    B. Deactivate all assigned attributes.

    C. Remove all objects of that class.

    D. Nothing.

14. In which of the following methods can a schema modification be made? (Choose all that apply.)

    A. The AD Users and Computers console

    B. A third-party application

    C. A Windows Scripting Host (WSH) script

    D. By executing the SCHMMGMT file

15. Which of the following considerations should be made when modifying the schema?

    A. Validity of OID strings to be used.

    B. Replication traffic.

    C. Disk space utilization.

    D. Existing classes may suffice.

MICROSOFT CERTIFIED SYSTEMS ENGINEER

Part III

Networking
Services

MICROSOFT CERTIFIED SYSTEMS ENGINEER

20

TCP/IP

I n April of 1996, in a visionary statement, Bill Gates noted "almost everyone agrees that the potential of the Internet to improve personal computing is inspiring." (source: NetWorld+Interop '96, at http://www.interop.com/) Four months earlier, he had announced Microsoft's intention to fully integrate Internet functionality into Microsoft's entire software line. The fortunes of a company having the size and competitive clout of Microsoft, run by a single decision-maker, allowed it to literally change the course and direction of its product development overnight.

Prior to making the decision to provide Internet functionality into its product line, Microsoft followed a more proprietary approach, developing new software products designed to leverage new functionality off of existing Microsoft products and the products of other competing software vendors. This was clearly illustrated with the development of Windows NT 3.1 (released July 1993).

Designed primarily as an operating system for network servers, workstations, and software development machines, Windows NT 3.1 was designed to operate in a mixed network environment. Version 3.1 and its successor version 3.5 (code-named "Daytona") were both designed to install NWLink by default as the Network layer protocol. NWLink is Microsoft's implementation of lower-level NetWare protocols, which includes IPX, SPX, RIPX, and NBIPX, by default. This is primarily because Novell NetWare had the largest market share for PC-based network operating systems at the time, and NetWare's native Network layer protocol was IPX, a Novell proprietary descendant of the Xerox XNS protocol.

Perhaps foreshadowing Microsoft's decision to make its products Internet ready, Windows NT 3.51 (released June 1995) was modified to include the installation of TCP/IP along with NWLink as default protocols. Commonly referred to as "the protocol of the Internet," Transmission Control Protocol/Internet Protocol (TCP/IP) standards allow computers utilizing a variety of operating systems to directly communicate with each other. Windows NT 4.0 (released July 1996) also continued the practice of installing TCP/IP and NWLink as default protocols.

Effective with the release of Windows 2000 , Microsoft's flagship network operating system no longer includes NWLink as an installation default protocol. The decision to implement TCP/IP as the single default protocol reflects Microsoft's Internet-centric product development policy.

The Role of TCP/IP in Networking

TCP/IP is in actuality a family of utilities and protocols (sometimes called a *suite*). When properly configured in what is commonly referred to as a "TCP/IP stack," the protocols provide the capability for host-to-host communications. The term *host* includes more than just computers. Other common hosts on a local area network include printers, print servers, fax servers, and other peripheral devices directly connected to the network.

With the release of the Windows 2000 operating system, Microsoft went beyond the advances in performance and ease of administration that were incorporated in Windows NT 3.5 and Windows NT 4.0, as a result of a complete rewrite of the TCP/IP stack. These advances primarily focused on providing improved management capabilities necessary in large enterprise networking environments, and recognition of the key position the Internet will play in networking environments in the future.

TCP/IP Stack Design Goals

Microsoft's goals in designing its network operating system around a TCP/IP stack were to make it

- Standards-compliant
- Interoperable
- Portable
- Scalable
- Versatile
- Easy to administer using standardized tools
- Adaptable

Microsoft designed the TCP/IP suite for Windows 2000 so that it will be easy to integrate this network operating system into large-scale corporate, government, and public networks; providing the ability to operate over these networks in a secure manner. As an Internet-ready operating system, Windows 2000 supports the following features:

- Logical and physical multihoming

- Internal IP routing capability

- Internet Group Management Protocol (IGMP) version 2 (IP Multicasting)

- Duplicate IP address detection

- Multiple default gateways

- Dead gateway detection

- IP Security (IPSec)

- Quality of Service (QoS)

- ATM Services

- Virtual Private Networks (VPNs)

- Layer 2 Tunneling Protocol (L2TP)

In addition, Windows 2000 has the following performance enhancements:

- Protocol stack tuning, including increased default window sizes

- TCP scalable window sizes (RFC 1323 support, off by default)

- Selective acknowledgments (SACK)

- Round Trip Time (RTT) and Retransmission Timeout (RTO) calculation improvements

- Improved performance for management of large numbers of connections

What Are TCP/IP Protocols?

In some ways, the TCP/IP protocols and utilities can be compared to a carpenter's tools. Each tool is used for a particular purpose. The hammer is used to drive nails. The saw is used to cut wood. TCP protocols and utilities provide specific functionality. FTP is an example of a connection-oriented protocol utilized for file transfers between hosts. The Packet Internet Groper (PING) utility is an example of a utility that is used to determine whether a host is accessible over the network (or Internet).

In order to develop an understanding of the available functionality associated with the TCP/IP protocol stack, the seven-layer OSI model provides useful reference points. Because many of the protocols span multiple OSI layers, a TCP/IP model has been created to provide a more effective representation of where each protocol functions. Figure 20-1 provides a comparison of the two models.

The Application layer of the TCP/IP model roughly corresponds to the OSI model's Application and Presentation layers. Software application programs gain access to the network through this layer, using TCP/IP protocols such as File Transfer Protocol (FTP), Hypertext Transfer Protocol (HTTP), Simple Mail Transport Protocol (SMTP), and Trivial File Transfer Protocol (TFTP). Simple Network Management Protocol (SNMP), Dynamic Host Configuration Protocol (DHCP), Point-to-Point Protocol (PPP), Serial Line Interface Protocol (SLIP), and Point-to-Point Tunneling Protocol (PPTP), are also resident at this layer of the TCP/IP model.

The Transport layer of the TCP/IP model generally corresponds to the Session and Transport layers of the OSI model. Transmission Control

---

FIGURE 20-1

Comparison of the OSI seven-layer and TCP/IP four-layer models

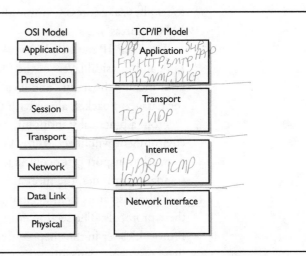

Protocol (TCP) and User Datagram Protocol (UDP) reside at this layer of the model. Network services utilizing TCP/IP as their transport protocol use either TCP or UDP, depending upon the nature of the service. TCP is generally defined as a connection-oriented protocol. It provides assured package delivery based on a process of delivery acknowledgment by the receiving host.

UDP is defined as a connectionless protocol. Delivery is defined more in terms of "best attempt." It can be compared to mailing a letter. When sender places a letter in a U.S. Mailbox, properly addressed with postage prepaid, the legal presumption is that delivery will be accomplished. But, just as in law where presumptions are not always factually correct, there will be times in a networking environment where packet delivery fails. In those circumstances where UDP is utilized, the responsibility for discovery of delivery errors or omissions falls on higher-level protocols or the network application itself.

The Internet layer of the TCP/IP model is roughly equivalent to the Networking layer of the OSI model. Internet Protocol (IP), Address Resolution Protocol (ARP), Internet Control Message Protocol (ICMP), and IGMP all reside at this layer of the model. IP provides logical network and host addressing that enable the TCP/IP transport protocol's routable functionality. ICMP and IGMP provide specific messaging functions. ARP is utilized to provide the mapping of a host's logical address (IP address) to its physical address (commonly referred to as the host's "burnt-in MAC address").

The TCP/IP model's Network Interface layer corresponds to the Data Link and Physical layers of the OSI model. Functions associated with this layer include the nature and location of header and trailer information in the datagram packet, along with the location of data in the packet.

From a practical standpoint, networks operating in a Windows 2000 environment will likely utilize TCP/IP as the primary (and possibly only) network transport protocol. As the migration of networks to this transport standard continues, the more important it becomes for network engineers and administrators to understand the purpose and function of each of these protocols. The section entitled "Using TCP/IP as a Base Network Protocol," later in the chapter, details the functions associated with each of these protocols, describing their installation, configuration, and use in a Windows 2000 networking environment.

Developing a TCP/IP Implementation **Strategy**

In this section, we walk through the steps in analyzing a TCP/IP workstation configuration in Exercise 20-1. Then we examine a scenario that involves troubleshooting a complex multiprotocol network environment and devising an implementation strategy.

EXERCISE 20-1

Analyzing a TCP/IP Workstation Configuration

Using the *ipconfig /all* command at the ms-dos prompt, identify the following:

1. Your computer's:

   Hostname:
   DNS Server:
   NetBIOS Scope ID:
   Ethernet Adapter Type:
   Adapter Address:
   IP Address:
   Subnet Mask:
   Default Gateway:
   DHCP Server:
   Primary WINS Server:
   Lease Expires Date:

2. At the ms-dos prompt, ping the following IP addresses and describe the results:

   127.0.0.1:
   Your IP Address:
   Your DHCP Server's IP Address:

3. Identify the transport protocols installed on your computer (TCP/IP, NetBEUI, etc.).

In a hostile office environment, where the topic of conversation over the past few months has been whether the network will continue to be the principal obstacle to getting work out, you've been called in to see if you can diagnose the problem. You've been told that the troubles started after the decision was made by IT staff to migrate over to a complete Microsoft Windows 2000 environment, utilizing TCP/IP as the base protocol. Unfortunately, the performance expectations have gone unfulfilled, resulting in user complaints associated with slow network response. Studies have shown that not only is user frustration heightened when application response time increases, user response time also increases. This result stems from effects on short-term memory and human attention span.

The first step in your efforts to seek a solution to the problem is to log on to a typical workstation during the expected peak usage time (10:00 A.M.–12:00 P.M.), and view system response time yourself. With the suspicious network manager standing behind you, it becomes quickly evident why users complain. Even simple tasks like searching the network neighborhood for a distant server becomes a time-consuming task. An obvious but often overlooked starting point is the configuration setting of the workstation where you are sitting.

A selection of the Network and Dial-up Connections applet on the Control Panel, followed with another selection of the Local Area Connections applet and a click on Properties, goes a long way toward explaining a primary cause for workstation response delays. The workstation is configured to use NetBEUI, NWLink (IPX/SPX), and TCP/IP. Additionally, the binding order for these three protocols places NetBEUI in first position, followed by NWLink, and then TCP/IP.

The reason for this multiprotocol arrangement has more to do with lack of adequate training than anything else. Windows 95 was designed by default to install both NetBEUI and IPX/SPX, and the installation configuration parameters utilized when Windows 2000 Professional was installed on the network workstations were likely adopted from the Windows 95 settings. The focus on the TCP/IP network implementation was more likely directed at the network's server environment rather than at the workstation. Further explanations might include a general distrust of the nonbroadcast nature of a properly implemented TCP/IP environment, and a belief that these other protocols provided a redundancy so workstations could communicate in the event of failure of the TCP/IP environment.

Your recommendation for a quick fix, designed to provide a noticeable improvement to network responsiveness, is the removal of unwanted protocols (NetBEUI and IPX/SPX). While you expect some resistance to this suggestion, particularly from IT staff personnel who don't understand how TCP/IP works, a demonstration on how workstation response time is improved with the protocol removals shows the benefits of operating with a single transport protocol.

Having produced some improvement doesn't mean that the job is done. Workstation response, while improved, is still slow. Your next focus will extend beyond the workstation to the network. You ask for and receive a network diagram. With reasonably priced network diagramming tools available, you are somewhat surprised at receiving a hand-drawn network diagram. Perhaps this is an omen of things to come.

The fact that the diagram shows the existence of four routers pleases you. What *doesn't* please you is the discovery that all 1500 hosts on the network are in the same subnet. Why, you ask yourself, would someone buy routers and then use them as bridges? The answer again is the lack of adequate training. If there was ever a time that planning should have preceded implementation, this was it.

Situations like this are all too commonplace. Where network planning is only an afterthought, substandard network performance, addressing conflicts, and security problems are just a few of a number of possible consequences. The planning stage for TCP/IP implementation is extremely important. The conclusions reached as a result of TCP/IP planning will likely impact the network layout. It should be completed before network diagramming is completed. Important issues associated with IP planning include

- Utilization of public versus private IP addressing
- Utilization of naming services (WINS and DNS)
- Utilization of dynamic IP addressing services (DHCP)
- Utilization of subnetting to segment the network

Public Versus Private IP Addressing

When deciding on an IP network-addressing scheme, an initial decision requires choosing either public or private addressing. Public addresses are assigned to the network either by an Internet Service Provider (ISP) or from an entity designated by the Internet Corporation for Assigning Names and

Numbers (ICANN). Internet addresses are doled out by the ICANN to ISPs, based on the particular ISP's demonstrated needs. Getting a full IP network range is almost impossible, even for the largest of companies.

The difficulties associated with obtaining enough registered IP addresses to meet the network's needs, coupled with the difficulties associated with providing LAN security where network resources are visible to the public Internet, justify utilization of a private addressing scheme for LANs. IP address ranges have been reserved from the pool of public Internet addresses for private addressing. Specified in Internet Request for Comments (RFC) 1918, their use is optional but suggested by the Internet community. The address ranges are shown in Table 20-1.

One of the features that comes with using the private IP addresses as specified in RFC1918 is that the major router vendors and users agree that requests going to or from these addresses are discarded. When using private IP addresses, you'll use some type of proxy or Network Address Translation (NAT) server to convert the private IP address range(s) on your local network to a public IP address that can be routed.

Utilization of Naming Services (WINS and DNS)

Unlike Windows NT, Windows 2000 Server uses DNS (Domain Name System) as the primary name resolution method by default. In fact, it is required if you are going to implement Active Directory services. This change is designed to utilize the LDAP-based Windows NT Active Directory. Every Windows NT domain is represented by a DNS domain name. A typical example of a Windows 2000 Server domain name might be senate.congress.gov. Prior to Windows 2000 Server, domains were represented by NetBIOS names, and the old NetBIOS name remains after migration for access by older clients.

TABLE 20-1   List of Internet IP Addresses Available for Private Addressing

IP Address Class	Address Range Beginning	Address Range Ending
Class A addresses	10.0.0.0	10.255.255.255
Class B addresses	172.16.0.0	172.31.255.255
Class C addresses	192.168.0.0	192.168.255.255

Since each Windows NT domain has a corresponding DNS domain representation, users can use DNS to contact the directory servers. In addition, any client or server can have a DNS name.

Where Active Directory services is implemented, Windows 2000 requires a DNS server that supports the service locator record type defined in RFC 2052 (SRV records). SRV records are similar in nature to the utilization of MX records, where several different servers can advertise a similar service.

The format of an SRV record is *Service.Proto.Name TTL Class SRV Priority Weight Port Target.* Table 20-2 defines each of the items in an SRV record.

TABLE 20-2	Identity	Description
List of Items in an SRV Record	Service	The symbolic name of the desired service as defined in Assigned Numbers or locally.
	Proto	The protocol. TCP and UDP are the likely values inserted into this field. However, any name defined by Assigned Numbers or locally can be used.
	Name	The domain name for this record.
	TTL	The standard DNS time-to-live.
	Class	The standard DNS class IN.
	Priority	The priority of this target host (this is similar to an MX record). A client must attempt to contact the target host with the lowest-numbered priority it can reach; target hosts with the same priority are tried in pseudo-random order.
	Weight	A load-balancing mechanism used when selecting a target host among those that have equal priority—a host should be chosen first by its weight. A weight of 0 is used when no load balancing is needed.
	Port	The port on the target host of this service.
	Target	The domain name of the target host (this is the same as an MX record). There is at least one A record for this name.

Handwritten annotations:
- e.g. ldap (next to Service)
- tcp (next to Proto)
- escc.gov.uk (next to Name)
- 0 (next to TTL)
- IN (next to Class)
- "SRV" goes in here → (next to Priority)
- 0 (next to Priority)
- 0 (next to Weight)
- 389 (next to Port)
- Markm.escc.gov.uk (next to Target)

= ldap.tcp.escc.gov.uk 0 IN 00 389 Markm.escc.gov.uk

A typical SRV record for domain senate.congress.gov would be ldap.tcp.senate.congress.gov 0 IN SRV 0 0 389 smithj.senate.congress.gov.

In addition, special DNS entries are used to identify subsets of domain controllers that have special roles. For example, a typical SRV record for a domain controller that is named Gold would be ldap.tcp.gold.condcs.senate. congress.gov 0 IN SRV 0 0 389 smithj.senate.congress.gov.

In Windows NT 3.*x* and 4.0 environments, servers are configured to use NetBIOS names for both machine and domain names. When you migrate to Windows 2000 Server, you need to have DNS names. Probably the best way to accomplish migration is to create NetBIOS names that are compatible with standard DNS names.

Standard DNS characters are the letters A–Z, numbers 0–9, and the dash (-). Be aware that DNS names are case insensitive. If existing NetBIOS names are constrained to the preceding character set, use the same name in a DNS or NetBIOS context. Where NetBIOS names do not meet the DNS standard, they should be changed if possible before migration begins.

With Windows 2000, the option of using full Unicode names in DNS is possible. Unicode is 16-bit character encoding that contains all of the characters in common use in the world's major languages. It provides an unambiguous representation of text across a range of scripts, languages, and platforms. The Unicode scheme is capable of encoding all known characters and is used as a worldwide character-encoding standard. Unicode is supported by all 32-bit versions of Microsoft Windows and by 32-bit OLE technology.

Windows 2000 Server DNS supports Unicode Character Support based on UTF-8 encoding. The UTF-8 encoding allows complete use of non-ASCII character sets. One limitation to its use in a DNS environment is the fact that Unicode has only limited support on Windows 95 and Windows 98.

Windows 2000 Server contains an implementation of Dynamic DNS (DDNS)that follows RFC 2136. DDNS allows clients and servers to register domain names and IP address mappings. This feature, unavailable with Windows NT Server, frees administrators from the time-consuming process of manually updating DNS entries. While it is possible to use Windows 2000 DNS without DDNS, the network administrator's workload will increase significantly because of the work involved in manually updating DNS information.

The NETLOGON service on a Windows NT domain controller uses DDNS to maintain all the DNS entries used to access the Active Directory. Clients and servers register their DNS address records when they boot.

The Dynamic Host Configuration Protocol (DHCP) server that shipped in Windows 2000 Server is able to optionally register pointer (PTR) records that map IP addresses to DNS names. For non-DDNS clients, the DHCP server can register both a host name and PTR record.

The design approach will vary for a Windows 2000 Server DNS architecture, depending on the current DNS environment. Key points associated with the planning state for the DNS namespace include

- Every Windows 2000 Server domain uses a DNS domain name for its domain controller location information.

- The host names of the computers in a domain *are not required to be related* to the Directory DNS name.

- DNS zones can be integrated into the Active Directory multimaster replication.

- Use of standard RFC host names if DNS interoperability is important.

- The Windows Internet Name Service (WINS) will coexist with DNS until all computers are migrated to Windows 2000 Server.

In a new DNS deployment, the easiest approach may be to establish DDNS zones that correspond to each Windows NT domain as a preliminary step. The second step would be to place each host in the DNS zone that corresponds to the NT domain where the host is a member. The Active Directory DNS integration should be enabled so that all DNS data is safely stored and replicated in the Active Directory.

In existing environments where a large existing DNS structure supports a heterogeneous environment, such as a university campus, it should not be necessary to do a major redesign to upgrade to Windows 2000 Server and DDNS. Complex existing environments where client domains do not correspond to Windows NT domains will operate effectively using standard

DNS zone transfer mechanisms. New DNS zones in the enterprise can be created containing the DDNS data for the new Windows 2000 Server domains. By keeping these domains dynamic, all domain controller updates will be automated.

The process of migrating from NT domains to a single Windows 2000 domain can be complex, and the migration tools available today may not be as useful as hoped. It may be better to maintain this *mixed mode* for some time until migration can be accomplished in a deliberate and well-planned way. Some limitations exist in this mixed mode. For example, nested groups are not supported in mixed mode.

With Windows 2000 Server, trees have a contiguous namespace. This namespace can be in one zone or in individual zones on a per-domain basis. In a large, highly decentralized company, more zones are effective. In a smaller, centralized company, fewer zones work well. This is because smaller zones reduce replication traffic.

Establishing zones based on the physical structure of the company generally keeps the local DNS information close to the region that requires the DNS name most often. However, a large centralized company with a corresponding large zone structure requires DNS zone transfer over a much larger area. Obviously, this increases traffic. These are the same considerations you must examine when deciding on the scope of domain replication traffic.

As mentioned earlier, WINS will continue to be included in Windows 2000 Server, but is not required in a pure Windows 2000 Server environment. WINS primary attribute relates to backward client compatibility. It will continue to be used for down-level clients, such as Windows for Workgroups, Windows 95, and servers that use NetBIOS. Over time, the use of WINS will decrease as clients and servers are migrated to a pure DNS environment.

The DNS/WINS integration feature that is provided in Windows NT 4.0 can be used to map the WINS NetBIOS namespace into DNS. This process works in situations where a specific host entry does not exist in the DNS server's database, and it has been configured to query the WINS server to learn whether the host's name appears in the WINS database. If an appropriate entry is found, the DNS server returns the IP address for that host to the DNS client making the inquiry.

[handwritten margin note: APIPA – Substitute for DHCP on lan < 5 hosts.]

Utilization of DHCP

With its expanded role in Windows 2000, DHCP is one of the most important client services. Its primary new feature is the ability to automatically configure an IP address and subnet mask when the client is started on a small private network without a DHCP server available to assign addresses. Known as Automatic Private IP Addressing (APIPA), it provides a substitute for the implementation of DHCP services on small networks (single LAN environments with five or fewer hosts). A component of plug-and-play networking, it works by automatically assigning unique reserved IP addresses to hosts on private local area networks (LANs). This frees users from having to manually configure host IP addresses, or deploy and manage DHCP or DNS. The theory behind APIPA is that it allows for network growth by seamlessly integrating with a DHCP server, should one be added later.

Another new feature is support for Media Sense. This feature of NDIS 5.0 provides a mechanism where changes in the media type are sensed (e.g., Token Ring to Ethernet), and the transport protocols are automatically bound to the network interface card (NIC). This feature can improve the roaming experience for portable device users.

When a Windows TCP/IP client is installed and set to dynamically obtain TCP/IP protocol configuration information from a DHCP server (instead of being manually configured with an IP address and other parameters), the DHCP client service is engaged each time the computer is restarted. Previous Windows clients (except for Windows 2000 and Windows 98 clients) would attempt to obtain an IP address from a DHCP server. If they were unable to obtain an IP address, the user was notified of this failure, and the Windows client would periodically attempt to contact a DCHP server for an address. Until an IP address was obtained, the client could not communicate via TCP/IP.

The Windows 2000 client service now uses a two-step process to configure the client with an IP address and other configuration information.

1. When the client is installed, it attempts to locate a DHCP server and obtain a configuration from it.

2. If this attempt to locate a DHCP server fails, the Windows 2000 DHCP client autoconfigures its stack with a selected IP address from

the ICANN-reserved Class B network 169.254.0.0, with the subnet mask 255.255.0.0. The DHCP client tests (using an ARP) to make sure that another host on the network has not already chosen the IP address. If it is in use, it selects another IP address (it does this for up to 10 addresses). Once the DHCP client has selected an address that is not in use, it configures the interface with this address. It continues to check for a DHCP server in the background every five minutes. When a DHCP server is found, the autoconfiguration information is abandoned, and the configuration offered by the DHCP server is used instead.

If the DHCP client has previously obtained a lease from a DHCP server, the following modified sequence of events occurs:

1. If the client's lease is still valid (not expired) at boot time, the client tries to renew its lease with the DHCP server. If the client fails to locate a DHCP server during the renewal attempt, it tries to ping the default gateway that is listed in the lease. If pinging the default gateway succeeds, the DHCP client assumes that it is still located on the same network where it obtained its current lease, and continues to use the lease. By default, the client attempts to renew its lease in the background when half of its assigned lease time has expired.

2. If the attempt to ping the default gateway fails, the client assumes that it has been moved to a network that has no DHCP services currently available (such as a home network), and autoconfigures itself as described earlier. Once autoconfigured, it continues to try to locate a DHCP server every five minutes, in the background.

With the implementation of NDIS 5.0, Media Sensing was added as a feature to Windows 2000. It provides a mechanism for the NIC to notify the protocol stack when media connect and media disconnect events occur. Windows 2000 TCP/IP utilizes these notifications to assist in automatic configuration activities. For example, in earlier versions of the Windows client operating systems, when a portable computer was located and DHCP-configured on an Ethernet network, and then moved to another network without rebooting, the protocol stack received no indication of the move. As a result, the computer's TCP/IP configuration parameters were not relevant to the new network. Additionally, if the computer was shut off, carried home and rebooted, the protocol stack was not aware that the NIC was no longer connected to a network, and again, stale configuration parameters remained.

Media Sense support allows the protocol stack to react to events and invalidate stale parameters. For example, when a computer running Windows 2000 is unplugged from the network (assuming the NIC supports Media Sense), after a damping period implemented in the stack (currently 20 seconds), TCP/IP automatically invalidates the parameters associated with the network that has been disconnected. The IP address will no longer allow sends, and routes associated with the interface are invalidated.

To provide users with information relating network connectivity, the network connection status can be made visible on the taskbar by selecting a connection, right-clicking it, clicking Properties, and then selecting the "Show icon in taskbar when connected" check box.

Utilization of Subnetting to Segment the Network

Viewed often as overly complex, the concept of subnetting a network for traffic segmentation purposes is extremely important for the network professional to understand. TCP/IP is by nature a routable protocol. To make routing work effectively, some sort of organizational structure for the network must be implemented. Subnetting provides a vehicle for organizing.

To properly understand IP addresses and subnet masks, you should think of them both as 32-bit binary numbers. Each IP address and each subnet can be written as four groups of eight binary digits (ones and zeroes), separated by periods (called dots). In the subnet mask, when represented in binary notation, the 1 bits identify the network, and the 0 bits identify the interface address. For example, the IP address 131.107.2.100, with a subnet mask of 255.255.240.0, in binary format would each be written as

```
IP Address    10000011  01101011  00000010  01100100

Subnet Mask  11111111  11111111  11110000  00000000

                       Network Number       Host Number
```

This example illustrates a Class B network that is subnetted into 16 (14) valid subnets, each with a large number of valid hosts (4094).

The first step in subnetting a network is to determine an appropriate subnet mask. An IP address is made up of a network ID and a host ID. A network ID is a number shared by every PC on the network. TCP/IP looks at the network ID to see if a packet is destined for a PC on the local network or on a remote network. The host ID is a number that's unique to each host on the network (PCs, network printers, router interfaces, and so on). The subnet mask tells TCP/IP where the network ID ends and the host ID begins.

In the previous example, the first 20-bits of the IP address identify the network identification. The remaining 12 bits identify the host address. Rather than have a single Class B network, 14 valid separate networks are created from this single Class B address. You can identify the address class by looking at the first few bits in an address. Table 20-3 identifies the address class together with its starting bits.

Each physical section (segment) of a network is usually assigned a unique block of IP addresses. This is accomplished by assigning the segment a network address and subnet mask. Every interface connected to that network segment is then assigned an address from within the block of addresses, and it is also configured using the subnet mask. Sometimes, multiple blocks of IP addresses will coexist on a single network segment,

TABLE 20-3		
Identification of Starting Bits for Subnet Classes	**Address Class**	**Starting Bits**
	Class A	01
	Class B	10
	Class C	110
	Class D	1110
	Class E	11110

utilizing the same physical cabling network but operating as separate logical network segments.

When designing and configuring a subnet, a network address and subnet mask are defined for each block of IP addresses. The network address defines the start of the IP address block, and the subnet mask determines how large the block is. The subnet mask also determines which portion of the IP address is used to identify the network, and which part of the IP address is used to identify the host or interface.

When you segment your network, it may be appropriate to come up with alternative values for the host ID portion of the IP address that will allow better regulation of traffic flow. To calculate this alternative subnet mask, the process begins with counting the number of segments on your network. Once the number of segments has been determined, the next process is converting this number to binary.

The next step is converting the number of segments on the network to binary form. For example, if there are six potential segments on the network, the binary equivalent for this number is 110. This number (110) utilizes 3 bits. In our example of a Class B network (131.107.0.0) with a default subnet mask of 255.255.0.0, the subnet mask could be modified to 255.255.224.0, providing six available subnets for the network.

Each subnet is interconnected to other subnets on the network through routers. Routers act as a sort of "traffic director," passing packets from a source subnet to another router, and ultimately to the subnet where the recipient station resides. Routers do this by examining the destination network ID, and then checking their routing table to ascertain where the packet should be forwarded to.

A Router's table can be configured statically, providing it with information about where packets need to be forwarded. Router tables can also be configured dynamically. Routers communicate with other routers on the network, learning from their neighbor routers about the location of distant networks. They communicate using routing protocols like RIP (Routing Information Protocol), RIP2, OSPF (Open Shortest Path First), and other routing protocols.

Using TCP/IP as a Base Network Protocol

From a network administrator's prospective, TCP/IP is not as easy to
configure and implement and use as other available protocols. With
NetBEUI aside, there are no configuration entries the administrator must
make when installing this protocol. IPX/SPX (NWLink) is almost
completely autoconfiguring.

In situations where TCP/IP is not installed during the installation
process, or when the protocol needs to be reinstalled, the process of
installing the protocol is relatively simple. The easiest way to begin this
procedure is to right-click the Network and Dial-Up Connections applet on
the desktop, and select Properties from the drop-down menu. Alternatively,
from the Control Panel, left-click on the Network and Dial-up
Connections applet (see Figure 20-2).

FIGURE 20-2

Network and Dial-up
Connections applet on the
Control Panel

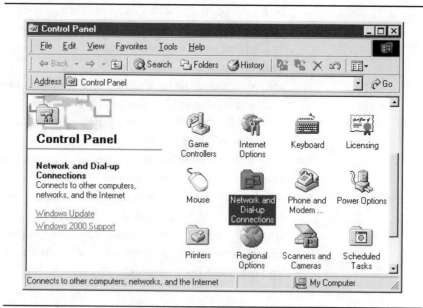

From the Network and Dial-up Connections dialog box (Figure 20-3), click the Local Area Connection applet. This will result in accessing the Local Area Connection Status property sheet shown next.

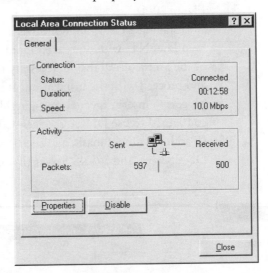

Network and Dial-up
Connections

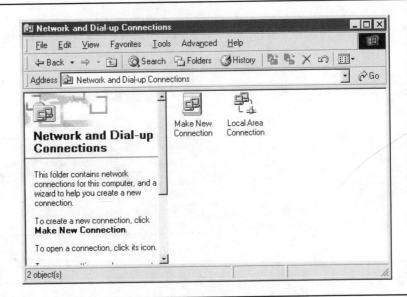

The next step involves simply clicking Properties on the General tab of the Local Area Connection Status property sheet. This selection results in the appearance of the Local Area Connection Properties sheet (see Figure 20-4).

Installing TCP/IP in Windows 2000 is similar to the process in Windows NT, with one exception: no reboot is required after installation of the protocol. All that is necessary is to click Install on the Properties sheet and proceed with the installation. It is necessary during the installation process to insert expected configurable information if the computer is not configured to use DHCP services. Configuration items including the host's IP address, subnet mask, and the IP addresses for the Default Gateway, DNS Server, and WINS Server (if applicable).

FIGURE 20-4

Local Area Connection
Properties sheet

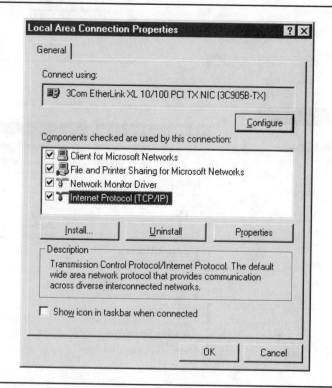

The Local Area Connection Properties sheet (Figure 20-4) is also the access point for reconfiguring TCP/IP settings on a machine already configured to use the protocol. Access the settings by clicking Properties on the sheet. This selection results in the appearance of the Internet Protocol (TCP/IP) Properties sheet (see Figure 20-5).

The top part of this Properties sheet is similar in appearance to the TCP/IP Properties sheet in Windows NT 4.0. However, it differs in the lower part where information relating to DNS servers is present. This change reflects the importance of DNS services in a Windows 2000 environment, and its requisite presence.

FIGURE 20-5

Internet Protocol (TCP/IP)
Properties sheet

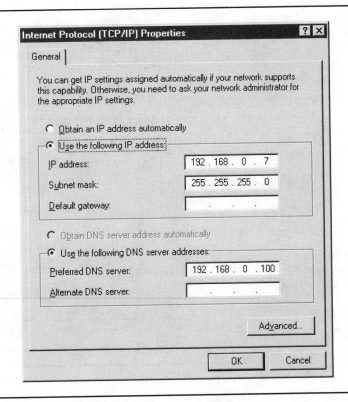

Additional settings for TCP/IP-related services are accessed by clicking Advanced on the Internet Protocol TCP/IP properties sheet. Figure 20-6 shows the advanced property sheets used to add additional host IP addresses and provide IP addressing information for additional default gateways (routers) and DNS servers. The property sheet utilized for advanced DNS settings contains a number of configuration parameters, including the process to be used when appending DNS suffixes to the Host's fully qualified domain name (FQDN).

FIGURE 20-6

IP Settings tab of the
Advanced TCP/IP Settings
properties sheet

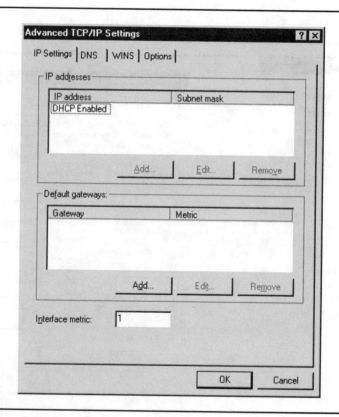

Figure 20-7 shows that the property sheet utilized for advanced DNS settings contains a number of configuration parameters, including the process to be used when appending DNS suffixes to the Host's FQDN.

The WINS tab of the Advanced TCP/IP Settings properties sheet (Figure 20-8) provides an opportunity to identify hosts on the network providing WINS services. As mentioned earlier, the need for WINS services primarily relates to migration issues and the inability of early Microsoft clients such as Windows 9x and Windows for Workgroups to exist in a pure TCP/IP environment. Ideally, the choice "Disable NetBIOS over TCP/IP" should be selected when WINS services are not required. This choice can be

---

FIGURE 20-7

DNS tab of the Advanced TCP/IP Settings properties sheet

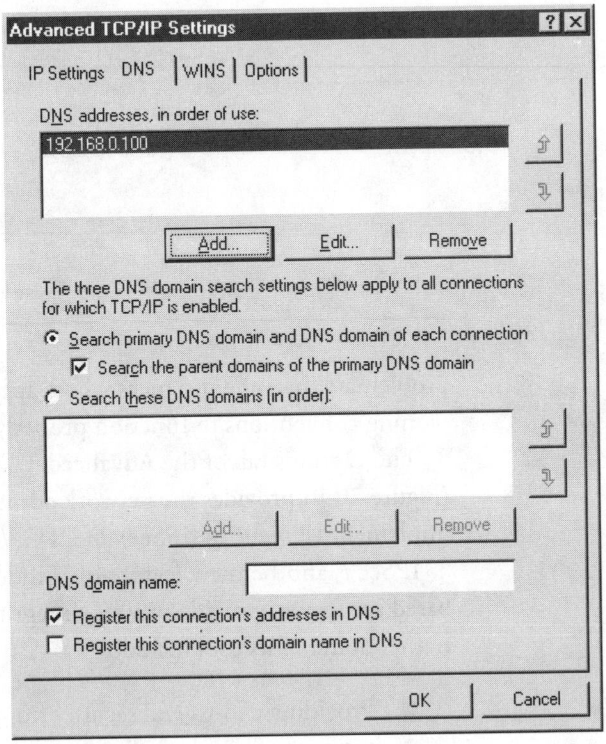

FIGURE 20-8

WINS tab on the Advanced TCP/IP Settings properties sheet

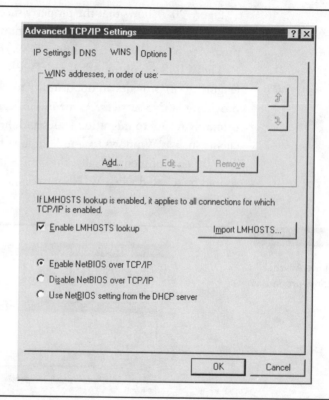

problematic in some instances where applications still rely on NetBIOS naming conventions to function properly in a network environment.

The Options tab of the Advanced TCP/IP Settings properties sheet (Figure 20-9) provides the network administrator with the opportunity to implement IP security (IPSec) and TCP/IP filtering.

IPSec is another new feature in Windows 2000. It uses a cryptography-based security to provide privacy, integrity, and authenticity for network traffic. Some of its uses include:

- Providing end-to-end security from host to host (client to server, server to server, and client to client), using IPSec transport mode.

- Secure access for remote users by providing a client-to-RAS server over the Internet secure connectivity using L2TP secured by IPSec.

FIGURE 20-9

Options tab on the
Advanced TCP/IP Settings
properties sheet

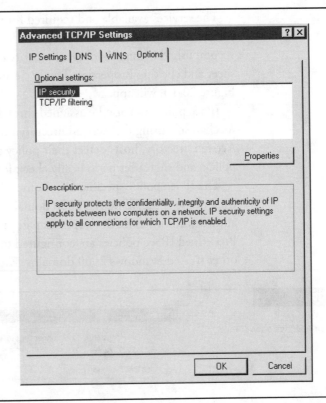

■ Secure LAN gateway to LAN gateway connections, across a private
WAN or the Internet, using L2TP/IPSec tunnels.

Because IPSec is provided at the IP layer, its services are available to
the upper-layer protocols in the stack and, transparently, to existing
applications. IPSec provides on-the-fly configuration capabilities,
enabling a system to

■ Select security protocols

■ Decide which algorithm(s) to use for the service(s)

■ Establish and maintain cryptographic keys for each security
relationship.

english?

The services available and required for traffic are configured using IPSec policy. IPSec policy may be configured locally on a computer. This is accomplished by highlighting IP security on the Options tab properties sheet and clicking Properties. The IP Security properties sheet, shown in Figure 20-10, will appear.

IPSec policy can also be assigned through Windows 2000 Group Policy mechanisms using the Active Directory directory services. When using the Active Directory, hosts detect their policy assignment at startup, retrieve the policy, and thereafter periodically check for policy updates.

The IPSec policy specifies how computers trust each other. The easiest trust to use is the Windows 2000 domain trust based on Kerberos, an authentication service developed as part of Project Athens at MIT. Predefined IPSec policies are configured to trust computers in the same or other trusted Windows 2000 domains. Each IP datagram processed at the

FIGURE 20-10

IP Security properties sheet

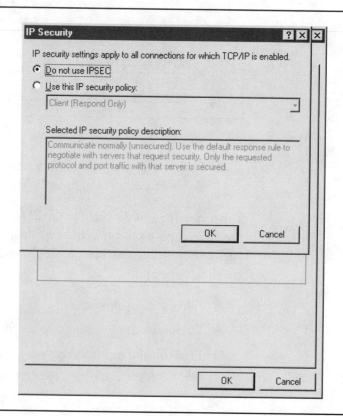

IP layer is compared to a set of filters that are provided by the security policy that is maintained by a domain administrator for a computer, user, group, or the whole domain. IP can do one of three things with any datagram:

- Provide IPSec services to it
- Allow it to pass unmodified
- Discard it

The steps involved in configuring IPSec involve describing traffic characteristics on which to filter (source/destination IP address, protocol, port, etc.). The next step is to specify what service characteristics to apply to traffic that matches the filters implemented.

Once the policy has been put in place, traffic that matches the filters uses the services provided by IPSec. When IP traffic is directed at one host by another, a Security Association (SA) is established, and traffic begins to flow.

The other configurable option on the Options tab (Figure 20-9) is TCP/IP filtering. Highlighting this option and clicking Properties results in the appearance of the TCP/IP Filtering properties sheet (Figure 20-11).

FIGURE 20-11

TCP/IP Filtering
properties sheet

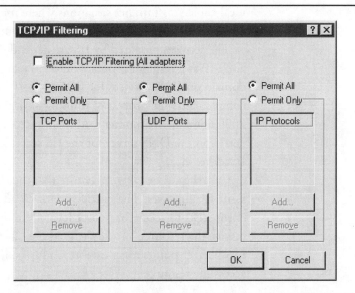

This sheet provides an additional IP security feature. The host machine can be configured to permit specific types of traffic associated with TCP/IP protocols by identifying the type of traffic or a specific port designation. For example, an Internet Information Server (IIS4.0) could be configured to allow only HTTP traffic to access it by identifying HTTP as the only permitted protocol.

HEADSTART OBJECTIVE 20.04

Using TCP/IP for an Intranet

While other Web server candidates exist for a corporate intranet, the likely candidate in a Windows 2000 domain environment for providing intranet services is a Windows 2000 server configured with Microsoft's Internet Information Server (IIS). This robust product is designed specifically to run on a server configured with either the Windows NT or Windows 2000 network operating system. IIS is also designed to leverage itself off of the security services provided by each of these operating systems, making it an ideal choice for intranet situations where user access to specific Web resources varies greatly, depending on an employee's job function.

The services provided by IIS are dependent upon the installation of TCP/IP as a resident protocol on the server. Reliance by a Windows 2000 domain on DNS services for FQDN-to-IP address resolution further complements the process of running a corporate intranet inside a Windows 2000 domain environment. All that is necessary is to provide appropriate entries in the DNS server for the IIS server's Web sites and their respective IP addresses.

Care should be taken to ensure that the IIS server is configured with static IP addresses. The need for static IP addressing is obvious. Each time a client seeks to access a resource located on the intranet server, it must first resolve the resource location's IP address. If that IP address changes and the DNS server points to an incorrect address, the client will not be able to access the resource.

Again this looks like NT it.

IIS can be installed as part of the default installation process, or can be installed later utilizing the Option Pack. You can install IIS components after the initial installation without using the option pack by using the Add/Remove Software applet. IIS is installed by default only if IIS 4.0 was previously installed on a machine that is being upgraded to Windows 2000.

Wm 2K uses IIS 5!

HEADSTART OBJECTIVE 20.05

Connecting to the Internet

The methods associated with Internet connectivity are largely dependent upon the goals to be accomplished. For stand-alone workstations, utilization of Microsoft's dial-up services can easily accomplish this goal. The configuration process, not unlike the typical Microsoft Wizard approach used in previous Windows products, is accessed through the Network and Dial-up Connections property sheet (Figure 20-2). Selecting the Make a New Connection applet results in the appearance of the Internet Connection Wizard's opening screen

When establishing an Internet connection for the first time, the Wizard gives you three choices. The first relates to situations where you do not have an existing Internet account, want to select an ISP from Microsoft's list of ISPs, and will be utilizing dial-up service via a modem. The second situation is when you already have an ISP in place and will be utilizing a dial-up service via a modem. The final choice is when you will be manually configuring your dial-up settings or will accessing the Internet via your LAN connection.

Figure 20-12 appears when you select the last selection from the Internet Connection Wizard screen.

To connect thought a LAN, select the second radio button. The process of setting up a connection through a phone line and a modem is a little more difficult. If that choice is selected, three setup screens shown in Figures 20-13, 20-14, and 20-15 walk you through the dial-up connection setup.

FIGURE 20-12

Setting Up Internet
Connection screen

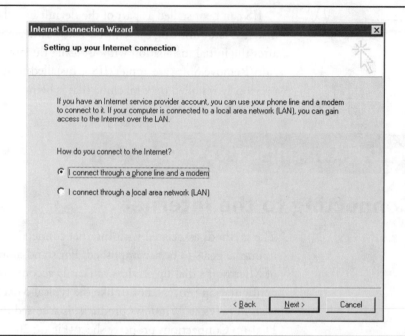

FIGURE 20-13

Internet Account
Connection (Step 1) screen

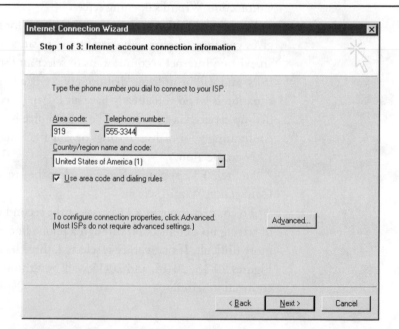

FIGURE 20-14

Internet Account
Connection (Step 2) screen

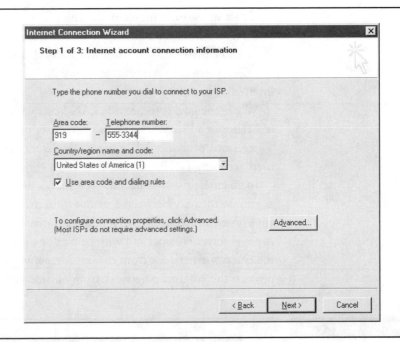

FIGURE 20-15

Internet Account
Connection (Step 3) screen

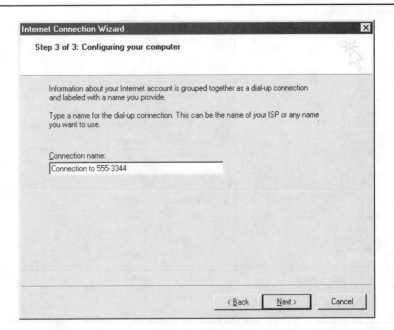

Other steps configurable in the Internet setup process provide the ability to configure Internet mail access. In order to complete this process, you must know the FQDN of your ISP's SMTP and POP3 (Post Office Protocol Version 3) servers (see Figure 20-16, where that information is inserted).

Where the goal is to provide LAN hosts with Internet access, utilization of Microsoft's Proxy Server or a third-party proxy server is recommended. The reasons primarily relate to security issues associated with unknown users accessing LAN resources if Internet connectivity is "wide open."

In an enterprise that uses the Internet, a proxy server is a server that acts as an intermediary between a workstation user and the Internet so that the enterprise can ensure security, administrative control, and caching service. A proxy server is associated with or part of a gateway server that separates the enterprise network from the outside network, and a firewall server that protects the enterprise network from outside intrusion.

FIGURE 20-16

E-mail Server account
connection screen

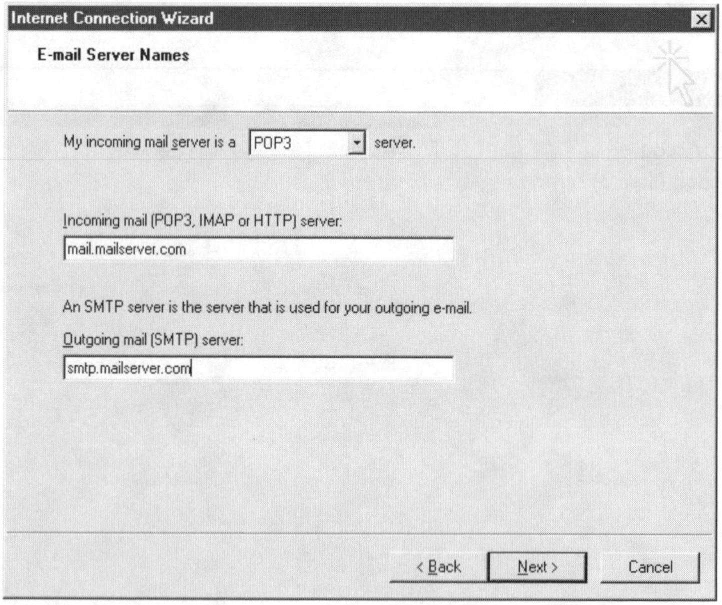

A proxy server receives a request for an Internet service (such as a Web page request) from a user. If it passes filtering requirements, the proxy server, assuming it is also a cache server, looks in its local cache of previously downloaded Web pages. If it finds the page, it returns it to the user without needing to forward the request to the Internet. If the page is not in the cache, the proxy server, acting as a client on behalf of the user, uses one of its own IP addresses to request the page from the server out on the Internet. When the page is returned, the proxy server relates it to the original request and forwards it to the user.

To the user, the proxy server is invisible; all Internet requests and returned responses appear to be directly connected with the addressed Internet server. An advantage of a proxy server is that its cache can serve all users. If one or more Internet sites are frequently requested, these are likely to be in the proxy's cache, which will improve user response time. In fact, there are special servers called *cache servers*. A proxy can also do logging.

HEADSTART OBJECTIVE 20.06

Developing a TCP/IP Management Strategy

Developing a TCP/IP management strategy is somewhat dependent upon the management tools that will be used. Microsoft's own System Management Server provides a number of management tools well suited for an enterprise network environment. Third-party products such as IBM's Tivoli and Hewlett-Packard's OpenView provide extensive management capabilities. Windows 2000 also comes with some "built-in" products, including Performance Monitor and Network Monitor. Those two products, along with utilities provided with Microsoft's version of TCP/IP, are described later in the chapter. The decision to implement additional tools will likely be based on a number of issues. In a large enterprise environment where administrative tasks need to be accomplished remotely, the appropriate decision may be to purchase third-party management products.

Performance Monitor and Network Monitor are both accessed through the Microsoft Management Console (MMC). This product provides a common console framework for management applications. The unified user interface for hosting administrative tools is designed to simplify the problems associated with each different management tool having an entirely different look. This "same-look" concept results in a number of benefits, including reduced training time for administrators, since all tools will function in the same user environment. It is anticipated that third-party management tool developers will adopt this standard interface.

Network Monitor

Windows 2000 Server includes a reduced version of Microsoft's Network Monitor 2.0. Network Monitor is a software-based protocol tracing and analysis tool. Microsoft's Systems Management Server product contains the full version of this product.

The primary difference between this version and the Systems Management Server version is that the limited version can only capture frames that would normally be seen by the computer that it is installed on, rather than all frames that pass over the network (which requires the adapter to be in promiscuous mode). It also does not support connecting to remote Network Monitor Agents.

Performance Monitor

Microsoft's Performance monitor provides a number of functions, for example:

- It is used to monitor system resources.
- It can be configured to send alerts to administrators.
- It can generate graphs and logs to view information collected over a period of time.

With Windows 2000, Performance Monitor provides a number of counters that relate specifically to the TCP/IP protocol suite. Tables 20-4, 20-5, and 20-6 identify important counters, together with the specific protocol they were designed to monitor.

TABLE 20-4	Counter	Description
Performance Monitor Counters for IP	Datagrams Forwarded/sec	The rate of input datagrams for which this entity was not their final IP destination, as a result of which an attempt was made to find a route to forward them to that final destination
	Datagrams Outbound Discarded	Number of output IP datagrams for which no problems were encountered to prevent their transmission to their destination, but which were discarded (for lack of buffer space)
	Datagrams Outbound No Route	Number of IP datagrams discarded because no route could be found to transmit them to their destination
	Datagrams Received Address Errors	Number of input datagrams discarded because the IPaddress in their IP header's destination field was not a valid address to be received at this entity
	Datagrams Received Delivered/sec	Rate at which input datagrams are successfully delivered to IP user protocols (including ICMP)
	Datagrams Received Discarded	Number of input IP datagrams for which no problems were encountered to prevent their continued processing, but which were discarded (e.g., for lack of buffer space)
	Datagrams Received Header Errors	Number of input datagrams discarded due to errors in their IP headers, including bad checksums, version number mismatch, other format errors, time-to-live exceeded, and errors discovered in processing their IP options
	Datagrams Received Unknown Protocol	Number of locally addressed datagrams received successfully but discarded because of an unknown or unsupported protocol
	Datagrams Received/sec	Rate at which IP datagrams are received from the interfaces, including those in error
	Datagrams Sent/sec	Rate at which IP datagrams are supplied to IP for transmission by local IP user-protocols (including ICMP)
	Datagrams/sec	Rate at which IP datagrams are received from or sent to the interfaces, including those in error

TABLE 20-4		
Performance Monitor Counters for IP *(continued)*	Fragment Reassembly Failures	Number of failures detected by the IP reassembly algorithm (for whatever reason: timed out, errors, etc)
	Fragmentation Failures	Number of IP datagrams that have been discarded because they needed to be fragmented at this entity but could not be (e.g., because their Don't Fragment flag was set)
	Fragmented Datagrams/sec	Rate at which datagrams are successfully fragmented at this entity
	Fragments Created/sec	Rate at which IP datagram fragments have been generated as a result of fragmentation at this entity
	Fragments Reassembled/sec	Rate at which IP fragments are successfully reassembled
	Fragments Received/sec	Rate at which IP fragments that need to be reassembled at this entity are received

TABLE 20-5	Counter	Description
Performance Monitor Counters for TCP	Connection Failures	Number of times TCP connections have made a direct transition to the CLOSED state from the SYN-SENT state or the SYN-RCVD state, plus the number of times TCP connections have made a direct transition to the LISTEN state from the SYN-RCVD state
	Connections Active	Number of times TCP connections have made a direct transition to the SYN-SENT state from the CLOSED state
	Connections Established	Number of TCP connections for which the current state is either ESTABLISHED or CLOSE-WAIT
	Connections Passive	Number of times TCP connections have made a direct transition to the SYN-RCVD state from the LISTEN state
	Connections Reset	Number of times TCP connections have made a direct transition to the CLOSED state from either the ESTABLISHED state or the CLOSE-WAIT state

Segments Received/sec	Rate at which segments are received, including those received in error
Segments Retransmitted/sec	Rate at which segments are retransmitted; that is, segments transmitted containing one or more previously transmitted bytes
Segments Sent/sec	Rate at which segments are sent, including those on current connections, but excluding those containing only retransmitted bytes
Segments/sec	Rate at which TCP segments are sent or received using the TCP protocol

Address Resolution Protocol (ARP)

ARP performs IP address to Media Access Control (MAC) address resolution. When each outgoing IP datagram is encapsulated in a frame, its source and destination MAC addresses must be added. ARP is responsible for determining the destination MAC address for each frame.

ARP compares the destination IP address on every outbound IP datagram to the ARP cache for the NIC that the frame will be sent over. If there is a matching entry, the MAC address is retrieved from the cache. If not, ARP broadcasts an ARP Request Packet on the local subnet, requesting

Counter	Description
Datagrams No Port/sec	Rate of received UDP datagrams for which there was no application at the destination port
Datagrams Received Errors	Number of received UDP datagrams that could not be delivered for reasons other than the lack of an application at the destination port
Datagrams Received/sec	Rate at which UDP datagrams are delivered to UDP users
Datagrams Sent/sec	Rate at which UDP datagrams are sent from the entity
Datagrams/sec	Rate at which UDP datagrams are sent or received by the entity

that the owner of the IP address in question reply with its MAC address. The ARP Request Packet includes the IP address of the sending host. If the packet is going through a router, ARP resolves the MAC address for that next-hop router, rather than the final destination host. When an ARP reply is received, the ARP cache is updated with the new information, and it is used to address the packet at the Link layer.

IPConfig

This utility displays local host TCP/IP configuration details. By utilizing the IPConfig /all command and the command-line prompt, configuration details for the host can be viewed. Figure 20-17 shows the display when this command is run. Similar to the Winipcfg utility found in Windows 95 and Windows 98, it does not provide the graphical user interface, but provides the same information.

NETSTAT

This utility displays current TCP/IP statistics, including the status of existing connections. It also displays listening ports, which provides

---

FIGURE 20-17

Results from IPConfig

```
Command Prompt                                                    _ □ ✕
C:\>IPCONFIG /ALL

Windows 2000 IP Configuration

        Host Name . . . . . . . . . . . . : SIERRACOLLEGEW2000
        Primary DNS Suffix  . . . . . . . :
        Node Type . . . . . . . . . . . . : Hybrid
        IP Routing Enabled. . . . . . . . : No
        WINS Proxy Enabled. . . . . . . . : No
        DNS Suffix Search List. . . . . . : SIERRA.CC.CA.US

Ethernet adapter Local Area Connection:

        Connection-specific DNS Suffix  . : SIERRA.CC.CA.US
        Description . . . . . . . . . . . : 3Com EtherLink XL 10/100 PCI
(3C905B-TX)
        Physical Address. . . . . . . . . : 00-10-5A-12-D7-1E
        DHCP Enabled. . . . . . . . . . . : No
        IP Address. . . . . . . . . . . . : 192.168.0.7
        Subnet Mask . . . . . . . . . . . : 255.255.255.0
        Default Gateway . . . . . . . . . :
        DNS Servers . . . . . . . . . . . : 192.168.0.100
```

information as to whether services are using the correct ports. The netstat –a command displays all current TCP and UDP connections, as well as the source and destination service ports. Additional information can be utilized by using different netstat switch syntax. Information about differences in switch syntax can obtained by typing the command **netstat /?.**

Packet Internet Groper (PING)

This utility provides the ability to troubleshoot TCP/IP connectivity. With it you can verify that TCP/IP is running on a host machine, bound to the NIC, configured properly, and communicating across the network to a remote host. PING utilizes the ICMP protocol to send echo requests and echo reply messages that determine whether a distant IP address is valid. You can ping an IP address, and where name resolution to IP address service is available (WINS, DNS, hosts file, or lmhosts file), you can ping utilizing a host name.

NSLOOKUP

This utility queries the DNS server, providing information relating to the status of a host, and returning information about its IP address. It is particularly useful when you need to know either the host's IP address (or hostname if you know its IP address). NSLOOKUP is used primarily as a troubleshooting tool. Like other utilities, it contains a number of functions that can be reached by modifying the command's syntax.

Nslookup.exe can be run in two modes: interactive and noninteractive. Noninteractive mode is useful when only a single piece of data needs to be returned. The syntax for noninteractive mode is:

nslookup [-option] [hostname] [server]

To start Nslookup.exe in interactive mode, simply type **nslookup** at the command prompt:

C:\> nslookup

Default Server: sierracollegew2000.sierra.cc.ca.us

Address: 192.168.0.100

>

Typing **help** or **?** at the command prompt will generate a list of available commands. Anything typed at the command prompt that is not recognized as a valid command is assumed to be a host name, and an attempt is made to resolve it using the default server. To interrupt interactive commands, press CTRL+C. To exit interactive mode and return to the command prompt, type **exit** at the command prompt.

TRACERT

The TRACERT utility uses ICMP to trace the path from a computer to a specified destination IP address, identifying all intermediate hops between them. This utility is useful for determining router or subnet connectivity problems. The TRACERT utility can be configured utilizing command syntax to provide specific useful information. Command syntax can be ascertained by typing the command **tracert /?**.

ROUTE

The ROUTE command displays the current routing table, revealing the routes and number of hops a packet takes to reach the destination hosts. The ROUTE utility allows you to add, change, or delete routes. You can also clear the routing table.

h e a d s
⑪P

With Microsoft's recent decision to retire the 070-059 exam, the jury is still out on how much content will exist relative to TCP/IP on the four core exams associated with MCSE certification for Windows 2000. It is safe to say that you must have an understanding of IP addressing schemes, including knowing how to determine the subnet mask you will need to satisfy a designated minimum host and subnet requirements given a specific scenario.

ACCELERATING TO WINDOWS 2000

Accelerating to Windows 2000

Windows 2000 includes automatic IP addressing in situations where the workstation or server has been configured to obtain an IP address from a DHCP server, but no DHCP server can be successfully contacted. In situations such as this, a Class B IP address from the 169.254.0.0 network will be automatically assigned. The problem associated with this arrangement is that while the host machine will be able to use TCP/IP as its transport protocol, it will not be able to access resources on the network because it belongs to another network.

Microsoft appears to have initiated this automatic configuration to make is easier for network configuration with smaller peer-to-peer networks utilizing TCP/IP as the base protocol. Without this automated address assignment process, configuration for peer-to-peer networks where no DHCP server was available required IP addresses to be statically configured. This workaround provides a substitute method. In larger networks where DHCP services are available, it may be best to modify or turn this service off. It can be found via a search utilizing the regedit tool, at

IPAutoconfigurationSubnet

Key: *Tcpip\Parameters,*
Tcpip\Parameters\Interfaces\<interface>

Value Type: *REG_SZ-String*

Valid Range: *A valid IP subnet*

Default: *169.254.0.0*

Description: *This parameter controls the subnet address used by autoconfiguration to pick an IP address for the client. See the "Automatic Client Configuration" section of this chapter for details. This parameter can be set globally or per interface. If a per-interface value is present, it overrides the global value for that interface.*

CHAPTER SUMMARY

While everything Microsoft does relative to defining certification requirements is subject to change, it appears that the MCSE certification requirements for Windows 2000 will not include a specific exam associated with TCP/IP. This decision likely rests with Microsoft's perception that the TCP/IP suite of utilities and protocols is effectively part of the Windows 2000 operating system. The fact that there will not be a specific exam associated with TCP/IP doesn't mean that you can become certified by not knowing as much about TCP/IP as you were required to know to satisfy the requirements to become MCSE, as the program existed for earlier versions of Microsoft's network operating systems. The reverse is true.

You should anticipate that TCP/IP-related questions will exist on all of the core certification exams. This chapter provides detailed information associated with the implementation of a TCP/IP network environment. Additionally, it discusses specific services provided by Windows 2000, and how the TCP/IP protocols and utilities fit into the overall picture.

This chapter details the role of TCP/IP in the Windows 2000 network environment. It outlines the development of a TCP/IP implementation strategy where it is being used as the base network protocol. The focus then shifts to utilizing TCP/IP for intranet development and Internet connectivity. It concludes with a discussion relating to the development of a TCP/IP management strategy.

TWO-MINUTE DRILL

- ❑ NWLink is Microsoft's implementation of lower-level NetWare protocols, which includes IPX, SPX, RIPX, and NBIPX, by default.

- ❑ Commonly referred to as "the protocol of the Internet," Transmission Control Protocol/Internet Protocol (TCP/IP) standards allow computers utilizing a variety of operating systems to directly communicate with each other.

- ❑ With the release of the Windows 2000 operating system, Microsoft went beyond the advances in performance and ease of administration that were incorporated in Windows NT 3.5 and Windows 4.0, as a result of a complete rewrite of the TCP/IP stack.

❑ Microsoft designed the TCP/IP suite for Windows 2000 so that it will be easy to integrate this network operating system into large-scale corporate, government, and public networks; providing the ability to operate over these networks in a secure manner.

❑ The Application layer of the TCP/IP model roughly corresponds to the OSI model's Application and Presentation layers.

❑ The Transport layer of the TCP/IP model generally corresponds to the Session and Transport layers of the OSI model.

❑ The Internet layer of the TCP/IP model is roughly equivalent to the Networking layer of the OSI model.

❑ The TCP/IP model's Network Interface layer corresponds to the Data Link and Physical layers of the OSI model.

❑ The planning stage for TCP/IP implementation is extremely important. The conclusions reached as a result of TCP/IP planning will likely impact the network layout.

❑ Public addresses are assigned to the network either by an Internet Service Provider (ISP) or from an entity designated by the Internet Corporation for Assigning Names and Numbers (ICANN).

❑ IP address ranges have been reserved from the pool of public Internet addresses for private addressing. Specified in Internet Request for Comments (RFC) 1918, their use is optional but suggested by the Internet community.

❑ WINS will continue to be included in Windows 2000 Server, but is not required in a pure Windows 2000 Server environment.

❑ TCP/IP is not as easy to configure and implement and use as other available protocols. With NetBEUI aside, there are no configuration entries the administrator must make when installing this protocol. IPX/SPX (NWLink) is almost completely autoconfiguring.

❑ While other Web server candidates exist for a corporate intranet, the likely candidate in a Windows 2000 domain environment for providing intranet services is a Windows 2000 server configured with Microsoft's Internet Information Server (IIS).

❑ Microsoft's own System Management Server provides a number of management tools well suited for an enterprise network environment. Third-party products such as IBM's Tivoli and Hewlett-Packard's Open View provide extensive management capabilities. Windows 2000 also comes with some "built-in" products, including Performance Monitor and Network Monitor.

SELF TEST

The following questions will help you measure your understanding of the material presented in this chapter. Read all of the choices carefully, as there may be more than one correct answer. Choose all correct answers for each question.

1. Which is not a layer of the TCP/IP model?

   A. Application

   B. Internet

   C. Presentation

   D. Network Interface

2. What are the minimum addressing requirements associated with the installation of TCP/IP on a Windows 2000 workstation? (Choose all that apply.)

   A. IP Address

   B. Gateway Address

   C. Subnet Mask

   D. DNS Server

3. Which command can you use with Windows 2000 to ascertain the lease term of your IP address?

   A. Winipcfg

   B. Winipcfg /all

   C. Ipconfig

   D. Ipconfig /all

4. Which IP addresses listed below are included in the ranges reserved for private addressing and not available as registered addresses on the Internet? (Choose all that apply.)

   A. 10.1.1.3

   B. 172.16.21.3

   C. 192.168.33.21

   D. 91.1.1.1

5. Utilization of Automatic Private IP Addressing (APIPA) is recommended for?

   A. Networks with five or fewer hosts where no DHCP service is available

   B. Networks with more than 1500 hosts where DHCP service is not consistently available

   C. Networks connected by leased lines

   D. Only in stand-alone workstations

6. The Media Sensing capability of Windows 2000 describes its ability to

   A. Simultaneously access two networks utilizing different network interface cards (NICs).

   B. Provide remote users with the ability to transport their laptop computers between two different networks, and the operating system will automatically determine whether the network uses Token Ring or Ethernet.

   C. The operating system will be able to identify whether unshielded twisted pair or thinnet is being used as the network's wire media.

   D. To tune and optimize memory.

7. How many valid subnets and valid hosts are available on the Class C network

having a subnet mask of
255.255.255.240?

A. 14 subnets with 14 hosts each

B. 16 subnets with 16 hosts each

C. 32 subnets with 240 hosts each

D. 240 subnets with 32 hosts each

8. Which of the following must be unique to
a specific host on the network?

A. The host portion of its IP address

B. The network portion of its IP address

C. Its subnet mask

D. The name of any designated shared file

9. Which of the following are routing
protocols? (Choose all that apply.)

A. RIP

B. TCP

C. IP

D. OSPF

10. An IP address with a bit pattern that
begins with the 110 is defined as a Class
____ address?

A. Class A

B. Class B

C. Class C

D. Class D

11. Which of the following values can be
automatically configured using DHCP?
(Choose all that apply.)

A. Host IP address

B. Host Default Gateway

C. Mail Server

D. Subnet Mask

12. IPSec can be implemented in a Windows
2000 network to

A. Provide automatic DNS addressing.

B. Provide a cryptography-based security.

C. Identify which hosts are utilizing the
Windows 2000 operating system.

D. None of the above.

13. With Windows 2000, TCP/IP filtering
can be used to specifically permit or deny
TCP/IP traffic, based on? (Choose all that
apply.)

A. Content

B. IP Protocol

C. TCP Port number

D. UDP Port number

14. Which product must you install to obtain
full functionality from Microsoft Network
Monitor?

A. Internet Information Server

B. System Management Server

C. Performance Monitor

D. Proxy Server

15. Address Resolution Protocol is used to

A. Resolve IP addresses to a host's MAC
address.

B. Resolve IP addresses to a host's
NetBIOS name.

C. Resolve a host's NetBIOS name to its
IP address.

D. Resolve a host's Fully Qualifying
Domain Name (FQDN) to its IP
address.

MICROSOFT CERTIFIED SYSTEMS ENGINEER

21

DHCP
Networking

CERTIFICATION OBJECTIVES

W ith Transfer Control Protocol/Internet Protocol (TCP/IP) so prominent in the Internet, local area networks (LANs), and wide area networks (WANs), managing Internet Protocol (IP) information plays a big role in the duties of a system engineer. In order for a computer to access the Internet or a TCP/IP network, it must be properly configured with the necessary IP information. This includes information such as the IP address; name servers, such as the Domain Naming Service (DNS) and Windows Internet Naming Service (WINS); gateway addresses; and the subnet class of the network.

If the network uses DNS, or WINS, it must also have the addresses of the corresponding DNS and WINS servers. Before the Dynamic Host Configuration Protocol (DHCP) existed, the administrator had to give each computer an individual IP address and the gateway, DNS, and WINS information. This was an extremely time-consuming, especially in an expanding environment. A new workstation or a workstation that was moved to a different subnet could require that a member of the IT staff go to the computer and configure the TCP/IP information manually.

The addition of DHCP has greatly eased administration in this area. With a network equipped with DHCP, manually configuring IP information on a device has been minimized. With DHCP, the only TCP/IP information that the administrator must manually enter is for servers that require static IP addresses. This chapter describes the benefits of DHCP, as well as the role it plays in a network and the convenience brought to it.

HEADSTART OBJECTIVE 21.01

The Role of the Dynamic Host Configuration Protocol (DHCP) in an Enterprise Network

Starting in Windows NT 3.5, the DHCP service was a core network service. DHCP is based on BOOTP, which allowed diskless workstations to boot up and access the TCP/IP network. A DHCP-configured client can access the network by requesting and receiving TCP/IP information such as that listed in Table 21-1.

TABLE 21-1	IP address	The IP address of the client.
DHCP TCP/IP Options	Subnet mask	The subnet mask of the client.
	Default gateway address	The IP address of the gateway.
	DNS server address	The address of the DNS server.
	WINS server address	The address of the WINS server.
	WINS/NBT node type	The type of NetBIOS being used by the client. Options available are broadcast (B-Node), peer (P-Node), mixed (M-Node), and hybrid (H-Node).
	NetBIOS scope ID	The NetBIOS scope ID. NetBIOS over TCP/IP can only communicate with other clients that have the same scope ID.

Once the DHCP server receives a request, it refers an IP address from a pool of available IP addresses from the scope that is defined in its database. A *scope* is a grouping of available IP addresses that DHCP clients can request. It is used to minimize the administration associated with the many IP addresses. This is analogous to groups used to group users in a NT domain. Scope settings pass down to the IP addresses within the scope. You can only have one scope per logical subnet.

Lease Process

To better understand DHCP, you must be aware of what occurs during the lease process. The lease process consists of a four-phase process: DHCPDISCOVER, DHCPOFFER, DHCPREQUEST, and DHCPACK. There is a fifth optional phase, DHCPNACK.

DHCPDISCOVER

During DHCPDISCOVER, a client broadcasts to the network trying to communicate with the DHCP server so that the client can discover the IP address of a DHCP server and request the address. The broadcast contains the client's network hardware address, or MAC address, and the computer name. Since the client does not know where the DHCP server is located, and because the requesting computer does not have an IP address, its source IP address is 0.0.0.0 and its destination IP address is 255.255.255.255.

Since broadcasts cannot be routed, often a DHCP relay agent in every subnet will route DHCP broadcasts to the nearest DHCP server. Many network hardware vendors (e.g., Cisco) have implemented DHCP relay agents into their products. Cisco has a setting called a Helper Address, which is similar in function to the Microsoft DHCP Relay Agent.

DHCPOFFER *Server contacts Client*

Once the DHCP server is located, the second phase DHCPOFFER occurs. When the DHCP server receives the request from the client, it broadcasts to the client (since it already knows the network hardware address and the computer name) the following configuration information:

- The network address of the client
- The IP address
- The subnet mask
- The lease length
- The IP address of the DHCP server

Once the DHCP server broadcasts the configuration message, it reserves the IP so that it won't be offered to another client asking for a new IP. When the client accepts the IP information, the third phase occurs.

DHCPREQUEST

In the third phase, the client broadcasts a message telling the DHCP server that it accepts the IP configuration information offer. If other DHCP servers offer their IP addresses and their information is denied, they release the IP that was previously reserved, and the IP is now back into the pool of available IP addresses.

DHCPACK

The DHCPACK phase follows the DHCPREQUEST phase. In this phase, the DHCP server broadcasts a response to the client's acceptance of its IP information. This response is the final broadcast and it returns other TCP/IP configuration data such as WINS and/or DNS servers.

DHCPNACK

The DHCPNACK phase occurs when the DHCPREQUEST fails, such as when the client is trying to lease an old address that is being used or is no longer available. The server sends a negative broadcast, called the DHCPNACK, and the lease process starts over.

heads UP

An easy way to remember the different phases of the DHCP process is to use DHCP-D.O.R.A.N: D for Discover, O for Offer, R for Request, A for Acknowledgement (ACK), and N for Negative Acknowledgement (NACK).

Lease Renewal and IP Release

The IP address that is leased to the client by the DHCP server is not permanent. After 50 percent of the lease time is up, the client sends a DHCPREQUEST to the DHCP server to renew its lease. If the DHCP server allows it to, it will update the lease time in its internal database and send out the DHCPACK with the updated lease time. If after 50 percent of the lease time is up the DHCP client cannot contact the DHCP server, it tries again after 75 percent of the leftover time has lapsed, or 87.5 percent of the total lease time. If the lease expires or a DHCPNACK is received, the client's present IP address is released, and the DHCP lease process begins again.

Windows 2000 and earlier versions of Windows NT include a utility called ipconfig. The ipconfig utility is used to display the IP configurations and other IP options. Figure 21-1 shows the IP configuration usage. The major options are release, renew, flushdns, registerdns, displaydns, showclassid, and setclassid. Their descriptions are shown on the screen.

The client can force a release and renewal of its IP address by using the command-line program called ipconfig. Ipconfig with the /renew switch will attempt to start the lease process or renew the lease time.

on the job

Users often think their IP addresses are static when they use DHCP with a long lease. This is wrong. DHCP does not mean the IP address is often changed, it means the IP information is dynamically configured.

FIGURE 21-1

Ipconfig usage

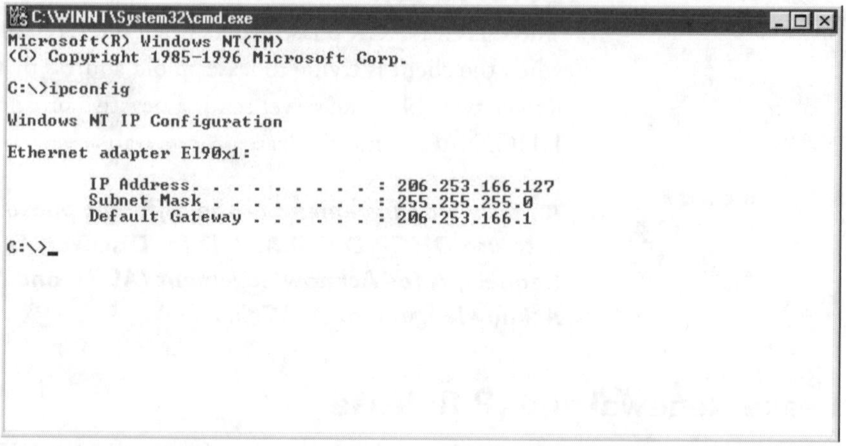

```
C:\WINNT\System32\cmd.exe                                          _ □ ×
Microsoft(R) Windows NT(TM)
(C) Copyright 1985-1996 Microsoft Corp.

C:\>ipconfig

Windows NT IP Configuration

Ethernet adapter E190x1:

        IP Address. . . . . . . . . : 206.253.166.127
        Subnet Mask . . . . . . . . : 255.255.255.0
        Default Gateway . . . . . . : 206.253.166.1

C:\>_
```

DHCP Versus Manual IP Configuration

Management of an enterprise network is a lot less stressful with DHCP. DHCP is such an important service that it is no longer a question of why you should implement it, but rather why not. With DHCP, the TCP/IP information is automatically given to the client computer when it boots.

- Workstations no longer need to be configured for TCP/IP when the OS is installed.

- Workstations no longer need to have their IP and default gateway address changed when they are moved.

- DHCP greatly simplifies the task of setting the IP information. TCP/IP information is centrally managed in the DHCP server, which reduces the chances of error by having the information in one place. Errors in IP information can cause problems that are difficult to trace. By managing DHCP information in the DHCP server, changes in IP configuration are made in one place, not on each client.

- DHCP is very effective on large networks where there are many clients. In a smaller network with five or less clients, it may not be worth the effort to set up a DHCP server. In that situation, static IP addresses would suffice.

Developing a DHCP Implementation Strategy

After you are familiar with how DHCP works and how it affects your network, you should implement DHCP if it is beneficial for you to do so. If you do decide to implement DHCP, you must first plan how DHCP is going to be set up in your network—DHCP affects how many computers interact and careful planning is a must.

Requirements

Which server

For a computer to run the DHCP server, any version of NT after 3.5 will be sufficient. The Windows 2000 server must have a static IP address. The server running the DHCP service can use a dynamic IP address but it is not recommended. The DHCP server must have a static IP address so that it is impossible for its own IP address to change, thus forcing its clients to reregister because they can't find the server.

This is confusing

When the DHCP service is installed, it must be set with a DHCP scope. The scope can also have certain IP addresses excluded from the range. In addition to excluding IP addresses, reservations can be set. *Reservations* are IP addresses that are reserved for certain computers. This is often used for servers that must use a set IP address, as well as for computers that are constantly moving around. They must have one IP address while in one subnet and another IP address in another subnet. This is explained later in this chapter.

In order for a client to be DHCP-enabled, it must be running one of the following operating systems:

- Windows NT 3.51 or later
- Windows 2000
- Windows 95 or later
- Windows for Workgroups 3.11 running TCP/IP-32
- MS-DOS with the Microsoft Network Client 3.0 with the real mode TCP/IP driver
- LAN Manager 2.2c, except for the OS/2 version

Installing DHCP Service

The first step in implementing DHCP is to install the DHCP service. Before you install it, however, make sure the requirements listed in the preceding section for running the DHCP server are fulfilled. The following exercise shows you how to install the DHCP service on Windows 2000.

Installing the DHCP Service

1. Go to the Control Panel and double-click Add/Remove Programs.

2. Click Add/Remove Windows Components and then Components, as shown in Figure 21-2.

3. When the Windows Component Wizard appears, click Next.

4. Select Networking Services, and click Details.

Add/Remove Windows components

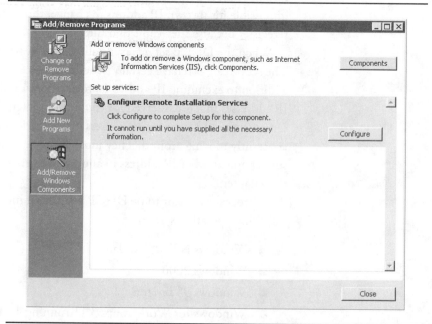

5. Within the Optional Networking Components dialog box, in the Subcomponents of Networking Options list, click Dynamic Host Control Protocol (DHCP) as shown next. Click OK.

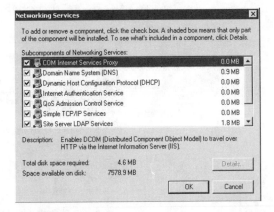

6. Click Next, and you will be prompted for the location of the Windows 2000 setup files, such as your Windows 2000 CD. Type the path of your setup files.

7. Once Windows 2000 installs all the files, click Finish. The entire procedure is completed.

Configuring DHCP on the Windows 2000 Client

Configuring DHCP on the Windows 2000 Client is a much easier task than installing the service on the server. Exercise 21-2 shows you how to configure your Windows 2000 client from a static IP, since Windows 2000's default configuration is DHCP.

EXERCISE 21-2

Configuring DHCP on the Windows 2000 Client

1. Go to the Control Panel and double-click Network and Dial Up Connections.

2. Double-click Local Area Connection.

3. The Local Area Connection Status dialog box appears. Click Properties.

4. The Local Area Connection Properties dialog box appears. Highlight the Internet Protocol (TCP/IP) and then click Properties as shown next.

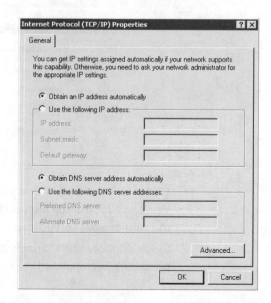

5. You will now see the Internet Protocol (TCP/IP) Properties. Click on "Obtain an IP address automatically" and then click OK.

HEADSTART OBJECTIVE 21.03

Developing a DHCP Management Strategy

Once you are familiar with implementing DHCP, you need to come up with a management solution. Incorporating DHCP is not just a matter of installing the services. To fully institute DHCP, you need to evaluate the total network structure.

Number of DHCP Servers

Although there is no limit to many how many clients a DHCP can serve, most networks should have at least one online DHCP server and one backup for every 10,000 clients. It is best to have as few DHCP servers as possible, and to have DHCP centrally located for management, monitoring, and control.

Additional Subnets

Since DHCP broadcasts cannot be routed, you need a DHCP broadcast forwarder such as Microsoft's DHCP Relay Agent to forward DHCP broadcasts to the DHCP. In order to enable the DHCP relay agent on Windows 2000, you must have a dual-homed system. Dual-home systems have two or more network cards to route from one subnet to another. However, multiple IP addresses can be bound to a single NIC, also creating a multi- or duel-homed system. Exercise 21-3 shows how to set up the DHCP Relay Agent.

EXERCISE 21-3

How to Enable a DHCP Relay Agent on a Dual-Homed System

1. Click Start | Control Panel | Routing and Remote Access.
2. Click Server Name | IP Routing | DHCP Relay Agent.
3. Right-click DHCP Relay Agent. Then click New | Interface.
4. Click the interface you want to add, then click OK.
5. In the DHCP Relay Properties dialog box, check Relay DHCP packets.
6. Click OK.

Another way to be able to use DHCP for additional subnets is to have a local DHCP server servicing its own subnet. The local DHCP will have the correct TCP/IP configuration to service its own subnet. Every logical subnet must have its own scope. This is changed from the previous version of Windows NT. In Windows NT 4.0, each physical subnet was restricted to one scope. With Windows 2000, a physical subnet can be broken up into many logical subnets. Each logical subnet can have only one scope. However, multiple scopes can be fitted into a scope grouping called a *superscope*. A superscope allows you to effectively manage all the scopes within one physical entity, while allowing the flexibility of more than one scope.

exam
ⓦatch

Each scope is independent of other scopes. Scopes cannot share IP addresses.

Creating Scope

Once the DHCP service is installed on the Windows 2000 server, you are ready to assign IP addresses to clients, right? Wrong. In order for the DHCP service to be able to give out IP addresses, the administrator must assign at least one scope for each DHCP server. The scope, as defined earlier, is a range of IP addresses that the DHCP server can assign. The scope must also exclude static IP addresses that exist within its range. This is done so that the same IP address is not used twice, a situation that can cause difficult-to-trace problems in the network. You can install more than one scope in the server; however, you can only have one per IP subnet. A single DHCP server can serve multiple subnets by having a workstation that is used as a DHCP Relay Agent. It can also use superscoping to service multiple IP subnets on a single physical subnet. A DHCP Relay Agent forwards DHCP broadcasts outside the subnet so that the DHCP server can receive them.

Table 21-2 lists the different parameters you need to be familiar with when you have to create a scope for the DHCP server.

TABLE 21-2

DHCP Scope Options

Parameter	Description
Name	The scope's name
Comment	A comment on the scope (optional)
IP Address Range From Address	The starting IP in a range
IP Address Range To Address	The ending IP in a range
Mask	The subnet mask assigned to clients
Exclusion Range Start Address	The starting IP in group of IP addresses that are excluded in the scope
Exclusion Range End Address	The ending IP in a group of IP addresses that are excluded in the scope
Lease Duration Unlimited	Parameter that specifies a lease that doesn't expire
Lease Duration Limited To	The lease duration

Exercise 21-4 shows you how to create a DHCP scope.

Creating a DHCP Scope

1. Click Start | Program Files | Administrative Tools | DHCP.

2. In the DHCP window, right-click your server. Click New | Scope.

3. In the Create Scope Wizard's welcome screen, click Next. In the screen that appears next, specify the name of the scope and the optional comment. Click Next.

4. The next screen asks you to specify the address range as shown in Figure 21-3. Specify the range of IP addresses and the length of the subnet mask or the mask. Click Next.

5. The next screen asks you to specify the exclusion range. Click Next after you specify your IP exclusion range, if any.

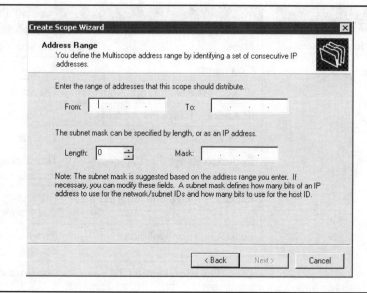

FIGURE 21-3

Setting Address Range in
Create Scope Wizard

6. The next screen asks you to specify the lease duration. Click Next
   and then click Finish.

7. In the DHCP Window, right-click the entry for the scope. Click
   Task | Activate.

Lease Times

The last factor in the management aspect of incorporating DHCP service
into your network is the lease time. The main factors in deciding the lease
time for dynamic configured IP addresses are the needs of the clients and
the number of free addresses available. If a main group of users has laptops
or moves their computers from time to time, it is prudent to have shorter
lease times so that the IP addresses are released quicker and sent back to
the pool to be used again. If many free addresses are available, longer lease
durations can decrease the number of DHCP broadcasts on the network.
If few free addresses are available, shorter lease durations are warranted.

QUESTIONS AND ANSWERS

What type of lease time should I set if I have a lot of moving clients?	Shorter leases. The quicker the IP addresses are released, the quicker they can be reused for another client.
What type of lease time should I set if I only have a few addresses?	Either long or short will be okay. Having shorter leases on a few clients doesn't cause much unnecessary traffic. Longer leases won't improve the network significantly.
What type of lease time should I set if I have many clients and even more addresses?	Long lease. The more clients you have, the longer you set the lease. The shorter the lease, the more often the clients send out renewal broadcasts.
What type of lease time should I set on a DHCP server?	This is a trick question. None. A DHCP server should have a static IP so clients can locate it..

ACCELERATING TO WINDOWS 2000

One of the most important themes of Windows 2000 is lowered cost of ownership. With the zero-administration initiative, time spent for administration is expected to dramatically decrease. Windows 2000 will require less time and have a much lower cost of ownership. DHCP plays a part in the zero-administration initiative. It includes many new features that showcase the new initiative, such as the improved management interface, support for Windows NT name-space, behavior with no DHCP server found, support for Active Directory, auditing capabilities, and support for multicast.

Management with the MMC

With Windows 2000, DHCP is managed within the Microsoft Management Console, or the MMC. The MMC was first introduced with NT Option Pack. Using the MMC leverages the familiarity you have with the other snap-ins available within MMC, such as SQL Server 7 and Internet Information Server 4. With the MMC, all your administrative tasks can be done in one place. Another enhancement with including the DHCP server as a snap-in within the MMC is the more icon-centric user interface. Icons are used for

ACCELERATING TO WINDOWS 2000

warnings and to show error states that the DHCP service is running out, or free addresses within a scope.

DNS Interoperability

WINS was very tightly integrated in previous versions of Windows NT. In essence, it was the core name server for Windows NT. NetBIOS over TCP/IP was used to resolve names.

The WINS database integrated with DHCP, so that the WINS name always followed the IP address. When DNS needed a lookup for an IP address, it had to access the WINS dynamic database of IP addresses. This was very inefficient because DNS did not function independently. In Windows 2000, the DNS has become the primary way to resolve names. The DNS is automatically updated whenever the IP address is assigned. Therefore, when a computer is moved to another subnet, the host name stays the same.

Behavior with No DHCP

In earlier versions of Windows NT when clients could not locate the DHCP server, the user was shown an error message and no network resources were accessible. This required users to renew their IP every few minutes by typing **IPCONFIG /RENEW**—a waste of time and resources. This problem is fixed in Windows

2000. When Windows 2000 DHCP-enabled clients cannot locate the DHCP server, the Microsoft Automatic Private IP Address (APIPA), which is built into every Windows 2000 computer, assigns an IP that does not conflict with the rest of the network. The APIPA uses the block of addresses that the Internet reserves for private networks. (It uses IP 168.254.0.0 to 169.254.255.254 with a subnet mask of 255.255.255.0.) The client then tries to contact a DHCP server every five minutes until it is located. Although the client won't be able can't access remote network resources, it is able to access resources on the private local network.

Active Directory Controlled Service

The DHCP service is a very important service and it is very problematic if not used correctly.

In earlier versions of Windows NT, a server could be equipped with the DHCP service. No authority was required.

Clients looking for the closest DHCP server may broadcast to it, and the unauthorized DHCP service may return faulty TCP/IP information that hasn't been set by the administrator. This can cause the client to be unable to access the network resources and is difficult to trace. Windows 2000 now uses the Active Directory to verify the existence of the

ACCELERATING TO WINDOWS 2000

DHCP service on the server. Whenever the DHCP service is started on Windows 2000, it contacts the Active Directory to see if it is an authorized DHCP server. If the server is not on the list of authorized DHCP servers, Active Directory halts the DHCP service. This helps to alleviate the problem of rogue DHCP servers causing unpredictable network problems.

Audit Logging

Windows 2000 has auditing to allow the administrator to monitor the DHCP server. However, auditing introduces another problem: logging. Since Windows 2000 now has disk quotas, it is much easier for the logs to fill up the available disk space. Windows 2000 reduces the problems by introducing registry keys to change the logging settings for the DHCP's audit log. To edit the values, edit the key: HKEY_LOCAL_MACHINE\SYSTEM\CurrentControlSet\Services\DHCP Server\Parameters. The values for the registry key parameters are

- DhcpLogFilePath
- DhcpLogMinSpaceOnDisk
- DhcpLogDiskSpaceCheckInterval
- DhcpLogFileMaxSize

The DhcpLogFilePath key, which is of data type REG_SZ, lets the user specify the full path to the log file. The DhcpLogMinSpaceOnDisk, which is of data type REG_DWORD, allows the administrator to specify the amount of disk space left before the audit logging is stopped. The DhcpLogDiskSpaceCheckInterval, which is of data type REG_DWORD, is the number of times the log is written before the free space is checked. DhcpLogFileMaxSize, which is of data type REG_DWORD, is the maximum size of the log file in megabytes. The default is 7 megabytes.

Multicast DHCP

DHCP has always had support for unicast communication. *Unicast* means that a message is meant for one user. The Windows 2000's DHCP service now includes support for multicast DHCP. Clients equipped with a multicast IP address can send messages to other multicast members within the group. Multicast messages use the Class D range of IP address, which goes from 224.0.0.0 to 239.255.255.255. DHCP now supports multicast through MDHCP, or multicast DHCP. Although this function is part of the DHCP service, it acts independently from unicast scopes.

Similar to unicast DHCP, MDHCP is configured through the use of scopes. The multicast scopes are created with the Multicast Scope Wizard.

Remember that multicast DHCP and unicast DHCP are different, even though they exist within DHCP. Multicast IP is mainly used for messaging a group within an intranet. Unicast IP is used for point-to-point transfer of data.

CHAPTER SUMMARY

DHCP is used to dynamically configure TCP/IP information on a client. With DHCP, often-moved computers or changing networking configurations such as WINS or DNS servers no longer require manual configuration by the administrators of the network. With DHCP, a smaller pool of IP addresses is needed because not all of the IP addresses are used at all times. During the DHCP lease process, a four-phase process coordinates how the client requests an IP and how the DHCP server responds to such requests. The phases are DHCPDISCOVER, DHCPOFFER, DHCPREQUEST, and DHCPACK. In order for the computer to run the DHCP server in Windows 2000, it has to be a Windows 2000 server. The Windows 2000 server must have a static IP. When the DHCP service is installed, it must be set with a DHCP scope. A scope is a range of IP addresses that are available to be assigned to clients. The scope can also have certain IP addresses excluded from the range. The requirements for clients to be DHCP-enabled are

- Windows NT 3.51 or later
- Windows 2000
- Windows 95 or later
- Windows for Workgroups 3.11 running TCP/IP-32
- MS-DOS with the Microsoft Network Client 3.0 with the real mode TCP/IP driver
- LAN Manager 2.2c, except for the OS/2 version

Once the administrator decides how to implement DHCP, he or she must decide the management aspect of it. Since DHCP broadcasts are not routable, a dual-homed Windows 2000 may be present as a DHCP Relay Agent in every subnet, or a DHCP server must exist in the subnet to service the subnet locally. Since DHCP is set up by logical subnet, one or more scopes must correspond to each IP subnet. Another crucial factor before you set up the DHCP server is the lease time. Decrease the lease time if a large portion of the clients have portable computers, move their computers often, or there are many clients on the network

One of the most important themes of Windows 2000 is zero administration. With the zero-administration initiative, time spent for administration is expected to dramatically decrease. Windows 2000 requires less time and will has a much lower cost of ownership. DHCP plays a big part in the zero-administration initiative. It includes many new features that showcase the new initiative, such as the improved management interface, support for Windows NT name space, behavior with no DHCP server found, support for Active Directory, auditing capabilities, and support for multicast.

TWO-MINUTE DRILL

❑ Starting in Windows NT 3.5, the DHCP service was a core network service. DHCP is based on BOOTP, which allowed diskless workstations to boot up and access the TCP/IP network.

❑ A *scope* is a grouping of available IP addresses that DHCP clients can request.

❑ The lease process consists of a four-phase process: DHCPDISCOVER, DHCPOFFER, DHCPREQUEST, and DHCPACK. There is a fifth optional phase, DHCPNACK.

❑ An easy way to remember the different phases of the DHCP process is to use DHCP-D.O.R.A.N: D for Discover, O for Offer, R for Request, A for Acknowledgement (ACK), and N for Negative Acknowledgement (NACK).

❑ After 50 percent of the lease time is up, the client sends a DHCPREQUEST to the DHCP server to renew its lease.

❑ The ipconfig utility is used to display the IP configurations and other IP options.

❑ With DHCP, the TCP/IP information is automatically given to the client computer when it boots.

❑ In order for a computer to run the DHCP server, it has to be a Windows 2000 server. The Windows 2000 server must have a static IP address.

❑ When the DHCP service is installed, it must be set with a DHCP scope. The scope can also have certain IP addresses excluded from the range.

❑ Although there is no limit to many how many clients a DHCP can serve, most networks should have at least one online DHCP server and one backup for every 10,000 clients.

❑ Since DHCP broadcasts cannot be routed, you need a DHCP broadcast forwarder such as Microsoft's DHCP Relay Agent to forward DHCP broadcasts to the DHCP.

❑ In order for the DHCP service to be able to give out IP addresses, the administrator must assign at least one scope for each DHCP server.

❑ The main factors in deciding the lease time for dynamic configured IP addresses are the needs of the clients and the number of free addresses available.

❑ Multicast IP is mainly used for messaging a group within an intranet. Unicast IP is used for point-to-point transfer of data.

SELF TEST

The following questions will help you measure your understanding of the material presented in this chapter. Read all of the choices carefully, as there may be more than one correct answer. Choose all correct answers for each question.

1. Jason is the CTO of NT2000 Corp. He has decided to implement DHCP into his network. He wants to only have the client receive the IP address and subnet mask automatically. What TCP/IP configuration can he set manually on the DHCP client? (Choose all that apply.)

   A. IP Address

   B. Subnet mask

   C. Domain Name System (DNS) server address

   D. Windows Internet Name Service (WINS) server address

2. What are the four phases in a successful DHCP lease process? (Choose all that apply.)

   A. DHCPDISCOVER

   B. DHCPOFFER

   C. DHCPREQUEST

   D. DHCPACK

   E. DHCPNACK

3. Lucille, the network administrator of NT 2000 Corp., is confused. DHCP is installed on one subnet. The clients on the same subnet as the DHCP server are able

to access the Internet. However, when a DHCP-enabled client tries to configure itself and get an IP on a remote subnet, it does not work. It is able to communicate with the rest of the clients on that subnet. What is wrong?

   A. Router is down.

   B. Router is misconfigured.

   C. DHCP Relay Agent does not exist on the local subnet.

   D. DHCP server is not working correctly.

4. An FTP server, using IP 128.56.45.221, is shut off. Three weeks later, it is unable to get the same IP. Lucille can't figure out why it is taking so long to get the DHCP response and why it is unable to get the same IP. What can Lucille do to work around this? (Choose all that apply.)

   A. Use static IP.

   B. Nothing she can do.

   C. Continue using DHCP.

   D. Make the lease on the server to last indefinitely.

5. When the DHCP server is not detected, the Windows 2000 client will manually set itself with a private network IP. What can Jon do to manually try to renew the IP address?

   A. Use ipconfig /restore.

   B. Use ipconfig /resurrect.

C. Use ipconfig /renew.

D. Use winipcfg.

6. What TCP/IP configuration should be set for running the DHCP service on a Windows 2000?

A. A dynamic IP

B. A static IP

C. A dynamic DNS server address

D. A static DNS server address

7. Which of the following clients are Windows 2000 DHCP ready? (Choose all that apply.)

A. Windows 95 or later

B. Windows for Workgroups 3.11 running TCP/IP-32

C. MS-DOS with the Microsoft Network Client 3.0 with the real mode TCP/IP driver

D. LAN Manager 2.2c, except for the OS/2 version

8. Ian has 7000 clients in his network. How many DHCP servers should he install?

A. One

B. Two

C. Three

D. Four

9. Fiona needs to route DHCP broadcasts to remote subnets. She installed Windows 2000 but she is unable to add the DHCP Relay Agent. What is needed on a computer for the DHCP Relay Agent to be available?

A. Two network cards

B. Two operating systems

C. Two instances on DHCP installed

D. DHCP service

10. Alex has a DHCP server with a static IP address of 129.56.24.15. It has a range of IP addresses from 129.56.24.5 to 129.56.24.45. All clients are able to access the DHCP server. Once in a while, a new client is not be able to access the Internet, or the DHCP server is unable to access network resources. How should Alex fix this problem?

A. Use all static IP addresses.

B. Install all the newest service packs and try again.

C. Make sure he excludes the IP of the DHCP server in the range of IP addresses available to the DHC-enabled clients.

D. Make sure he includes the IP of the DHCP server in the range of IP addresses available to the DHCP enable clients.

11. Marty is running a network of 4000 clients. Two thousand of them are contractors,+ and they move often from subnet to subnet doing changes in different departments. One day, Marty walks in and realizes he is running out of IP addresses. What can he set to ensure

the most IP addresses are available at one time while maintaining the same subnet address?

A. Disable DHCP and use all static IP addresses.

B. Decrease the lease time.

C. Increase the least time.

D. Use a proxy server.

12. A computer that only has the TCP/IP protocol and is DHCP enabled is able to access other computers on the same subnet, but the DHCP is unreachable. How is it able to do that?

A. It is using a nonroutable protocol, such as NetBEUI.

B. It is using NWLink.

C. It is using a set of IP addresses that it assigns itself.

D. It can't.

13. David has a client who is an aspiring MCSE. Last year, the client installed a DHCP server to prepare for his Supporting and Implementing Windows NT Server 4.0 test. The new DHCP server brought the entire network to a grinding halt. How can David prevent that from happening to him?

A. Upgrade to Windows 2000 and control authority to run DHCP services.

B. Put a DHCP server on every local subnet.

C. Disable all the DHCP Relay Agents.

D. Upgrade to Windows 2000.

14. With Windows NT 4, the server always crashed when the DHCP auditing log got too big. There was nothing an administrator could do to work around it except to manually move or delete the logs. What registry keys must the administrator set to prevent this in Windows 2000? (Choose all that apply.)

A. DhcpLogFilePath

B. DhcpLogMinSpaceOnDisk

C. DhcpLogDiskSpaceCheckInterval

D. DhcpLogFileMaxSize

15. How do you configure multicast scopes in Windows 2000?

A. Set them in the DNS settings.

B. Set them in the WINS Settings.

C. Set them in the gateway settings.

D. Use the Multicast Scope Wizard.

22

DNS Networking

With the introduction of Active Directory as the primary security provider and resource management system in Windows 2000 networks, the importance of the Domain Name System (DNS) has soared to new heights. No longer is DNS the "add-on" service that was of secondary importance in Windows NT 4.0 networks, where it was primarily used to support non-WINS clients (such as UNIX servers).

In this chapter, we take a look at how DNS is used in the Windows 2000 Enterprise network. After examining how the DNS works, we move our attention to the planning phase, and assess what is required before implementing DNS in our Windows 2000 network. This includes how to install DNS on our Windows 2000 server. After completing installation, we work through our plan and get to the task of managing a DNS server.

Role of DNS in an Enterprise Network

DNS is a method used to map "friendly" names to IP addresses. Think of DNS as a phonebook, where host names are paired up with their IP addresses. This is similar to the Windows Internet Name Service (WINS). A WINS server matches up or resolves NetBIOS names to IP addresses.

During the early development of the Internet, this process of name resolution (where host names and IP addresses are matched up) was accomplished via a file called Hosts. The Hosts file was a raw text file that contained the names and IP addresses of all the computers that were on the Advanced Research Projects Agency Network (ARPAnet) at that time (the ARPAnet was a forerunner of the Internet).

There was a big problem with using the Hosts file. Since it was a static text file, someone had the job of updating it manually. After the file was updated, each computer on the ARPAnet had to download a copy of the Hosts file. This Hosts file was kept on a central computer at the Stanford Research Institute (SRI). Traffic on the SRI computer that housed the

Hosts file became a significant bottleneck. A better way to resolve host names to IP addresses had to be developed.

A Distributed Database

It became clear that no one person or entity could possibly keep track of the tens of millions of computers on the Internet. You wouldn't want to be the person typing in thousands of new host names and IP addresses every day! Another problem was that a single text file containing millions of entries would take forever to search. It could take hours to resolve your URL request to an IP address.

The DNS is a *distributed* database. Rather than having a single enormous database that contains all the host name and IP address combinations on the Internet, the database is broken up, and the responsibility for maintaining each piece of the database is given to the DNS administrator of each domain. Your enterprise network will have a domain name, and it will be the organization's responsibility for maintaining its part of this database. Each organization will maintain a list of resources in its own subdomains.

This diffusion of responsibility allows for a great deal of flexibility to the DNS administrator of the enterprise domain, and improves the speed of name resolution by orders of magnitude.

Domains and Their Inhabitants

Domains are "containers"—they can contain other domains (subdomains), as well as other objects. Let's look at how these domains and the objects that inhabit them are arranged.

How Domains Are Organized

Domains are organized in a hierarchical structure, just like the folder structure that you see in your Windows 2000 Explorer window. Each domain can contain hosts and/or other domains. This is similar to your computer's folder structure: A folder can contain either files or other folders, or both. In the case of DNS, the files represent host computers, and folders represent other domains. Figure 22-1 depicts this hierarchical arrangement of DNS.

FIGURE 22-1

The inverted tree structure is illustrated by the branching out of the top-level domains from the root, and further branching of subdomains underneath

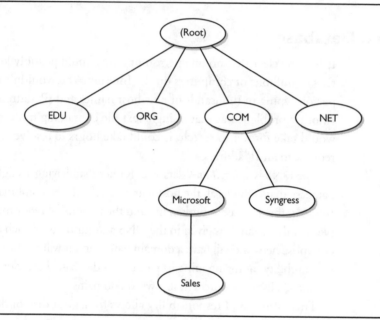

At the top of the hierarchy is Root. The root domain is often represented as "." (a period or dot). Just underneath the root domain are the Top-Level domains. Frequently encountered top-level domains include .com, .net, .org, .edu, .mil, and .gov. Top-level domain names are assigned by the Internet Society (ISOC).

The domain names just under the top-level domains are Second-Level domains. Examples of second-level domains include microsoft.com, syngress.com, and osborne.com. The assignment of second-level domain names had been the sole responsibility of Network Solutions until 1999. The responsibility of registering second-level domains for use on the Internet is now shared by other entities. These entities are referred to as *Domain Registrars.*

The top- and second-level domains represent the only centralized aspects of DNS on the Internet. Once a company receives approval for a second-level domain name, it becomes that company's responsibility to manage the domain name space underneath it.

Domains located under the second-level domains are loosely referred to as *subdomains*. As the DNS administrator, you are responsible for designing, allocating, and maintaining subdomains.

Each domain contains *resource records*, which represent the computer host names and IP addresses contained in that domain. As we will discuss later in the chapter, several subdomains can be managed from a single DNS server. A group of domains managed from a single DNS server is referred to as a *zone*.

Host Names

A rose by any other name is definitely not the same when we're talking about computer names. Prior to Windows 2000, Microsoft networks were based on the NetBIOS naming standard, and accessed the networking protocols via the NetBIOS session layer interface. Because NetBIOS programs *must* know the NetBIOS name of the target computer in order to establish a session, each computer required a NetBIOS name. On TCP/IP-based networks, the NetBIOS name has to be resolved to an IP address. That resolution led to additional broadcast traffic on the network.

Applications written specifically for TCP/IP networks use the WinSock interface rather than the NetBIOS interface. WinSock applications do not need to know the name of the destination host in order to establish a session. However, we can use host names to make it easier for us to remember the locations of network resources. Host names are not required to establish a session between two computers using the WinSock interface; only the destination IP address is required to create a session. While NetBIOS names are an integral and required component in NetBIOS networking, host names are there to make it easier for us to remember how to access another computer on the network.

Fully Qualified Domain Names

In NetBIOS networking the cardinal rule is, "let no two computers share the same NetBIOS name." Bad things happen if this rule is violated, such as the computer attempting to use a duplicate NetBIOS name being unable to initialize its networking components and therefore not being able to access the network.

Using DNS, two computers can share the same host name on the network. This includes the biggest network of them all, the Internet. We can do this because DNS is a hierarchical namespace (in contrast to the "flat" namespace used in NetBIOS networking).

The Fully Qualified Domain Name (FQDN) includes the host name and the domain membership of that computer. In this way we can have two computers THAT share the name "blah." Here are FQDNs for two computers with the host name of "blah":

blah.somedomain.com

blah.yourdomain.com

Even though two computers share the same host name, they live in two different neighborhoods (domains). It's comparable to street addresses: We can have two homes share the same house number, such as 123, because one house is on 123 Main Street and the other is on 123 Elm Street.

This is how we get tens of thousands of computers on the Internet that all have the same host name of "www." All these hosts named "www" exist in different domains. This also explains why we occasionally see URLs that have unusual host names, such as "www2." This typically signifies that a corporation is maintaining more than one Web server on the Internet.

How Host Name Resolution Works

Host name resolution starts with the *resolver*. The resolver is software included in the WinSock application that is used to query DNS servers for the IP address of a particular host's FQDN. Programs with resolver components include Web browsers (such as Microsoft Internet Explorer) and dedicated FTP programs (such as the command-line FTP program found in Windows 2000).

Recursive and Iterative Queries

When you type the FQDN in the address bar of your Web browser, you send a query or question to your Preferred DNS server. This query essentially states: "Tell me the IP address of this FQDN that I sent to you." The DNS server you sent the query to *must* answer your question either positively or negatively. It has two choices: a definitive answer (the IP address), or "I don't know." This type of query is known as a *recursive* query. However, this is not the only type of query DNS can use.

If I ask you a question—such as "who was the 17th president of the United States?"—you might think that you have only two choices: give me the right answer, or tell me that you don't know. This represents a recursive query. But do you have another option?

Of course you do. You can tell me, "Go ask George, he's the history buff; he might know." You have this option if I issue to you an *iterative* query. With iterative queries, the DNS server receiving the iterative query has the option of making "a best effort" attempt at answering the question posed to it. This best effort typically involves sending back to the resolver (usually the requesting host's preferred DNS server) the IP address of a DNS server that might have the information sought after: the IP addresses of the destination host.

Stepping through the DNS Name Resolution Query Process

Let's now follow the sequence of events after you type the FQDN of a destination host you want to connect to in the address bar in your Web browser. In this example, we want to connect to a Web server at blah.somedomain.com.

1. Type the FQDN of the computer blah.somedomain.com in the address bar of your Web browser, and then press ENTER. After you press ENTER, a recursive query is sent to your configured Preferred DNS server.

2. Your Preferred DNS server then checks its database to see if it has an address record for the host you are seeking (we'll cover address records later). The server first checks its cache to see if it recently

successfully resolved the same request. If the IP address is not in its cache, and if the DNS server is not *authoritative* (does not contain records for the target domain) for the domain in which your destination host is located, it then sends an iterative query to a root name server.

3. The root name server does not contain an address record for blah.somedomain.com. However, the root DNS server does contain the IP address of the DNS servers that are authoritative for all of the top-level domains, which includes the .com domain. The IP address of the .com DNS server is sent to the DNS server that initiated the iterative query.

4. Your Preferred DNS server now connects to the .com domain's DNS server. The .com domain DNS server checks its address records to see if it has the IP address for blah.somedomain.com, and it doesn't. In a best effort attempt, it forwards to the requesting DNS server the IP address of the somedomain domain's DNS server.

5. Your Preferred DNS server then makes a connection to the somedomain DNS server. The somedomain DNS server checks its database to see if it has an address record for blah.somedomain.com. Since blah is located in the somedomain domain, there is an address record for blah. The somedomain DNS server responds to your Preferred DNS server that issued the iterative query with the IP address of host machine blah.

6. Your Preferred DNS server now completes the recursive query you initiated by sending to your Web browser (resolver) the IP address of blah.somedomain.com. You are now able to establish a connection to the destination host. If the somedomain .com DNS server did not have a record for host blah, your Preferred server would have completed the recursive query by returning to you an error message.

Notice that both the requesting host and the Preferred server acted as resolvers in the preceding process.

Developing a **DNS** Implementation **Strategy**

In developing our DNS implementation strategy we have to consider three main elements:

- The domain names that we will use for our organization
- The creation and planning of our DNS zones
- The types of DNS servers we want to deploy, and their placement

Let's examine each of these considerations.

Planning Domain Names for Your Organization

When deciding on a domain name for your organization, you must be acutely aware of the influence these decisions will have on your Active Directory. The Active Directory namespace will mirror your DNS namespace, so careful planning here is a must.

Each domain in a URL is limited to 63 characters, and this includes the period. The length of a URL cannot exceed 255 characters. When you are planning your domain names, be sure that the full path to any single host does not exceed the 255-character limit. If you choose long domain names, such as:

Advancedresourceallocationandmanagementsouth.mygreatandstupendou scorp.com

it won't be long before your URLs become too long.

Keep your domain names meaningful and short. Your users will use these domain names to get to resources on your network. Make it easy for them to find these resources, and life at the help desk will be a lot more pleasant.

In addition to keeping your domain names meaningful and short, be sure to limit the number of subdomains in your organization. Guidelines vary, but Microsoft recommends limiting the depth of your domain tree to less than six levels deep. This eases administration and reduces user error when entering URL information into their WinSock applications.

Legal DNS Characters

The characters available for use in your domain names are: A–Z, a–z, 0–9, and the hyphen. Do *not* use underscores in your domain or host names. Perhaps one of the most egregious errors administrators make is assigning a NetBIOS name to their computer that has an underscore, and then attempting to extend this practice to the machine's host name. A hyphen can be used in place of the underscore. If you use just these "legal" characters, you will avoid potential incompatibilities with other, non-Windows 2000 DNS servers. The Windows 2000 DNS server supports the use of the Unicode character set. This means that you can use extended characters, such as foreign language characters. If you plan to deploy DNS solely on your intranet and will not be interacting with non-Windows 2000 DNS servers, then you may choose to include Unicode characters in your domain names.

The Windows 2000 DNS server is not case sensitive. Although RFC 1035 supports case sensitivity, our servers will not support this. Avoid mixed case in all your Internet and intranet implementations. All URL information should be accessible via lowercase-only naming. Doing this avoids the sorrowful situation of users not being able to connect to a resource because they cannot recall all the mixed cases in a complex URL.

Special Guidelines for Organizations Connected to the Internet

If your company chooses to maintain an Internet presence, you will have to decide how your internal domain name system will integrate with your Internet presence. You do *not* want to expose your internal domain for perusal by those on the Internet. This represents a major security risk. If an

Internet user has access to your internal domain records, the knowledge of your host names and IP address structures gives them the "key to the mint."

There are a couple of options available in this circumstance:

■ **Use the same second-level domain name for both your internal and external (Internet available) resources**   The major advantage to this approach is that it seems easy. Certain complications arise if internal users attempt to access your external servers via a firewall or proxy. However, these can be solved by mirroring external servers on the intranet.

The major disadvantage of this approach is that you need to maintain two different zones for the same second-level domain. One zone would be used by your internal DNS servers, and the second zone applied to the Internet DNS servers. Managing these two distinct zones and keeping track of what's internal and external could seriously cut into your "rubber-band shooting time."

■ **Use two different second-level domain names for your organization**   The advantage of this approach is that you maintain separate and distinct namespaces for your external and internal resources. This significantly reduces the risk of Internet users gaining access to your internal resources via DNS queries. Your internal second-level domain would not be public knowledge.

For example, if your Internet presence was associated with blah.com, you could assign your internal resources to the second-level domain blahcorp.com. Resource records would be managed separately for the blah.com and the blahcorp.com DNS servers, with little chance for confusion between the two.

This is the preferred solution. If you choose this approach, be sure to register your internal second-level domain with a domain registrar. Although this is not required, it will keep your options open in the future and may avoid some embarrassing situations like when the CEO goes home and mistakenly types in the URL www.blahcorp.com and sees somebody else's Web site!

Naming Your Subdomains

There are different naming schemes you can apply to your subdomains. You could name your subdomains by business unit. For example, you could have a marketing domain, a sales domain, a quality assurance domain, a manufacturing domain, a personnel domain, and so forth. However, this may be disadvantageous in corporate environments that experience frequent restructuring. Yesterday's "personnel department" may become "human resources" today and "organic assets" in the future. You will have to restructure your domain scheme whenever these sociopolitical changes take place.

The preferred method of domain organization is to use geographical references. East will always be East, West always West, Texas always Texas, and Dallas always Dallas. When organizing your domains geographically, you avoid the consequences of corporate restructuring. Another major advantage is that zones are managed at a physical location; thus, categorizing your zones by location facilitates zone management.

If you require granular management by business unit, assign each business unit to an individual organizational unit (see the chapters on the Active Directory for a discussion of organization units).

In summary: Keep your domain names simple, easy to remember, short, and within the DNS guidelines as defined by RFC 1035. Try to name subdomains based on geographic considerations rather than by business unit. Remember that the Windows 2000 DNS server is not case sensitive, although certain UNIX implementations of DNS are case sensitive. Instruct your Web developers never to use mixed-case naming as a general rule to significantly improve ease of usability.

Planning Your DNS Zones

Until this point, we've focused on domain names. These domain names can be top-level domains, second-level domains, or subdomains. Resources will be affiliated with their domain membership. However, the way we manage domains and the resources located within the domains is through DNS *zone files.*

Forward and Reverse Lookup Zones

A DNS zone file is a database file that contains the resource records for a domain or set of domains. Each domain or set of domains included in a zone file are said to be members of the same DNS zone. There are two basic types of zones: Forward lookup and Reverse lookup. Forward lookup zones allow a resolver to obtain the IP address of a host when the host name is known. A Reverse lookup zone allows the resolver to obtain the host name when an IP address is known. Let's first focus on forward lookup zones.

ASSIGNING DOMAINS TO ZONES AND FORWARD LOOKUP ZONES Look at the example in Figure 22-2. The .com domain is the top-level domain. The second-level domain is our corporate subdomain, blah. We have operations in Dallas, Seattle, and Boston. We have decided to partition the blah domain into three domains: blah.com, west.blah.com, and east.blah.com. The west.blah.com domain will contain resource records for those machines located in Seattle, the east.blah.com domain will contain resource records for machines in Boston, and the blah.com domain will contain resource records for resources at our headquarters in Dallas.

FIGURE 22-2

The three domains shown are divided into two separate zones

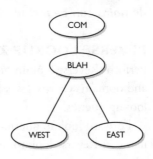

Our main operations are in Dallas. The majority of our employees and computer personnel are located there. The Seattle location has mainly programmers and systems administration staff; our consulting services are there as well. The Boston Location has sales and marketing personnel. There are no full-time computer professionals on site in Boston.

In order to assure accurate and timely management of our DNS servers, we will manage our corporate domains using two zones. One zone will include both the blah.com and the east.blah.com domains, and the second zone will include only the west.blah.com domain.

The zone that contains both the east.blah.com and the blah.com domains will be named the blah.com zone. Blah.com is the zone's root domain, and the name of the zone is derived from the root domain of the zone. The west.blah.com domain is contained in the west.blah.com zone, since it is the root domain of the zone. If we were to create subdomains of the west.blah.com domain, they could be part of the west.blah.com zone.

This is how we distribute the responsibility for maintaining domain resource records to personnel capable of maintaining them. Do not confuse domains with zones. Resources are located in individual domains. Zones represent physical zone files where the domain and resource information is stored.

These are Forward lookup zones, where hosts look up to resolve FQDN to an IP address.

heads
⓪P

Remember that domains are administered via zone files, and multiple domains can be included in a single zone (zone file).

REVERSE LOOKUP ZONES   Reverse lookup zones allow us to perform Reverse lookup queries. Many diagnostic tools such as nslookup and domain security assessment programs make extensive use of Reverse lookup queries.

Forward lookup queries seek to resolve an IP address from a known host name. A Reverse lookup query does the opposite: it seeks to resolve a host name from a known IP address. Forward lookup zone files are not designed to accomplish this type of query. In order to perform a Reverse lookup query, we need to create a new zone: a Reverse lookup zone.

The Reverse lookup zone is contained in a special zone-level domain known as in-addr.arpa. The in-addr.arpa domain works in just the same way as our Forward lookup domains. The subdomains of the in-addr.arpa domain are based on the dotted quad representation of each Network ID, but the order of the octets is reversed.

For example, let's say that you have a Network ID of 131.107.0.0. The name of the Reverse lookup zone is 107.131.in-addr.arpa. If you have a Network ID of 192.168.20, the Reverse lookup zone is 2.168.192.in-addr.arpa. A Network ID of 10.1.0.0 has a Reverse lookup zone of 1.10.in-addr.arpa.

The Reverse lookup zones are created independently of the Forward lookup zones. Pointer (PTR) records populate the Reverse lookup zone. You can manually enter PTR records for each computer, or have a PTR record created automatically each time you enter an A record into a Forward lookup zone.

Resource Records

How do we populate our zones and the domains that reside in them? We create DNS database entries. Each entry into the DNS database is referred to as a *resource record*. Table 22-1 lists some important resource record types.

When we add a specific host to a domain, we add an A record. If we have a mail server, we would add that server's name and IP address with an MX record. A single computer can have multiple records of different types. For example, your Web server's host name on the Internet would most likely be named "www." However, internally you may want to refer to it by another name, such as bigserver. You would enter an A record for bigserver and then create a CNAME record for www. Both records would map to the same IP address.

TABLE 22-1   Important Resource Record Types

Resource Record Type	Name	Description
SOA	Start of Authority	The SOA identifies which DNS server is authoritative for the data within this domain. The first record in any zone file is the SOA.
NS	Name server	An NS record lists the DNS servers that will return authoritative answers for the domain. This includes the Primary DNS server for the zone, and any other DNS servers to which you delegate authority for the zone.
A	Address	The A record contains the host name to IP address mapping for the particular host. The majority of the records in the zone will be A records.
SRV	Service	The SRV record records which services are running on a particular host. This is similar to the service identifier in NetBIOS environments. If a particular host is looking for a server to authenticate with, it will check for a SRV record to find an authenticating host.
CNAME	Canonical Name	This is an alias for a computer with an existing A record. For example, if you have a computer called bigserver that is going to be your Web server, you could create a CNAME for it, such as "www."
MX	Mail Exchanger	MX identifies the preferred mail servers on the network. If you have several mail servers, an order of precedence will be run.
HINFO	Host Information	HINFO records provide information about the DNS server itself. This might include CPU, operating system, interface type, and other aspects of the server. Consider this a primitive resource tracking method.
PTR	Pointer	The PTR record is created to allow for Reverse lookups. Reverse lookups are valuable when doing security analysis and checking authenticity of source domains for e-mail.

Zone File Limitations and Zone Transfers

Why not just put all your resources records into one zone? This seems like the easy way to do things—everything in one place. However, while it may seem easy, management would be a nightmare. A large corporation may have over 20,000 computers, and managing a database that large can lead to an increased probability of human error when zone database entries are made. It would also slow database queries to a crawl.

Think about it this way: What would happen if you ran a law office, and put all of your papers in one big file folder? Imagine that you have 300 pending cases and all of your legal briefs are in this single folder. How long would it take you to find the information you need for the "jones" case? What you should do is put each case in a separate file folder to make it easier and faster to find the "resource" you require. The same principles apply when we assign our resources to domains. Each domain is a separate file folder containing resource records for computers in that domain.

You are limited to 65,553 records per zone, and a single server can have no more than 1000 zones. While you might come up against these limitations, there is an even more compelling reason to avoid too vigorous "collapsing" of your zones. The most pressing issue is that of *zone transfer*.

ZONE TRAFFIC   As we'll see when we talk about deployment of DNS servers, we need to plan some degree of fault tolerance into our zone strategy. If the single server that houses the zone file goes offline, then host name resolution stops for machines configured only for that DNS server. The zone file where actual changes are made is referred to as the *primary* zone file. This is the actual file that is changed when you update it with resource records.

To provide for fault tolerance, we create a *secondary* zone that will exist on Secondary DNS servers. These Secondary DNS servers will maintain a *read-only* copy of the zone file.

The process of copying the primary zone file from the Primary DNS server to the Secondary DNS server is *zone transfer*. If a single zone file becomes very large, the process of zone transfer will consume large amounts of bandwidth. When planning your zones, take into account the potential size of each zone file and the nature of the link between your Primary and Secondary DNS servers.

Delegating Authority for a Zone

Let's say that you are sitting at a client workstation somewhere in the blah.com domain. Your Preferred DNS server is authoritative for the blah.com and the east.blah.com domains. Now, you issue a request from your Web browser to resolve www.syngress.com. What happens? Your blah.com DNS server issues an iterative query to an Internet root server, which returns the IP address of the .com server, which then returns the IP address of the syngress.com server, which finally returns the IP address of host www at syngress.com, www.syngresss.com.

The question is, how did all these servers know which server was authoritative for each respective subdomain? This is accomplished via *domain delegation.*

Our blah.com zone is authoritative for both the blah.com and the east.blah.com domains. If a host name query is received requesting name resolution for a host in the blah.com domain, our DNS server for this zone will be able to resolve the host to an IP address and return the IP address to the requesting host. But what if a client issues a query for a host on the west.blah.com domain to the DNS server authoritative for the blah.com zone?

The blah.com zone's DNS server must have a mechanism for referring the client to a DNS server authoritative for its subdomain, the west.blah.com domain. What we must do is create an NS record in the blah.com domain indicating which server is authoritative for the west.blah.com domain. The NS record will include the name of the domain being referred to (in this case, west.blah.com) and the host name of the DNS server authoritative for the west.blah.com domain.

GLUE RECORDS However, the NS record only indicates the name of the DNS server authoritative for the west.blah.com domain. It does not include the DNS server's IP address. We must create a second record, an A record, which will include the name of the DNS server authoritative for the west.blah.com domain and its IP address. The A record is referred to as a *glue record* because it associates the host name in the NS record with an IP address of the A record. It "glues" together the name server's host name and IP address.

Whenever you split your domains into subdomains, you must include on all parent domains delegation information, which will include NS records for authoritative servers and their corresponding glue records. Remember to include the primary DNS server and all Secondary DNS servers for the zone.

Planning DNS Server Types and Locations

Now that we've defined our corporate namespace and organized our domains into zones, we can begin planning our DNS server deployment.

In order to properly deploy our DNS servers, we need to define the types of DNS servers available, what their purposes are, and the advantages of using one type over another.

There are six types of DNS servers:

- Primary
- Secondary
- Caching-Only
- Forwarding
- Slave
- Dynamic

After describing the types of servers, we'll take a look at strategies in properly deploying them across our enterprise.

Primary DNS Servers

The Primary DNS server is where the primary read/write copy of a particular zone file is located. This server then is authoritative for the domain or domains that the zone files it houses contain. Because this server is authoritative, it can directly respond to client DNS queries regarding the IP address for a specific host.

Primary DNS servers share some characteristics with all DNS servers, including:

- **Zone database information is stored in the <systemroot>\ system32\dns directory**   All zone files are stored in this directory. Zone files have the .dns file extension.

- **The ability to boot from either the registry or a boot file**   By default, the Windows 2000 DNS server obtains operating information from the Registry. This information is derived from the administrator entering information via the GUI interface provided by Windows 2000 DNS server. You can choose to administer from a file called BOOT if you prefer not to use the GUI interface. To do so, you will have to edit the following registry key:

```
HKEY_Local_machine\System\CurrentControlSet\Services\DNS\Parameters\BootMethod
```

Change the registry key back to its previous setting if you choose to boot from the registry again.

- **Caching of previously resolved queries**   All DNS servers, regardless of type, have the ability to cache previously resolved queries. Remember, a DNS server can both receive and issue queries. When a DNS server issues an iterative query to another DNS server, the results obtained from these queries are placed in the DNS server's cache. You won't find a file dedicated to the server's cache, because this information is stored in memory. If you reboot the server, the entire contents of the cache are lost. DNS servers perform best when not required to reboot frequently.

- **The cache.dns file**   The cache.dns file contains the host names and IP addresses of the root DNS servers on the Internet. During an iterative query, a DNS server seeks out one of these root servers for name resolution. The cache.dns file is located in the same directory as the zone files.

For our fictional domain, blah.com, we assign a Windows 2000 computer as the Primary DNS server for the blah.com zone. Recall that the blah.com zone is authoritative for both the blah.com and the east.blah.com domains. It is authoritative because the server does not need to issue an iterative query to any other server in order to return to the client the IP address of hosts within either the blah.com or the east.blah.com domains.

A Primary DNS server can be also be a Secondary DNS server. The same server software is installed for both. What makes a computer a Primary or a Secondary DNS server is the type of zone files it contains. Any DNS server can contain either or both Primary or Secondary zone files.

For example: In the west.blah.com domain there is a server that is the Primary DNS server for the west.blah.com domain. That is because we have decided to let the DNS administrators in Seattle manage their own domain resource records. In addition to being authoritative for the west.blah.com domain, we would like this same machine to have a copy of the blah.com zone file. The will minimize name resolution traffic across the WAN and provide a measure of fault tolerance for the Primary DNS server of the blah.com zone. This same computer is now the Primary DNS server for the west.blah.com zone and the Secondary server for the blah.com zone.

Which leads us to the next subject: How do we provide for fault tolerance for our zone information? Our corporation is highly dependent on name resolution services for both intranet and Internet access. In order to provide this measure of fault tolerance, we would configure a Secondary DNS server.

Secondary DNS Servers

Secondary DNS servers provide for

- **Fault Tolerance** A Secondary DNS server houses a copy of the zone database file. It receives this copy during a process known as *zone transfer*, during which the Primary DNS server for the zone transfers a copy of the zone file to the Secondary DNS server. If the Primary DNS server for the zone goes offline, clients can be configured to access the Secondary server for the zone. This maintains name resolution services without interruption.

- **Load Balancing** Load balancing involves balancing or distributing the query load among multiple DNS servers. If all client computers were to access a single Primary DNS server for name resolution services, that server could become easily overwhelmed by name query traffic. By implementing a Secondary DNS server we can take some of the processing duties away from the Primary DNS server and distribute them to Secondary DNS servers.

- **Bandwidth Conservation** In our example of the blah.com domain, we chose to let the west.blah.com DNS administrators maintain their own zone information. The Primary DNS server for the west.blah.com domain is located in Seattle. Because a large number of name queries for the blah.com and the east.blah.com domains source from the Seattle site, we would choose to make the DNS server a Secondary DNS server for the blah.com zone (recall that the blah.com zone is authoritative for both the blah.com and the east.blah.com domains). When hosts located in Seattle issue a host name query for hosts located in the blah.com zone, they will not need to send the query across the WAN. These host name resolution requests can be handled locally in Seattle.

Fault tolerance, load balancing, and bandwidth conservation are strong reasons for implementing Secondary DNS servers. Always plan for Secondary DNS servers. If you plan to maintain your own DNS servers on the Internet, your Domain Registrar will require you to have at least one Primary and one Secondary DNS server for your second-level domain.

Zone Transfers

Whenever a Secondary DNS server starts up, it checks in with the Primary server for the zone to see if there are any updates to the zone. If there are, the entire zone file is sent to the Secondary DNS server. If there are no changes, the zone is not transferred.

REFRESH INTERVAL The Secondary DNS server will periodically *refresh* its zone file in order to obtain updates to the zone. This *refresh interval* is defined by the Primary DNS server zone properties. The refresh interval is included in the SOA record on the Primary DNS server. In addition to obtaining information about the refresh interval from the Primary DNS server's SOA record, the Secondary server gets information regarding updates to the zone file. This is communicated via a *serial number*.

The SOA record contains a version number, known as the *serial number*. The serial number is incremented whenever there is a change in the zone file. If the Secondary DNS server reads on the SOA record that the version of the zone database it has contains a lower serial number than the one on the SOA on the Primary server, the Secondary DNS server will request that the entire new zone file be sent to it.

ZONE SECURITY   By default, any DNS server can make itself a secondary to any Primary DNS server. The Secondary just has to issue a request for the zone file, and the Primary will send it. As you can see, this can represent a significant security problem. If users can obtain a copy of your internal DNS information, they have the IP addresses of your internal computers, as well as the roles of many of those computers on your network.

One way to circumvent this situation is to allow only "authorized" Secondary DNS servers to obtain updates. In order to accomplish this, we reverse the responsibility for initiating updates. Out of the box, the Secondary DNS server initiates the zone transfer process. What we want to do is have the Primary DNS server trigger updates instead.

This can be accomplished by creating a notify list on the zone properties sheet. By using the notify list, we tell the Primary server to notify the Secondary DNS server when changes take place in the zone database. When a change takes place, the Primary DNS server sends a message to only configured DNS servers to send a pull request to the Primary DNS server. In this way, Joe Hacker can't just set up his DNS server at home to be a secondary to our DNS server. Only DNS servers whose IP addresses appear in the notify list will receive zone transfers.

Caching-Only Servers

All DNS servers cache the results of the queries they have issued. The difference between a Caching DNS server, and a Primary or Secondary DNS server, is that the Caching server does not contain any zone information. Everything a Caching server knows comes from the results of previous queries it has issued.

Recall that all DNS servers have the cache.dns file that contains the IP addresses of all the root servers on the Internet. In Windows 2000, this file is referred to as the "root hints" file, and you can view its contents in the properties of the DNS server. The Caching-only server uses this list to begin building its cache, and then adds to the cache as it issues iterative queries in response to the recursive queries clients have sent to it.

Caching-only servers are useful because

■ **They do not generate zone transfer traffic**   Caching-only servers are not authoritative for any zone, and therefore are in no need of zone information. Hence, there is no need for zone transfers.

■ **They can be used at locations on the far side of a slow WAN link**   Small office locations located remotely across a slow WAN link benefit from Caching servers because they do not generate zone transfer traffic. It also reduces over time the need to reach across the WAN for host name resolution.

■ **They are especially useful as forwarders**   There is no risk of someone obtaining zone information from a Caching-only server. Therefore, Caching-only servers make excellent candidates for forwarders. We cover forwarders in the next section.

Fowarders and Slave Servers

A DNS Forwarder is a DNS server that accepts requests to resolve host names from another DNS server. Caching-only servers make good forwarders. A Forwarder can be used to protect an internal DNS server from access by users on the Internet.

Here's how a Forwarder works:

1. A client sends a recursive query to its Preferred DNS server. The request is for a host located on a zone that the server is not authoritative.

2. The DNS server now needs to resolve the host name for the client. We can configure the Preferred DNS server to forward all requests for which it has no authority to another DNS server, which is the Forwarder.

The vocabulary gets a little confusing here. The client's Preferred server is "forwarding" the request to the "forwarder." We then would name the client's Preferred server the "forwarding" DNS server, and the DNS server that receives the "forwarding" server's request is the "forwarder."

3. The Forwarder attempts to resolve the FQDN. If it is successful at obtaining the IP address of the destination host, it returns this IP address to the "forwarding" server, which in turn returns the IP address to the client that initiated the request.
   If the Forwarder cannot resolve the host name to an IP address, the forwarding DNS server will attempt to resolve the request itself via iterative queries.

Note here that the client's Preferred DNS server gave the Forwarder first shot at resolving the IP address. Only if the Forwarder is unsuccessful will the client's Preferred DNS server attempt to resolve the request itself.

SLAVE SERVERS   There is a type of forwarding process that prevents the Preferred server from attempting to resolve the host name to an IP address if the Forwarder fails. When we configure the forwarding server to not attempt to resolve the host name on its own if the Forwarder is unsuccessful, we call the forwarding comsuter a *Slave* server. The Slave server will accept the response the forwarder provides to it, and will relay the response from the Forwarder to the client directly without attempting to resolve the name itself.

FORWARDERS AND FIREWALLS   The Slave server/Caching-only Forwarder combination is very helpful in maintaining the security of our zone data. We can use this combination to prevent users on the other side of a firewall from having access to information on our Internal DNS server.

For example, at blah.com we have an internal DNS server that we use to resolve DNS requests for resources inside our corporate environment. As long as the requests are for only hosts in our internal network, DNS requests represent no security risk. However, what happens when users on the Internal network need to access resource on the Internet?

Let's say a user wants to connect to www.stuff.com. When the recursive request hits our internal DNS server, which is authoritative for only blah.com and east.blah.com, what does the DNS server do? It begins the iterative query request in order to resolve the Internet host name. In the process, the DNS servers on the Internet must send their responses to our Internal DNS machine through the firewall. This exposes our internal DNS server, and its zone data, to users on the Internet. How can we avoid this potentially harmful situation?

We can place a Caching-only Forwarder on the outside of the firewall and configure our internal DNS server to be a Slave server. Now when one of our clients issues a name resolution request for an Internet host to our internal DNS server, the internal DNS server forwards the request to the Forwarder on the outside of the firewall. The Forwarder attempts to resolve the FQDN to an IP address. If successful, it returns the IP address to our internal DNS server, which in turn returns the IP address to the client that issued the request. If the Forwarder is unsuccessful, it reports that to our internal server, which then reports to the client that the host was not found. Our internal Slave server will *not* attempt to resolve the host name itself.

At no time does an Internet DNS server send a response to our internal DNS server when we use the Slave server/Caching-only forwarder combination. In this way, our internal zone records are safe.

Dynamic DNS Servers

Dynamic DNS (DDNS) servers are new to Windows 2000. Traditional DNS servers required that the DNS administrator enter Address Records manually. If we wanted dynamic updates of host name/IP address combinations (which are required if we want to implement DHCP), we could integrate an NT 4.0 DNS server with WINS, which would provide us with a pseudo-Dynamic DNS. I say "pseudo" because the WINS server doesn't track host names; it tracks NetBIOS names. This was good enough for previous Windows operating systems because they were NetBIOS based. Windows 2000 is not NetBIOS based, and NetBIOS names are to be deemphasized in favor of true host names. A DDNS server registers host name/IP address combinations dynamically.

Only Windows 2000 clients can register with a DDNS system. When a Windows 2000 host starts up, it reports its IP address and host name to the

DDNS. If DHCP is used on the network, the DHCP server itself updates the DDNS server with the current IP address for the particular host name.

DNS Server Placement Considerations

Now that we have learned about how to create our domain name structure, zones, and the types of DNS servers available, it's time to decide where to place our DNS servers for optimal client response times for host name resolution.

In a routed environment, you should have at least one DNS server on each subnet. If your segments are connected via fast connections, you might consider placing DNS servers in central locations. However, if the link goes down to the DNS server on the remote subnet, you'll be without host name resolutions services until it is restored.

If you have remote sites connected to your main site via a slow WAN link, consider using only a Caching DNS server at the remote site. By implementing the Caching server solution, you avoid the potential for congestion during zone transfers. Over time, the cache will increase in size and greatly reduce the need to reach over the WAN for name resolution queries.

DNS servers were designed with at least a Primary and Secondary in mind. Place the Primary server for each zone in a location convenient for the DNS administrators. Then locate your Secondary servers on subnets that generate large amounts of host name resolution traffic. You might also consider adding a Secondary on the same subnet as a Primary if the volume of name resolution traffic is so high that load balancing on the local segment would be of value.

You can speed up host name resolution in a large corporate network by including a Caching-only server designated as a Forwarder to which all Primary and Secondary DNS forward their queries. Configure the forwarding machines as Slave servers, and after a short time your Forwarder will have a large cache that will minimize the need to leave the internal network for name resolution requests.

If you place this Caching-only Forwarder on the outside of the corporate firewall, you enhance the security of your network. Configure your internal servers as Slave servers, and no DNS server on the Internet will touch any of your internal machines.

Your company will likely have a strong Internet presence. If it doesn't have one now, it will in the future. Employees will need access to the Internet, and with that access they are going to require reliable name resolution services. You also must keep your internal resources safe from Internet intruders. One of the best things you can do for yourself and your company now is to become proficient at implementing a firewall solution. Microsoft Proxy Server 2.0 is both a firewall and proxy server and is invaluable at providing the protection you need. If your users require host name resolution of resources outside the corporate domain, place a Caching-only Forwarder on the far side of the firewall. Then configure your internal forwarding server as a Slave. You can configure Microsoft Proxy Server 2.0 to allow your forwarding and Forwarder servers to dialog safely.

Installing the DNS Service

You can install DNS during the Windows 2000 installation process, or you can defer installing it until later. Let's go through the procedure for installing the DNS Service after Windows 2000 has already been installed.

1. Open the Windows Components Wizard.

2. Click Next.

3. Under Components, scroll down to Networking Services, and click it.

4. Click Details.

5. Under Subcomponents of Networking Services, click Domain Name System (DNS), and then click OK.

6. Type the full path to the Windows 2000 distribution files and click Continue.

7. Required files are copied to your hard disk, and server software can be used after restarting the system.

This completes the planning and installation section. Next we look at the specifics of managing the DNS server that is installed.

Developing a DNS Management Strategy

We've covered a lot of ground. You learned about DNS, DNS server types, and some deployment strategies. You've also installed the DNS Service. Now that we have the DNS Service installed, it's time to manage that installation. There are several tasks we must complete in order to manage our installation:

- Create a Forward lookup zone
- Create a Reverse (Inverse) lookup zone
- Configure zone properties
- Create resource records
- Configure clients to point to their Preferred DNS server

Let's begin!

Creating a Forward Lookup Zone

Now that we've installed our DNS server, the next step is to configure a zone. There are two types of zones: Primary and Secondary. In this exercise, you will configure a new primary zone where the top-level domain for the zone will be BLAH. Note that a DNS server can be authoritative for multiple zones. Our server QONOS already contains a zone file for the FEDERATION Domain. We will add our BLAH Domain to QONOS.

EXERCISE 22-1

Creating a Domain

Log on with an Account that is a member of the Administrators Group for that machine. Typically, this will be the Administrator Account. However, you may have changed the name of the default Administrator Account for security purposes.

1. Click Start. Point to Programs | Administrative Tools | Computer Management and click that with the left mouse button.

2. Under Services and Applications you will see an entry for the DNS server. We have already added QONOS, as shown in Figure 22-3. Expand the computer name on your machine by clicking the + sign if there is one. At this time, you don't have any zones configured, so now let's create a new zone.

FIGURE 22-3   Windows 2000's Computer Management tool

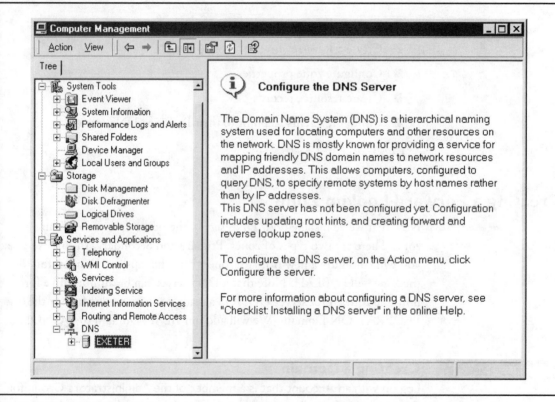

3. Right-click the computer name, and then point to New Zone.

4. The Welcome to the New Zone Wizard starts. The Wizard will walk us through the process of creating the new zone. Click Next.

5. We want to create a Standard primary zone, so select this option, shown in Figure 22-4. Click Next.

FIGURE 22-4   Choose the zone type in the New Zone Wizard

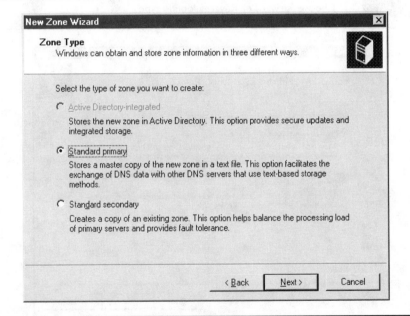

6. The Wizard now asks whether we want to create a Forward lookup zone or a Reverse lookup zone, as shown in Figure 22-5. Always create your Forward lookup zone prior to creating the Reverse lookup zone. The Reverse lookup zone will contain the pointer records for resources in your Forward lookup zone. Click Next.

7. Type the name of your new zone (see Figure 22-6). This DNS server will be authoritative for the blah second-level domain, where the .com domain is the top-level domain. Click Next.

Choose Forward or Reverse lookup type

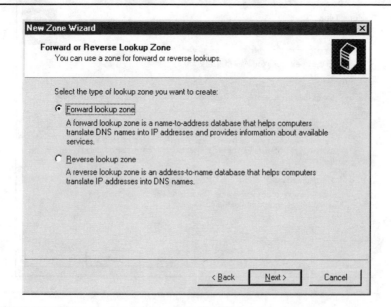

FIGURE 22-6   Naming the new zone

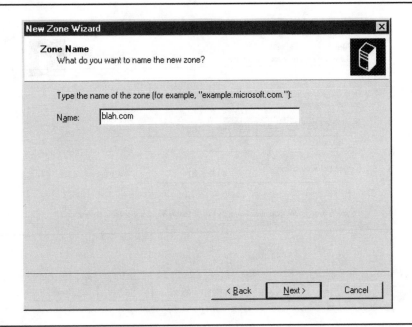

8. By default, the Wizard creates the new zone file based on the domain name, and then appends the .dns extension, as shown in Figure 22-7. This file will be stored in the <systemroot>\system32\dns folder. This zone file can easily be transferred to another DNS server if you need to. Click Next.

9. When you have finished answering the Wizard's questions, it will present back to you the data it has received. If everything looks good, click Finish. If you need to make corrections, click Back. Click Finish.

FIGURE 22-7   Creating or selecting a zone file

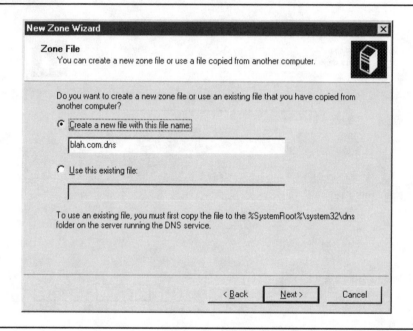

10. After you click Finish, return to the Computer Management Window (see Figure 22-8). You should now see a folder for Forward Lookup Zones. Expand that folder by clicking on the + sign. blah.com now appears as a Forward lookup zone. Congratulations! You have configured your Forward lookup zone and you are now ready to configure your resource records.

FIGURE 22-8   The Computer Management screen

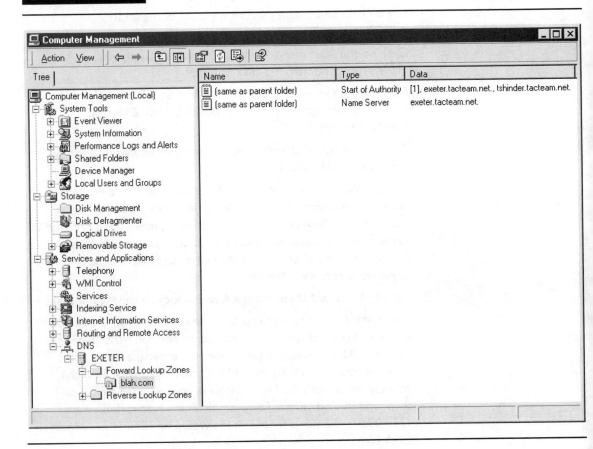

Creating a Reverse Lookup Zone

Now let's configure our Reverse lookup zone. Our computers on the blah.com domain are located on Network ID 192.168.1.0 and use the default Class C subnet mask, 255.255.255.0.

Configuring a Reverse Lookup Zone

1. Log on with an account that is a member of the local Administrators Group.

2. Click on the Start menu. Point to Programs | Computer Management and then left-click on that.

3. Right-click on your computer name in the Scope pane of the Computer Management Console. Point to New Zone and left-click on that.

4. The Wizard will start again, just like when you configured the Forward lookup zone. Click Next.

5. You are asked whether you want to create a Standard Primary, Standard Secondary, or Active Directory Integrated zone. Since this is the first Reverse lookup zone created, make this a Primary Zone. If you have Active Directory installed, you should select Active Directory integrated to take advantage of the benefits of Active Directory. Click Next.

6. Tell the Wizard that you want a Reverse lookup zone. Click Next.

7. The Wizard now requires you to enter the Network ID that will be serviced by this Reverse lookup zone. You can either type the Network ID and subnet mask, or directly enter the name of the zone file yourself (see Figure 22-9). If you should want to type it yourself, begin with the Network ID in reverse, then a period, then type **in-addr.arpa**. For example, if my Network ID were 131.107.0.0, the Reverse lookup file would be 107.131.in-addr.arpa. Click Next.

8. The Wizard asks you to confirm the name of the file it will create. Unless you have an old Reverse lookup file that you are importing, select the default entry. Click Next.

9. The last screen confirms the data you entered. Click Finish.

10. Return to the Computer Management screen to confirm the creation of your new Reverse lookup zone.

FIGURE 22-9 Configuring the Reverse lookup zone

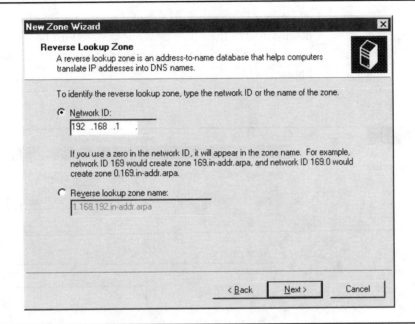

Configuring Zone Properties

With both our Forward and Reverse lookup zones created, we can now take on the task of configuring the Primary Forward lookup zone we created. There are two steps: manipulate the properties of our Forward lookup zone, and then add resource records.

1. Log on as a user with Administrative privilege.

2. Right-click the Forward lookup zone that you just created. Point to Properties and left-click.

3. There are five tabs. The first is the General tab, shown in Figure 22-10. Listed here is the name of your zone file. You can allow your DNS server to accept dynamic updates by clicking the down arrow in the Allow dynamic updates? list box. Click the down arrow and select Yes. Select the Start of Authority tab, shown in Figure 22-11.

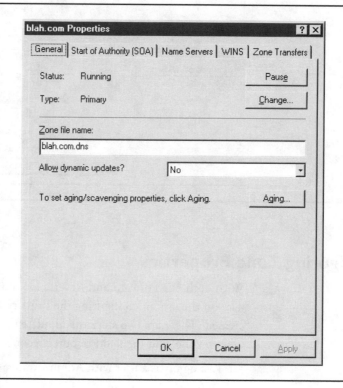

Designating the SOA

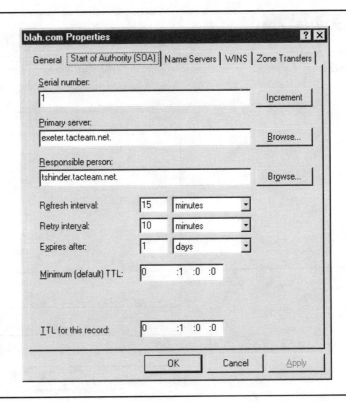

4. Here you can change the Refresh interval, Retry interval and expiration time. You can also adjust the Time to Live (TTL) for cached queries. The TTL determines how long the cache query results will be valid. Make no changes here and then select the Name Servers tab, shown in Figure 22-12.

FIGURE 22-12

Listing the Secondary
name servers

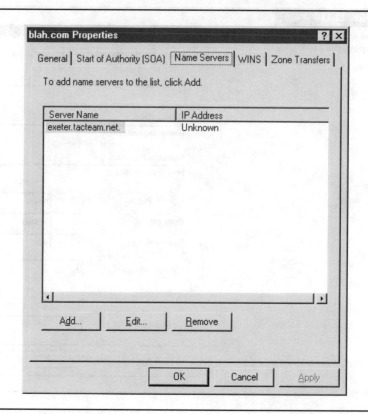

5. Here you list the Secondary name servers that will receive records
   from this Primary name server. Click Add and type the host name
   and IP addresses of your Secondary name servers. Next, select the
   WINS tab, shown in Figure 22-13.

FIGURE 22-13

Enabling WINS for
non-Windows 2000 clients

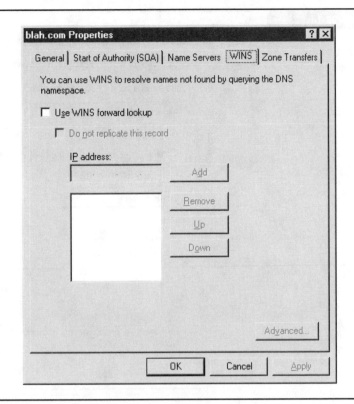

6. If you have clients that need to resolve NetBIOS names, but they
themselves cannot be made WINS clients, you can configure DSN
to query a WINS server to resolve the NetBIOS name to an IP
address. Computers such as UNIX clients fit into this category. Put
a check in the "Use WINS forward lookup" box and enter the IP
address of a WINS server. Then click Add. Select the Zone
Transfers tab, shown in Figure 22-14.

FIGURE 22-14

Configuring zone
transfer options

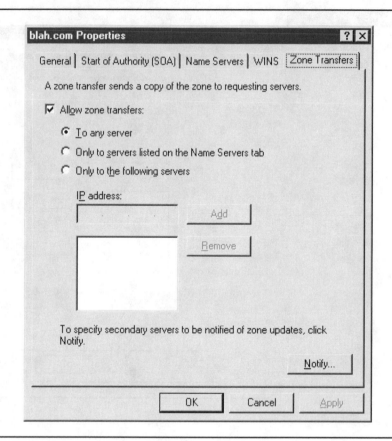

7. On the Zone Transfer property sheet, you can configure to
   whom zone transfers can be sent by clicking the Notify button, as
   shown in Figure 22-14. This brings up the property sheet shown
   in Figure 22-15. You have the option to send them to anybody, or
   to only servers listed on the Servers tab, or specific servers whose
   IP addresses you can add here. These servers will initiate the zone
   transfer themselves. If you want the Primary server to notify (and
   therefore initiate the zone transfer) the Secondary servers of Zone
   updates you can click Notify.

FIGURE 22-15

Configuring notification
options

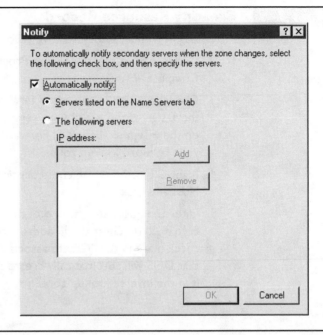

8. Notice that the check mark for "Automatically notify" is checked by
   default for the servers listed on the Name Servers tab. If you require
   automatic notification of alternate servers, click the "The following
   servers" and add their IP addresses.

You have completed configuring your zone properties. Let's now add
some resource records.

Creating Resource Records

Now we need to populate our zone with resource records. A Address
records are the most common type of record you will enter. Let's go over
the procedure of entering A records.

EXERCISE 22-3	**Creating Resource Records**

1. Log in with an Administrative account.

2. Click the Start menu. Point to Programs │ Administrative Tools │ Computer Management.

3. Click the + sign to the left of DNS to expose your server. Click the + sign to the left of your server to expose your zones. Click on the + sign to the left of Forward Lookup Zones to expose your Forward lookup zones.

4. Right-click on the blah.com Forward lookup zone. Point to New Host and click.

5. Enter the host name **neuro** of the new computer as shown in Figure 22-16. Enter the IP address of the host. Be sure to put a check mark in the "Create associated pointer (PTR) record" so that DNS will automatically create this record for you and place it in the Inverse lookup zone.

FIGURE 22-16	

Entering resource records for host computers

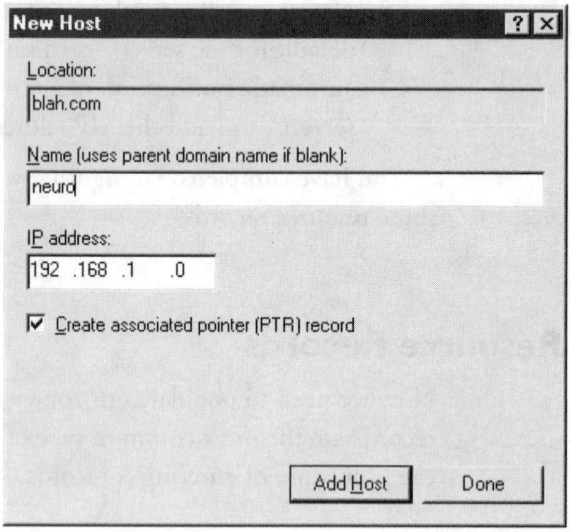

6. You have now entered a resource record for host neuro at blah.com. Go to a command prompt and type

   nslookup neuro.blah.com

   You should see the host name successfully resolved.

   Congratulations! You have successfully created your first A record.

Configuring the Client's Preferred DNS Server

The last step in our DNS configuration plan is to set up the clients to communicate with our DNS server. There are two ways to do this:

- Configure DHCP to automatically configure the client's DNS server settings. This is the preferred method.

- Configure the client individually. This is required in some instances where the machine must have a static IP address and therefore is not a DHCP client.

In this exercise we configure our DNS server to use itself as its own DNS server to resolve host names to IP address. The DNS client configuration works the same on all Windows 2000 clients that require manual DNS configuration.

EXERCISE 22-4

Configuring a Client's Preferred DNS Server

1. Log on with an account that has Administrative Privileges.

2. Right-click My Network Places, point to Properties, and left-click.

3. This opens the Network and Dial-up Connections window. You should see at least two icons: one for Make New Connection and another for Local area Connection. Right-click "Local area Connection," point to Properties and left-click .

4. The Local Area Connection Properties dialog box appears. Scroll through the list and find Internet Protocol (TCP/IP). Click once on the text (not on the check mark or you may remove it inadvertently), and then click the Properties just underneath it to bring up the TCP/IP properties sheet as shown in Figure 22-17.

FIGURE 22-17

Configuring TCP/IP
properties and setting the
DNS servers

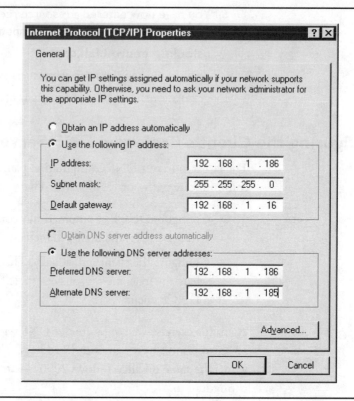

5. Select the option "Use the following DNS server addresses"
    and type the IP addresses for your DNS server. For fault
    tolerance, type the IP address of an Alternate DNS server,
    just in case the Primary should go offline.

6. Click OK, and then click OK again. You have successfully configured
    your DNS client.

EXERCISE 22-5

Analyzing a DNS Strategy

You have been asked to design a DNS strategy for BigEarth Incorporated.
BigEarth manufactures bulldozers and other earth-moving equipment. The
company has about 10,000 users located in four major locations. There

are 8000 employees in Dallas, and 500 users each in San Francisco, Seattle, Austin, and San Antonio. BigEarth also maintains a small branch office of 20 users in Carson City, Nevada. The major sites are connected via T1 links. The Carson City office is connected to Dallas via a 56 Kbps frame relay.

The bulk of the systems administration talent is in Dallas. Central corporate databases and e-mail systems are located in Dallas, and all sites need reliable access to these resources

The Austin and San Antonio operations are complimentary, and staff shuttle back and forth between those two facilities frequently. However, most of the experienced DNS administrators are stationed in Austin. For the most part, they operate independently from the other locations. The same is true for the Seattle location. The Seattle location has an experienced administrative staff onsite.

The situation in San Francisco is quite different. There are predominantly sales and marketing personnel located at this site. There are no reliable or experienced DNS administrators. All their systems support sources from the Dallas operation.

Dallas also supports the Carson City, Nevada office. There are no computer professionals at this location. The Dallas IT department manages systems remotely as well.

With this information consider the following:

1. How many DNS second-level domains would you configure? What would you name these domains?

2. How many subdomains would you configure? What would you name these domains?

3. How many zones would you create? What would be the names of these zones, as defined by the root domain for each zone?

4. How many Primary DNS servers would you place? Where would you place them?

5. How many Secondary DNS servers would you place? Where would you place these?

6. How many Caching-only servers would you place?

7. Would you use Forwarders? If so, why? Under what circumstances would you absolutely want to implement forwarding, and what type of forwarding?

ACCELERATING TO WINDOWS 2000

Much of the material we've covered bears some similarity to what we had available in Windows NT 4.0. However, there are some cool things available only in Windows 2000.

Incremental Zone Transfers

The default method of zone transfer is to copy the entire zone file from the Primary to the Secondary DNS server. This process consumes large amounts of bandwidth when the zone file grows. In Windows 2000, you can initiate incremental zone transfers that will only send updates to the Secondary server when changes to the Primary zone take place. This feature is only available when DNS is integrated with the Active Directory

Active Directory Integration

Rather than keeping discrete zone files on Primary and Secondary DNS servers, you can integrate DNS with the active directory. When you integrate the DNS with the Active Directory, the zone information is stored in the Active Directory. This streamlines the replication process of zone data significantly. You do not need to designate Primary and Secondary DNS servers. All domain controllers participate in a Multi-Master model, and share information with each other.

When a new domain controller is added, the zone is automatically copied to the computer.

Integration simplifies the planning process. Rather then creating your Active Directory tree and zone information separately, you create them in a central location. Seeing the "big picture" is much easier when everything is in one place.

Dynamic Updates

Traditional DNS management meant sitting in front of the DNS management console and entering all of your resource records manually. A Windows 2000 DNS server is able to accept dynamic updates from Windows 2000 client computers. Down-level clients can still query a Windows 2000 DNS server, but these clients cannot dynamically update their A record information.

SRV Records

SRV resource records provide information about which computers in the domain are domain controllers in an Active Directory integrated DNS environment. This information serves a similar purpose as the 16th hexadecimal byte used as service identifiers in NetBIOS names. In the future, well-known TCP/IP services may be included as SRV records.

QUESTIONS AND ANSWERS

How do I register my second-level domain for use on the Internet?	You must contact a Domain Registrar to register your second-level domain on the Internet.
Can I still integrate DNS with WINS for my legacy NetBIOS-based machines?	Yes. Even though Windows 2000 DNS server supports DDNS, you can still enable NetBIOS name resolution services by enabling WINS Forward lookup on your DNS servers.
What is an Active Directory Integrated DNS server? What advantages does this have?	Rather than storing zone information in a zone file, an Active Directory-enabled DNS server stores zone information in the Active Directory. One of the major advantages of the Active Directory-enabled DNS server is the ability to perform incremental zone transfers. The Active Directory Integrated DNS server will update Secondary DNS servers with only new information since the previous zone transfer. This can significantly reduce zone transfer-related network traffic.
Am I required to have Secondary zones?	No. If your situation limits your computing resources, you can get by with a single Primary DNS server. However, you will lack fault tolerance and lose host name resolution while your Primary DNS server is offline.
Will my Windows NT 4.0 clients automatically update their A records in a DDNS server?	No. Down-level clients (all Microsoft operating systems prior to Windows 2000) are not able to dynamically register their IP addresses with a DDNS server. However, they can still register their NetBIOS names with a WINS server. NetBIOS name resolution can take place via the DDNS server when WINS Forward lookups are enabled.

CHAPTER SUMMARY

DNS is a distributed database of host names and IP addresses. Host names can be used by WinSock programs to identify hosts on TCP/IP-based networks. In order to improve the speed and efficiency of DNS management, groups of computers sharing similar corporate and geographical characteristics placed into domains. Only the root and top-level domains are managed centrally. You should name your domains based on geographic consideration rather than on business unit labels. Domain names can be up to 63 characters, and an entire URL path is limited to 255 characters (including the periods). Limit the number of subdomains to less than five. Finally, make your domain names as intuitive and meaningful as possible.

Domains are managed via *zone files*. Zone files are stored on a DNS server. Multiple domains can be stored in a single zone file. Place domains that are going to be managed in a central location in a central zone file. This would be the case when you need to need to manage a remote domain from your location. The server that stores the read/write copy of the zone file is called the Primary DNS server. Information related to host names and their IP addresses is entered into the DNS server via resource records. An A record lists a host name and its IP address.

There are other types of DNS servers: Secondary, Caching-only, and Forwarders. Secondary DNS servers are used for both fault tolerance and load balancing. These DNS servers receive read-only copies of the zone database from the Primary DNS server for the particular zone. By default, Secondary DNS servers call the Primary DNS server for a copy of the zone database every 60 minutes. This is called the *refresh interval.* A Caching-only DNS server contains no zone files. This server builds up its cache of host names and IP addresses after completing iterative queries. A Forwarder is a DNS server that accepts requests for host name resolution from another DNS server to perform iterative requests. Using Caching-only forwarders outside of a firewall will protect your network from intruders seeking information about your internal DNS structure. Iterative queries utilize a file named cache.dns, also known as the *cache hints* file. This file contains the IP addresses of the Internet's root name servers.

Management of the DNS server is done via the Microsoft Management Control (MMC). You can manage the DNS via the GUI interface or by directly editing the Boot file. Via the GUI interface you can control which Secondary DNS servers receive updates. You add resource records via the MMC. You also create your domains and subdomains from here. WINS forwarding can be enabled from the GUI.

Integrating DNS with the Active Directory allows for hosts to dynamically update their IP address in the DNS. Another advantage of

Active Directory is that zone information is stored in the Active Directory. This allows for multiple master DNS (multiple Primary) servers. Windows 2000 DNS servers integrated into the Active Directory are able to send incremental updates of zone information.

TWO-MINUTE DRILL

- ❏ DNS is a method used to map "friendly" names to IP addresses.
- ❏ The DNS is a *distributed* database.
- ❏ Domains are "containers;" they can contain other domains (subdomains), as well as other objects.
- ❏ Applications written specifically for TCP/IP networks use the WinSock interface rather than the NetBIOS interface.
- ❏ In NetBIOS networking the cardinal rule is, "Let no two computers share the same NetBIOS name."
- ❏ The Fully Qualified Domain Name (FQDN) includes the host name and the domain membership of that computer.
- ❏ When deciding on a domain name for your organization, you must be acutely aware of the influence these decisions will have on your Active Directory. The Active Directory namespace will mirror your DNS namespace, so careful planning here is a must.
- ❏ Keep your domain names meaningful and short.
- ❏ The characters available for use in your domain names are: A–Z, a–z, 0–9, and the hyphen. Do *not* use underscores in your domain or host names.
- ❏ A DNS zone file is a database file that contains the resource records for a domain or set of domains.
- ❏ If you have remote sites connected to your main site via a slow WAN link, consider using only a Caching DNS server at the remote site.
- ❏ You can speed up host name resolution in a large corporate network by including a Caching-only server designated as a Forwarder to which all Primary and Secondary DNS forward their queries.

SELF TEST

The following questions will help you measure your understanding of the material presented in this chapter. Read all of the choices carefully, as there may be more than one correct answer. Choose all correct answers for each question.

1. You have a mixture of client machines on your network. These client machines include Windows 98, Windows NT 4.0 workstations, and Windows 2000 Professional workstations. You are implementing an Internet Information Server 5.0 Web Server to host your corporate intranet. What service should you install to allow for host name resolution?

   A. DHCP

   B. FTP

   C. DNS

   D. WINS

2. You have installed a Primary and a Secondary DNS server to resolve host names on your intranet. You would like to provide name resolution services for hosts on the Internet. What type of DNS server should you implement for this task?

   A. Another Secondary server

   B. Another Primary server

   C. A Forwarder that also contains zone information

   D. A Caching-only Forwarder

3. You have installed Internet Information Server 5.0 on a machine with the host name bigboy.corp.com. You have installed the FTP and the WWW services on this machine. What resource record type would you add so users can refer to this machine as www.corp.com and ftp.corp.com?

   A. AFSDB

   B. CNAME

   C. MB

   D. MG

4. You are in the process of putting together your DNS Domain structure and have not yet commissioned any DNS servers. Some of the users would like to access resources on your intranet via their Web browsers. What could they use in the place of the DNS server?

   A. A HOSTS file

   B. FTP Server Service

   C. NetBT

   D. RIP for IP

5. You are planning a TCP/IP based Windows 2000 network. What service should you install to allow for host name resolution?

   A. DHCP

   B. DNS

   C. NNTP

   D. RIP

   E. WINS

6. You have installed a DNS server on your network. Fault tolerance is a primary concern, as you want your users to be able to continue host name resolution for your intranet in case the server crashes. What type of server would you implement?

   A. Caching-only server

   B. Forwarder

   C. Resource Imaging server

   D. A Secondary server

7. A user on a Windows 2000 Professional computer named W2KPRO1 on SubnetQ cannot connect to a Windows 2000 server computer on SubnetW with the command NET USE F: \\Bigsrv.blah.com\data. Using another Windows 2000 Professional computer on SubnetA, you succeed in making the same connection with the command NET USE F:\\ Bigsrv.blah. com\data. What is the most likely cause of the problem?

   A. W2KPRO1 is not set up with the IP address of the DNS server.

   B. W2KPRO1 is not set up with the IP address of the WINS server.

   C. The DNS server has no entry for Bigsrv.blah.com.

   D. The DNS server is not set up for WINS resolution.

8. You administer a TCP/IP network running 200 Windows 2000 computers and 5 Linux servers. The 200 Windows

2000 computers are all DNS-enabled clients. How can you resolve host names to IP addresses with a minimum use of static name resolution?

   A. By creating a centralized LMHOSTS file on a Windows NT server computer

   B. By setting up Active Desktop Services

   C. By setting up DNS to use WINS

   D. By setting up a Dynamic DNS server

9. You manage a network that employs DHCP, DNS, and WINS. You discover that IP address to host name resolution is not working properly. What is the best way to troubleshoot this problem?

   A. Examine the Reverse lookup file using the nslookup utility.

   B. Flush the DNS server's cache using NBTSTAT –n.addr.arpa.

   C. Run nbtstat.exe on the Browser service.

   D. Run netstat.exe –wins.nl on the WINS server.

10. Your network has both Windows 98 and Windows 95 clients. You are running four Web servers on your intranet. What service would you install so that these Windows 9x machines can connect to your Web servers via their Fully Qualified Domain Names (FQDNs).

    A. DHCP

    B. DNS

    C. FTP

11. You would like to use the feature of DDNS. What clients are able to register with a DDNS server?

    A. Windows 95.

    B. Windows 3.11.

    C. Windows 98.

    D. Windows 2000.

12. Which file does a DNS zone root server on your intranet use to resolve host names on the Internet?

    A. cache.dns

    B. domain.dns

    C. HOSTS.dns

    D. place.in-addr.arpa

13. How can you make non-Microsoft TCP/IP clients use WINS to resolve NetBIOS names?

    A. Enable the DHCP server to resolve FQDNs.

    B. Enable the DNS server to use the WINS server for name resolution.

    C. Under name resolution on the client computer, list DNS first, then SMTP.

    D. Under name resolution on the client computer, list SNMP first, then DNS.

14. Your UNIX Hosts cannot resolve NetBIOS names of computers on remote subnets. How could you configure DNS to aid non-WINS hosts to resolve NetBIOS names?

    A. Install a WinProxy Relay Unit.

    B. Configure the DNS server for WINS forwarding.

    C. Configure DNS for NetBIOS broadcast interception mode.

15. You have just installed the DNS service on a Windows 2000 server computer. You need to add a resource record for your domain's mail server. Which resource record must you add?

    A. CNAME

    B. MX

    C. PTR

    D. WKS

MICROSOFT CERTIFIED SYSTEMS ENGINEER

23

WINS
Networking

T his chapter examines the features of the Windows Internet Naming Service (WINS) server provided with Windows 2000. It teaches the fundamentals of providing name resolution with WINS, while providing considerations to use when implementing WINS in different environments. Finally, this chapter presents advice relating to the ongoing management of a WINS network.

HEADSTART OBJECTIVE 23.01

The Role of WINS in an Enterprise Network

WINS is a NetBIOS Name Server (NBNS) that provides NetBIOS (Network Basic Input/Output System) name resolution to workstations and servers running Windows NT or Windows 9x. Microsoft's goal is to phase out NetBIOS, which will lead to the decommissioning of WINS servers. However, WINS is still required on networks that must support down-level clients, such as those running Windows 3.x, Windows 9x, and Windows NT. In Windows 2000, the Dynamic Domain Naming System (DNS) replaces WINS as the primary standard method of name resolution. This chapter covers much of the material found in the Windows NT 4.0 exams; however, the Windows 2000 exam will focus primarily on the new features and the understanding of when to use WINS as opposed to Dynamic DNS.

WINS is based on the Requests for Comments (RFC) standards for a NetBIOS Name Server: 1001 and 1002. These standards define the specific requirements of an NBNS, and detail the NetBIOS name resolution process. The resolution process, or the method in which a machine resolves an IP address, is discussed in the next section.

NetBIOS and WINS Basics

NetBIOS provides a standard interface by which applications can communicate with a variety of network protocols (e.g., TCP/IP). It is used heavily in Windows NT, and used only for down-level support in Windows 2000. The NetBIOS standard was designed to maximize efficiency on PC networks, on which computers are constantly being brought online and taken offline without any notification, by eliminating or centralizing as much of the administrative overhead as possible.

A common misconception is that NetBIOS relies on NetBEUI, a protocol supported by Windows operating systems. In fact, NetBIOS can function with any protocol, and does not require that NetBEUI be installed on the server at all.

The NetBIOS Naming Standard

All networked Windows computers, including Windows 3.*x*, Windows 95, and Windows NT, must be assigned a NetBIOS name, which is the computer name assigned to that workstation or server. The name can be up to 15 characters in length, and must be unique on the network.

Unlike DNS, which uses a hierarchical namespace, NetBIOS uses a flat namespace. This means that all NetBIOS names consist of a single part. This is different from DNS, in which names are fully qualified in a *name.domain.domain* format.

The NetBIOS Naming Standard actually allows for a 16-character name. In Windows networking, the 16th character of a NetBIOS name is a hexadecimal value that is automatically appended to the name based on the type of registration. This is known as the *identifier byte.* When a WINS entry is stored, the gap between the computer name and the identifier byte is padded with spaces; however, most WINS views will not display this gap. Table 23-1 shows some of the common identifier bytes, and their designations.

Advantages of WINS

WINS serves as a central database for NetBIOS names to IP address mappings. When a configured WINS client needs to look up a NetBIOS name, it can query the WINS server for the information. There are two other ways that a client can be configured to resolve a NetBIOS name:

- LMHOSTS File
- Local Broadcast

Identifier Byte	Designation
<00h>	Workstation or Workgroup
<1Ch>	Windows NT Domain Name
<1Bh>	Windows NT Domain Master Browser
<20h>	File Server
<03h>	Used by the Messenger service—can be a computer name or a user name
<1Fh>	Used by the NetDDE service
<06h>	A server providing Remote Access via RAS

LMHOSTS FILE   A workstation can be configured to use a local text file called LMHOSTS to resolve name to IP mappings. This file is located in the <System Root>\System32\Drivers\Etc folder, and follows a straightforward format. Refer to the LMHOSTS.SAM file in <System Root>\System32\Drivers\Etc folder for a complete description on the syntax used in the LMHOSTS file.

LMHOSTS files have inherent disadvantages in that they are located on each machine in the network and are static, not dynamic. This means that if a network relies solely on LMHOSTS files for NetBIOS name resolution, each file must be manually edited if an entry needs to be changed or added. When it comes time to update a resource mapping, it is usually not practical to have to touch every workstation and server in order to do so.

BROADCASTS   A workstation can also be configured to resolve NetBIOS names through a local broadcast. Broadcasts can lead to excessive network utilization, and are usually used after another resolution method fails.

WINS Name Resolution Process

The WINS Name Resolution Process refers to the steps involved with a client registering and removing its NetBIOS name and IP address with the WINS server, as well as the steps involved with the querying of the information of the WINS server to perform NetBIOS name queries. The name resolution process is divided into four main events:

- Name Registration
- Name Renewal
- Name Refresh
- Name Query

These events define the name resolution process, and are discussed in detail in the following sections.

Name Registration

The Name Registration request is the process by which a client registers its information with a WINS server. When a client boots, it sends a name registration request to the primary WINS server configured on the client. The request includes the client's IP address, the computer name, and information about specific NetBIOS services running on the machine. If the client receives a positive response, the name-to-IP address mapping is stored in the WINS database to be used by other clients when performing queries against the registered name. The registering client also receives a Time To Live (TTL) that sets the lease period for that name. When the TTL expires, the client must renew the lease. There are some circumstances in which the client can receive either a negative response or no response at all. This is due to either the server being unavailable, which will lead to no response from the server, or a duplicate name existing in the database, which will lead to a negative name registration response.

SERVER UNAVAILABLE   In the event that the WINS server to which a client is sending a name registration request is unavailable, the client will not receive a registration response. This may happen due to a server being offline, or a client being configured with the wrong IP address for the Primary WINS server. The client will try the name registration request a total of three times, and will then attempt to contact the Secondary WINS server for registration.

DUPLICATE ENTRY IN DATABASE   It is also possible that a client will attempt to register its name with a WINS server when an entry already exists with that same name. In this case, the WINS server sends a name query request to the client with the existing registration. The WINS server attempts this query request a total of three times. If the existing client fails to respond, the newly registering client receives a positive acknowledgement and the entry is updated with the new IP address. If the existing client does respond, the new client receives a negative acknowledgement, is not registered in the WINS database, and receives a "Duplicate Name on Network" error. Depending on the client used, this error message is either displayed on the screen (Windows 3.x, 9x) or logged to the Event Log (Windows NT, 2000).

Name Renewal

A Name Renewal occurs when a client first needs to renew its lease with WINS. In this process, the WINS client sends a *Name Refresh* request to the WINS server. A positive response from a WINS server results in the client receiving a new TTL, and the lease is renewed on the server.

The concept of Name Renewal is simple enough; however, the way in which a client renews its lease is unique. A client first attempts to contact the Primary WINS server to renew its lease when one-eighth of the TTL has expired. In most cases, the client receives a positive response at this point and the lease is renewed. In these cases, the client only uses one-eighth of its lease time before renewing.

If a client attempts to renew its lease but does not receive a response, it continues to attempt to contact the Primary WINS server every *N* time increments (where *N* is one-eighth the TTL) until a response is received or the lease expires. Then, if half the TTL expires, the client switches over to the Secondary WINS server. The client sends Name Refresh requests to the secondary server every two minutes, until half the TTL is expired again. At that point, the client switches back to the Primary WINS server.

The initial TTL of a WINS client is 16 minutes. Therefore, a WINS client first attempts to send a Name Refresh request after only two minutes. The interval for subsequent name refreshes is defined by the Renewal Interval setting defined on the WINS server. The default Replication

[Handwritten margin notes: Default Replication = 6 Days Interval. Def Refresh = 18 hours Request.]

Interval for a WINS server is six days (144 hours), so by default a WINS client sends Name Refresh requests every 18 hours (one-eighth of 144).

With this process of continually attempting to renew a lease, it is unusual for a client to be unsuccessful with a lease renewal. The only time that this may occur is if there is a network outage that lasts longer than half the defined lease period, which is unlikely when long lease periods are configured on the WINS server.

Name Release

When a WINS client is correctly shut down, it sends a Name Release request to the WINS server. This request includes the name and IP address, and notifies the WINS server to remove the mapping entry from the database. The WINS server sends a positive acknowledgement if the removal is successful. A negative acknowledgement is only received if the entry doesn't exist. The client ignores the response to a name release, however, so a negative response does not prevent the client from shutting down.

Name Query

A WINS client initiates the Name Query process when it needs to communicate with a WINS server to determine the IP address of the client (the name query occurs when a client needs to talk to another node). The client sends the NetBIOS name that it is attempting to find to the WINS server. The WINS server responds with the IP address if it exists in the database. If the Primary WINS server does not respond after three attempts, the client attempts to contact the Secondary WINS server. If all WINS servers fail to resolve, the client uses another method to resolve the name, usually a broadcast. Before attempting to resolve a NetBIOS name in any other manner, a client always checks its local NetBIOS Name Cache to see if the mapping is there.

The order of the resolution methods is defined by the client's *node type*. The various node types are as follows:

■ Broadcast (B-Node)

■ Point-to-Point (P-Node)

- Hybrid (H-Node)
- Mixed Mode (M-Node)

The illustrations in the following sections depict only the standard NetBIOS lookup methods. In the full NetBIOS resolution process, HOSTS and DNS are also queried after the standard resolution process takes place.

The complete order of NetBIOS name resolution on an H-Node client can easily be remembered using the phrase, "Can We Buy Large Hard Drives?"

NetBIOS Name **C**ache
WINS
Broadcast
LMHOSTS
HOSTS
DNS

BROADCAST NODE   The Broadcast Node, or B-Node, uses broadcasts as the primary method of resolving a NetBIOS name. This is the most simplistic node type, as a WINS server is not required. The B-Node client sends a name query to the broadcast address, and any client with the requested name responds to the broadcast. This process is shown in Figure 23-1. The inherent disadvantage of using B-Node on large networks is the network utilization overhead involved. Since a WINS server is not being queried, each client must analyze every name query request to determine whether to send a response.

POINT-TO-POINT NODE   The Point-to-Point Node, or P-Node, resolution type uses the WINS server as the method for resolving a NetBIOS name, as shown in Figure 23-2. P-Node is generally used when the administrator wants to entirely eliminate NetBIOS-related broadcast traffic from the network. The disadvantage of using P-Node is that is does not make allowances for when WINS is unable to resolve the name (i.e., when the server is unavailable), because it does not use broadcasts at all.

FIGURE 23-1

The B-Node
resolution process

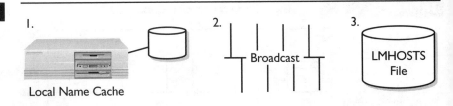

MIXED NODE   The Mixed Node, or M-Node, resolution method
(shown in Figure 23-3) uses a combination of the B-Node and P-Node
methods detailed earlier. A client configured to use M-Node first attempts
to find a workstation using a broadcast and if it does not receive a positive
name query response, it then sends a name query request to the Primary
WINS server. This node type is generally not used in large local networks
due to the network traffic generated by a NetBIOS query broadcast.

M-Node is often useful on enterprise networks in which there are
multiple locations with a domain controller at each. Using M-Node, a
client first searches the local subnet for a Domain Controller before
querying WINS. If a client queries WINS first, it may be given a Domain
Controller in a completely different location, thereby eliminating the
benefit of having local Domain Controllers.

HYBRID NODE   The Hybrid Node, or H-Node, is the default node
type on a WINS client. H-Node, like M-Node, uses both broadcasts and
WINS server queries to resolve a NetBIOS name. H-Node simply performs
broadcasts and WINS server queries in the reverse order of the M-Node
type, by first querying the WINS server and then using broadcasts if it gets
a negative response or no response from WINS. The H-Node resolution
process is depicted in Figure 23-4.

**DETERMINING AND CONFIGURING A CLIENT'S NODE
TYPE**   To determine which node type a specific client is using, the
ipconfig /all | more command can be issued from the local Windows 2000

FIGURE 23-2

The P-Node
resolution process

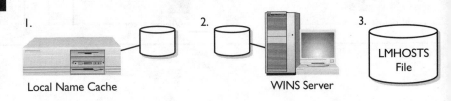

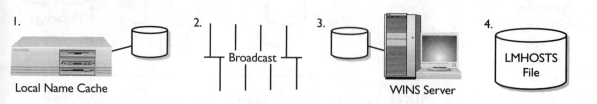

FIGURE 23-3   The M-Node resolution process

Command Prompt. The IP configuration of the computer will be displayed, and will contain a line similar to the following:

Node Type . . . . : Hybrid

A client's node type can be modified on a local workstation by changing the NodeType registry value to the appropriate value based on the listings in Table 23-2. The registry change is made in the following location on workstations running NetBIOS over TCP/IP (NetBT):

HKEY_LOCAL_MACHINE\SYSTEM\CurrentControlSet\Services\ NetBT\Parameters.

WARNING: Incorrectly using the Registry Editor to directly modify the registry can cause serious problems that may require reinstallation of the operating system. Modify the registry at your own risk, and do so only after creating a current Emergency Repair Disk (ERD).

FIGURE 23-4   The H-Node resolution process

ACCELERATING TO WINDOWS 2000

Windows Internet Naming Service (WINS) in Windows 2000 introduces a number of new features and improvements over the previous WINS service found in Windows NT 4.0. Some of the most notable improvements and additions are

- Manual tombstoning
- Improved search and filter capabilities
- Persistent connections between replication partners
- Database export function
- Ability to specify multiple WINS servers on a client

Manual Tombstoning

Tombstoning in WINS refers to the marking of an entry for deletion. In earlier versions of WINS, tombstoning did not always function correctly when replication was involved. This has been addressed in Windows 2000, and the administrator now has the ability to manually tombstone a record instead of simply deleting it.

Improved Search and Filter

To put to rest a common complaint by network administrators, WINS in Windows 2000 allows you to find a specific record without having to scroll through the entire WINS database, which was a painful process on large networks. This "quick find" feature allows the administrator to specify just the first few letters and WINS will return all the results beginning with the specified string. This can be useful on a network on which the first few letters of the computer name designate a location or department, to return all records with the specified designation.

Filtering can also be used against a WINS database to view only records of a specific type. For example, you can enable a filter that will display only the <1Ch> entries in the database, which will show only the Windows NT domain names that are registered with WINS.

Persistent Connections between Replication Partners

In Windows 2000, administrators have the ability to allow replication partners to maintain persistent connections with one another. This is different from earlier WINS versions in which a connection had to be reestablished every time replication was to take place. The ability for replication partners to maintain persistent connections eliminates the network and processor overhead involved in

ACCELERATING TO WINDOWS 2000

reestablishing a connection, resulting in faster replication performance.

Database Export Function

The new console-based WINS manager provides the ability to export the WINS database to a comma-delimited (CSV) file. This file can then be opened in Excel or imported into a database, such as Access or SQL Server Desktop Edition, to facilitate greater querying and reporting capabilities.

Ability to Specify Multiple WINS Servers

The ability to configure a client with the IP addresses of multiple WINS servers is new to Windows NT users, but was also implemented in Windows 98. In Windows NT 4.0 and Windows 95, only a Primary WINS server and Secondary WINS server could be configured. Windows 2000 introduces the ability to specify up to 12 WINS servers to allow for increased fault tolerance. If both the Primary and Secondary WINS servers fail to resolve a name query, the request is sent to the additional servers in order.

HEADSTART OBJECTIVE 23.02

Developing a WINS Implementation Strategy

To be successful with a WINS implementation, you must first determine the strategy. This includes the understanding of when to use WINS, how to install WINS, and knowledge of how replication should be configured. A

TABLE 23-2

Node Type Registry Values

NodeType Registry Value	Node Type
REG_DWORD: 0x1	Broadcast Node (B-Node)
REG_DWORD: 0x2	Point-to-Point Node (P-Node)
REG_DWORD: 0x4	Mixed Node (M-Node)
REG_DWORD: 0x8	Hybrid Node (H-Node)

WINS implementation strategy must also make considerations for static mappings and WINS proxy agents.

Deciding Whether to Implement WINS

A WINS server must be configured for any network running down-level clients (Windows NT 4.0 or Windows 9*x*) that are configured to use WINS for NetBIOS name resolution. A WINS server is *not* required when a network consists only of Windows 2000 clients, or clients configured to use only the B-Node resolution method. In an all-Windows 2000 network, WINS is not needed and only DNS is required.

On a native Windows 2000 network, Windows 2000 clients can register with a Dynamic DNS server. This differs from Windows NT 4.0, in which only WINS could manage dynamic name to IP address mappings, and DNS entries had to be manually added.

heads
⊕p

Throughout Windows 2000, you will see fields that allow you to specify a NetBIOS name for an object (i.e., a computer or domain). These names are registered with WINS, and are required by WINS clients that do not use DNS for most Windows networking functions (such as querying for a domain controller).

Developing a Replication Strategy

When multiple WINS servers are configured on a network, it is often desired that servers maintain the same information. That is, if a client registers on one server but another client queries a different server for the name, a positive response will be sent. The technology used to maintain consistent databases between multiple WINS servers is called *WINS Replication*.

Replication Modes

Replication occurs between two WINS servers when either the defined Replication Interval expires, or when the Update Count Threshold limit is exceeded. The Replication Interval specifies the maximum amount of time that can pass between replications. This timer is reset whenever replication occurs, regardless of why it occurs. The Update Count Threshold sets the maximum number of changes that can be made to the database before replication occurs.

Table 23-3 discusses the two methods by which replication can be configured on a WINS server. A single WINS server can use either or both of these modes to replicate with its partner. WINS servers that use both replication methods are known as *Push/Pull partners*.

Considerations for WANs

Managing WINS replication effectively on a routed network is critical. If a Replication Interval or threshold is set too low when replication is occurring on a slow WAN link, replication may potentially use all of the network bandwidth the majority of the time.

As a general rule, use shorter Replication Intervals and thresholds on fast WAN links and local networks, and use longer Replication Intervals and thresholds on slow WAN links.

The Replication Intervals that you choose should also be based on what is considered acceptable time for a WINS registration to be propagated to all WINS servers on a network. The time it takes for an entry addition or modification to be replicated to all WINS servers on the network is known as the *convergence time*. The convergence time is the sum of all of the Replication Intervals. In reality, replication of an entry usually occurs long before the convergence time—the convergence time is simply the maximum time it may take.

TABLE 23-3	Replication Mode	Description
Push and Pull Replication	Push Replication	A WINS server is configured to "push" database changes to its partner when the Update Count Threshold limit is exceeded or replication is manually initiated by the administrator.
	Pull Replication	A WINS server is configured to "pull" entries with a higher version ID from its WINS partner when the specified time interval is reached or replication is manually initiated by the administrator.

In Figure 23-5, a client is registering with WINS server 1. WINS server 1 is a push/pull partner with WINS server 2 with a Replication Interval of 30 minutes. WINS server 3 is a pull partner of WINS server 2, with a Replication Interval of twice per day.

In this example, the convergence time would be 12 hours 30 minutes, the sum of both Replication Intervals.

Replication Models

There are many ways to configure WINS replication in a network spanning multiple locations. The most common replication models are the Central Replication Model and the Chained Replication Model.

THE CENTRAL REPLICATION MODEL The Central Replication Model is usually the most practical means of implementing WINS replication. This model works best in networks that have a single "hub" location, to which other sites have a direct link. The Central Replication Model is less susceptible to database inconsistencies or high convergence times, since a single server propagates changes to all other servers on the WAN. An example of the Central Replication Model is shown in Figure 23-6.

THE CHAINED REPLICATION MODEL The Chained Replication Model is used on networks that are designed in a linear layout,

| FIGURE 23-5 | Example of WINS Replication Intervals |

Atlanta, GA	Atlanta, GA	London, England
WINS Server 1	WINS Server 2	WINS Server 3
Local Link 30 Minute interval Push/Pull Replication	Slow WAN Link Replicates twice daily Server 3 Pull Replication	

FIGURE 23-6

An example of the Central
Replication Model

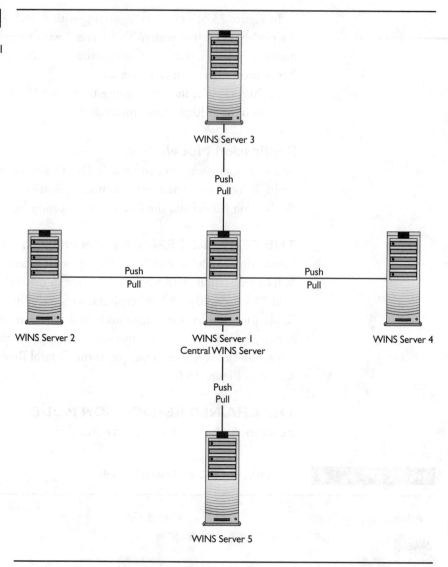

WINS Server 3

Push
Pull

WINS Server 2   Push
Pull   WINS Server 1
Central WINS Server   Push
Pull   WINS Server 4

Push
Pull

WINS Server 5

where it is practical for a server to pass replication to other servers in a
chained manner. In Chained Replication Models, the servers at both ends
of the chain should be push/pull partners with one another to ensure
consistency. The Chained Replication Model is shown in Figure 23-7.

The following are sample scenarios for implementing WINS replication.

QUESTIONS AND ANSWERS

There are three locations all linked to one another via 56K WAN links.	Implement a longer Replication Interval, such as once or twice per day.
WINS servers at 15 locations are all connected by WAN to the corporate office.	Implement a Central Replication Model, with replication occurring between the central office and all other WINS servers on the WAN.
There are four locations, each chained with T1 connections.	Implement the Chained Replication Model, and ensure that the locations at each end of the chain are push/pull partners.
A low convergence time is essential on the corporate high-speed WAN.	Implement a low Replication Interval, such as every 15 minutes, depending on the acceptable convergence time. Consider central replication, depending on the WAN topology.

Installing WINS

Before you can begin configuring clients to use WINS to resolve NetBIOS names, you must configure a Windows NT or Windows 2000 server as a WINS server. In Windows 2000, WINS is installed using the Windows Components Wizard, as shown in Figure 23-8. The exercise in this section

FIGURE 23-7   An example of the Chained Replication Model

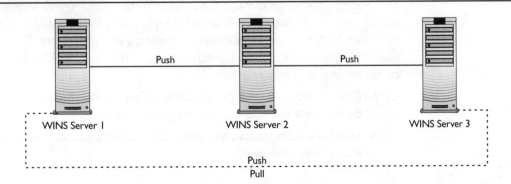

FIGURE 23-8

Installing the WINS Service

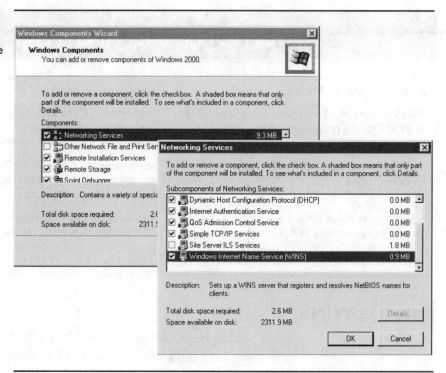

focuses on installing the WINS Server service on a Windows 2000 server computer.

EXERCISE 23-1

Installing WINS Server

This exercise takes you through the steps of installing the WINS Server service on your Windows 2000 server computer. You will need the Windows 2000 Server CD to complete the steps in this exercise. This exercise requires that you be logged on to your Windows 2000 server computer as a local administrator.

1. Open Control Panel (Start | Settings | Control Panel) and double-click the Add/Remove Programs applet.

2. Select the Add/Remove Windows Components button in the left area of the window.

3. Click Components.

4. Select Network Services from the list and click Details.

5. Select the check box next to Windows Internet Name Service (WINS) and click OK. If this check box is already enabled, you may skip to the end of this exercise.

6. Click Next in the Windows Components Wizard window. If you have Terminal Services installed, a window will appear prompting for the Terminal Services mode. Leave the default, and click Next.

7. The Configuring Components window will appear with a progress bar, and may remain for a few minutes.

8. Click Finish after you have successfully completed the component configuration.

WINS Proxy Agents

A WINS Proxy Agent is a client computer configured to accept broadcast NetBIOS name queries and then query the WINS server for the information. When a non-WINS client (such as B-Node or UNIX) sends a NetBIOS name request to the broadcast address, the WINS Proxy Agent checks its local name cache for the information and, if the entry is there, sends a response back to the requesting client. If the name is not in the name cache, the Proxy Agent queries the WINS server and, assuming it gets a positive response, it then stores the name in its local name cache for subsequent name query broadcasts. WINS Proxy Agents are used when there is no local WINS server, and a B-Node client needs to resolve mappings stored in a remote WINS server. A WINS Proxy Agent is not required in situations where broadcasts are being routed (usually not recommended), or when clients are directly communicating with a WINS server for name query requests.

The WINS Proxy Agent can be enabled on a WINS client by creating a registry value called EnableProxy and setting it to REG_DWORD: 1. The EnableProxy value is stored in the following registry path:

HKEY_LOCAL_MACHINE\SYSTEM\CurrentControlSet\ Services\Netbt\Parameters

Static Mappings

While WINS clients register their names and IP addresses with the WINS server for other clients to resolve, it may be necessary for WINS clients to resolve NetBIOS names for clients that are not registered with the same WINS server or are not using WINS name registration at all. This is accomplished by adding static mappings to the WINS database.

A new static mapping is added to the WINS database by right-clicking Active Registrations in the WINS console, and selecting New Static Mapping, as shown in Figure 23-9.

A few different types of static mappings may be added to the WINS database, each serving a different purpose. The types of static mappings are detailed in Table 23-4.

Adding a static mapping to the WINS database

New Static Mapping

General

Static Mapping

You can add static name-to-address mappings to the WINS database, but only for computers that cannot register dynamically in WINS. Static mappings can replicate throughout your WINS environment and write over records on other servers.

Computer name:

NetBIOS scope (optional):

Type: Unique

Unique
Group
Domain Name
Internet Group
Multihomed

IP address:

OK   Cancel   Apply

TABLE 23-4	Static Mapping Type	Description
Types of Static Mappings	Unique	A single NetBIOS name registration with a single IP address (most common).
	Group	A group of multiple machines, each with its own IP address. A group can store an unlimited number of machines. A client communicates with group members by using broadcast packets.
	Domain Name	An entry for a Windows NT domain name. This static entry type can be an array of multiple IP addresses, one for each primary or backup domain controller on the domain. These entries are created with a <1Ch> identifier byte.
	Internet Group	An Internet Group mapping is similar to a Group mapping; however, it is limited to only 25 members. Internet Groups are used to group resources, such as printers, to facilitate easier browsing. Internet Group entries are stored with a <20h> identifier byte.
	Multihomed	A multihomed entry must be created for a computer if the computer has multiple network cards. This enables WINS to recognize all IP addresses as a single computer, and not duplicate entries. A multihomed entry can have up to 25 IP addresses.

on the
job

In general, try to keep the number of static mapping in a WINS database to a minimum. Static mappings often involve a great deal of administrative overhead, and can cause additional hassle in the event that a database must be rebuilt.

HEADSTART OBJECTIVE 23.03

Developing a WINS Management Strategy

Once WINS is implemented on a network, it must be effectively managed to avoid potential problems with the database or loss of information due to a failure. This section teaches you how to administer WINS, back up the WINS database, initiate scavenging, and examine WINS server statistics.

Backing Up and Restoring the WINS Database

It is a good idea to make frequent backups of the WINS database. This is especially important if you have many static mappings in your database that are not documented elsewhere.

The following two exercises step you through backing up and restoring the WINS database.

EXERCISE 23-2

Backing Up the WINS Database

This exercise requires that you are running a Windows 2000 Server computer with the WINS service installed, and that you are logged on as a local administrator.

1. Open the Computer Management Console by right-clicking My Computer and selecting Manage.

2. Expand Services and Applications and select WINS.

3. From the Action menu, select Back Up Database.

4. Make sure that the root C:\ folder is selected for the backup destination, and click OK.

5. You should receive a message stating, "The database backup was completed successfully."

6. To verify that the WINS backup performed in the previous steps was completed successfully, open Windows Explorer and verify that the C:\Wins_bak folder exists with a subfolder called "New." If the directory structure does not exist, repeat the exercise and verify that the correct destination is chosen and that the backup completes successfully.

EXERCISE 23-3

Restoring the WINS Database Backup

1. Stop the WINS Service by right-clicking WINS in the Computer Management Console, and selecting All Tasks | Stop. You will receive a message saying "Attempting to stop the Windows Internet Name Service (WINS) service on computer <computer name>."

2. Verify that WINS is selected in the Computer Management Console, and select Restore Database from the Action menu.

3. Make sure the default path of C:\ is selected, and click OK.

4. The WINS service will start up, and you will receive a message saying "The database restore was completed successfully."

heads
⓵p

Remember, you must stop the WINS Service on a server prior to attempting to restore a database backup. Database backups can, however, be performed with WINS running.

Database Scavenging

Database Scavenging refers to the process of "cleaning" the WINS database; that is, either deleting or tombstoning entries for which specific intervals have expired.

EXERCISE 23-4

Manually Initiating Database Scavenging

1. Right-click My Computer and select Manage to open the Computer Management Console.

2. Expand Services and Applications and select WINS.

3. From the Action menu, select Scavenge Database. A message will appear informing you that the scavenge request has been queued. Click OK.

4. Open the Windows Event Log from Start | Programs | Administrative Tools | Event Viewer.

5. Select the System Event Log.

6. Verify that a 4328 event exists, indicating that the Database Scavenging operation was initiated. You may need to refresh the log using the F5 key.

Analyzing WINS Statistics

The WINS Service in Windows 2000 gathers statistics on most events that happen, including registration and query events, as well as the times of database events. The statistics window for the WINS Service is shown in Figure 23-10.

FIGURE 23-10

The WINS
Statistics window

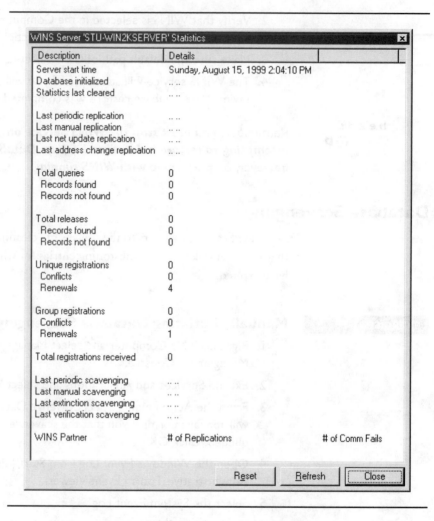

The statistics collected by WINS are often useful when attempting to troubleshoot a problem with the WINS server. Statistics are available on a WINS server by right-clicking WINS in the Computer Management Console, and selecting Display Server Statistics. Table 23-5 examines each individual WINS statistic in detail.

TABLE 23-5	Statistic Name	Information Provided
WINS Server Statistics	Server Start Time	Displays the Date and Time the WINS Service was last started
	Database Initialized	Displays the Date and Time that static mappings were last imported into the database
	Statistics Last Cleared	The Date and Time that WINS statistics were last cleared by clicking Reset in the WINS statistics window
	Last Periodic Replication	The last time replication was initiated due to the defined Replication Interval being reached
	Last Manual Replication	The last time WINS replication was manually initiated
	Last Net Update Replication	The last time WINS replication was initiated by a network request
	Last Address Change Replication	The last time WINS replication was initiated due to the number of changes in the version ID being reached
	Total Queries: Records Found	Total positive responses returned to name query requests since statistics were last cleared
	Total Queries: Records Not Found	Total negative responses returned to name query requests since statistics were last cleared
	Total Releases: Records Found	Total release attempts where the record was found in the database
	Total Releases: Records Not Found	Total release attempts where the record was not found in the database
	Unique Registrations: Conflicts	The number of client attempts to register a name that already existed in the database
	Unique Registrations: Renewals	The number of unique name registration renewals

TABLE 23-5

WINS Server Statistics
(continued)

Statistic Name	Information Provided
Group Registrations: Conflicts	Similar to Unique Conflicts, the number of conflicts occurred for Group registration types
Group Registrations: Renewals	The number of group name registration renewals
Total Registrations Received	The total number of name registrations
Last Periodic Scavenging	The Date and Time that the database was last scavenged due to the renewal interval being reached
Last Manual Scavenging	The last time database scavenging was initiated by an administrator by selecting Scavenge in the console
Last Extinction Scavenging	The Date and Time that the database was last scavenged due to the extinction interval being reached
Last Verification Scavenging	The Date and Time that the database was last scavenged due to the verification interval being reached

CHAPTER SUMMARY

WINS provides a means for down-level clients such as Windows NT 4.0 and Windows 9*x* workstations to resolve NetBIOS names to IP addresses. A NetBIOS name query can be performed a number of ways, including broadcast, LMHOSTS lookup, and WINS query.

WINS Replication is the technology by which database changes are propagated to other WINS servers on the network, and can be implemented using either or both Push and Pull mechanisms. Replication can be configured in different models, including the Central and Chained models.

Maintaining a WINS server includes routine backups and scavenging of the database, as well as the knowledge of how to analyze WINS statistics to assist with troubleshooting or general performance analysis.

✓ TWO-MINUTE DRILL

- ❏ WINS is a NetBIOS Name Server (NBNS) that provides NetBIOS (Network Basic Input/Output System) name resolution to workstations and servers running Windows NT or Windows 9x.

- ❏ NetBIOS provides a standard interface by which applications can communicate with a variety of network protocols (e.g., TCP/IP).

- ❏ All networked Windows computers, including Windows 3.x, Windows 95, and Windows NT, must be assigned a NetBIOS name, which is the computer name assigned to that workstation or server

- ❏ The WINS Name Resolution Process refers to the steps involved with a client registering and removing its NetBIOS name and IP address with the WINS server, as well as the steps involved with the querying of the information of the WINS server to perform NetBIOS name queries.

- ❏ The Name Registration request is the process by which a client registers its information with a WINS server.

- ❏ When a WINS client is correctly shut down, it sends a Name Release request to the WINS server.

- ❏ The Broadcast Node, or B-Node, uses broadcasts as the primary method of resolving a NetBIOS name.

- ❏ The Hybrid Node, or H-Node, is the default node type on a WINS client.

- ❏ When multiple WINS servers are configured on a network, it is often desired that servers maintain the same information.

- ❏ The Central Replication Model is usually the most practical means of implementing WINS replication.

- ❏ A WINS Proxy Agent is a client computer configured to accept broadcast NetBIOS name queries and then query the WINS server for the information.

SELF TEST

The following questions will help you measure your understanding of the material presented in this chapter. Read all of the choices carefully, as there may be more than one correct answer. Choose all correct answers for each question.

1. Which of the following clients can register their NetBIOS name with WINS? (Choose all that apply.)

   A. Windows 98

   B. Windows NT 4.0

   C. Windows 2000

   D. UNIX

2. What is the length of a NetBIOS name?

   A. 13 characters

   B. 15 characters

   C. 16 characters

   D. 23 characters

3. What identifier byte is used to designate a Windows NT domain name?

   A. <1Bh>

   B. <1Ch>

   C. <1Dh>

   D. <1Eh>

4. Where is the LMHOSTS file stored?

   A. <System Root>\System32

   B. <System Root>\System32\WINS

   C. <System Root>\ System32\Drivers\TCPIP

   D. <System Root>\System32\Drivers\Etc

5. Which step of the name resolution process is initiated when a WINS client shuts down?

   A. Name Query

   B. Name Release

   C. Name Removal

   D. Name Tombstone

6. A WINS client is configured to access a primary and secondary WINS server, and is using the M-Node type. An attempt to resolve a name results in no response. After querying the Primary WINS server, which will the client next attempt for a resolution response?

   A. The Secondary WINS server

   B. The LMHOSTS file

   C. A Local Broadcast

   D. The Local Name Cache

7. Using a default configuration, after how long will a WINS client first attempt to renew its lease?

   A. 2 minutes

   B. 16 minutes

   C. 18 hours

   D. 6 days

8. Which of the following shows the complete order of the NetBIOS Name Resolution process on an H-Node system?

A. Local Name Cache, LMHOSTS File, Broadcast, DNS, HOSTS, WINS

B. Local Name Cache, WINS, Broadcast, LMHOSTS, HOSTS, DNS

C. Local Name Cache, LMHOSTS, HOSTS, WINS, Broadcast, DNS

D. Local Name Cache, Broadcast, WINS, DNS, HOSTS, LMHOSTS File

9. What is the easiest way to determine the Node Type of the local client?

A. The NodeType value in the Registry

B. By issuing the ipconfig /all | more command from a command prompt

C. In Network | TCP/IP Properties

D. Viewing the entry's properties in WINS

10. Server A, Server B, and Server C are all WINS servers configured for replication. Server A is a Push/Pull partner of Server B with a 30-minute replication interval, and Server B is a push replication partner of Server C with a 15-minute replication interval. What is the convergence time for replication?

A. 15 minutes

B. 30 minutes

C. 45 minutes

D. 60 minutes

11. A server in Columbus, OH pushes database changes to servers in Newark, NJ, Boston, MA, and Atlanta, GA. Which replication model is implemented on this network?

A. Central Replication

B. Chained Replication

C. Pull Replication

D. Push Replication

12. The WINS Proxy Agent is used primarily to assist which of the following clients with name resolution?

A. B-Node

B. P-Node

C. M-Node

D. H-Node

13. For which type of client would you configure a multihomed entry?

A. A mobile user

B. A server with multiple names

C. A server with multiple network interfaces

D. A server acting as a Windows NT domain controller

14. You are attempting to restore a WINS database backup to a WINS server; however, the Restore Database option in the Action menu is grayed out. What is the most likely cause for not being able to select the Restore option?

A. A backup has not been performed on this server.

B. The backup files are missing from the WINS directory.

C. The user logged on does not have the appropriate permissions.

D. The WINS service has not been stopped.

15. As an administrator of a WINS server, you want to determine the total number of queries that have been attempted against the database that have returned negative responses. Which of the following statistics will you use?

A. Total Releases: Records Not Found
B. Total Queries: Records Not Found
C. Unique Registrations: Conflicts
D. Name Queries: Negative Responses

MICROSOFT CERTIFIED SYSTEMS ENGINEER

24

RAS and RADIUS Networking

A s organizations and users become more versatile, the ability to move around and still access network resources becomes more of a necessity than a convenience. Sales consultants need direct access to up-to-date company information such as current price and items in stock. Executives require the ability to check e-mail and stock information via a remote connection. Home users wish to access Internet services such as online banking and research information. These are only a few of the countless scenarios in which remote access is used today.

As networks and services become more sophisticated, additional security and reduced administrative overhead are both required to maintain a lower cost of ownership within any organization. Windows 2000 meets and exceeds these requirements by providing a robust and extremely versatile Remote Access Service (RAS). In addition, RADIUS services have also been added to provide a secure and efficient authentication method to meet the industry's growing security concerns. This architecture offers a scalable, reliable infrastructure to support the needs of large organizations to provide secure remote access services.

HEADSTART OBJECTIVE 24.01

The Role of RAS in an Enterprise Network

In any enterprise network, RAS servers are becoming more commonplace every day. These services have been built into Windows 2000 as part of the Routing and Remote Access components to provide seamless network integration. Services are available both for servers and clients to set up remote solutions such as Internet gateways, Virtual Private Network (VPN) gateways, or remote dial-up servers.

RAS servers are used to provide network services as if a user was physically attached. For example, when a user is out of town, he or she may dial into a RAS server and, once attached, access network applications. E-mail is a very common example of a network application that is used in this manner. Other examples include internal Web services or file and print services. Even network drive mappings that are used while in the office can be accessed as if the computer is on the local network. This provides an incredible level of flexibility for users to move around and still be able to access the resources they require.

Developing a RAS Implementation Strategy

When implementing RAS, you must fully understand the various configuration options and the overall architecture. With Windows 2000, many new features and options have been added to provide a scalable remote access solution. In addition to several remote access protocols that are supported, various connections types ranging from VPN hosts to servers acting as network routers can be configured. RAS servers can be configured for client dial-up access or to provide secure communication channels between servers. You must also understand the strategies involved in managing a remote access solution. All of these factors play a critical role in effectively implementing and maintaining Windows 2000 RAS servers.

RAS Protocol Support and Connection Types

RAS in Windows 2000 supports various connection types and protocols. Each is an important consideration when creating a RAS implementation strategy. Protocols are used as a communication language when exchanging data between two computers. These are generally determined by the network protocol and operating systems of the client and host computers. For example, some protocols that are supported in Windows 2000 can only communicate with a specific Network layer protocol such as TCP/IP, while others provide greater flexibility.

Windows 2000 RAS supports three different types of protocols. The most commonly used is the Point-to-Point Protocol (PPP). This protocol is used so heavily because it is an industry standard protocol that is very versatile. PPP supports any combination of Network layer protocols, including TCP/IP, NetBEUI, and IPX/SPX, while the other supported RAS protocols are more dependent upon a single network protocol. This RAS protocol is currently widely used by organizations such as Internet Service Providers (ISPs) and corporations to provide low-cost, analog dial-in solutions for users, and is supported by Microsoft's newer operating systems, including Windows 95/98, Windows NT, and Windows 2000.

The next available protocol is the Serial Line Interface Protocol (SLIP). SLIP is an older protocol used primarily to connect to legacy UNIX systems. It was designed to work only with the TCP/IP network protocol and is not in use much in today's computing environments. Although Windows 2000-based clients maintain support for SLIP, Windows 2000 RAS servers do not support this as a remote access solution.

The last available protocol supported by Windows 2000 is Microsoft RAS. This is a proprietary protocol used in older versions of Windows based on the NetBIOS API. Clients connecting to the RAS server connect using NetBEUI (the network protocol), and the server provides a gateway to the network. These are found in older Microsoft clients, including Windows 3.1 and MS-DOS.

heads
TP

Be sure to know the remote access protocols that are available in Windows 2000, and the main uses of each one. Also, know the two connection types and how they are used.

Another factor with RAS includes the type of connections that are available. The two different connection types that can be used are Dial-Up Networking, or access through a VPN. Dial-Up Networking is used by a client to make a physical connection via a network such as the Public Switched Telephone System into a remote access server. For example, a user may use his or her home phone line to connect to an ISP to use services such as the Web or e-mail.

The second connection type available in Windows 2000 is VPN services. This is a virtual connection created over a network such as the Internet that is encrypted and secured. An example of a VPN connection may include a user dialing in to an ISP and then making a VPN connection using a special tunneling protocol into an internal company RAS Server. These are becoming common for organizations to provide an efficient, secure connection for corporate users to access resources within an intranet.

RAS Installation

To set up RAS, you must first verify that all communications hardware is installed and functioning properly. Hardware components may include items such as Network Interface Cards, ISDN modems, or analog modems. These devices are used to provide the physical network connection required to support network services, and are configured in the Device Manager. Device Manager is available by navigating to Start | Settings | Control Panel | System. Within the System applet, choose the Hardware tab and select Device Manager as shown in Figure 24-1.

FIGURE 24-1

The Device Manager is used to configure hardware components required for Remote Access Services

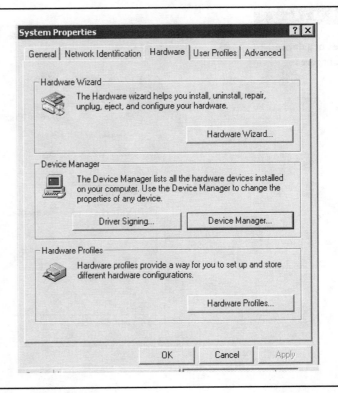

Once Device Manager has been selected, the hardware devices installed in the computer can be configured. By right-clicking a device, the properties can be displayed. As shown in Figure 24-2, a network interface card, or NIC, can be modified as required to meet the needs of the RAS server.

Once the appropriate devices are installed, you must configure the network protocols to be used. These will determine the RAS protocol that will be used to connect to other computers. Network protocols may include TCP/IP, IPX/SPX, or NetBEUI. These protocols must be set up appropriately on both the host and client computers to communicate correctly.

The next step is to activate and configure Routing and Remote Access. While this service is installed by default, it must be enabled in order to utilize its services. To configure Routing and Remote access, select Start |

FIGURE 24-2

Properties of a device can be configured

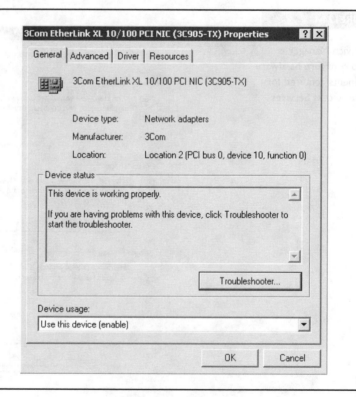

Programs | Administrative Tools | Routing and Remote Access. Next select the appropriate server, right-click the object, and select Configure and Enable Routing and Remote Access as shown in Figure 24-3.

Once selected, a Wizard dialog begins to configure the options for this server. Several configuration options are available, including an Internet Router, a VPN server, or a RAS Server. These options use various connection types and protocols types, and are displayed in Figure 24-4.

Once selected, follow the prompts for the configuration option selected, including configuring network protocols to use for remote access. Options will vary, depending upon the configuration selected. For example, the Internet connection server may prompt to install Internet Connection Sharing services (ICS); however, the manually configured server will immediately complete and will require configuration changes once installed. Once the Wizard has finished, the last step is to start the Routing and Remote Access server.

FIGURE 24-3

To start Routing and Remote Access, this option must be selected

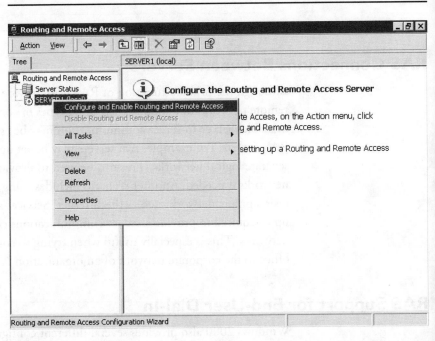

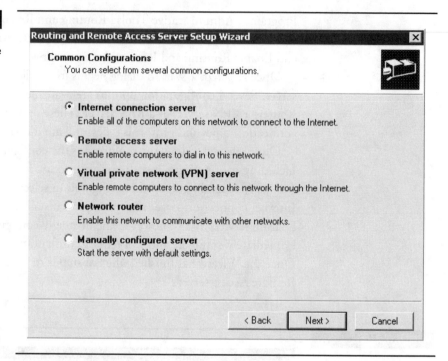

RAS Connections Between Servers

Although the primary function of RAS is to provide an interface to a
remote network for a mobile user, other types of configurations are
available. Server-to-server communication may be established by using
RAS Servers. For example, two servers may be set up as routers between two
separate logical networks. This can be used to provide a gateway between
networks if needed. Another scenario includes using two servers connected
over a public network such as the Internet. Services such as VPN can be set
up if required to provide a secure communications channel between two
networks. This is especially useful when trying to connect a secluded remote
office to the corporate network of an organization.

RAS Support for End-User Dial-In

Windows 2000 also provides several different configuration options for
Routing and RAS for end users. Included is the ability to set up a dial-up

server to allow users to access network resources as if they were local. A dial-up server is usually configured with a modem of some kind that is connected to a public network such as the Public Switched Telephone System. Users then use a modem from their current location to dial up the remote server over the telephone system. A connection is established over the public network, and resources are now available to the end user. Although this scenario has become the most common for RAS, with the new features and options available in Windows 2000, it provides the capability to do much more.

Developing a RAS Management Strategy

When implementing RAS servers, the management strategy for each server must be considered carefully. Two different methodologies can be used when managing RAS servers. First, the older manner of administration that was most commonly seen is distributed administration. This was based upon the idea that each server maintained its own account database and provided authentication on its own. Older versions of Microsoft Windows NT provided this level of service for remote access. Although this works in some organizations, growing businesses need the ability to manage these systems more effectively.

The second manner of administering these servers is by using a centralized database. Several different technologies have been created to meet this need, including the Remote Authentication Dial-In User Service (RADIUS). This allows an administrator to manage a single database of users that can handle hundreds of remote access servers. ISPs are a prime example of the type of organizations that require this level of functionality. A second advantage of a centralized administration model is the ability to provide multiple points of access to the network. For example, if a user normally dials in to the network from home, he or she would use a particular phone number. If that user went out of town, he or she would still have to dial this same number if the systems were distributed and not tied together. This would result in long-distance charges incurred by the user. Within a centralized environment, this would not happen. A user can dial in to the network using a local access point, thereby not incurring this additional expense. Therefore, the ability to dial in to different points of access within the network allows users to also use a local number and provides them with the flexibility to meet their needs without additional costs.

As new and upcoming technologies emerge that provide these abilities, they are becoming more common in remote access solutions. For example, Windows 2000 provides support for centralized administration by offering services such as RADIUS to allow this solution to meet the needs of growing enterprise customers.

HEADSTART OBJECTIVE 24.03

The Role of RADIUS in an Enterprise Network

As remote access grows in popularity and usage, the need for secure communications becomes more prevalent each day. Security and scalability are both ongoing issues that the computer industry must battle in every area. As users begin to rely more heavily on these services, new technologies are being developed to better the overall experience. RADIUS was created to meet these needs.

Developed by Lucent Technologies, RADIUS is a protocol used to provide secure authentication and accounting services for large-scale remote access networks. An authentication server uses the RADIUS protocol to provide a central point for multiple dial-up users to validate against within a network of distributed remote access servers. This allows the security and authentication process to be separated from the physical devices making the connection. In addition, it does not tie users to particular remote access servers. For example, a user may dial in to different remote access servers, depending upon his or her current location. RADIUS can be used to access a single secure database to authenticate the user against by allowing connections through various remote access servers. The physical device that is being used to connect the user only has to maintain the information required to authenticate the user against the database. This provides a scalable, secure solution, while not increasing the functionality for the end-user.

heads **⊕p**

Know what RADIUS is used for, along with its major benefits, including security and scalability.

Protocol Basis

When remote access servers authenticate users, a secure method is required for communicating with the authentication server. A special protocol known as RADIUS is used to verify that communications between these two servers are secure. The process by which RADIUS works is fairly simple.

A remote access server would be set up as a RADIUS client. It would then access an authentication and accounting server that would provide validation for the user logging on to the network. Windows 2000 includes a RADIUS client to allow the servers to be used in environments that depend upon this protocol to meet the business needs. Although RADIUS is used to communicate between the remote access server and a RADIUS host, the computer connecting to the remote access server must still use an authentication protocol that is understood by RADIUS services. Windows 2000 supports several different authentication protocols, including Extensible Authentication Protocol (EAP), Password Authentication Protocol (PAP), and Challenge Handshake and Response (CHAP). In addition, many different options are available, such as allowing multiple encryption types and forcing the most secure protocol to be used first. Each protocol has advantages over others, such as level of security, industry support, and ease of use. Understanding which protocols can be used is important to implementing the appropriate remote access solution when using RADIUS services.

Designing a RADIUS Implementation

When implementing RADIUS, several components must be considered prior to initial installation. The two components required for any RADIUS implementation are the client and host components. Windows 2000 includes the RADIUS client as part of its available remote access services. In addition, the Internet Authentication Service (IAS) has been included to provide RADIUS host capabilities. IAS provides the authentication, auditing, and accounting of RADIUS clients within Windows 2000. IAS also provides extensive management capability to the remote access services that already exist, as illustrated in Figure 24-5.

Figure 24-5 shows how the Internet Authentication Server fits into a remote access strategy. Selecting Network Services from the Add/Remove Control Panel applet is used to install IAS.

Address Management

When using RADIUS services, you must configure connections between RAS servers acting as clients and the Internet Authentication Server. Once a

FIGURE 24-5

The IAS server acts as the RADIUS host in this implementation

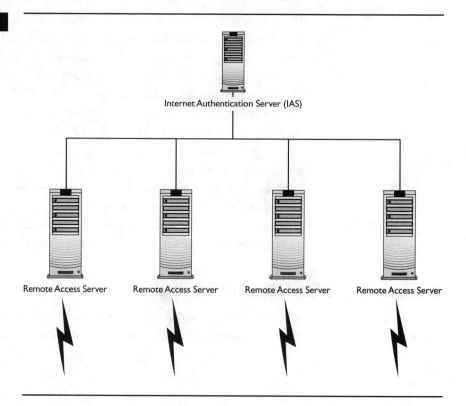

Internet Authentication Server (IAS)

Remote Access Server   Remote Access Server   Remote Access Server   Remote Access Server

client has been configured, authentication services will be used for remote access clients. One important part of configuring a client is address management. Several components must be configured correctly to enable RADIUS services through the IAS server. To start the client setup process, right-click the client's folder in the IAS management console and select New Client. A Wizard appears that walks you through the process of creating this client. You are prompted for the friendly name and protocol to use, as shown in Figure 24-6. RADIUS is selected for the protocol by default.

Enter the client name to use and click Next. The information that is requested next includes the client IP address or DNS name, the vendor of the client remote access server, and the shared secret information. The client IP address or DNS name is used to resolve the address of the client when communicating. The vendor of the client defines the remote access server that is being used, and the shared secret is used to verify secure encrypted

FIGURE 24-6

Enter the client name to use for this connection

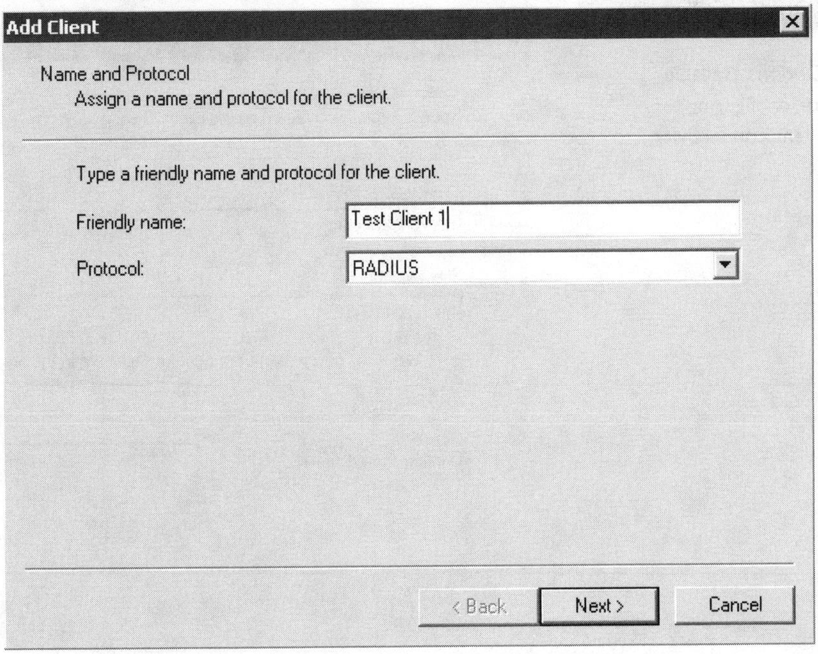

communications between the RADIUS client and the IAS server. Figure 24-7 illustrates the available options.

Once the options are selected, click Finish to complete the client setup process.

Designing for RADIUS Management

When using RADIUS, the management structure defined by its definition is primarily centralized. RADIUS services use a centralized authentication and auditing server such as IAS included with Windows 2000. When designing a remote access solution, it is important to keep RADIUS management in mind. This allows you to customize the solution to better suit the architecture that RADIUS uses.

Other factors also come into play when developing a RADIUS management strategy. Because RADIUS servers maintain security information about users, you must be careful in securing the server from intruders. Several recommendations can be made to further protect the server from internal and external violations. The most important

FIGURE 24-7

Options available for configuring client connectivity

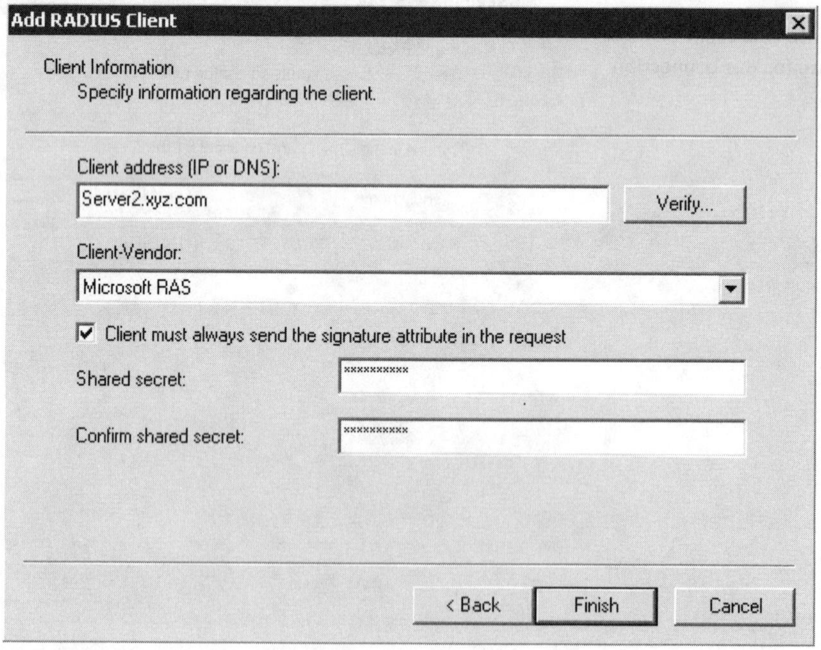

recommendation is dedicating a server to handle only RADIUS requests. This prevents other applications or users from tampering with security. Physically secure the server to verify that no one can interfere with it. Try to use the most secure authentication protocols possible. You can also disable any authentication protocols that will not be used. Place the RADIUS server behind a firewall. This helps to prevent traffic from even arriving at the server, especially from outside sources.

ACCELERATING TO WINDOWS 2000

Although Microsoft has provided RAS in prior releases of Windows NT, Windows 2000 includes many new features and options. These can be leveraged to provide a more scalable, stable remote access solution for your users. New features include integration with the Windows 2000 Active Directory. Active Directory can be used to provide authentication services in addition to access to network resources. Additional administration can be performed and controlled with Active Directory.

Other new features include addition protocol support, such as EAP and MS-CHAP 2. EAP provides new authentication options that provide more secure access and can utilize new industry security features such as smart cards. In addition, EAP provides additional plug-ins to Windows 2000 for use with features such as RADIUS. Another protocol provided is MS-CHAP 2. MS-CHAP 2 is a newer release of MS-CHAP and is primarily designed for VPN connections. The Bandwidth Allocation Protocol (BAP) has also been added to Windows 2000 to provide

an efficient method of allocating bandwidth during multilink PPP connections. For example, when creating multiple PPP connections, only two lines may be required during low traffic times, while four or more may be required to handle larger loads. BAP can automatically create these connections if needed by monitoring traffic usage and making decisions based on these statistics. Another protocol provided with Windows 2000 is Layer 2 Tunneling Protocol (L2TP). This supplies the foundation for VPN services by working in cooperation with the IPSec, or IP Security policies.

Other features include items such as IP multicast support and RADIUS support. IP multicast provides more flexibility in offering IP network-related services, while RADIUS provides a secure robust architecture for authentication services. Remote access policies have also added some new functionality that provides more options when configuring client access, such as account lockout or available hours. These new options and features allow administrators a greater level of control and flexibility when using RAS with Windows 2000.

Although you may be familiar with the RAS provided in previous versions of Windows, be sure to understand the new options that are available in Windows 2000 prior to implementing these features. Although Windows 2000 provides a more secure and stable remote access solution, features that are used improperly can cause more problems than they solve.

CHAPTER SUMMARY

As companies are providing more services to meet the growing needs of their user communities, the need for remote access services almost becomes a requirement. Users are becoming more dependent on network resources to perform their jobs. Windows 2000 includes several new and improved features that allow organizations to meet these requirements. RAS servers provide a means of allowing network users to access applications and resources as if they were on the local network. E-mail and shared files are good examples of resources accessed through RAS.

When implementing RAS solutions, several factors must be considered. First, several different remote access protocols can be used. Point-to-Point Protocol (PPP) is the most common due to its extensibility and support of multiple network protocols such as TCP/IP, IPX/SPX, and NetBEUI. Another support RAS protocol, the Serial Line Interface Protocol (SLIP), was designed for older UNIX systems and only uses the TCP/IP network protocol. The last protocol supported is MS RAS. This protocol is used in older Windows-based systems such as Windows 3.1 and MS-DOS. In addition, it uses NetBIOS-based services to communicate.

Two connection types are also available when using RAS: conventional dial-up connections and VPN connections. Dial-up networking clients create a physical connection to a port, such as a modem located on the remote access server. This is then used to provide communication with the rest of the network. VPN services are used to create a logical communication path across public networks such as the Internet. These are commonly used to access a remote corporate network across the Internet after connecting to an ISP.

To set up RAS, you must first install the associated hardware, such as an ISDN modem or analog modem. This is done by using the Add/Remove Hardware and the Device Manager. Once completed, the network protocol must be set up to allow communication between the RAS clients and the rest of the network. Next, you must activate the Routing and Remote Access services by specifying the configuration options to use for this server, such as network router, VPN server, or Internet connection server. These can be used to specify different connectivity between servers and clients as required by the organization.

When creating a RAS implementation strategy, you must take into account the management strategy that will be used. For example, RAS servers can be administered centrally through a single database or distributed through the organization. Although this will differ, depending on the business requirements, it needs to be considered prior to implementation if possible. Solutions such as the Remote Authentication Dial-In User Service (RADIUS) can be used to implement a centralized secure management strategy.

RADIUS is a communications protocol used between an authentication server and remote access server acting as a RADIUS client to provide authentication and auditing for remote access users. It can utilize a variety of encryption protocols, such as the Extensible Authentication Protocol (EAP), the Password Authentication Protocol (PAP), or the Challenge Handshake and Response protocol (CHAP). Other options are available to further customize the security available with RADIUS services.

Windows 2000 includes a RADIUS server-based component known as the Internet Authentication Server or, IAS. This solution is used to create a RADIUS infrastructure by using Windows 2000. This eliminates the need for third-party software. In addition, IAS can integrate with Active Directory to further ease the burden of administration. Within the IAS management snap-in, clients must be configured to create a secure communications channel.Configuration options include the client address, the RADIUS client vendor, and the shared secret that verifies that communications between the client and host are secure.

When creating a RADIUS management strategy, keep several factors in mind. First, the architecture is a centralized database that must communicate with the distributed remote access servers. Next, certain security precautions should be taken to protect the information stored in the RADIUS host. For example, be sure to physically secure the server from being tampered with. Also, create a dedicated RADIUS server for IAS to minimize the impact of applications or other users on the system.

TWO-MINUTE DRILL

❑ RAS servers are used to provide network services as if a user was physically attached.

❑ The two different connection types that can be used with RAS are Dial-Up Networking or access through a VPN.

❑ The second connection type available in Windows 2000 is VPN services.

❑ To set up RAS, you must first verify that all communications hardware is installed and functioning properly.

❑ Developed by Lucent Technologies, RADIUS is a protocol used to provide secure authentication and accounting services for large-scale remote access networks.

❑ When using RADIUS services, you must configure connections between RAS servers acting as clients and the Internet Authentication Server.

SELF TEST

The following questions will help you measure your understanding of the material presented in this chapter. Read all of the choices carefully, as there may be more than one correct answer. Choose all correct answers for each question.

1. Remote Access Servers are a component of what Windows 2000 feature set?

    A. Internet Information Server

    B. Certificate Services

    C. Remote Installation Services

    D. Routing and Remote Access Services

2. Which Remote Access Server protocol supports multiple Network layer protocols?

    A. IAS

    B. PPP

    C. SLIP

    D. MS RAS

3. What remote access protocol was developed primarily for UNIX systems and supports the TCP/IP network protocol?

    A. PPP

    B. IAS

    C. SLIP

    D. MS RAS

4. What remote access protocol is used for older Microsoft clients such as Windows 3.1 and MS-DOS?

    A. PPP

    B. IAS

    C. SLIP

    D. MS RAS

5. What does VPN stand for?

    A. Virtual Private Network

    B. Virtual Public Network

    C. Virtual Private Name

    D. Virtual Public Name

6. What tool is used to manage the hardware required for RAS servers?

    A. Administrative Tools

    B. Hardware Setup

    C. Add/Remove Programs applet

    D. Device Manager

7. What Remote Access configuration option would be selected to install the Internet Connection Sharing services?

    A. Network router

    B. Internet server

    C. Internet connection server

    D. Manually configured server

8. What kind of management strategy can be used when implementing Remote Access Services?

    A. Centralized

    B. Distributed

    C. Centralized and distributed

    D. None of the above

9. What does RADIUS stand for?

   A. Remote Authentication Dial-In User Service

   B. Remote Access for Dial-In User Setup

   C. Remote Administration for User Dial-In Services

   D. None of the above

10. Which of the following protocols is not supported in Windows 2000 RADIUS services?

    A. Extensible Authentication Protocol (EAP)

    B. HyperText Transport Protocol Secured (HTTPS)

    C. Password Authentication Protocol (PAP)

    D. Challenge Handshake and Response Protocol (CHAP)

11. What component in Windows 2000 is used to provide RADIUS host services?

    A. Internet Information Services

    B. Certificate Services

    C. Remote Installation Services

    D. Internet Authentication Services

12. What is used by the Internet Authentication Server to verify that communications between the RADIUS host and client are secure?

    A. Client IP address

    B. Vendor Type option

    C. Shared Secret

    D. None of the above

13. Which of the following are not factors when considering the management strategy for RADIUS services?

    A. Physical Security

    B. Dedicated Server

    C. RADIUS Server placed behind a firewall

    D. None of the above

14. Which of the following are new features included with the Windows 2000 implementation of Routing and Remote Access Services?

    A. Internet Information Server 5.0

    B. Certificate Services

    C. Layer 2 Tunneling Protocol

    D. Terminal Services

MICROSOFT CERTIFIED SYSTEMS ENGINEER

25

Connection Manager Networking

HEADSTART OBJECTIVES

25.01   The Role of Connection Manager
        in an Enterprise Network

25.02   Designing a Connection Manager
        Implementation

25.03   Designing for Connection Manager
        Management

The Windows 2000 Connection Manager is client dialer software that provides a custom user interface for dialing and accessing the Internet and corporate resources. It virtually eliminates the need for your users to manage their own access configuration. Connection Manager is designed to allow your company to provide a graphical user interface so that others can connect to your company's network using your predefined connection features. This customization is accomplished via the Connection Manager Administration Kit (CMAK) Wizard. The Wizard has an easy-to-use graphical interface that lets you specify custom elements for your service, and then builds your customized installation package for you.

Connection Manager supports local and remote connections to your service using a network of access points (such as those available worldwide through Internet Service Providers (ISPs)). You can also use Connection Manager to establish virtual private network connections to your service (secure connections through the Internet).

In addition, the Connection Manager supports branding (customization of the icons, graphics, and messages, to identify your organization), automatic running of custom applications at specified points during connection, running multiple instances of Connection Manager, multiple user support, and custom phone books. You can even create a self-installing executable file that your users can download or that you can distribute on disk to simplify the distribution process.

In this chapter, we look at all these features, how to plan and implement a Connection Manager service, and the day-to-day management of Connection Manager connections.

HEADSTART OBJECTIVE 25.01

The Role of Connection Manager in an Enterprise Network

Most of Microsoft's documentation of the Connection Manager seems to assume that it will be used for connection to an online service or ISP. There are, however, numerous uses for this feature in any large company or other enterprise network environment, especially given its support of Virtual Private Networking (VPN), which allows for creation of a secure tunnel through the Internet to the organization's LAN.

More and more companies are currently employing telecommuters who need to connect to the company network from home, as well as the more traditional traveling employees who have a need to access company resources while on the road. Add to this the number of executives and others who take work home and can benefit from an after-hours connection. The advantages of being able to distribute software that will let them all get connected easily, without having to manually configure network settings and protocols, becomes apparent.

Advantages for Users

With the Connection Manager client software, users no longer have to be computer savvy to install the correct components and connect to the company's network through a regular direct dial-up connection or through a VPN via an ISP. Many employees who need access to network files and other resources are not knowledgeable about configuration tasks, and may be afraid to make changes to their operating systems' networking properties.

A major reason for the popularity of online services such as America Online is the "no-brainer" aspect of installation and configuration, which they advertise heavily. Using Connection Manager makes it as easy for these users to get online to the company's network as installing those "anyone can do it" services.

Advantages for Administrators

A policy of having users connect to the company network through the Connection Manager software gives administrators more control over remote access to the network. Connection Manager gives you a fine degree of control, allowing you to set up the software the way you want it, even mandating that certain programs run at various points during the installation or upon connection.

Advantages for Technical Support Personnel

In those organizations where remote access is used at many levels of the company hierarchy, technical support staffs devote many hours to helping users set up and troubleshoot their connectivity problems. It can be frustrating on both sides, when support personnel are attempting to guide nontechnical users through the process of installing and configuring the components required to make a dial-in connection. In some cases, support personnel may even be required to visit the remote site to accomplish the task.

Using Connection Manager saves time and money by reducing the amount of support time necessary for remote access users.

HEADSTART OBJECTIVE 25.02

Designing a Connection Manager Implementation

Designing a Connection Manager implementation is a four-phase process. Microsoft's CMAK covers all phases thoroughly, including

1. Planning, which includes a planning worksheet to simplify design and implementation of your plan

2. Developing custom elements

3. Running the CMAK Wizard and creating a service profile

4. Preparing for integration, delivery, and installation

Phase One: Planning

Properly planning the implementation of a Connection Manager deployment will make your job much easier when you get to the action phases and begin to create your service profiles, integrate Connection Manager as part of your network connectivity methodology, deliver the

Connection Manager package to your customers, and finally install the Connection Manager on users' machines.

The worksheet included in the following exercise outlines Microsoft's recommended steps in planning the implementation of Connection Manager in your organization.

EXERCISE 25-1

Analyzing a Connection Manager Strategy

Prior to implementing Connection Manager to provide connectivity to your network or service, you should complete the following check list (this is information you will need to have on hand when you run the CMAK Wizard):

1. Determine whether you will create a new service profile or edit an existing profile (you should create a service profile for each target audience).

2. Specify a service name to identify your service to the users. Connection Manager can display a maximum of 31 to 45 characters (depending on the characters and capitalization used). This name appears at several points when the user runs your service.

3. Specify a file name to be given to the files created by the CMAK Wizard when building the service profile. The file name can be up to 8 alphanumeric characters. Do not use extended character sets, and be sure the service and file names are different from all other service and file names that you provide to your customers. If two service profiles on the same computer have the same service or file name, the associated connection icons do not work correctly.

4. Determine whether you wish to merge features from existing profiles. If you have information in existing service profiles that you need in the service profile you are building, you can use the CMAK Wizard to merge much of the information from existing profiles into the profile you are building.

5. Determine if you wish to specify a line of information to be displayed in the logon dialog box. This line of text can be a maximum of approximately 50 characters, and commonly would consist of contact information for technical support or similar

information. If you do not specify a line of text, this area of the logon dialog box will be left blank.

6. Determine whether you need to specify a realm name. Realm names are used for network routing and authentication. They provide the identification necessary to forward authentication requests to the server that holds the user's credentials.

7. Determine whether you will need to incorporate custom network and dial-up connection entries and, if so, the options you want to use for each.

8. Determine whether you wish to support VPN connections using Point-to-Point Tunneling Protocol (PPTP) or Layer 2 Tunneling Protocol (L2TP). If so, you will need to know the server address, and (if not using DHCP to allow the server to assign addresses) you will need to specify a primary and secondary DNS and WINS address for the VPN connection.

9. Determine whether you wish to incorporate connect actions, which provide additional programs that start seamlessly during the connection to your service. If so, you will need to know the name, path, and parameters of the program to run.

10. Determine whether to use the default icons for the logon dialog box and phone book or whether to provide a custom bitmap.

11. Specify any phone book file that you wish to include with the service profile (this should be an 8-character name with the extension .pbk).

12. Determine whether you wish to customize other elements of Connection Manager, such as the help files, user support documentation, and additional files to include with the profile to help users implement your service.

Once you have gathered all the information necessary to create your Connection Manager service profile, you can run the CMAK Wizard to create and customize the profile.

But before you proceed, take a look at the following table for answers to some frequently asked questions about the necessary system requirements for installing the Connection Manager software on users' computers.

QUESTIONS AND ANSWERS

What operating systems can I use with the Microsoft Connection Manager?	Windows 95, Windows 98, Windows NT 4.0, or Windows 2000
How much free disk space is required to install Connection Manager software?	A minimum of 1MB (disk-space requirements can vary, based on the elements included in the service profile)
What protocols must be installed on the user computer to run Connection Manager?	TCP/IP (for peer connections in a network, TAPI (for dialing support), and PPTP or L2TP (to establish a VPN connection)
What other components are required on the user computer?	At least one service profile (the set of customized files needed to install and use Connection Manager to connect to your service), which you build using the CMAK Wizard Microsoft Connection Manager version 1.2 (which you can include with the service profile that you provide to your customers) Network and Dial-Up Connections to connect to a remote computer or network

Phase Two: Developing Custom Elements

Connection Manager supports *branding*. This refers to customization of the installation package that you deliver to your customers. You can make the Connection Manager interface display the identity of your organization by adding your company logo and custom information. You are able to decide which features you want to include, and fine-tune the appearance of the Connection Manager to your customers or users.

You'll need to design and develop a phone book and any other custom elements you want, such as graphics, text, and related programs. The CMAK Wizard will take you through the process of building each custom profile, and you can then use the advanced customization techniques if necessary to complete the customization process.

The planning worksheet that you completed earlier provides you with the information you need to perform the customization process. Use it as a guideline as you proceed through the next phase, running the CMAK Wizard.

Phase Three: Running the CMAK Wizard

Once you've made the decisions regarding which features you wish to make available to your users and how you want to customize them, Microsoft makes it easy to accomplish all this by providing the CMAK Wizard to walk you through the steps.

The first step is to select the source to use in building the service profile. If you are creating a new profile from scratch, simply choose the "Create a new service profile" radio button. If you wish instead to edit an already-existing profile, you will need to select the service name of the profile in the Wizard's drop-down box.

Next, you must give the new service profile a name, and designate a file name for the service profile and any associated files (see Figure 25-1). The profile name can be up to 40 characters, not including the following: * \ / : ? " < > | [ ]. The file name should be limited to 8 alphanumeric characters. Do not include any of the following: ! , ; <space> * = \ / : ? ' " < > | . % + [ ] $ #.

You may merge other service profiles into this one if you wish. This allows you to make several dissimilar networks appear to be a single, cohesive service. If you wish to merge other profiles, select the profiles to be merged in the dialog box shown in Figure 25-2.

When you create a service profile, the CMAK Wizard copies all files referenced in the service profile, including the merged service-profile files, into the \Program Files\CMAK\Profiles*ServiceProfileFileName* folder for that service profile.

When you use the CMAK Wizard to merge features, the resulting service profile includes references to the existing (merged) service profiles.

FIGURE 25-1

Specifying the service
and file names for the
service profile

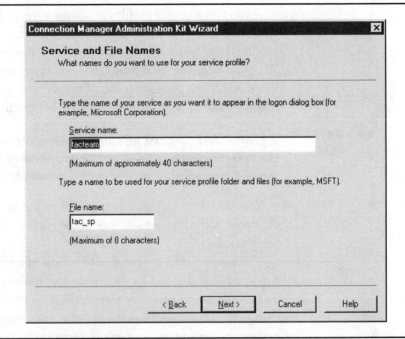

FIGURE 25-1

Specifying the service
and file names for the
service profile

FIGURE 25-2

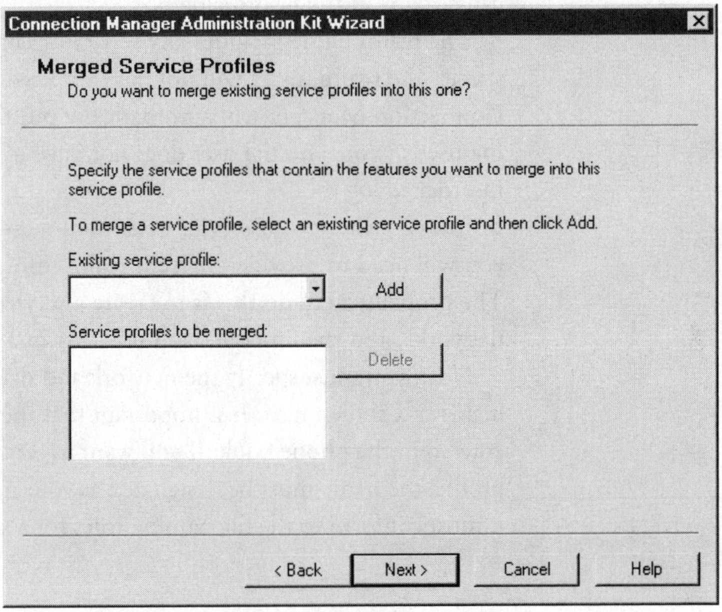

Adding an existing service
profile to be merged with
the new one

If you edit a service profile containing a merged service profile, the CMAK Wizard will try to use the latest version of the merged service profile. If the Wizard cannot find the merged service profile in the \Program Files\CMAK\Profiles*MergedServiceProfileFileName* folder, it will then use the current version of the merged service profile that was originally stored with the service profile being edited.

heads

① p

A profile that contains information from other service profiles is called the referencing profile. A service profile that has its information merged into another service profile is called a merged profile.

You can add contact information for technical support, which will be displayed in the logon dialog box, directly above the Connection Status information.

The support information should consist of approximately one line of text (up to 50 characters). This part of the logon dialog box will be left blank if you choose not to enter any text on this page of the CMAK Wizard.

If your network requires the use of a realm name for routing and authentication (the realm name provides identification necessary to forward authentication requests to the server that holds the user's credentials), you can enter it in the next dialog box.

The realm name includes any separator characters, such as @ or /. If you specify the realm, users will not have to provide it themselves; instead the Connection Manager will automatically put the realm name before or after the user's name and the user does not have to understand network routing in order to log on.

In cases where your service uses more than one network or ISP for access, you will need to provide different realm information for each network/ISP. The proper way to do this is to create a service profile for each of the networks, and then merge them together in a *referencing* profile.

Next, you must specify the network and dial-up connection entries in the dialog box shown next. It is important that they be entered exactly as they are entered in the phone book. If you want to set up a default for your service profile, the name must be designated as your *ServiceProfileServiceName*, and it must conform to the file naming rules for a service profile.

You can let the server assign the DNS and/or WINS addresses, or you can use specific DNS and/or WINS addresses, which are entered in the dialog box shown in the figure above. If you want to assign specific addresses to the Network and Dial-up Connections entry, you can specify both primary and secondary DNS and WINS IP addresses. You can also associate a Network and Dial-up Connections script (.scp) file with this entry if your service requires it.

Next, you must choose whether to implement support for VPN. VPN connections allow you to establish a remote connection to a private network over the Internet, by using a tunneling protocol. Connection Manager supports the use of either PPTP or L2TP To use L2TP, you must use the Advanced Customization Techniques to edit the service profile files (L2TP cannot be enabled through the CMAK Wizard).

Setting up the profile to support VPN connections adds an Internet Logon tab to the Properties dialog box. On this tab, users type the username and password for the ISP. In the logon dialog box, users type a private network user name, password, and logon domain.

You can use the CMAK Wizard to include Connect Actions in your service profiles. This will automatically start programs when users connect to your service, which will then run seamlessly. To designate connect actions, see Figure 25-3.

FIGURE 25-1

Specifying Connect Actions
(programs to run when a
user connects)

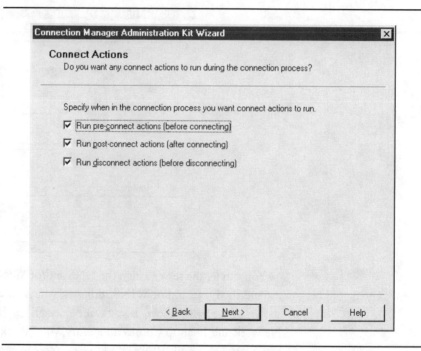

There are four points during the connection process when a program
can be designated to run. These are categorized as follows:

- **Pre-connect actions**   Run as soon as a user connects.

- **Pre-tunnel actions**   Applicable only to VPN connections and run
  between the establishment of a connection with the Internet server
  and the establishment of a secure tunnel to the VPN server. This
  could be, for example, a program designed to verify user credentials
  for accessing a corporate server behind a firewall. (You will note in
  Figure 25-3 that pre-tunnel actions are not shown as an option.
  This choice appears only if you have set up VPN support).

- **Post-connect actions**   Run immediately after establishing a connection (if using a VPN, they will run immediately after establishing the tunnel).

- **Disconnect actions**   Run immediately before disconnecting from the service. This is most often used to collect information such as the total time spent logged on to the service.

Auto-applications that you specify in the CMAK Wizard run every time the user connects to the service. This is true whether the connection is a dial-up or a direct connection. Auto-applications are similar to post-connect actions, except that the latter are DLLs, while auto-applications are normally .exe files. A .DLL cannot be run as an auto-application.

You can specify standard or custom programs to run as auto-applications. A common example is including a commercially available e-mail program to run as an auto-application.

The next two dialog boxes allow you to customize the look of the Connection Manager dialog box by adding your own logo or other bitmap.

You can include a phone book in the service profile if you wish. To do so, simply browse to the phone book file (which will have a .pbk extension). You also have the option of not including a phone book in your service profile, but downloading the phone book (and upgrades) to your users later. To do so, follow the instructions in the Wizard (see Figure 25-4).

By using the advanced customization feature to edit the service profile, you can also control which service types (such as modem or ISDN) appear in the Phone Book dialog box, change the message displayed during phone book updates, and/or control the delay before downloading phone book updates.

FIGURE 25-2

Adding a phone book
to the service profile
(optional)

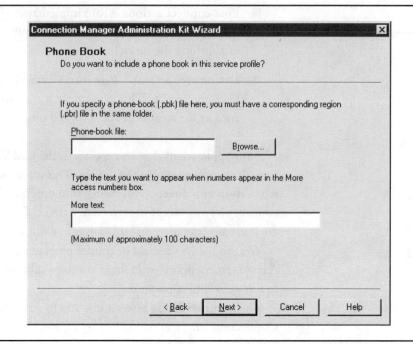

You can customize the program icon, the title-bar icon, and the
status-area icon if you wish (or you can use Microsoft's default icons).
If you want to use your own custom icons, type in the path and file name,
or browse for the .ico files to be used (see Figure 25-5).

The icons you use must be 16-color icons. It is recommended that you
create icons that are similar to each other to unify the appearance of the
service profile. You should also create icons that match the size and overall
shape of the default icons.

You can use an icon editor, available on the web, to create your custom icons.

The program icon is the largest of the three, and is used as the desktop
icon for the Connection Manager program. The smaller title-bar icon will
appear at the left edge of the title bar in the Connection Manager logon
dialog box and in pop-up dialog boxes. When the Connection Manager
program is running, this icon is displayed on its program button on the
taskbar. The small status area icon will be displayed at the far right of the
taskbar when a connection has been established.

FIGURE 25-3

Customizing Connection
Manager icons

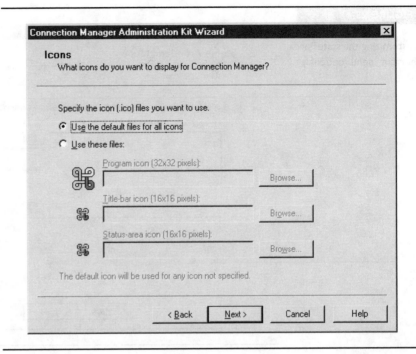

If you want to use the same icon in place of all three default icons, it will be scaled to fit the assigned area when it is displayed, but note that the image might distort due to the resizing.

You also have the ability to customize the status-area icon menu. This will determine what programs can be chosen when a user right-clicks the status area icon (see Figure 25-6).

In Windows 2000, the default commands on the status-area shortcut menu are as follows:

- Status
- Disconnect
- Open Network Connections

You use the CMAK Wizard to customize the shortcut menu by specifying which, if any, additional commands appear on the menu.

FIGURE 25-4

Customizing the status-area
shortcut menu (optional)

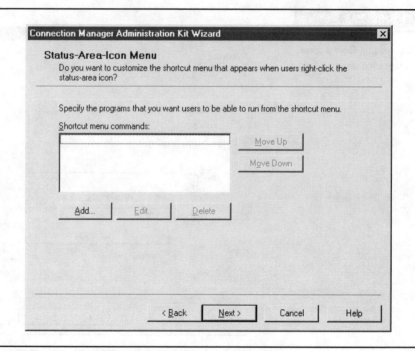

You can also designate a customized Help file for those users who connect
to your network or service.

If you want to include custom Windows Help files for your users, you
must prepare the files before you run the CMAK Wizard. Your CMAK
folder contains all the source files for the default Help. To create custom
Help files, you should copy the default Help source files, including the
project (.hpj) file, rename them, and then edit the renamed files.

Next, you will be asked if you want to include the Connection Manager
1.2 software in the service profile.

Your users will have to have Connection Manager 1.2 installed on their
computers in order to run a Connection Manager 1.2. service profile. If

they don't already have it installed, you can include the software in your service profile, and the software will be installed when the user installs the service profile.

You can include your own license agreement that users must accept when they install your service profile. To do so, enter the path and file name of the agreement (which must be in plain text format) as shown in Figure 25-7.

If the user does not accept your license agreement, the Connection Manager software will not be installed.

Use a text-editor program (such as Notepad) to create your license agreement as a text (.txt) file. To avoid formatting problems, do not use hard returns at the end of lines. Line-wrapping for the license agreement is done automatically when the service profile is built.

FIGURE 25-5

Adding a license agreement to the service profile

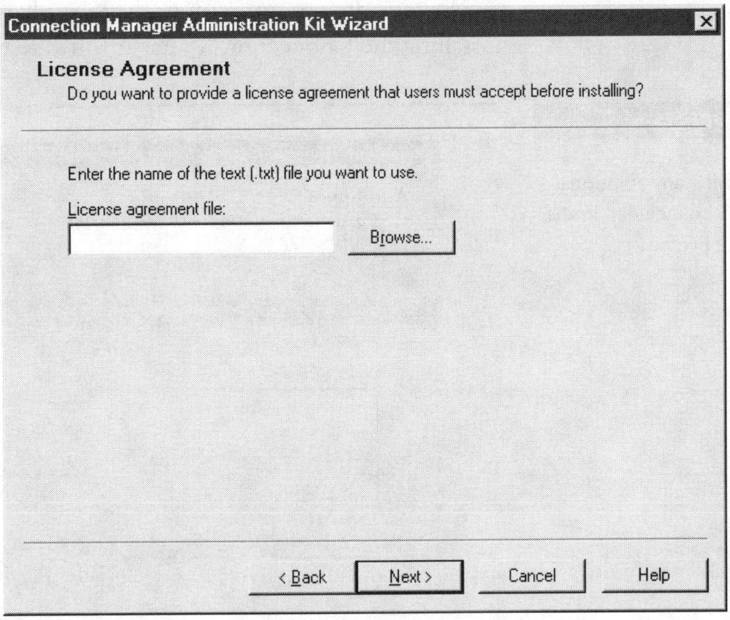

If any other files need to be included with the service profile, you get a last chance to add them in the next CMAK dialog box (see Figure 25-8).

These additional files can be files used for connect actions (only one program file can be specified in the Connect Action dialog box, so any additional files needed to run the program can be added here as Additional Files), or any other files needed to help users implement your service.

Finally, the dialog box shown in Figure 25-9 will signal that you have completed all the information required by the Wizard, and your service profile is now ready to be built.

After you click Next, you will see a command screen as the Wizard creates your profile.

As the last step in the process, the CMAK Wizard will display the final dialog box, which includes the location of the self-installing executable file that contains your new service profile, which can now be distributed to your users.

Now it's time to move on to the next phase: integrating, delivering, and installing the Connection Manager software to your service's users.

FIGURE 25-6

Specifying any additional files to be included in the service profile

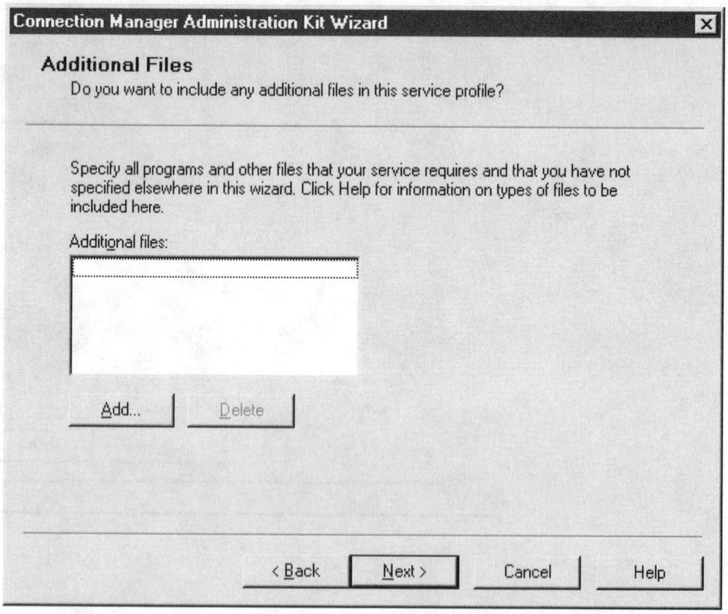

FIGURE 25-7

Finishing the CMAK
Wizard service profile
creation process

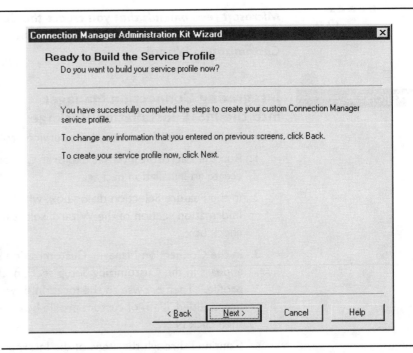

Integration, Delivery, and Installation

Now that you have finished creating a service profile, the Connection
Manager and your service profile can be delivered and installed on their
own, or they can be integrated with an Internet Explorer Administration
Kit (IEAK) installation package (which can be created with the IEAK
Wizard).

Using the IEAK to Integrate Connection Manager and the Service Profile into an IEAK Custom Installation Package

You can use IEAK to create an installation package, and include the
Connection Manager service profile in the package. Then your users
can install both Connection Manager and Internet Explorer in a single
procedure.

The IEAK supports incorporating a Connection Manager service profile
in the Internet Explorer installation package that you create with the Internet
Explorer Customization Wizard.

heads
① p *Microsoft recommends that you create the Connection Manager service profile first, and test it before you start the Internet Explorer Customization Wizard.*

Integrating Connection Manager into the MSIE Installation Package

After you have created and tested the service profile, follow these steps:

1. Run the Microsoft Internet Explorer Customization Wizard to create an installation package.

2. In the Feature Selection dialog box, which appears in the Gathering Information section of the Wizard, select the Connection Manager check box.

3. In the Connection Manager Customization dialog box, which appears in the Customizing Setup section, click on "Use custom profile." Then browse to the location of your service profile in the box entitled "Path of custom profile box." Select the profile, and then click Next.

4. Continue through the steps of the Internet Explorer Customization Wizard and complete creation of the Internet Explorer installation package (which now contains the Connection Manager service profile).

Using Your Own Installation Package to Install Connection Manager

You can use command-line parameters to integrate Connection Manager in an installation package and deliver it to your users in one of the following ways:

■ Distribute and install the Connection Manager service profile over a corporate network using Microsoft Systems Management Server (SMS) to automatically handle the process without user intervention.

■ Integrate the Connection Manager service profile with another product's installation package and install them both in a single process.

Post the Connection Manager service profile to a Web site so users can access and install the service profile in a standard way.

The Connection Manager installer, cmstp.exe, supports command-line parameters that can be used to install a service profile, remove a service profile, or remove the Connection Manager software. To display Help for the command-line installation parameters, type **cmstp.exe /?.**

Installing the Connection Manager Software from the Self-Executing (.exe) File

To install the Connection Manager software alone, simply run the .exe file created by the CMAK Wizard. A new icon will appear in your Network and Dialup Connections properties window (see Figure 25-10).

Clicking on the new icon will start the Connection Manager software, and you will see the logon dialog box, shown in Figure 25-11.

FIGURE 25-8   The Connection Manager icon (tacteam) appears in the Network and Dial-up Connections properties window

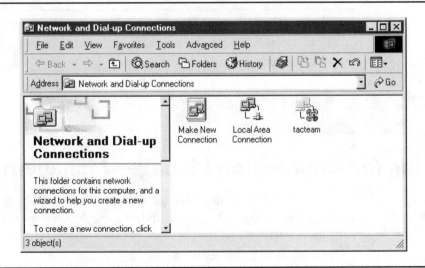

The Microsoft Connection Manager logon screen for the newly created tacteam service profile

The user now has only to enter a valid user name and password for your service or network, and then click Connect.

Designing for Connection Manager Management

Managing your Connection Manager implementation will be easy if you begin with proper planning, and design the deployment to fit your network's or service's needs.

Some issues to be addressed include

- Make sure that the appropriate version of Connection Manager is installed on the users' computers.

- Check to see that the latest version of Network and Dial-up Connections is installed on users' machines.

- Be sure the latest service pack is installed.

- Ensure that the proxy settings are correct.

- Make certain that all required network protocols, including TCP/IP, IPX, and NetBEUI (depending on your network's configuration), are installed and configured correctly on the users' computers.

- If your service profile supports VPN connections, be sure that PPTP is installed and configured correctly and completely. (In Windows 2000, the CMAK Wizard will automatically install PPTP. To use L2TP, you must edit the service profile using the advanced configuration techniques.)

- Finally, ensure that the required Network and Dial-up Connections entry is available on the users' computers.

For information on troubleshooting Connection Manager, the Windows 2000 Resource Kit and the Internet Explorer 5 Resource Kit (published by Microsoft Press) contain detailed, useful information and tools to assist in problem-solving.

on the job

If your company has nontechnical computer users who need access to the network, whether employees or customers, implementing the Connection Manager to aid them in establishing the dial-up or VPN connection will benefit everyone. Distributing the Connection Manager software integrated into a customized Internet Explorer package is excellent advertising for your company, especially when you incorporate the company logo and your own custom icons. This package can be written onto CDs, which can then be customized with labels and jewel cases featuring your company name and logo. If you distribute the software this way, remember to include clear installation instructions and tech support phone numbers on the case and/or in a text README file to ensure that all users will have the information available in case they need help installing the software.

ACCELERATING TO WINDOWS 2000

Windows 2000 includes Connection Manager version 1.2, which supports a variety of features that simplify and enhance implementation of connection support for both administrators and users, including

- **Branding** Complete customization so that you can incorporate your own logo, icons, menu shortcuts, phone books, and otherwise truly make the Connection Manager software interface your company's own.

- **Connect-actions and auto-applications** Now it's easy to run programs when and in the way you want, at various points during the user's connection.

- **Multiple-user support for each service profile** Users who share the same

computer can share the same service profile, while still connecting with their individual usernames and passwords, without having to re-enter the information each time.

- **Simplified distribution** The CMAK Wizard makes it easy to create Connection Manager software that can be distributed alone or integrated into an Internet Explorer custom package.

- **VPN support** Windows 2000's implementation of Connection Manager now automatically installs PPTP for VPN (via the CMAK Wizard), and also supports the newest version of tunneling protocol, L2TP (installed via advanced configuration techniques).

CHAPTER SUMMARY

Microsoft's newest version of Connection Manager and the easy-to-use Connection Manager Administration Kit (CMAK) provide a way for online services, ISP, and companies running enterprise networks to give their users a quick-and-simple way to get connected.

By creating custom service profiles, an organization can provide its users with software that takes much of the work out of connectivity issues for administrators, users, and technical support personnel.

In addition, Connection Manager's customization features give a company or organization the opportunity to fine-tune the connection process to whatever degree is desired, and to present the most professional image possible to those who utilize the service.

TWO-MINUTE DRILL

❑ The Windows 2000 Connection Manager is client dialer software that provides a custom user interface for dialing and accessing the Internet and corporate resources.

❑ Connection Manager supports *branding*. This refers to customization of the installation package that you deliver to your customers.

❑ A profile that contains information from other service profiles is called the *referencing* profile. A service profile that has its information merged into another service profile is called a *merged* profile.

❑ In cases where your service uses more than one network or ISP for access, you will need to provide different realm information for each network/ISP. The proper way to do this is to create a service profile for each of the networks, and then merge them together in a *referencing* profile.

❑ The IEAK supports incorporating a Connection Manager service profile in the Internet Explorer installation package that you create with the Internet Explorer Customization Wizard.

❑ The Connection Manager installer, cmstp.exe, supports command-line parameters that can be used to install a service profile, remove a service profile, or remove the Connection Manager software.

SELF TEST

The following questions will help you measure your understanding of the material presented in this chapter. Read all of the choices carefully, as there may be more than one correct answer. Choose all correct answers for each question.

1. Which of the following is true of Connection Manager?

   A. It supports only local connections to your network or service.

   B. It supports only remote connections to your network or service.

   C. It supports both local and remote connections to your network or service.

   D. It supports neither local nor remote connections to your network or service.

2. What is branding?

   A. The ability to run commercially available applications while Connection Manager is running

   B. The ability to customize graphics, icons, and text on the Connection Manager interface

   C. The ability to run more than one instance of Connection Manager at a time

   D. The ability to allow users who share a computer to use the same service profile

3. Which of the following would be an effective utilization of the Connection Manager software for an enterprise organization?

   A. To allow employees who telecommute or take work home to connect to the company network easily and quickly without configuring their own settings

   B. To allow customers access to parts of the company's network

   C. To allow sales personnel who are on the road to connect to the company's network easily, even if they are not technically savvy

   D. All of the above

4. Which of the following is *not* one of the four stages of implementing Connection Manager (according to Microsoft)?

   A. Planning, which includes a planning worksheet to simplify design and implementation of your plan

   B. Installing the TCP/IP protocol on the user machines

   C. Running the CMAK Wizard and creating a service profile

   D. Preparing for integration, delivery, and installation

5. What is the maximum number of characters for the designated file name to be used by the files created in the CMAK Wizard?

   A. 45

B. 5

C. 18

D. 8

6. What are realm names used for? (Choose all that apply.)

   A. Network routing

   B. Identifying your company in the logon dialog box

   C. Authentication

   D. Identifying the author of the Connection Manager software

7. When you enable VPN support, if you don't use a DHCP server to assign IP addresses, what addresses must you specify in the CMAK Wizard dialog box? (Check two.)

   A. The name of a Terminal server

   B. The IP address of a DNS server

   C. The IP address of a WINS server

   D. The IP address of a TCP/IP server

8. Which of the following is a valid phone book file name?

   A. phonebookfile.pbk

   B. phonefile.phb

   C. phfile.phb

   D. phonefle.pbk

9. Which of the following protocols is used for establishing a VPN connection? (Check all that apply.)

A. IPX

B. PPTP

C. SLIP

D. LTPT

10. What is a service profile called when it contains information from other service profiles?

    A. A merged profile

    B. A merging profile

    C. A referencing profile

    D. A multiple profile

11. Which of the following terms refers to programs designated to run when users connect to your service, at one of four points in the connection process?

    A. Seamless applications

    B. Connect actions

    C. Auto-programming

    D. Four-point programs

12. How do auto-applications differ from connect actions?

    A. Auto-applications run asynchronously, and connect actions run synchronously.

    B. Auto-applications run as DDLs, and connect actions do not.

    C. Auto-applications run prior to connection, but not during a connection.

    D. Auto-applications must be started by the user, and connect actions are not.

13. Which of the following is true of custom icons that you use with Connection Manager? (Choose all that apply.)

    A. They should be 256 colors.

    B. The same .ico file should be used for all the icons for best results.

    C. They should be 16 colors.

    D. They should all be similar in design and appearance, but different sizes.

14. If more than one file is needed for a connect action, how do you specify the second and subsequent files?

    A. Enter them all in the Connect Action dialog box.

    B. Enter the first three in the Connect Action dialog box; then enter the rest in the Additional Files dialog box.

    C. Enter the first one in the Connect Action dialog box; then enter the rest in the Additional Files dialog box.

    D. You cannot use connect actions that require more than one file to run.

15. How can the Connection Manager software and a service profile be integrated with the distribution of Internet Explorer?

    A. The Connection Manager Wizard supports incorporating an IEAK package into your Connection Manager package.

    B. The Internet Explorer Administration Kit Wizard supports incorporating a Connection Manager package into the IEAK package.

    C. You can incorporate the Connection Manager software into the IEAK package using the Connection Manager Wizard, but the service profile will have to be distributed separately.

    D. You cannot integrate the distribution of Connection Manager and Internet Explorer.

26

Internet Routing

CERTIFICATION OBJECTIVES

Using Windows 2000 Server as a Router

If all machines could directly connect with every other machine, then each machine could simply keep a record of the IP address and intercommunication would be easy. Rarely can all machines be connected this way. More commonly, networks are broken up into related sets; by floor, building, office, corporate group, geographical region, or whatever you fancy. When the network is made up of many smaller networks, connections between them are handled by a host machine called a router, gateway, or bridge.

In Windows 2000 Server, Microsoft has moved all of the IP Routing services from the familiar Services Tab in the Network control panel into the Routing and Remote Access Service. This service is fully integrated with the rest of the operating system, turning the Windows 2000 Server into a full feature software router.

Enabling the Routing Service

To start the service, Launch Start | Programs | Administrative Tools | Routing and Remote Access, as displayed in Figure 26-1.

While Windows 2000 Server installation defaults to installing the Router and Remote Access service, it is initially in a disabled state. To activate the service, right-click Server Status and select "Add Server," as shown next. Select "This Computer" and then click OK.

FIGURE 26-1   Routing and Remote Access service

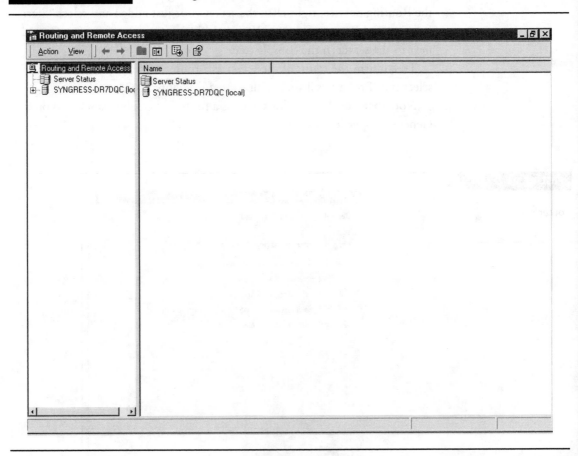

The host computer is now ready to be configured as a router. To enable the Routing Service, right click the server your just added and select "Start Routing and Remote Service." You should see a green arrow point upward next to the server in the console tree.

To confirm the status of the server as a router, right click the server and select the "Properties Tab," as illustrated in Figure 26-2.

Note that the "Enable this server as a router" check box is selected on the General Properties tab.

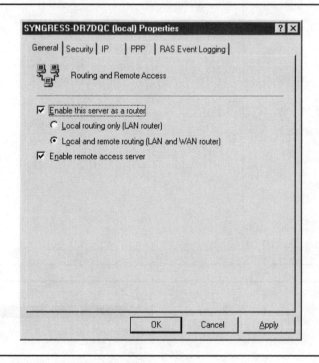

Gateway, Router, and Bridge

The term *router* is sometimes generically used to imply packet forwarding and protocol translation. Strictly speaking, this is a *gateway*, which is one step up from a pure router. A gateway provides router and protocol translation. Both a router and a gateway forward packets, also called *datagrams*, around a network; this is true routing. A *bridge* provides selective connection between LANs where only packets destined for the other side cross the bridge.

Interior and Exterior Gateways

In the big picture of networks, there are small networks connected to large networks, which are in turn connected through backbone networks to each other. For instance, if the small networks are all the offices in each city, then the city is the large network. The backbone or core connections between the cities and other countries make up the entire network. The Internet was a major development ground for protocols to manage these networks.

Rather than having every router know about every other router, they are organized into interior and exterior, or small groups with borders, and these borders are connected by the *backbone*.

Interior Protocols

Router Internet Protocol (RIP) is a common Interior Gateway Protocol (IGP) used by neighboring networks to communicate with each other. RIP messages are sent frequently to all adjacent routers from every other router providing basic route and hop information.

To configure RIP select "RIP" from the console tree, and then right click the interface you want to configure in the details pane, as shown in Figure 26-3.

FIGURE 26-3 Configuring RIP

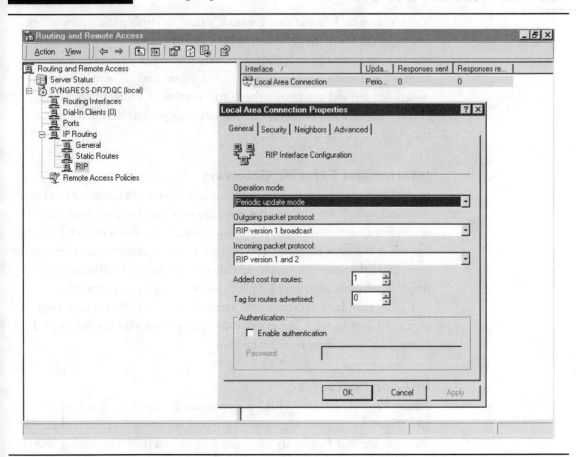

Windows 2000 Server as a Router (Gateway)

Any multihomed (multiple Network Interface Cards) Windows 2000 Server system can be configured as a router, not only for the same protocol, such as TCP/IP, but for other protocols as well, like IPX/SPX using RIP for IPX/SPX, or between topologies like Ethernet and Token Ring.

With two or more network interfaces, Windows 2000 Server can transfer, and translate for the protocol or topology if necessary, packets received at one interface but destined for some other network reachable by one or more of the other interfaces. This is called routing. The protocol that is used to send a packet must provide some routing information within it. A packet is considered routable by the protocol used. TCP/IP and IPX/SPX are routable protocols. NetBEUI is not considered a routing protocol although some specialized, high performance, dedicated routers can forward NetBEUI packets. This is not recommended because it floods both networks with broadcast messages.

HEADSTART OBJECTIVE 26.03

Understanding Routing

The postal system uses a similar concept to deliver letters. The address on an envelope or package (IP destination on a data packet) determines the letter's destination. If the letter's destination is local to the sender (same network, the Network Mask is used to determine this), then the sender can drop it off directly, in the same office, or locality (Local Area Network). If the address is not local, the letter is sent to the post office (the router), which then uses its internal forwarding system (routing table) to decide where next to send it (best or next route).

The postal code can be interpreted to represent what country, city, and street a letter is destined for. Similarly, the network number from an IP packet determines the remote area destination and whether to route or forward the packet to the destination.

HEADSTART OBJECTIVE 26.04

How Routing Works

For a network protocol to be routable, the protocol software design must provide a mechanism for determining whether a packet is local or not. If it is not local, it is sent on to the router or gateway. The router is programmed to forward the packet like the post office would forward a letter through the postal system to the final destination.

Routing a Packet on the Internet

Let's look at the packet information when the destination address is on a remote network and see how IP does routing. Workstation 160.45.100.1 wants to send a packet to the destination host at 160.20.10.105.

The workstation checks the destination address with the ANDing process and determines that the packet needs to be routed. The workstation RARPs to the default gateway and receives the IP address of the gateway. It then addresses the packet with the newly obtained address.

Packet information:
Source hardware address	11 (created the packet)
Source IP address	160.45.100.1
Destination hardware address	5
Destination IP address	160.20.0.3

IP on the gateway inspects the destination address and says, "This isn't for me." It then forwards the packet to network 160.20.

IP on network 160.20 uses ARP to obtain the hardware address for 160.20.10.105.

Receiving the hardware address, the packet is sent out with the newly obtained address.

Packet information:
Source hardware address	5 (created the packet)
Source IP address	160.45.100.1
Destination hardware address	13
Destination IP address	160.20.0.3

Once on the 160.20 network, the NIC recognizes itself and grabs the packet off the wire.

Looking at the packet information, you see that the hardware addresses are changing as the packet goes on its journey. The IP addresses are never changed.

If the two network cards use different topologies, like Ethernet and Token Ring, then this is called a gateway. A gateway will translate the packets between these topologies.

DEDICATED COMPUTERS   Dedicated routers are machines that provide only routing and translation services between networks and topologies. Additional services may include security and routing path optimization software such as Border Gateway Protocol (BGP),= or Open Shortest Path First (OSPF).

Most dedicated routers are not multiuser systems that provide file and print services like Windows 2000 Server would; for example, there is usually no monitor or keyboard attached. Terminal access to dedicated routers is usually via a telnet session across the network or from a dial-in port on the router itself. Some routers do have terminal ports, not video ports like a PC, but just the dumb terminal ports that support terminals with a VT100 or better display emulation. Some of the well-known brand names for routers include Bay Networks, Cisco, Digital, Fore Systems, IBM, and Cabletron Systems.

These routers have their own built-in language for managing their features. They are dedicated to routing functions only and can be programmed for many different features along with advanced routing features. Windows 2000 Server provides a few of the many possible features available on these dedicated routers.

Mixing routing vendors usually means losing some of the functionality that is proprietary in nature to each manufacturer, forcing you to use the lowest common denominator between them.

Gateway

The term *gateway* is used to identify the network interface that can transfer or route a packet from one network to another network interface on another network. Gateways are routers that can also translate the packet format between topologies. For instance, a Token Ring NIC and an Ethernet NIC would require packet translation to the different formats. Pure routers simply use software to forward a packet between interfaces.

Multihomed Hosts

Multihomed means there are two or more network interfaces on one machine. This is common on routers and switching equipment. Many Network Operating Systems using TCP/IP (Windows 2000 Server, Novell, Banyan, UNIX, and others) also provide this routing service between network interfaces. Each network card or modem connection has a network interface number specific to the network to which it is attached. Routing is the transferring of a packet from one LAN to another via a software program, the routing software.

Multiple Cards with Two Different IP Addresses

Each network interface card gets an IP address specific to the network to which it is attached. Some administrators like to use the last few addresses for their router connections and some like to use the first few addresses for routers and possibly servers. It makes no difference technically. The second network card acts as the default gateway for remote packets for the first network card and vice versa. The routing software then takes care of the actual packet transfer. In TPC/IP networks, the Network Mask is used to determine whether a packet should be routed. The packet is routed if the network number for the destination host does not match the network number of the local host.

Single Adapter Systems

There is a special case of a single card acting as a router to two sets of networks that actually share the same local area cabling media.

In the case of the single network interface card you would have to have two distinct network IP addresses assigned to it, one for each network to be accessed. Static routes should be added to the interface so that packets from either network interface will use the other IP address on the same card as their default gateway. This is also known as a *logically multihomed network interface.*

Static and Dynamic Routing

Early routers had to be programmed with exactly which networks they could route between which interfaces, especially if there were many network interfaces. This configuration method is called *static routing.* Pre-set routing tables are loaded from a disk file or EPROM into the router software at boot time or after any reset or reboot.

Dynamic routing sends special route information packets between routers. RIP is the most widely used dynamic routing protocol. Dynamic routing protocols advertise the routes they are familiar with and pass on the metrics, number of other routers, or hops, required to get from their host to another network, either directly or indirectly through another router.

Features of Static Routing

Static routing refers to a specific table of routes input by you. This requires you as the router manager to manually configure the specific routing information for each interface. Each network card can be programmed with explicit routes to allow and or disallow specific routes. This gives the administrator explicit control over each interface. Additionally, you as the administrator can add the costs associated with routes as well as other related metrics to manage the flow of traffic between networks.

Features of Dynamic Routing

Dynamic routing protocols advertise the routes they are familiar with and pass on the metrics, number of other routers, or hops, required to get from their host to another network, either directly or indirectly through another router. No further set up is required for all the interfaces, they learn from the other routers over time. However, dynamic routing generates continuous traffic from the routers with route update information and they can be attacked from external sources with falsified RIP packets, which requires much more security and attention by a security officer, or you, for corruption and attacks.

HEADSTART OBJECTIVE 26.05

Routing Tables

Each independent router port has a routing table. In a simple scenario with two networks only, the routing table would contain one entry for each card pointing to the other network interface as the gateway. This is a simplified description, as there are other routes that are not discussed in detail, such as references to internal interfaces, network, and broadcast addresses.

To view the IP Routing Table, right click Static Routes in the console tree and select All Tasks | Show IP Routing Table, as illustrated in Figure 26-4.

To add a new static route to the Routing Table, right click again on Static Routes in the console tree and select New | Static Route, which will open the Static Route dialog box (shown next) and enter in the applicable values.

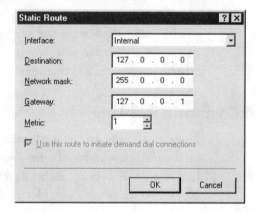

FIGURE 26-4   Viewing the Routing Table

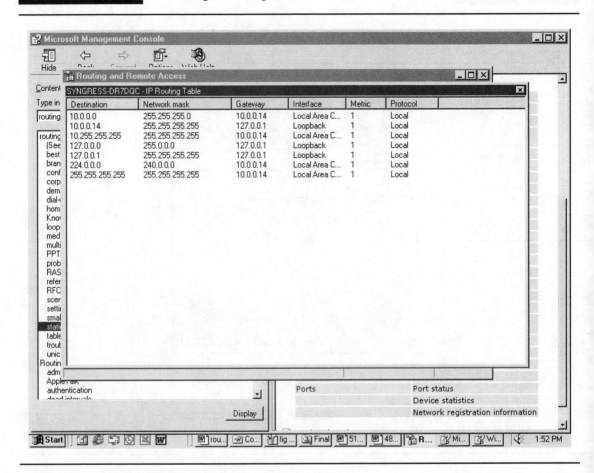

OSPF

Open Shortest Path First (OSPF) is used for IP routing in very large networks. OSPF is far more complex to configure and manage than RIP, but it is also far more efficient in managing network resources once it is up and running. To add OSPF, right click "General" under IP Routing on the console tree, and select New | Routing Protocol. Select OSPF, as shown in Figure 26-5.

FIGURE 26-5   Adding the OSPF protocol.

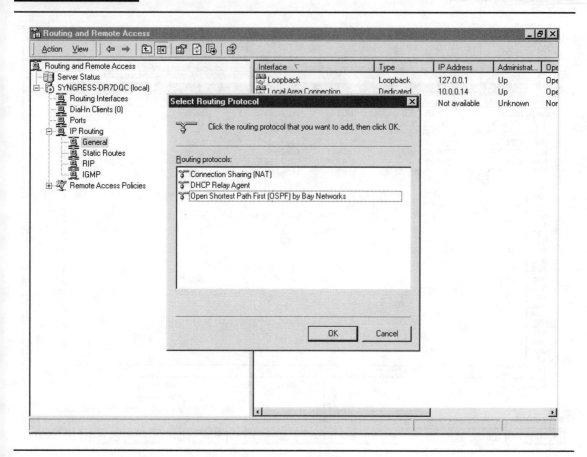

Subnet Broadcast

The broadcast address for every subnet is the network number combined with all the client bits being set to one, or the last address in the network range. The broadcast address is used by many protocols to send a general query to all machines on the network so that one or more of them may respond. For example, the Address Resolution Protocol (ARP) uses a broadcast to the network to locate the IP address of a local host.

BRIEF OVERVIEW OF IP NUMBERING   IP (current version) addressing uses 32 bits conveniently broken into 4 octets, or 4 sets of 8 bits. A Network Number represents one combination of some of those 32 bits, from 2 minimum to 30 maximum. Generally, there are 3 well known groups called Class A, B, and C address ranges. The Class A addresses each have 24 bits that can be used for client numbers or over 16 million IP addresses; the network number in the first 8 bits does not change. The Class B network address is contained in the first 16 bits and the last 16 bits are used for client addresses, allowing for a total of 65,533 values. A Class C network address is in the first 24 bits and the last 8 bits are used for the client addresses.

Example of addresses in each basic class (using default masks):

Class A 1-126 first octet value (127 reserved for Loopback)
12.33.234.23   255.0.0.0   12.0.0.0 Network   33.234.23 Client
58.38.94.123   255.0.0.0   58.0.0.0 Network   38.94.123 Client

Class B 128-191 first octet value
162.3.24.73   255.255.0.0   162.3.0.0 Network   24.73 Client
144.223.4.5   255.255.0.0   144.223.0.0 Network   4.5 Client

Class C 192- 223 first octet value
212.78.231.59   255.255.255.0   212.78.231.0 Network   59 Client
212.78.231.60   255.255.255.0   212.78.231.0 Network   60 Client

Classes D and E range from 224 to 254 in the first octet and are reserved for special uses.

BROADCAST ADDRESS   In a Class A network, the 24 bits for the clients represent all the numbers between 1 and $2^{24}-1$. The zero address, like 12.0.0.0, is reserved as the network number. The last address, where all the client bits are set to the value 1, is the broadcast address, 12.255.255.255.

DEFAULT MASK The *default mask* is a number that identifies all the bits that represent the network number part of the IP address. For a Class A address, 255.0.0.0 is the default mask. This implies that all of the first 8 bits represent the network number. For a Class B address, the first 16 bits indicate the network number; the mask is 255.255.0.0 by default. For a Class C network, the first 24 bits define the network number and the mask is 255.255.255.0 by default.

SUBNETTING Subnetting allows you to further break up a standard Class A, B, or C network into smaller sections. By using some of what are normally considered the client bits as part of the network mask, then you can subdivide larger groups into smaller groups of IP addresses.

You can subnet using all but the first bit and last 2 bits of the client addresses. The Class A addresses allow 2 to 22 bits, Class B allow 2 to 14 bits, and Class C allow 2 to 6 bits of the client bits to be used in subnetting the network.

If you use the first 3 bits from any Class A, B, or C network address and include this as part of the subnet, your network masks become

- 255.224.0.0 for Class A
- 255.255.224.0 for Class B
- 255.255.255.224 for Class C

The following section is a more complete example of subnetting various address classes using 2 bits. If you use the first 2 bits from any Class A, B, or C network address and include this as part of the subnet, your network masks become

- 255.192.0.0 for Class A
- 255.255.192.0 for Class B
- 255.255.255.192 for Class C

This creates 4 blocks from the original set of addresses for any class since the 2 bits have 4 possible combinations: 00, 01, 10, and 11. Unfortunately, you should not use any block that uses all zeros or all ones. This excludes the 00 and 11 address blocks. You end up with the 01 and 10 blocks or 2 subnets. The formula for the number of groups created is 2^n-2 (2 to the power of n less 2) where n is the number of bits used to create the subnets. This is summarized in Table 26-1.

| **TABLE 26-1** | Subnet Client Addresses, Network Number, and Broadcast Addresses for Each Network Class |

Basic Class A Network has $2^{24}-2$ clients (~16 million)				
Network	Using Netmask	First Client	Last Client	Broadcast Address
12.0.0.0	255.0.0.0	12.0.0.1	12.255.255.254	12.255.255.255
Class A Network with two subnets of $2^{22}-2$ clients (~4 million) each				
12.64.0.0	255.192.0.0	12.64.0.1	12.127.255.254	12.127.255.255
12.128.0.0	255.192.0.0	12.128.0.1	12.191.255.254	12.191.255.255
Basic Class B Network has $2^{16}-2$ clients (64K) clients				
Network	Using Netmask	First Client	Last Client	Broadcast Address
162.2.0.0	255.255.0.0	162.2.0.1	162.2.255.254	162.2.255.255
Class B Network with two subnets of $2^{14}-2$ clients (~16K) each				
162.2.64.0	255.255.192.0	162.2.64.1	162.2.127.254	162.2.127.255
162.2.128.0	255.255.192.0	162.2.128.1	162.2.191.254	162.2.191.255
Basic Class C Network has 2^8-2 = 254 clients				
Network	Using Netmask	First Client	Last Client	Broadcast Address
212.3.6.0	255.255.255.0	212.3.6.1	212.3.6.254	212.3.6.255
Class C Network with two subnets of 2^6-2 clients (62) clients each				
212.3.6.64	255.255.255.192	212.3.6.65	212.3.6.126	212.3.6.127
212.3.6.192	255.255.255.192	212.3.6.129	212.3.6.190	212.3.6.191

Network Broadcasts

The network broadcast address is the last address available for a given network; all client bits are set to the value 1. This address is used to send general query packets to all hosts on the network. Broadcast packets are used extensively in all network protocols to establish information about zero or more hosts. Any packet using this address as the destination address forces every host on the network to interpret the request and reply if the request pertains to that host. This is similar to requesting a show of hands from everyone in a theater lineup who has a ticket. This would be considered a broadcast message that everyone listens to, whether or not they respond. For example, a broadcast message might be to request the hardware address for a given host name.

Local Loopback

There is one specialized network address that is reserved on every machine to represent the "software." This is called the *local loopback address*. On every machine, the Class A network 127.0.0.0 is used to represent the TCP/IP software. You can ping the loopback to test if your software is running. Normally, the loopback is numbered 127.0.0.1 but any numbers after the 127. are acceptable, for example, 127.23.45.67. Just remember the octet numbers vary between 0 and 255. IP addresses use 8-bit numbers and can never exceed the value 255.

Local Network

Your local network is defined as all hosts using the same network number. In Table 26-1 the Class A network is 12.0.0.0 and all the local hosts are the IP addresses from 12.0.0.1 to 12.255.255.254. The broadcast address is the last address of this network, 12.255.255.255.

The assumption is that all host numbers for your local network are reachable directly; no gateway is needed. This defines a local area network. You could have 16 million connections on one Class A local area network but it would not be efficient. Nor would 64 thousand nodes on a Class B network be efficient, although you could try. You could not do this using one Ethernet segment as there is a limitation to number of nodes and overall wire length; but, with enough bridges and repeaters, you might be able to do it.

CHAPTER SUMMARY

Most of the administrative tasks associated with IP routing have been moved from the Network control panel to the Routing and Remote Access service, which is launched from the Administrative Tools program group. The host computer can be enabled as a network router by adding the server to Routing and Remote Access and enabling it as a router. Router Internet Protocol (RIP) is used by neighboring networks to communicate with each other. RIP messages are sent frequently to all adjacent routers from every other router providing basic route and hop information. A gateway provides router and protocol translation. Both a router and a gateway forward packets, also called *datagrams*, around a network; this is true routing. A *bridge* provides selective connection between LANs where only packets destined for the other side cross the bridge. The broadcast address for every subnet is the network number combined with all the client bits being set to one, or the last address in the network range. Early routers had to be programmed with exactly which networks they could route between which interfaces, especially if there were many network interfaces. This configuration method is called *static routing*. *Dynamic routing* sends special route information packets between routers. RIP is the most widely used dynamic routing protocol. Open Shortest Path First (OSPF) is used for IP routing in very large networks. OSPF is far more complex to configure and manage than RIP, but it is also far more efficient in managing network resources once it is up and running.

TWO-MINUTE DRILL

- ❑ In Windows 2000 Server, Microsoft has moved all of the IP Routing services from the familiar Services Tab in the Network control panel into the Routing and Remote Access Service.

- ❑ The term *router* is sometimes generically used to imply packet forwarding and protocol translation. Strictly speaking, this is a *gateway*, which is one step up from a pure router. A gateway provides router and protocol translation.

- ❑ Both a router and a gateway forward packets, also called *datagrams*, around a network; this is true routing.

❑ A *bridge* provides selective connection between LANs where only packets destined for the other side cross the bridge.

❑ Router Internet Protocol (RIP) is a common Interior Gateway Protocol (IGP) used by neighboring networks to communicate with each other.

❑ Any multihomed (multiple Network Interface Cards) Windows 2000 Server system can be configured as a router, not only for the same protocol, such as TCP/IP, but for other protocols as well, like IPX/SPX using RIP for IPX/SPX, or between topologies like Ethernet and Token Ring.

❑ For a network protocol to be routable, the protocol software design must provide a mechanism for determining whether a packet is local or not.

❑ *Multihomed* means there are two or more network interfaces on one machine.

❑ *Dynamic routing* sends special route information packets between routers.

❑ The *default mask* is a number that identifies all the bits that represent the network number part of the IP address.

SELF TEST

The Self Test questions will help you measure your understanding of the material presented in this chapter. Read all the choices carefully, as there may be more than one correct answer. Choose all correct answers for each question.

1. What must you configure for static routing?

    A. RIP for Internet Protocol

    B. Enable IP Forwarding

    C. RIP for IPX/SPX

    D. Enable ROUTE service

2. What does OSPF stand for?

    A. Operating System Protocol Forwarder

    B. Offer and Selection Permanent Frame

    C. Open Shortest Path First

    D. Open Secure Path Frame

3. What does RIP provide?

    A. Static Routing

    B. Dynamic Routing

    C. Static Routing Information Display

    D. Dynamic Routing Information Display

4. How many IP addresses can be maintained for one network interface?

    A. 1

    B. 2

    C. 5

    D. 255

5. What is the default Network Mask for a Class B network?

    A. 255.255.255.255

    B. 255.255.255.0

    C. 255.255.0.0

    D. 255.0.0.0

6. What is the default Network Mask for six subnets in a Class B network? (Hint: Subnets is 2^n-2 where n is the number of bits.)

    A. 255.255.255.248

    B. 255.255.255.240

    C. 255.255.224.0

    D. 255.192.0.0

7. How many bits does IP version 4.x use.

    A. 8

    B. 16

    C. 32

    D. 128

8. How many bits in a Class A network address can be used for client numbers?

    A. 16

    B. 24

    C. 32

    D. 128

9. What is the total number of client address values available in a Class B network address?

    A. 16 million

    B. 64,000

    C. 65,533

    D. 128

10. Which of the following is an acceptable loopback address?

    A. 127.23.45.67

    B. 255.255.255.0

    C. 12.0.0.1

    D. 255.255.255.192

MICROSOFT CERTIFIED SYSTEMS ENGINEER

27

VPN

You may have already heard about Virtual Private Networks (VPNs)—one of the hottest new technologies in the networking world. You may also have some questions about it. What is a VPN, and how does it work? Is it worth the time and effort? Will it save your company money? This chapter helps to explain this new tool that takes advantage of Internet connectivity to give your organization a cost-effective way to extend its LAN. Both Windows NT and the Windows 9x operating systems are capable of establishing a VPN connection. However, Windows 2000 is ushering in the next era of network operating systems by providing the ability to establish a secure connection "tunnel" through the Internet in a way that is easier to implement than ever before.

The MCSE 2000 certification exams cover many Internet connection-related areas, and VPN is likely to show itself in one or more of these new exams. Be prepared to encounter this topic, and be sure you understand what is required to implement and manage virtual private networking in your enterprise.

The Role of VPN in an Enterprise Network

First, let's look at exactly what a VPN is, how it works, and where this technology fits into the modern enterprise network. Then we'll examine how to plan and implement one in your own business.

What Is a Virtual Private Network?

Virtual Private Network: Let's break the phrase down into its component parts. "Network" is just that, a computer network. The definition of a network may vary (there are business networks, home networks, phone networks, cable networks, etc.), but the standard definition of a network is two or more (sometimes a great many more) computers and peripherals connected together via cabling or wireless media for the purpose of sharing resources. (For more information on the basics of networking, a good starting place is *MCSE Networking Essentials Study Guide*, for Exam 70-58, by Syngress and Osborne/McGraw-Hill.) In this discussion of VPNs, you need to understand that the "Network" you're joining has a physical presence somewhere, and you may not necessarily "see" all the pieces. This leads to our discussion of the "Private" and "Virtual" aspects of VPN.

Private Networking Over Public Media

"Private" is the part that makes VPNs special, and so useful. You and/or others will be participating in a network that will consist of only authorized users—even though you are connecting through the very public global Internet. You will typically be required to supply authentication information (a valid user name and password) just as when you log on to your company's private network onsite. With a VPN, the privacy is maintained by the process of *tunneling*, or encapsulating one protocol inside another, and by encryption.

Virtual Networking

This brings us to the "Virtual" part. The VPN connection to the company's network will allow users to print, access files, browse the Internet, and all the other things they can do from their individual workspaces at the office. Yet, they may be doing all this from their homes or hotel rooms. That's what makes it virtual.

To the user, the "virtuality" of the network is almost completely transparent; there is no difference (other than possibly the speed of the data transfer) between working with network resources from a remote location and working with them from a computer that is physically cabled to the LAN. Only the way the connection is established and maintained differs.

Suppose your company's home office is in Houston and you are in a hotel room in Seattle preparing for an important meeting with Bill Gates.

You used to have to dial in to a modem pool via a 1-800 number. Now, you establish a connection to a national Internet Service Provider (ISP) by making a local phone call. After you establish the connection, you dial in to your corporate headquarters. How can you do this?

Basic Requirements

VPN makes use of three components:

- A client computer with a modem or other Internet connection device (router, ISDN, etc.)

- A dial-up account with an ISP (including local or national ISPs such as Earthlink, AT&T, or dallas.net), or a dedicated connection to the Internet (DSL, ISDN, or frame relay)

- A destination server within the corporate network with a permanent or on-demand connection to the Internet

If you have a Windows 2000 Server (running the appropriate services, which we discuss later in the chapter), a laptop or desktop PC, and the means to connect to the Internet, you can implement a VPN. However, you may still be asking yourself why you would want to do this.

Benefits of Using Virtual Private Networking

Here's an example of how virtual private networking can benefit you and your organization: Let us assume you're a traveling salesperson and have to upload your orders daily to the company's Sales server (located in Houston). Your company has 35 modems for its 75 salespeople. The Sales staff is tasked with uploading their sales reports daily. They access these dial-up servers via a 1-800 number (there are some direct-dial numbers, but there will be long-distance charges if the salesperson isn't in Houston). The company can run up a large phone bill using conventional dial-up methods. If money isn't a problem, you still have to concern yourself with the low reliability of modems and the fact that only 35 of the salespeople can access the server simultaneously. These are problems that a VPN can resolve fairly easily.

A Windows 2000 VPN server (or servers) will most likely have a direct connection to the Internet using a high-speed link such as a T1 line or ISDN, and a network card that connects it to your company's network. Your client computer will have a modem (or other device allowing connection to the Internet) and a Dial-Up Networking connection to your ISP. Establishing the VPN connection is a two-step process. You first dial the modem number of your provider and make a connection. After you've successfully connected, you create another connection to connect to the VPN server. However, this second connection doesn't dial a phone number. It has been configured instead with the unique IP address or Fully Qualified Domain Name (FQDN) of the VPN server. Using the connection to the Internet that you've already established, your laptop will "tunnel" through that connection and find the VPN server (which is also connected to the Internet).

Does this implementation solve our salesperson's problems? Well, let's see what we've accomplished. All 75 salespeople can connect if they all have ISP accounts and phone lines. There's really no "logical" limitation on the number of users that can connect to the VPN server. The only "physical" limitation comes from the amount of bandwidth available to your VPN server (a 128 Kbps ISDN line will not be able to support as many connections as a 1.54 Mbps T1 line). The modems can be eliminated, which could save a lot of money in long-distance fees, not to mention maintenance costs for the equipment itself.

Can you see the possibilities now? VPN technology has been around for a while, but only recently has it begun to become popular in the corporate networking world. With an increasing number of employees working from home, businesses are trying to find ways to keep them connected *and* save money. Plus, there's the advantage of being able to connect to your network from anywhere in the world, and still maintain a high level of security.

The benefits of a VPN are obvious. If you're now convinced that your company needs to build one, read on for some details about the specific technologies (PPTP and L2PT), and the additional ammunition you'll need to convince your boss (or yourself) that a VPN is reliable, secure, cost-effective, and—with Windows 2000—easier than ever to construct.

Point-to-Point Tunneling Protocol

An entire book could be written on the Point-to-Point Tunneling Protocol (PPTP). PPTP is one of a handful of methods that can be used for creating a VPN. Since this chapter is focused on how VPN technology relates to the MCSE exams, we'll concentrate on two of them: PPTP and L2TP, the tunneling protocols supported by Microsoft Windows 2000.

What is PPTP? It is a simple extension of the Point-to-Point Protocol (PPP) data link layer protocol that is used to allow a "point-to-point" connection between two nodes via serial lines. PPTP allows traditional routable or nonroutable network protocols such as TCP/IP, IPX/SPX, and NetBEUI to be transported over lines your users will be using to connect to your network. The tunnel is actually created by the encapsulation (and, at the receiving end, decapsulation) of the PPTP packets as they are transferred from one machine to another. The PPP frames are encrypted within the PPTP packets, which allows for highly secure communications.

User Authentication

Having PPTP installed on a server doesn't automatically mean that anyone can connect to it from the Internet (the virtual network wouldn't be very "private" if they could). PPTP will handle the data that is sent and received; but, before a connection can be established, the user's credentials must be verified. The network to which the user is connecting uses standard Microsoft authentication in this case. (Windows 2000 will also allow RADIUS authentication for VPN users—see Chapter 24, "RAS and RADIUS Networking".) Windows 2000 will require the user to submit the logon name and the password before any connection to the network is allowed. Users will find the authentication process very similar to the typical logon routine. The only difference is that this time the user is not in the office, but could be miles or continents away.

For the exams, be aware that Microsoft has added client functionality into the Windows 2000 products as well as Windows NT 4.0, Windows 95, and Windows 98. It is not necessary to have a detailed knowledge of the inner workings of PPTP and how each frame is packaged, or the details of the encapsulation and encryption processes. What *is* necessary to understand is the step-by-step procedure of what happens when a user attempts to connect.

on the **!** **j**ob

It will be beneficial, in planning the implementation of VPN connections to your network, to draw a diagram of the network as it currently exists. This diagram can be as simple as line drawings with balloons for computer and networking components, or can involve third-party software specially designed for detailed diagramming (such as Visio). Understanding the details of your network and how users connect to the servers will be invaluable when troubleshooting network problems. For the creation of a VPN, you need to know exactly how and where the users are currently logging on to the network (such as through a modem pool). Once you have it all down on paper, you can then break up the network into areas that can be refined or reworked to increase efficiency and reduce cost. In this example, the RAS modem pool on a diagram would indicate an area you might want to investigate for possible replacement. Consider all the options (maybe a VPN isn't the only or best solution here), and make a decision that will get the job done and will be supportable by administrator(s) and cost-effective to management.

How Remote Access Works

Before we examine the VPN connection process more deeply, let's look at the old tried-and-true method of dialing up to a Windows server using Remote Access Service (RAS). RAS allows a user to dial directly via a point-to-point connection to a server.

Figure 27-1 shows a typical server running Windows 2000 and functioning as a RAS server. It has a modem pool and is connected to the Houston company's network. Our fictional user, Lisa, is working from her hotel room in Seattle, and wants to connect to the company network to check her mail and upload some files.

Lisa is running Windows 2000 Professional on her laptop. She dials the 1-800 number to connect to the Houston server. She is prompted for her

FIGURE 27-1 A typical server running Windows 2000 with RAS

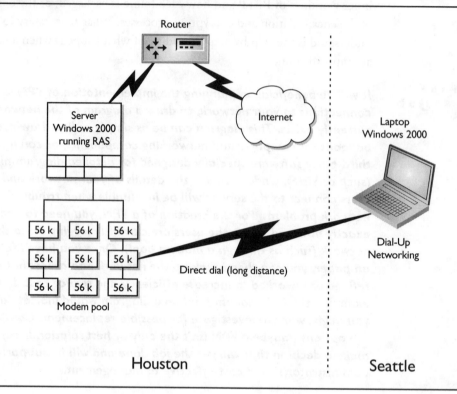

Houston   Seattle

user name and password, and if all goes well, she will be authenticated and allowed to work on the network.

Two important points need to be made here regarding her connection:

- The 1-800 number is expensive, especially if she needs to stay connected for a significant period of time.

- The modem she dialed in to is a 28.8 Kbps, so although she has a 56 Kbps on her laptop, data will be transferred at the lower connection speed.

How does VPN connection compare, based on the preceding three points? Let's look at Figure 27-2.

In Figure 27-2, we have the same Windows 2000 Server running the Routing and Remote Access Service, but this time it has a PPTP device driver installed. It has a direct connection to the Internet through a router on the network (and a high-speed T1 connection to boot). Lisa still has her Windows 2000 Professional laptop and modem, but this time she's in Tampa and has connected to her ISP's local dial-up number. Her laptop is also configured as a VPN client.

FIGURE 27-2	Windows 2000 Server with RAS and PPTP

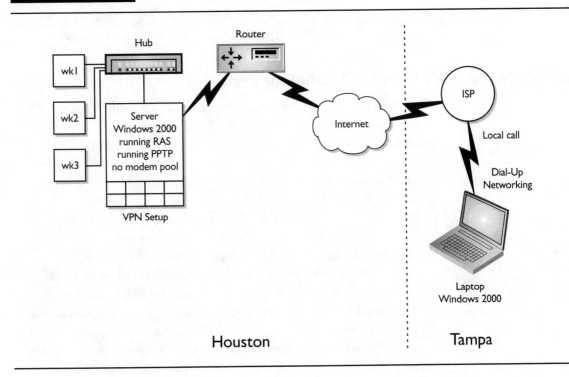

Here are three important points about this second connection:

■ Since she's dialing a local phone number for her ISP, the cost is minimal to her and the company, making this a more cost-effective solution.

■ Her connection speed to her ISP is 53 Kbps (56K modems very rarely connect at 56 Kbs), and this will not be bottlenecked by slow modems at the server end, making this a higher-performance solution.

■ No data will flow until the VPN server has authenticated her, making connection at least as secure as the dial-up connection.

Now that you understand how RAS and VPN differ, you can understand why the PPTP is such an important component. It provides the security that makes a low-cost, high-speed connection over the Internet feasible.

L2TP: Microsoft's Newest Tunneling Protocol

While virtual private networking is not a new concept with Windows 2000, its implementation in Microsoft's new operating system differs from its previous incarnation in Windows NT 4.0. PPTP was the only VPN protocol supported by NT, but Windows 2000 gives you a choice: a VPN can be established using either PPTP, or its new and improved implementation, Layer 2 Tunneling Protocol (L2TP).

Like PPTP, L2TP encapsulates PPP frames, which in turn encapsulate IP, IPX, or NetBEUI protocols. This allows users to remotely run applications that are dependent upon specific network protocols.

By using the new Internet Protocol Security (IPSec) authentication and encryption protocol in Windows 2000, data transfer through an L2TP-enabled VPN is as secure as within a single LAN at a corporate site. L2TP over IPSec provides the primary VPN services of encapsulation and encryption of private data. Note that it is possible to have a non-IPSec-based (nonencrypted) L2TP connection where the PPP frame is sent in plaintext, but this is not recommended for VPN connections over the Internet because communications of this type are not secure.

L2TP has some limitations. Because the L2TP specifications did not include parameters for user authentication and client IP addressing, different vendors chose to extend the protocol in proprietary fashion. Because of this, interoperability is a limiting factor. In addition to the interoperability issue is a problem with using L2TP in networks that employ Network Address Translation (NAT). L2TP does not function on networks that use NAT.

The next sections give you the basics of how to install PPTP, and how to get it to work for you and for the users you support who are just itching to work from home.

heads
①P

Because VPNs are becoming very popular with businesses, systems administrators are expected to know how to install them quickly and cheaply. The first step is to be sure that your server hardware is adequate. Remember that the data encryption process is processor intensive. Be sure your CPU configuration is up to the task of supporting this extra processing overhead. For exam questions involving VPNs, remember that PPTP is a protocol, and Routing and Remote Access is a service.

HEADSTART OBJECTIVE 27.03

Planning a **VPN** Implementation **Strategy**

If you've come to the conclusion that a VPN would be a welcome addition to your network, then you'll want the details of planning an implementation. You need to understand everything involved in building a simple VPN before tackling a corporate-wide network. If you can design and build a single VPN server and get it working properly, then you will be able to implement virtual private networking throughout your enterprise. For a large or small network, the process is the same.

Server Hardware and Configuration

Let's look at the server requirements first:

■ A machine running Windows 2000 Server or Advanced Server (preferably with a high-end processor and plenty of RAM)

■ TCP/IP installed on the server

■ Routing and Remote Access Service installed on the server

■ PPTP or L2TP protocol installed on the server

■ PPTP or L2TP ports configured

■ Connection to the Internet (preferably with high-speed access)

Look at Figure 27-3. It shows a Windows 2000 Server connected to a company's network and to the Internet (via the router). It has a unique IP address that will be made known to the users attempting a VPN connection.

The Windows 2000 server was configured by the system administrator, (who, undoubtedly wishing to save him/herself some grief, made sure the server machine complied with the Hardware Compatibility published by Microsoft). The administrator will next install the RAS. If you're not familiar with RAS, see Chapter 24, "RAS and RADIUS Networking," for more details on its installation and configuration.

FIGURE 27-3

Diagramming a simple network set up for VPN connection

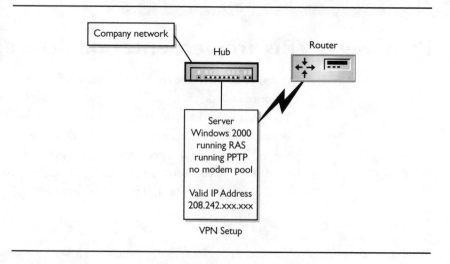

Installing the Tunneling Protocol

L2TP is installed with the Routing and Remote Access service. By default, L2TP is configured for five L2TP ports. You can enable L2TP ports for inbound remote access and demand-dial routing connections by using the Routing and Remote Access Wizard.

Installing Routing and Remote Access Services

1. Open Routing and Remote Access by choosing Start | Programs | Administrative Tools | Routing and Remote Access.

2. Right-click on the server you wish to configure and choose Configure and Enable Routing and Remote Access.

3. This invokes the Routing and Remote Access Wizard. Click Next on the opening splash screen, and you will be given five choices for configuring routing and remote access, including the option to make this computer a VPN server. Select this option and click Next.

4. Now you will be asked to designate the client protocols that will be used for VPN access and verify that they are installed on the server. Click Next.

5. The next dialog box will ask you to specify the type of Internet connection you will be using with this server (see Figure 27-4). Select the appropriate choice, and click Next.

6. Next you will be required to decide whether to let a DHCP server automatically assign IP addresses to remote clients, or be given the option to specify a range of addresses that may be assigned. If you have a DHCP server, select the first option. Click Next.

7. The dialog box shown in Figure 27-5 allows you to choose whether to use Remote Authentication Dial-In User Service (RADIUS) to provide a central authentication database for multiple remote access servers. Make your choice, and click Next.

8. Finally, you will see a screen that indicates that you have completed the steps necessary for the Wizard to configure routing and remote access on your server.

FIGURE 27-4

Designating the Internet connection type that the server will use

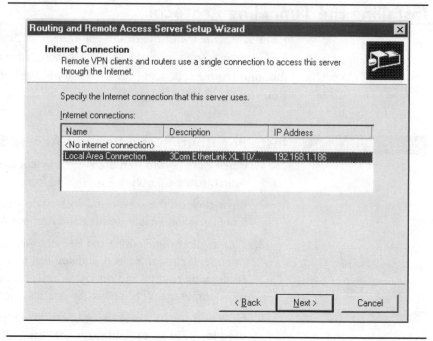

FIGURE 27-5

The Wizard lets you choose whether to use RADIUS to manage multiple remote access servers

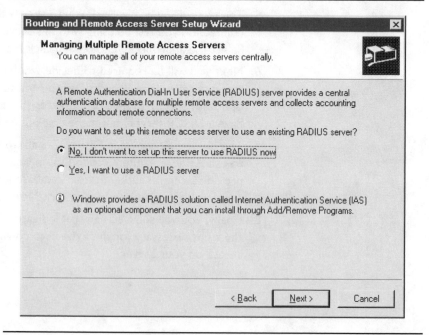

FIGURE 27-6

The Routing and Remote
Access MMC after
installation of remote
access services

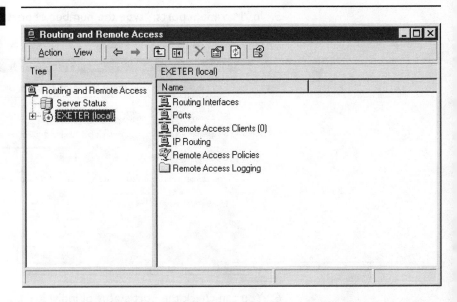

Once you have completed the Setup Wizard, it may take a few moments
for the remote access service to be initialized and start. Once it is started,
the objects shown in the right pane of the Routing and Remote Access
MMC (shown in Figure 27-6) will appear.

The Routing and Remote Access Service has now been successfully
installed, and the server configured to act as a VPN server.

PPTP or L2TP ports can be added through the Routing and Remote
Access MMC.

EXERCISE 27-2

Adding PPTP or L2TP Ports

1. Open Routing and Remote Access by choosing Start | Programs |
   Administrative Tools | Routing and Remote Access

2. In the console tree, click Ports.

3. Right-click Ports, and then click Properties.

4. In the Ports Properties dialog box, double-click either WAN
   Miniport (PPTP) or WAN Miniport (L2TP), to configure.

5. In "Maximum ports," type the number of ports (the default is 128), as shown next, and then click OK.

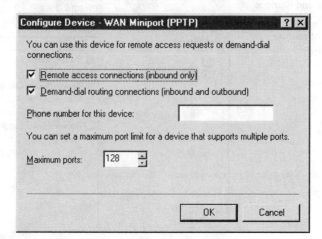

6. You can check the port status of individual ports by first clicking on Ports in the right pane of the MMC to expand the ports listing and then double-clicking on the port you wish to check, as shown next.

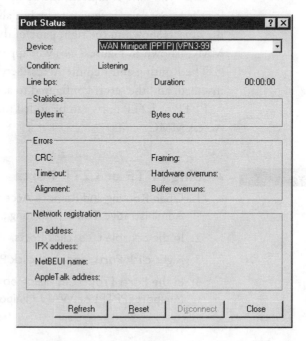

Now your VPN server is ready for users to connect securely to your private network over the Internet.

Configuring the Client Computer to Use the VPN

Prior to making a connection, you must first configure the client computer to connect to a VPN server using the virtual VPN adapter.

There are four components on the client machine that are needed for VPN to work:

■ An operating system that supports VPN connections. Microsoft operating systems include Windows 9*x*, Windows NT 4.0, and Windows 2000.

■ Installation of the Microsoft VPN virtual adapter (this takes place during the Connection Setup Wizard).

■ The TCP/IP protocol must be installed in order to establish the tunnel.

■ A network connection device (modem, Ethernet adapter, ISDN, etc.).

An ISP will be required if the client will be creating a tunnel via the Internet.

You are not limited to using TCP/IP as your networking protocol. The secure tunnel is established using TCP/IP as the networking protocol. However, the transport protocol that you use to communicate with the destination network can be NetBEUI or IPX/SPX.

Let's now go through the process of installing the VPN client.

EXERCISE 27-3

Installing and Configuring the VPN Client Software

1. Log on under any account with local administrator privileges.

2. Right-click the My Network Places icon on the desktop, and then click Properties.

3. You are now in the Network and Dial-up Connections window. Click the Make New Connection icon.

4. The Network Connection Wizard starts up and gives you the welcome screen. Click Next.

5. At this point, you will choose your connection type. Select the "Connect to a private network through the Internet" option and click Next.

6. The Wizard now asks if you would like to establish a RAS connection to an ISP before implementing the tunnel. Click No if you are using a dedicated connection to the Internet. If you do not have a dedicated connection, select "Automatically dial this initial connection," and then click the down arrow and select the dial-up account that will be used to establish the connection to the local ISP. In this case, select "Do not dial the initial connection," and click Next.

7. What is your VPN server's FQDN or IP address? If your VPN server has a dedicated IP address, enter that into the text box. If your VPN server has a dynamically assigned IP address, you can still connect to it via its FQDN. It should look like Figure 27-7. Click Next.

8. You can now choose who can use this VPN connection. Select "For all users" and click Next.

FIGURE 27-7

Entering the IP address or FQDN of the VPN server

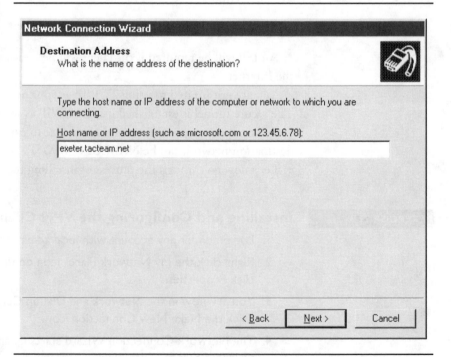

9. If you would like to allow other computers on the network to use this connection, you can place a check mark in the "Enable Internet Connection Sharing for this connection" box. If you choose to allow other users to access this connection over the network, you can choose whether on-demand dialing is enabled. In this case, leave the "Enable Internet Connection Sharing for this connection" empty and click Next.

10. You're just about finished. Type the name of this connection. Make it meaningful for the user. Select the "Add shortcut to my desktop" option. Click Finish.

You have successfully completed created a VPN connection!

HEADSTART OBJECTIVE 27.04

Planning a VPN Management Strategy

Now that you've built the VPN server, you need to test its functionality. Be sure to test client connections to the server from different access points and from a variety of platforms before putting the server into production. Thoroughly test your VPN client and server functionality prior to going online.

Let's look at some other issues to consider when developing a VPN management strategy.

Fault Tolerance

Understand that, at this juncture, you have a single point of failure. If the VPN server fails, all your users who depend on the VPN for their connections to the network are in limbo. If you kept your RAS modem pool, that could provide a measure of fault tolerance. A more cost-effective solution would be to build a backup VPN server *or* a second live VPN server. Either solution will work and will make you the hero—instead of the villain—when the original VPN server grinds to a halt.

Capacity Planning

Earlier in the chapter, it was mentioned that the VPN puts a small load on the server's processor(s). Due to the overhead of the encryption process, the server must utilize additional processor cycles. Consider performing server load testing prior to the widespread release of the server's active status. Microsoft will likely provide tools to provide "load stress" simulations in the future. Be sure to look for these after the release of Windows 2000.

You can determine if your VPN server is slowing down by using the Performance monitoring tool provided with Windows 2000. This tool allows you to monitor many system components and variables (too many to count), and you will want to monitor the processor statistics. When the percent processor time remains over 80 percent for an extended period, it may be time to upgrade the processor or install additional processors.

You can use the RAS Ports and RAS total performance objects to assess VPN server usage. If you are using RADIUS authentication and accounting, several performance objects are available. Some RADIUS performance objects include IAS Account Clients, IAS Accounting Server, IAS Authentication Clients, and IAS Authentication Server. You can click Explain to get details on these counters. Figure 27-8 demonstrates some of the IAS objects available. For more details on RADIUS authentication, see Chapter 24 on RADIUS networking.

heads
⊕P

Performance Monitor (now just called "Performance" in Windows 2000, and accessed through the Administrative Tools menu) is one of the subjects often covered on Microsoft Exams. It doesn't pertain to only VPNs, but you should be prepared for questions on what system components can be monitored and how. Familiarize yourself with the Performance Monitoring tool by using it to track some basic components on your server. Monitoring memory, processors, and hard drives are all possible candidates for Windows 2000 exam questions. It is one of the most powerful tools that Microsoft provides to an administrator for gathering information about performance issues.

FIGURE 27-8

IAS Accounting objects

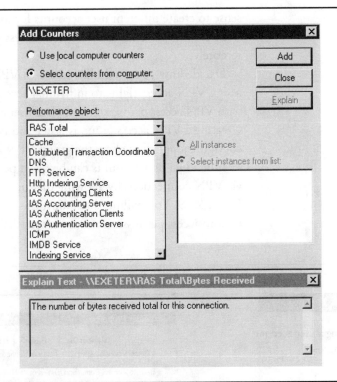

FIGURE 27-8

IAS Accounting objects

VPN Client IP Addressing Assignments

The VPN clients will require an IP address in order to participate in network activities. You can install a DHCP server and allow it to assign VPN clients their IP addresses, or you can create a static address pool dedicated to VPN client computers. Be sure to include both a WINS and a DNS server for IP addressing information to be delivered to the VPN clients.

VPN User Authentication

User accounts used to access the network via VPN are usually the same as those used when the user is connected to the network locally. It makes little sense to create different user accounts for local and VPN access—unless you want users to have fewer or different access privileges when connecting remotely.

Decide how you would like to assign VPN access. You can either assign VPN access rights to individual accounts, or you can create a group with VPN access permission and place user accounts into that group. Creating a VPN access group is faster and more efficient. You will need to configure a policy to allow the group VPN access.

Individual user accounts can be given permission to access the network via VPN connections by allowing dial-in permissions as depicted in Figure 27-9. You will need to adjust the remote access policy to grant remote access permissions to those with dial-in permissions enabled.

FIGURE 27-9

Configuring a user account for VPN access

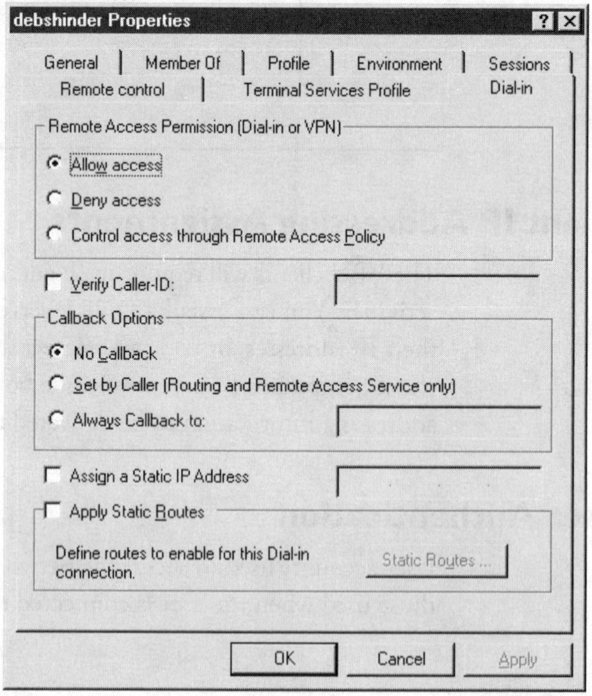

This represents some of the major aspects of VPN management. Other management considerations might include your organization's use of SNMP to monitor the VPN server remotely, using Enterprise Management tools.

ACCELERATING TO WINDOWS 2000

Windows 2000 provides the following new features for virtual private networks:

- **Layer Two Tunneling Protocol (L2TP)** You can now create Virtual Private Networks (VPNs) using either PPTP or L2TP. Support for L2TP is new in Windows 2000. L2TP utilizes the ability of the IPSec protocol, which provides encryption for L2TP. However, standards for IPSec have not been widely accepted. This poses a limiting factor when trying to adopt L2TP in a multivendor environment. Another limiting factor is that L2TP cannot be used in environments utilizing Network Address Translation (NAT). It is, however, an ideal intranet solution for networks standardized on Windows 2000.

- **Remote access policies** You can get tighter control over your remote access solution by using the new Remote Access Policies available in Windows 2000. If you need to create separate security parameters for VPN users

versus dial-in users, you can create a Remote Access Policy that will differentiate the two groups.

- **VPN Server and Client Creation Wizards** VPN Client and Server creation and configuration in Windows NT 4.0 was far from intuitive. In Windows 2000, simple, easy-to-use Wizards walk you through the process of creating your VPN.

- **Extensible Authentication Protocol (EAP)** EAP allows the administrator to "plug in" different authentication security providers outside of those included with Windows 2000. EAP allows your organization to take advantage of new authentication technologies including "smart card" logon and Certificate-based authentication. EAP information can be communicated to a RADIUS server if RADIUS authentication and accounting is enabled in your VPN solution.

QUESTIONS AND ANSWERS

How many inbound connections can a single VPN server have?	Inbound connections are limited by your hardware and connection capabilities. There are no built-in limitations to the number of ports you can create.
Can I create a single outbound VPN connection that all the users on my network can use?	Connection sharing is an option available in Windows 2000. All users on your network can connect via a single outbound VPN connection. Autodial is available if dial on demand is required.
What operating systems can I use as VPN clients?	Microsoft operating systems that support VPN client software include Windows 95/98, Windows NT 4.0, and Windows 2000.
What protocol must the client use in order to connect to a network via VPN?	TCP/IP must be installed in order to support the tunnel. However, if the destination network uses another protocol, such as NetBEUI or IPX/SPX, these LAN protocols can be used as the client transport protocol.
How much more will I have to spend to get the VPN software that goes with Windows 2000?	You don't have to pay more! VPN Server software is included with Windows 2000.

CHAPTER SUMMARY

The Windows 2000 MCSE exams may ask you questions about the theories and concepts involved in building a VPN, but on the job, what your boss cares about is whether you can put the knowledge into practice and build one for your company's network. Knowing that RAS and PPTP (or L2TP) are core components of a working VPN server will help you answer certain questions on the exams. But, more importantly, knowing the procedure for installing and configuring those components will help you actually get a VPN server up and running on your network.

In this chapter, we've tried to provide you with both the theories and the practical step-by-step procedures. We discussed what virtual private networking is and how it works, and we examined the basic requirements in terms of hardware and software for establishing a VPN. We compared the protocols that can be used for the creation of a private "tunnel," and then we went through the process of installing and configuring the components for a typical VPN server.

Be sure you understand the functions of each service and protocol used by a VPN server, and how they work together to provide a client with a connection. One last piece of advice: Now that you've read about it, go out and do it. Get your hands dirty (figuratively speaking). That's the best way to learn, both for the MCSE exams and for the ultimate test: real-life networking.

 # TWO-MINUTE DRILL

❑ The MCSE 2000 certification exams cover many Internet connection-related areas, and VPN is likely to show itself in one or more of these new exams.

❑ The definition of a network may vary (there are business networks, home networks, phone networks, cable networks, etc.), but the standard definition of a network is two or more (sometimes a great many more) computers and peripherals connected together via cabling or wireless media for the purpose of sharing resources.

❑ PPTP is a simple extension of the Point-to-Point Protocol (PPP) data link layer protocol that is used to allow a "point-to-point" connection between two nodes via serial lines.

❑ Remote Access Service (RAS) allows a user to dial directly via a point-to-point connection to a server.

❑ PPTP was the only VPN protocol supported by NT, but Windows 2000 gives you a choice: a VPN can be established using either PPTP, or its new and improved implementation, Layer 2 Tunneling Protocol (L2TP).

❏ By using the new Internet Protocol Security (IPSec) authentication and encryption protocol in Windows 2000, data transfer through an L2TP-enabled VPN is as secure as within a single LAN at a corporate site.

❏ If you can design and build a single VPN server and get it working properly, then you will be able to implement virtual private networking throughout your enterprise.

❏ You can enable L2TP ports for inbound remote access and demand-dial routing connections by using the Routing and Remote Access Wizard.

❏ PPTP or L2TP ports can be added through the Routing and Remote Access MMC.

❏ Prior to making a connection, you must first configure the client computer to connect to a VPN server using the virtual VPN adapter.

❏ You are not limited to using TCP/IP as your networking protocol. The secure tunnel is established using TCP/IP as the networking protocol. However, the transport protocol that you use to communicate with the destination network can be NetBEUI or IPX/SPX.

❏ If you kept your RAS modem pool, that could provide a measure of fault tolerance. A more cost-effective solution would be to build a backup VPN server *or* a second live VPN server.

❏ You can determine if your VPN server is slowing down by using the Performance monitoring tool provided with Windows 2000.

❏ Be sure to include both a WINS and a DNS server for IP addressing information to be delivered to the VPN clients.

❏ User accounts used to access the network via VPN are usually the same as those used when the user is connected to the network locally.

SELF TEST

The following questions will help you measure your understanding of the material presented in this chapter. Read all of the choices carefully, as there may be more than one correct answer. Choose all correct answers for each question.

1. What makes a VPN "private"?

    A. It does not allow any communication into or out of the user's PC.

    B. It uses a protocol that allows encrypted, point-to-point connections.

    C. Only one user can access a server at a time.

    D. Nothing that is typed in during a VPN session appears on the user's monitor.

2. Which statement is true?

    A. RAS is not as expensive as VPN.

    B. VPN requires a special modem on a laptop/PC.

    C. VPN can provide an alternative to modem pools.

    D. RAS uses PPP to create a VPN.

3. Which components could be used to create a VPN? (Choose all that apply.)

    A. ISDN adapter

    B. 56 Kbps modem

    C. DSL

    D. Router

4. Which statement is false?

    A. VPNs can save a company money.

    B. A VPN server does not necessarily have to connect to the Internet.

    C. RAS uses modem pools to provide users with dial-up connections.

    D. AOL is an Internet Service Provider.

5. What is a major drawback of traditional dial-up methods?

    A. Can be used over the Internet

    B. Requires ISDN lines

    C. High cost

    D. New technology

6. Which statement(s) is true?

    A. You must connect to an ISP first before establishing a VPN connection via the Internet.

    B. After establishing an Internet connection, you next dial up the VPN server.

    C. You can use L2TP to connect on a network that uses NAT.

    D. PPTP does not use encryption for authentication.

7. What must first be installed before PPTP can be added to a Windows 2000 server?

    A. Modem

    B. Routing and Remote Access Service

    C. IPSec

    D. Router

8. How many connections can be made to a VPN server?

   A. 10

   B. 128

   C. 1,024

   D. Limited only by hardware and connection type limitations.

9. Name two authentication Providers for Windows 2000 VPN connections.

   A. RADIUS

   B. Windows 2000 Security

   C. DIAMETER

   D. R2D2

10. A user is attempting to connect to a VPN server. What information could you provide to allow connection to the server? (Select all that might apply.)

    A. IP address of client machine

    B. IP address of VPN server

    C. Phone number for VPN server modem

    D. The Fully Qualified Domain Name

11. Which tool can you use to see who is logged on through the VPN?

    A. Routing and Remote Access Console

    B. Server Manager

    C. Performance Monitor

    D. PPTP Manager

12. Which tool can be used to monitor the VPN server processor for overutilization?

    A. RAS Administrator

    B. Performance snap-in

    C. Administrator Tools

    D. Processor Monitor

13. What tool do you use to create a client connection to a VPN server?

    A. RAS Administrator

    B. RAS tools

    C. Network Connection Wizard

    D. Network Properties dialog box

14. What are some important things to consider when planning a management strategy for your VPN network?

    A. Fault Tolerance

    B. Capacity Planning

    C. Authentication Methods

    D. IP Address assignments

15. Which of the following Microsoft operating systems can be a VPN client? (Choose all that apply.)

    A. Windows 3.11

    B. Windows 95/98

    C. Windows NT Workstation

    D. Windows 2000 Professional

28

Proxy Server

Proxy servers provide a much needed set of services in today's enterprise networks. Microsoft Proxy Server runs only on Windows NT Server computers, and its integration with the operating system and the Windows NT domain model gives it some unique advantages over most other proxy servers in Windows environments. This chapter explains the role of a proxy server in general, the specific added value of Microsoft Proxy Server, and how to implement and manage Proxy Server.

This chapter is not intended to be a complete study guide for the Proxy Server 2.0 exam—an entire book is needed to cover all of the items necessary. This chapter is meant to cover the major concepts and provide some technical details on implementing and managing Proxy Server.

HEADSTART OBJECTIVE 28.01

The Role of Proxy Server in an Enterprise Network

A proxy server can provide several functions for an enterprise network to facilitate and manage Internet access by client PCs. A proxy server, in simple terms, works in the following way:

1. The client browser (e.g., Internet Explorer), configured to use the proxy server for all requests that are not on the local network, requests a URL.

2. The proxy server analyzes the request to establish that the user, protocol, and remote host are not in violation of any of the configured permissions.

3. If the request is not rejected in step 2, the proxy server then fetches the URL and returns the file to the client. The client never establishes communication with the remote host. All contact with remote hosts is restricted to the proxy server.

Proxy servers can also *reverse proxy* to allow Web servers on your network to publish without ever establishing communications with computers beyond your network. All of your clients can access your internal Web servers directly, and the proxy server will handle URL requests coming from the Internet. The proxy server must be configured to route specific URL requests to the appropriate Web servers.

Since the clients and servers on your network never actually communicate with Internet hosts, computers on your network, with the exception of the proxy server, do not need a registered IP address. Networks using private IP addresses (e.g., 10.0.0.0 and 192.168.0.0 networks) do not need to obtain registered IP addresses for clients. This can also be accomplished with a router or server running NAT (network address translation), which is available on Windows 2000 Server. However, NAT is different from a proxy server because it works at a lower level of protocols in the OSI model. While a proxy server functions at the layer containing HTTP and FTP, NAT works only at the IP level. NAT simply changes the addresses on packets while a proxy server actually acts like an HTTP or FTP server.

Additionally, your client PCs do not even need to have TCP/IP installed for some applications. Microsoft Proxy Server supports clients using the IPX protocol, which is primarily used in Novell NetWare networks. Proxy servers are typically configured with two or more network adapters, one of which is assigned a registered Internet IP address. A proxy server uses a local address table (LAT) to determine what IP addresses are on the internal network, enabling it to distinguish between internal and external requests.

Fault Tolerance and Scalability

In addition to simply proxying Internet requests, there are a number of elements that are necessary for a proxy server to be suitable for enterprise use. The first of these is fault tolerance. Large networks need reliable network services to avoid costly downtime. Businesses, organizations, and government entities are becoming increasingly dependent on Internet connections, and a proxy server solution that cannot provide fault tolerance has no place in a modern enterprise network.

A proxy server solution can be designed so that an array comprised of two or more proxy servers provides fault tolerance and scalability. Clients configured with a list of IP addresses that includes all array members will automatically use another array member if one is not available. Microsoft Proxy Server clients update their configuration files at every initialization or every six hours, so changing one file on the server updates all clients. This is important since it allows the clients to be easily updated as an organization's proxy needs grow and servers are added.

When configured in arrays, Microsoft Proxy Server computers will maintain a distributed cache, which increases performance for clients. This scalability feature gives added value to the use of arrays in addition to their fault tolerance capabilities.

Microsoft Proxy Server also benefits from the plethora of fault-tolerant hardware available for Windows NT Server. Configuring proxy servers with RAID disk subsystems, fault-tolerant network adapters, and multiprocessor-capable systems will help ensure maximum uptime and scalability.

Proxy Server can also be configured to use a backup route to the Internet. If the primary link to the Internet fails, Proxy Server will use the backup route. For instance, if a proxy server is configured to use an upstream array, it can be configured to access the Internet directly if the array is not reachable.

Manageability

Another important attribute of a proxy server used in enterprise networks is manageability. If an organization using multiple proxy servers in an array needs to make a configuration change, it is important that changes can be made to the array as one unit instead of changing each server. Microsoft Proxy Server automatically synchronizes most configuration parameters between array members. However, certain parameters that are likely to be different from server to server are not synchronized. These parameters include cache size, cache location, enable caching flag, and log directories.

Proxy Server also includes a backup and restore function that enables administrators to easily manage the configuration of a server. Proxy Server writes its entire configuration to a backup file that, if needed, can be restored if the current configuration loses integrity or the server is replaced.

Command-line utilities can be used for many proxy server configuration tasks in addition to the GUI administration tools. This important feature enables administrators to use scripts to automate some of the maintenance chores.

Logging is a critical component of almost any enterprise application, and proxy servers are no exception. Proxy Server logs information to either text files or ODBC data sources.

Caching

Proxy servers that utilize HTTP and FTP caching can improve performance significantly. Microsoft Proxy Server's Web Proxy service caches both of these protocols, and when configured in an array, the cache index for each array member is available to all others. If an HTTP request is not cached on the server that receives the request, but the request is cached on another array member, the server will either refer the client to the proxy server that has the request in its cache or retrieve it from the other server for the client. Since cached requests are fulfilled from the internal network, client performance is improved.

Caching also preserves the bandwidth that is available between the Internet and the network. Requests that are fulfilled from cache do not use this bandwidth. Using properly configured cache settings and having plenty of disk space available for the cache can achieve significant performance improvement and bandwidth savings.

Firewall Capabilities

A good proxy server must be able to provide firewall functionality for enterprise networks. Microsoft Proxy Server provides dynamic packet filtering, packet alerts, packet logging, and domain filters to fill this need. Proxy Server filters both inbound and outbound packets, and opens ports only as needed. Alerts can be configured to warn administrators via e-mail or pager of certain events, including packets sent to an unused port. An administrator can also retain a security audit trail by using the packet-logging feature. Events can be written to a packet log or to the Windows NT System Event Log.

Microsoft Proxy Server also enables you to specify domain filters. These filters can block access to all domains except the ones listed, or allow access to all domains except the ones listed. Domain filters can be specified by domain names, IP addresses, or IP subnets. If a client requests a URL from a domain that is not permitted to a domain filter, an error message is returned. It is necessary to specify a filter for both IP addresses and domain names to control access to sites via WinSock Proxy.

A number of third-party plug-ins are available for Proxy Server to assist with blocking unwanted traffic, scanning for viruses, and other functions. Microsoft maintains information on some of these on the Proxy Server Web site (www.microsoft.com/proxy), and several of them are available there for evaluation download.

WinSock and SOCKS Support

Applications that communicate on the Internet commonly use either the WinSock or the SOCKS interface. These session layer interfaces must be supported by a proxy server for the applications to function properly. Proxy Server 2.0 includes services to proxy both WinSock and SOCKS applications.

Reverse Hosting and Proxying

Many organizations want to have HTTP servers on the internal network—behind the proxy and firewall. This can be accomplished by *reverse hosting* and *reverse proxying* services on the proxy server.

Reverse hosting is accomplished by binding a service on an internal server to a specific IP port on the proxy server's external network adapter. Traffic sent to that port from the Internet will be passed to the internal server, and the Internet client never knows that a proxy server is involved. Using reverse hosting limits you to using port 80, for example, for only one internal Web server. Since that port is bound to a server, all inbound traffic on port 80 will go to that server and can't be routed to any other servers.

heads ⏏️P

Some of the study materials available for Proxy Server 2.0 do not cover
how to configure reverse hosting for SMTP and other servers behind
Proxy Server. However, this is an item that is included in exam questions.

Reverse proxying allows you to use port 80 for a number of internal Web
servers, and Proxy Server maintains a list of "request path" and "route to" URLs.
Whenever a client requests a specific URL, the request is intercepted by the proxy
server, which then requests the appropriate URL from an internal server based on the
"route to" information for the URL requested by the client. Again, the client never
knows that a proxy server is involved. In the example in Table 28-1, a client requesting
http://www.thisco.com, http://www.thatco.com, or http://www.otherco.com will
resolve those host names via DNS. All three host names will resolve to the IP
address of the proxy server. When the proxy server receives a request for
www.thisco.com, it makes an HTTP request to the internal server named
ganymede, and then returns the results of that request to the client. As you can
see, requests to the beeswax directory can be routed to an entirely different
server than requests to the root and other subdirectories.

HEADSTART OBJECTIVE 28.02

Microsoft Proxy Server Services

Microsoft Proxy Server provides three distinct services—Web Proxy,
WinSock Proxy, and Socks Proxy—that combine to make it a complete
proxy solution for almost any network.

Security, Array, Auto Dial, and Plug-in settings affect all three services
(Figure 28-1). Buttons to configure each of these are present on the Service

TABLE 28-1		
	Request Path	**Route to**
Sample Table for Reverse Hosting with Proxy Server 2.0	http://www.thisco.com/	http://ganymede/
	http://www.thisco.com/beeswax/	http://callisto/
	http://www.thatco.com/	http://ios/
	http://www.otherco.com/	http://europa/

FIGURE 28-1

Options affecting multiple proxy services are Security, Array, Auto Dial, and Plug-ins

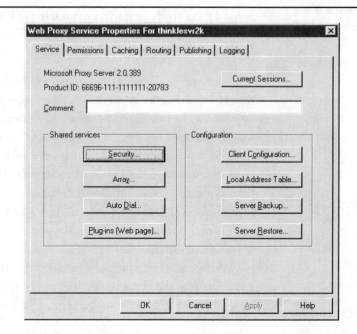

Properties page for all three services. The security settings include packet filters, domain filters, alerts, and logging options.

Packet filters are the primary firewall feature of Proxy Server. By defining packet filters, administrators can control exactly which packets can be passed from the Internet through the proxy server based on protocol, local port, remote port, local address, and remote address.

Domain filters are an easy way to deny or grant access to Internet sites (Figure 28-2). The Web Proxy and WinSock Proxy services share the domain filters set in the shared Security configuration. The Socks Proxy service has its own permissions configuration that allows you to grant or deny access based on domain, source or destination IP address, and port.

Alerts can be set for rejected packet, protocol violation, and disk full events. Alerts can be sent to the Windows NT Event Log, by SMTP mail, or both. Logging can be configured as regular or verbose, and can be grouped in daily, weekly, or monthly files. Logging can also be sent to a SQL/ODBC database, but Proxy Server will not log to both file and database at the same time. In addition to the shared logging, each service has its own log with the same options, and each can be set independently.

FIGURE 28-2

Denying access to Internet
sites through domain filters

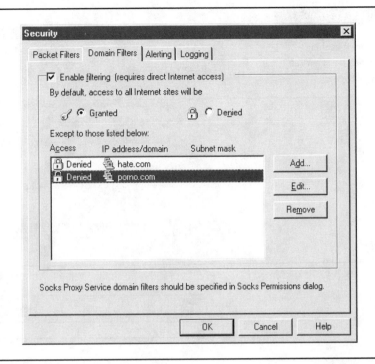

Web Proxy

Proxy Server's Web Proxy service handles HTTP, HTTPS, FTP, and Gopher
traffic between client PCs and Internet hosts. The Web Proxy service utilizes
caching to improve client response times and to conserve bandwidth on the
Internet link. Caching can be configured in a number of ways, from completely
disabled to a very aggressive, large cache (see Figure 28-3). Active caching is a
feature that updates the items in the cache when the service is idle. With active
caching disabled, items are not updated until a client requests them.

The maximum size of cached objects and Time To Live (TTL) settings
can also be configured (see Figure 28-4). The TTL values keep the service
from updating a cached item that is not changed very often. Cache filters
can also be set to either never cache or always cache URLs from specific sites
and subdirectories (see Figure 28-5).

Web Proxy includes the ability to internally publish HTTP and FTP by
either reverse proxying or reverse hosting (see Figure 28-6). User-level
security can be set on each Web Proxy protocol, and access can also be

FIGURE 28-3

Configuring caching
properties on the Web
Proxy service

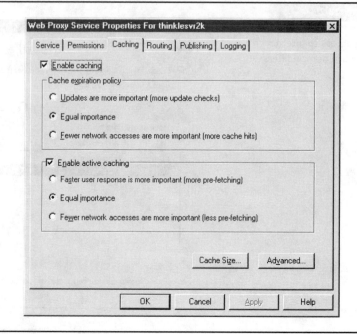

FIGURE 28-4

The TTL and size limit
settings for cache objects

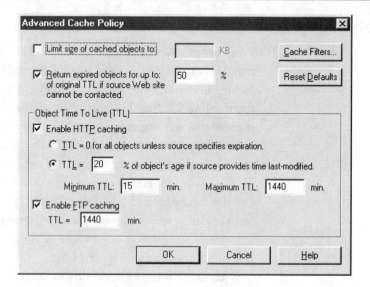

FIGURE 28-5

Configuring Web Proxy
cache filters

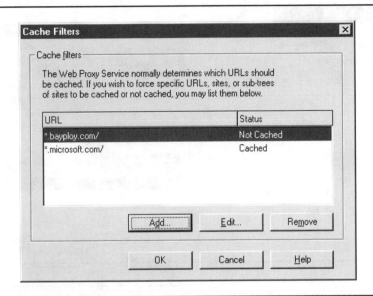

filtered by domain or IP address. All client access can be logged to a text file
or database, and Web Proxy will work with any CERN compliant browser
regardless of the client operating system.

on the **job**

*IIS 4.0's FTP publishing service is not compatible with reverse proxying
via Proxy Server 2.0. Although this information is not found in the
Microsoft documentation, it is a well-known fact and is published in
the Proxy FAQ titled "Tips from the Proxy Gurus" maintained at
http://proxyfaq.networkgods.com. Microsoft's official Proxy FAQ is at
http://support.microsoft.com/support/proxy/faq.*

The Web Proxy service also allows filtering of Internet sites so
administrators can restrict access to sites that violate company policy.
Domain filters are implemented through the shared security settings and
affect the Web Proxy and WinSock Proxy services.

WinSock Proxy

Telnet, mail, news, and IRC are some applications that use the Windows
Sockets interface. The Proxy Client directs WinSock communications to

FIGURE 28-6

Configuring publishing via
reverse proxying

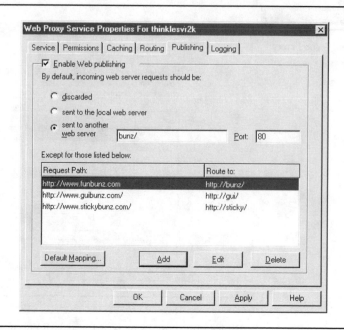

the proxy server, which forwards the communication on to its intended
destination. When the remote server responds, it responds to the proxy
server, which forwards the data to the client. The result is that these
applications work as if the client and remote server are directly connected
to each other. The function that Proxy Server performs is similar to NAT,
but Proxy Server adds the ability to control access to each defined WinSock
protocol by NT user group (see Figure 28-7).

The WinSock Proxy service supports both TCP/IP and IPX/SPX on
the internal network.. It also supports Windows NT Challenge/Response
authentication, and is compatible with applications written to the WinSock
1.1 specifications.

WinSock protocol definitions can be added, modified, or deleted (see
Figure 28-8). Several protocol definitions for popular WinSock application are
installed by default, and administrators can add new ones as necessary. Since
the definitions are set with initial and subsequent port connections,
connections from external clients are not allowed to pass through to internal
servers.

FIGURE 28-7

Configuring access control
for WinSock protocols

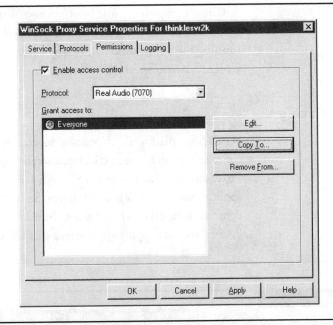

FIGURE 28-8

Editing a WinSock protocol

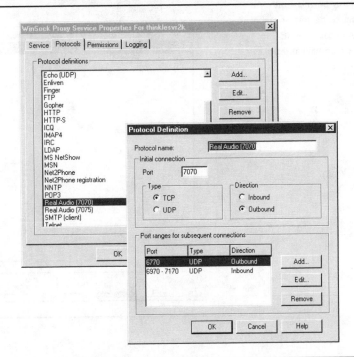

Client computers must be running a Windows operating system for the WinSock Proxy service to work properly. However, the Internet server running the application can be any common operating system such as UNIX, Macintosh, or Windows.

Socks Proxy

SOCKS is a platform-independent session-level interface used for communication between client and server applications. Proxy Server's Socks Proxy service, which supports SOCKS 4.3a, provides access to Internet applications to non-Windows clients. Security can be configured to permit or deny access based on IP addresses, domains, and ports (Figure 28-9). The Socks Proxy does not support applications that use UDP or clients using IPX/SPX.

FIGURE 28-9

Socks Proxy permissions can be set to permit or deny traffic based on IP address or domain and port numbers

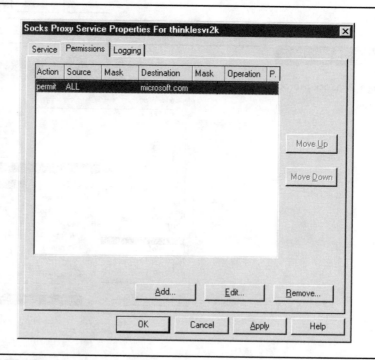

ACCELERATING TO WINDOWS 2000

Proxy Server Version 2.0 includes several improvements and features that were not available in the first version.

Distributed Caching

Proxy Server 2.0 is capable of distributing the cache among a number of servers. This provides performance improvements for clients because they have a much larger cache available to service their requests. Distributed caches can be set up with both proxy server arrays and chains.

- **Array-Based Caching** A distributed cache in a proxy array is one logical cache, parts of which exist on each array member. When a client requests an object that is contained anywhere within the array's cache, it will be redirected to the server with the cached content. The server that received the original request will retrieve the object for the client, as shown in Figure 28-10.

- **Chain-Based Caching** In a proxy chain, a proxy server is configured to use another proxy server to access the Internet. Accordingly, if the downstream proxy server requests an object that is in the upstream server's cache, the upstream server fulfills the

request from cache just as it would for a client. The difference between array-based caches and chain-based caches is that the downstream server in chain-based caching has no information regarding what is in the upstream server's cache. In an array, all members know what objects are in the array's cache.

Chain-based caching works with proxy arrays as well as individual servers. A downstream server or array can be configured to use an upstream server or array, as shown in Figure 28-11.

- **CARP** A new protocol developed by Microsoft, Cache Array Routing Protocol (CARP), is implemented in Proxy Server 2.0. Proxy servers use CARP, an Internet Engineering Task Force draft standard, to perform chain and array caching.

Firewall Features

Proxy Server 2.0 includes significant new firewall and security features. These enhancements make it much more secure than version 1 and are necessary in order to consolidate firewall and proxy services on one device.

- **Dynamic Packet Filtering** Firewalls are configured with rules to allow and deny

ACCELERATING TO WINDOWS 2000

specific packets. The ports that are allowed can be opened permanently or dynamically. When dynamic packet filtering is used, the filtering device opens the port when needed and closes it when communication is complete. Proxy Server 2.0 utilizes dynamic packet filtering for both inbound and outbound ports, reducing the number of vulnerable ports in either direction.

■ **Security** Proxy Server can now be configured to alert administrators via pager or e-mail in response to certain events. Alerts can also be sent to a log file or logged in the Windows NT System Event Log. Thresholds for packets sent to an unused port and dropped packets, for example, can be set to trigger alerts. Client authentication, including Windows NT challenge/response and SSL tunneling, are carried through the entire route in proxy arrays and chains.

Administration

Several administrative functions have been added and improved with Proxy Server 2.0.

■ Command-line utilities can be used for a number of admin tasks, and are particularly useful since they can be used in scripts.

■ An entire proxy array can be administered from one server, which will be a great benefit to large Proxy Server sites.

■ Java Scripts can be used to configure clients.

■ Proxy Server 2.0 has a backup and restore function that saves all Proxy Server configuration information to a file.

Other Enhancements

■ Server proxying is supported, which allows Proxy Server to listen on specific ports and forward incoming traffic to a designated client. This is commonly used to forward SMTP traffic to an organization's mail server.

■ Support for SOCKS 4.3a.

■ Support for third-party plug-ins.

■ Improved performance using HTTP version 1.1.

FIGURE 28-10

A server that receives a request for an object contained within the array's cache will retrieve the object for the client.

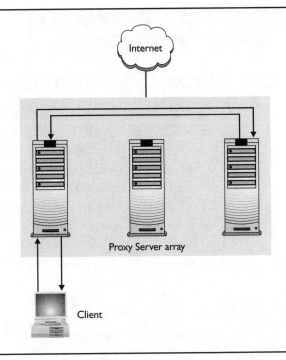

Proxy Server array

Client

FIGURE 28-11

A downstream server or array can be configured to use an upstream server or array.

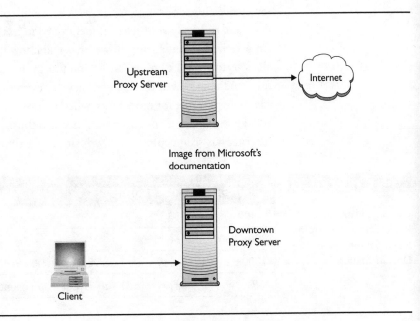

Upstream Proxy Server

Internet

Image from Microsoft's documentation

Downtown Proxy Server

Client

Developing a Proxy Server Implementation Strategy

There are many tasks to be completed to successfully implement a proxy server within a network. There are three key areas, however, that require the most attention: hardware sizing, security settings, and client deployment.

Microsoft has an Update Wizard you will need for Proxy Server 2.0 to operate on Windows 2000. Instructions and download links are currently located at http://www.microsoft.com/proxy/Support/win2kbeta3.asp. It is not known at this time whether a new update will be issued for the release version of Windows 2000. For up-to-date information, check the Proxy Server Web site at http://www.microsoft.com/proxy.

Hardware Sizing

Microsoft has published hardware recommendations for Proxy Server (see Table 28-2). Hardware sizing is particularly important because an undersized server will cause poor response times. Users will notice this and call the help desk, and suddenly your name is mentioned in less than complimentary ways. An oversized server is great; however, we all know that budgets do not always allow us to get a dream machine. Don't forget to plan for *both* types of growth, users and usage. Even though you may not expect more users, people continue to use the Internet for more tasks, whether job-related or not.

The Proxy Server documentation was published in 1997, and the Internet has seen explosive growth since that time, with many multimedia

TABLE 28-2	Clients	Processor	RAM
Obsolete Hardware Recommendations from Proxy Server Documentation	0-300	133 MHz	32MB
	300-2000	166 MHz	64MB
	2000+	Array with 1 server per 2000 clients, 166 MHz	64MB
	ISP	Array with 1 server per 1000 clients, 166 MHz	64MB

and other bandwidth-intensive uses expanding. Accordingly, these hardware recommendations are *de facto* obsolete. The highest CPU speed mentioned is 166 MHz, which was high end when Proxy 2.0 was released. However, the high demands of a corporate intranet require a lot more processing power and RAM than the minimum requirements. Objects retrieved from cache utilize less CPU time than objects obtained from the Internet, so more aggressive cache settings can be used if you find that your CPU is being overworked.

Disk space recommendations for Proxy Server 2.0 are as follows:

- 10MB to install Proxy Server
- 100MB + .5MB per client for the Web Proxy Cache

If a proxy array is used, it is also beneficial to have high-speed network connections between servers. Another item not mentioned in the recommendations is using a RAID array. This will improve performance considerably for objects being retrieved from cache, as well as provide much-needed fault tolerance.

Security Configuration

As you have noticed throughout this chapter, there are a number of ways to configure security in Proxy Server. For this reason, it is important that you determine the specific requirements of management and IT regarding security, so that you can implement them properly. Some of the questions that need to be answered are:

- Where does Proxy Server fit into our network security plan?
- Are we going to use Proxy Server to deny access to certain Internet sites?
- Are we going to enforce policies regarding use of the Internet with Proxy Server?
- Do we want to restrict WinSock and SOCKS application usage?
- Are there other security concerns that Proxy Server cannot fulfill?
- Do we want to use dynamic packet filtering?

Getting answers to all of these questions will enable you to set Proxy Server security with confidence. Making assumptions about security needs could result in breached security or help desk calls ("I can't use IRC!"), both of which will result in reconfiguring Proxy Server.

Client Deployment

The Microsoft Proxy client is very easy to install; the difficult part is getting it installed on every client PC on the network. This can be accomplished a number of ways, and if you are managing a large network you probably already have a software distribution method in place.

The following scenarios answer some common questions you may encounter about Proxy Server.

Proxy Server creates an MSPCLNT share on the server when it is installed. Client PCs can simply run the SETUP.EXE and accept the defaults. For a quiet installation that requires no user action, see Table 28-3 and Figure 28-12. Some options for getting the client installed on PCs if you don't have a software distribution method in place are as follows:

- Commands can be put in logon scripts that check to see if the Proxy client is installed, and run the silent installation command line if it is not.

- Shortcuts with the silent install command can be e-mailed to users.

QUESTIONS AND ANSWERS

One of my users messed up some of the files in the Proxy client directory. How do I correct the problem?	Uninstall and reinstall the Proxy client. Trying to find which file was modified and then repairing it will probably take much longer.
What do users need to know to set up WinSock applications to use Proxy Server?	Nothing! The Proxy client redirects all WinSock API calls to the proxy server, which handles them accordingly.
What are the client license issues for Proxy Server?	Unlike most Microsoft Backoffice applications, Proxy Server requires no client access licenses. The only licenses necessary are for servers.

FIGURE 28-12

Proxy client installation
options can be set to
automatically configure
Web browsers.

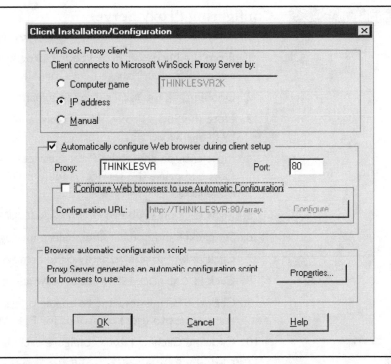

- A link to a batch file can be placed on an intranet page.

If you are setting up a Proxy Server array, you will need to edit the
mspclnt.ini file on the server. See the Proxy Server documentation regarding
the entries in this file and the changes you need to make. Be sure to test any
changes you make before deploying the client to users.

TABLE 28-3

Client Installation
Command Lines

Action	Client	Command
Silent Install, Reboot	32-bit	Setup /qt
Silent Install, Reboot	16-bit	Setup /q1
Uninstall, Reboot	32-bit	Setup /qt /u
Uninstall, Reboot	16-bit	Setup /q1 /u

Configuring Proxy Server

This exercise assumes that you have already installed Proxy Server 2.0.

1. From the Microsoft Proxy Server program group in the start menu, select Microsoft Management Console.

2. Double-click the local server to expand its Internet services.

3. Note the Socks Proxy, Web Proxy, and WinSock Proxy items added by Proxy Server.

4. Right-click on any of the Proxy services and note that you can start, stop, and pause the service. Additionally, the Properties menu item is available.

5. Right-click on Web Proxy and click SECURITY.

6. Set packet and domain filters, alert and log settings as desired.

7. Click ARRAY to join an array or to remove a server from the array.

8. Click LOCAL ADDRESS TABLE to view and edit the local address table.

9. Click the Permissions tab to enable or disable access control and to grant access to users or groups for FTP, Web, Secure, and Gopher.

10. Click the Caching tab to configure caching properties.

11. Click the Routing tab to configure direct or upstream server/array Internet access.

12. Click the Publishing tab to configure internal publishing via reverse proxying.

13. Click the Logging tab to configure the Web Proxy logs.

14. Right-click WinSock Proxy and Socks Proxy and select Properties to configure.

HEADSTART OBJECTIVE 28.04

Developing a Proxy Server Management Strategy

After you have successfully installed Proxy Server on your network, you want to make sure that it continues to run smoothly and meets the current and future needs of the network. You want to be sure you are monitoring the proxy services, disk space, CPU and network adapter utilization, preferably setting up alerts to inform you of any problems. Additionally, you want to analyze utilization on your proxy servers on a regular basis and note any trends that indicate future performance problems.

Command-Line Tools

Proxy Server provides two command-line tools to make management tasks easier. The WspProto command is used to manage WinSock protocol definitions. With the RemotMsp command, administrators can perform the following tasks on a local or remote proxy server:

- Start, stop, and view status of proxy services
- Back up and restore Proxy Server configuration
- Enable and disable Web Proxy and WinSock Proxy access control
- Enable and disable caching, Internet publishing, array synchronization
- Join, remove, synchronize, or view status of an array

You may want to use the AT command to write status information to files on a daily basis. These can be quickly checked each day to make sure that all services are running.

Logs

The logs generated by Proxy Server should be analyzed on a regular basis to determine if hacking attempts are being made or to see if clients are repeatedly attempting to access filtered sites. In addition to "catching" someone doing something wrong, you may find that you have filtered a site for which a user has a legitimate need to access. This would be more likely to occur if you have installed a plug-in that enters filters automatically. Setting your logs to the "verbose" setting will give you more detailed information. Remember that there are logs for each of the three Proxy services in addition to the shared security log.

Event Logs

Proxy Server makes use of the Windows NT Event Viewer like all other Backoffice applications. Proxy Server logs service failures and other information. Additionally, thresholds for protocol violations, rejected packets, and disk full events can be configured to log to the Event Log and/or send SMTP mail. Third-party utilities are available that monitor the Event Log and alert you if any specific event occurs.

Change Policies

As new applications are introduced or the needs of your network change due to growth or new functions, you will benefit from having policies and procedures for the necessary changes. Items affected include:

- WinSock protocol changes
- Domain filter changes
- Hardware upgrades/replacements
- Group access permission changes
- Internal publishing changes

Test Server

As with any server application, it is always a good idea to have equipment available to test proposed changes. It is very common for administrators to make untested changes to production servers only to find that the changes cause problems or don't work as expected. Since Proxy Server's hardware requirements are minimal, a desktop PC running Windows NT 4.0 Server or Windows 2000 Server can function adequately in this role.

Resources

A few valuable resources are very available if you need assistance with configuration or troubleshooting Proxy Server.

- The Proxy Server Web site at http://www.microsoft.com/proxy
- "Tips from the Proxy Gurus" maintained at http://proxyfaq.networkgods.com
- Microsoft's official Proxy FAQ at http://support.microsoft.com/support/proxy/faq
- The microsoft.public.proxy newsgroup available on msnews.microsoft.com
- The Microsoft Knowledge Base at http://support.microsoft.com

CHAPTER SUMMARY

Many large networks have proxy servers to control Internet access and provide security. Like all enterprise applications, the proxy solution must be fault-tolerant, scalable, robust, and easy to manage. For many users, Internet access is necessary to their jobs, so the reliability and performance of the proxy server are very important to the productivity of the organization.

There are a number of usability features that are important for proxy servers to be able to meet the needs of a large network. These include support for WinSock and SOCKS applications, reverse hosting and reverse proxying, caching, and firewall capabilities. Consolidation of all of these features into one application running on one server is a very cost effective solution for an organization.

With its Web Proxy, WinSock Proxy, and Socks Proxy services, Microsoft Proxy Server 2.0 is capable of handling the most challenging enterprise network needs. With the ability to set up Proxy Server arrays, administrators have a method of balancing the work load, increasing performance, and providing fault tolerance. With a supported automated install, clients can be using the proxy server in minutes without intervention from desktop support staff. Numerous filter and permission configuration options make it possible to finely tune the Security and Access permissions to enforce Internet usage policies and prevent outside network attacks.

✓ TWO-MINUTE DRILL

❑ Microsoft Proxy Server runs only on Windows NT Server computers.

❑ A proxy server can provide several functions for an enterprise network to facilitate and manage Internet access by client PCs.

❑ Proxy servers can also *reverse proxy* to allow Web servers on your network to publish without ever establishing communications with computers beyond your network.

❑ In addition to simply proxying Internet requests, there are a number of elements that are necessary for a proxy server to be suitable for enterprise use. The first of these is fault tolerance.

❑ When configured in arrays, Microsoft Proxy Server computers will maintain a distributed cache, which increases performance for clients.

❑ If an organization using multiple proxy servers in an array needs to make a configuration change, it is important that changes can be made to the array as one unit instead of changing each server.

❑ Proxy servers that utilize HTTP and FTP caching can improve performance significantly. Microsoft Proxy Server's Web Proxy service caches both of these protocols, and when configured in an array, the cache index for each array member is available to all others.

❑ Proxy Server filters both inbound and outbound packets, and opens ports only as needed. Alerts can be configured to warn administrators via e-mail or pager of certain events, including packets sent to an unused port.

❑ A number of third-party plug-ins are available for Proxy Server to assist with blocking unwanted traffic, scanning for viruses, and other functions.

❑ Proxy Server 2.0 includes services to proxy both WinSock and SOCKS applications.

❑ Reverse hosting is accomplished by binding a service on an internal server to a specific IP port on the proxy server's external network adapter.

❑ Reverse proxying allows you to use port 80 for a number of internal Web servers, and Proxy Server maintains a list of "request path" and "route to" URLs.

❑ Proxy Server's Web Proxy service handles HTTP, HTTPS, FTP, and Gopher traffic between client PCs and Internet hosts. The Web Proxy service utilizes caching to improve client response times and to conserve bandwidth on the Internet link.

❑ The Proxy Client directs WinSock communications to the proxy server, which forwards the communication on to its intended destination.

❑ SOCKS is a platform-independent session-level interface used for communication between client and server applications.

❑ Microsoft has an Update Wizard you will need for Proxy Server 2.0 to operate on Windows 2000.

❑ Hardware sizing is particularly important because an undersized server will cause poor response times.

❑ Making assumptions about security needs could result in breached security or help desk calls ("I can't use IRC!"), both of which will result in reconfiguring Proxy Server.

❑ Proxy Server creates an MSPCLNT share on the server when it is installed. Client PCs can simply run the SETUP.EXE and accept the defaults.

❑ After you have successfully installed Proxy Server on your network, you want to make sure you are monitoring the proxy services, disk space, CPU and network adapter utilization, preferably setting up alerts to inform you of any problems.

❑ Proxy Server provides two command-line tools to make management tasks easier: the WspProto command and the RemotMsp command.

❑ The logs generated by Proxy Server should be analyzed on a regular basis to determine if hacking attempts are being made or to see if clients are repeatedly attempting to access filtered sites.

❑ Proxy Server makes use of the Windows NT Event Viewer like all other Backoffice applications.

SELF TEST

1. Which item is not a common feature of proxy servers?

   A. Firewall capabilities

   B. Caching

   C. Routing

   D. Reverse hosting

2. What two fields are used by Web Proxy to accomplish reverse proxying?

   A. Request path

   B. URL

   C. Route to

   D. Proxy path

3. Which of the following three services are used by Proxy Server?

   A. Web Proxy service

   B. FTP Proxy service

   C. WinSock Proxy service

   D. Socks Proxy service

4. What is the most powerful firewall feature of Proxy Server?

   A. Domain filters

   B. Socks Proxy service

   C. Distributed caching

   D. Packet filters

5. Domain Filters set in the shared Security properties affect what Proxy Services?

   A. Web Proxy

   B. WinSock Proxy

   C. Socks Proxy

   D. None

6. Proxy Server can generate alerts for what three events?

   A. CPU utilization

   B. Rejected packets

   C. Protocol violation

   D. Disk full

7. What protocols are handled by the Web Proxy service? (Choose all that apply.)

   A. HTTP

   B. FTP

   C. NNTP

   D. Gopher

8. Which type of caching is not a function of Proxy Server?

   A. Client-based caching

   B. Chain-based caching

   C. Single server caching

   D. Array-based caching

9. What protocol is used between Proxy Servers to maintain the distributed cache?

   A. HTTP

   B. CARP

   C. FTP

   D. SMB

10. What three items are most important for a successful Proxy Server implementation?

    A. Security considerations

    B. Hardware sizing

    C. User training

    D. Client deployment

11. How much disk space is recommended for the Web Proxy Cache for 1500 clients?

    A. 1.5GB

    B. 75MB

    C. 750MB

    D. 3GB

12. What two features does a RAID disk array provide?

    A. Improved performance

    B. Fault tolerance

    C. Security

    D. Lower cost

13. What is the command line to silently install the Proxy client on Windows 95?

    A. Setup /qt

    B. Setup /q1

    C. Setup /u

    D. Setup /s

14. What is the GUI application used for Proxy Server administration?

    A. Proxy Server Administration Console

    B. Microsoft Management Console

    C. Server Manager

    D. User Manager

15. What two command-line utilities are available to manage Proxy Server?

    A. ProxAdmn

    B. WspProto

    C. RemotMsp

    D. RemotWsp

29

Managing Internet Information Services

CERTIFICATION OBJECTIVES

Microsoft Internet Service Manager

The Internet Service Manager (ISM) is the primary tool used to manage the Internet Information Services (IIS). You can manage any IIS server from anywhere in the world using Internet Service Manager, not just your local IIS server computer. The IIS configuration parameters are stored in a database called the *metabase*. Most of the metabase parameters are set using the IIS. The metabase offers the following advantages:

- Speed
- More flexibility
- Easier to expand
- Scriptable
- Easier for remote administration

Start the ISM by launching Start | Programs | Administrative Tools | Internet Services Manager. This in turn launches the MMC, resulting in the screen in Figure 29-1. You can also click on an .msc file in Windows 2000 Server Explorer to launch ISM.

Service Manager Views

When you start IIS, it connects you to the local machine and the Internet Information Services and the Component Services. You can view which servers are connected by expanding the Internet Information Services folder.

FIGURE 29-1   Internet Information Services Main Screen

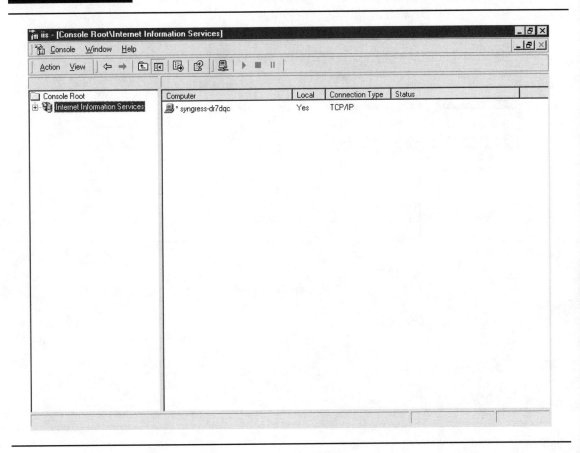

You can view which services are installed on that server by clicking on the plus (+) key to the left of the server to expand the tree or by double-clicking the server icon or name. See Figure 29-2.

You can add other servers to the console display so that you can manage their services from this console as well. You add servers by a right-click on

FIGURE 29-2

Viewing the server and installed services

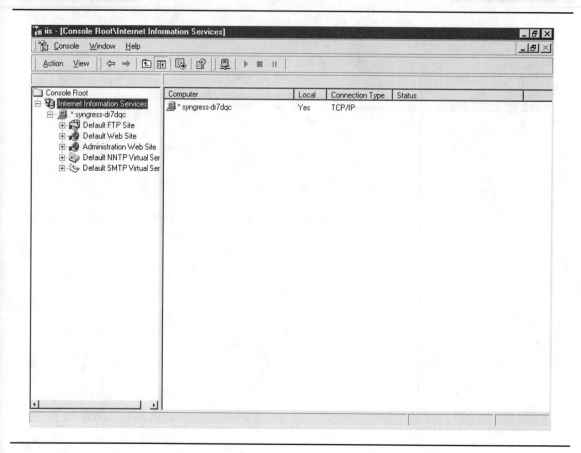

either the Internet Information Services folder or any server icon displayed. Then select Connect from the pop-up dialog box and enter the name of the server. After a brief pause, the new server is displayed under the Internet Information Services folder. Figure 29-3 illustrates the MMC with two servers connected.

FIGURE 29-3 MMC with two servers connected

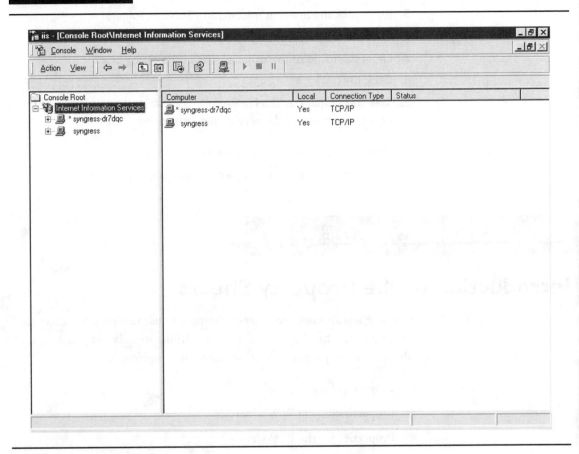

EXERCISE 29-1

Expanding MMC

Purpose: To add another server to the console.
   Complete this procedure from both computers.

1. Ensure that you are logged on as Administrator.

2. Open the MMC.

3. Expand the Internet Information Services folder.

4. Which servers are listed?

5. Right-click the Internet Information Services folder.

6. Click on Connect in the pop-up menu.

7. Enter the name of the other server in the dialog box.

8. Click OK.

9. Save this console as the file named "console with server*xx*" where *xx* is the number of the server that you added.

Answer to the question in the exercise:

4. Server*xx*, depending upon which computer you are using.

HEADSTART OBJECTIVE 29.03

Introduction to the Property Sheets

Each service has an associated *property sheet.* You use this property sheet to set the parameters for the particular service. In the installation you have set up, there are three property sheets of immediate interest:

- Properties for the server
- Properties for the WWW service
- Properties for the FTP service

WWW

The Web provides information in a graphical format, complete with images, rich-text formatting, and multimedia. The Web also provides an ingenious way of moving around within documents or jumping to other Web sites using *hyperlinks.* Click on a hyperlink and you're on another Web page. This has become so popular that Microsoft has enabled all of its Office products with Web technology.

You do not actually "go" to the Web page as in a login, telnet, or FTP session. Your Web browser requests a Hypertext Markup Language

(HTML) page from the remote site specified by the Uniform Resource Locator (URL). As your browser interprets this HTML document while downloading it from the remote site, it may encounter requests for other objects such as pictures. As each picture request is interpreted, the browser may indicate, by a percentage value changing in the bottom line or a filling bar graph, that further downloading is occurring. You can always click the Stop button to discontinue any further downloading of pictures if you are happy with the text-only output. Hyperlinks are usually embedded URLs that, when clicked on, result in the specified Web page being downloaded and interpreted.

The Web can tie together many servers throughout the world or within your organization into what appears to users as unified information content. With this power, the Web is preferable to storing information in the form of files on different servers. The Web technology brings information to life. It puts a premium on the information content and not where the information is stored.

HEADSTART OBJECTIVE 29.04

WWW Service

Hypertext Transfer Protocol (HTTP) was the protocol that led to the World Wide Web. HTTP grew out of a need for a standards-based protocol to simplify the way in which users access information on the Internet. It is a generic, stateless, object-oriented protocol. HTTP is at the application layer of the protocol model. HTTP categorizes data, allowing systems to be built independently of the data being transferred.

Virtual Servers

The WWW service supports a concept called *virtual servers*. A virtual server can be used to host multiple domain names on the same physical Internet Information Server. You need a unique IP address for each virtual server that you host.

heads ⓊP
Each virtual server requires a unique IP address that is assigned to the Network Interface Card (NIC).

Virtual Directories

The WWW and FTP services also support *virtual directories.* A virtual directory is a directory that appears to be in ftproot, the home folder. A virtual directory can be on any server in the same Windows 2000 Server domain. Virtual directories created on other servers should be referenced by their Universal Naming Convention (UNC) names.

heads ⓊP
Virtual directories may be located on local drives or on remote servers. You should refer to remote drives by the UNC.

HEADSTART OBJECTIVE 29.05

HTTP Communication

HTTP is a client/server model. There must be a server-side application and a client-side application. The client and the server interact to perform a specific task.

When a client clicks on a hyperlink, the HTTP protocol performs the following:

1. The client browser uses HTTP to communicate with the server.

2. A connection is established from the client to the server. The server monitors TCP port 80 by default.

3. Once the connection is made, the requested message is sent to the server. The requests are typically for a resource file.

4. Server sends a response message to the client, along with the data the client requested.

5. The server closes the connection unless the client's browser has configured a keep-alive option.

HTTP Requests

The client communicates with the server in the form of a simple request method. This request method consists of a URL and a protocol version. Below is an example of an HTTP request:

Get http://www.microsoft.com/cert_train/iis HTTP 1.0

The above request contains the following elements:

- **get**   Specifies the request method.
- **URL**   //www.microsoft.com/cert_train/iis specifies which object to get.
- **HTTP 1.0**   The version of the protocol to be used.

The following elements may be used in an HTTP request:

- **Request**   Such as "get."
- **Resource**   The URL path to the object.
- **Message**   The message makes a simple request into a full request and can include additional information such as a MIME (Multipurpose Internet Mail Extensions), request modifiers, and client information.
- **Response**   The HTTP response message.

HTTP Server Response Messages

The client sends a request to the HTTP (Web) server. The server receives the request and responds with a status message. The message includes the protocol version and a success or error code. A MIME message follows containing server information, entity information, and possibly body content. Table 29-1 contains examples of server status messages.

heads ⓤp   *Know what the syntax of the request is. Know what a URL is and how to construct it.*

TABLE 29-1	Message	Type	Description
HTTP Server Response Messages	2xx	Success	The request was successfully received.
	3xx	Redirection	Further action must be taken to complete the request.
	4xx	Client error	The request contains bad syntax or the request cannot be fulfilled.
	5xx	Server error	The server has failed to fulfill a valid request.
	1xx1	Informational	This series has been reserved for future use. It is not currently used.

MIME Type Configuration

If your server has files that use different file formats, your server must have a MIME mapping for each different file type or extension. If you don't have this, your client's browser may not be able to retrieve the file. You set these mappings from the HTTP Headers tab in the property sheet, as illustrated next.

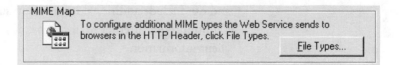

To configure additional MIME mappings, click the New Type button in the File Types dialog box. In the File Types dialog box, enter the extension that is associated with the file in the Associated Extension box. In the Content Type (MIME) box, enter the MIME type followed by the filename extension in the form MIME *type /filename extension,* as illustrated in Figure 29-4. If you are using files with a .my_file extension and do not map this file as a MIME type, then when a client requests the file it will be identified as the default MIME type, which is typically binary.

Creating MIME mappings

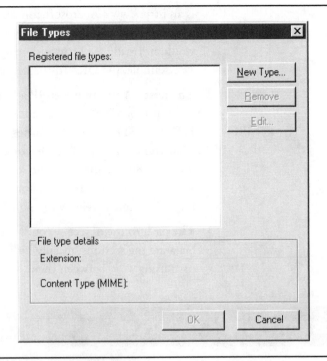

HTTP Clients and URLs

You need an HTTP client to attach to the Web server. The client is called a *browser* and the default browser for Windows 2000 Server is Microsoft Internet Explorer 5.0 (IE).

To access a resource on the Web server, you specify three items:

1. **How access is to occur** The default in IE is HTTP protocol; if you enter a URL like www.microsoft.com, the browser assumes that this

is an http://www.microsoft.com request. You can still use the FTP protocol from your browser by simply specifying ftp: where you would normally see http: and using the appropriate FTP site URL. For example, the URL ftp://sunsite.unc.edu/ accesses an FTP site.

2. **The host** You can use an IP address, a fully qualified domain name (FQDN), or a NetBIOS computer name. You separate the protocol, HTTP or FTP, with "//," slashes that go the opposite direction from what you use in a DOS path (for example). By default, the browser uses port 80 to connect to the server. If you have configured the server to monitor a different port, use a ":" after the host name, followed immediately by the port number the server is monitoring.

3. **The path to the object** You must use the entire path to the object. Separate the sections, usually indicating subdirectory names, in the path using a "/" between them.

HEADSTART OBJECTIVE 29.07

HTTP Ports and Connections

The HTTP server monitors port 80 for client connections, as illustrated in Figure 29-5. You change this port by modifying the port number from the Default Web Site Properties sheet or by changing the values in the Services file located in the <winnt_root>\system32\drivers\ect folder. Changing the port number on the server requires that the clients specify the same port number when they attempt to connect. This may act as a small security screen because the client needs to know which port is in use but, as in the case with FTP, this is not much of an obstacle to an experienced hacker.

EXERCISE 29-2

Connecting to Your HTTP Server

Purpose: To demonstrate the ability of your browser to connect to the Web server. You will also modify the TCP port and reconnect to the server specifying the new port number.

Do this exercise from either computer.

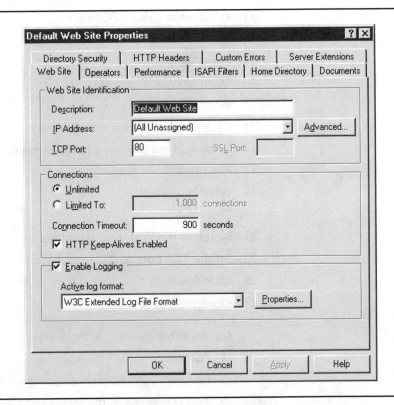

FIGURE 29-5

Modifying the HTTP port

1. Ensure you are logged on as Administrator.

2. Start Internet Explorer.

3. In the Address box, type **Serverxx**, where **xx** is the number of your server.

4. Press ENTER. Your browser should connect to your server.

5. Close IE.

6. Open Internet Service Manager.

7. Expand your server so that you can see the Default Web Site.

8. Right-click the Default Web Site.

9. Click Properties.

10. Ensure that the Web Site is selected.

11. What is the default TCP port?

12. Modify the TCP port number to 3300.

13. Click Apply.

14. Open Internet Explorer.

15. What message did you get?

16. Click OK to clear the error message.

17. In the Address box, type **http://serverxx:3300**.

18. Press ENTER.

19. What happened?

20. Close IE.

21. Switch to the Web property sheet.

22. Set the TCP port to 80.

23. Click Apply.

24. Close the MMC.

Answers to the questions in the exercise:

10. Port 80.

15. Internet Explorer cannot open the Internet site...

19. You connected to the server using TCP port 3300.

HEADSTART OBJECTIVE 29.08

Configuring WWW Services

You configure the Web services using three property sheets. Which property sheet you use depends upon what object you wish to change. The property sheets are

- Master

- Default

- File

Master

When Internet Information Services is installed, properties are applied to the Master Properties sheet, which is illustrated in Figure 29-6. You select the Master Properties sheet by right-clicking on the server icon and selecting Properties.

Default

Each IIS installation creates a Default Web Site. This site initially has the same properties as specified on the Master Properties sheet. You select the Default Web Site Properties sheet by right-clicking the Default Web Site node and selecting Properties. Figure 29-7 illustrates the Default property sheet.

FIGURE 29-6

Master Properties sheet for WWW service

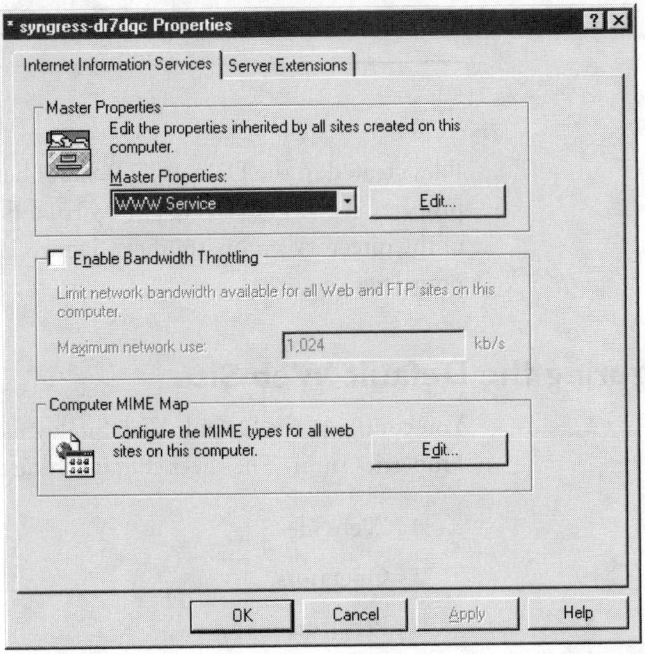

FIGURE 29-7

Default Web Site
Properties sheet

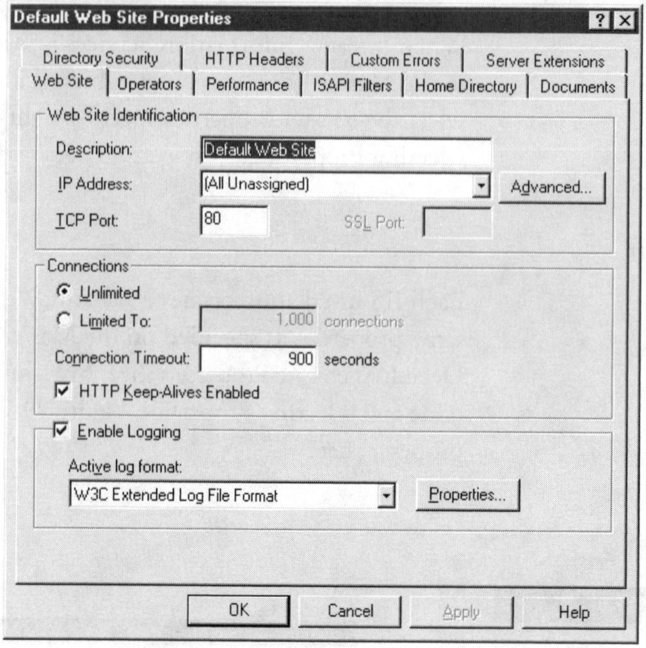

File

Files created in the Default FTP Site inherit the properties of that site's property sheet. Files created in a virtual FTP directory inherit the properties of the directory's property sheet. Figure 29-8 contains an example of a file's properties.

Configuring the Default Web Site

You configure the Default Web Site by using the Default Web Site Properties sheet. The sheet contains nine tabs:

- Web Site
- Operators
- Performance
- ISAPI Filters
- Home Directory

FIGURE 29-8

Properties sheet for
file ie.gif

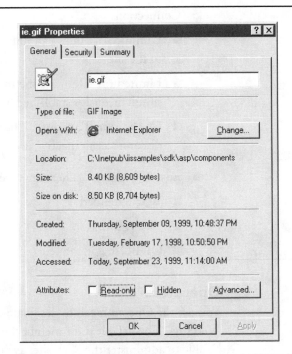

- Documents
- Directory Security
- HTTP Headers
- Custom Errors

Web Site

You use the Web Site tab, illustrated in Figure 29-7, to set general parameters about the site including

- Web site identification

  - **Description**   A name you choose for your site.

  - **IP Address**   The IP address for this site.

  - **TCP Port**   The port the server monitors for connections.

  - **SSL**   Port used by the Secure Sockets Layer transmission.

- Connections

  - **Unlimited**   Allows an unlimited number of connections to the site

  - **Limited to**   Restricts the number of sessions that can be simultaneously established at the site

  - **Connection Timeout**   The number of seconds before the server disconnects an inactive user

- **Enable Logging**   There are three log formats:

- W3c Extended

- NCSA common

- ODBC logging

Operators

You use the Operators tab to designate users you want to administer specific Web sites. The default is for members of the local administrators group to be able to administer the Web site, as illustrated in Figure 29-9.

Performance

You use the Performance tab to

- Adjust performance tuning to the number of expected daily connections. This is different than the maximum number of simultaneous connections you will allow. For example, you can set the maximum number of simultaneous connections to 25,000 and set the anticipated number of daily connections to more than 100,000. However, that means that you expect more than 100,000 daily users to connect to your site, but you will only allow 25,000 to be connected at any one time.

- Check the Enable Bandwidth Throttling box to restrict the Web site. The value here overrides the value set at the server computer, even if the value set at the site is higher.

FIGURE 29-9

Assigning operators
for a site

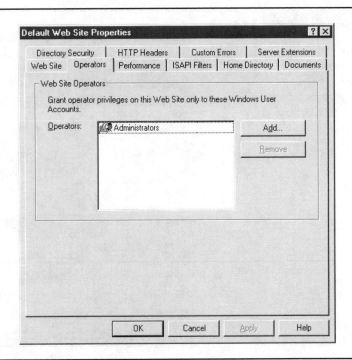

HTTP Keep-Alives is enabled by default. This allows the client to keep an open connection with the server, instead of opening a connection for each new request. This is enabled by default. Without this enabled, each time a client gets a new page from your site, it opens a connection, get the pages, and closes the connection. This is how Web sites work without this enhancement. Figure 29-10 illustrates the Performance tab.

ISAPI Filters

You use the ISAPI tab to set Internet Server Application Programming Interface (ISAPI) filters. ISAPI can be used to run remote applications. You do this by requesting a URL that is mapped to a filter, which activates the application. ISAPI programs run inside a single process and memory space. If you use CGI scripts, each time a CGI script runs, it initializes its process, spawns a thread, and allocates memory. This all takes time and machine

FIGURE 29-10

Configuring site
performance and
keep-alives

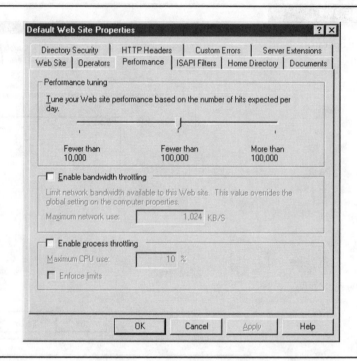

Default Web Site Properties

Directory Security | HTTP Headers | Custom Errors | Server Extensions
Web Site | Operators | Performance | ISAPI Filters | Home Directory | Documents

Performance tuning

Tune your Web site performance based on the number of hits expected per day.

Fewer than
10,000

Fewer than
100,000

More than
100,000

☐ Enable bandwidth throttling

Limit network bandwidth available to this Web site. This value overrides the
global setting on the computer properties.

Maximum network use: 1,024 KB/S

☐ Enable process throttling

Maximum CPU use: 10 %

☐ Enforce limits

OK   Cancel   Apply   Help

resources. ISAPI calls are faster and consume fewer resources. Figure 29-11
illustrates the ISAPI Filters tab.

Home Directory

You use the Home Directory tab to change settings and properties for your
home directory. Figure 29-12 contains the Home Directory tab. When you
install IIS, it creates a home directory called wwwroot in the \inetpub
folder. You can have a home directory

- In a folder on the local server
- In a folder shared on another computer
- From a URL redirection

You can set access permissions as follows:

- **Read**   Web clients can read and download files.

FIGURE 29-11

Configuring ISAPI filters

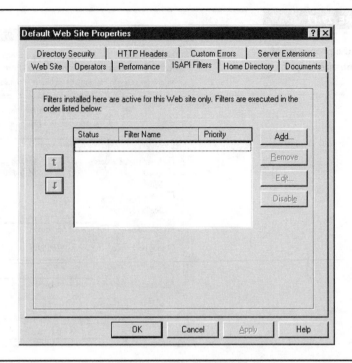

Write Web clients can upload files to the enabled folder. They can change the contents in a write-enabled file. To do this, the client must be using a browser that supports the PUT feature of the HTTP 1.1 standard.

The content control properties are in effect when you are using a local folder or using a folder from a network share. These properties are

Log Access Record all visits to a folder or a file.

Director Browsing Allowed Show the user a hypertext listing of the folders and files so that the client can navigate through the directory structure. This listing is automatically sent to the client when the browser request does not contain a specified file name or there is no default document in the folder.

FIGURE 29-12

Setting the properties of
the home directory

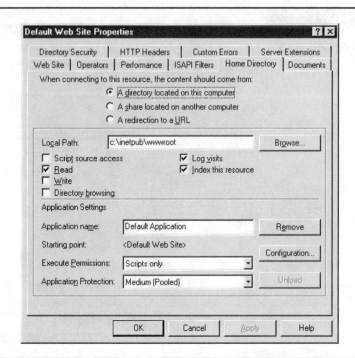

- **Index This Directory** Instruct Microsoft Index Server to include this directory in a full text search of your Web site.

- **FrontPage Web** Create a Microsoft FrontPage Web site for this directory.

With respect to Application Settings in the Home Directory dialog box, an application is defined as all the folders and files contained within a folder marked as an application starting point, until another application starting point is reached. To make a folder an application starting point, click the Create button. You have the following choices for applications:

- **Run in Separate Memory** This option causes the application to run in its own memory space as a separate process on the Web server. Running in its own memory space causes the application to be protected from other processes.

■ **Permissions**   This option controls how applications can be run in this folder. You have the following choices:

■ **None**   Any programs or scripts can run in this folder.

■ **Script**   The script engine can run in this folder without setting the Execute permission.

■ **Execute**   Applications can run in this folder, including script and executables (Windows 2000 Server binaries).

Documents

You use the Documents tab to select which default document you will show the user when the browser does not specify a particular HTML file. The default document file name should be "Default.htm." Figure 29-13 illustrates the Documents tab.

Documents tab

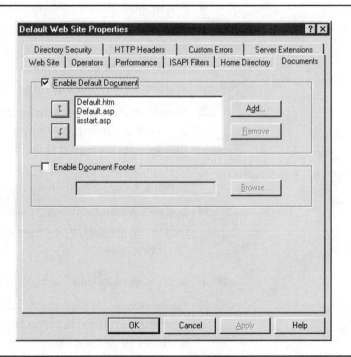

You can specify more than one default document by using the Add button. This causes the Web server to go down the list of documents in the order listed until it finds one of the listed documents in the folder.

You can enable Document Footer to have the Web server automatically insert a footer for you. This file can contain HTML formatting instructions for identifying your Web page, but this file should not be an HTML document. This file should only include tags necessary for formatting the appearance of your footer. You must provide a complete path and file name for the footer file.

Directory Security

Use the Directory Security tab to configure your Web server's security features, as illustrated in Figure 29-14. This dialog box includes

- Anonymous Access and Authentication Control. Click the Edit button to select the following options:

  - **Anonymous Access**   Always allow this.

  - **Basic Authentication**   If you select this option, and Allow Anonymous Access is disabled, the user is required to submit a valid set of Windows 2000 Server account credentials. The associated password is sent in clear text.

  - **Windows 2000 Server Challenge/Response**   A user name and password is required if Anonymous Access is disabled, and this access is controlled by NTFS security. The password is encrypted and the client browser must support Windows 2000 Server Challenge/Response.

  - **Secure Communications**   Select the Key Manager button to initiate the process of receiving a Secure Sockets Layer (SSL) certificate.

- IP Address and Domain Name Restrictions

  - **Grant Access**   This is the default. Grants access to all computers. You restrict access by denying access to specific IP addresses or domain names.

  - **Deny Access**   This turns off access. You must grant access by specific IP address or domain name.

FIGURE 29-14

Setting Web access using
the Directory Security tab

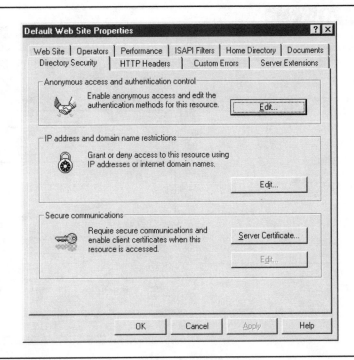

HTTP Headers

Use the HTTP Headers tab (illustrated in Figure 29-15) to set the values
returned to the browser in the header of the HTML page.

Select Enable Content Expiration to include expiration information.
This causes the browser to compare the current date to the date in the
document. If the date is good, the browser uses the locally cached copy.
If the date is old, it does not use the locally cached copy; it attempts to
get an updated page.

The Custom HTTP Header option allows you to send a custom header
from your server to the client's browser. Use the Add button to specify
the header.

MIME Map is used to set information about files kept on the server.
You need to create a map to map specific applications to certain file
extensions. For example, you want to match the WINZIP application to
files with the .ZIP extension. If you do not create this map, the client's
browser might not know how to interpret the file type when it is received.

FIGURE 29-15

HTTP Headers tab

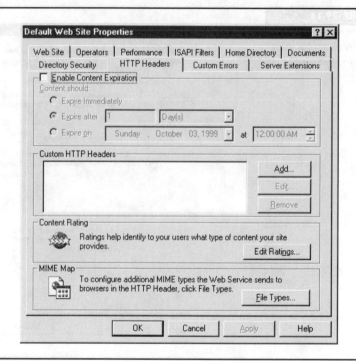

The client then has to decode the file manually using a utility program. While this is not difficult, it is nice just to get the file and use it.

Custom Errors

The Custom Errors property sheet shows the messages that are returned to the browser in the event of an HTTP error. You can use the default HTTP 1.1 error messages supplied, or create your own custom error messages. Figure 29-16 illustrates the Custom Errors tab.

Configuring the WWW Server

Purpose: To configure the Web server.

Do this exercise on either computer.

1. Ensure that you are logged on as Administrator.

2. Open the MMC.

3. Expand your server, if not already expanded.

4. Right-click Default Web Site.

FIGURE 29-16

Custom Errors tab

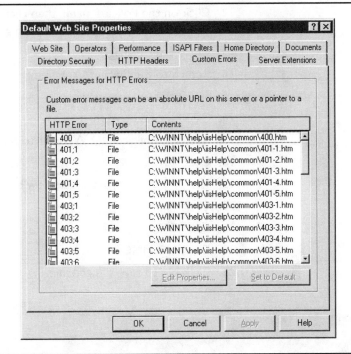

5. Click Properties.

6. In the Description box, change the description to be *your name's* Web Site.

7. In the Connections section, click the radio button for Limited To.

8. In the box to the right, set the connection limit to 5. In a real environment, you would not normally set the limit so low.

9. Click Apply.

10. Open User Manager.

11. Create a new user with the following properties:

- Username: Webmgr

- Full Name: Web Manager

- Description: Account to be used for other Web management

- Password: Blank (null)

- Clear the check box User Must Change Password at Next Logon.

- Check the box Password Never Expires.

12. Click on the Policies menu, then click User Rights. Modify the User Right, Log on locally, to include the group Everyone.

13. Close User Manager.

14. Return to the Default Web Site Properties.

15. Select the Operators tab.

16. Click the Add button.

17. Add the user account Webmgr to the Add Names box.

18. Click OK.

19. The Webmgr account should now be included in the Operators box.

20. Click Apply.

21. Click OK.

22. Close the MMC.

23. Click No to save the console.

HEADSTART OBJECTIVE 29.09

FTP

File Transfer Protocol (FTP) uses the Transmission Control Protocol (TCP) to transfer files between the FTP client and the FTP server. FTP was one of the earliest protocols used on the Internet. The HTTP servers have supplanted much of the work that was done in the past by FTP. HTTP servers are convenient for clients to download files but they do not support uploading of files. To do that, you must still use the FTP protocol.

To transfer files over the Internet, one computer must be functioning as an FTP server and one computer must be an FTP client. Using Windows NT, your computer can be both an FTP server and an FTP client. The client issues commands to the server and the server responds. File transfers are always initiated by the client and never by the server. It is not possible for the server to send files automatically to the client.

heads **⓪p** *The client must always initiate the connection to the server. In this respect, the server is always passive.*

HEADSTART OBJECTIVE 29.10

TCP

FTP uses the TCP protocol to do all of its work. TCP is a *connection-oriented protocol.* A connection-oriented protocol establishes a session between the client and the server before any information is exchanged. This session remains established until it is torn down, typically by the process that initiated the session. This is a bidirectional connection; traffic can travel in both directions during the session. One feature of a connection-oriented protocol is that the protocol itself provides for error recovery and is more reliable. Because the TCP protocol performs error correction, the application using TCP does not have to provide for error correction. The programmer is free to concentrate on the application's semantics without having to also incorporate mechanisms to ensure that the other party reliably receives data. This reliable receipt of information is also called *guaranteed end delivery.*

TCP Features

The most important features of the TCP protocol include

■ **Acknowledgment** When sending a packet, the sending computer expects to "hear back" from the receiving computer that it received the data packet. This is called an *acknowledgement (ACK).* If the sending computer does not get an ACK from the receiving computer, the sending computer assumes that the receiving computer never received the data packet and retransmits the packet. The sender continues to resend the packet until it receives an ACK, or the process times out.

■ **Checksum** The *checksum* is a calculation done by the sending computer and is attached to the data packet. When the receiving computer gets the packet, it calculates the checksum on the data and compares that value to the checksum value contained in the packet (the one calculated by the sending computer). If the two values are the same, the receiver assumes that the data was transmitted without error. If the two values are different, the receiving station sends a *negative acknowledgement* (*NACK*) back to the sender. The sender recalculates the checksum and retransmits the packet. This process is repeated until the packet is received error free (the checksum values match) or the process times out.

■ **Flow Control** When two computers are transmitting packets back and forth, there must be some agreement about when to stop if one side gets too many packets. This process is called *flow control.* If packets are received faster than the computer can process them, data will be lost. By invoking flow control, the receiving computer can ask the sending computer to stop transmitting until it has time to catch up. When the receiving is ready for more packets, it "turns off" flow control and the sending computer starts sending packets again until it is done sending packets, or until it gets a stop sending (flow control) message from the receiving computer.

■ **Retransmission** Retransmission is the term used when the sender resends data packets that it sent previously. If the receiving station sends a NACK, then the sending station retransmits the packet. If the sending station does not get an ACK, it assumes the packets were lost or corrupted and resends the packets. It continues to send the packet until it no longer receives a NACK or until it receives an ACK. This is automatically done by the protocol without user intervention and generally without the user even being aware that it is happening.

■ **Sequencing** When data is being sent, it is divided up into segments and put in an "envelope" called a packet. The actual data is most likely put into multiple packets and sent on to its destination. The path to the destination can be different for each data packet. Packets can arrive in an order different than the order in which they were sent. If the receiving computer reassembles the data from the out-of-order packets, then the data is useless. To prevent this, the protocol assigns a sequence number to each packet as it is sent. When the packets arrive, the receiving computer reassembles them in the order indicated by the sequence numbers.

Trivial File Transfer Protocol (TFTP)

Trivial File Transfer Protocol (TFTP) is distinct from FTP. TFTP uses the UDP (User Datagram Protocol) as its transport protocol. UDP is a *connectionless protocol.* TFTP differs from a connection-oriented protocol like TCP in the following ways:

- No guarantee of end delivery. TFTP does not provide for error-checking in the protocol so there is no guarantee that what you send will be received without errors.

- TFTP does not set up a bidirectional session with the other end. Think of this as a "send and forget" type of protocol. It does not wait for an ACK from the receiving station and, therefore, has no idea if the packet was ever received.

- TFTP is faster than TCP since it doesn't have the overhead of setting up a session and going through acknowledgments and error control.

- Because it can be less reliable than TCP, TFTP should be used only for traffic that is not critical and where speed is more important than data reliability.

- You can still use UDP if you include error-handling procedures in your application.

heads
⑪P *Internet Information Services is not a TFTP server. You can use Windows 2000 Server as a TFTP client.*

Managing the FTP Service

Managing the FTP service is done through the Microsoft Management Console (MMC) and the Internet Service Manager (ISM). You can stop and start the FTP service from the ISM. Figure 29-17 contains the MMC window that shows the FTP service stopped. You can also start and stop the FTP service using the Services applet in the Control Panel.

FIGURE 29-17   Stopping and starting the FTP service

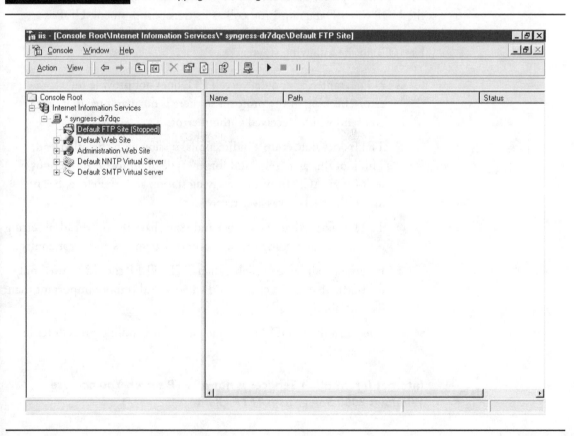

FTP Ports

A *socket* represents the endpoint of a network connection. Two numbers identify TCP sockets:

- **IP address**   The IP address identifies the computer on the network.
- **TCP port number**   The TCP port number identifies a process or application at the computer.

An example of such a number is 201.200.199.250(20).

A *TCP port* is the address of a server on an Internet Protocol (IP) network. When an application uses TCP, it calls an assigned port for access. For example, the FTP service always monitors TCP port 21 for activity.

TCP ports are divided into two general categories: *well-known ports* and *dynamic ports*. A TCP port can be referred to by several different names, including

- TCP port number
- Port address
- TCP port
- Port number
- Port
- Data port

These terms all refer to a TCP port.

TCP ports can be numbered from 0 to 65,535. Port numbers 0 through 1023 are reserved for server-side use and never change. Port numbers 0 through 1023 are called well-known ports because they never change. These well-known ports are preassigned by the Internet Assigned Numbers Authority (IANA). You can always expect FTP to monitor port 21 in a standard configuration.

Ports 1024 through 65,535 are reserved for client-side applications. These port numbers are assigned dynamically by the operating system when an application makes a request for service. An application may be assigned a given port number on one occasion and another port number on a different occasion, even though the application may be performing the same function on both occasions.

A server-side application that uses TCP always has at least one preassigned, or well-known, port number. By way of example, FTP uses two port numbers for its service:

- Port 20 for data
- Port 21 for control

These well-known port numbers can be found in RFC (Request for Comments) 1700, which can be accessed at www.internic.net. RFC is the way the Internet defines standards. Listed below are some well-known port numbers. You can see these port numbers listed in the <winnt_root>\system32\drivers\etc\Services file (see Table 29-2).

TABLE 29-2	Service Name	Port Number	Description
Well-Known Ports for TCP and UDP	echo	7/tcp	
	echo	7/udp	
	discard	9/tcp	sink null
	discard	9/udp	sink null
	systat	11/tcp	
	systat	11/tcp	users
	daytime	13/tcp	

TABLE 29-2	Service Name	Port Number	Description
Well-Known Ports for TCP and UDP *(continued)*	daytime	13/udp	
	netstat	15/tcp	
	qotd	17/tcp	quote
	qotd	17/udp	quote
	chargen	19/tcp	ttytst source
	chargen	19/udp	ttytst source
	ftp-data	20/tcp	
	ftp	21/tcp	
	telnet	23/tcp	
	smtp	25/tcp	mail
	time	37/tcp	time server
	time	37/udp	time server
	rlp	39/udp	resource # resource location
	name	42/tcp	name server
	name	42/udp	name server
	whois	43/tcp	nickname # usually to sri-nic
	domain	53/tcp	name server # name-domain server
	domain	53/udp	name server
	name server	53/tcp	domain # name-domain server
	name server	53/udp	domain
	mtp	57/tcp	# deprecated
	bootp	67/udp	# boot program server

TABLE 29-2
Well-Known Ports for TCP and UDP *(continued)*

Service Name	Port Number	Description
tftp	69/udp	
rje	77/tcp	netrjs
finger	79/tcp	
link	87/tcp	ttylink
supdup	95/tcp	
hostnames	101/tcp	hostname # usually from sri-nic
iso-tsap	102/tcp	
dictionary	103/tcp	webster
x400	103/tcp	# ISO Mail
x400-snd	104/tcp	
csnet-ns	105/tcp	
pop	109/tcp	Post office
pop2	109/tcp	# Post Office
pop3	110/tcp	Post office
portmap	111/tcp	
portmap	111/udp	
sunrpc	111/tcp	
sunrpc	111/udp	
auth	113/tcp	authentication
sftp	115/tcp	
path	117/tcp	
uucp-path	117/tcp	

TABLE 29-2			
Well-Known Ports for TCP and UDP *(continued)*	**Service Name**	**Port Number**	**Description**
	nntp	119/tcp	usenet # Network News Transfer
	ntp	123/udp	ntpd ntp # network time protocol (exp)
	nbname	137/udp	
	nbdatagram	138/udp	
	nbsession	139/tcp	
	NeWS	144/tcp	news
	sgmp	153/udp	sgmp
	tcprepo	158/tcp	repository # PCMAIL
	snmp	161/udp	snmp
	snmp-trap	162/udp	snmp
	print-srv	170/tcp	# network PostScript
	vmnet	175/tcp	
	load	315/udp	
	vmnet0	400/tcp	
	sytek	500/udp	
	biff	512/udp	comsat
	exec	512/tcp	
	login	513/tcp	
	who	513/udp	whod
	shell	514/tcp	cmd # no passwords used

Service Name	Port Number	Description
syslog	514/udp	
printer	515/tcp	spooler # line printer spooler
talk	517/udp	
ntalk	518/udp	
efs	520/tcp	# for LucasFilm
route	520/udp	router routed
timed	525/udp	timeserver
tempo	526/tcp	newdate
courier	530/tcp	rpc
conference	531/tcp	chat
rvd-contro	531/udp	MIT disk
netnews	532/tcp	readnews
netwall	533/udp	# -for emergency broadcasts
uucp	540/tcp	uucpd # uucp daemon
klogin	543/tcp	# Kerberos authenticated rlogin
kshell	544/tcp	cmd # and remote shell
new-rwho	550/udp	new-who # experimental
remotefs	556/tcp	rfs_server rfs# Brunhoff remote filesystem
rmonitor	560/udp	rmonitord # experimental
monitor	561/udp	# experimental
garcon	600/tcp	

	Service Name	Port Number	Description
TABLE 29-2 Well-Known Ports for TCP and UDP *(continued)*	maitrd	601/tcp	
	busboy	602/tcp	
	acctmaster	700/udp	
	acctslave	701/udp	
	acct	702/udp	
	acctlogin	703/udp	
	acctprinte	704/udp	
	elcsd	704/udp	# errlog
	acctinfo	705/udp	
	acctslave2	706/udp	
	acctdisk	707/udp	
	kerberos	750/tcp	kdc # Kerberos authentication—tcp
	kerberos	750/udp	kdc # Kerberos authentication—udp
	kerberos_m	751/tcp	# Kerberos authentication
	kerberos_m	751/udp	# Kerberos authentication
	passwd_ser	752/udp	# Kerberos passwd server
	userreg_se	753/udp	# Kerberos userreg server
	krb_prop	754/tcp	# Kerberos slave propagation
	erlogin	888/tcp	# Login and environment passing
	kpop	1109/tcp	# Pop with Kerberos

Service Name	Port Number	Description
phone	1167/udp	
ingreslock	1524/tcp	
maze	1666/udp	
nfs	2049/udp	# sun nfs
knetd	2053/tcp	# Kerberos de-multiplexor
eklogin	2105/tcp	# Kerberos encrypted rlogin
rmt	5555/tcp	rmtd
mtb	5556/tcp	mtbd # mtb backup
man	9535/tcp	# remote man server
w	9536/tcp	
mantst	9537/tcp	# remote man server, testing
bnews	10000/tcp	
rscs0	10000/udp	
queue	10001/tcp	
rscs1	10001/udp	
poker	10002/tcp	
rscs2	10002/udp	
gateway	10003/tcp	
rscs3	10003/udp	
remp	10004/tcp	
rscs4	10004/udp	

	Service Name	Port Number	Description
TABLE 29-2 Well-Known Ports for TCP and UDP *(continued)*	rscs5	10005/udp	
	rscs6	10006/udp	
	rscs7	10007/udp	
	rscs8	10008/udp	
	rscs9	10009/udp	
	rscsa	10010/udp	
	rscsb	10011/udp	
	qmaster	10012/tcp	
	qmaster	10012/udp	

HEADSTART OBJECTIVE 29.13

FTP Connections

FTP is a client/server process and uses two connections: the *control connection* and the *data connection.* These connections may have one of two states:

- **Passive open**   A state waiting for transmission
- **Active open**   A state initiating the transmission

The control connection starts the process between the client and the FTP server. The control connection uses port 21 on the server side and an open port on the client side that is greater than 1023. This connection is maintained for the duration of the session.

The control connection is managed by a set of programs known as the *Protocol Interpreter.*

The data connection is managed by a set of programs known as the Data Transfer Process.

The server maintains a passive open state at port 21 listening for an FTP connection request from the client. When a request arrives, the server sets up the control session and receives FTP commands from the client. This session remains until the user types **Bye** or **Quit**.

The data transfer connection gets set up only when there is data to transfer between the server and the client. After the data transfer is complete, the connection is closed. The next time data is to be transferred, a new data connection is established. The control connection remains open through multiple data transfers. The server data port is always 20.

HEADSTART OBJECTIVE 29.14

FTP Commands

FTP commands are issued from the FTP command line. For example, to transfer a file from the server to you, you enter the command **get** *filename.* Table 29-3 lists some of the common FTP commands.

heads
⓵p

You do not need to know all of the FTP commands for the exam, but you should know what open, dir, get, put, bye, and quit do. You should also know how to get to the DOS prompt and back.

FTP Return Codes

When you enter a command, the FTP server returns a return code or a series of return codes. These codes identify the status of your command. Table 29-4 contains a partial list of return codes and their associated messages. A complete list may be found in RFC 640.

TABLE 29-3

FTP Commands

Command	Description
!	Returns to the DOS or UNIX shell. FTP is still in session. Type **exit** to return to FTP.
?	Displays descriptions for FTP commands
!command	Executes a DOS or UNIX command without leaving the FTP session.
bye	Ends the FTP session with the server and exits FTP.
dir	Lists the server's files and directories.
get, mget	Copies one or more files (using wildcards if necessary) from the server to your computer.
help	Displays descriptions for FTP commands
mkdir	Creates a directory on the server. You need to have the appropriate permission to create a directory.
put, mput	Copies one or more files (using wildcards if necessary) from your computer to the server.
quit	Ends the FTP session with the server and exits FTP.

*put and get do not support wildcards, while mput and mget do support wildcards.

TABLE 29-4

Standard FTP
Return Codes

Code	Description
119	Terminal not available.
120	Service ready in *nnn* minutes.
125	Data connection already open; transfer starting.
150	File status OK; about to open data connection.
151	User not local.
152	User unknown.
200	Command OK.
211	System status or system help reply.
212	Directory status.
213	File Status.
214	Help message.

Code	Description
220	Service is ready for new user.
221	Service closing Telnet connection.
225	Data connection open; no transfer in progress.
226	Closing data connection; requested action successful.
227	Entering passive mode.
230	User logged on.
250	Request file action OK.
331	User name OK, password needed.
350	Requested file action pending further information.
421	Service not available.
425	Can't open data connection.
426	Connection closed; transfer aborted.
450	Requested file action not taken.
530	Not logged in.
532	Need account for storing files.
550	Requested action not taken.

When you enter an FTP command, a return code and its associated message appears after the command. Figure 29-19 contains an example of command usage and the resulting return codes.

EXERCISE 29-4

Entering FTP commands

Purpose: To gain experience using FTP commands. To observe various return codes.

Do this step from Server01 only.

1. Ensure that you are logged on as Administrator

2. Using Windows 2000 Server Explorer, select the \interpub\ftp root folder.

FIGURE 29-18

FTP command and
return codes

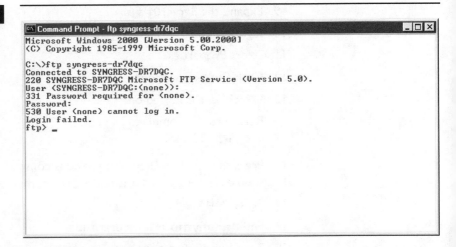

```
Command Prompt - ftp syngress-dr7dqc                                    _ □ ×
Microsoft Windows 2000 [Version 5.00.2000]
(C) Copyright 1985-1999 Microsoft Corp.

C:\>ftp syngress-dr7dqc
Connected to SYNGRESS-DR7DQC.
220 SYNGRESS-DR7DQC Microsoft FTP Service (Version 5.0).
User (SYNGRESS-DR7DQC:(none)):
331 Password required for (none).
Password:
530 User (none) cannot log in.
Login failed.
ftp> _
```

3. Right-click the right side pane.

4. Click New.

5. Click Text Document.

6. Type **From_Server01** in the dialog box. Press ENTER to create the file.

7. You are done.

Do this step only from Server02.

1. Ensure that you are logged on as Administrator.

2. Open a command prompt.

3. Type **ftp server01** and press ENTER.

4. Which return code was returned?

5. Enter **anonymous** for a user name.

6. Press ENTER to supply a null password.

7. Which return codes were returned?

8. Open Internet Service Manager. (Refer to earlier chapters if you do not remember how to do this.)

9. Expand the Server01 site.

10. Right-click the Default FTP Site.

11. Select Properties.

12. Click Current Sessions.

13. Which user is logged on?

14. Return to the command prompt.

15. Type **Bye**.

16. Press the up arrow key. The previous command, **ftp server01**, should be displayed. If it is not displayed, then type **ftp server01**.

17. Press ENTER.

18. Enter **anonymous** for a username.

19. Type **Fred@fun.com** and press ENTER.

20. Return to the MMC, Default FTP Site Properties.

21. Click Current Sessions.

22. Which user is logged on?

23. Return to the command prompt.

24. Change directories to the \inetpub\ftproot folder.

25. Type **dir** and press ENTER.

26. What do you see listed?

27. Type **get From_Server01.txt** and press ENTER.

28. Type **bye** to quit the FTP session. Close the command prompt.

29. Click the Cancel button in the Default FTP Site Properties.

Answers to the questions in the exercise:

4. 220 server01...

7. 331 Anonymous access allowed... and 230 Anonymous user logged in.

13. Anonymous.

22. Fred@fun.com.

26. From_Server01.txt file name.

HEADSTART OBJECTIVE 29.15

Configuring the FTP Service

Configuring the FTP service is done from the various property sheets. The property sheets are Master, Default, and File. Which property sheet you use depends on what you need to accomplish. The property sheets are similar to those found in the WWW Service.

Master Properties Sheet

When Internet Information Services is installed, properties are applied to the Master Properties sheet, illustrated in Figure 29-19. You get to this sheet by right-clicking on the server icon and selecting Properties.

FIGURE 29-19

Master Properties sheet

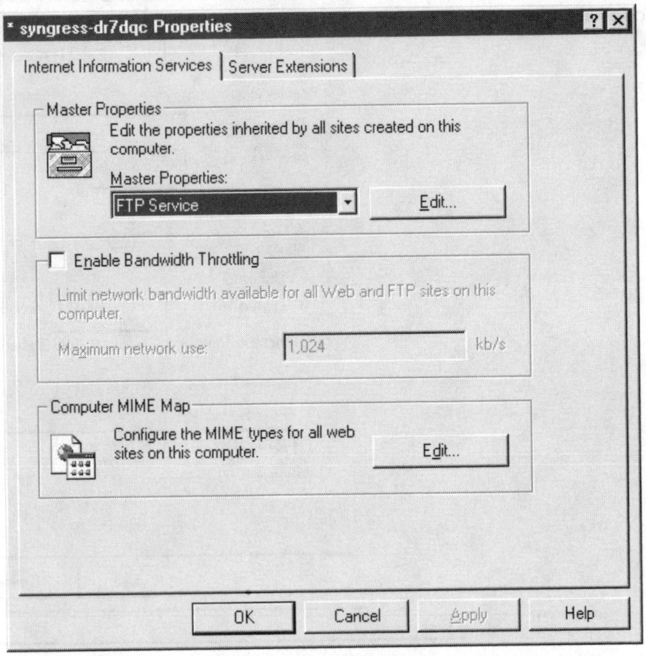

You configure the FTP and the WWW property sheets from this dialog box. Every virtual FTP site that you create inherits the properties set in the Master Properties sheet. Clicking the Edit button brings up the service Master Properties sheet as illustrated in Figure 29-20.

There are six tabs:

- **FTP Site**   Use this tab to set connection limits and logging options.
- **Security Accounts**   Use this tab to set the account used for anonymous logins. You can allow Anonymous Connection or Allow Only Anonymous Connections. You can also set Enable Password Synchronization so that if you change the password here, it also changes in the SAM database.

FIGURE 29-20

Master Properties tabs

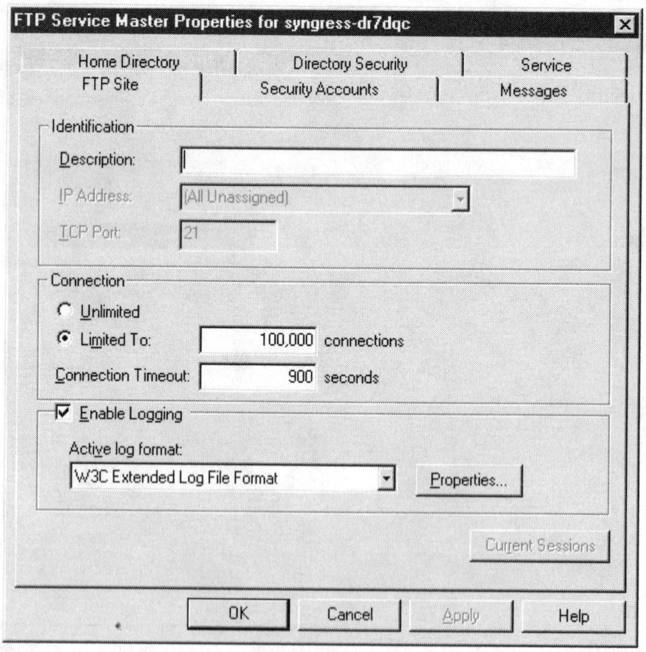

You can enter **Messages** to be sent to users on the server when

- They connect.
- They exit.
- The site has the maximum number of connections already.

- **Home Directory**   You can set the designated Home Directory for read and write access and you can set the Directory Listing Style.

- **Directory Security**   The default is to grant access to everyone and restrict by IP addresses or domains. You can deny access to everyone and then allow access by exception.

- **IIS 3.0 Admin**   You can use this tab to select one, but only one, IIS 4.0 FTP site to be managed by the ISM that is used with IIS 3.0.

Default FTP Site

Each IIS installation creates a Default FTP Site. This site initially has the same properties as specified on the Master Properties sheet. You select the Default FTP Site Properties sheet by right-clicking the Default FTP Site node and selecting Properties. Figure 29-22 illustrates this property sheet.

There are five tabs on this property sheet. They are

- FTP Site
- Security Accounts
- Messages
- Home Directory
- Directory Security

From the FTP Site tab, you can change the listening port of the FTP server. By changing the port, the FTP client has to specify the connection port at the time of connection. Otherwise, the client cannot connect since the default port for the FTP client is port 21. This can give your site a small measure of extra security.

FIGURE 29-21

Default FTP Site
Properties tabs

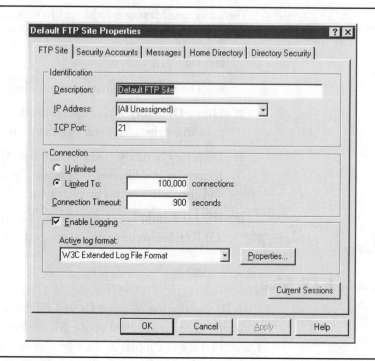

Files

Files created in the Default FTP Site inherit the properties of that site's property sheet. Files created in a virtual FTP directory inherit the properties of the directory's property sheet.

Virtual Directories

A *virtual directory* is a directory that appears to be in the ftproot, or home, folder. A virtual directory can be on any server in the same Windows 2000 Server domain. Virtual directories created on other servers should be referenced by their Universal Naming Convention (UNC) names.

Virtual Servers

A *virtual server* can be used to host multiple domain names on the same physical Internet Information Services. You need a unique IP address for each virtual server that you host.

Configure the FTP Service

Purpose: To configure the Default FTP Site using the property sheets.
Complete this exercise from both computers.

1. Ensure that you logged on as Administrator.

2. Open Internet Service Manager.

3. Right-click the Default FTP Site node.

4. Click Properties.

5. In the Description box, Type **your name FTP Site**
(where **your name** is the site name).

6. Click the Messages tab.

7. Enter a message of your choice for a Welcome message.

8. Click Apply.

9. Open a command prompt.

10. Establish an FTP session with your server.

11. Log on as anonymous.

12. Did you get your welcome message?

13. Type **put c:\boot.ini** and press ENTER.

14. What message did you get?

15. Switch back to the Default FTP Site Properties sheet.

16. Click the Home Directory tab.

17. Check the Write box.

18. Click Apply.

19. Switch to the command prompt.

20. Type **put c:\boot.ini** and press ENTER.

21. What message did you get?

22. Type **dir** and press ENTER.

23. Which files do you see?

Answers to the questions in the exercise:

12. Hopefully you saw the message that you entered.

14. Access denied.

21. Opening ASCII mode... and Transfer complete...

23. You should see the boot.ini file and one other if you were
successful in a previous exercise.

FTP Security

Users can log on using the user name "anonymous." You can restrict your site to only anonymous logons but this precludes users from attempting to log on to the FTP site using their Windows 2000 Server account.

You can also use Windows 2000 Server user accounts. Keep in mind that the user name and password for FTP logins are transmitted in clear text over the Internet. In many cases, this is undesirable.

You can also change the port that the server listens on for connections. By default, the FTP server listens on port 21 and the FTP client attempts to connect to port 21. If you change this port at the FTP server, then the computer attempting to make the connection has to manually supply the port number in order to complete the connection. Determining which port your FTP server is using to make a connection is not difficult to an experienced hacker, but it can be quite vexing to others who are trying to get unauthorized access to your site.

EXERCISE 29-6

Using FTP Security

Purpose: To implement some of the FTP security features.
  Complete this exercise from either computer.

  1. From the previous exercise, you should still have open a command prompt and the property sheet for your FTP site.
  2. Switch to the property sheet.
  3. Select the Security Accounts tab.
  4. Click Allow Only Anonymous connections.
  5. Switch to the command prompt.
  6. Type **ftp serverxx** and press ENTER.
  7. Enter **Administrator** as the user and press ENTER.
  8. Press ENTER to accept a blank password.
  9. Which message did you get?

10. Type **Bye** and press ENTER.

11. Type **ftp serverxx** and press ENTER.

12. Type **anonymous** and press ENTER.

13. Press ENTER to accept a blank password.

14. Were you able to log on as anonymous?

15. Type **Bye** and press ENTER.

16. Switch to the FTP site property sheet in MMC.

17. Select the FTP Site tab.

18. In the TCP Port dialog box, enter the number 5683.

19. Click Apply.

20. Switch to the command prompt.

21. Type **ftp serverxx** and press ENTER.

22. Which message did you receive?

23. Type **open serverxx 5683** and press ENTER.

24. Type **anonymous** and press ENTER.

25. Press ENTER to accept a blank password.

26. Were you able to log on as anonymous?

27. Type **Bye** and press ENTER.

28. Switch to the property sheet of the FTP site server.

29. Change the port number back to 21.

30. Click OK.

31. Close the MMC.

32. Answer No if you are asked to save the console settings.

Answers to the questions in the exercise:

9. Login failed.

14. Yes.

22. ftp: connect:connection refused.

26. Yes. When you specify the port number where the FTP server is listening, you get a connection and can log in.

CHAPTER SUMMARY

Internet Information Services (IIS) has objects and tasks associated with it. Objects, such as the FTP service and the WWW service, have properties. The properties are managed from the Internet Service Manager (ISM).

The Web server is a graphical client/server application. On one end is a Web server and on the other end is a client browser. The communication method is the HTTP protocol, a stateless, object-oriented protocol. The client establishes a connection with the server. The client makes this request by specifying the exact resource. The resource request is in the form of a URL. If the client does not specify a file name at the end of the URL, the server sends the default page. If there is no default page in the folder and the server is configured to allow directory browsing, the client receives a directory listing. If there is no home page and directory browsing is not allowed, then the client receives an error message from the server.

You manage the server properties using various property sheets. You must be an administrator or have been given operator permission to change the property sheets.

The FTP service is used to transfer files between the FTP server and an FTP client. The FTP service uses the TCP protocol as its transport protocol. The TCP protocol is robust and provides for automatic error detection.

You manage the FTP service from the MMC using the Internet Service Manager (ISM). You can manage all of the FTP servers in your organization from the ISM. FTP servers listen on port 21 for connections. You can change that port if you wish, but your clients need to know the nonstandard port number in order to connect.

You configure the FTP services using property sheets. You communicate with the FTP server using commands. The server sends you return codes indicating what the server did in response to your command. You can configure your FTP server to be more flexible by configuring the service for virtual directories and virtual servers.

TWO-MINUTE DRILL

- ❑ You manage the Internet Information Services with the Internet Service Manager (ISM).
- ❑ ISM is a snap-in to Microsoft Management Console (MMC).
- ❑ IIS servers can be administered locally.
- ❑ IIS servers can be administered remotely.
- ❑ HTTP 1.1 supports both put and get operations.
- ❑ A virtual directory may be on a local drive.
- ❑ A virtual directory may be on a remote drive.
- ❑ Refer to a virtual directory on a remote server by the UNC.
- ❑ IIS supports virtual servers.
- ❑ You can have multiple virtual servers on one physical server.
- ❑ Virtual servers can be assigned to one IP address.
- ❑ Virtual servers can be assigned a unique IP address to each virtual server.
- ❑ HTTP is a client/server process.
- ❑ The WWW server monitors TCP port 80.
- ❑ Each time the browser makes a request, a new connection is made.
- ❑ Enabling keep-alives prevents client connections from being closed after a request.
- ❑ The client communicates with the Web server with a simple request.
- ❑ The request specifies a Uniform Resource Locator (URL).
- ❑ The client request can also specify the protocol.
- ❑ The server responds with a status message.
- ❑ You need to configure MIME mappings to associate file extensions (file types).
- ❑ You can connect to the FTP site using the browser.
- ❑ FTP is a client/server process.
- ❑ Use FTP to transfer files between the server and the client.
- ❑ The client must initiate the connection.
- ❑ FTP uses the TCP protocol.

❑ TCP protocol is connection-oriented.

❑ TCP protocol performs automatic error correction and packet retransmission.

❑ TFTP is a command-line utility that uses the UDP protocol.

❑ IIS is not a TFTP server.

❑ You can manage any FTP server using the ISM interface.

❑ You can start and stop the FTP service from ISM.

❑ The FTP server monitors port 21 for a connection.

❑ TCP ports are divided into two broad categories: Well-known ports are numbered 0 through 1023 and have assigned functions. Dynamic ports are numbered from 1024 through 65,535 and are assigned as needed by processes.

❑ Some of the dynamic ports are used by companies to support their products or processes.

❑ A data transfer connection is set up on port 20.

❑ The data transfer connection is closed after the data transfer.

❑ The FTP connection is open until closed by the client.

❑ The FTP connection can be closed by the server if the connection timeout limit is exceeded (inactivity timeout).

❑ The FTP server sends the client a return code to indicate the status of the command issued by the client.

❑ You configure the FTP service using property sheets.

❑ The Master Properties sheet is created at installation.

❑ Virtual servers inherit the properties of the Master Properties sheet.

❑ Files inherit the properties of the FTP site.

❑ A virtual directory is a folder that appears to the client as though it is in the ftproot folder, but it is not.

❑ Virtual directories may be on any local drive and any server in the Windows 2000 Server domain.

❑ A virtual server can be used to host multiple domain names on the same physical IIS server.

❑ You can restrict the FTP server to allow only anonymous login.

❑ You can change the TCP port number your server monitors for a connection.

SELF TEST

The Self Test questions will help you measure your understanding of the material presented in this chapter. Read all the choices carefully, as there may be more than one correct answer. Choose all correct answers for each question.

1. What protocol does the WWW use?

    A. FTP

    B. HTTP

    C. IPX

    D. Hyperlink

2. Which of the following statements is true about a virtual server?

    A. IIS can host multiple virtual servers.

    B. A virtual server appears on the network and then disappears.

    C. Each virtual server must have its own IP address.

    D. Each virtual server must have its own network card.

3. Which port does the WWW service monitor for a client connection?

    A. 20

    B. 21

    C. 70

    D. 80

4. Which characteristics are necessary for you to specify access to a resource on a Web server?

    A. How access is to occur

    B. The MAC address of the server

    C. The host

    D. A path to the object

5. You receive a call from a user stating that he is trying to connect to your Web server and receives the error message, "Internet Explorer cannot open the Internet site…" What may be causing this to happen?

    A. The user does not have TCP/IP loaded.

    B. The default gateway is down.

    C. He is trying to access the Web server using the wrong TCP port number for the server.

    D. The Web server is down.

6. You want to restrict the amount of bandwidth your Web server might use on the network. What is the best way to accomplish this?

    A. Use a slower network card.

    B. Enable bandwidth throttling in the Performance tab.

    C. Limit the number of concurrent users at the server.

    D. Keep the server busy with other processes so that it has less time to service Web requests.

7. Which of the following statements is correct about keep-alives?

    A. Keep-alives keep the server running in the event of a power outage.

    B. A keep-alive restarts a file copy in the event you are accidentally disconnected from the server.

C. Keep-alives have something to do with life insurance.

D. Keep-alives maintain the client connection so that the client's browser doesn't have to make a connection with each request.

8. To transfer files using FTP, what must be in place?

   A. A default gateway

   B. An FTP server

   C. A WWW server

   D. An FTP client

9. Which protocol does FTP use?

   A. TFTP

   B. IPX

   C. TCP

   D. NetBIOS

10. Which of the following are features of the TCP protocol?

   A. It provides error correction.

   B. It does not provide error correction.

   C. It provides flow control.

   D. It supports TFTP.

11. Which port does the FTP service monitor for a connection request?

   A. 20

   B. 21

   C. 1024

   D. Any available port

12. Which ports does the FTP service use to transfer files?

   A. 20

   B. 21

   C. Any port above 1023 set by the client

   D. 2

13. Which of the following is not an FTP command?

   A. Dir

   B. Bye

   C. Get

   D. Copy

14. You are preparing to set up several virtual servers on your IIS computer. You want these virtual servers to have properties in common. Which property sheet should you modify?

   A. Default

   B. Master

   C. IIS

   D. MMC

15. You want to set your FTP server to only allow anonymous connections. How can you accomplish this?

   A. Disable the IUSR_*servername* account.

   B. Create an anonymous account in User Manager.

   C. Select the Connections tab and clear all users from the Allowed to Connect box.

   D. Select the Security Accounts tab and check the Allow Only Anonymous Connections box.

MCSE
MICROSOFT CERTIFIED SYSTEMS ENGINEER

Part IV

Appendixes

A

Self Test
Answers

Chapter I Answers

1. Which platform is Windows 2000 architecture most similar to?

   A. Windows 3.*x*

   B. Windows NT

   C. Windows 95

   D. Windows 98

   B. Windows NT. Windows 2000 is basically an upgrade version of the Windows NT 4.0 platform. The two platforms share a common heritage, and as such are based on the same core registry and security architecture. Although Windows 2000 does include many new features and improvements, it is still more compatible with the NT platform than with any other.

2. Which operating system is the Windows 2000 version of Windows NT Server 4.0, Enterprise Edition?

   A. Windows 2000 Professional

   B. Windows 2000 Server

   C. Windows 2000 Advanced Server

   D. Windows 2000 Datacenter Server

   C. Windows 2000 Advanced Server is the Windows 2000 upgrade from Windows NT Server 4.0, Enterprise Edition. Both operating systems are designed for use by medium-to-large networks that require server clustering.

3. Which operating system in the Windows 2000 platform can support up to 10,000 simultaneous users?

   A. Windows 2000 Professional

   B. Windows 2000 Server

   C. Windows 2000 Advanced Server

   D. Windows 2000 Datacenter Server

   D. Windows 2000 Datacenter Server can support up to 10,000 simultaneous users. It is the high-end operating system in the Windows 2000 platform, and is intended for use on networks with very large databases and large ISPs.

4. Which operating systems include Plug and Play (PnP) support? (Choose all that apply.)

   A. Windows 95

   B. Windows 98

   C. Windows NT 4.0

   D. Windows 2000

   A, B, and **D.** Windows 95, Windows 98, and Windows 2000 all provide PnP support (the ability of the OS to dynamically assign system resources and load drivers for devices). Windows 2000 improves on PnP technology with a new feature called ACPI. PnP, which was introduced in Windows 95 and carried into Windows 98, was never available in the Windows NT platform.

5. Which component in Windows 2000 is responsible for assigning PnP resources to devices?

   A. Resource Arbitrator

   B. Configuration Manager

C. Kernel mode Manager

D. User mode Manager
   C. The Kernel mode Manager is responsible for assigning PnP resources to devices in Windows 2000. The Resource Arbitrator and Configuration Manager are components of the Windows 95 and Windows 98 PnP architecture. The User mode Manager, while found in Windows 2000, is used to provide the user with an interface for managing and configuring PnP devices.

6. What is the name of the Windows 2000 technology that places PnP capability and Power Management under complete control of the operating system?

   A. Advanced Configuration and Power Interface

   B. Advanced Power Management

   C. Windows Driver Model

   D. Code Signing
      A. Advanced Configuration and Power Interface. Also known as ACPI, this technology improves on the BIOS-dependent nature of PnP and Power Management in the computer. In fact, Advanced Power Management is the name of the Windows 95 power management technology.

7. Which of the following file systems does Windows 2000 support? (Choose all that apply.)

   A. FAT16

   B. FAT32

C. NTFS 4.0

D. NTFS 5.0
   A, B, C, and **D.** Windows 2000 supports FAT16, FAT32, NTFS 4.0, and NTFS5.0. FAT16 and FAT32 were traditionally used in the Windows 9*x* platform, and NTFS is the file system native to the NT 4.0 platform. NTFS 5.0 is the native file system of Windows 2000, but retains the ability to support the other file systems for backward compatibility.

8. What is the name of the new Windows 2000 technology that provides roaming access capabilities and allows users to access their files even when the network or server is down?

   A. Kerberos

   B. Intellimirror

   C. Distributed Link Tracking

   D. None of the above
      B. Intellimirror. This technology places a copy of server-based documents, settings, and applications on the user's workstation. Because a copy of this information is kept on the server, a user can retrieve it from any workstation in the network (roaming access). Because a copy is also kept on the workstation, a user can access his or her information, even when the network is down or the server is unavailable. As soon as the server becomes available, changes to the user's files and settings are automatically updated on the server.

9. How much memory can be addressed by the Windows 2000 Professional operating system?

   A. 64MB

   B. 2GB

   C. 4GB

   D. 64GB

   C. Windows 2000 Professional can address up to 4GB of memory. This is the same amount addressable by its predecessor, Windows NT Workstation 4.0. Windows 2000 Server can also address up to 4GB of memory, and Advanced and Datacenter servers can address a whopping 64GB!

10. Which *new* Windows 2000 Server feature allows administrators to end all processes related to a process that is causing a problem?

    A. Task Manager

    B. Process Manager

    C. Kill Process Tree

    D. Server Recovery Console

    C. Kill Process Tree. Earlier versions of Windows NT allowed administrators to end single processes. However, processes spawned by the original one would continue to run, although there was no need for them anymore. With the Kill Process Tree feature, when an administrator ends one process, all related processes are also ended, thus freeing up computer resources and avoiding errors.

11. Which of the following are improvements in the Windows 2000 Advanced Server operating system? (Choose all that apply.)

    A. Enhanced Server clustering

    B. COM+ services

    C. Improved fail-over protection

    D. Increased SMP support

    A, B, and **C.** Windows 2000 Advanced Server includes enhanced server clustering, COM+ services, and improved fail-over protection. These improvements lead to higher availability, less downtime, and better load balancing on a multidomain network.

12. Active Directory focuses on objects in terms of their:

    A. Containers

    B. Namespace

    C. Attributes

    D. Forests

    C. Active Directory focuses on objects' attributes. This allows administrators to easily organize objects into containers based on their similarities rather than their physical locations. It also improves search capabilities for users by allowing them to search for objects based on their attributes or functions rather than their domains or pathnames.

13. Which Active Directory feature provides each domain controller with portions of the directory that pertain only to that domain's accessible objects?

A. Transitive trust

B. Redundant replication

C. Mirroring

D. Multimaster replication

   D. Multimaster replication. Active
   Directory will automatically filter out
   portions of the main directory that
   pertain to each domain, and store
   copies of that information in each
   domain controller. This reduces the
   amount of information that each
   domain controller must manage. That
   is, each domain controller is only
   responsible for storing information
   about the objects on the network that
   it uses.

14. A single hierarchical path of domains
    within a network is called a:

    A. Container

    B. Tree

    C. Forest

    D. Domain path

       **B. A single hierarchical path of
       domains within a network is called a
       tree.** A tree is an unbroken path
       between some parent domain in the
       network to some distant child
       domain. For example, suppose that
       "North America" is the parent domain
       for other domains associated with
       Canada, USA, and Mexico. The USA
       domain contains the New York
       domain. The New York tree consists
       of New York, USA, and North
       America. Canada and Mexico do not
       belong to the same linear path, so they
       are not part of the New York tree, but

rather are different branches of the
North America tree.

15. What is the name given to domain trees
    that can access each other's resources, but
    do not share domain names or security
    configurations?

    A. Container

    B. Tree

    C. Forest

    D. Parent Domain Path

       C. Forest. A forest consists of
       individual trees that have no
       similarities other than their ability to
       access each other's resources. For
       example, the company
       largecompany.com may have access to
       the resources of another company,
       smallcompany.com. These two
       companies (and their networks) are
       separate in every way except that they
       can share resources through a global
       catalog, and therefore share an Active
       Directory.

Chapter 2 Answers

1. Lucille plans to install Windows 2000 but
   the video card she just got is nowhere to
   be found on the Hardware Compatibility
   List. What can she do?

   A. Nothing. If it's not on the HCL, it
      won't work.

   B. Get another video card

   C. Check the hardware manufacturer for
      updated drivers for the video card.

D. Use the Windows 95 drivers that came with the card.
C. The HCL is not always up to date, so the video card might still be compatible with Windows 2000. Check the hardware manufacturer to see if they have Windows 2000 drivers for the video card. Windows 2000 cannot use Windows 95 drivers.

2. Marty, an administrator, is in the middle of a Windows 2000 installation and just remembered that he forgot to add the computer to the domain. The nearest Windows 2000 machine is very faraway and he would prefer to not walk so far. What should he do?

A. Stretch his legs for a few minutes. He's got a long walk ahead of him.

B. Enter his login/password when prompted.

C. Nothing. Windows 2000 is automatically added to the domain in every installation.

D. Add the computer to a workgroup with the same name as the domain.
B. The only two ways to add the computer to the domain are to either add the computer manually or enter the login/password of an account that has the privilege of adding computers to the domain. Adding the computer to a workgroup doesn't give it access to any domain.

3. There are 50 Windows 2000 Professional Clients accessing a Windows 2000 Server's print services. There are 40 clients accessing the same server's FTP services. How many Per Seat Client Access Licenses should the Windows 2000 Server have?

A. 10

B. 40

C. 50
C. You only need 40 Per Seat Client licenses. FTP, telnet, and Web access does not count toward the Client Access License.

4. When can you partition the space on your hard disk?

A. During the install

B. Right after the installation

C. Anytime after the installation

D. Before the installation
A, B, C, D. You can partition your hard drive before, during, and anytime after Windows 2000 is installed.

5. What type of file systems does Windows 2000 support?

A. FAT

B. FAT32

C. NTFS

D. HPFS
A, B, C. Windows 2000 supports FAT, FAT32, and NTFS.

6. David is installing a dual-boot system with Windows 2000 and Windows 95. After installing Windows 2000, he realizes all the applications he installed on Windows 95 are not available in Windows 2000. What can he do?

A. Make shortcuts to the application's executables.

B. Import Windows 95 registry to Windows 2000.

C. Reinstall all applications.

D. Export the Windows 2000 registry to Windows 95.
C. You need to reinstall all applications on dual-boot system in order for them to be available on both operating systems. The registry for Windows 95 and Windows 2000 are not compatible, so they cannot be imported and exported.

7. Billy wants to install Windows 2000 over the network for a workstation that currently has no operating system on it. How can he install Windows 2000 if he can't access the distribution server?

A. Boot off a network client disk.

B. Install a network card with a BOOT ROM.

C. Do a push installation.

D. Do a pull installation.
A. In order to access a distribution server on a PC without an operating system, you need to boot the PC with a network client boot disk.

8. Ryan is doing a Windows 2000 network installation. What switch does he use to specify the source of the distribution files?

A. /a

B. /r

C. /rx

D. /s
D. Ryan uses the /s switch to specify the source of the distribution files.

9. What is the name of the answer file that the Setup Manager Wizard uses?

A. Unattend.txt

B. Attend.txt

C. Answer.txt

D. Autoanswer.txt
A. The Setup Manager Wizard uses the unattend.txt.

10. What folder do you copy from the Windows 2000 CD when you need to do network installations for Digital Alpha computers?

A. i386

B. x386

C. iAlpha

D. Alpha
D. You need to copy the Alpha folder from the Windows 2000 when you do network installation for Digital Alpha computers.

11. Felix is setting up Windows 2000 so it can be set up on multiple computers. He is installing boot and temporary files on multiple drives. What switch should he use with winnt32.exe to ensure the proper files are copied to each drive and set as active?

A. /unattend

B. /source

C. /s

D. /syspart

D. The /syspart switch copies temporary and boot files to a specified target drive and marks it active.

12. Oscar decided to use disk duplication to do mass installation of Windows 2000. His computer is working fine, so he decides to use it as the reference computer. After he installs a few computers, he discovers that all the workstations can access his e-mail. How can he fix this?

A. Change his password.

B. Reconfigure all the workstations.

C. Reinstall the computers with files from a different reference computer.

D. Deny e-mail access from all the workstations

A, B, C, D. All of these are viable fixes. The best cure is prevention. To prevent this in the future, ensure the reference computer has few user-specific settings.

13. Louis decides to use the System Preparation Tool. However, he wants to ensure that he is never prompted for any messages. Which switch should he use?

A. /quiet

B. /nosidgen

C. /pnp

D. /reboot

A. The /quiet switch runs sysprep in the silent mode where no messages are displayed. The /nosidgen switch runs sysprep.exe without generating a SID.

Normally, you each computer has to have an individual SID, or security identifier. Use this option only to make a clone of the computer as a backup or to allow the end user to customize the computer. The /pnp switch forces Plug and Play to refresh when the computer reboots to redetect all the hardware devices in the computer. The /reboot switch reboots the computer after sysprep.exe runs.

14. How is the Remote Installation Preparation Wizard different from the System Preparation Tool?

A. The Remote Installation Preparation Wizard is for remote installations only.

B. The System Preparation Tool is for remote installations only.

C. The Remote Installation Preparation Wizard removes user-specific settings.

D. The System Preparation Tool removes user-specific settings.

C. The Remote Installation Preparation Wizard goes one step farther by removing anything unique to that client, such as the SID, computer name, and hardware settings.

15. When Windows 2000 won't start or install, what is the first thing you should do?

A. Reinstall Windows 2000.

B. Ensure all hardware is Windows 2000 compatible.

C. Reboot the computer.

D. Reseat the hardware and reboot.
B. Ensure all hardware is Windows 2000 compatible.

Chapter 3 Answers

1. What is the difference between the System Preparation Tool and the Remote Installation Preparation Wizard?

   A. Nothing.

   B. The Remote Installation Preparation Wizard removes anything unique to the client.

   C. The System Preparation Tool removes anything unique to the client.

   D. The Remote Installation Preparation Wizard adds unique items to the client.
   B. The Remote Installation Preparation Wizard removes anything unique to that client, such as the SID, computer name, and hardware settings. This allows computers with multiple hardware configurations to use the same image.

2. You have just copied many installed images on to the RIS server. Why do the remote boot images not add up?

   A. Windows 2000 is incorrectly reporting the space for the RIS image.

   B. The images you have uploaded are incomplete.

   C. Windows 2000 uses the groveler agent to eliminate redundant files across many images.

   D. You may have an incomplete image.
   C. When there are many copies of the operating system, there are many overlapping files. This can quickly consume the hard disk space on the RIS server. Single Instance Store fixes this by having a groveler agent scan the hard disk regularly and link redundant files.

3. What components must your network have to ensure the RIS will function correctly?

   A. DHCP Servers

   B. DNS Servers

   C. Active Directory Servers

   D. RIS Servers
   A, B, C, D. To ensure the RIS, your network must have all the components listed.

4. Unlike Windows NT, services such as the RIS server must be authorized. How do you authorize the RIS server?

   A. Type in your login/password when prompted.

   B. Proper permission is given when the RIS is installed.

   C. Ensure client accessing service has permission to access the RIS service.

   D. You must authorize it within the Active Directory.
   D. The RIS allows you to control access of the client computers to the RIS servers. In order for the clients to be able to contact a certain RIS server, it must be authorized within the Active

Directory. If the RIS server is not authorized, clients trying to request that RIS server will not get a response.

5. Where can you change the properties of the distribution point?

   A. Component Services

   B. Data Sources

   C. Active Directory Users and Computers

   D. Computer Management
   C. In the Active Directory Users and Computers, you can change many properties of the distribution point, such as installation choices and troubleshooting tools.

6. Which option in the Client Installation Wizard do you set if you want the most streamlined and painless client installation?

   A. Automatic Setup

   B. Custom Setup

   C. Restart a Previous Setup Attempt

   D. Maintenance and Troubleshooting
   A. Automatic Setup. This setup minimizes user error and minimizes the number of help desk calls. This setup is the ideal choice when the workstations are all the same.

7. Which option in the Client Installation Wizard do you set if you want to restart a client installation that has been prematurely aborted?

   A. Automatic Setup

   B. Custom Setup

   C. Restart a Previous Setup Attempt

   D. Maintenance and Troubleshooting
   C. Restart a Previous Setup Attempt. This is used so that the user is not prompted for questions that were answered in the previous setup attempt.

8. Which option in the Client Installation Wizard do you use to access third-party tools?

   A. Automatic Setup

   B. Custom Setup

   C. Restart a Previous Setup Attempt

   D. Maintenance and Troubleshooting
   D. Maintenance and Troubleshooting. Use this option to access third-party maintenance and troubleshooting tools

9. You want to create an unattend.txt file for an automated installation of Windows 2000. Your colleague is new to Windows 2000. He wants to create the unattend.txt by hand. What new feature should you tell him about in Windows 2000 that allows for easier generation of an unattend.txt file?

   A. None. Create the file yourself.

   B. Copy the file from the CD-ROM and modify it yourself.

   C. Use the Windows 2000 Setup Manager.

   D. Use the Windows 2000 winnt32 tool.
   C. The Windows 2000 Setup Manager is a new tool to Windows 2000. It uses an easy-to-follow GUI to allow for generation of an unattend.txt file by prompting you with questions.

10. After your colleague decides to use the Windows 2000 Setup Manager, he is mildly surprised that the Setup Manager does more than just generate an unattend.txt file. What other file does Windows 2000 Setup Manager generate that allows for an unattended installation?

    A. A new setup.exe

    B. A new winnt32.exe

    C. A batch file that runs the Windows 2000 setup program

    D. A new winnt.exe
    C. Windows 2000 Setup Manager creates two files that allow an unattended installation: the unattended answer file, called unattend.txt, and a batch file that launches the Windows 2000 setup program with the answer file as the command-line argument.

11. You are running sysprep to clone hard drives to another computer. Unfortunately, each computer has hardware that is usually not detected during the Windows 2000 installation. What switch should you use to ensure all hardware is detected?

    A. /nosidgen

    B. /pnp

    C. /nopnp

    D. /sidgen
    B. The /pnp switch forces a plug-and-play scan of all the hardware after the installation is finished.

12. You do not have a PXE boot ROM and you need to enable remote client installation. How do you create a remote installation boot floppy?

    A. Run the RBFG.exe from the RIS server.

    B. Run the RBFG.exe from a client connected to the RIS.

    C. Run the RBFG.exe on a computer with administration tools installed.

    D. Run the RBFG.exe on a Windows 2000 Server.
    A, B, C, D. To create a remote installation boot floppy, run the RBFG.exe from the RIS server, on a client connected to the RIS server, or on a computer with the administration tools installed that includes Windows 2000 Server.

13. When you boot up using the RIS and the BOOTP message shows up on the client, but the computer cannot get past this part, what can you do to troubleshoot it?

    A. Ensure the server is available and the service has started.

    B. Ensure the DHCP server is authorized in the Active Directory.

    C. Ensure there is an active IP address scope.

    D. Ensure the router between the client and DHCP server is allowing DHCP packets to go through.
    A, B, C, D. During this step, the client is requesting an IP address. If it does not pass this step, it means the

client is unable to receive the IP. The main thing to look at it is the DHCP server. All four relate to making sure the DHCP server is up and running.

14. When you boot up using the RIS and the DHCP message shows up on the client, but the computer cannot get past this part, what can you do to troubleshoot it?

   A. Ensure the remote installation server is available and the RIS has started.

   B. Ensure the RIS server is authorized in the Active Directory.

   C. If you have a remote boot client, ensure the client is supported by checking the PXE ROM version on the client computer.

   D. Ensure the router between the client and the RIS is allowing the DHCP request and response to go through.
   A, B, C, D. After the client gets past the BOOTP screen and shows DHCP, it has successfully obtained an IP address. If it does not pass this step, it means the client cannot contact the RIS server. All four relate to ensuring the RIS is working correctly.

15. After the client changes to BINL or prompts the user to press F2, it means the client has contacted the RIS server and is waiting for the first image file. If you are unable to get a response from the RIS server, or the client times out, what should you do?

   A. Restart the RIS server.

   B. Ensure DHCP is working.

   C. Ensure Domain Controller is up.

   D. Reboot the computer.
   A. If you are unable to get a response from the RIS server, or the client times out, stop and restart the RIS server.

Chapter 4 Answers

1. Which of the following file systems are supported by Windows 2000? (Choose all that apply.)

   A. NTFS

   B. FAT

   C. HPFS

   D. UDF
   A, B, D. The OS/2 High Performance File System (HPFS) has not been supported since Windows NT 3.51.

2. Which of the following file systems can be used to format a volume in Windows 2000? (Choose all that apply.)

   A. FAT16

   B. FAT32

   C. NTFS

   D. UDF
   A, B, C. UDF is implemented in Windows 2000 as a Read-Only file system for accessing data on Digital Versatile Disc (DVD) media only.

3. As an administrator of a Windows 2000 server, you have been given the task of selecting a file system for the server's single

partition. The partition must be formatted as 6GB, will hold the Windows 2000 system files, must support Long File Names (LFNs), and must allow for file/directory-level security. Which of the following file systems will support this? (Choose all that apply.)

A. FAT16

B. FAT32

C. NTFS

D. DES
   C. NTFS is the only file system supported in Windows 2000 that supports file/directory level security. DES is not a file system.

4. You are attempting to compress data stored on a 6GB FAT32 volume; however, the Compression option is disabled. What is most likely the cause of the problem?

A. Encryption has been enabled on one or more directories on the volume.

B. The partition size is too large.

C. You do not have the Compress permission to the root folder.

D. Compression cannot be used on FAT32 volumes.
   D. Compression can only be enabled on NTFS volumes. Encryption cannot be enabled on FAT32. There is no maximum size for a compressed partition. There is no such thing as the Compress permission, only a Compression attribute.

5. Which of the following shows the correct UNC name syntax to be specified when connecting to a share?

A. servername.sharename

B. \\servername\sharename

C. \\sharename\servername

D. sharename.servername
   B. A UNC path follows the format \\servername\sharename.

6. As an administrator of several Windows 2000 servers, you want to provide your users with a method to access files from several servers through a single logical directory hierarchy. Which of the following technologies will you implement?

A. DES

B. EFS

C. UDF

D. DFS
   D. DFS is the Distributed file system, and is used to provide a logical hierarchical view of file resources to end users.

7. The C:\Marketing directory is shared as Marketing on the Departments server. The only permission assigned to the Marketing share is Ray:Change. The C:\ drive is formatted with NTFS , and the Marketing directory has the following Security permissions: Marketing: Full Control, Ray:Read. What are Ray's Effective permissions when accessing the

Marketing data through the \\Departments\Marketing share?

A. Full Control

B. Read

C. Change

D. No Access

C. Change. Ray is granted only Change access through the share. Although he has Full Control to the file/directory structure through the Marketing group, the share restricts his access back to Change only.

8. The Payroll directory has been moved from C:\, an NTFS volume, to D:\, a FAT32 volume on the Departments server. The Payroll share has been reconfigured to point to D:\Payroll, and security is set on the share as Payroll: Full Control. The Payroll Directory permissions were set to Payroll:Change prior to the move. What are the Effective permissions for members of the Payroll group accessing the data through the \\Departments\Payroll share?

A. Full Control

B. Change

C. Read

D. No Access

A. Payroll users have Full Control through the share. Regardless of previous NTFS permissions, the data now resides on a FAT32 volume, which does not support File/Directory permissions.

9. Betty is a member of the Managers group on the Departments server. The Managers directory has been shared from C:\, an NTFS volume as Managers. The only permission on the share is Managers: Change. On the Managers directory, the following permissions are in effect: Managers: Full Control, Betty: Deny for all permissions. What are Betty's Effective permissions to the Managers data when accessing it through the \\Departments\Managers share?

A. Change

B. No Access

C. Full Control

D. List Data

B. Betty has been denied all permissions to her user account, which overrides any other permissions that have been granted based on group membership.

10. How can encryption be enabled on a Windows 2000 NTFS directory?

A. By entering ENCRYPT /FS:NTFS from a command prompt

B. By using ATTRIB +E <filename>

C. By adding All Users with the Encrypt permission

D. By enabling the Encrypt Advanced attribute in the file Properties window

D. None of the other options are valid.

11. You have enabled the Auditing Policy on your local computer, and have enabled

auditing for the delete event on the Inventory directory. You suspect that someone has deleted critical data out of this folder. How can you find out which user deleted the file?

A. View the Security Event Log

B. View the Auditing Event Log

C. View the contents of the Master File Table

D. View the AUDIT.LOG file in the C:\WINNT\Logs directory
A. Auditing results are stored in the Security Event Log, accessible through the Computer Management Console.

12. You plan to bring a new server online with a larger storage capacity than your existing machine. Both servers will be online running Windows 2000, and you plan to copy the data across the network from one server to the other. You have hundreds of customized quota entries on the old Windows 2000 server. What is the best way to ensure that quota entries are populated on the new server?

A. Export the quota configuration using the Quota Entries console, and import it on the new server.

B. Export the quota configuration using QEXPORT, and import it on the new server using QIMPORT.

C. Back up the quota to tape using the Windows 2000 backup program.

D. You must recreate all quota entries manually.

A. Exporting and Importing the quota entries using the console is the easiest option to migrate the quota configuration.

13. What type of encryption is used on the Encrypting File System (EFS)?

A. DES+

B. DES-X

C. AES

D. DFS
B. DES-X is the encryption mechanism employed by EFS.

14. When should you defragment your hard drive? (Choose all that apply.)

A. At least every month

B. After deletion of large amounts of data

C. When disk write performance is slow

D. When disk read performance is slow
A, B, C, D. All answers are correct. Defragmentation should occur at least every month, and should be run after a large amount of data is deleted. A fragmented hard drive can cause slow disk read and write performance.

15. You currently have Windows 2000 installed on a FAT32 volume, but you would like to convert to NTFS to allow for the implementation of file/directory level security. Which is the easiest method to convert your FAT32 volume to NTFS?

A. CHKDSK C: /CONVERT:NTFS

B. CONVNTFS C:

C. CONVERT C: /FS:NTFS

D. FAT32 cannot be converted to NTFS
   C. The CONVERT utility is used to convert a FAT32 volume to NTFS.

Chapter 5 Answers

1. Which of the following is included with Windows 2000?

   A. System Policy Editor
   B. Group Policy
   C. Both of the above
   D. Neither of the above
      C. Both System Policy Editor, for creating NT 4.0-style policies for down-level clients, and the new Group Policy feature are included with Windows 2000. It is recommended that you use Group Policy whenever possible instead of NT system policies. Also note that NT and Windows 9x policies are not compatible with Windows 2000, and cannot be applied to a Windows 2000 machine.

2. Which of the following purposes can be served by Group Policy? (Choose all that apply.)

   A. Control of a user's desktop environment
   B. Redirection of special folders to a network location
   C. Management of security settings
   D. Assignment of scripts to run at computer startup

A, B, C, D. All of these purposes, and more, can be accomplished by the use of Group Policy.

3. Who should apply and configure Group Policy?

   A. All administrators.
   B. Designated Group Policy administrators only.
   C. All domain users should configure their own policies.
   D. None of the above.
      B. Best practice is for only designated Group Policy administrators to apply and configure Group Policy. Group Policy is set for a specific SDOU (site, domain, or organizational unit) and because it has such a broad effect, it is important that those who set up and administer it have special training and knowledge in this area.

4. What is the term used to refer to the Group Policy management application that is added to your custom MMC for managing Group Policy?

   A. Plug-in
   B. Applet
   C. Snap-in
   D. Tool
      C. MMC management applications are called Snap-ins, and are added to a console by choosing the "Add/Remove snap-in" option on the Console menu.

5. Group policies themselves are stored in which of the following, in much the same way word processing data is stored in an individual document?

    A. GTPs

    B. GPCs

    C. GPFs

    D. GPOs

    D. The policies are stored in Group Policy Objects, or GPOs. There is no such thing as a GTP, although GTP refers to the Group Policy Template, which is a folder structure containing the information for a particular GPO. A GPC is a Group Policy Container that contains GPO properties such as version and status information.

6. What type of GPO resides on Windows 2000 member servers and workstations running Windows 2000 Professional?

    A. Nonlocal policies

    B. Local policies

    C. Domain policies

    D. Active Directory policies

    B. Windows 2000 nondomain controllers (member servers and workstations running Windows 2000 Professional) have just one local policy GPO. As the name implies, they affect only the local computer. Nonlocal policies are stored on domain controllers, and are applied to sites, domains, or organizational units (SDOUs).

7. What is the folder name for the Group Policy Template folder as it appears in the Sysvol directory?

    A. An eight-character name designated by the administrator.

    B. "GPT," followed by a 32-bit binary number, which is randomly assigned by the system.

    C. A hexadecimal number that represents the GUID for the GPO to which it applies.

    D. Poltemp, followed by a decimal number assigned to each GPT in sequence (e.g.,. Poltemp1, Poltemp2, etc.).

    C. The folder name is the hexadecimal number that represents the Globally Unique Identifier for the GPO to which the GPT applies. An example: {A3A1B867-E344-74F3-00A4DE200 C52}.

8. Which of the following is true of the \USER subfolder in the GPT? (Choose all that apply.)

    A. It contains the Registry.pol file with the Registry settings applied to users.

    B. It contains the .ADM files.

    C. It contains several subfolders.

    D. It contains the scripts and related files for startup and shutdown scripting.

    A, C. The \USER folder contains the Registry.pol file with Registry settings applied to users, and has several subfolders, such as \USER\APPLICATIONS and

\USER\SCRIPTS. The .ADM files are contained in the \ADM subfolder, and the scripts for startup and shutdown (which applies to the computer, not the user) are contained in the \MACHINE\SCRIPTS subfolder.

9. Which of the following are modes in which an MMC console can be saved? (Choose all that apply.)

   A. User mode

   B. Editor mode

   C. Control mode

   D. Author mode

   A, D. Saving the console in Author mode will provide full functionality, including the ability to add and remove Snap-ins. Saving the console in User mode restricts functionality. There are no Editor or Control modes.

10. When you add the Group Policy Snap-in to a console, the GPO that the Snap-in will control by default is which of the following?

   A. The default domain GPO

   B. The local computer GPO

   C. The site GPO

   D. The organizational unit GPO

   B. By default, the new Snap-in will control the local computer policies. To change this, you must click BROWSE in the Wizard and choose a GPO that you want the Snap-in to control.

11. Which of the following check boxes must be checked in order to force Child containers to inherit policies from their higher-level objects?

   A. Force Inheritance

   B. Prevent Inheritance

   C. No Override

   D. High-Level Container Priority

   C. The No Override check box will prevent higher-level policies from being overridden, thus forcing the Child Container object to inherit the policies of its higher-level objects. Prevent Inheritance does just the opposite, specifying that higher-level policies will not be inherited. There are no such check boxes as Force Inheritance or High-Level Container Priority.

12. Which of the following security areas should be modified to control password configuration policies?

   A. User rights

   B. Account policies

   C. Password policies

   D. NTFS permissions

   B. Account policies govern password length, expiration, history, and configuration, as well as Kerberos and account lockout policies. User rights govern what users can do with the computer, such as the right to log on locally or the right to shut down the computer. NTFS permissions govern access to specific objects. There is no such thing as password policies, per se.

13. Which of the following is a special folder that can be redirected to a network location via Group Policy folder redirection? (Choose all that apply.)

    A. My Documents

    B. Winnt (system root folder)

    C. Sysvol

    D. Start menu
       A, D. The My Documents folder (along with its subfolder, My Documents\My Pictures) and the Start menu folder can be redirected. Other such special folders include Applications Data and the Desktop folder. The Winnt system root folder and the Sysvol folder are not included in this group.

14. If you assign multiple logon scripts, in what order are they processed?

    A. Alphabetical order based on the script's file name.

    B. The order in which you assigned them.

    C. The order in which you specify by moving them up or down in the dialog box.

    D. All are run simultaneously.
       C. Multiple logon scripts are processed in the order specified by the administrator. This is down by moving them up or down in the dialog box when you add scripts.

15. Disabling the unused parts of a GPO will have what effect?

    A. It will speed up the startup and logon process for all users.

    B. It will speed up the startup and logon process for the users and computers subject to that GPO.

    C. It will slow the startup and logon process for the users and computers subject to that GPO.

    D. It will have no effect on performance.
       B. Disabling the unused parts of the GPO (those listed as "Not Configured") will speed up startup and logon for any users or computers subject to that GPO, since these parts will not have to be processed.

Chapter 6 Answers

1. Identify the first phase of the software life cycle.

    A. Deployment

    B. Preparation

    C. Test Lab and Development

    D. Pilot
       B. The four phases of the software life cycle are Preparation, Deployment, Maintenance, and Removal.

2. Which of the following file types relate to applications package in Windows Installer?

    A. .IPF

    B. .MWI

    C. .MSI

    D. .ZAP
       C. Applications packaged using Windows Installer are stored with a .MSI extension.

3. A Group Policy Object (GPO) *cannot* be assigned to which of the following? (Choose all that apply.).

   A. Domain

   B. Site

   C. Organizational Unit (OU)

   D. User

   D. Group Policy Objects (GPOs) can be assigned only to a Domain, Site, or Organizational Unit. A GPO cannot be assigned directly to a user object; however, users inherit policies enabled on a higher level.

4. When assigning an application to a computer, which of the following is true?

   A. The application is automatically installed when the user logs on.

   B. The application is automatically installed when the computer starts.

   C. The application is added to the Start menu in preparation for installation.

   D. The application is added to Add/Remove Programs in preparation for installation.

   B. When assigning an application to a computer, the application is installed automatically when the computer starts. The advertisement for the application does not appear in the Start menu or Add/Remove Programs.

5. When publishing an application to a user, which of the following is true?

   A. The application is automatically installed when the user logs on.

   B. The application is automatically installed when the computer starts.

   C. The application is added to the Start menu in preparation for installation.

   D. The application is added to Add/Remove Programs in preparation for installation.

   D. Published applications will appear in the Add/Remove Programs window.

6. As an administrator, you must decide how Microsoft Excel should be deployed to your enterprise. Every user in the Finance department requires the application for day-to-day operations. Some users in Information Technology also need the application. Both departments are in the same tree and domain, but each its own OU. What is the best way to deploy the application using Group Policy?

   A. Assign the application to the domain using a single GPO.

   B. Publish the application to the domain using a single GPO.

   C. Create a GPO for both OUs. Assign the package to the Finance OU, and publish it to the Information Technology OU.

   D. Create a GPO for both OUs. Publish the package to the Finance OU, and assign it to the Information Technology OU.

   C. In this scenario, deployment would best be handled by assigning the application to Finance users and publishing it to Information

Technology. Using this method, all Finance users will have the application installed by default, and it will still be available for users in Information Technology in the Add/Remove Programs applet.

7. How is deployment of a non-Windows Installer application managed using Group Policy?

   A. A .ZAP file must be created.

   B. A .MST file must be created.

   C. It can be deployed in the same method as any other application.

   D. A non-Windows Installer application cannot be deployed using Group Policy.
   A. A non-Windows Installer application can be deployed using Group Policy; however, a .ZAP file must first be created. Applications that use .ZAP files can only be published, and do not run with elevated privileges on the client.

8. Users at remote sites are complaining of slow performance when installing required applications across the WAN. You are currently using a single GPO to assign software to all users at the domain level. What should you do to increase performance?

   A. Assign the software to computers instead of users.

   B. Assign software at the site level, using individual Distribution Points for each site.

   C. Stagger user logon hours, to reduce concurrent WAN traffic.

   D. Publish the application instead of assigning it.
   B. You should bring the source of the application closer to the user on the network by configuring multiple Distribution Points. Multiple GPOs can then be created and assigned on a site level, each using its own Distribution Point for the individual site.

9. What is the easiest way to remove an application that was previously assigned using Group Policy?

   A. Create an Uninstall package in Windows Installer, and make it assigned.

   B. Delete the package in the Group Policy console, and select the Uninstall option.

   C. Send a memo to the users requesting that they remove the application using Add/Remove Programs.

   D. Manually remove the application from each workstation while logged on as a local administrator.
   B. A previously assigned application can be removed from all computers or users to which it was assigned by deleting it in Group Policy Editor and selecting the "Immediately uninstall software from users and computers" option.

10. Which of the following sections of a .ZAP file is required?

    A. [Application]

    B. [Ext]

    C. [CLSIDs]

    D. [ProgIDs]
       A. The [Application] section of a .ZAP file contains information such as the name of the application and the setup executable to be launched.

11. You have assigned an application to the users at your site. However, when users attempt to launch the installer from the Start menu, they receive an "Access Denied" message. What is the probable cause of the problem?

    A. Users are not local administrators.

    B. Users do not have access to the Distribution Point share.

    C. The policy does not apply to the user.

    D. The application was created using a .ZAP file.
       B. Users must have at least Read permissions to the Distribution Point share and directory structure.

12. Which of the following are limitations of deploying software using .ZAP files? (Choose all that apply.)

    A. Applications can only be published.

    B. Applications can only be assigned.

    C. Users must have local permissions to install software.

    D. GPOs can only be created at the OU level.
       A, C. When deploying software using .ZAP files, the applications can only be published and not assigned. Also, since they do not use Windows Installer, .ZAP files do not run with elevated privileges, so the user must have the required permissions to install the software.

13. A published application will open three types of files; however, when users attempt to launch any one of the file types, the application is not being automatically installed. Which of the following are potential causes of the problem? (Choose all that apply.)

    A. The package does not have any associated file types defined.

    B. The administrator has not specified file types in package properties.

    C. The "Auto-install this application by file extension activation" option is disabled.

    D. The file type is already assigned to another published application that uses the same extension with a higher precedence.
       A, C, D. For an application installation to be initiated based on the launching of a file extension, the list of extensions must be specified in the package. The "Auto-install this application by file extension

activation" deployment property must be enabled. It is also possible that another application has already been installed that has a higher precedence for that particular file extension; In this case, the new application would not be installed.

14. To assign a category to a software package, you must first:

    A. Define the categories internally in the package.

    B. Define the categories in Software Settings properties.

    C. Create the categories on all client workstations.

    D. Create the categories in the package properties.
    B. Before a package can be assigned to a category, the categories must be created in the Software Settings properties window in the File Extensions tab.

15. Group Policy can be used to deploy software to which of the following clients? (Choose all that apply.)

    A. Windows 95/98

    B. Windows NT 4.0 Workstation

    C. Windows 2000 Professional

    D. Windows 2000 Server
    C, D. Only Windows 2000 supports installation of software through Group Policy.

Chapter 7 Answers

1. Which of the following is one of the two modes in which Terminal Services can be installed on the server?

    A. Remote control

    B. Remote access

    C. Remote administration

    D. Remote logon
    C. Terminal Server can be installed in either remote administration mode, in which administrators can connect to the server to control and administer it from anywhere on the network, or in application server mode, in which users connect to the Terminal server to run applications.

2. What tool is used to remotely control a user's terminal session?

    A. Terminal Services Client Connection Manager on the client machine

    B. Terminal Services Manager on the server machine

    C. Terminal Services Configuration tool on the server machine

    D. Terminal Services Remote Manager on the client machine
    B. The Connection Manager on the client machine is used to create a new connection to a Terminal server on the network. The Terminal Services Configuration tool on the server is

used to disable or enable a connection, and to configure server settings. There is no such tool as Terminal Services Remote Manager.

3. If your attempt to remotely control a user session fails, which of the following would be a likely explanation for the failure? (Choose all that apply.)

   A. The video card on the client machine does not support the resolution used at the session you are trying to remotely control.

   B. Your processor is incompatible with the processor in the machine on which the session is running that you are trying to remotely control.

   C. You do not have Full Control permissions required to remotely control the session.

   D. You do not have the "remotely control terminal sessions" user right.
   A, C. If your video card does not support the resolution used at the session you are trying to remotely control, or if you do not have Full Control permissions, the remote control attempt will fail. Processor compatibility is not an issue, and there is no such thing as the "remotely control terminal sessions" user right.

4. Which of the following is the minimum recommended hardware configuration for acceptable performance from a Terminal server?

   A. 64MB of RAM, and an additional 4 to 8MB RAM for each user, and a Pentium processor

   B. 32MB of RAM, and an additional 1 to 2MB RAM for each user, and an X486 processor

   C. 128MB of RAM, and an additional 4MB RAM for each user, and a Pentium II or higher processor

   D. 256MB of RAM, and an additional 2 to 4MB RAM for each user, and a Pentium processor
   A. 64MB of RAM, and an additional 4 to 8MB RAM for each user and a Pentium processor is recommended for an acceptable level of performance from a Terminal server. However, depending on the number of users running sessions simultaneously and the applications they are using, your particular installation may require more memory and a higher-speed processor than the minimum.

5. Which of the following is recommended for increased performance if you have several application programs that use a great deal of resources? (Choose all that apply.)

   A. Install them all on the same Terminal server.

   B. Disable unnecessary features.

   C. Install them on separate Terminal servers.

   D. Restrict access to only certain users and groups.

B, C, and D. Disabling unnecessary features will cause the programs to use fewer system resources, and installing them on separate Terminal servers will spread the load over all the systems. Restricting access to only those users and groups who really need to use the program will ensure that the resource-intensive programs are not being run unnecessarily, thus putting a heavier load on the system.

6. Which type of user places the lightest load on the server's resources?

   A. Typical users

   B. Task-based users

   C. Advanced users

   D. Power users

   B. Task-based users place the lightest load on the Terminal server's resources, because they generally open only one program at a time, and the programs they use are often less resource intensive (such as word processing applications). Advanced users (also sometimes called "power users") place the heaviest load on system resources, because they usually open multiple programs and perform resource-intensive activities (such as complex database queries).

7. Which of the following is considered a best practice when deploying Terminal Services as an application server in the typical network environment?

   A. Install the applications you want to use with Terminal Services first, before you enable the Terminal Services on the server.

   B. Put the Terminal Services applications on a FAT16 partition, not on a partition formatted with NTFS.

   C. Install the Terminal Services on a domain controller, not on a member or stand-alone server.

   D. None of the above.

   D. None of the choices is correct. It is considered best practice to install Terminal Services before installing the applications, as they will generally not work correctly in a multisession environment otherwise. You should install the Terminal Services applications on an NTFS partition, for heightened security. Terminal Services should be installed on a stand-alone server rather than a domain controller, due to the heavy load on system resources that the in controller's duties require.

8. The Terminal Services Licensing is a required component that licenses clients on a Terminal server if you are running in which mode?

   A. Licensed mode

   B. Remote administration mode

   C. Application server mode

   D. Terminal user mode

   C. The two modes in which Terminal Services can be run on the server are remote administration mode and application server mode. The licensing component is required only when running in application server mode.

9. Which of the following is NOT one of the choices you are given in the Network Client Administrator dialog box?

A. Make installation disk set.

B. Make emergency repair disk.

C. Copy client-based network administration tools.

D. View remoteboot client information.
B. The four choices given are 1) Make network installation startup disk, 2) Make installation disk set, 3) Copy client-based network administration tools, and 4) View remoteboot client information. There is no option to create an emergency repair disk in the Network Client Administrator dialog box.

10. Which of the following can be done from the Terminal Services Configuration MMC? (Choose all that apply.)

A. You can choose whether to delete temporary folders on exit.

B. You can enable or disable Active Desktop.

C. You can send a message to Terminal Services users.

D. You can change Terminal server mode from remote administration to application server.

A, B, and D. In addition to choosing whether to delete temporary folders on exit, enabling or disabling Active Desktop, and changing the Terminal server mode, you can use the Terminal Services Configuration tool to specify whether to use temporary folders per session, and enable or disable Internet Connector licensing. To send messages to Terminal Services users, you use the Terminal Services Manager tool.

11. Which of the following pieces of information do you need to have at hand when you create a new connection in Terminal Services Client Connection Manager? (Choose all that apply.)

A. The name or IP address of the Terminal server.

B. The username and password with which you will log on.

C. The IP address of the client machine.

D. The screen resolution at which you wish to run the terminal screen.
A, B, D. When you create the connection, you will be asked to supply the name or IP address of the Terminal server to which you wish to connect, a username and password with which you will log on, and the screen resolution at which you wish to run the terminal screen. It is not necessary to know the IP address of the client machine to make the connection.

12. When an administrator resets a client's session, what happens?

   A. The session continues as before, and the client is unaware that the session was reset.

   B. The session is disconnected, but can be reactivated by the user.

   C. The session is not disconnected, but a message is sent to the user notifying him that the session was reset, and all unsaved data at the time of the reset is lost.

   D. The session is closed and can no longer be activated by the user.
   D. When the connection to the server is broken for any reason, the administrator can either place the user's session into the disconnected state (in which case, it will be activated when the connection is reestablished) or reset the session. If the session is reset, it is closed and can no longer be activated by the user.

13. Which of the following are ways to install an application on the Terminal server so as to run in the multisession environment? (Choose all that apply.)

   A. Use the Install Programs tab on the Terminal Services Manager properties sheet.

   B. Use the Add/Remove Programs applet in Control Panel.

   C. Use the Change User command at the command line.

   D. Use the Multi-session Applications button on the toolbar of the Terminal Services Configuration tool.

   B, C. Programs can be added through the Add/Remove Programs applet, or the administrator can use the Change User command at a command prompt. Keep in mind that some programs installed using the Change User command won't work at first because of the locked-down state of the system. Some 16-bit programs must be able to write to the directory where the program .ini file is stored. Some 32-bit programs create registry entries that are needed for proper operation.

14. What is the command-line command that an administrator can use to shut down the computer remotely?

   A. shutdown

   B. srvshtdn

   C. tsshutdn

   D. termserv powerdwn
   C. An administrator can use the tsshutdn command at the command line to shut down the Terminal server remotely. To reboot, the /reboot switch can be added, and the /powerdown switch can be used to power off the server if the computer supports software control of AC power.

15. Which of the following is true regarding connecting an OS/2 client to the Microsoft Terminal Server?

   A. It is impossible to use OS/2 clients with Terminal Server.

   B. Terminal Server supports OS/2 clients with no necessity for third-party software or special configuration.

C. OS/2 clients can connect to Terminal Server by installing the OS/2 Client services software included on the Windows 2000 CD.

D. OS/2 clients can connect to Terminal Server by using Citrix Metaframe software with Microsoft Terminal Server.
D. Citrix Metaframe allows you to use non-Windows client operating systems such as OS/2, UNIX, and Macintosh with the Windows 2000 Terminal Server. There is no OS/2 client services software on the Windows 2000 CD, and Terminal Server does not support OS/2 clients without the third-party add-on.

Chapter 8 Answers

1. Manual assignment of IP addressing information has which disadvantages?

   A. Increased probability of human error when entering the numerical information.

   B. Automatic assignment of IP addresses to properly configured clients.

   C. Reduction in paperwork required by the network administrator.

   D. Allows central administration of IP address assignments.
   A. Increased probability of human error when entering the numerical information. All the other answers represent advantage of using DHCP to assign IP addressing information.

2. New features available in the Windows 2000 DHCP server include: (Choose all that apply.)

   A. Enhanced DHCP logging capabilities and improved checks to prevent loss of logging information in the event of a potential "disk full" condition.

   B. The ability to create Multicast Scopes to allocate multicast addresses to servers and applications that require these.

   C. Detection of unauthorized or "rogue" DHCP servers on the network, and the ability to shut down DHCP servers automatically on these rogue DHCP servers.

   D. The ability to back up the DHCP server database information.
   A, B, and C. These all are new features in the Windows 2000 implementation of the DHCP server. The ability to back up the DHCP server database was available with previous versions of the Microsoft DHCP server.

3. The default lease period for IP addressing information from the Windows 2000 DHCP is:

   A. 4 days

   B. 6 days

   C. 8 days

   D. 16 days
   C. The default lease period for the Windows 2000 DHCP server is 8 days. You can change this to any value

you like in the DHCP management MMC console. Shorter lease periods should be used for networks that are short of IP addresses, or that have many clients that join and leave the network on a frequent basis (such as laptop users).

4. What are the four components in the dialog between a DHCP client and server during the process of IP address assignment?

   A. DISCOVER, OFFER, REQUEST, ACKNOWLEDGEMENT

   B. REQUEST, DISCOVER, OFFER, ACKNOWLEDGEMENT

   C. OFFER, REQUEST, ACKNOWLEDGEMENT, RELEASE

   D. RELEASE, RENEW, ABANDON, DISCOVER

   A. DISCOVER, OFFER, REQUEST, ACKNOWLEDGEMENT. All the other answers are incorrect. The DHCP client on initialization broadcasts the DHCPDISCOVER message to the local segment. The DHCPOFFER message is returned by all DHCP servers that receive the DISCOVER message. The DHCP client issues the DHCPREQUEST message to the DHCP server, requesting that it keep the lease offered to it. The DHCPACKNOWLEGEMENT is sent back to the DHCP client acknowledging its request and also to return DHCP Options.

5. Several of your users report to you that they intermittently receive error messages on their screens indicating that a duplicate address has been detected on the network. You network contains primary Windows 2000 and Windows NT computers, along with three UNIX servers. What is the most likely cause of the problem?

   A. The users are in error and there is no problem.

   B. The UNIX servers are using static IP addresses, and their IP addresses have not been excluded from the Scope.

   C. Duplicate IP addresses on the network are common with DHCP.

   D. The Windows 2000 TCP/IP stack has an *autoresolve* mechanism that can allow for duplicate IP addresses on the network, and therefore there will be no problems in this situation

   B. The UNIX servers are using static IP addresses and their IP addresses have not been excluded from the Scope. If there are any computers on the subnet that have static IP addresses, you will need to exclude them from the Scope of IP addresses handed out by the DHCP server. If you fail to exclude them, the DHCP server will hand these out to DHCP clients. Duplicate IP addresses on the network will cause the second computer to receive the IP address to fail during initialization of its TCP/IP stack. Generally, you are able to avoid duplicate IP addresses on the network by using DHCP. There is no

autoresolve mechanism in
Windows 2000.

6. What are the major groupings of DHCP
Options?

A. Server Options

B. Scope Options

C. Client Options

D. Class Options
A, B, C, and D. Server Options,
Scope Options, Client Options, and
Class Options. Server Options apply
to all Scopes on a particular DHCP
server. Scope Options apply only to a
particular Scope. Client Options are
applied only to a defined reserved
client. Class Options are applied to all
computers that identify themselves to
the DHCP server as members of a
particular class. Scope Options
override Server Options, and Client
Options override Scope Options.
Class Options are always applied if a
computer is identified as a member of
a particular class.

7. After installing a Windows 2000 DHCP
server, you find that you get numerous
error messages from the service control
manager informing you that the DHCP
service has been shut down. What can you
do that might correct this situation?

A. Increase the number of Scopes on the
DHCP server

B. Remove duplicate Scope Options if
they appear in different Scope on the
same DHCP server

C. Authorize the DHCP server in the
Active Directory

D. Reinstall Windows 2000
C. Authorize the DHCP server in the
Active Directory. Windows 2000
DHCP servers are able to participate
in rogue server detection. If a
Windows 2000 DHCP server is
detected on the network, it will be
checked against a list of Authorized
DHCP servers in the Active
Directory. If the machine's IP address
is not in the Authorized list, its
DHCP services will be shut down.
The other answers are bogus and
obviously incorrect.

8. You have mostly Windows NT 4.0
Workstations on your network. How can
you have these machines' dynamically
update their Address (A) records and
Pointer (PTR) records in a Dynamic DNS
(DDNS) Server?

A. Install the Windows 2000 DNS
redirector on all the Window NT
machines.

B. Make the Windows NT computers
clients of a Windows 2000 DHCP
server.

C. This cannot be done.

D. Configure the Windows 2000 DDNS
server for Windows NT compatibility.
B. Make the Windows NT computers
clients of a Windows 2000 DHCP
server. If you do this, the DHCP
server will register and tell the DNS
server to create Address (A) records

and Pointer (PTR) records for the NT clients. There is no DNS redirector, and there is no "compatibility mode."

9. User Classes included with Windows 2000 DHCP servers include:

    A. Default User Class

    B. Microsoft Dynamic BOOTP Class

    C. Microsoft RRAS Class

    D. Microsoft Linux Class
       A, B, and C. Default User Class, Microsoft Dynamic BOOTP Class, and Microsoft RRAS Class. Microsoft does not include a Linux User Class.

10. Vendor Classes included with Windows 2000 DHCP servers include:

    A. DHCP Standard Options

    B. Microsoft Options

    C. Microsoft Windows 2000 Options

    D. Microsoft Windows 98 Options
       A, B, C, and D. DHCP Standard Options, Microsoft Options, Microsoft Windows 2000 Options, and Microsoft Windows 98 Options are all included "out of the box."

11. Microsoft Vendor-Specific Options include:

    A. Disable BOOTP dynamic assignment

    B. Disable NetBIOS over TCP/IP (NetBT)

    C. Release DHCP lease on shutdown

    D. Default router metric base
       B, C, and D. Disable NetBIOS over TCP/IP (NetBT), Release DHCP

lease on shutdown, and Default router metric base are all Microsoft Vendor-Specific Options. Microsoft has not yet defined a Disable BOOTP Dynamic Assignment Option.

12. You have moved your Windows 2000 Professional computer that is configured as a DHCP client to another subnet. The computer has been turned off for three months. There is no DHCP server on the new subnet. When the computer tries to communicate with other computers on the new subnet, you find that it is unable to establish a session. What is the most likely cause of the problem?

    A. The other computers are down-level machines, and therefore cannot connect to Windows 2000 computers.

    B. The Windows 2000 computer cannot communicate with its domain controller, and therefore will not initialize its networking protocols.

    C. The Windows 2000 Professional computer has autoconfigured its IP address with a network ID different from the network ID that it is now located on.

    D. The Windows 2000 computer requires a DHCP server on its segment in order to start its networking protocols.
       C. The Windows Professional computer has autoconfigured its IP address with a network ID different than the network ID that it is now located on. Since all local computers

will appear as if they are on remote networks, IP will attempt to forward packets to a default gateway. Down-level machines have no difficulty establishing sessions with Windows 2000 computers. Windows 2000 computers do not require communication with domain controllers prior to initializing networking protocols. A DHCP server is not required by Windows 2000 machines to start their network stack.

13. What are some of the advantages of WINS servers maintaining persistent connections?

   A. Replication partners are able to immediate perform push updates.

   B. Fewer processor cycles are committed to establishing and tearing down sessions.

   C. Re-replication of deleted objects is eliminated.

   D. Tombstoned objects reactivate spontaneously.
   A, B. Replication partners are able to immediately perform push updates, and fewer processor cycles are committed to establishing and tearing down connections. Preventing re-replication of deleted objects is the function of tombstoning. Tombstoned objects do not reactivate spontaneously.

14. How many secondary WINS servers can you configure for a Windows 2000 WINS client?

   A. 1

   B. 4

   C. 12

   D. 256
   C. 12.

15. What is the difference between WINS and DNS?

   A. A WINS server maps IP addresses to NetBIOS names, and a DNS server maps host names to IP addresses.

   B. WINS servers can dynamically update their databases, and Windows 2000 DNS servers have static databases.

   C. WINS has been eliminated in Windows 2000.

   D. DNS maintains a list of NetBIOS names, and WINS confirms host MAC addresses.
   A. A WINS server maps IP addresses to NetBIOS names, and a DNS server maps host names to IP addresses. Windows 2000 DDNS server are able to dynamically update their address records.

Chapter 9 Answers

1. Which of the following is NOT a new feature of disk management with Windows 2000?

   A. Dynamic Volumes

   B. Disk Administration Utility

   C. Less Downtime

D. Remote Disk Management
B. Disk Administration Utility.
Windows NT 4.0 had a Disk
Administrator. There is a new Disk
Manager utility that is different from
the Disk Administrator' however,
administration in itself existed, so it is
not a new feature of Windows 2000.

2. Which of the following file system types
are supported with Windows 2000?
(Choose all that apply.)

A. FAT

B. NTFS

C. HPFS

D. FAT32
A, B, D. FAT, FAT32, and NTFS are
all supported with Windows 2000.
HPFS, which is not widely used
anymore, is not supported. This file
system type was supported with
Windows NT 3.51, but not with
Windows NT 4.0 and Windows
2000.

3. Which of the following is a new benefit of
NTFS 5?

A. Per-disk, per-user disk quota

B. Permissions assignments on folders

C. Unreadable by a FAT boot disk

D. Transactional tracking
A. Per-disk, per-user disk quota. In
previous versions of Windows NT,
there was no support to limit the
amount of space a user had available.
This created problems for

administrators. Now administrators
have control over how much space
their users consume on their volumes.

4. In order to configure automated
defragmentation with Windows 2000,
what do you have to do?

A. Use the Computer Management
Utility.

B. It is not possible at all, even with a
third-party utility.

C. A third-party utility must be acquired.

D. None of the above.
C. A third-party utility must be
acquired. The technology of
Diskeeper is included with Windows
2000, but it is a manual utility. To
automate the process, you must
purchase the full retail version.

5. What service, introduced with Windows
NT 4.0, allows an administrator to take
shares from diverse locations and
incorporate them into one directory?

A. UDF

B. DFS

C. MSCS

D. EFS
B. DFS. Distributed File Services. To
help centralize data for users so they
will no longer have to connect to
multiple servers, Windows 2000 uses
DFS, or Distributed File Services.

6. Which RAID level has a parity block for
fault tolerance and requires at least three
drives to function?

A. RAID 0

B. RAID 1

C. RAID 2

D. RAID 5

D. RAID 5. RAID 5 is Drive Striping with Parity. There must be at least three drives, and the data is striped across them along with a parity block that is based on the data on the other drives.

7. What two ways can you open the Computer Management utility? (Choose two.)

A. Through Control Panel

B. It starts automatically

C. Shortcut on desktop

D. Shortcut under Administrative Tools

A, D. The Computer Management utility can be accessed from the Control Panel or from the Administrative Tools shortcut under the Start menu.

8. What is the new type of disk in Windows 2000 that is not backward compatible?

A. Basic Disk

B. RAID Configuration

C. Dynamic Disk

D. All formats are backward compatible.

C. Dynamic Disk. Dynamic Disks are not backward compatible, nor are they accessible by other operating systems such as Windows 9x. Being able to dynamically change the size, span, stripe, or mirror on the fly without

creating server downtime adds benefits for network administrators.

9. What steps need to be taken to upgrade a Basic Disk to a Dynamic Disk?

A. Right-click on any volume on the disk and choose Upgrade to Dynamic.

B. Right-click on the disk and choose Upgrade to Dynamic Disk.

C. Right click on the Storage folder and choose Dynamic Upgrade from the Tools pull-down menu.

D. This is not possible. Dynamic Disks must be made dynamic at installation.

B. Right-click on the disk and choose Upgrade to Dynamic Disk. This is done in the Computer Management utility.

10. You try to upgrade to a Dynamic Disk and receive an error. The drive you are trying to upgrade is a 4.3GB hard disk and has a 4.3GB partition on it that is almost full. Why can't you upgrade this disk to a Dynamic Disk?

A. 4.3GB drives cannot be upgraded to Dynamic Disks.

B. There needs to be 1MB of unallocated space at the end of the drive.

C. The drive needs to have 1MB available at the beginning of the drive.

D. You cannot upgrade Basic Disks to Dynamic Disks.

B. There needs to be 1MB of unallocated space at the end of the drive. This is for administrative information that the disk management routines use. The logical Disk Manager stores information here about the drive.

11. You are trying to upgrade a Basic Disk to a Dynamic Disk and have the following information on the disk: 9.1GB, 16MB unallocated at end of drive, sector size is 1024KB. Why can't you upgrade this disk?

    A. 9.1GB drives cannot be dynamic.

    B. There is not enough space at the end of the drive.

    C. The sector size is wrong.

    D. You should be able to upgrade this drive.
    C. The sector size is wrong. One stipulation of Dynamic Disks is that they must have sectors no larger than 512 bytes. Sector sizes on IDE drives are preset at the factory. You can change this value on SCSI drives. The cluster size is not to be confused with the sector size. Cluster size is determined on format.

12. How do you access the Quota configuration for a drive?

    A. Use the Control Panel.

    B. Right-click on the drive and choose Properties, and then the Quota tab.

    C. Right-click on a drive and choose Quota.

    D. Through the Disk Administrator utility.
    B. Right-click on the drive and choose Properties, and then the Quota tab. This is where the quota information is configured.

13. Which RAID level has two drives that are identical copies of each other?

    A. RAID 0

    B. RAID 1

    C. RAID 2

    D. RAID 5
    B. RAID 1. RAID 1 is drive mirroring, and each drive is an exact mirror of the other, giving us fault tolerance. If one drive fails, the other drive can be used to keep the system running.

14. What services allow for fault tolerance by having two servers share the same storage, so if one fails, the other can pick up and keep the network running?

    A. MCS

    B. MSCS

    C. EFS

    D. NTFS
    B. MSCS. Microsoft Cluster Services allow multiple servers to share the same storage, while one is a standby in the event the other fails.

15. What type of disk has partitions and not volumes, is not resizable without server reboot, and does not allow configuration of mirrors or stripe sets without server reboot?

    A. Dynamic

B. Simple

C. Basic

D. With Windows 2000, all disk types
    are configurable without server reboot.
    C. Basic. Basic Disks are those that
    have partitions and are not
    configurable dynamically like
    Dynamic Disks.

Chapter 10 Answers

1. Which of the following is a form of disk
    fault tolerance supported by Windows
    2000 Server? (Choose all that apply.)

    A. RAID Level 0

    B. RAID Level 1

    C. RAID Level 4

    D. RAID Level 5
        B, D. RAID Level 0, disk striping
        with no parity, is supported by
        Windows 2000 Server, but is not fault
        tolerant, so A is incorrect. RAID Level
        4, disk striping with large blocks, is a
        fault-tolerance method but is not
        supported by Windows 2000 Server,
        so C is incorrect. Only RAID Level 1,
        disk mirroring/duplexing, and RAID
        Level 5, disk striping with parity, are
        fault-tolerance methods supported by
        Windows 2000 Server.

2. Which of the following is true of disk fault
    tolerance in Windows 2000?

    A. Fault-tolerant volumes can be created
        in both Windows 2000 Professional
        and Windows 2000 Server.

    B. Fault-tolerant drives can only be
        created on dynamic disks.

    C. Implementing disk fault tolerance
        removes the need to do regular
        backups.

    D. Fault-tolerant volumes are created
        using the Device Manager component
        of the Computer Management
        Console.
        B. Fault-tolerant volumes can only be
        created in Windows 2000 on dynamic
        disks. Fault-tolerant volumes cannot
        be created in Windows 2000
        Professional, only in Server, so A is
        incorrect. Fault tolerance does not
        take the place of regular backups, so C
        is incorrect. Fault-tolerant volumes are
        created in the Disk Management
        component of the Computer
        Management Console, not the Device
        Manager, so D is incorrect.

3. What is the minimum and maximum
    number of disks used in a stripe set with
    parity?

    A. Minimum of 1, maximum of 3

    B. Minimum of 2, maximum of 10

    C. Minimum of 3, maximum of 32

    D. Minimum of 4, no limit on maximum
        C. A minimum of 3 disks is required
        as the data spans at least 2 disks, and
        parity information is written on the
        third. The maximum number of disks
        supported by a Windows 2000 stripe
        set is 32. It would be impossible to
        create a redundant set with only 1
        disk, so A is incorrect. Two is the

minimum number of disks required for a stripe set without parity, so B is incorrect. You do not have to have 4 disks to create a stripe set with parity, so D is incorrect also.

4. Which of the following files will need to be edited to point to the second disk in a mirror set if the first disk fails and the operating system files are stored on the mirrored partition?

A. ARC.dll

B. config.sys

C. w2000os.com

D. boot.ini
D. config.sys is used with MS-DOS to initialize the operating system, so B is incorrect. ARC.dll and w2000os.com do not exist, so A and C are incorrect. boot.ini is the file used by Ntldr in Windows 2000 to locate the Winnt root directory and must be edited if the location of the directory changes.

5. Which of the following is the Windows 2000 fault-tolerance driver?

A. ftdisk.sys

B. ftolerant.dll

C. ftdriver.com

D. ntdetect.com
A. ftolerant.dll and ftdriver.com do not exist, so B and C are incorrect. ntdetect.com is used in the loading of the operating system to detect the hardware configuration, so D is

incorrect. ftdisk.sys is the name of the Windows 2000 fault-tolerance driver.

6. Which of the following advanced startup options is available only in Windows 2000 Server?

A. VGA Mode

B. Safe Mode with Networking

C. Debugging Mode

D. Safe Mode with Command Prompt
C. VGA Mode and Safe Mode (along with its Networking and Command Prompt variations) are available in both Windows 2000 Professional and Windows 2000 Server, so A, B, and D are incorrect. Debugging Mode and Directory Services Restore Mode are available only in Windows 2000 Server.

7. In which of the following cases might the Last Known Good configuration allow you to load an operating system that has been rendered unbootable?

A. You have changed the refresh rate in your display adapter settings to an unsupported rate.

B. You have installed a new device driver that is incompatible or corrupt and have not been able to log on since the installation.

C. You have accidentally deleted the winnt system root directory.

D. You have changed the location of the operating system files to a different partition.

B. The Last Known Good configuration is a copy of the configuration with which a user last logged on successfully, and will not contain the reference to the new device driver installed during the last session. The VGA Mode would be used to boot into the operating system if your display settings are incorrect, so A is incorrect. Last Known Good cannot restore a deleted system directory; the ASR would be used in this case, so C is incorrect. Changing the location of the operating system files will require you to edit boot.ini, so D is incorrect.

8. Which of the following statements is true of the Windows 2000 Recovery Console? (Choose all that apply.)

   A. The Recovery Console can only be run by administrators.

   B. The Recovery Console is run by selecting Administrative Tools from the Start menu.

   C. The Recovery Console can be installed on your computer and will thereafter show up as a choice in the boot menu.

   D. The Recovery console can be used to repair a faulty master boot record.
   A, C, and D. Only those who are logged on with administrative privileges can run the Recovery Console. The Recovery Console can either be run from the Windows 2000 setup disks or CD, or it can be installed on your computer and will then show up as a boot menu option.

The Recovery Console can be used for many administrative tasks, including repair of a faulty master boot record. The Recovery Console does not show up under Administrative Tools in the Start menu, however, so B is incorrect.

9. Which of the following commands can be used to open the Backup and Restore Wizard?

   A. runbackup.exe

   B. backup.exe

   C. ntbackup.exe

   D. w2000backup.exe
   C. Although we are running the backup utility in Windows 2000, the name of the executable program is still the same as in Windows NT: ntbackup.exe. You can start the Backup and Restore Wizard by running it at the command line, or by clicking Start | Programs | Accessories | Backup. All the other choices are incorrect.

10. In which of the following backup methods are all marked files backed up, but the markers not cleared?

    A. Incremental

    B. Differential

    C. Daily

    D. Copy
    B. In an incremental backup, the marked files are backed up and the markers are cleared. In a daily backup, only the files that have been changed that day are backed up. In a copy

backup, all selected files and folders are backed up and markers are not used to determine which files to back up. Thus A, C, and D are incorrect.

11. Which of the following options is/are available in the Backup Wizard when asked to specify what to back up? (Choose all that apply.)

    A. Back up everything on the computer

    B. Only back up System State data

    C. Back up device driver files only

    D. Back up selected files, drives, or network data

    A, B, and D. You may elect to back up everything, back up selected files, drives, or network data, or back up only the System State data (which includes the Active Directory on domain controllers). There is no option to back up device driver files only, so C is incorrect.

12. What happens next when you choose Later on the "when to back up" page of Backup Wizard?

    A. The Wizard closes, and you can reopen it later and start where you left off.

    B. The Task Scheduler starts, and you are asked for a user name and password.

    C. The Wizard pops up a dialog box asking you for a time and date to do the backup.

    D. The Backup automatically starts one hour later.

    B. Choosing Later automatically invokes the Task Scheduler, and a user name and password are required with

permissions to perform the backup. The other answers are incorrect.

13. How do you restore data from backup tapes or files?

    A. Run the Recovery Console and choose Restore.

    B. Open the Disk Management tool and choose Regenerate Data.

    C. Select the files to be restored in Windows Explorer, right-click on them, and select Restore to Original Location.

    D. Select the data to be restored and open the Restore Wizard.

    D. The Recovery Console is used when you are unable to boot into the computer, to perform administrative tasks. The Disk Management tool is used to regenerate data when a hard disk fails. There is no Restore to Original Location option when you right-click on a file in Explorer. Thus, answers A, B, and C are incorrect.

14. Which of the advanced startup options attempts to load Windows 2000 Professional or Server with only basic drivers?

    A. VGA Mode

    B. Debugging Mode

    C. Safe Mode

    D. Basic Driver Mode

    C. VGA Mode uses a generic video driver but loads all other drivers. Debugging Mode is used for debugging and is only available in Windows 2000 Server. There is no such thing as Basic

Driver Mode. Thus, answers A, B, and D are incorrect.

15. Which of the following is true of an ARC path in the boot.ini file that begins with SCSI(1)?

A. The winnt directory is located on a drive that uses the first SCSI controller with the SCSI BIOS enabled.

B. The winnt directory is located on a drive that uses the first SCSI controller with the SCSI BIOS disabled.

C. The winnt directory is located on a drive that uses the second SCSI controller with the SCSI BIOS enabled.

D. The winnt directory is located on a drive that uses the second SCSI controller with the SCSI BIOS disabled.

D. "SCSI" is used only to refer to a SCSI controller with the BIOS disabled. A SCSI controller with the BIOS enabled will have an ARC path that begins with "Multi." Numbering of all parameters except Partition begins with 0, thus the number (1) indicates the second controller.

Chapter 11 Answers

1. Which of the following is the most important piece to ensuring a successful upgrade?

A. Network infrastructure

B. Planning

C. Security

D. Installation

B. Planning. Planning a network upgrade is the most important piece to ensuring a successful upgrade.

2. What is one component when planning an upgrade that could be documented and would include hubs, routers, switches, and multiple locations?

A. Network infrastructure

B. Protocol plan

C. Device database

D. None of the above

A. Network infrastructure. Network infrastructure is the details of your network from hubs, switches, etc. Also included in this are certain components that are more software related, such as DNS or other name resolution methods.

3. If you want to make sure you can build the network from the ground up, what should you have in place?

A. Active Directory Services

B. Floppy backup of network

C. Disaster Recovery Plan

D. Workstations and Servers

C. Disaster Recovery Plan. This item, if overlooked, can cause major delays or downtime during an upgrade.

4. What are the three areas that Microsoft breaks its servers into?

A. Enterprise

B. Small Business

C. Divisional

D. Departmental
A, C, and D. Microsoft breaks the server platforms into three distinct areas: Enterprise, Divisional, and Departmental. Each of these is broken down based on size.

5. Which of the three server models is the one the corporate IT people do not administer and take responsibility for?

A. Enterprise

B. Small Business

C. Divisional

D. Departmental
D. Departmental servers are usually not as robust as Divisional or Enterprise servers. Departmental servers are the ones that stand out the most. These are not handled by the Enterprise support team. These types of servers are usually for storage of larger items, such as graphics or special projects.

6. What is one key component to plan for when upgrading that would include the backup software, possibly virus protection, or others.

A. Server Farms

B. Server Domain Controller

C. Server Applications

D. Third-Party Suites.
C. Server Applications. If a server application does not make it in the year 2000, then you have to determine

if the app needs to be upgraded or changed.

7. In order to keep consistency across the network and ensure that corporate needs are met, what should you have documented before upgrading?

A. Hard drive sizes

B. Machine types

C. Network Standards

D. Amount of RAM
C. Network Standards. Some standards are as simple as naming servers in a certain fashion. Others include where applications or data are stored . Other items might have to do with backup rotation and plan, virus protection configuration, or even server location and WAN layout.

8. If your users dial in to your network from home, you should already have this documented. How are they accessing the network, what are they using?

A. DNS

B. Remote Access

C. IP Addressing

D. WINS
B. Remote Access. Some people need to start from a starting diagram. Along with this are the standards of the logical pieces of the network. This will include machine naming, IP addressing, Remote Access, and DNS configuration, among others. If these items are not well documented and the network layout does not hold up to the

standards, productivity will suffer especially, from a support perspective.

9. What is the new service that allows for a large database of network objects, including users, printers, server, etc.? This new service was first available in previous versions.

A. Active Directory

B. Windows Directory Services

C. Windows ZAK

D. NSD
   A. Active Directory. With the other domain models, the process becomes a little different. The reason for this is that a root domain has to be established. Active Directory uses DNS, which uses the hierarchical structure starting from a root. Active Directory is going to be hierarchical, so a root domain has to be established.

10. Which of the following is not one of the five roles a Domain Controller can fill?

A. Domain Naming Master

B. Schema Master

C. PDC Emulator

D. Backup Domain Controller
   D. Backup Domain Controller. The one difference that stands out is that there are five different roles that can be served: Domain Naming Master, Schema Master, Primary Domain Controller emulator, Relative Identifier Master, and Infrastructure Master.

11. How many total Schema Masters can there be in any Active Directory Forest?

A. 1

B. 2

C. 3

D. 10
   A. 1. There can only be one Schema Master in the forest. This is true with other roles also.

12. What Domain Controller role handles changes and configuration of groups and group-to-user relations?

A. Infrastructure Manager

B. Primary Domain Controller

C. Schema Master

D. Domain Naming Master
   A. Infrastructure Manager. The Infrastructure Manager handles changes and configuration of groups and group-to-user relations. There must be one of these in your domain.

13. In order to have redundancy in the network, what does Windows 2000 use for a replacement to the Backup Domain Controller?

A. Multimaster replication

B. Multidomain replication

C. Multidomain Controller replication

D. Multisite replication
   A. Multimaster replication. This is the replacement for the Backup Domain Controller (BDC) in Windows NT 4.0. Multimaster replication keeps the information synchronized across all Domain Controllers. This ensures that there is fault tolerance in the event of server failure.

14. How will Windows 2000 organize network objects in the forest into a hierarchical structure?

    A. With Organizational Pieces

    B. With Organizational Units (OUs)

    C. With Organizational Groups

    D. With Organizational Roles
    B. With Organizational Units. With Domains, you can have hundreds and hundreds of network objects. You can use the Organizational Unit to separate different locations. Some people, depending on the size of the network, will use different domains for different geographic locations.

15. What new utility can administrators use to preconfigure user settings for client workstations?

    A. Setup Configurator

    B. Setup Scripts

    C. Setup Manager

    D. Installation Manager
    C. Setup Manager. One focus of Windows 2000 Professional is ease of installation. Installation scripts are more powerful and make administrators' jobs even easier. The new Setup Manager allows an administrator to configure settings for a user. All the user has to do is log on the first time with Windows 2000, and a customized profile is automatically updated on the workstation.

Chapter 12 Answers

1. The name resolution and location service used by Active Directory is:

    A. WINS

    B. HOSTS file

    C. DNS

    D. HTTP
    C. DNS. WINS is the NetBIOS-name-to-IP-address name resolution service used as the preferred name resolution method in Windows networks prior to Windows 2000. The HOSTS file is a text file that maps host names to IP addresses, but grows unmanageable in large networks. HTTP is hypertext transfer protocol, used by Web browsers.

2. The term that best describes an object into which you can put other objects is:

    A. Hierarchy

    B. Container

    C. Site

    D. Schema
    B. A hierarchy is a tree-like structure in which there is a parent-child relationship between objects at successive levels. A site is one or more IP subnets, typically connected by a fast link. A schema is a set of definitions of objects and their properties.

3. What is the type of namespace in which the name of the child object in the

hierarchy always includes the parent domain's name?

A. Disjointed namespace

B. Distinguished namespace

C. Conventional namespace

D. Contiguous namespace
   D. Contiguous namespace. A disjointed namespace is one in which the names of the parent object and of a child of the same parent are not directly related. A distinguished name is a unique identification, which includes the name of the domain in which the object resides and the hierarchical path to the object. There is no such thing as a conventional namespace in this context.

4. The trust relationship between a parent and child object in a contiguous namespace is:

A. One-way: parent domain trusts child domain.

B. One-way: child domain trusts parent domain.

C. Two-way: parent and child domains trust each other.

D. By default, there is no trust relationship between the parent and child domains.
   C. In Windows 2000 Active Directory domains, a two-way transitive trust exists between the parent and child domains. In Windows NT networks, all trust relationships between domains were one-way and had to be established

explicitly by the administrator, as none existed by default.

5. The .com, .net, and .org domains commonly seen on the Internet are known as:

A. Domain extensions

B. Top-level domains

C. Root domains

D. Second-level domains
   B. Top-level domains. Although the dot followed by three letters looks similar to the file extension used in the DOS file naming convention, this has nothing to do with the domain hierarchy. The root domain on the Internet is the unnamed domain above the top-level domains, represented by a dot. Second-level domains are those organization names that are registered by companies and individuals with a domain registration authority and reside within the top-level domains.

6. A group of objects in the Active Directory with the same types of attributes or characteristics is called a:

A. Class

B. Container

C. Distribution group

D. Global catalog
   A. Class. A container is an object into which other objects can be placed. A distribution group is a nonsecurity group, used to send e-mail or messages

to more than one user at a time. The global catalog is the compilation of information about all the objects in a tree or forest.

7. A "friendly" name for a user account that consists of a shortened version of the user name and the domain tree where that account resides is called the:

A. Globally Unique Identifier (GUID)

B. Relative Distinguished Name (RDN)

C. Distinguished Name (DN)

D. User Principal Name (UPN)
D. User Principal Name (UPN). The GUID is a number assigned to the object at the time of its creation. The RDN represents a part of the DN that is an attribute of an object. The DN is the LDAP unique identifier that contains the name of the domain in which the object resides and the complete path to the object.

8. Which of the following is a DNS naming convention (all that apply)?

A. Characters A–Z and a–z are allowed.

B. Numerical characters 0–9 are allowed.

C. Names should be long and complex to ensure their uniqueness.

D. Underscores should be used to connect words.
A, B. Characters A–Z and a–z, along with numerical characters 0–9, are allowed under DNS naming standards. However, names should be simple and precise, so they will be easier to remember. Hyphens, not underscores, should be used to connect words.

9. Which of the following is *not* a good reason to create multiple domains?

A. The organization spans international borders, and the office in each country wishes to conduct administrative tasks in its native language.

B. You wish administration to be centralized.

C. You want to reduce the amount of replication traffic.

D. Managers wish to separate resources due to internal political considerations.
B. Centralized administration would be a good reason to create only a single domain, not multiple domains. However, the need for administration in different languages, reduction of replication traffic, and a wish to separate and distinguish between resources are all acceptable reasons for creating multiple domains.

10. Which of the following is true of the practice of using the same namespace for external (Internet) resources and the internal network (all that apply)?

A. You will only have to register one domain name.

B. There will be no need for separate DNS zones to resolve internal and external names.

C. You will have to address security issues to keep external users from accessing the internal network.

D. It often proves to be more complicated to administer than establishing separate and distinct namespaces for internal and external resources.

A, C, and D. It is true that you will only have to register one domain name, which represents a small initial cost savings. It is also true that security will be more of an issue, and a firewall may be necessary to keep external users out of the internal resources. For those reasons, it is indeed often more complicated to administer a network that combines the internal and external resources in one namespace. In fact, you will need to set up separate DNS zones for resolution of internal and external names to prevent confusion.

11. The purpose of DNS is to:

A. Resolve NetBIOS names to IP addresses

B. Resolve Fully Qualified Domain Names (FDQNs) to IP addresses

C. Resolve computer hardware addresses to IP addresses

D. Automatically assign names to newly created objects

B. Resolution of Fully Qualified Domain Names (FDQNs) to IP addresses. DNS has long served this role on the Internet and in UNIX-based networks. Resolution of NetBIOS names to IP addresses is done by WINS, which was the

preferred name resolution method in Windows NT networks. Resolution of hardware addresses to IP addresses is a function of ARP in a TCP/IP network. There is no service that automatically assigns names to newly created objects.

12. Which of the following is used by Active Directory to publish the addresses of servers?

A. RFCs

B. Zone transfers

C. SRV RRs

D. NetBIOS names

C. The Active Directory uses SRV RRs, or Service Resource Records, to publish the names of servers so that they can be located even if all you know is the domain name. RFCs are Requests for Comments, which are published standards available on the Internet. Zone transfers are a way of replicating information between DNS servers. NetBIOS names are used by down-level clients to identify computers on the network.

13. Which of the following is true of DNS when used with Active Directory (all that apply)?

A. Microsoft's DNS server is the only one that works with Active Directory.

B. Dynamic DNS is required if you wish to use Active Directory.

C. If a static DNS server is used, records must be entered manually.

D. There are no advantages to using Microsoft's DNS server.

C. A static DNS server can be used with Active Directory, but records will have to be entered manually, which is time-consuming and prone to errors. It is not true that Microsoft's DNS server is the only one that will work with Active Directory. Any RFC-compliant DNS server will work. However, it is not true that there are no advantages to using Microsoft's DNS server. Microsoft DNS servers will replicate DNS information to other Microsoft DNS servers as part of the Active Directory replication process instead of using zone transfer, which is more efficient. Finally, Dynamic DNS is not required, but is recommended, so that records will be automatically entered in the DNS database.

14. One or more IP subnets, connected by fast links, make up a:

   A. Site

   B. Directory

   C. Domain

   D. Forest

   A. Sites define the physical structure of the network. A directory is a collection of objects within the directory service. A domain is a container object that forms an administrative unit. A forest is a group of two or more domain trees within a network.

15. Which of the following is true of sites (all that apply)?

   A. Sites can be used to control user logon location.

   B. Each site requires a Primary Domain Controller.

   C. Sites are the smallest unit of administrative authority.

   D. Creating sites can help reduce replication traffic.

   A, D. You can separate logons in one physical area from those in another by creating separate sites; Active Directory will be searched for a domain controller that is local to that site. Creating sites can also help reduce replication traffic, as replication between sites is compressed and can be scheduled to occur at a time when there is less network traffic. Sites are not the smallest unit of administrative authority, and each site does not require a PDC; the Windows 2000 Active Directory domain model replicates to all domain controllers as peers. The concept of PDCs and BDCs applies to down-level (Windows NT 3.*x* and 4.0) domain models.

Chapter 13 Answers

1. For a hierarchical structure without multiple domains, what would you use to organize the network?

   A. Organizations

B. Groups

C. Organizational Units (OUs)

D. Units of Organization
    C. Organizational Units. When you
    are planning the domain structure,
    you have to consider if you will have
    multiple domains, or one domain with
    OUs that group similar objects
    together. This is where the hierarchical
    structure comes into play.

2. Which of the following is not a default
   container with Windows 2000?

   A. Built-In

   B. Users

   C. Computers

   D. Accounting
       D. Accounting. There are Users,
       Computers, and Groups containers.
       The Accounting container could exist
       but is has to be created.

3. What is the biggest factor in determining
   your network object layout?

   A. Number of Organizational Units

   B. Overall Size of the Network

   C. Number of Login Scripts

   D. Novell Directory Services
       B. Overall Size of the Network. When
       designing your directory structure, you
       have to take into consideration how
       you want to divide the company
       structure. The size of your organization

can make a difference in how you
want the general layout to be.

4. When you have a NetWare 4.*x* and
   Windows 2000 mixed environment, what
   is the biggest concern?

   A. Size of the network

   B. Different Types of Directory Services

   C. Bindery Emulation

   D. NetWare Client
       B. Different Types of Directory
       Services. In many environments today,
       you will find a mix of NetWare and
       Microsoft networking products. With
       this in mind, you have to consider the
       interaction of the different directory
       services. NetWare and Microsoft have
       similar Directory Service methods, but
       they are vastly different at the core.
       This means you have to decide how
       they will interact with each other, or if
       one will be the primary directory
       controlling the other.

5. Which Control Panel applet allows for
   integration between NetWare and
   Windows 2000?

   A. Gateway Service for NetWare

   B. Gateway Service for Novell

   C. Gateway Service for NDS

   D. Gateway Service for NOS
       A. Gateway Service for NetWare.
       Once the decisions are made, you have
       to decide which tools you will use.

There are different tools available for migrating from NetWare to working together with NetWare. These include services for NetWare to connect to the NetWare directory and use both Windows NT and NetWare servers and networks simultaneously. The migration tools allow for moving from NetWare Directory Services to Microsoft's Directory Services.

6. When there is a large number of objects, what do you want to plan for when designing your network?

   A. Large quantity of users in one container, with a small number of objects in other containers.

   B. Lopsided network layout.

   C. Equal layout of objects throughout the domain.

   D. Duplicate users throughout the network.
   C. Equal layout of objects throughout the domain. A massive number of users can make for a challenging decision when it comes to laying out your network design in terms of directory. You don't want to have a directory that isn't laid out in a fashion of equilibrium. What I mean is, you don't want a lopsided tree. This can make administration harder, but the biggest factor is replication of information. Having a lopsided tree can mean lengthy synchronization time.

7. What can be used as a guideline to assist in layout of the network?

   A. Administrative Model

   B. List of users

   C. Physical Diagram of all objects on the network

   D. Department List
   A. Administrative Model. The administrative model of the company is used as a guideline as of the most common ways that networks are laid out in terms of directory services,. This is very similar in look and feel to the DNS layout we discussed earlier in this chapter.

8. What can you use when planning to help you visual your network layout in hierarchical fashion?

   A. Diagrams showing the layout

   B. Written documents with user information

   C. Printer configuration print-outs

   D. BIOS configuration pages from Workstations
   A. Diagrams showing the layout. Remember, the planning stage is the most critical. When deciding how to lay out your network, you need to document and diagram the object model. The object model is basically a diagram showing the branching out of each organizational unit or domain. This is one of the first things you have to do before you begin to design your network.

9. If you want to have a person at each location help you administer the network, what would you do?

   A. Make that person an administrator on the network.

   B. Make that person an administrator of his or her location container.

   C. Keep that person as a general user and have him or her contact IS for help.

   D. Give that person multiple user accounts for administering the network, and one for each location.

   B. Make that person an administrator of his or her location container. Another factor that can make a difference in the layout of your network is whether you will have container administrators. In other words, you can have someone administer a certain portion of the network directory tree, and this can help decide how to organize the objects in your network. This may be based again on location, job function, or other certain terms. Remember, the goal is always to make administration easier and less time consuming.

10. Select the design goals discussed in this chapter. (Choose all that apply.)

    A. Single User Sign-On

    B. Changes in the Administrative Model

    C. Centralized Locations

    D. Centralized Adminstration

    A, B, and D. Single User Sign-On, Changes in the Administrative Model, Centralized Administration. *Single User Sign On*: This is important in corporate settings where you have users who may sign on from various locations. All users want to do is sit down at a workstation and sign on. They do not want to worry about where they are on the network. *Centralized Administration*: Effective administration means you do not have to duplicate tasks when maintaining your users. There are going to be some tasks, such as the initial creation of users, that will require repeat steps, but having to add users twice to different locations on the network so they can log on is not effective planning, nor is it centralized in nature for an administrator. *Changes in Administrative Models*: The design and layout of network objects should be able to change in terms of meeting the administrative model. For example, if the company is restructured, your network model can accommodate these changes. Another possibility is if the company merges with another company. Even if the other company is prepared to merge existing networks, having your network ready will make the migration to one network easier.

11. If you are only going to have Windows 2000 domain controllers on your network, what type of network do you have?

    A. Mixed

    B. Native

C. Multi

D. Master
   B. Native. The native domain only has Windows 2000 domain controllers. Once you convert to a native domain, you cannot go back to a mixed environment. This is very important to remember.

12. If you have an environment that will contain both Windows NT 4.0 and Windows 2000 servers as domain controllers, what domain model would you use?

   A. Native

   B. Native Mixed

   C. Mixed

   D. Mixed Native
      C. Mixed. The mixed domain model can contain both Windows NT 4.0 domain controllers and Windows 2000 domain controllers.

13. What is the master database copy of the directory called?

   A. Master Database

   B. Global Catalog

   C. Global Database

   D. Master Catalog
      B. Global Catalog. The master database is known as the Global Catalog (GC). The other domain controllers receive a replicated copy of the database.

14. If you have a mixed environment domain model, what role must one of your Windows 2000 domain controllers assume?

   A. Primary Domain Controller

   B. Backup Domain Controller

   C. Domain Controller Master

   D. Primary Domain Controller Emulator
      D. Primary Domain Controller Emulator. In order for a Windows NT 4.0 domain controller to receive the replicated information, there must be a PDC Emulator to send the information out.

15. If you have both NetWare and Windows 2000 servers on your network, what is the main consideration with this scenario?

   A. Determining which Network Operating System directory you will use

   B. Make sure all NetWare boxes are on Token Ring.

   C. Native versus Mixed domain model

   D. Gateway Services for NetWare
      A. Determining which Network Operating System directory you will use. Centralized administration is the reasoning for this; managing two directories raises the total cost of ownership.

Chapter 14 Answers

1. Which of the following is the executable that creates a domain controller?

   A. WINNT.EXE

   B. WINNT32.EXE

   C. DCPROMO.EXE

   D. ACTDRWZD.EXE

   C. The executable application that is used to create a domain controller from a member server or stand-alone server is DCPROMO.EXE, also known as the Active Directory Wizard.

2. What type of server will a Windows 2000 Server become by default when using a fresh install?

   A. Server

   B. Domain Controller

   C. PDC

   D. BDC

   A. By default, each time a Windows 2000 server is installed, it becomes a member server.

3. Which of the following commands or utilities converts the Windows 2000 Server's file system to NTFS?

   A. NTFS.EXE

   B. CONVERT /FS:NTFS

   C. Disk Administrator

   D. DISK /FS:NTFS

   B. The command CONVERT /FS:NTFS will convert a Windows 2000 Server's file system to NTFS.

4. When running the Active Directory Wizard on the first Windows 2000 domain controller in your organization, what selection would be made for the Create or Join Forest screen?

   A. Create a new forest

   B. Copy an existing forest

   C. Join an existing forest

   D. Move to a new forest

   A. The selection for the first Windows 2000 domain controller would be to create a new forest.

5. During the Active Directory Wizard, which type of server must be available on the network?

   A. DHCP

   B. NetWare

   C. Web

   D. DNS

   D. A DNS server must be available on the network during the Active Directory Wizard, or else the Wizard will install the DNS service itself.

6. What is the recommended configuration for the location of log files and database files for the Active Directory?

   A. Log files and database files on two separate servers

   B. Log files with the database files on same partition

C. Log files and database files on separate physical disks

D. Do not install Log files, but include database files on system partition
   C. It is recommended that log files and database files are stored on separate physical disks.

7. What command will demote a domain controller to a member server?

   A. DEMOT.EXE

   B. DCPROMO.EXE

   C. WINNT.EXE

   D. WINNT32.EXE
      B. DCPROMO.EXE is used both to promote and demote a domain controller.

8. What type of administration can make use of delegation of administration using Organizational Units (OUs)?

   A. Centralized

   B. Single Administration

   C. Schema Admins

   D. Decentralized
      D. Decentralized administration can make use of delegation of administration using OUs.

9. Which type of group can contain users, Global groups, and Universal groups?

   A. Nested groups

   B. User groups

   C. Domain Local groups

   D. Universal groups

   C. Domain Local groups can contain users, Global groups, and Universal groups.

10. Which tab on a user's properties will let an administrator change password and security options for that user?

    A. Organization

    B. Account

    C. Profile

    D. General
       B. The Account tab contains options for password and security in the User properties.

11. If an organization has more than a million users, each with their own assigned computer, should the organization implement more than one domain?

    A. Yes

    B. No
       A. Since a domain can contain roughly a million objects, then this organization should probably implement more than one domain.

12. If a company has more than one namespace that it wishes to implement, can it use a single domain?

    A. Yes

    B. No
       B. If a company wants to use more than one namespace in its domain design, it will need a different domain for each DNS namespace.

13. Which of the following describe Kerberos trusts in the Active Directory? (Choose all that apply.)

    A. Bidirectional
    B. Unidirectional
    C. Transitive
    D. Nontransitive
       A, C. A Kerberos trust relationship is both bidirectional and transitive.

14. Which utility can be used to enable users in one forest to access resources in another forest?

    A. TRUSTS.EXE
    B. Active Directory Users and Computers
    C. Active Directory Domains and Trusts
    D. KERBEROS.EXE
       C. The Active Directory Domains and Trusts console is used to enable users in one forest to access resources in another forest.

15. Trench and Coats are two companies that are planning to merge. Each has a Windows 2000 Active Directory domain, trench.com and coats.com, respectively. Can Trench and Coats merge the domains?

    A. Yes
    B. No
       B. No. Domains cannot be merged. However, there are utilities that can migrate user accounts and resources from one domain to another.

Chapter 15 Answers

1. Which of the following statements is true of Active Directory transitive trusts?

    A. Administrative authority flows down the tree by default, giving the administrator of a parent domain the authority to control child domains.
    B. Domains are security boundaries, and by default an administrator of one domain has no administrative authority in other domains unless it is specifically granted.
    C. Two-way transitive trust relationships are not supported by Windows 2000.
    D. None of the above.
       B. Two-way transitive trusts are established by default between domains in a tree, but the trust relationship affects user access to resources; it does not extend administrative privileges across domains.

2. What is the maximum length limit for Windows 2000 passwords?

    A. 14 characters.
    B. 15 characters
    C. 128 characters
    D. There is no limit.
       C. 128 characters. 14 characters was

the practical limit for NT 4.0 passwords (the maximum accepted by the password field in the user account properties). 15 characters is the limit imposed on computer names (often called the "NetBIOS" name, although the NetBIOS name actually is composed of 16 characters since it incorporates an invisible hexadecimal identifier at the end).

3. What is the Microsoft-recommended level at which administrative control should be assigned whenever possible?

   A. Forest level
   B. Object level
   C. Tree level
   D. OU level
   D. By creating Organizational Units (OU), placing those objects you want a specific user or users to control in them, and assigning administrative authority to the user(s), delegation of authority is simplified. Administration at higher levels gives too much broad authority to too many persons, and assignment of control at the object level can be tedious and time-consuming.

4. Which of the following is assigned to a user account at the time of logon, and contains information about that user's group memberships, permissions, and rights?

   A. Access Control List
   B. Access Token
   C. Security Identifier

   D. GPO
   B. The security database information stored in Active Directory is checked when a user logs on and an Access Token is assigned, which lasts for that logon session. The Access Control List (ACL) is assigned to each object containing information about what groups and users have what permissions for that object. The Access Token is compared to the ACL when a user tries to access an object.

5. The Integral subsystem in the Windows 2000 architectural model contains which of the following? (Choose all that apply.)

   A. Server service
   B. Executive services
   C. Security subsystem
   D. Hardware Abstraction Layer
   A, C. The Server service, Workstation service, and Security subsystem are all part of the Integral subsystem in the User Mode portion of the architecture. Executive services and HAL are both parts of the Kernel Mode.

6. Which of the following is true of security groups? (Choose all that apply.)

   A. Security groups cannot be used for such purposes as sending a message to a group; that is exclusively the function of distribution groups.

   B. Security groups are used by the Windows 2000 operating system, while distribution groups are used by applications.

C. Windows 2000 security groups can be nested inside other groups.

D. A group can be designated as both a security group and a distribution group at the same time.
B, C. Security groups can be used for distribution purposes like distribution groups. The latter are used by applications, while the former are used by Windows 2000. A group is designated via a radio button as either a security or a distribution group in its Properties sheet.

7. Which of the following is a type of security group that can be used only when Windows 2000 runs in native mode, and was not used in Windows NT 4.0?

A. Universal group

B. Domain global group

C. Domain local group

D. None of the above
A. While global and local groups are familiar to NT 4.0 administrators (although their function is different in Windows 2000), there was no Universal group in NT, and it can be used in Windows 2000 only when running in native mode.

8. What tool is used to create groups in Active Directory?

A. User Manager for Domains

B. Active Directory Users and Computers

C. Directory Manager

D. Domain Tree Administrator
B. Active Directory Users and Computers. User Manager for Domains was the administrative tool used in NT 4.0 to create users and groups. Directory Management was the name of a Snap-in used in an early beta version of Windows 2000. There is no such thing as the Domain Tree Administrator.

9. The Windows 2000 feature that allows you to run an administrative application as an administrator although you are logged on to a nonadministrative account, using the Run As command, is known as which of the following?

A. Administrative Emulation

B. Dual Logon

C. Secondary Logon

D. There is no such feature.
C. By using secondary logon, an administrator can avoiding staying logged on to an administrative account for routine tasks, but can easily run those programs requiring administrative privileges in administrative context by selecting Run As in the right-click context menu and typing in the appropriate administrative username and password.

10. Which of the following is NOT one of the standard NTFS file permissions?

A. Write

B. List Contents

C. Modify

D. Full Control

B. List contents. A, C, and D are all permissions that can be assigned to files or folders; however, List Contents is a folder permission only.

11. Which of the following is true of NTFS and shared folder permissions?

A. NTFS permissions apply only when accessing the object through the network share, not when accessing from the local machine.

B. NTFS permissions apply only when accessing the object from the local machine, not when accessing through the network share.

C. Shared folder permissions apply only when accessing the object through the network share, not when accessing from the local machine.

D. Shared folder permissions apply only when accessing the object from the local machine, not when accessing through the network share.

C. Shared folder permissions only apply when accessing the object through the network share, not to normal access at the local machine. (It is, however, possible to access a shared folder through the network share even though it is on the local machine. Rarely would you want to do this, but in this case, shared folder permissions would apply.)

12. Which of the following is used to assign Active Directory permissions in Windows 2000?

A. The Security tab in the object's Properties sheet.

B. The Sharing tab in the object's Properties sheet.

C. The Active Directory Permissions Assignment Snap-in.

D. Disk Administrator.

A. The Security tab in the object's Properties sheet. The Sharing tab pertains to Shared Folder permissions. There is no Active Directory Permissions Assignment Snap-in. Disk Administrator was an NT 4.0 tool used to partition, format, modify, and monitor the computer's physical disks and logical drives.

13. Which two of the following are the steps required to audit object access in Windows 2000?

A. Enable auditing in the Users and Computers Snap-in.

B. Enable auditing using the Group Policy Editor Snap-in.

C. Configure auditing for specific objects using the Group Policy Editor Snap-in.

D. Configure auditing for specific objects using the Security tab on the object's Properties sheet.

B, D. Auditing must first be enabled using the Group Policy Editor (which can be added to a custom MMC for ease of use). Then auditing is assigned to each object to be audited through the Security tab on its Properties sheet.

14. Where does the Group Policy Template (GPT) reside on a domain controller?

    A. In the root directory of the c: drive.

    B. In the sysvol directory in the root directory of the system volume.

    C. In the sysvol subdirectory in the systemroot directory.

    D. In the systemroot/system32/GPT subdirectory on the boot volume.
       C. The GPT on a domain controller is stored in the sysvol subdirectory, located in the systemroot directory (usually winnt).

15. Which of the following is considered a "best practice" in assigning permissions? (Choose all that apply.)

    A. The Deny permission should be used liberally to restrict access.

    B. For every directory object, there should be at least one user who has Full Control.

    C. Administrative permissions should be granted at the OU level if possible.

    D. You should track permissions assignments to keep records of what permissions have been assigned.
       B, C, and D. For every directory object, there should be at least one user who has Full Control. Administrative permissions should be granted at the OU level if possible. You should track permissions assignments to keep records of what permissions have been

assigned. However, Microsoft recommends that the Deny permission be used sparingly, and that group assignments be made more carefully to grant the access and administrative control you desire.

Chapter 16 Answers

1. What are the benefits of using multimaster replication? (Choose two.)

   A. Single point of failure

   B. Redundancy

   C. Optimizes performance

   D. Immediate synchronization
      B, C. Multimaster replication provides redundancy and optimizes performance.

2. Which of the following represent partitions of the Active Directory database?

   A. Domains

   B. Global Catalog

   C. Schema and configuration

   D. All of the above
      D. Each separate domain, the Global Catalog, and the schema and configuration are all partitions of the Active Directory database.

3. What is a grouping of IP subnets called?

   A. Site

   B. Site Link

   C. Connection

D. Site Link Bridge
A. A site is a grouping of IP subnets, and are usually considered to be a grouping of well-connected IP subnets that have fast reliable connectivity between them.

4. What are Connection objects used for?

A. Inter-site replication

B. Bridging two links together

C. Establishing the IP subnet

D. Intra-site replication
D. Connection objects are used for intra-site replication.

5. What characteristics represent intra-site replication? (Choose all that apply.)

A. Uses SMTP transport

B. Uses RPCs over IP transport

C. Automatically generated via Connection objects

D. Relies on site links and site link bridges
B, C. Intra-site replication uses RPCs over IP transport, and is automatically generated by the KCC through Connection objects.

6. Which of the following is used to generate the replication topology?

A. KCC

B. RPC

C. IP

D. SMTP
A. The KCC, or Knowledge Consistency Checker, runs as a service on each domain controller and generates the replication topology.

7. Which of the following tools can help troubleshoot replication?

A. The Active Directory Replication Troubleshooter

B. Active Directory Sites and Services

C. Knowledge Consistency Checker

D. Active Directory Replication Monitor
D. The Active Directory Replication Monitor can help troubleshoot replication problems.

8. What happens to a domain controller if the administrator never creates a site topology?

A. It cannot be installed.

B. It is automatically demoted to a member server.

C. It is placed into a site called "default-first-site-name."

D. It is placed into a "waiting" container.
C. If no sites are ever created, new domain controllers are automatically placed within a site called the "default-first-site-name."

9. Which of the following is compressed?

A. Inter-site replication

B. Intra-site replication

C. Connection objects

D. Sites
A. The inter-site replication traffic is compressed before it is sent across a site link.

10. How can inter-site replication be prevented from occurring across a site link?

   A. It can't

   B. Change the cost of a site link to 0

   C. Change the frequency of replication to 10,080

   D. Change the schedule of availability
   D. Inter-site replication can be prevented from occurring across a site link by changing the schedule of availability. The administrator must remove all the time that replication should not occur from the schedule, and the site link will not be available during those times.

11. Which object's properties enable the selection of bridgehead servers?

   A. Server

   B. Site

   C. Site link

   D. Site link bridge
   A. The Server object's properties enable its designation as a bridgehead server for inter-site replication.

12. True or False: If an organization has two forests, it can use the same sites to handle both forests' replication traffic.

   A. True

   B. False
   B. False. Sites are designated on a per-forest basis. If an organization has two forests, they will each have their own sets of sites and will most likely be duplicated.

13. Where do workstations attempt logon first?

   A. Within the site of the user who is logging on

   B. Within the workstation's site, indicated by its IP subnet

   C. Anywhere within the forest

   D. Anywhere within its own domain
   B. Workstations attempt to log on to domain controllers within the workstation's own site, which is indicated by the IP subnet assigned to the workstation.

14. What is the minimum recommended number of domain controllers to place within a site?

   A. 0

   B. One

   C. Two

   D. Three
   C. The minimum recommended number of domain controllers to place within a site is two.

15. If a site is not directly connected to the rest of the forest's network, what transport should it use?

   A. IP

   B. SMTP

   C. RPC

   D. KCC
   B. Sites that are not directly connected to the rest of the forest should use the SMTP transport.

Chapter 17 Answers

1. Which of the following tools can analyze and clean up core directory structures?

   A. Disk Management snap-in

   B. ntdsutil.exe

   C. dirclean.exe

   D. replmon
   B. The Disk Management tool is used to manage the partitioning, formatting, and upgrading of the physical disks. There is no such thing as dirclean.exe. Replmon is the graphical interface tool used to monitor replication events. ntdsutil.exe serves many functions, including directory structure analysis and cleanup.

2. What is the purpose of the LostAndFound container?

   A. It is a desktop folder in which you can deposit miscellaneous files.

   B. It is part of the Recycle Bin.

   C. It is used by the directory replication process as a "holding" place for objects when the service cannot determine where the object should be placed.

   D. It is used by the administrator as a shared folder where users can look for objects when they have forgotten the object's location.
   C. The LostAndFound container is the replication service's repository for objects that have been created in, or moved to, a location that is missing after replication. The administrator should periodically check this container, found in the Active Directory Users and Computers domain tree, and move or delete the "lost" objects.

3. Which of the following resource kit utilities can be used to monitor the replication process? (Choose all that apply.)

   A. REPADMIN

   B. DSASTAT

   C. NETDOM

   D. NTDS.DIT
   A and B. NETDOM is used to move computers and join them to domains. NTDS.DIT is the file in which the Active Directory database is stored. Both REPADMIN and DSASTAT are used for monitoring aspects of the replication process.

4. How can you publish printers shared by non-Windows 2000 computers in the Active Directory? (Check all that apply.)

   A. Use the pubprn script.

   B. Use the PMON utility.

   C. Use the DS MMC.

   D. Non-Windows 2000 printers cannot be published in the Active Directory.
   A and C. Non-Windows 2000 printers can be published in Active Directory in one of two ways. The simplest method is with the pubprn script, which is located in the system 32 directory. Alternately, you can use the DS MMC snap-in. PMON is a utility that allows you to monitor per-process CPU and memory usage.

5. Which of the following is used to move a subtree of objects from one domain to a different domain in the same forest?

   A. MOVEDOM

   B. TREEMOVE

   C. MOVETREE

   D. NETDOM
      C. The MOVETREE utility allows you to move a subtree to a different domain. MOVEDOM and TREEMOVE do not exist. NETDOM is used to move computer accounts to a new domain, and join computers to domains.

6. When the database file is updated, the fastest method is to write to the first available database pages. However, this causes which of the following problems?

   A. Fragmentation of the database

   B. Deletion of some of the data

   C. Inability to find the data, which is placed in the LostAndFound container

   D. None of the above
      A. The database becomes fragmented. Active Directory performs an online defragmentation as part of its regular self-cleaning process, or an administrator can force an offline defragmentation, which will free up space on the disk.

7. What happens to an object's permissions when you move it to a different OU?

   A. It retains all permissions it had in the original OU.

   B. It loses the permissions specifically assigned to it in the original OU but retains those that were inherited.

   C. It retains the permissions that were specifically assigned to it in the original OU but does not retain those it inherited.

   D. It loses all permissions it had in the original OU.
      C. Those permissions specifically assigned to the object are retained, but it loses any inherited permissions when it is moved to a new OU.

8. Which resource kit tool is used to replace instances of a SID on ACLs when you move accounts and need to update the ACL?

   A. ACLUPDATE.EXE

   B. SIDUPDATE.EXE

   C. SIDWALK.EXE

   D. SYSDIFF.EXE
      C. There are no such utilities as ACLUPDATE.EXE and SIDUPDATE.EXE. SYSDIFF.EXE is used to install applications as part of an automated install process.

9. What is the Windows 2000 backup program called?

   A. W2000bu.exe

   B. ntbackup.exe

   C. backw2k.exe

   D. nt5backup.exe
      B. The Windows 2000 backup utility has the same name as its counterpart

in NT 4.0; however, it includes several new features and improved functionality.

10. Which of the following would you back up in order to back up the Active Directory information?

A. Replication data

B. LDAP data

C. System State data

D. Directory data
C. The directory services information is backed up as part of the System State data, which also includes Registry and other critical system data.

11. Which of the following is true of authoritative restore? (Choose all that apply.)

A. To restore System State data on a domain controller, you must start the computer in Directory Services Restore mode.

B. An authoritative restore can be done only on a Primary domain controller.

C. You use the ntdsutil.exe tool to do an authoritative restore.

D. You use the adrestore.exe tool to an authoritative restore.
A and C. In Windows 2000, all domain controllers are equal; there are no primary domain controllers. There is no adrestore.exe tool; the ntdsutil.exe tool is used with authoritative restore. The computer must be started in

Directory Services Restore mode to do an authoritative restore.

12. In which domain mode would your Windows 2000 server operate if there are still Windows NT domain controllers on your network?

A. NT emulation

B. Native

C. Hybrid

D. Mixed
D. Until all domain controllers are Windows 2000 machines, you must use Mixed mode to allow the down-level servers to perform as BDCs. When you have upgraded all DCs to Windows 2000, you can switch to Native mode, which allows you to take advantage of features such as universal groups. There are no such domain modes as NT emulation and hybrid.

13. Which of the following allows you to accurately see the size of the ntds.dit file?

A. Refresh the Explorer window.

B. Reboot the computer.

C. Use the Windows Explorer Properties dialog on the partition where the ntds.dit file is located.

D. Right-click the file name and select "update file size."
B and C. Rebooting the computer closes the file and the reported size will be updated when you reopen it. The Properties dialog box always reports the correct file size. There is no

"update file size" selection in the right-click context menu, and refreshing the Explorer window will not update the reported file size.

14. What is the recommended limit for number of security-principal objects per domain in a Mixed-mode environment?

    A. 10,000

    B. 40,000

    C. 75,000

    D. Approximately 1.3 million
    B. Microsoft recommends that if you have NT Server domain controllers participating in your domain, you limit the number of security objects to 40,000 due to limitations on the size of the SAM (Security Account Manager) database.

15. Which of the following enhances performance on domain controllers that must handle high request rates?

    A. Place the Active Directory database file and log files on the same hard disk.

    B. Place the database file and operating system files on the same hard disk, but place the log files on a separate disk.

    C. Place the database, operating system, and log files on three separate hard disks.

    D. The placement of the files has no effect on performance.
    C. If you have multiple physical hard disks in your system, you can increase performance by placing the Active Directory database files, the operating system files, and the log files on three separate hard disks.

Chapter 18 Answers

1. Why should your Active Directory deployment plan include identification of existing directory services being used in your network?

    A. So all existing directory services can be eliminated.

    B. So you can develop a plan for migrating or synchronizing other directory services across the enterprise.

    C. So you will know whether it is possible to implement Active Directory, since it can't be used if other directory services are already in place.

    D. There is no need to identify existing directory services.
    B. You need to identify other directory services being used in your network, such as Novell NetWare NDS or Microsoft Exchange directory services, so a plan can be developed for either migrating to Active Directory or synchronizing the services across the enterprise.

2. Which of the following should be included in the assessment phase of your Active Directory deployment plan? (Choose all that apply.)

A. A diagram of the existing NT network, showing trust relationships between domains.

B. Identification of users who have multiple accounts.

C. The organization's administrative model.

D. The serial numbers of all hardware devices on the network.
   A, B, and C. One of the first steps in the assessment phase is to diagram the network, including a diagram of the domain model showing all current trust relationships. It is important to identify where users have multiple accounts so you can plan to consolidate them if possible. You must collect information about the organization's administrative model to guide you in delegating administrative authority in the new Active Directory structure. Although the IT department should keep records of serial numbers of network hardware, this information is not important in planning the Active Directory deployment.

3. Which of the following is true of Windows 2000 domain controllers?

A. A domain can have only one domain controller.

B. A domain must have at least two domain controllers.

C. A domain can have one or more domain controllers.

D. One domain controller can control multiple domains.
   C. A domain can have one or more domain controllers. Each domain must have at least one, and a domain controller is specific to one domain; it cannot controller multiple domains.

4. Why might you take one of your NT domain's BDCs off the network prior to upgrading the PDC to Windows 2000?

A. A PDC cannot be upgraded if there are BDCs on the network.

B. The BDC taken offline will have the SAM of the original NT domain intact, in case you need to revert to the old domain model.

C. All BDCs must be demoted to member servers before you can upgrade an NT domain to Windows 2000.

D. There is no reason to take the BDC offline.
   B. Taking the BDC offline is one method of providing a recovery option if the Windows 2000 deployment encounters problems and you wish to reinstate the NT domain. The BDC could then be brought back online and promoted to PDC.

5. Which of the following statements is false? (Choose all that apply.)

A. Building a large, complex network with NT was easier than doing so with Windows 2000, because Active

Directory is difficult to configure across the enterprise.

B. Active Directory makes it easier to organize network resources logically, as opposed to NT's directory services.

C. The hierarchical namespace used by Active Directory makes it more scalable than the flat namespace used by NT.

D. NT's directory services used the domain tree concept.

A, D. Windows 2000 with Active Directory makes it easier to build large, complex networks, as opposed to using the old Windows NT domain models. NT's directory services did not use the domain tree concept, which is hierarchical in nature, but Windows 2000's Active Directory does.

6. Which of the following is one of the basic units of organization in Active Directory? (Choose all that apply.)

A. Domains

B. Forests

C. Schemas

D. Member servers

A, B. Domains and Forests are basic units of organization used in Active Directory, along with sites, trees, and organizational units (OUs). The schema is the set of specifications governing objects and their attributes, and member servers are computers running the server operating system, which are not domain controllers.

7. The repository for information about all of the objects that reside in Active Directory containers, used to locate resources on the network, is called the:

A. Name server

B. Directory index

C. Global catalog

D. Object log

C. The global catalog (GC) holds the information about Active Directory objects that allows users to search and locate network resources, regardless of where those objects physically reside on the network.

8. Which of the following is true of sites? (Choose all that apply.)

A. Sites are used to reduce replication traffic across slow links.

B. Sites are used only in small LANs, which are contained in one geographic location.

C. A site is associated with one or more TCP/IP subnet with a high-bandwidth connection.

D. Sites can be used to isolate logon authentication requests.

A, C, and D. Sites are associated with one or more TCP/IP subnet connected by a fast link, and can be used for reducing replication bandwidth and isolating authentication requests. Sites are used most often in large enterprise-level networks as there is no use for them in a small, contained LAN.

9. Which of the following is not a reason to create multiple domains?

    A. Offices in different countries where users need to use different languages.

    B. A requirement for different domain policies.

    C. A need to isolate or balance replication traffic.

    D. A centralized administrative model.
    D. The need for different languages or different domain policies in different parts of the network is a common reason for creating multiple domains, as is the need to isolate or balance the replication traffic. However, a centralized administrative model would favor a single domain structure, while decentralized administration favors creation of multiple domains.

10. Which domain in a tree is considered that tree's "root" domain?

    A. The domain specified by the administrator using the "set root" command.

    B. The first domain created in the tree.

    C. The domain with the largest number of Active Directory objects.

    D. The domain with the name starting with the lowest letter of the alphabet.
    B. The first domain to be created in a new tree becomes the root domain for that tree. There is no "set root" command in Windows 2000, and number of objects and alphabetical

order of names have no bearing on which domain is the root of the tree.

11. Which of the following pairs of domains have a contiguous namespace? (Choose all that apply.)

    A. tacteam.net, team-one.net

    B. tacteam.net, team-one.com

    C. tacteam.net, team-one.tacteam.net

    D. team-one.tacteam.net, team-one.federation.net
    C. Only the domain pair tacteam.net and team-one.tacteam.net share a contiguous namespace. Tacteam.net is the parent domain, and team-one.tacteam.net is the child domain, which includes the parent's namespace in its own. (The pair team-one.tacteam.net and team-one.federation.net are child domains of the same name that reside in two different domain trees).

12. Which of the following is true of Windows 2000 domains? (Choose all that apply.)

    A. The administrator of a parent domain also has administrative privileges in all child domains.

    B. There is an implicit, two-way trust between domains within the same tree.

    C. The domain is a basic line of demarcation for administrative purposes.

    D. Windows 2000 multiple domain models are more difficult to manage in an enterprise environment than NT multiple domain models.

B, C. Users within a domain tree can access resources in other domains (if they have the proper permissions), because an implicit, two-way transitive trust exists between the domains of the tree. The domain, however, is the basic line of demarcation for administrative purposes; administrators of a parent domain do not have administrative privileges in child domains (unless explicitly assigned). The two-way trusts make Windows 2000 multiple domain models easier to manage.

13. Which of the following statements is true of organizational units (OUs)? (Choose all that apply.)

A. OUs can contain users and groups, but cannot contain resources such as printers and shared folders.

B. OUs can contain other OUs.

C. Administrative authority can be delegated on the OU level.

D. Deep OU hierarchies are not recommended because they can negatively impact performance.

B, C. and D. OUs can contain users, groups, printers, shared folders, and other resources, as well as other OUs. A primary reason for using OUs is the ability to delegate authority at the OU level. There is no limit on how deep your OU hierarchy can be, but deep hierarchies are not recommended, as the search through multiple levels can negatively impact performance.

14. What is an advantage of placing a domain controller at each Active Directory site?

A. User logon authentication requests can all be serviced by a local computer.

B. Users will not be able to access resources outside their sites, thereby enhancing security.

C. A domain controller at each site is required in order for users at all sites to access Active Directory objects.

D. IT costs will be lower, because there will be less wear and tear on the server machines.

A. Placing a domain controller at each site ensures that all users will be able to log on and be authenticated by a local computer, thus reducing logon traffic across slow WAN links. Users will still be able to access resources outside their sites, and a domain controller is not required at each site for users to access Active Directory objects as long as they are able to log on to the network. Physical wear and tear on the server machines would not be affected.

15. Which of the following is true of a well-designed test lab? (Choose all that apply.)

A. It can be used for experimenting with the technology without endangering the production network.

B. It will cost a great deal of money and requires a large amount of dedicated personnel.

C. It should be dismantled once Windows 2000 directory services have been deployed throughout the enterprise.

D. It can be used for validating the compatibility of server and client applications.

A, D. The test lab serves many purposes, including experimentation with technology, comparing design solutions, validating compatibility of server and client applications, and fine-tuning the rollout process. It can also be used in an ongoing role after the deployment of Windows 2000, for testing proposed changes and troubleshooting, and it does not necessarily have to be expensive or require dedicated personnel.

Chapter 19 Answers

1. Every object created in Active Directory is an instance of a:

A. Attribute

B. Object

C. Schema

D. Class

D. Every object in Active Directory is an instance of a class. The class contains attributes that define the properties of the object.

2. Class Definition Objects are stored in Active Directories as instances of:

A. The classSchema class

B. The attributeSchema class

C. The classSchema attribute

D. The attributeSchema attribute

B. Class Definition Objects are instances of the classSchema class.

3. Attribute Syntaxes are used to

A. Restrict the range of values that may be entered

B. Restrict the type of values that may be entered

C. Restrict permissions to the attribute

D. Restrict which classes can use the attribute

B. Attribute syntaxes define the type of values that may be entered for that attribute of an object (e.g., Case-Insensitive-String).

4. The schema is stored in which of the following locations?

A. CN=Schema,CN=Configuration, DC=*Domain*,DC=*Domain*

B. The %SystemRoot%\SCHEMA.INI file

C. The Windows NT Registry

D. The schema is only stored in cache

A. The schema is stored within Active Directory in the Configuration container.

5. There are always at least how many copies of the schema on a domain controller?

A. 1

B. 2

C. 3

D. 4

B. There is always at least one copy in cache on a domain controller, and one copy within the Active Directory. There may be multiple copies in cache if clients are maintaining process threads to older schema revisions.

6. Which of the following represents an attribute?

A. User

B. Computer

C. Organizational Unit (OU)

D. LogonHours

D. LogonHours is an attribute of the User class, used to specify the login time restrictions for a user object.

7. In a custom user class, you are currently storing each user's phone number as a 7-number string. You want to require 10 numbers, so that an area code is also assigned to each user. How would you make this change?

A. Modify the class

B. Modify the attribute

C. Create a new class and attribute

C. Create a new attribute and assign to the existing class

B. Only the attribute must be modified. The syntax rule can be changed to require 10 numbers.

8. Microsoft Active Directory is based on which standard?

A. X.5

B. X.25

C. X.400

D. X.500

D. Active Directory is based on the X.500 standard for a directory service.

9. Valid OIDs must be obtained from

A. An OID naming authority, such as ANSI

B. The InterNIC

C. OIDGEN.EXE

D. Microsoft

A. A valid OID is unique on the Internet, and must be obtained from a proper naming authority, such as the American National Standards Institute (ANSI).

10. There is a single Schema Operations Master per

A. Site

B. Domain

C. Tree

D. Forest

D. Only one Schema Operations Master may exist in a single forest.

11. Before loading the Active Directory Schema Snap-in component into a new or existing console, what must first be done on the client computer?

A. The SCHMMGMT.DLL file must be registered using REGEDT32.

B. The SCHMMGMT.DLL file must be registered using REGSVR32.

C. The ADSIEDIT.DLL file must be registered using REGEDT32.

D. The ADSIEDIT.DLL file must be registered using REGSVR32.
B. The SCHMMGMT.DLL file is the component that provides the Active Directory Schema MMC Snap-in, and must be registered using REGSVR32 for the Snap-in to be available for addition to a console.

12. Which of the following types of classes may be created in the schema? (Choose all that apply.)

A. Structural

B. Auxiliary

C. Abstract

D. 88
A, B, and C. The type 88 class is used only for backward compatibility with the 1988 X.500 standard, and cannot be created in the schema.

13. What must you do prior to deactivating a class?

A. Delete all assigned attributes

B. Deactivate all assigned attributes

C. Remove all objects of that class

D. Nothing
D. You do not need to remove or deactivate attributes, or delete instantiated objects when removing a class from the schema.

14. In which of the following methods can a schema modification be made? (Choose all that apply.)

A. The AD Users and Computers console

B. A third-party application

C. A Windows Scripting Host (WSH) script

D. By executing the SCHMMGMT file
B, C. Schema modifications are not made in the AD Users and Computers console. SCHMMGMT is a .DLL file that must be registered prior to running the Active Directory schema console, another method by which schema modifications can be performed.

15. Which of the following considerations should be made when modifying the schema?

A. Validity of OID strings to be used

B. Replication traffic

C. Disk space utilization

D. Existing classes may suffice
A, B, and D. Disk space utilization is not really an issue when modifying the schema. Consider replication issues before placing an attribute on the Global Catalog Server (GCS), and consider modifying existing classes and attributes before adding a new one. OID strings should be registered with a valid naming authority, such as ANSI.

Chapter 20 Answers

1. Which is not a layer of the TCP/IP model?

    A. Application

    B. Internet

    C. Presentation

    D. Network Interface

    C. Presentation. While the Presentation layer exists in the OSI model, it does not exist in the TCP/IP model. Functions associated with this OSI layer are handled by the Application and Transport layers of the TCP/IP model.

2. What are the minimum addressing requirements associated with the installation of TCP/IP on a Windows 2000 workstation? (Choose all that apply.)

    A. IP Address

    B. Gateway Address

    C. Subnet Mask

    D. DNS Server

    A, C. You need to configure the IP address as unique on the network. You also need to configure the subnet mask (or accept the default subnet mask) so that all hosts on the network will be able to communicate.

3. Which command can you use with Windows 2000 to ascertain the lease term of your IP address?

    A. Winipcfg

    B. Winipcfg /all

    C. Ipconfig

    D. Ipconfig /all

    D. Winipcfg is only available with Windows 95 and Windows 98. Ipconfig will not show you the remaining lease term. You need to add the /all switch to the command line to obtain this information.

4. Which IP addresses listed below are included in the ranges reserved for private addressing and not available as registered addresses on the Internet? (Choose all that apply.)

    A. 10.1.1.3

    B. 172.16.21.3

    C. 192.168.33.21

    D. 91.1.1.1

    A, B, C. Only D does not fit within the range of IP addresses available for private addressing (see Table 20-1).

5. Utilization of Automatic Private IP Addressing (APIPA) is recommended for?

    A. Networks with five or fewer hosts where no DHCP service is available.

    B. Networks with more than 1500 hosts where DHCP service is not consistently available.

    C. Networks connected by leased lines.

    D. Only in stand-alone workstations.

    A. APIPA's suggested utilization is limited to small networks where no DHCP server is available.

6. The Media Sensing capability of Windows 2000 describes its ability to:

    A. Simultaneously access two networks utilizing different network interface cards (NICs).

    B. Provide remote users with the ability to transport their laptop computers between two different networks and the operating system will automatically determine whether the network uses Token Ring or Ethernet.

    C. The operating system will be able to identify whether unshielded twisted pair or thinnet is being used as the network's wire media.

    D. To tune and optimize memory.
    B. Media Sensing eliminates the problems associated with roaming users connecting up to a different network (e.g., Token Ring to Ethernet).

7. How many valid subnets and valid hosts are available on the Class C network having a subnet mask of 255.255.255.240?

    A. 14 subnets with 14 hosts each

    B. 16 subnets with 16 hosts each

    C. 32 subnets with 240 hosts each

    D. 240 subnets with 32 hosts each
    B. In a Class C network, the subnet mask 255.255.255.240 provides 16 subnets (only 14 of which are valid) and 16 hosts (only 14 of which are valid).

Rubbish: Read the question! It Asks for valid then gives an answer that includes invalid hosts.

8. Which of the following must be unique to a specific host on the network?

    A. The host portion of its IP address

    B. The network portion of its IP address

    C. Its subnet mask

    D. The name of any designated /'shared file
    A. The host portion of its IP address must be unique on the network.

9. Which of the following are routing protocols? (Choose all that apply.)

    A. RIP

    B. TCP

    C. IP

    D. OSPF
    A, D. Routing Information Protocol (RIP) and Open Shortest Path First (OSPF) are two common routing protocols.

10. An IP address with a bit pattern that begins with the 110 is defined as a Class ____ address?

    A. Class A

    B. Class B

    C. Class C

    D. Class D
    C. When the first 3 bits are 110, this designates a Class C address.

11. Which of the following values can be automatically configured using DHCP? (Choose all that apply.)

    A. Host IP address

B. Host Default Gateway

C. Mail Server

D. Subnet Mask
    A, B, and D. Each of these can be
    automatically configured through
    DHCP service.

12. IPSec can be implemented in a Windows
    2000 network to:

    A. Provide automatic DNS addressing

    B. Provide a cryptography-based security

    C. Identify which hosts are utilizing the
        Windows 2000 operating system

    D. None of the above
        B. Provide a cryptography-based
        security. This is the only possible
        answer.

13. With Windows 2000, TCP/IP filtering
    can be used to specifically permit or deny
    TCP/IP traffic, based on? (Choose all
    that apply.)

    A. Content

    B. IP Protocol

    C. TCP Port number

    D. UDP Port number
        B, C, D. The TCP/IP Filtering
        Properties sheet specifies TCP Ports,
        UDP Ports, and IP Protocols as the
        available filtering items.

14. Which product must you install to obtain
    full functionality from Microsoft Network
    Monitor?

    A. Internet Information Server

B. System Management Server

C. Performance Monitor

D. Proxy Server
    B. System Management Server, as one
    of its utilities, includes a fully
    functional version of Network
    Monitor.

15. Address Resolution Protocol is used to?

    A. Resolve IP addresses to a host's
        MAC address

    B. Resolve IP addresses to a host's
        NetBIOS name

    C. Resolve a host's NetBIOS name to its
        IP address

    D. Resolve a host's Fully Qualifying
        Domain Name (FQDN) to its IP
        address
        A. Resolve IP addresses to a host's
        MAC address. This is the only
        appropriate answer.

Chapter 21 Answers

1. Jason is the CTO of NT2000 Corp. He
    has decided to implement DHCP into his
    network. He wants to only have the client
    receive the IP address and subnet mask
    automatically. What TCP/IP
    configuration can he set manually on the
    DHCP client? (Choose all that apply.)

    A. IP Address

    B. Subnet mask

    C. Domain Name System (DNS)
        server address

D. Windows Internet Name Service (WINS) server address

C, D. DHCP is able to do the IP address and subnet mask configuration dynamically. The Domain Name System (DNS) and Windows Internet Name Service (WINS) can be either dynamically set with DHCP or be manually set on the client side.

2. What are the four phases in a successful DHCP lease process? (Choose all that apply.)

A. DHCPDISCOVER

B. DHCPOFFER

C. DHCPREQUEST

D. DHCPACK

E. DHCPNACK

A, B, C, and D. The four phases in a successful DHCP lease process are DHCPDISCOVER, DHCPOFFER, DHCPREQUEST, and DHCPACK. The DHCPNACK occurs during an unsuccessful lease process.

3. Lucille, the network administrator of NT 2000 Corp., is confused. DHCP is installed on one subnet. The clients on the same subnet as the DHCP server are able to access the Internet. However, when a DHCP-enabled client tries to configure itself and get an IP on a remote subnet, it does not work. It is able to communicate with the rest of the clients on that subnet. What is wrong?

A. Router is down.

B. Router is misconfigured.

C. DHCP Relay Agent does not exist on the local subnet.

D. DHCP server is not working correctly.

C. During DHCPDISCOVER, a client broadcasts to the network trying to communicate with the DHCP server. DHCP broadcasts are not forwarded to other subnets unless a DHCP Relay Agent is installed on the subnet.

4. An FTP server, using IP 128.56.45.221, is shut off. Three weeks later, it is unable to get the same IP. Lucille can't figure out why it is taking so long to get the DHCP response and why it is unable to get the same IP. What can Lucille do to work around this? (Choose all that apply.)

A. Use static IP.

B. Nothing she can do.

C. Continue using DHCP.

D. Make the lease on the server to last indefinitely.

A, D. The DHCPNACK phase occurs when the DHCPREQUEST fails, such as when the client is trying to lease an old address that is being used or is no longer available. The server sends a negative broadcast called the DHCPNACK and the lease process starts all over again. When you set the FTP server with a static IP, it never needs to use DHCP. Lucille can use a reservation where the IP correlates to

(handwritten note: C / Must be Correct if DIS.)

the computer. She could also use a reservation instead of a static assignment. This is permanent, and a record exists of the assignment.

5. When the DHCP server is not detected, the Windows 2000 client will manually set itself with a private network IP. What can Jon do to manually try to renew the IP address?

A. Use ipconfig /restore

B. Use ipconfig /resurrect

C. Use ipconfig /renew

D. Use winipcfg
   C. Jon should use ipconfig /renew to renew his IP address. Winipcfg is an application that can be used to renew an IP, but it only exists in Windows 95/98.

6. What TCP/IP configuration should be set for running the DHCP service on a Windows 2000?

A. A dynamic IP

B. A static IP

C. A dynamic DNS server address

D. A static DNS server address
   B. A static IP must be set on the Windows 2000 server so that DHCP can function correctly. The DNS configuration is not critical to the performance on the DHCP service on Windows 2000.

7. Which of the following clients are Windows 2000 DHCP ready? (Choose all that apply.)

A. Windows 95 or later

B. Windows for Workgroups 3.11 running TCP/IP-32

C. MS-DOS with the Microsoft Network Client 3.0 with the real mode TCP/IP driver

D. LAN Manager 2.2c, except for the OS/2 version
   A, B, C, and D. All the clients are Windows 2000 DHCP ready.

8. Ian has 7000 clients in his network. How many DHCP servers should he install?

A. One

B. Two

C. Three

D. Four
   B. Ian should install two DHCP servers. Most networks should have at least one online DHCP server and one backup for every 10,000 clients.

9. Fiona needs to route DHCP broadcasts to remote subnets. She installed Windows 2000 but she is unable to add the DHCP Relay Agent. What is needed on a computer for the DHCP Relay Agent to be available?

A. Two network cards

B. Two operating systems

C. Two instances on DHCP installed

D. DHCP service
   A. In order for the DHCP Relay Agent to be available, the system must be dual homed—it must have two or more network cards.

10. Alex has a DHCP server with a static IP address of 129.56.24.15. It has a range of IPs from 129.56.24.5 to 129.56.24.45. All clients are able to access the DHCP server. Once in a while, a new client is not be able to access the Internet, or the DHCP server is unable to access network resources. How should Alex fix this problem?

A. Use all static IPs.

B. Install all the newest service packs and try again.

C. Make sure he excludes the IP of the DHCP server in the range of IPs available to the DHC- enabled clients.

D. Make sure he includes the IP of the DHCP server in the range of IPs available to the DHCP enable clients.
   C. Although using all static IPs can solve the problems of the network, it is not a good fix. Most likely the problem is that the DHCP server is giving out its own IP to clients, and that is causing an IP conflict on the network that can prevent one or both computers from accessing TCP/IP resources.

11. Marty is running a network of 4000 clients. Two thousand of them are contractors and they move often from subnet to subnet doing changes in different departments. One day, Marty walks in and realizes he is running out of IP addresses. What can he set to ensure the most IP addresses are available at one time while maintaining the same subnet address?

A. Disable DHCP and use all static IP addresses.

B. Decrease the lease time.

C. Increase the least time.

D. Use a proxy server.
   B. Marty should decrease the lease time so that the IP addresses are returned quicker to the pool. A proxy server is used to access the Internet with one real-world IP. Access to the proxy server still requires a pool of intranet IP addressees.

12. A computer that only has the TCP/IP protocol and is DHCP enabled is able to access other computers on the same subnet, but the DHCP is unreachable. How is it able to do that?

A. It is using a nonroutable protocol, such as NetBEUI.

B. It is using NWLink.

C. It is using a set of IP addresses that it assigns itself.

D. It can't.
   C. Windows 2000 address the problem of not being able to access network resources when the DHCP server is unavailable by having default behavior without DHCP. When Windows 2000 DHCP-enabled clients cannot locate the DHCP server, the Microsoft Automatic Private IP Address (APIPA) assigns an IP that does not conflict with the rest of the network. The APIPA uses the block of addresses that the Internet

reserves for private networks (168.254.0.0 to 169.254.255.254 with a subnet mask of 255.255.255.0). The computer is able to access computers that have APIPA assigned IP addresses.

13. David has a client who is an aspiring MCSE. Last year, the client installed a DHCP server to prepare for his Supporting and Implementing Windows NT Server 4.0 test. The new DHCP server brought the entire network to a grinding halt. How can David prevent that from happening to him?

   A. Upgrade to Windows 2000 and control authority to run DHCP services.

   B. Put a DHCP server on every local subnet.

   C. Disable all the DHCP Relay Agents.

   D. Upgrade to Windows 2000.
   A. There is nothing he can do to prevent this. Windows 2000 now integrates with Active Directory. Whenever the DHCP service is started on Windows 2000, it contacts the Active Directory to see if it is an authorized DHCP server. If the server is not on the list of authorized DHCP servers, Active Directory will halt the DHCP service.

14. With Windows NT 4, the server always crashed when the DHCP auditing log got too big. There was nothing an administrator could do to work around it

except to manually move or delete the logs. What registry keys must the administrator set to prevent this in Windows 2000? (Choose all that apply.)

   A. DhcpLogFilePath

   B. DhcpLogMinSpaceOnDisk

   C. DhcpLogDiskSpaceCheckInterval

   D. DhcpLogFileMaxSize
   B, D. The DhcpLogFilePath key lets the user specify the full path to the log file. The DhcpLogMinSpaceOnDisk allows the administrator to specify the amount of disk space left before the audit logging is stopped. The DhcpLogDiskSpaceCheckInterval is the number of times the log is written before the free space is checked. DhcpLogFileMaxSize is the maximum size of the log file in megabytes.

15. How do you configure multicast scopes in Windows 2000?

   A. Set them in the DNS settings.

   B. Set them in the WINS Settings.

   C. Set them in the gateway settings.

   D. Use the Multicast Scope Wizard.
   D. The Multicast Scope Wizard within DHCP is used to configure multicast scopes in Windows 2000.

Chapter 22 Answers

1. You have a mixture of client machines on your network. These client machines include Windows 98, Windows NT 4.0

workstations, and Windows 2000 Professional workstations. You are implementing an Internet Information Server 5.0 Web Server to host your corporate intranet. What service should you install to allow for host name resolution?

A. DHCP

B. FTP

C. DNS

D. WINS

C. DNS. To access resources on the Internet Information Server 5.0 Web Server, clients will be using their Web browsers. Web browsers are WinSock applications. WinSock applications use host name resolution. DHCP assigns IP addressing information to client machines; it does not resolve host names. FTP is used for file transfer. WINS is used for resolving NetBIOS names. WINS should undergo the process of decommissioning after a Windows 2000 deployment.

2. You have installed a Primary and a Secondary DNS server to resolve host names on your intranet. You would like to provide name resolution services for hosts on the Internet. What type of DNS server should you implement for this task?

A. Another Secondary server

B. Another Primary server

C. A Forwarder that also contains zone information

D. A Caching-only Forwarder

D. A Caching-only Forwarder. In order to protect your internal resources you want to use forwarders. However, forwarders are able to house zone information. To protect your intranet, you should implement only Caching-only forwarders if they are going to interact with DNS servers on the Internet.

3. You have installed Internet Information Server 5.0 on a machine with the host name bigboy.corp.com. You have installed the FTP and the WWW services on this machine. What resource record type would you add so users can refer to this machine as www.corp.com anf ftp.corp.com?

A. AFSDB

B. CNAME

C. MB

D. MG

B. CNAME. The CNAME record allows you to create an alias for a computer that already has another host name. This is useful when you are running multiple services on a single computer, and users are accustomed to using traditional names such as FTP, WWW, MAIL, or NEWS. *Andrew File System Database (AFSDB) server record.* Indicates the location of either of the following standard server subtypes: an AFS volume location (cell database) server, or a Distributed Computing

Environment (DCE) authenticated name server. It also supports other user-defined server subtypes that use the AFSDB resource record format. (RFC 1183). *Mailbox (MB) record.* Maps a specified domain mailbox name to a host that hosts this mailbox. (RFC 1035). *Mail group (MG) record.* Adds domain mailboxes, each specified by a mailbox (MB) record in the current zone, as members of a domain mailing group that is identified by name in this record. (RFC 1035).

4. You are in the process of putting together your DNS Domain structure and have not yet commissioned any DNS servers. Some of the users would like to access resources on your intranet via their Web browsers. What could they use in the place of the DNS server?

A. A HOSTS file
B. FTP Server Service
C. NetBT
D. RIP for IP

   A. Hosts File. A Hosts file is a plain text file that contains host name to IP address mappings. The FTP server service lives on the FTP server and will not help resolve host names to IP addresses. NetBT is a session layer interface that allows NetBIOS applications to participate on TCP/IP based networks. RIP is the Routing Information Protocol, which is used

by routers to automatically upgrade neighboring routers' routing tables.

5. You are planning a TCP/IP based Windows 2000 network. What service should you install to allow for host name resolution?

A. DHCP
B. DNS
C. NNTP
D. RIP
E. WINS

   B. DNS. Unlike all previous versions of Microsoft operating systems, Windows 2000 computer names represent host names. Microsoft networking components are WinSock applications and are no longer dependent on the NetBIOS interface to function correctly on TCP/IP based networks. NNTP is the Network News Transfer Protocol, which is used to relay messages between NNTP servers and clients. WINS is used to resolve NetBIOS names. WINS was an integral component of all prior Microsoft operating systems because of their dependence on NetBIOS. This is no longer that case, and Microsoft recommends removing NetBIOS components as soon as possible in order to complete the transition to a uniform TCP/IP based environment.

6. You have installed a DNS server on your network. Fault tolerance is a primary concern, as you want your users to be able

to continue host name resolution for your intranet in case the server crashes. What type of server would you implement?

A. Caching-only server

B. Forwarder

C. Resource Imaging server

D. a Secondary server

D. A Secondary server. The purpose of Secondary DNS servers is fault tolerance. Forwarders are servers that respond to requests from forwarding servers to resolve host names, typically host names on the Internet. A Caching-only server does not contain resource records and caches the results of iterative queries it has performed previously. Placing a Caching-only forwarder on the far side of a firewall is good protection from hackers accessing your intranet zone file information.

7. A user on a Windows 2000 Professional computer named W2KPRO1 on SubnetQ cannot connect to a Windows 2000 server computer on SubnetW with the command NET USE F: \\Bigsrv.blah.com\data. Using another Windows 2000 Professional computer on SubnetA, you succeed in making the same connection with the command NET USE F:\\ Bigsrv.blah.com\data. What is the most likely cause of the problem?

A. W2KPRO1 is not set up with the IP address of the DNS server.

B. W2KPRO1 is not set up with the IP address of the WINS server.

C. The DNS server has no entry for Bigsrv.blah.com.

D. The DNS server is not set up for WINS resolution.

A. W2KPRO1 is not set up with the IP address of the DNS server. Since the second Windows 2000 Professional computer could connect to Bigsrv.blah.com, there must be an entry in the DNS for that server. Bigsrv.blah.com is a host name, and therefore WINS would not be involved with name resolution of the server. The only possibility in this scenario is that W2KPRO1 is not configured with a DNS server to query for host name resolution.

8. You administer a TCP/IP network running 200 Windows 2000 computers and 5 Linux servers. The 200 Windows 2000 computers are all DNS-enabled clients. How can you resolve host names to IP addresses with a minimum use of static name resolution?

A. By creating a centralized LMHOSTS file on a Windows NT server computer

B. By setting up Active Desktop Services

C. By setting up DNS to use WINS

D. By setting up a Dynamic DNS server

D. A new feature of Windows 2000 DNS servers is the ability to dynamically register host name and IP address mappings. This virtually eliminates the need for static address mapping on the DNS server.

However, Linux servers are not capable of taking advantage of DDNS, and therefore you would have to manually configure A records for your Linux hosts. An LMHOSTS file maps NetBIOS names to IP addresses. Active Desktop Services does not exist. There is no need to configure DNS to use WINS because our goal is to resolve host names to IP addresses. WINS dynamically tracks NetBIOS names and IP addresses

9. You manage a network that employs DHCP, DNS, and WINS. You discover that IP address to host name resolution is not working properly. What is the best way to troubleshoot this problem?

A. Examine the Reverse lookup file using the nslookup utility.

B. Flush the DNS server's cache using NBTSTAT –n.addr.arpa.

C. Run nbtstat.exe on the Browser service.

D. Run netstat.exe –wins.nl on the WINS server.
   A. Examine the Reverse lookup file using the nslookup utility. You can use the nslookup utility to run diagnostics on your DNS server and zone database file. You can perform both Forward and Inverse lookup using nslookup. The NBTSTAT command is used to assess NetBIOS-over-TCP/IP node statistics. Netstat provides protocol statistics and current TCP/IP connections.

10. Your network has both Windows 98 and Windows 95 clients. You are running four Web servers on your intranet. What service would you install so that these Windows 9*x* machines can connect to your Web servers via their Fully Qualified Domain Names (FQDNs).

A. DHCP

B. DNS

C. FTP
   B. DNS. The purpose of DNS is to resolve host names to IP addresses. DHCP provides IP addressing information to DHCP clients on system startup. FTP is the File Transfer Protocol that allows cross-platform file transfers.

11. You would like to use the feature of DDNS. What clients are able to register with a DDNS server?

A. Windows 95.

B. Windows 3.11.

C. Windows 98.

D. Windows 2000.
   D. Only Windows 2000 clients can register their host names and IP addresses with the DDNS server automatically.

12. Which file does a DNS zone root server on your intranet use to resolve host names on the Internet?

A. cache.dns

B. domain.dns

C. HOSTS.dns

D. place.in-addr.arpa

A. cache.dns. The cache.dns file (also known as the *root hints* file) contains the IP addresses of the Internet Root name servers. When your intranet DNS server performs an iterative query to resolve a host name on the Internet, it first queries one of the root DNS servers. The <domain>.dns file is the zone file for a specific defined zone. There is no HOSTS.dns. There is no place.in-addr.arpa file.

13. How can you make non-Microsoft TCP/IP clients use WINS to resolve NetBIOS names?

A. Enable the DHCP server to resolve FQDNs.

B. Enable the DNS server to use the WINS server for name resolution.

C. Under name resolution on the client computer, list DNS first, then SMTP.

D. Under name resolution on the client computer, list SNMP first, then DNS.

B. Enable the DNS server to use the WINS server for name resolution. A Windows 2000 DNS server can be configured to query WINS servers in order to resolve NetBIOS names for down-level clients (client operating systems that predate Windows 2000). DHCP servers cannot resolve FQDNs. SMTP is the Simple Mail Transfer Protocol and is an application-layer protocol used for Internet e-mail. SNMP is Simple Network Management Protocol and is used to communicate information via MIBs (Management Information Bases) to SNMP Management software to monitor network resources. Recall that MIBs are the mechanisms used by the SNMP Agent to collect the information required by SNMP Management Software.

14. Your UNIX Hosts cannot resolve NetBIOS names of computers on remote subnets. How could you configure DNS to aid non-WINS hosts to resolve NetBIOS names?

A. Install a WinProxy Relay Unit.

B. Configure the DNS server for WINS forwarding.

C. Configure DNS for NetBIOS broadcast interception mode.

B. Non-WINS clients typically use DNS for host name resolution. These non-WINS clients can obtain the IP addresses of NetBIOS hosts if the DNS server is configured for WINS forwarding. There are no WinProxy Relay Units or NetBIOS broadcast interception modes.

15. You have just installed the DNS service on a Windows 2000 server computer. You need to add a resource record for your domain's mail server. Which resource record must you add?

A. CNAME

B. MX

C. PTR

D. WKS

B. MX. *Mail Exchanger record.*
Provides message routing to a
specified mail exchange host that is
acting as a mail exchanger for a
specified DNS domain name. MX
records use a 16-bit integer to indicate
host priority in message routing where
multiple mail exchange hosts are
specified. For each mail exchange host
specified in this record type, a
corresponding host address (A) type
record is needed. (RFC 1035).
CNAME Alias record. Indicates an
alternate or alias DNS domain name
for a name already specified in other
resource record types used in this
zone. The record is also known as the
canonical name (CNAME) record
type. (RFC 1035). *Pointer (PTR)
record.* Points to a location in the
domain name space. PTR records are
typically used in special domains to
perform Reverse lookups of
address-to-name mappings. Each
record provides simple data that
points to some other location in the
domain name space (usually a
Forward lookup zone). Where PTR
records are used, no additional section
processing is implied or caused by
their presence. (RFC 1035). *Well
Known Service (WKS) record.*
Describes the well-known TCP/IP
services supported by a particular
protocol on a particular IP address.
WKS records provide TCP and UDP
availability information for TCP/IP
servers. If a server supports both TCP

and UDP for a well-known service, or
if the server has multiple IP addresses
that support a service, then multiple
WKS records are used (RFC 1035).

Chapter 23 Answers

1. Which of the following clients can register
   their NetBIOS name with WINS?
   (Choose all that apply).

   A. Windows 98

   B. Windows NT 4.0

   C. Windows 2000

   D. UNIX

   A, B, and C. All of the listed
   Windows operating systems are
   capable of registering a NetBIOS
   name with a WINS server. Windows
   2000, however, is not dependent on
   NetBIOS name resolution for network
   functionality. UNIX machines cannot
   register with a WINS server.

2. What is the length of a NetBIOS name?

   A. 13 characters

   B. 15 characters

   C. 16 characters

   D. 23 characters

   C. A NetBIOS name consists of 16
   characters: up to 15 for the computer
   name (with missing characters padded
   with spaces), and 1 character used for
   the identifier byte.

3. What identifier byte is used to designate a
   Windows NT domain name?

   A. <1Bh>

B. <1Ch>

C. <1Dh>

D. <1Eh>

> **B.** The <1Ch> identifier byte is used to designate a domain name. All other options are also valid identifier bytes, used for other purposes.

4. Where is the LMHOSTS file stored?

A. <System Root>\System32

B. <System Root>\System32\WINS

C. <System Root>\System32\Drivers\TCPIP

D. <System Root>\System32\Drivers\Etc

> **D.** The LMHOSTS file is stored in the <System Root>\System32\Drivers\Etc path. This is also the location of the sample LMHOSTS file, LMHOSTS.SAM.

5. Which step of the name resolution process is initiated when a WINS client shuts down?

A. Name Query

B. Name Release

C. Name Removal

D. Name Tombstone

> **B.** A Name Release request is sent to the WINS server when a WINS client shuts down, informing it to remove the entry from the database.

6. A WINS client is configured to access a primary and secondary WINS server, and is using the M-Node type. An attempt to resolve a name results in no response. After querying the Primary WINS server,

which will the client next attempt for a resolution response?

A. The Secondary WINS server

B. The LMHOSTS File

C. A Local Broadcast

D. The Local Name Cache

> **A.** A client configured with multiple WINS servers will attempt to query the Secondary WINS server after a request to the Primary WINS server has timed out.

7. Using a default configuration, after how long will a WINS client first attempt to renew its lease?

A. 2 minutes

B. 16 minutes

C. 18 hours

D. 6 days

> **A.** The default Refresh Timeout on a new WINS client is 16 minutes. However, the client will first attempt to renew the lease after one-eighth of the TTL, or 2 minutes. Once the client receives a positive response to its initial refresh request, it will obtain a TTL equal to the Renew Interval defined on the server (the default is 6 days).

8. Which of the following shows the complete order of the NetBIOS Name Resolution process on an H-Node system?

A. Local Name Cache, LMHOSTS File, Broadcast, DNS, HOSTS, WINS

B. Local Name Cache, WINS, Broadcast, LMHOSTS, HOSTS, DNS

C. Local Name Cache, LMHOSTS, HOSTS, WINS, Broadcast, DNS

D. Local Name Cache, Broadcast, WINS, DNS, HOSTS, LMHOSTS File
B. The H-Node resolution process will first attempt to query WINS after checking its local name cache and before initiating a broadcast. If no response is received, the client will check LMHOSTS, HOSTS, and DNS. Remember: "Can We Buy Large Hard Drives?"

9. What is the easiest way to determine the Node Type of the local client?

A. The NodeType value in the Registry

B. By issuing the ipconfig /all | more command from a command prompt

C. In Network | TCP/IP Properties

D. Viewing the entry's properties in WINS
B. Although this could be determined by analyzing the registry, the ipconfig command is the easiest method of determining the node type currently in use.

10. Server A, Server B, and Server C are all WINS servers configured for replication. Server A is a Push/Pull partner of Server B with a 30-minute replication interval, and Server B is a push replication partner of Server C with a 15-minute replication interval. What is the convergence time for replication?

A. 15 minutes

B. 30 minutes

C. 45 minutes

D. 60 minutes
C. 45 minutes. The convergence time is calculated by determining the sum of all replication intervals.

11. A server in Columbus, OH pushes database changes to servers in Newark, NJ, Boston, MA, and Atlanta, GA. Which replication model is implemented on this network?

A. Central Replication

B. Chained Replication

C. Pull Replication

D. Push Replication
A. The Central Replication Model is demonstrated in this example, since a single server propagates changes to multiple WINS servers. Push and Pull are types of replication, not replication models.

12. The WINS Proxy Agent is used primarily to assist which of the following clients with name resolution?

A. B-Node

B. P-Node

C. M-Node

D. H-Node
A. B-Node clients use broadcasts to resolve NetBIOS names. A WINS Proxy Agent intercepts broadcasts and uses its internal name cache to send a response. If the entry is not in the local name cache, the proxy agent queries its WINS server for the information.

13. For which type of client would you configure a multihomed entry?

    A. A mobile user

    B. A server with multiple names

    C. A server with multiple network interfaces

    D. A server acting as a Windows NT domain controller
    C. The multihomed static entry type allows the administrator to enter multiple IP addresses for a single machine name.

14. You are attempting to restore a WINS database backup to a WINS server; however, the Restore Database option in the Action menu is grayed out. What is the most likely cause for not being able to select the Restore option?

    A. A backup has not been performed on this server.

    B. The backup files are missing from the WINS directory.

    C. The user logged in does not have the appropriate permissions.

    D. The WINS service has not been stopped.
    D. A restore operation cannot be completed until the WINS service has been stopped, At which point, the restore option will become available in the Action menu.

15. As an administrator of a WINS server, you want to determine the total number of queries that have been attempted against the database that have returned negative responses. Which of the following statistics will you use?

    A. Total Releases: Records Not Found

    B. Total Queries: Records Not Found

    C. Unique Registrations: Conflicts

    D. Name Queries: Negative Responses
    B. The Total Queries: Records Not Found statistic captures information about the number of negative name query responses issued.

Chapter 24 Answers

1. Remote Access Servers are a component of what Windows 2000 feature set?

    A. Internet Information Server

    B. Certificate Services

    C. Remote Installation Services

    D. Routing and Remote Access Services
    D. Routing and Remote Access Services. Remote Access Servers are an integral part of the Windows 2000 Routing and Remote Access strategy. These servers provide the physical interface for clients to connect via dial-up or VPN solutions.

2. Which Remote Access Server protocol supports multiple Network layer protocols?

    A. IAS

    B. PPP

    C. SLIP

D. MS RAS

B. PPP. The Point-to-Point Protocol supports multiple Network layer protocols, such as TCP/IP, IPX/SPX, and NetBEUI.

3. What remote access protocol was developed primarily for UNIX systems and supports the TCP/IP network protocol?

A. PPP

B. IAS

C. SLIP

D. MS RAS

C. SLIP. The Serial Line Interface Protocol is an older remote access protocol that was designed for UNIX systems. This protocol is no longer widely in use and is found on legacy systems.

4. What remote access protocol is used for older Microsoft clients such as Windows 3.1 and MS-DOS?

A. PPP

B. IAS

C. SLIP

D. MS RAS

D. MS RAS. This protocol is used in older Windows-based operating systems and is based on NetBIOS-based network services. This is usually only used to provide backward compatibility with these legacy Windows systems.

5. What does VPN stand for?

A. Virtual Private Network

B. Virtual Public Network

C. Virtual Private Name

D. Virtual Public Name

A. Virtual Private Network. Virtual Private Networks are used to provide a secure communication channel over a public network such as the Internet. Although a newer technology, it is widely in use today.

6. What tool is used to manage the hardware required for RAS servers?

A. Administrative Tools

B. Hardware Setup

C. Add/Remove Programs applet

D. Device Manager

D. Device Manager. This applet, found in the Control Panel under System, is used to manage the hardware used for Routing and Remote Access services such as modems, network cards, or ISDN devices.

7. What Remote Access configuration option would be selected to install the Internet Connection Sharing services?

A. Network router

B. Internet server

C. Internet connection server

D. Manually configured server

C. Internet connection server. To install Internet Connection Sharing, or ICS, the Internet connection server configuration option is chosen. This allows multiple users on the same network to use this Internet connection.

8. What kind of management strategy can be used when implementing Remote Access Services?

   A. Centralized

   B. Distributed

   C. Centralized and distributed

   D. None of the above
   C. Centralized and distributed. With RAS servers, options are available for both management strategies. They depend upon the business requirements and model of the organization implementing them.

9. What does RADIUS stand for?

   A. Remote Authentication Dial-In User Service

   B. Remote Access for Dial-In User Setup

   C. Remote Administration for User Dial-In Services

   D. None of the above
   A. Remote Authentication Dial-In User Service. RADIUS is a protocol used to provide a scalable, secure remote access solution.

10. Which of the following protocols is not supported in Windows 2000 RADIUS services?

    A. Extensible Authentication Protocol (EAP)

    B. HyperText Transport Protocol Secured (HTTPS)

    C. Password Authentication Protocol (PAP)

    D. Challenge Handshake and Response Protocol (CHAP)
    B. HyperText Transport Protocol Secured (HTTPS). Although HTTPS is used for secure communications by other services, it is not supported in RADIUS services.

11. What component in Windows 2000 is used to provide RADIUS host services?

    A. Internet Information Services

    B. Certificate Services

    C. Remote Installation Services

    D. Internet Authentication Services
    D. Internet Authentication Services. Internet Authentication Services (IAS) is used to centrally authenticate and audit user logins for RADIUS implementation. IAS is the RADIUS host component included with Windows 2000.

12. What is used by the Internet Authentication Server to verify that communications between the RADIUS host and client are secure?

    A. Client IP address

    B. Vendor Type option

    C. Shared Secret

    D. None of the above
    C. Shared Secret. The shared secret is a phrase or set of characters that are used to identify the two computers to each other during communication.

13. Which of the following are not factors when considering the management strategy for RADIUS services?

    A. Physical Security

    B. Dedicated Server

    C. RADIUS Server placed behind a firewall

    D. None of the above
       D. None of the above. All of the options listed are important factors when considering what will be used and managed in any organization.

14. Which of the following are new features included with the Windows 2000 implementation of Routing and Remote Access Services?

    A. Internet Information Server 5.0

    B. Certificate Services

    C. Layer 2 Tunneling Protocol

    D. Terminal Services
       C. Layer 2 Tunneling Protocol. The Layer 2 Tunneling Protocol, or L2TP, is a security protocol used in VPN solutions to provide a secure communications channel.

Chapter 25 Answers

1. Which of the following is true of Connection Manager?

    A. It supports only local connections to your network or service.

    B. It supports only remote connections to your network or service.

    C. It supports both local and remote connections to your network or service.

    D. It supports neither local nor remote connections to your network or service.
       C. It supports both local and remote connections to your network or service, using a network of access points (such as those available worldwide through ISPs).

2. What is branding?

    A. The ability to run commercially available applications while Connection Manager is running.

    B. The ability to customize graphics, icons, and text on the Connection Manager interface.

    C. The ability to run more than one instance of Connection Manager at a time.

    D. The ability to allow users who share a computer to use the same service profile.
       B. Branding refers to customizing the Connection Manager interface by using your company's logo, special graphics, icons, and text identifying your organization that your employees or customers use to establish the connection to your network.

3. Which of the following would be an effective utilization of the Connection

Manager software for an enterprise organization?

A. To allow employees who telecommute or take work home to connect to the company network easily and quickly without configuring their own settings.

B. To allow customers access to parts of the company's network.

C. To allow sales personnel who are on the road to connect to the company's network easily, even if they are not technically savvy.

D. All of the above.

D. All of the above. Microsoft's Connection Manager can accomplish all of these objectives, making it easy for both employees and customers to connect to the company's network from other business locations, from home, or on the road, without requiring that the users be technically savvy or configure their own dial-up or VPN settings.

4. Which of the following is *not* one of the four stages of implementing Connection Manager (according to Microsoft)?

A. Planning, which includes a planning worksheet to simplify design and implementation of your plan.

B. Installing the TCP/IP protocol on the user machines.

C. Running the CMAK Wizard and creating a service profile.

D. Preparing for integration, delivery, and installation.

B. The second stage of planning, according to Microsoft, is developing custom elements. Planning, running the CMAK Wizard, and preparing for integration, delivery, and installation are the other three specified stages. The Connection Manager software will automatically install the required protocols on user machines if they are not present.

5. What is the maximum number of characters for the designated file name to be used by the files created in the CMAK Wizard?

A. 45

B. 5

C. 18

D. 8

D. The file name can be up to 8 alpha-numeric characters. None of the following characters should be used: ! , ; <space> * = \ / : ? ' " < > | . % + [ ] $ #.

6. What are realm names used for? (Choose all that apply.)

A. Network routing

B. Identifying your company in the logon dialog box

C. Authentication

D. Identifying the author of the Connection Manager software

A, C. Realm names are required by some networks or services, to be used for routing and authentication. They are not used to identify the company in the logon dialog box, and they are not used to identify the author of the Connection Manager software.

7. When you enable VPN support, if you don't use a DHCP server to assign IP addresses, what addresses must you specify in the CMAK Wizard dialog box? (Choose two.)

A. The name of a Terminal server

B. The IP address of a DNS server

C. The IP address of a WINS server

D. The IP address of a TCP/IP server
B, C. A DHCP server can automatically assign DNS and WINS server addresses, but if you do not have a DHCP server on the network or do not wish to use DHCP to assign addresses, you must designate a DNS and WINS server manually in the CMAK Wizard dialog box. There is no need to designate a Terminal server in order to establish a VPN, and there is no such thing as a TCP/IP server.

8. Which of the following is a valid phone book file name?

A. phonebookfile.pbk

B. phonefile.phb

C. phfile.phb

D. phonefle.pbk
D. A phonebook file should be limited to 8 characters, and should have a .pbk extension.

9. Which of the following protocols is used for establishing a VPN connection? (Choose all that apply.)

A. IPX

B. PPTP

C. SLIP

D. LTPT
B. Point-to-Point Tunneling Protocol (PPTP) is used to establish a VPN connection. Windows 2000 also supports L2TP for VPNs, not LTPT. SLIP is an older WAN (dial-up) protocol, and IPX is used mostly in connecting to Novell NetWare networks.

10. What is a service profile called when it contains information from other service profiles?

A. A merged profile

B. A merging profile

C. A referencing profile

D. A multiple profile
C. A service profile that contains information from other service profiles is known as a referencing profile. The profile that has its information merged into another is called the merged profile.

11. Which of the following terms refers to programs designated to run when users connect to your service, at one of four points in the connection process?

A. Seamless applications

B. Connect actions

C. Auto-programming

D. Four-point programs
B. Connect actions. Programs that you can specify to run at one of four points during the user's connection session are called connect actions. They can be pre-connect, pre-tunnel, post-connect, or disconnect actions.

12. How do auto-applications differ from connect actions?

A. Auto-applications run asynchronously, and connect actions run synchronously.

B. Auto-applications run as DDLs, and connect actions do not.

C. Auto-applications run prior to connection, but not during a connection.

D. Auto-applications must be started by the user, and connect actions are not.
A. Auto-applications run asynchronously, while connect actions run synchronously. Connect actions run as DDLs. Auto-applications can run during a connection, and do not have to be started by the user.

13. Which of the following is true of custom icons that you use with Connection Manager? (Choose all that apply.)

A. They should be 256 colors.

B. The same .ico file should be used for all the icons for best results.

C. They should be 16 colors.

D. They should all be similar in design and appearance, but different sizes.
C, D. Your custom icons should be designed to be similar in appearance for a uniform look, and they should be 16-color .ico files. Although it is possible to use the same file for all icons, there may be some distortion due to resizing, so this is not recommended.

14. If more than one file is needed for a connect action, how do you specify the second and subsequent files?

A. Enter them all in the Connect Action dialog box.

B. Enter the first three in the Connect Action dialog box, then enter the rest in the Additional Files dialog box.

C. Enter the first one in the Connect Action dialog box, then enter the rest in the Additional Files dialog box.

D. You cannot use connect actions that require more than one file to run.
D. Only one file can be entered in the Connect Actions dialog box for each connect action. If more than one is required, the rest must be entered in the Additional Files dialog box near the end of the Wizard.

15. How can the Connection Manager software and a service profile be integrated with the distribution of Internet Explorer?

A. The Connection Manager Wizard supports incorporating an IEAK package into your Connection Manager package.

B. The Internet Explorer Administration Kit Wizard supports incorporating a Connection Manager package into the IEAK package.

C. You can incorporate the Connection Manager software into the IEAK package using the Connection Manager wizard, but the service profile will have to be distributed separately.

D. You cannot integrate the distribution of Connection Manager and Internet Explorer.
B. The IEAK supports incorporation of Connection Manager and a service profile into the Internet Explorer package. This is done using the Internet Explorer Administration Kit Wizard.

Chapter 26 Answers

1. What must you configure for static routing?

A. RIP for Internet Protocol

B. Enable IP Forwarding

C. RIP for IPX/SPX

D. Enable ROUTE service
B. Enable IP Forwarding

2. What does OSPF stand for?

A. Operating System Protocol Forwarder

B. Offer and Selection Permanent Frame

C. Open Shortest Path First

D. Open Secure Path Frame
C. Open Shortest Path First

3. What does RIP provide?

A. Static Routing

B. Dynamic Routing

C. Static Routing Information Display

D. Dynamic Routing Information Display
B. Dynamic Routing-use the ROUTE command to display route information.

4. How many IP addresses can be maintained for one network interface?

A. 1

B. 2

C. 5

D. 255
C. 5 IP addresses per network interface.

5. What is the default Network Mask for a Class B network?

A. 255.255.255.255

B. 255.255.255.0

C. 255.255.0.0

D. 255.0.0.0
C. 255.255.0.0

6. What is the default Network Mask for six subnets in a Class B network? (Hint: Subnets is 2**n-2 where n is the number of bits.)

A. 255.255.255.248

B. 255.255.255.240

C. 255.255.224.0

D. 255.192.0.0
   C. 255.255.224.0—requires 3
   bits for 6

7. How many bits does IP version 4.x use.

   A. 8

   B. 16

   C. 32

   D. 128
      C. 32 bits

8. How many bits in a Class A network addresses can be used for client numbers?

   A. 16

   B. 24

   C. 32

   D. 128
      B. 24 bits

9. What is the total number of client address values available in a Class B network address?

   A. 16 million

   B. 64,000

   C. 65,533

   D. 128
      C. 65,533

10. Which of the following is an acceptable loopback address?

    A. 127.23.45.67

    B. 255.255.255.0

C. 12.0.0.1

D. 255.255.255.192
   A. 127.23.45.67

Chapter 27 Answers

1. What makes a VPN "private"?

   A. It does not allow any communication into or out of the user's PC.

   B. It uses a protocol that allows encrypted, point-to-point connections.

   C. Only one user can access a server at a time.

   D. Nothing that is typed in during a VPN session appears on the user's monitor.
      B. It uses a protocol that allows encrypted point-to-point connections. More than one user can access a server using VPN, and VPN will allow a user's PC to communicate to a network.

2. Which statement is true?

   A. RAS is not as expensive as VPN.

   B. VPN requires a special modem on a laptop/PC.

   C. VPN can provide an alternative to modem pools.

   D. RAS uses PPP to create a VPN.
      C. VPN can provide an alternative to modem pools. RAS is typically more expensive if long-distance calls are made. VPN does not require a special

modem. PPP does not provide the security necessary for a VPN.

3. Which components could be used to create a VPN? (Choose all that apply.)

   A. ISDN adapter

   B. 56 Kbps modem

   C. DSL

   D. Router

   A, B, C, and D. All the above devices can be used to connect to the Internet. An Internet connection is a basic component of all VPNs.

4. Which statement is false?

   A. VPNs can save a company money.

   B. A VPN server does not necessarily have to connect to the Internet.

   C. RAS uses modem pools to provide users with dial-up connections.

   D. AOL is an Internet Service Provider.

   D. AOL is an online service that uses proprietary protocols and interfaces in order to access their private network. Like other online services, AOL provides a "portal" to the Internet via their private network, but connections to AOL do not comply with standard Internet technologies and specifications.

5. What is a major drawback of traditional dial-up methods?

   A. Can be used over the Internet

   B. Requires ISDN lines

   C. High cost

   D. New technology

   C. Conventional RAS connections via direct dial-up often lead to high phone bills for the company. By using VPN over the Internet, telecommunications costs are slashed.

6. Which statement(s) is true?

   A. You must connect to an ISP first before establishing a VPN connection via the Internet.

   B. After establishing an Internet connection, you next dial up the VPN server.

   C. You can use L2TP to connect on a network that uses NAT.

   D. PPTP does not use encryption for authentication.

   A, B. The creation of a VPN connection via the Internet is a two-step process. First, you dial up an ISP and establish a PPP connection. Next, you dial the VPN Server. L2TP cannot be used with NAT.

7. What must first be installed before PPTP can be added to a Windows 2000 server?

   A. Modem

   B. Routing and Remote Access Service

   C. IPSec

   D. Router

   B. The Routing and Remote Access Service must be installed prior to implementing a VPN server using either PPTP or L2TP. A connection to the network is required. A modem is not required if connections are to be established via dedicated lines.

8. How many connections can be made to a VPN server?

A. 10

B. 128

C. 1024

D. Limited only by hardware and connection type limitations.
D. Microsoft has not hard-coded any logical limits to the number of simultaneous VPN connections. The only limitations are those related to hardware and connection type characteristics.

9. Name two authentication Providers for Windows 2000 VPN connections.

A. RADIUS

B. Windows 2000 Security

C. DIAMETER

D. R2D2
A, B. VPN client connections can be authenticated either via RADIUS or conventional Windows 2000 authentication providers.

10. A user is attempting to connect to a VPN server. What information could you provide to allow connection to the server? (Choose all that apply.)

A. IP address of client machine

B. IP address of VPN server

C. Phone number for VPN server modem

D. The Fully Qualified Domain Name
B, D. You can connect to the VPN server by using either the IP address or the Fully Qualified Domain Name (FQDN). The IP address of the client machine and the phone number for the VPN server modem (if indeed, it has a modem) are not required.

11. Which tool can you use to see who is logged on through the VPN?

A. Routing and Remote Access Console

B. Server Manager

C. Performance Monitor

D. PPTP Manager
A. Routing and Remote Access Console. Server Manager is a Windows NT component. Performance Monitor is for watching your server's behavior. PPTP Manager doesn't exist.

12. Which tool can be used to monitor the VPN server processor for overutilization?

A. RAS Administrator

B. Performance Snap-in

C. Administrator Tools

D. Processor Monitor
B. Performance Console. There is no RAS Administrator in Windows 2000, although this tool was used in Windows NT. Administrator Tools and Processor Monitor do not exist.

13. What tool do you use to create a client connection to a VPN server?

A. RAS Administrator

B. RAS tools

C. Network Connection Wizard

D. Network Properties dialog box
C. Network Connection Wizard. The other options do not exist.

14. What are some important things to consider when planning a management strategy for your VPN network?

A. Fault Tolerance

B. Capacity Planning

C. Authentication Methods

D. IP Address assignments
A, B, C, and D. All of these are important when designing a VPN management strategy.

15. Which of the following Microsoft operating systems can be a VPN client (Choose all that apply)?

A. Windows 3.11

B. Windows 95/98

C. Windows NT Workstation

D. Windows 2000 Professional
B, C, and D. Microsoft Windows 95, 98, NT, and 2000 Professional all have built-in support for acting as VPN clients. Windows 3.11 (Windows for Workgroups) is not supported as a VPN client.

Chapter 28 Answers

1. Which item is not a common feature of proxy servers?

A. Firewall capabilities

B. Caching

C. Routing

D. Reverse hosting
C. Routing. While it is possible to use a proxy server as a router, it is not a task normally assigned to proxy servers. The additional load of routing would have an adverse impact on the performance of the proxy server, and vice versa.

2. What two fields are used by Web Proxy to accomplish reverse proxying?

A. Request path

B. URL

C. Route to

D. Proxy path
A, C. The request path is the path in the URL that is requested by the client. Route to is where the Web Proxy retrieves the object, which will be returned to the client.

3. Which of the following three services are used by Proxy Server?

A. Web Proxy service

B. FTP Proxy service

C. WinSock Proxy service

D. SOCKS Proxy service
A, C, D. The three services provided by Proxy Server are Web Proxy, WinSock Proxy, and SOCKS Proxy. FTP proxying is handled by the Web Proxy service.

4. What is the most powerful firewall feature of Proxy Server?

    A. Domain filters

    B. Socks Proxy service

    C. Distributed caching

    D. Packet filters
        D. Packet filters allow administrators to specify exactly what types of packets are allowed to pass through the server.

5. Domain Filters set in the shared Security properties affect what Proxy Services?

    A. Web Proxy

    B. WinSock Proxy

    C. Socks Proxy

    D. None
        A, B. Setting domain filters will affect all the Web Proxy and WinSock Proxy services. Permission settings on the Socks property allow filtering specific domains as well.

6. Proxy Server can generate alerts for what three events?

    A. CPU utilization

    B. Rejected packets

    C. Protocol violation

    D. Disk full
        B, C, and D. Alerts can be sent to the Windows NT Event Log or via SMTP mail for rejected packets, protocol violations, and disk full events. Proxy server does not have an option to monitor CPU utilization, although Windows NT/2000 Performance Monitor can be used for that purpose.

7. What protocols are handled by the Web Proxy service? (Choose all that apply.)

    A. HTTP

    B. FTP

    C. NNTP

    D. Gopher
        A, B, and D. The Web Proxy service is used for the HTTP, HTTPS, FTP, and Gopher protocols.

8. Which type of caching is not a function of Proxy Server?

    A. Client-based caching

    B. Chain-based caching

    C. Single server caching

    D. Array-based caching
        A. Most Web browsers maintain a cache on the client, but this is not a function of Proxy Server.

9. What protocol is used between Proxy Servers to maintain the distributed cache?

    A. HTTP

    B. CARP

    C. FTP

    D. SMB
        B. CARP (Cache Array Routing Protocol) was developed by Microsoft to perform array and chain-based content caching.

10. What three items are most important for a successful Proxy Server implementation?

    A. Security considerations

    B. Hardware sizing

    C. User training

D. Client deployment

A, B, and D. The bulk of your planning time should be dedicated to proper hardware sizing, security configuration issues, and a client deployment plan. There is virtually no user training needed, except maybe to tell users to not change their browser's connection configuration.

11. How much disk space is recommended for the Web Proxy Cache for 1500 clients?

A. 1.5GB

B. 75MB

C. 750MB

D. 3GB

C. 750MB. Microsoft recommends having enough disk space for the cache to hold .5MB for each client. 1500 × .5MB = 750MB.

12. What two features does a RAID disk array provide?

A. Improved performance

B. Fault tolerance

C. Security

D. Lower cost

A, B. A RAID array provides fault tolerance and better performance than disks that aren't in an array. However, RAID does not make the system more secure, and it costs much more than JBD (just a bunch of disks).

13. What is the command line to silently install the Proxy client on Windows 95?

A. Setup /qt

B. Setup /q1

C. Setup /u

D. Setup /s

A. Setup /qt is the command line to silently install the Proxy client on a 32-bit client. The /q1 switch is used for 16-bit clients, and the /u switch is used to uninstall.

14. What is the GUI application used for Proxy Server administration?

A. Proxy Server Administration Console

B. Microsoft Management Console

C. Server Manager

D. User Manager

B. Proxy Server utilizes the Microsoft Management Console for administration. Proxy services are included under the Internet Information Services with Web and FTP sites.

15. What two command-line utilities are available to manage Proxy Server?

A. ProxAdmn

B. WspProto

C. RemotMsp

D. RemotWsp

B, C. WspProto is the command-line tool used to configure WinSock protocols. RemotMsp is used to start, stop, and view Proxy Server services, back up and restore the configuration, and manage arrays.

Chapter 29 Answers

1. What protocol does the WWW use?

    A. FTP

    B. HTTP

    C. IPX

    D. Hyperlink
    B. HTTP. FTP is a service. IPX is a transport protocol and has nothing to do with Internet technologies.

2. Which of the following statements is true about a virtual server?

    A. IIS can host multiple virtual servers.

    B. A virtual server appears on the network and then disappears.

    C. Each virtual server must have its own IP address.

    D. Each virtual server must have its own network card.
    A, C. Each virtual server must have its own IP address but you can use a single NIC to host many virtual servers.

3. Which port does the WWW service monitor for a client connection?

    A. 20

    B. 21

    C. 70

    D. 80
    D. Port 80. FTP uses ports 21 and 20.

4. Which characteristics are necessary for you to specify access to a resource on a Web server?

    A. How access is to occur

    B. The MAC address of the server

    C. The host

    D. A path to the object
    A, C, and D. How access is to occur, the host, and a path to the object. While the communication will eventually need the MAC address, the ARP protocol takes care of this for you; you do not need to specify it.

5. You receive a call from a user stating that he is trying to connect to your Web server and receives the error message, "Internet Explorer cannot open the Internet site…" What may be causing this happening?

    A. The user does not have TCP/IP loaded.

    B. The default gateway is down.

    C. He is trying to access the Web server using the wrong TCP port number for the server.

    D. The Web server is down.
    C. This is the best possible answer of the choices given. Either the client is specifying the wrong port number or your server is not monitoring port 80.

6. You want to restrict the amount of bandwidth your Web server might use on the network. What is the best way to accomplish this?

    A. Use a slower network card.

    B. Enable bandwidth throttling in the Performance tab.

    C. Limit the number of concurrent users at the server.

D. Keep the server busy with other processes so that it has less time to service Web request.
B. Enable bandwidth throttling in the Performance tab. Using a slower network card is not a good idea. Limiting the number of concurrent users might have the desired effect and it might not.

7. Which of the following statements is correct about keep-alives?

A. Keep-alives keep the server running in the event of a power outage.

B. A keep-alive restarts a file copy in the event you are accidentally disconnected from the server.

C. Keep-alives have something to do with life insurance.

D. Keep-alives maintain the client connection so that the client's browser doesn't have to make a connection with each request.
D. Keep-alives maintain the client connection so that the client's browser doesn't have to make a connection with each request.

8. To transfer files using FTP, what must be in place?

A. A default gateway

B. An FTP server

C. A WWW server

D. An FTP client
B, D. FTP is a client/server process.

You don't need a default gateway if you are on the same network segment.

9. Which protocol does FTP Use?

A. TFTP

B. IPX

C. TCP

D. NetBIOS
C. TCP. TFTP and NetBIOS are not transport protocols.

10. Which of the following are features of the TCP protocol?

A. It provides error correction.

B. It does not provide error correction.

C. It provides flow control.

D. It supports TFTP.
A, C. TCP provides error correction and flow control. TFTP uses UDP, not TCP.

11. Which port does the FTP service monitor for a connection request?

A. 20

B. 21

C. 1024

D. Any available port
B. The FTP service monitors port 21 for connections. It uses port 20 for data connections.

12. Which ports does the FTP service use to transfer files?

A. 20

B. 21

C. Any port above 1023 set by the client

D. 2

A. The FTP service monitors port 21 for the connection and uses port 20 for data transfer connections.

13. Which of the following is not an FTP command?

A. Dir

B. Bye

C. Get

D. Copy

D. Copy is DOS command. It is also used by other operating systems.

14. You are preparing to set up several virtual servers on your IIS computer. You want these virtual servers to have properties in common. Which property sheet should you modify?

A. Default

B. Master

C. IIS

D. MMC

B. The Master property sheet provides inheritance for all FTP servers created. IIS is the server and MMC is the management console.

15. You want to set your FTP server to only allow anonymous connections. How can you accomplish this?

A. Disable the IUSR_*servername* account

B. Create an anonymous account in User Manager.

C. Select the Connections tab and clear all users from the Allowed to Connect box.

D. Select the Security Accounts tab and check the Allow Only Anonymous Connections box.

D. Select the Security Accounts tab and check the Allow Only Anonymous Connections box. If you disable the IUSR account, no one will be able to log on. Creating an anonymous user is not necessary; that is what the IUSR account is for. There is no Connections tab.

B

About the
Web Site

Access Global Knowledge

As you know by now, Global Knowledge is the largest independent IT training company in the world. Just by purchasing this book, you have also secured a free subscription to the Global Knowledge Web site and its many resources. You can find it at: http://access.globalknowledge.com

You can log on directly at the Global Knowledge site, and you will be e-mailed a new, secure password immediately upon registering.

What You'll Find There. . .

The wealth of useful information at the Global Knowledge site falls into three categories:

Skills Gap Analysis

Global Knowledge offers several ways for you to analyze your networking skills and discover where they may be lacking. Using Global Knowledge's trademarked Competence Key Tool, you can do a skills gap analysis and get recommendations for where you may need to do some more studying. (Sorry, it just might not end with this book!)

Networking

You'll also gain valuable access to another asset: people. At the Access Global site, you'll find threaded discussions, as well as live discussions. Talk to other MCSD candidates, get advice from folks who have already taken the exams, and get access to instructors and MCTs.

Product Offerings

Of course, Global Knowledge also offers its products here, and you may find some valuable items for purchase—CBTs, books, or courses. Browse freely and see if there's something that could help you take that next step in career enhancement.

Glossary

Accelerate Graphics Port (AGP)   An Intel-created high-speed graphics port providing direct display adapter and memory connection (with the memory at twice the PCI bus speed).

Account Domain   The account domain is the one in which the user resides.

Account Policies   Configures policies for passwords, account lockout, and Kerberos.

Acknowledgement (ACK)   When sending a packet, the sending computer expects to "hear back" from the receiving computer that it received the data packet. This is called an acknowledgement (ACK).

Active Directory   A Windows 2000 or Windows NT 5.0 hierarchical directory service. It is designed to help administrators organize network resources and allow users easy access to those resources, while providing tight security within the network. The Active Directory database has been tested for up to 1.5 million objects.

Active Directory Policies   Configures security on specific Directory objects.

Address Resolution Protocol (ARP)   An IP (Internet Protocol) that maps Internet addresses dynamically to the actual addresses on a Local Area Network (LAN). ARP performs IP address to Media Access Control (MAC) address resolution. When each outgoing IP datagram is encapsulated in a frame, its source and destination MAC addresses must be added. ARP is responsible for determining the destination MAC address for each frame. ARP compares the destination IP address on every outbound IP datagram to the ARP cache for the NIC that the frame will be sent over.

Advanced Configuration and Power Interface (ACPI)   ACPI combines Plug and Play capability with Power Management, and places these functions under complete control of the operating system.

Advanced Research Projects Agency Network (ARPAnet)   A Wide Area Network (WAN) supported by the U.S. Department of Defense (DoD) Advanced Research Projects Agency (DARPA) and intended to support advanced scientific research. Its broader communication function was taken over by the National Science Foundation NETwork (NSFNET).

Advanced Startup Options   Provides ability to load the operating system when files used in the normal boot process have been damaged or corrupted.

American National Standards Institute (ANSI)   A U.S.-based organization for establishing many data communications and terminal standards and standards for the information processing industry such COBOL and FORTRAN.

Application Launching & Embedding (ALE)   Application Launching & Embedding (ALE) makes it easy to integrate Windows- and Web-based applications without rewriting the code, thereby saving time and money.

Array Controller   An array controller is a Small Computer System Interface (SCSI) controller that has software routines built into the chipset that allows it to mirror, or stripe drives automatically so the operating system does not have to worry about it.

Attribute Definition Objects   Similar to Class Definition Objects, Attribute Definition Objects are used to store information about the available attributes in the directory. When an attribute is created, a definition object is instantiated in the attributeSchema class.

Attributed Indexing Similar to indexing in a database, an attribute can be indexed to allow for faster searching. You should index an attribute when frequent searches are performed that need to order information based on the attribute value. Indexed attributes should typically be unique for most objects—there is no use indexing an attribute that maintains consistently identical values for all objects. Also, only single-value attributes should be indexed.

Attributes Attributes are "flags" on a file or directory that enable specific system options. These attributes can be enabled on the General tab of a file or directory's Properties window, or by using the attrib command from a command prompt (the first four only).

Audit Results Audited information about an object's access is stored in the Security Event Log of the server on which the file resides. It is therefore possible in a DFS hierarchy for audit results to be distributed among multiple servers, depending on where the physical object is located. The audit results stored in the Event Log will be stored for a period of time defined by the properties of the Security Event Log.

Auditing Auditing is used to track specific events that occur on a Windows 2000 computer, including those initiated by users and those performed by the system.

Authoritative Restore Authoritative Restore ensures that all DCs have the same information after an Active Directory restoration.

AutoComplete Helps with the entry of long Internet and network locations by automatically completing entries with previously used ones.

Automatic Client Configuration Automatic Client Configuration, or Automatic Private IP Addressing, is a new feature that was initially available in Windows 98. The feature has been extended to Windows 2000 and allows DHCP client computers to self-configure their IP addressing information in the event a DHCP server is not available when the computer issues a DHCPDISCOVER message, or when it senses that it has been moved from a previous network via Windows 2000 media sensing capabilities. This system allows a DHCP client that is unable to obtain an IP address from a DHCP server to configure itself to temporarily use an IP address from a preassigned range.

Automatic Private IP Addressing (APIPA) Automatic Private IP Addressing, or Automatic Client Configuration, is a new feature that was initially available in Windows 98. The feature has been extended to Windows 2000 and allows DHCP client computers to self-configure their IP addressing information in the event a DHCP server is not available when the computer issues a DHCPDISCOVER message, or when it senses that it has been moved from a previous network via Windows 2000 media sensing capabilities. This system allows a DHCP client that is unable to obtain an IP address from a DHCP server to configure itself to temporarily use an IP address from a preassigned range.

Backbone In a Wide Area Network (WAN) such as the Internet, a high-speed, high-capacity medium that is designed to transfer data over hundreds or thousands of miles and connect usually shorter, slower circuits.

Balloon Help A Windows ToolTips variation that offers more extensive help on selected items. Instead of one- or two-word names of a screen feature, Balloon Help offers descriptions of the selected feature, and the options that the user can perform with it.

BIOS (Basic Input/Output System) A set of programs encoded in ROM on IBM PC-compatible computers programs handle startup operations such as POST and low-level control for hardware such as disk drives, keyboards, etc.

BOOTP Bootstrapping Protocol.

Branding   This refers to customization of the installation package that you deliver to your customers.

Bridge   A bridge provides selective connection between LANs where only packets destined for the other side cross the bridge.

Broadcast Node (B-Node)   The Broadcast Node uses broadcasts as the primary method of resolving a NetBIOS name. This is the most simplistic node type, as a WINS server is not required. The B-Node client sends a name query to the broadcast address, and any client with the requested name responds to the broadcast.

CDFS (CD-ROM File System)   The CDFS is a Read-Only file system that enables Windows 2000 to access data on CD-ROMs. The CDFS file implemented in Windows 2000 is fully ISO 9660 compliant. The ISO 9660 standard defines a method for storing data on a CD that can be accessed by various hardware platforms and operating systems, including UNIX and MacOS.

Central Replication Model   This is one of two ways to configure WINS replication in a network spanning multiple locations. The Central Replication Model is usually the most practical means of implementing WINS replication. This model works best in networks that have a single "hub" location, to which other sites have a direct link.

Chained Replication Model   This is one of two ways to configure WINS replication in a network spanning multiple locations. The Chained Replication Model is used on networks that are designed in a linear layout, where it is practical for a server to pass replication to other servers in a chained manner. In Chained Replication Models, the servers at both ends of the chain should be push/pull partners with one another to ensure consistency.

Checksum　The checksum is a calculation done by the sending computer and is attached to the data packet. When the receiving computer gets the packet it calculates the checksum on the data and compares that value to the checksum value contained in the packet (the one calculated by the sending computer). If the two values are the same, the receiver assumes that the data was transmitted without error. If the two values are different, the receiving station sends a negative acknowledgement (NACK) back to the sender.

Citrix MetaFrame　Citrix MetaFrame is server-based software designed to work with Microsoft's Windows 2000 Server with Terminal Services installed. The purpose of MetaFrame is to extend the Windows Terminal Services by providing additional client and server functionality. This includes support for heterogeneous computing environments, enterprise-scale management, and seamless desktop integration. Using MetaFrame with Terminal Services provides improved application manageability, access, performance, and security. Citrix MetaFrame system software, which incorporates Citrix's Independent Computing Architecture (ICA), provides a complete Server-based computing solution for multiuser Windows 2000 environments.

Class Definition Objects　Each class is actually an instance of the classSchema class. Objects in this class are known as Class Definition Objects.

Client Access License (CAL)　The CAL allows clients to access the Windows 2000's network services, shared folders, and printers.

Client Installation Wizard　The Client Installation Wizard starts when the computer boots. The user is then presented with four options: Automatic setup; custom setup; Restart a Previous Setup Attempt; and Maintenance and Troubleshooting.

Clusters Clusters are the areas of space broken down in the hard disk structure on a partition using the FAT file system.

Comma-Delimited File A data file, often in the ASCII format, for which the data items are separated by commas to speed data transfer to another program.

Component Object Model (COM) A Microsoft component software architecture, which defines a structure to help in building objects. COM can provide an interface between these objects.

Component Object Model Enhanced (COM+) Allows easier development for programmers.

Connection Failure The number of times TCP connections have made a direct transition to the CLOSED state from the SYN-SENT state or the SYN-RCVD state, plus the number of times TCP connections have made a direct transition to the LISTEN state from the SYN-RCVD state.

Connection Manager The Windows 2000 Connection Manager is client dialer software that provides a custom user interface for dialing and accessing the Internet and corporate resources. Connection Manager supports local and remote connections to your service using a network of access points. You can also use Connection Manager to establish Virtual Private Network connections to your service (secure connections through the Internet).

Connection-Oriented Protocol A connection-oriented protocol establishes a session between the client and the server before any information is exchanged.

Connections Active The number of times TCP connections have made a direct transition to the SYN-SENT state from the CLOSED state.

Connections Established   The number of TCP connections for which the current state is either ESTABLISHED or CLOSE-WAIT.

Connections Passive   The number of times TCP connections have made a direct transition to the SYN-RCVD state from the LISTEN state.

Connections Reset   The number of times TCP connections have made a direct transition to the CLOSED state from either the ESTABLISHED state or the CLOSE-WAIT state.

Container Object   Container objects that can contain other objects are known as container objects. A special type of container object that you can create in the Active Directory is the Organizational Unit (OU).

Containers   Containers are used to describe any group of related items, whether they are objects, other containers, domains, or an entire network.

Contiguous Namespace   A contiguous namespace is one in which the child object contains the name of the parent domain. A contiguous namespace in Windows 2000 is called a tree.

Convergence Time   The time it takes for an entry addition or modification to be replicated to all WINS servers on the network is known as the convergence time. The convergence time is the sum of all of the Replication Intervals.

CONVERT Program   CONVERT allows an administrator to convert existing FAT file systems to NTFS. The CONVERT utility is executed from a command prompt, and follows a specific syntax, where X: is the drive letter of the FAT16/FAT32 volume that you are converting.

Copy Backup   This type of backup can be done between other types without affecting the regular scheduled backups. All the selected files and folders are backed up when you do a Copy. Markers are not used to determine which files and folders to back up, and existing markers are not cleared.

Create Shared Folder Wizard   The Create Shared Folder Wizard is designed so that an administrator can easily configure a directory on a server for sharing. The first screen of the Create Shared Folder Wizard presents fields to choose the directory to be shared, the name of the share, and optionally, a comment to describe the share.

Daily Backup   This type of backup backs up the selected files and folders that have been changed during that day. It does not use the archive markers to determine which files and folders to back up (instead, it looks to the date marker), and it does not clear existing markers.

Data Encryption Standard (DES)   DES is a private key encryption scheme developed by IBM in the 1970s which has been adopted by the National Institute of Science and Technology (NIST).

Data Store   Data stores (another term for the directory) store information about Active Directory objects.

Database Scavenging   Database Scavenging refers to the process of "cleaning" the WINS database; that is, either deleting or tombstoning entries for which specific intervals have expired.

Default Mask   The default mask is a number that identifies all the bits that represent the network number part of the IP address. For a Class A address, 255.0.0.0 is the default mask. This implies that all of the first 8 bits represent the network number. For a Class B address, the first 16 bits indicate the network number; the mask is 255.255.0.0 by default. For a Class C network, the first 24 bits define the network number and the mask is 255.255.255.0 by default.

Defragmentation   Defragmentation refers to the process of organizing the clusters on the hard drive to reduce the time required to read a file. Servers that have a lot of creations and deletions, such as print servers that perform intense spooling, are more prone to fragmentation than others.

Datagram   A self-contained packet used in connectionless transmission protocols such as TCP/IP.

Delegation of Control Wizard   The Delegation of Control Wizard is designed to delegate authority over lower-level Organizational Units (OUs).

Deny Permission   Permissions can be granted or denied to specific users or groups. Being assigned Deny for permission is not the same as not having that permission at all. If a user or group is assigned Deny to a permission, they will never be able to access it, regardless of permissions obtained through group membership. Deny always overrides any other permissions.

Deployment Phase   The deployment phase of the software life cycle is actually divided into a few steps: Testing and Development Stage; Pilot Deployment Stage; and Production Deployment Stage. Following these stages of the deployment process provides a greater chance of a smooth rollout that does not interrupt the user by causing unnecessary downtime.

Design Goals   In order to make your network a success, you have to keep the user in mind when designing your layout of Active Directory. There are certain end results that you want to achieve to ensure that users have a much easier time using the network. You also want to make sure administration is productive. Design goals you may want to keep in mind include: Single-user sign on; Centralized administration; and Administrative model changes.

DHCPACKNOWLEDGMENT (DHCPACK)   The DHCP server sends the client a DHCPACKNOWLEDGEMENT message after the

DHCP server receives the DHCPREQUEST message from the client. A positive DHCPACKNOWLEDGEMENT message (DHCPACK) is sent to the client to confirm that the client has successfully leased an IP address.

DHCPDISCOVER   The DHCP client issues a DHCPDISCOVER message if the client has never obtained a lease before, or if the client must obtain an entirely new lease because it was not able to renew a previous one. The DHCPDISCOVER message is broadcast to the entire subnet. All DHCP servers on the subnet respond to the DHCPDISCOVER message.

DHCPINFORM   This DHCPINFORM message is part of a new and evolving DHCP specification. The DHCPINFORM message contains vendor-specific option types that can be interpreted by Microsoft DHCP servers. These included option types allow the new DHCP server to obtain information about the network from other DHCP servers extant on the segment. The DHCPINFORM message can submit queries to other DHCP servers.

DNCPNACK   The DHCPNACK phase occurs when the DHCPREQUEST fails, such as when the client is trying to lease an old address that is being used or is no longer available. The server sends a negative broadcast, called the DHCPNACK, and the lease process starts over.

DHCPOFFER   All DHCP servers respond to the client's DHCPDISCOVER message with a DHCPOFFER message. The DHCPOFFER message includes the IP address that the DHCP server offered to lease to the host. The client accepts the first offer it receives, and rejects any additional offers. The DHCP servers whose offers were rejected retract their offers.

DHCPREQUEST   After the DHCP client receives a DHCPOFFER message, it returns a DHCPREQUEST message to the issuing DHCP server. The message contains a request to the issuing DHCP server that the client would like to accept the offer and keep the IP address assigned to it.

Differential Backup   Files that have previously been marked are backed up in a differential backup. Markers are not cleared so there is no flag indicating that those files have been backed up. This means the same files will be backed up in subsequent differential backups.

Directory Service   A database that contains information about who and what is on the network, their attributes, and what their relationship is to each other.

Directory Services Restore Mode   Directory Services Restore Mode allows restoration of the Active Directory on domain controllers.

Disaster Recovery Wizard   The Disaster Recovery Preparation Wizard allows you to prepare a set of Disaster Recovery disks that can be used to fully recover a failed system.

Disk Defragmenter   Disk Defragmenter organizes the clusters that make up a file by grouping them, to the extent possible, into one location on the hard disk. Disk Defragmenter also consolidates clusters that are marked as free space, which speeds up performance when creating new files. Disk Defragmenter is able to defragment FAT16, FAT32, and NTFS partitions.

Disk Duplexing   Disk duplexing is when the data is written to two disks that are on different controllers.

Disk Encryption   Disk encryption can encrypt folders, subfolders, and files.

Disk Fault Tolerance   Recovery from failure of a hard drive that is part of a RAID set.

Disk Image Replication   Disk image replication copies the contents of the entire partition onto an image and replicates it on another machine.

This is one of the best ways to do mass installs because it's extremely powerful and comprehensive. With disk image replication, the contents of the entire hard partition are replicated.

Disk Quotas The amount of disk usage allocated to a user on a volume basis. With disk quotas, you can limit the use of the hard disk by the user. This eases administration worries of certain users using more than their fair share of space. Disk quotas are a new feature of NTFS v5 that allows administrators to control the amount of disk space that individual users are able to consume on a server.

Disk Striping Also called RAID 0. Supported by Windows NT and Windows 2000, but offers no fault tolerance. RAID 0 is many disks with the data striped across them. RAID 0 is different from RAID 5 in that there is no parity drive.

Distinguished Name (DN) The Distinguished Name (DN) must uniquely identify the object. The LDAP DN includes the domain name in which the object resides and the complete path to the object. The DN must be unique in the Directory.

Distributed File System (DFS) The DFS uses a single root share to facilitate hierarchical management of multiple shares. These shares can be on many different servers, but all appear to the end user as existing in one folder. DFS has the both the advantage of a central file storage location (a single drive mapping) for the end user, as well as a single point of share administration for the network administrator.

Distributed Link Tracking Preserves and updates shortcuts when files are moved or renamed by the user.

Domain A group of objects on a network that share the same security rights. Domains in a tree share a common configuration and must have contiguous domain names. Every domain contains one PDC.

Domain Forest   A domain forest consists of domain trees that have access to each other, but do not share intrinsic trust relationships and do not share domain names.

Domain Name System (DNS)   Text labels (separated by dots) are used for domain names because the actual IP address is difficult to work with. The DNS is responsible for mapping these domain names to the actual IP numbers in a process called resolution.

Domain Name System (DNS) Server   DNS server keeps a list of host names and their matching IP addresses.

Domain Naming Master   The Domain Naming Master is what handles the responsibility of adding and removing domains in the Forest. The Forest is similar to the Tree in NetWare. There are trees within a Windows 2000 network as well, so be sure to understand that the tree in NetWare is the Directory just as the forest in Windows 2000 is the directory.

Domain Operation   The Domain Operation Master is the main place for updates and changes to the security and permissions in the domain. This is similar to how Novell has one master replica, and other servers are read-and-write replicas.

Domain Tree   A domain tree is a hierarchical collection of the child and parent domains within a network. The domains in a domain tree have contiguous namespaces. Domain trees in a domain forest do not share common security rights, but can access one another through the global catalog.

Drive Striping with Parity   Also called RAID 5. There must be at least three hard drives for RAID 5 to be possible. Striping is when the data is striped across the drives and there is parity information along with the data. The parity information is based on a mathematical formula that comes up with the parity based on the data on the other drives.

Duplexing   Duplexing, unlike mirroring, does the same, but the second disk uses a separate disk controller.

Dynamic Domain Name System (DDNS)   The DDNS server provided by Windows 2000 allows computers to automatically register their hostnames and IP addresses in the form of an A record. The new functionality afforded by DDNS allows the widespread use of DHCP, and allows for the dynamic update of hostnames in the same fashion as WINS provided dynamic updates of NetBIOS name to IP address mappings.

Dynamic Host Configuration Protocol (DHCP)   The DHCP automatically assigns IP addresses to client stations when they log onto a TCP/IP network. DHCP eliminates manual IP address assignation.

Dynamic Link Library (DLL)   The MS-DOS file name extension attached to a collection of library routines.

Dynamic Routing   Dynamic routing sends special route information packets between routers. RIP is the most widely used dynamic routing protocol. Dynamic routing protocols advertise the routes they are familiar with and pass on the metrics, number of other routers, or hops, required to get from their host to another network, either directly or indirectly through another router.

Emergency Repair Process   The Emergency Repair Process repairs problems with the Registry, startup environment, system files, and boot sector that prevent the computer from starting.

Enable Indexing   Allows the Indexing Service to record catalog information for the file or directory, enabling faster searching of the hard disk. Indexing is enabled by default.

Encrypting File System (EFS)   With EFS enabled, the files are actually stored in an encrypted format, eliminating the ability to mount a partition on another system and bypass all security. EFS uses the Data Encryption Standard-X (DES-X) encryption technology.

Enterprise Server   Enterprise servers are usually located in the corporate data center. They serve the users by providing user home directories, print queues, or simple communication services. They may also be Web servers that serve the corporate intranet or extranet. These types of servers are backed up daily or at least weekly in most cases.

Extensible Authentication Protocol (EAP)   EAP allows the administrator to "plug in" different authentication security providers outside of those included with Windows 2000. EAP allows your organization to take advantage of new authentication technologies including "smart card" logon and Certificate-based authentication.

Fault Tolerance   Fault tolerance is the ability of the computer to recover from a catastrophe, such as a disk failure, without losing critical data. Fault tolerance is also the design of a computer to maintain its system's performance when some internal hardware problems occur.

File Allocation Table (FAT)   An area on a disk indicating the arrangement of files in the sectors. The FAT file system is the oldest of the file systems supported by Windows 2000, and has been implemented in Microsoft operating systems since the earliest versions of MS-DOS.

File Allocation Table 16 (FAT16)   The earlier version of the FAT file system implemented in MS-DOS is known as FAT16, to differentiate it from the improved FAT32.

File Allocation Table 32 (FAT32)   FAT32 is the default file system for Windows 95 OSR2 and Windows 98. The FAT32 file system was first implemented in Windows 95 OSR2, and was supported by Windows 98 and now Windows 2000. While FAT16 cannot support partitions larger than 4GB in Windows 2000, FAT32 can support partitions up to 2TB (Terabytes) in size. However, for performance reasons, the creation of FAT32 partitions is limited to 32GB in Windows 2000. The second major benefit of FAT32 in comparison to FAT16 is that it supports a significantly smaller cluster size—as low as 4K for partitions up to 8GB. This results in more efficient use of disk space, with a 15–30 percent utilization improvement in comparison to FAT16.

File Transfer Protocol (FTP)   An Internet protocol allowing the exchange of files. A program enables the user to contact another computer on the Internet and exchange files.

FireWire   Also known as IEEE 1394. An Apple/Texas Instruments high-speed serial bus allowing up to 63 devices to connect; this bus supports hot swapping and isochronous data transfer.

Flow Control   When two computers are transmitting packets back and forth, there must be some agreement about when to stop if one side gets too many packets. This process is called flow control.

Folder Redirection   Folder Redirection is an extension to Group Policy, which you can use to redirect certain Windows 2000 special folders to network locations. Folder Redirection is located under User Configuration in the Group Policy Console. Folder Redirection is an exciting new concept that can provide more fault tolerance for users' data, as well as greater convenience for those who work at different computers or sometimes log on from laptops.

Forwarder   A DNS Forwarder is a DNS server that accepts requests to resolve host names from another DNS server. Caching-only servers make good forwarders. A Forwarder can be used to protect an internal DNS server from access by users on the Internet.

Forward lookup query   Forward lookup queries seek to resolve an IP address from a known host name. A Reverse lookup query does the opposite: It seeks to resolve a host name from a known IP address.

Fully Qualified Domain Name (FQDN)   A full site name of a system rather than just its host name. The FQDN of each child domain is made up of the combination of its own name and the FQDN of the parent domain. The FQDN includes the host name and the domain membership of that computer.

Gateway   A gateway acts as an interface and connects two dissimilar Local Area Networks (LANs) or connects to a Wide Area Network (WAN) or mainframe. The term gateway is used to identify the network interface that can transfer or route a packet from one network to another network interface on another network.

Global Catalog (GC)   The Global Catalog (GC) is a partial replica of every object within a forest. It is an index for the Active Directory, provided for users to be able to query for resources on the network. The Global Catalog (GC) also contains information about all the objects in the directory. The GC allows users and administrators to find directory information without having to know which server or domain actually contains the data.

Global Catalog Server (GCS)   A GCS enables a server to fulfill queries about objects in all domains on your network.

Globally Unique Identifier (GUID)   The Globally Unique Identifier (GUID) is a unique numerical identification created at the time the object is created. An analogy would be a person's social security number, which is assigned once and never changes, even if the person changes his or her name, or moves.

Glue Record   The glue record associates the host name in the NS record with an IP address of the A record. Its "glues" together the name server's host name and IP address.

Group Policy   A group policy is a set of configuration settings that can be applied to an Active Directory object (or group of objects) to define the behavior of the object and its child objects. Group policies can serve many purposes, from application and file deployment to global configuration of user profile settings and restriction of access. Group Policy can run scripts at specified times, to fine-tune security settings, and, in short, to control the user environment to whatever degree is desired. Group Policy gives an administrator the power to enhance productivity throughout the organization by completely managing the users' desktop environment. Group policies are applied to two types of Active Directory objects: Users and Computers. Group policies can also be used to assign and run scripts at prescribed times, such as when a user logs on or when the computer is shut down.

Group Policy Container (GPC)   The GPC is a Directory Service object that includes subcontainers for Machine and User Group Policy information. The GPC contains Version information, Status information, List of components, and Class stores.

Group Policy Object (GPO)   GPOs are where the policies themselves are stored. If you think of the Group Policy Snap-in as the application program that creates group policies, just as Microsoft Word is an application that creates documents, the individual GPOs would be analogous to individual document files, each of which contains information.

Group Policy Template (GPT)   A GPT is a folder structure consisting of the GPT folder and a set of subfolders, which together contain all the Group Policy information for that particular GPO. The GPT is located in the system volume folder on the Windows 2000 domain controller(s). The folder name is the GUID (Globally Unique Identifier) of the GPO to which it applies, which is a hexadecimal number.

Groveler agent   The groveler agent scans the hard disk regularly and links redundant files.

HOSTINFO (HINFO)   HINFO records provide information about the DNS server itself. This might include CPU, operating system, interface type, and other aspects of the server. Consider this a primitive resource tracking method.

HTTP (HyperText Transfer Protocol)   HTTP is the protocol used by a WWW browser. Most URLs request resources via FTP.

Hybrid Node (H-Node)   The Hybrid Node is the default node type on a WINS client. H-Node, like M-Node, uses both broadcasts and WINS server queries to resolve a NetBIOS name. H-Node simply performs broadcasts and WINS server queries in the reverse order of the M-Node type, by first querying the WINS server and then using broadcasts if it gets a negative response or no response from WINS.

Hyperlink   In a hypertext system, a hyperlink is an underlined or otherwise emphasized word or phrase which, when clicked, takes the user to another document or site.

Incremental Backup   The incremental backup is similar to the differential in that marked files are backed up, but in this case, the markers are then cleared so that a subsequent incremental backup does not back up those same files again.

Infrastructure Manager   The Infrastructure Manager handles changes and configuration of groups and group-to-user relations. There must be one of these in your domain.

Instantiation   Objects created in a class are also known as instances of that class. The process of creating the object (that is, populating the values for the appropriate attributes), is therefore known as instantiation.

Intellimirror Intellimirror provides more availability and security to users' data, applications, and settings, and allows for roaming access. A mirrored copy of a user's work is always kept on both the workstation and the server. As the user works, the local copy of his or her files are edited, and the server copy is updated using a write-through cache. This mirrored copy on the server also provides a place for users to store reliable backups of their files Intellimirror is able to provide application shortcuts to the user, but installations are initiated only when the user invokes that application, not automatically at login time.

International Standards Organization (ISO) The ISO (also called the International Organization for Standardization) is one of two international bodies developing data communications and networking standards and promoting global trade.

Internet Engineering Task Force (IETF) The organization providing standard coordination and specification development of TCP/IP networking.

Internet Protocol (IP) This connectionless protocol aids in providing a best-effort delivery of datagrams across a network and was originally developed by the U.S. Department of Defense (DoD) for internetworking dissimilar computers across a single network.

Internet Protocol (IP) address A 32-bit address identifying networks and hosts within a network.

Internet Protocol Configuration (IPConfig) This utility displays local host TCP/IP configuration details. By utilizing the IPConfig /all command and the command-line prompt, configuration details for the host can be viewed.

Internet Protocol (IP) Numbering IP (current version) addressing uses 32 bits conveniently broken into 4 octets, or 4 sets of 8 bits. A

Network Number represents one combination of some of those 32 bits, from 2 minimum to 30 maximum.

Internet Protocol security (IPsec) Policies   Configures network IP security.

Internet Service Manager (ISM)   The Internet Service Manager (ISM) is the primary tool used to manage the Internet Information Services (IIS).

Interoperability   A computer process for interactivity with other computers across a network. Interoperability does not require data conversion or human intervention.

Interrupt ReQuest (IRQ)   A pathway that a hardware device uses to communicate with the processor. It is designed to interrupt a program for an Input/Output (I/O) function.

Intranet   A private network inside a company or organization using similar software from a public Internet but for restricted and internal use.

IPX (Internet Packet eXchange)   IPX is Novell NetWare's built-in networking protocol for Local Area Network (LAN) for internetworking of dissimilar computers across a single network. This connectionless protocol aids in providing a best-effort delivery of datagrams across a network.

Kerberos Security System   Kerberos speeds up network processes by integrating security and rights across network domains and also eliminates workstations' need to authenticate themselves repeatedly at every domain they access. Kerberos security also makes maneuvering around networks using multiple platforms such as UNIX or NetWare easier.

Kernel mode Manager   The Kernel mode Manager assigns resources, provides device drivers, and controls I/O communications and Power Management.

Kill Process Tree   A Windows 2000 Server utility that is able to end all processes related to the one being terminated by the administrator.

Knowledge Consistency Checker (KCC)   The KCC is a service that runs on each domain controller. It automatically creates Connection objects within the same site between domain controllers in that site, regardless of whether those domain controllers belong to the same domain. The KCC creates a bidirectional ring of connection objects between the domain controllers in the site.

Last Known Good Configuration   Last Known Good is used when the loading of a driver changes the Registry configuration, and the system doesn't like the change. The Last Known Good option allows you to revert to a previous configuration that did work.

Load balancing   The fine tuning process of a computer system, a network, or other subsystems. Load balancing involves balancing or distributing the query load among multiple DNS servers.

Local Area Network (LAN)   A system using high-speed connections over high-performance cables to communicate among computers within a few miles of each other, allowing users to share peripherals and a massive secondary storage unit, the file server.

Local Loopback Address   There is one specialized network address that is reserved on every machine to represent the "software." This is called the *local loopback address*. On every machine, the Class A network 127.0.0.0 is used to represent the TCP/IP software. You can ping the loopback to test if your software is running. Normally the loopback is numbered 127.0.0.1 but any numbers after the 127. are acceptable, for example, 127.23.45.67.

Just remember the octet numbers vary between 0 and 255. IP addresses use 8-bit numbers and can never exceed the value 255.

Local Network   Your local network is defined as all hosts using the same network number.

Local Policies   Configures auditing, user rights, and security options for the local machine.

Logically Multihomed Network Interface   In the case of the single network interface card you would have to have two distinct network IP addresses assigned to it, one for each network to be accessed. Static routes should be added to the interface so that packets from either network interface will use the other IP address on the same card as their default gateway. This is also known as a logically multihomed network interface.

LostAndFound   The LostAndFound utility container object acts as a "holding place" for objects unable to be placed by the file replication service.

LostAndFound container   The LostAndFound container is the replication service's repository for objects that have been created in, or moved to, a location that is missing after replication.

Mail Exchanger (MX)   MX, a type of record in a DNS table, identifies the preferred mail servers on the network. If you have several mail servers, an order of precedence will be run.

Maintenance Phase   The maintenance phase of the software life cycle refers to the ongoing process of keeping applications on the latest version, by applying the appropriate upgrades and fixes as they become available by the developer.

Master File Table (MFT)   The NTFS stores information about files in the Master File Table. Each file is assigned a record number, and each record in the MFT includes most information about the file, including size and attributes.

Media Access Control (MAC)   A sublayer in the Open System Interconnection (OSI) data link layer that controls access, control, procedures, and format for a Local Area Network (LAN).

Media Sense   Media sense refers to the capability of the operating system to detect when it has been disconnected and reconnected to a network. This functionality was provided with NDIS 4.0 and works with network interface cards that support this capability.

Metadata   Metadata is a definition or description of data.

Microsoft Management Console (MMC)   The MMC provides a standardized interface for using administrative tools and utilities. The management applications contained in an MMC are called Snap-ins, and custom MMCs hold the Snap-ins required to perform specific tasks. Custom consoles can be saved as files with the .msc file extension. The MMC was first introduced with NT Option Pack. Using the MMC leverages the familiarity you have with the other snap-ins available within MMC, such as SQL Server 7 and Internet Information Server 4. With the MMC, all your administrative tasks can be done in one place.

MIME (Multipurpose Internet Mail Extension)   MIME is the standard for how such tools as electronic mail programs and Web browsers transfer non-text files complete with sounds, graphics, and video over the Internet.

Mirroring   Also called RAID 1. RAID 1 consists of two drives that are identical matches, or mirrors, of each other. If one drive fails, you have another drive to boot up and keep the server going.

Mixed Node (M-Node)   The Mixed Node resolution method uses a combination of the B-Node and P-Node methods detailed earlier. A client configured to use M-Node first attempts to find a workstation using a broadcast, and if it does not receive a positive name query response, it then sends a name query request to the Primary WINS server. This node type is generally not used in large local networks due to the network traffic generated by a NetBIOS query broadcast.

Modifications   Modifications, also referred to as Transforms, are stored in .MST files in a similar format to .MSI files. One or more modification packages can be added to a software package in a GPO, and are applied in list order.

MOVETREE Utility   The MOVETREE resource kit utility gives you a way to move Active Directory objects across domains within a forest.

Multihomed   Multihomed means there are two or more network interfaces on one machine.

Multimaster Replication   Each domain on the network receives its own copy of the portions of the AD catalog that it needs to use. That is, each domain only receives information about the objects to which it has access. All domain replications of the global directory are synchronized, so when new objects are added or configured in the global catalog, each domain directory is automatically updated. This is the replacement the Backup Domain Controller of Windows NT 4.0. Multimaster replication keeps the information synchronized across all Domain Controllers. This ensures that there is fault tolerance in the event of server failure.

Name Registration   The Name Registration request is the process by which a client registers its information with a WINS server. When a client boots, it sends a name registration request to the primary WINS server configured on the client. The request includes the client's IP address as well as the computer name, and information about specific NetBIOS services running on the machine.

Name Renewal   A Name Renewal occurs when a client first needs to renew its lease with WINS. In this process, the WINS client sends a Name Refresh request to the WINS server. A positive response from a WINS server results in the client receiving a new TTL, and the lease is renewed on the server.

Namespace   A namespace is a characteristic of directory services representing a space in which a name is resolved, or translated into the information represented by that name. Consider a familiar example, the telephone directory. You use it to resolve names of people to their street addresses or telephone numbers.

Naming Conventions   Each Active Directory object must have a name, to identify it to users on the network. Several different naming conventions are supported, making it possible to search the Directory in different ways. For example, you can query by name, or by object attributes if you don't know the exact name of the object.

NetBIOS (Network Basic Input/Output System)   A program included in the MS-DOS versions 3.1 and later for linking personal computers in a Local Area Network (LAN). NetBIOS provides a standard interface by which applications can communicate with a variety of network protocols (e.g., TCP/IP). It is used heavily in Windows NT, and used only for down-level support in Windows 2000. The NetBIOS standard was designed to maximize efficiency on PC networks, on which computers are constantly being brought online and taken offline without any notification, by eliminating or centralizing as much of the administrative overhead as possible.

NETDOM   The NETDOM tool is designed to rejoin machine objects to the new domain. NETDOM also allows you to move computer accounts across domains without altering local groups.

NETSTAT   This utility displays current TCP/IP statistics, including the status of existing connections. It also displays listening ports, which provides information as to whether services are using the correct ports. The netstat –a command displays all current TCP and UDP connections, as well as the source and destination service ports.

NetWare   An operating system that also serves as an implementation and control approach developed by Novell to define the architecture and software modules needed for Local Area Network (LAN) operation for IBM PC compatibles and Macintoshes.

Network Broadcast   The network broadcast address is the last address available for a given network; all client bits are set to the value 1. This address is used to send general query packets to all hosts on the network.

Network Domain   A network domain is a group of objects on a network that belong together logically and share common security rights.

Network Interface Card (NIC)   A board with encoding and decoding circuitry and a receptacle for a network cable connection that, bypassing the serial ports and operating through the internal bus, allows computers to be connected at higher speeds to media for communications between stations.

Network Operating System (NOS)   The file server and workstation software that integrates the hardware on a Local Area Network (LAN), usually including such features as a menu-driven interface, security restrictions, facilities for sharing printers, central storage of network applications and information, remote log-in via modem, and support for diskless workstation.

Node   The point in a Local Area Network (LAN) where one or more functional units connect with each other; often applied to a workstation, though the term includes repeaters, file servers, and shared peripherals.

Normal Backup   A straightforward backup procedure in which all the files and folders you have selected are backed up. No markers are used to determine which files to back up, and any markers that exist are cleared by the backup program, which then marks each file as having been backed up. Normal backup gives you a complete backup set that is easy to restore. However, it uses more tape (or other media) than some of the other methods.

/nosidgen   Runs sysprep.exe without generating a SID. Normally, each computer must have an individual SID, or security identifier. Use this option only to make a clone of the computer as a backup or to allow the end user to customize the computer.

NSLOOKUP   This utility queries the DNS server, providing information relating to the status of a host, and returning information about its IP address. It is particularly useful when you need to know either the host's IP address (or hostname if you know its IP address). NSLOOKUP is used primarily as a troubleshooting tool.

ntdsutil Tool   The ntdsutil tool can analyze and clean up core directory structures, for example, when you have removed a domain controller from the network. The ntdsutil tool allows you to compact, move, repair, and check the integrity of the directory database.

NT File System (NTFS)   A Windows file system which employs the Unicode character set. NTFS allows 255-character file names and can aid in recovery from disk crashes.

NTFS Permissions   NTFS permissions are used to assign users or groups a specific set of permissions to a file or directory resource on an NTFS partition. NTFS permissions are used on volumes formatted with NTFS.

NT Media Services (NTMS)   NT Media Services works with various types of removable storage devices such as optical drives, tape libraries,

CD-ROM, and robotic loaders. NTMS will help with disaster recovery situations for administrators; previously, administrators had to rely on third-party solutions for disaster recovery.

Object　A data entity that can be manipulated as a whole, as in a document, a widget in a Graphical User Interface (GUI) environment, or a piece of stand-alone code in an object programming environment.

Object Identifier (OID)　The OID is used to identify the object within the schema to prevent potential conflicts that may occur when directories are combined.

Object Linking and Embedding (OLE)　A set of Microsoft standards for creating dynamic automatically updated links between documents and for embedding documents created by another. Changes made in a source document can be automatically reflected in a destination document. Embedding actually places the source document or part of it physically into the destination file, creating a compound file containing information needed by both the server and the client application.

Organizational Units (OUs)　OUs in Windows 2000 are objects that are containers for other objects, such as users, groups, or other organizational units. Objects cannot be placed in another domain's OUs. The whole purpose of an OU is to have a hierarchical structure to organize your network objects. You can assign a group policy to an OU. Generally, the OU will follow a structure from your company. It may be a location, if you have multiple locations. It can even be a department-level organization.

Original Equipment Manufacturer (OEM)　The company that manufactures a given piece of hardware, unlike a Value-Added Reseller (VAR) that changes, reconfigures, or repackages hardware for sale.

OS/2　A multitasking operating system for IBM PC and compatible computers that uses flat memory to emulate separate Disk Operating

System (DOS) machines; it can run DOS, Windows, and OS/2 programs concurrently, protecting the others if one program crashes and allowing dynamic exchange of data between applications.

Parent Domain   The parent domain (also called the root domain) is at the top of the tree, with its "children" and "grandchildren" at lower (and deeper) levels beneath it.

Parity   Parity is a mathematical formula used to check the integrity of data by comparing the number of odd or even bits in a series of numbers.

Partition   A section of storage on a hard disk, usually set aside before the disk is formatted. Every MS-DOS hard disk has at least one DOS partition, for instance, though some versions require more. Keep in mind that when you delete an existing partition, all data on that partition will be lost. During the installation, you must create and size the partition in which Windows 2000 will be installed.

Per Seat Licensing   Per Seat Licensing requires one CAL for each client computer that is accessing Windows 2000 Server. Per Server Licensing requires licenses for the maximum number of concurrent connections that is expected to access the Windows 2000 Server.

Permission Inheritance   Permission Inheritance can be blocked at any level of the directory structure to prevent child directories from inheriting the permissions of the parent. This is useful when you wish to have one set of permissions at the directory level, but a separate set of permissions for the files or subfolders.

PING (Packet INternet Groper)   PING is a common utility program used to determine whether a computer is connected to the Internet properly and provides the ability to troubleshoot TCP/IP connectivity.

Plug and Play (PnP)   A standard that requires add-in hardware to carry the software to configure itself in a given way supported by Microsoft Windows 95. Plug and Play makes, for instance, peripheral configuration software, jumper settings, and DIP switches unnecessary. PnP allows the operating system to load device drivers automatically and assign system resources dynamically (IRQs, I/O addresses) to computer components and peripherals. Windows 2000 moves away from this older technology with its use of Kernel-mode and User-mode PnP architecture. PnP autodetects, configures, and installs the necessary drivers in order to minimize user interaction with hardware configuration. Users no longer have to tinker with IRQ and I/O settings.

/pnp   Forces Plug and Play to refresh when the computer reboots to redetect all the hardware devices in the computer.

Pointer (PTR) Record   The PTR record is created to allow for Reverse lookups. Reverse lookups are valuable when doing security analysis and checking authenticity of source domains for email.

Point-to-Point Node   The Point-to-Point Node, or P-Node, resolution type uses the WINS server as the method for resolving a NetBIOS name. P-Node is generally used when the administrator wants to entirely eliminate NetBIOS-related broadcast traffic from the network. The disadvantage of using P-Node is that is does not make allowances for when WINS is unable to resolve the name (i.e., when the server is unavailable), because it does not use broadcasts at all.

Point-to-Point Protocol (PPP)   PPP is one of two standards for dial-up telephone connection of computers to the Internet, with better data negotiation, compression, and error connections than the other SLIP, but costing more to transmit data and unnecessary when both sending and receiving modems can handle some of the procedures.

Point-to-Point Tunneling Protocol (PPTP)   PPTP is a simple extension of the Point-to-Point Protocol (PPP) data link layer protocol that is used to allow a "point-to-point" connection between two nodes via serial lines. PPTP allows traditional routable or nonroutable network protocols such as TCP/IP, IPX/SPX, and NetBEUI to be transported over lines your users will be using to connect to your network..

Power Management   A microprocessor feature that reduces electricity consumption by turning off peripherals when they are not in use, common in portable computers where energy savings equal longer battery life.

Primary Zone File   The zone file where actual changes are made is referred to as the primary zone file. This is the actual file that is changed when you update it with resource records.

Print Subsystem   The print subsystem automatically propagates changes made to the printer attributes (location, description, loaded paper, and so forth) to the directory.

Proxy Autodiscovery   The proxy autodiscovery option is used by clients that have Internet Explorer 5.0 only. This option informs the client of the location of the Internet Explorer 5.0 automatic configuration file.

Proxy Server   The proxy server analyzes the request to establish that the user, protocol, and remote host are not in violation of any of the configured permissions.

Public Key Policies   Configures encrypted data recovery agents, trusted certificate authorities, etc.

Pull Replication   A WINS server is configured to pull entries with a higher version ID from its WINS partner when the specified time interval is reached or replication is manually initiated by the administrator.

Push Replication   A WINS server is configured to "push" database changes to its partner when the Update Count Threshold limit is exceeded or replication is manually initiated by the administrator.

Quality of Service (QoS)   A measure of network effectiveness based on a number of factors, including transit delay, cost, and the likelihood of packets being lost, duplicated, or damaged.

/quiet   Runs sysprep in the silent mode where no messages are displayed.

Ranges   Ranges are consecutively numbered IP addresses.

/reboot   Reboots the computer after sysprep.exe runs.

Recovery Console   The Recovery Console performs administrative tasks from a command-line utility that can be started from the Windows 2000 setup floppies or installed on your computer.

Redundancy   Redundancy means duplication or repetition of elements in equipment to provide alternative functional channels in case of failure.

Redundant Array of Inexpensive Disks (RAID)   A system storage method, common on network servers, using software working with several hard drives to assure data redundancy and security.

Redundant Array of Inexpensive Disks (RAID 0)   Also called Disk striping. Supported by Windows NT and Windows 2000, but offers no fault tolerance. RAID 0 is many disks with the data striped across them. RAID 0 is different from RAID 5 in that there is no parity drive.

Redundant Array of Inexpensive Disks (RAID 1)   Also called mirroring. RAID 1 consists of two drives that are identical matches, or mirrors, of each other. If one drive fails, you have another drive to boot up and keep the server going.

Redundant Array of Inexpensive Disks (RAID 5)   Also called Drive Striping with Parity. There must be three hard drives for RAID 5 to be possible. *Striping* is when the data is striped across the drives and there is parity information along with the data. The parity information is based on a mathematical formula that comes up with the parity based on the data on the other drives.

Refresh Interval   The Secondary DNS server will periodically refresh its zone file in order to obtain updates to the zone. This refresh interval is defined by the Primary DNS server zone properties. The refresh interval is included in the SOA record on the Primary DNS server.

Relative Distinguished Name (RDN)   The RDN represents part of a Distinguished Name (DN) that is an attribute of the object.

Relative Identifier Master (RID)   The Relative Identifier Master is the one server that handles the database and allocation of Relative IDs (RIDs). When each workstation is added, is has a Security Identifier, or SID. This was evident in Windows NT 4.0. The SID consists of the domain security ID and the relative ID. The domain security ID is the same on each workstation. The relative ID is specific to that workstation.

Remote Access Service (RAS) Server   RAS servers are used to provide network services as if a user was physically attached. For example, when a user is out of town, he or she may dial into a RAS server and, once attached, access network applications. E-mail is a very common example of a network application that is used in this manner.

Remote Authentication Dial-In User Service (RADIUS)
RADIUS is a protocol used to provide secure authentication and accounting services for large-scale remote access networks. An authentication server uses the RADIUS protocol to provide a central point for multiple dial-up users to validate against within a network of distributed remote access servers. RADIUS

allows an administrator to manage a single database of users that can handle hundreds of remote access servers.

Remote Installation Preparation (RIPrep)   These images are the customized images made from the base operating system, local installation of applications such as Microsoft Office, and customized configurations.

Remote Installation Preparation Wizard   This is similar to the System Preparation Tool, where a reference computer is created and an image is made from it. Remote Installation Preparation Wizard removes anything unique to a client such as the SID, computer name, and hardware settings. This allows computers with multiple hardware configurations to use the same image; you only need to prepare one image for one type of user.

Remote Installation Service (RIS)   The RIS, part of Windows 2000 Server, allows client computers to install Windows 2000 Professional from a Windows 2000 Server with the service installed.

Remote Procedure Call (RPC)   Software tool developed by a consortium of manufacturers for developers who create distributed applications that automatically generates code for both client and server. RPCs are a Session-layer application programming interface (API) that makes remote applications appear to be executing locally. RPCs are used over IP for the Active Directory, but are capable of executing over other protocol stacks.

Remote Storage Server (RSS)   The RSS constantly monitors the amount of storage space on the server's hard disk. When this space dips below the specified level, the RSS removes from the hard drive any data that has also been saved to a remote location.

Remote Windows Installation   Remote Windows Installation is a tool in Windows 2000 Server that enables remote boot clients to remotely install Windows 2000. With the new Remote Windows Installation, many remote installations can run simultaneously, which lowers administrative overhead.

Removal Phase   This phase is needed to effectively manage applications that are no longer needed by the business, or applications that have been retired for other reasons. In Windows 2000, a software object can be removed from a Group Policy in two ways: Forced removal and Optional removal.

Replication   Replication is the process of synchronizing the Active Directory partitions. When an administrator makes a change to an object, only the change and enough information to locate where that change occurred within the Active Directory partition is replicated. Replication is also used in WINS and DNS.

Request For Comment (RFC)   An Internet system, currently controlled by the Internet Architecture Board (IAB), that has become the chief method of promulgating standards.

Reservations   Reservations are IP addresses that are reserved for certain computers. This is often used for servers that must use a set IP address, as well as for computers that are constantly moving around.

Reserved Client   A reserved client is a computer that is always assigned the same IP addressing information by the DHCP server. This reserved client always obtains the same IP address that you configure in the DHCP manager.

Resolver   The resolver is software included in the WinSock application that is used to query DNS servers for the IP address of a particular host's FQDN. Programs with resolver components include Web browsers (such as Microsoft Internet Explorer) and dedicated FTP programs (such as the command-line FTP program found in Windows 2000).

Resource Domain   The resource domain is the domain in which the resource resides.

Resource Records   Resource records represent the computer host names and IP addresses contained in that domain.

Restricted Group Policies   Configures group membership for groups that are security sensitive (by default, this includes the Administrators group).

Retransmission   Retransmission is the term used when the sender resends data packets that it sent previously. If the receiving station sends a NACK, then the sending station retransmits the packet. If the sending station does not get an ACK, it assumes the packets were lost or corrupted and resends the packets. It continues to send the packet until it no longer receives a NACK or until it receives an ACK.

Reverse Hosting   Reverse hosting is accomplished by binding a service on an internal server to a specific IP port on the proxy server's external network adapter.

Reverse Lookup Query   Reverse lookup query does the opposite of a forward lookup query: The reverse lookup query seeks to resolve a host name from a known IP address.

Reverse Proxy   A reverse proxy allows Web servers on your network to publish without ever establishing communications with computers beyond your network.

Root Domain   The root domain (also called the parent domain) is at the top of the tree, with its "children" and "grandchildren" at lower (and deeper) levels beneath it.

RootDSE (Root Directory Specific Entry)   The RootDSE locates objects and can be used to access standard information about Active

Directory. RootDSE is a special node that can be queried by LDAP clients (LDAP version 4 and later) to discover the schema and Directory Information Tree (DIT).

ROUTE The ROUTE command displays the current routing table, revealing the routes and number of hops a packet takes to reach the destination hosts. The ROUTE utility allows you to add, change, or delete routes. You can also clear the routing table.

Router The term router is sometimes generically used to imply packet forwarding and protocol translation.

Safe Mode Safe Mode is used to load the operating system with only the minimal drivers and files necessary to start Windows 2000. If Windows is not starting because of a bad driver or configuration, Safe Mode may allow you to boot the operating system and make changes to the appropriate settings.

Schema A schema is the organization or structure for a database. The schema is the part of the Active Directory that defines what attributes objects of a particular class can have and which of those attributes are required. Schema also defines the classes of objects and attributes contained in the directory, the constraints and limits on instances of these objects, and the format of their names.

Schema Master The Schema Master is what controls the schema in the forest. From time to time, the schema will be updated. There can only be one Schema Master in the forest.

Scope A scope is a grouping of available IP addresses that DHCP clients can request. It is used to minimize the administration associated with the many IP addresses. This is analogous to groups used to group users in a NT domain. Scope settings pass down to the IP addresses within the scope. You can only have one scope per logical subnet.

SecureICA   SecureICA Services offer end-to-end RSA RC5 encryption for the ICA data stream to ensure security of data.

Security Account Manager (SAM)   SAM is a read-write copy of a domain's database.

Security ID (SID)   A number for each user and workgroup not assigned to any other.

Security Subsystem   The security subsystem provides for a secure logon process to the network, as well as access control on both directory data queries and data modifications.

Serial Line Internet Protocol (SLIP)   The standard (one of two) for how a workstation or personal computer can dial up a link to the Internet that defines the transport of data packets through an asynchronous telephone line, allowing computers not part of a Local Area Network (LAN) to be connected fully to the Internet.

Serial Number   The Start of Authority (SOA) record contains a version number, known as the serial number.

Setup Manager Wizard   Setup Manager Wizard helps you create unattended installation files. With the new Setup Manager Wizard, you can minimize the amount of user interaction during setup.

Server Application   The program that creates a source document in Object Linking and Embedding (OLE); from the source document, an object can be linked or embedded in one or more destination documents.

Service Location Resource Records (SRV RRs)   An SRV RR is a DNS record that maps to the name of a server offering that service, much like the "service identifier" character (the 16ᵗʰ character) of a NetBIOS name.

Share Permissions   Share permissions are Security permissions assigned to specific users or groups to allow access to a share. Share permissions are separate from NTFS permissions. Share permissions can be used in conjunction with File/Directory permissions on NTFS volumes. On FAT partitions, Share permissions are the only means of locking down directory access, as FAT does not support File/Directory-level permission assignments. Share permissions include only limited options for restricting access, and any permission applied to the share will play a role in calculating the user's Effective permissions. The disadvantage of relying solely on Share permissions is the inherent lack of granularity.

SIDWALKER   The SIDWALKER utility is designed to update the Access Control Entries. SIDWALKER also allows you to update the security identifier on Access Control Entries and create SID profile files.

Simple Mail Transfer Protocol (SMTP)   SMTP is used in the Internet to transfer e-mail between servers.

Simple Network Management Protocol (SNMP)   SNMP is a standard for managing hardware devices connected to a network, approved for UNIX use that lets administrators know, for example, when a printer has a paper jam or is low on toner, etc.

Simple Volumes   Simple Volumes can only exist on a Dynamic Disk, and cannot contain partitions or logical drives. Simple Volumes can be configured as FAT 16, FAT32, or NTFS. To have multiple file systems, you must have multiple volumes.

Single Instance Store   The Single Instance Store uses the groveler agent to scan the distribution point of the remote installation images. It ensures that only one master copy of a file exists. With many images, many files are duplicated in each. The Single Instance Store minimizes the space needed to store the images.

Site Link Bridges   Site link bridges provide multihop routing through site links that have at least one site in common.

Sites   A site is defined as an area where network connectivity is fast (high bandwidth). A site is associated with one or more TCP/IP subnets in the Active Directory. Sites are used to locate the resources that are in closest proximity to the user and to reduce replication traffic, as well as for the isolation of logons so that those requests from one branch office, for example, will always log on at a particular domain controller. Sites are typically created to represent parts of the internetwork that can communicate easily with each other. Their boundaries are usually WAN links.

Slave Server   A type of forwarding process prevents the Preferred server from attempting to resolve the host name to an IP address if the Forwarder fails. When we configure the forwarding server to not attempt to resolve the host name on its own if the Forwarder is unsuccessful, we call the forwarding computer a Slave server. The Slave server will accept the response the forwarder provides to it, and will relay the response from the Forwarder to the client directly without attempting to resolve the name itself.

Small Computer System Interface (SCSI)   A complete expansion bus interface that accepts such devices as a hard disk.

Socket   A socket represents the endpoint of a network connection and is the Internet address that combines an IP address and a port number.

SOCKS   SOCKS is a platform-independent session-level interface used for communication between client and server applications.

Software RAID   Software RAID is the ability to create fault-tolerant volumes.

Sparse File   A file that contains a large number of null or 0 values, such as a large database. Only parts of the file with the non-null values are saved to disk, thus reducing the size needed to store them. Sparse files are those that are small, and after a period of time are only taking up a minute amount of space on the volume. Support for sparse files will help in managing space on the hard drive better.

Sparse File Support   A design that allocates the minimum required hard disk space necessary for very large files.

Start of Authority (SOA)   The SOA identifies which DNS server is authoritative for the data within this domain. The first record in any zone file is the SOA.

Static Routing   Early routers had to be programmed with exactly which networks they could route between which interfaces, especially if there were many network interfaces. This configuration method is called static routing.

Striping   Striping is when the data is striped across the drives and there is parity information along with the data. The parity information is based on a mathematical formula that comes up with the parity based on the data on the other drives.

Subnet Broadcast   The broadcast address for every subnet is the IP network number combined with all the client bits being set to one, or the last address in the network range.

Subnetting   The practice of taking an assigned class A, B, or C IP network and subdividing it into smaller internal networks.

Suite   A family of TCP/IP utilities and protocols.

Superscope   Each logical subnet can have only one scope. However, multiple scopes can be fitted into a scope grouping called a *superscope*. A superscope allows you to effectively manage all the scopes within one physical entity, while allowing the flexibility of more than one scope.

Syspart   Syspart is similar to System Preparation Tool (Sysprep), except it is used for dissimilar computers.

System Services Policies   Configures startup and security settings for services.

System Preparation Tool (Sysprep)   Sysprep duplicates the contents of computers running Windows 2000 to other computers so the target computer does not need to have the operating system as well as all the applications installed. Sysprep automatically regenerates Security IDs (SID) to ensure each machine is not an exact duplicate. Sysprep is used to prepare a source computer prior to the disk being imaged.

System Volume (SYSVOL)   SYSVOL is a directory structure that is replicated to every domain controller. It contains the information required by the Active Directory for replication purposes, and also contains group policy information, scripts, and the NETLOGON folder. The default folder location is C:\WINNT\SYSVOL.

Take Ownership Permission   Take Ownership permission is usually only used by administrators, as users will automatically be granted ownership to the files that they create. Even if a user has ownership of a file, and an administrator does not have any assigned NTFS permissions (or is denied permissions by the user), the administrator can still take ownership of the file based on the Take Ownership *user right* assigned to administrators by the operating system. This security ownership model is designed to ensure that a user cannot lock an administrator out from accessing server file resources.

TCP (Transmission Control Protocol)   A specification for software that bundles and unbundles data into packets, manages network transmission of packets and checks for errors.

TCP/IP (Transmission Control Protocol/Internet Protocol)
A set of communications standards created by the U.S. Department of

Defense (DoD) in the 1970s that has now become an accepted way to connect different types of computers in networks because the standards now support so many programs.

Terminal Server   Terminal Server transmits the user interface to the client, and the client returns input (via keyboard and mouse) back to be processed by the server.

Terminal Services   Terminal Services provides net administrators with an effective and reliable way to distribute Windows-based programs with a network server and fully utilize older, less powerful hardware. Terminal Services application server delivers the Windows 2000 desktop and the most current Windows-based applications to computers that might not normally be able to run Windows 2000 at all. Since Terminal Services provides the capability for multiple sessions simultaneously, applications must be installed according to Microsoft's directions so that each session will be able to run a program on the server without disrupting the server or other sessions.

Tombstoned Objects   Tombstoned objects, which are a WINS concept, are those unused objects tagged to be deleted after a specified time period.

Tombstoning   Tombstoning refers to marking records as "extinct" in the WINS database. When a record is marked as extinct, it is no longer considered a valid record by the WINS database. A question that many have is, "why doesn't the WINS server just delete the record?" The reason why WINS doesn't delete the record rather than tombstone it is related to issues involved in the replication process.

Total Cost of Ownership (TCO)   Total Cost of Ownership is a major issue in evaluating whether to upgrade from older versions of Windows. Initial costs play a big part in the total costs.

TRACERT   The TRACERT utility uses ICMP to trace the path from a computer to a specified destination IP address, identifying all intermediate hops between them. This utility is useful for determining router or subnet connectivity problems. The TRACERT utility can be configured utilizing command syntax to provide specific useful information.

Traffic Director   The traffic director passes packets from a source subnet to another router.

Transactional Tracking   Transactional tracking is a method of tracking changes in the system. The better transactional tracking will make recovery from a long period of changes easier. Previous versions of transactional tracking only kept transactional tracking logs until the next server reboot.

Transforms   Transforms, also referred to as Modifications, are stored in .MST files in a similar format to .MSI files. One or more modification packages can be added to a software package in a GPO, and are applied in list order.

Trivial File Transfer Protocol (TFTP)   A simplified of the FTP, associated with the TCP/IP family, that does not provide password protection or a user directory.

tsshutdn Command   The tsshutdn command sends a notice to users that their Terminal sessions are going to be disconnected.

Tunneling   The process of encapsulating one protocol inside another.

Unicast   Unicast means that a message is meant for one user.

Uniform Resource Locator (URL)   A string of characters precisely identifying the type and location of an Internet resource.

Uninterruptible Power Supply (UPS)   A battery that can supply power to a computer system if the power fails; it charges while the computer is on and if the power fails provides power for a certain amount of time allowing the user to shut down the computer properly to preserve crucial data.

Universal Disk File Format System (UDF)   UDF is the successor of CDFS. UDF is compliant with ISO 13346, and was first implemented by Microsoft in the Windows 98 operating system. UDF is currently used in Windows 2000 for accessing Digital Versatile Disc (DVD) media, but may possibly be used in the future to provide a common storage area between Windows 2000 and other operating systems such as UNIX. Currently, however, Windows 2000 implements a Read-Only version of UDF.

Universal Naming Convention (UNC) path   The UNC path is specified for drive mappings performed on the client. The UNC path for a share consists of the server name and the share name, and is referenced in the format \\servername\sharename.

Universal Serial Bus (USB)   A bus that operates as a hardware interface for low-speed peripherals with a bandwidth up to 12 Mbits/sec. USBs support MPEG-1 and MPEG-2 device drivers; Windows 98 supports USBs completely.

User Datagram Protocol (UDP)   A TCP/IP protocol normally bundled with an IP-layer software that describes how messages received reach application programs within the destination computer

User mode Manager   The User mode Manager provides interfaces with PnP components such as Setup and Control Panel windows.

User Principal Name (UPN)   The UPN is a "friendly" name for a user account, which consists of a shortened version of the user name and domain tree name where that account resides. An example of a UPN is jsmith@mydomain.com. The UPN is a name for users that is in the form of an e-mail address. Each forest can support a single UPN namespace. That means that if the UPN namespace is domain.com, then users who want to use cyberdomain.com cannot.

Vendor Classes   Vendor Classes allow hardware and software vendors to identify their components to the DHCP server.

VGA Mode   VGA Mode will load Windows 2000 with only a basic generic VGA video driver. VGA Mode is used to boot into a system when the video display has been corrupted by improper display settings.

Virtual Device Driver (VxD)   A Microsoft Windows 95 32-bit program that manages a resource such as a sound card or printer and runs in the processor's protected mode so it is less likely to crash the system by creating conflict with other applications.

Virtual Directory   A virtual directory is a directory that appears to be in ftproot, the home folder. A virtual directory can be on any server in the same Windows 2000 Server domain. Virtual directories created on other servers should be referenced by their Universal Naming Convention (UNC) names.

Virtual Private Networking (VPN)   The VPN allows for creation of a secure tunnel through the Internet to the organization's LAN.

Virtual Server   A virtual server can be used to host multiple domain names on the same physical Internet Information Services. You need a unique IP address for each virtual server that you host.

Web Proxy   Web Proxy is a method of allowing users on one network access to the Internet.

Wide Area Network (WAN)   A network using high-speed long-distance common-carrier circuits or satellites to cover a large geographic area.

Windows 95   An operating system for running Windows applications on Intel-based 80386DX, 486, and Pentium microprocessors with a completely redesigned Graphical user Interface (GUI) that is easy to learn as well as to use. Windows 95 is not a true 32-bit operating system (like OS/2 Warp or Microsoft's own Windows NT) but incorporates Plug and Play capabilities for nearly automatic configuration of such accessories as sound cards and CD-ROM drives.

Windows 2000 Advanced Server   Formerly known as Enterprise Edition in earlier NT platforms, this OS is a more powerful version of Windows 2000 Server, designed for larger networks. Windows 2000 Advanced Server is built on the technology formerly used in Windows NT Server 4.0, Enterprise Edition.

Windows 2000 Datacenter Server   Windows 2000 Datacenter Server is the high-end operating system in the Windows 2000 platform and includes more advanced features than Windows 2000 Advanced Server. The Windows Datacenter Server can support over 10,000 users simultaneously and is designed for large-scale enterprise networks that will host large Internet Server Providers (ISPs), very large databases, and can perform large-scale engineering simulations. Windows 2000 Datacenter Server can support 10,000 users at once.

Windows 2000 Professional   This operating system is designed for standalone users, and for workstations on a network. The Windows 2000 Professional Operating System helps users upgrade from both the NT 4.0 and Windows 9x platforms

Windows 2000 Server   Also referred to as Windows 2000 Server Standard Edition, it is designed to provide the security and resources to workstations in a network.

Windows 2000 Server OS   The Windows 2000 Server OS provides network security and resources to workgroups, and it provides file and print services, as well as application, communication, and Web services.

Windows Backup Utility   Windows 2000's backup program lets you back up to files, which can be stored on hard disks, writable CDs, or removable media such as those components made by Iomega and Syquest. Windows Backup provides for manual or scheduled backup to tape or file, and quick-and-easy restoration of backup sets, files, and folders.

Windows Driver Model (WDM)   This model is compatible with that used in Windows NT, but will not support the VxD (virtual device) driver model used in Windows 9*x*, so many older 16-bit drivers will not run on Windows 2000 at all.

Windows Installer   Windows Installer addresses the issue of not having a standard installation routine by providing a standard technology that software developers can use to package an application for installation. Windows Installer also provides a cleaner method for software removal and a more efficient and more standardized process for uninstalling software, resulting in a lesser chance of a software removal leaving undesired files, or affecting other applications by removing shared .DLL components. Another benefit of Windows Installer is its ability, under certain circumstances, to repair an application if it detects a problem. For example, if a critical file in an application becomes corrupt or is deleted, Windows Installer has the intelligence to reload the affected file when you next attempt to launch the application.

Windows Internet Naming Service (WINS)   NetBIOS applications require knowledge of the NetBIOS name of a destination host before creating a session. However, TCP/IP is only concerned with destination IP addresses and is oblivious to NetBIOS names. We must, therefore, have some mechanism to resolve NetBIOS names to IP addresses in order for NetBIOS-based applications to function properly on a TCP/IP-based network. This is the primary function of WINS. WINS was the name resolution method of choice because of the reliance on NetBIOS.

Windows Internet Naming Service (WINS) Server A WINS server maintains a database of NetBIOS names and their corresponding IP addresses.

Windows NT A 32-bit operating for high-end Pentium, Alphas, and MIPS processors that combines high performance with personal productivity applications compatibility; designed for users such as scientists and other professional technical workers whose work is processor-intensive.

Workgroup A workgroup is used mainly for peer-to-peer networking. A workgroup is commonly a group of employees working together on an assigned project and whose productivity is enhanced by a Local Area Network (LAN) linkage for improved communication.

World Wide Web (WWW) A global hypertext system accessed by the Internet and navigated by clicking hyperlinks from one document to the next with the actual location of the document immaterial.

X.500 Directory Compliant Software Application X.500 is a scalable standard hat defines a distributed database concept to store information about people or objects, and how that information is made directly available from a local directory replica.

XNS (Xerox Network Service) The XNS is a multilayer protocol system by Xerox, adopted at least in part by other vendors that allows one workstation on a network to use files and peripherals of another as if they were local.

ZAP file   A .ZAP file is a text-based file that follows a similar format to the unattended text files used in Windows NT for installation of the operating system. A .ZAP file is not actually a software package; it simply initiates another setup program. If the setup program supports unattended installation, it is a good idea to include the necessary switches in the .ZAP file so that no user intervention is required. The primary limitation of .ZAP files is that they can only be published, and not assigned. Another limitation is that .ZAP packages do not run with elevated privileges, so the user installing the application must have the appropriate rights to the file system and registry as required by the application installation process.

Zone   A group of domains managed from a single DNS server is referred to as a zone.

Zone Transfer   The process of copying the primary zone file from the Primary DNS server to the Secondary DNS server is zone transfer.

INDEX

Custom Corporate Network Training

Train on Cutting Edge Technology   We can bring the best in skill-based training to your facility to create a real-world hands-on training experience. Global Knowledge has invested millions of dollars in network hardware and software to train our students on the same equipment they will work with on the job. Our relationships with vendors allow us to incorporate the latest equipment and platforms into your on-site labs.

Maximize Your Training Budget   Global Knowledge provides experienced instructors, comprehensive course materials, and all the networking equipment needed to deliver high quality training. You provide the students; we provide the knowledge.

Avoid Travel Expenses   On-site courses allow you to schedule technical training at your convenience, saving time, expense, and the opportunity cost of travel away from the workplace.

Discuss Confidential Topics   Private on-site training permits the open discussion of sensitive issues such as security, access, and network design. We can work with your existing network's proprietary files while demonstrating the latest technologies.

Customize Course Content   Global Knowledge can tailor your courses to include the technologies and the topics which have the greatest impact on your business. We can complement your internal training efforts or provide a total solution to your training needs.

Corporate Pass   The Corporate Pass Discount Program rewards our best network training customers with preferred pricing on public courses, discounts on multimedia training packages, and an array of career planning services.

Global Knowledge Training Lifecycle   Supporting the Dynamic and Specialized Training Requirements of Information Technology Professionals

- Define Profile
- Assess Skills
- Design Training
- Deliver Training
- Test Knowledge
- Update Profile
- Use New Skills

College Credit Recommendation Program   The American Council on Education's CREDIT program recommends 53 Global Knowledge courses for college credit. Now our network training can help you earn your college degree while you learn the technical skills needed for your job. When you attend an ACE-certified Global Knowledge course and pass the associated exam, you earn college credit recommendations for that course. Global Knowledge can establish a transcript record for you with ACE, which you can use to gain credit at a college or as a written record of your professional training that you can attach to your resume.

Registration Information

COURSE FEE: The fee covers course tuition, refreshments, and all course materials. Any parking expenses that may be incurred are not included. Payment or government training form must be received six business days prior to the course date. We will also accept Visa/MasterCard and American Express. For non-U.S. credit card users, charges will be in U.S. funds and will be converted by your credit card company. Checks drawn on Canadian banks in Canadian funds are acceptable.

COURSE SCHEDULE: Registration is at 8:00 a.m. on the first day. The program begins at 8:30 a.m. and concludes at 4:30 p.m. each day.

CANCELLATION POLICY: Cancellation and full refund will be allowed if written cancellation is received in our office at least six business days prior to the course start date. Registrants who do not attend the course or do not cancel more than six business days in advance are responsible for the full registration fee; you may transfer to a later date provided the course fee has been paid in full. Substitutions may be made at any time. If Global Knowledge must cancel a course for any reason, liability is limited to the registration fee only.

GLOBAL KNOWLEDGE: Global Knowledge programs are developed and presented by industry professionals with "real-world" experience. Designed to help professionals meet today's interconnectivity and interoperability challenges, most of our programs feature hands-on labs that incorporate state-of-the-art communication components and equipment.

ON-SITE TEAM TRAINING: Bring Global Knowledge's powerful training programs to your company. At Global Knowledge, we will custom design courses to meet your specific network requirements. Call 1 (919) 461-8686 for more information.

YOUR GUARANTEE: Global Knowledge believes its courses offer the best possible training in this field. If during the first day you are not satisfied and wish to withdraw from the course, simply notify the instructor, return all course materials, and receive a 100% refund.

In the US:

CALL: 1 (888) 762-4442

FAX: 1 (919) 469-7070

VISIT OUR WEBSITE:

www.globalknowledge.com

MAIL CHECK AND THIS FORM TO:

Global Knowledge

Suite 200

114 Edinburgh South

P.O. Box 1187

Cary, NC 27512

In Canada:

CALL: 1 (800) 465-2226

FAX: 1 (613) 567-3899

VISIT OUR WEBSITE:

www.globalknowledge.com.ca

MAIL CHECK AND THIS FORM TO:

Global Knowledge

Suite 1601

393 University Ave.

Toronto, ON M5G 1E6

REGISTRATION INFORMATION:

Course title _____

Course location _____ Course date _____

Name/title _____ Company _____

Name/title _____ Company _____

Name/title _____ Company _____

Address _____ Telephone _____ Fax _____

City _____ State/Province _____ Zip/Postal Code _____

Credit card _____ Card # _____ Expiration date _____

Signature _____